Association of Southeast Asian Nations (ASEAN)

Association of Southeast Asian Nations (ASEAN)

Second Edition

Konstantinos D. Magliveras
Gino J. Naldi

This book was originally published as a monograph in the International Encyclopaedia of Laws/Intergovernmental Organizations.

Founding Editor: Roger Blanpain
General Editor: Frank Hendrickx
Volume Editor: Jan Wouters

Wolters Kluwer

Chapter 3. The Institutional Architecture of ASEAN 119

§1. General Observations 119

§2. The ASEAN Summit 120

§3. The ASEAN Coordinating Council 154

Part III. Activities 157

Chapter 1. Settlement of Disputes 157

§1. Treaty of Amity and Co-operation in Southeast Asia 159

§2. Manila Protocol on Enhanced Dispute Settlement Procedure 160

§3. Dispute Settlement under the ASEAN Charter 163

§4. The Protocol to the ASEAN Charter on Dispute Settlement Mechanisms 165
I. Consultation 168
II. Good Offices, Mediation and Conciliation 170
III. Arbitration 173

Chapter 2. Human Rights 182

§1. ASEAN and Human Rights 182

§2. The Human Rights Record of ASEAN States 183

§3. The ASEAN Human Rights Declaration 189
I. The General Principles of the AHRD 194
II. Civil and Political Rights 197
III. Economic, Social and Cultural Rights 200
IV. Collective Rights 202

§4. Other ASEAN Declarations on Human Rights 205

§5. ASEAN Convention Against Trafficking in Persons 209

§6. ASEAN Intergovernmental Commission on Human Rights 215

§7. ASEAN Commission on the Promotion and Protection of the Rights of Women and Children 220

§8. ASEAN Committee on the Implementation of the ASEAN Declaration on the Protection and Promotion of the Rights of Migrant Workers 224

Chapter 3. Terrorism 226

§1. The ASEAN Convention on Counter Terrorism 226

§2. Comprehensive Plan of Action on Counter Terrorism 231

Chapter 4. Environment 233

§1. The ASEAN Agreement on Transboundary Haze Pollution 233

§2. ASEAN Action on Marine Debris 237

Part IV. ASEAN External Relations 241

Chapter 1. Introduction: The So-Called External Parties 241

Chapter 2. The Conclusion of ASEAN International Agreements 247

Chapter 3. ASEAN United Nations Relations 249

Chapter 4. ASEAN: Pacific Alliance Relations 253

Chapter 5. The South China Sea Dispute 255

Part V. ASEAN Economic Community 261

Chapter 1. Introduction: The Position of the AEC in the Structure of the ASEAN Charter – The AEC Council 261

Chapter 2. From Free Trade among Member States to the AEC 263

Chapter 3. The Establishment of the AEC and the Economic Community Blueprint 2025 269

§1. The Structure of the AEC 270

§2. Law-Making in the AEC: The Question of the Requirements for the Entry into Force of ASEAN Economic Treaties 272

Chapter 4. FTAs Between the Member States of ASEAN and Third States 277

§1. The FTA with South Korea 277

§2. The FTA with Australia and with New Zealand 279

§3. The Regional Comprehensive Economic Partnership (RCEP) 281

Part VI. Appraisal 285

Part VII. Addresses and Networks 291

Selected Bibliography 333

Table of Cases 341

Index 347

List of Abbreviations

AADMER	ASEAN Agreement on Disaster Management and Emergency Response
AANZFTA	ASEAN-Australia-New Zealand Free Trade Area
ACC	ASEAN Coordinating Council
ACCT	ASEAN Convention on Counter Terrorism
ACHR	American Convention on Human Rights
ACIA	ASEAN Comprehensive Investment Agreement
ACMECS	Ayeyawady–Chao Phraya–Mekong Economic Cooperation Strategy
ACMW	ASEAN Committee on the Implementation of the ASEAN Declaration on the Protection and Promotion of the Rights of Migrant Workers
ACTP	ASEAN Convention Against Trafficking in Persons
ACWC	ASEAN Commission for the Promotion and Protection of the Rights of Women and Children
ADMW	ASEAN Declaration on the Rights of Migrant Workers
AEC	ASEAN Economic Community
AEM	ASEAN Economic Ministers
AEMM	ASEAN – EU Ministerial Meeting
AFAS	ASEAN Framework Agreement on Services
AFTA	ASEAN Free Trade Area
AHA Centre	ASEAN Co-ordinating Centre for Humanitarian Assistance on Disaster Management
AHRD	ASEAN Human Rights Declaration
AJIL	American Journal of International Law
AIA	ASEAN Investment Area
AICHR	ASEAN Intergovernmental Commission on Human Rights
AIDS	Acquired Immunodeficiency Syndrome

List of Abbreviations

AJIL	American Journal of International Law
AKFTA	ASEAN-Korea Free Trade Agreement
AMLAT	ASEAN Treaty on Mutual Legal Assistance in Criminal Matters
AMMD	ASEAN Ministerial Meeting on Drug Matters
AMMTC	ASEAN Ministerial Meeting on Transnational Crime
AMRG	ASEAN Militaries Ready Group
APSC	ASEAN Political-Security Community
ARF	ASEAN Regional Forum
ASCC	ASEAN Socio-Cultural Community
ASEAN	Association of Southeast Asian Nations
ATIGA	ASEAN Trade in Goods Agreement
ATISA	ASEAN Trade in Services Agreement
AU	African Union
AYBIL	Australian Yearbook of International Law
BIMSTEC	Bay of Bengal Initiative for Multi-Sectoral Technical and Economic Cooperation
BYBIL	British Yearbook of International Law
CEDAW	UN Convention on the Elimination of Discrimination Against Women
CEPT	Common Effective Preferential Tariff
CETS	Council of Europe Treaty Series
CERD	International Convention on the Elimination of All Forms of Racial Discrimination
CJEU	Court of Justice of the European Union
CLMV	Cambodia–Laos–Myanmar–Vietnam
CMLR	Common Market Law Reports
CPTPP	Comprehensive and Progressive Agreement for Trans-Pacific Partnership
CRC	UN Convention on the Rights of the Child
CSO	Civil Society Organisation
DOC	Declaration on Conduct
Doc.	Document
EAC	East Africa Community
EAS	East Asia Summit
ECCC	Extraordinary Chambers of the Courts in Cambodia

ECHR	(European) Convention for the Protection of Human Rights and Fundamental Freedoms
ECJ	European Court of Justice
ECOSOC	United Nations Economic and Social Council
ECR	European Court Reports
EEC	European Economic Community
EHRR	European Human Rights Reports
EJIL	European Journal of International Law
EPG	Eminent Persons' Group
EU	European Union
ECtHR	European Court of Human Rights
FCDO	Foreign, Commonwealth and Development Office
FTA	Free Trade Area
GATT	General Agreement on Tariffs and Trade
GCC	Gulf Cooperation Council
GDP	Gross Domestic Product
HADR	Humanitarian Assistance and Disaster Relief
HLTF	High-Level Task Force
HIV	Human Immunodeficiency Virus
HRLR	Human Rights Law Review
IACHR	Inter-American Court of Human Rights
ICC	International Criminal Court
ICCPR	International Covenant on Civil and Political Rights
ICESCR	International Covenant on Economic, Social and Cultural Rights
ICJ	International Court of Justice
ICLQ	International and Comparative Law Quarterly
ICOE	Independent Commission of Enquiry
IDPs	Internally Displaced Persons
IGO	Intergovernmental Organisation
IHRR	International Human Rights Reports
IIMM	International Investigative Mechanism for Myanmar
ILO	International Labour Organization
ILR	International Law Reports
IRENA	International Renewable Energy Agency
LNTS	League of Nations Treaty Series
MoU	Memorandum of Understanding

MPAC	Master Plan on ASEAN Connectivity
NGO	Non-governmental Organisation
NILR	Netherlands International Law Review
NYUJIL & Pol	New York University Journal of International Law and Politics
OJ	Official Journal
PCA	Permanent Court of Arbitration
PDR	People's Democratic Republic
RCEP	Regional Comprehensive Economic Partnership
RECs	Regional Economic Communities
REIOs	Regional Economic Integration Organisations
RIAA	Reports of International Arbitral Awards
Res.	Resolution
SAARC	South Asian Association for Regional Cooperation
SADC	Southern Africa Development Community
SAEU	South Asian Economic Union
SAFTA	South Asian Free Trade Area
SEANWFZ	Southeast Asia Nuclear Weapons-Free Zone
SEOM	Senior Economic Officials Meeting
SGCA	Supreme Court of Singapore Court of Appeal
SIJORI	Singapore–Johor–Riau Growth Triangle
SLR	Singapore Law Reports
SYBIL	Singapore Yearbook of International Law
TAC	Treaty of Amity and Co-operation in Southeast Asia
TEU	Treaty on European Union
TFEU	Treaty on the Functioning of the European Union
TOR	Terms of Reference
TPP	Trans-Pacific Partnership
UDHR	Universal Declaration of Human Rights
UK	United Kingdom of Great Britain and Northern Ireland
UN	United Nations
UNCLOS	United Nations Convention on the Law of the Sea
UNESCO	United Nations Educational, Scientific and Cultural Organization
UNGA	United Nations General Assembly
UNHCR	United Nations High Commission for Refugees
UNSC	United Nations Security Council

UNSG	United Nations Secretary-General
UNTS	United Nations Treaty Series
USA	United States of America
VAP	Vientiane Action Programme
VCLT	Vienna Convention on the Law of Treaties
WTO	World Trade Organization
4IR	Fourth Industrial Revolution
5 PC	Five-Point Consensus

List of Abbreviations

Preface

The Association of Southeast Asian Nations (ASEAN) is a regional intergovernmental organisation (IGO) consisting of ten states first formed in 1967. Hence fifty-seven years old at present, ASEAN started life as a loose regional association of states concerned with protecting its members' economic, political and security interests. Over time, ASEAN has evolved into a rules-based international organisation. Although dedicated to deepening integration in the economic, political, socio-cultural, and security spheres, ASEAN operates, presently and for the foreseeable future, on the basis of intergovernmental cooperation and does not follow the supranational model of the Regional Economic Integration Organisations (REIOs), as exemplified by the European Union (EU). The states comprising ASEAN are rich in natural resources and, with a population of almost seven hundred million, have enormous human potential. ASEAN is one of the fastest growing markets in the world, and their export-oriented model of economic growth has lifted many of them up to economic importance not only in Asia but beyond. ASEAN's membership is thus made up of some of the world's lead-performing markets. However, wealth is not evenly distributed, while political as well as socio-economic conditions vary considerably between and within these states. ASEAN's growing economic power but also the tensions with China (primarily due to the precarious situation that has developed in the South China Sea) have attracted the attention of Western powers for many years now. But despite its important and growing influential role in the wider region, in Asia and beyond, arguably ASEAN is relatively unknown and underexplored in Western academic circles. This monograph aims at rectifying this lack of awareness by presenting an examination and analysis of ASEAN as an international organisation, its institutions, its activities, and its achievements, principally from a legal perspective. We trust that it will prove informative for academics and practitioners everywhere.

The law is stated as we understood it to be in September 2024. Several later events and developments have, however, been taken into accounted and noted. The arguments and submissions made in the present monograph are the authors' only.

Konstantinos D. Magliveras and Gino J. Naldi

Part I. History and Evolution

1. The Association of Southeast Asian Nations (ASEAN) is a regional intergovernmental organisation (IGO) established by treaty,[1] first founded in 1967,[2] dedicated to political, security, economic and socio-cultural cooperation in addition to maintaining and enhancing peace, security and stability.[3] It has a current membership of ten states, Brunei Darussalam, the Kingdom of Cambodia, the Republic of Indonesia, the Lao People's Democratic Republic (Laos PDR), Malaysia, the Republic of the Union of Myanmar (Burma), the Republic of the Philippines, the Republic of Singapore, the Kingdom of Thailand and the Socialist Republic of Vietnam (Vietnam),[4] drawn, as its name attests, from the geographical region of Southeast Asia.[5] These states have diverse ethnic, cultural, historical, political and religious makeup and experiences which are also reflected in their legal traditions.[6] Membership of ASEAN is open to other Southeast Asian states recognised by all the current members.[7] Timor-Leste may be admitted to membership in the near future, possibly by 2025. In November 2022, ASEAN agreed 'in principle' to admit Timor-Leste and to grant it observer status.[8] The following year, the ASEAN Summit adopted a roadmap to Timor-Leste's accession.[9]

In terms of their political composition, these states form a heterogeneous group, a mix of new democracies, guided, directed or controlled democracies and authoritarian

1. ASEAN Charter (20 Nov. 2007), 2624 U.N.T.S. 223, Art. 3. *See* generally, P. Sands & P. Klein, *Bowett's Law of International Institutions* 232–235 (Sweet & Maxwell 6th ed. 2009); P. Malanczuk, *Association of Southeast Asian Nations (ASEAN)*, in *Max Planck Encyclopedia of Public International Law* (October 2017), http://opil.ouplaw.com.
2. The founding members were Indonesia, Malaysia, the Philippines, Singapore, and Thailand.
3. ASEAN Charter Art. 1(1), (2).
4. ASEAN Charter Art. 4.
5. ASEAN Charter Art. 6(2)(a).
6. A. Harding, *Global Doctrine and Local Knowledge: Law in South East Asia*, 51 I.C.L.Q. 35, 42–44 (2002).
7. ASEAN Charter Art. 6(2). Papua New Guinea has an outstanding application for membership and has observer status.
8. ASEAN Leaders' Statement on the Application of Timor-Leste for ASEAN Membership, Phnom Penh, Cambodia, 11 Nov. 2022, https://asean.org/wp-content/uploads/2022/11/05-ASEAN-Leaders-Statement-on-the-Application-of-Timor-Leste-for-ASEAN-Membership.pdf.
9. Chairman's Statement of the 42nd ASEAN Summit, Labuan Bajo, Indonesia, 10–11 May 2023, para. 25, https://asean.org/wp-content/uploads/2023/05/FINAL-Chairmans-Statement-42nd-ASEAN-Summit-1.pdf.

or repressive regimes.[10] But none of these states can be described as a full democracy. Brunei is an absolute monarchy, a virtual personal fiefdom.[11] Cambodia, a constitutional monarchy, is a parliamentary democracy in name only, with regular if deeply flawed elections;[12] the reality is that an authoritarian regime holds sway.[13] Indonesia and the Philippines, both republics, are also young, multiparty democracies which face a number of challenges.[14] Thailand, also a constitutional monarchy, was considered a new democracy until May 2014 when the military took power in a coup. Limited democratic rule was established in 2019, but democratic values continue to be eroded.[15] Arguably, the most egregious example is the dissolution by the Constitutional Court of the party that won the most seats in the election held in 2023 for campaigning to amend the lèse-majesté law.[16] Laos and Vietnam, people's republics, are under one-party rule.[17] Myanmar, currently mired in civil war, had laboured under a repressive military regime until 2011 when a limited democratic opening, with the military still exercising considerable power, was allowed. However, this came to a violent end in February 2021 when the military once again seized power in a coup d'état and violent repression followed.[18] Myanmar has also been criticised for pervasive human rights abuses of civilians,[19] including Rohingya Muslims and other minorities.[20] Malaysia, a federal parliamentary constitutional monarchy, and

10. *See* Economist Intelligence Unit, *Democracy Index 2023*; U.S. State Department, 2023 Country Reports on Human Rights Practices, https://www.state.gov/reports/2023-country-reports-on-human-rights-practices/; A. Duxbury & T. Hsein-Li, *Can ASEAN Take Human Rights Seriously?* 66–90 (Cambridge University Press 2019).
11. Classified as 'not free', Freedom House, 'Freedom in the World 2024: Brunei', https://freedomhouse.org/country/brunei/freedom-world/2024.
12. EU Annual Report on Human Rights and Democracy in the World 2023 Country Updates, 181.
13. Classified as 'authoritarian', *Democracy Index 2023*, 47; and 'not free', Freedom House, 'Freedom in the World 2024: Cambodia', https://freedomhouse.org/country/cambodia/freedom-world/2024.
14. Classified as 'flawed democracies', *Democracy Index 2023*, *ibid.*; and 'partly free', Freedom House, 'Freedom in the World 2024: Indonesia', https://freedomhouse.org/country/indonesia/freedom-world/2024, and Freedom House, 'Freedom in the World 2024: Philippines', https://freedomhouse.org/country/philippines/freedom-world/2024.
15. EU Annual Report on Human Rights and Democracy in the World 2023 Country Updates, 219. Classified as 'flawed democracy', *Democracy Index 2023*, *ibid.*; and 'partly free', Freedom House, 'Freedom House, 'Freedom in the World 2024: Thailand', https://freedomhouse.org/country/thailand/freedom-world/2024.
16. Reuters, 'Thai court orders dissolution of anti-establishment election winner', 7 Aug. 2024, https://www.reuters.com/world/asia-pacific/thai-politics-edge-court-decides-fate-anti-establishment-party-2024-08-06/.
17. Classified as 'authoritarian', *Democracy Index 2023*, *ibid.*; and 'not free', Freedom House, 'Freedom in the World 2024: Laos', https://freedomhouse.org/country/laos/freedom-world/2024, and https://freedomhouse.org/country/vietnam/freedom-world/2024.
18. Classified as 'authoritarian', *Democracy Index 2023*, *ibid.*; and 'not free', Freedom House, 'Freedom in the World 2024: Myanmar', https://freedomhouse.org/country/myanmar/freedom-world/2024. The coup and the resulting violence were criticised in UNGA Res. 75/287, The situation in Myanmar, 18 Jun. 2021, and in UNSC Res. 2669 (2022), 21 Dec. 2022. *See also* Statement by the President of the Security Council, UN Doc. S/PRST/2021/5 (10 Mar. 2021). *See further* K. E. Eichensehr, '*Military Coup in Burma Draws International Condemnation and Pressure*', 115 A.J.I.L. 558 (2021).
19. EU Annual Report on Human Rights and Democracy in the World 2023 Country Updates, 207–208.
20. *See* UNGA Res. 79/182, Situation of human rights of Rohingya Muslims and other minorities in Myanmar, 17 Dec. 2024. Note the order of the International Court of Justice indicating provisional

Singapore, a parliamentary republic, may be classified as controlled democracies with regular multiparty elections which are not wholly free.[21]

The socio-economic development of these states also varies widely with marked inequality a signal feature, a combination of rich, high or upper middle-income and dynamic developed or developing market economies, such as Brunei, Singapore, Thailand and Malaysia, and relatively poor and emerging market economies experiencing rapid economic growth, such as Cambodia, and socialist-oriented market economies such as Laos and Vietnam, both fast-growing economies.[22] One assessment is that common features shared by these states are authoritarian government structures, a commitment to social stability and long-term economic planning.[23] Given their differences and the fact that forward movement has been based on finding common ground, progress has not always been easy or timely for ASEAN.

2. In the 1950s and 1960s, Southeast Asia was riven by conflict, particularly the wars in Indochina, insurgencies and a fear of the spread of communism which eventually led to the creation of ASEAN in 1967 by five founding members, Indonesia, Malaysia, the Philippines, Singapore and Thailand.[24] ASEAN was originally established pursuant to the ASEAN, or Bangkok, Declaration of 8 August 1967 as a loose regional association of states with political, cultural and economic goals, including advancing economic development and the promotion of regional peace and stability.[25] ASEAN thus engaged with other states with which it had close political and trading links, giving rise to Dialogue Partnerships with states such as Australia, Canada, China, India, Japan, New Zealand, Russia, South Korea, United Kingdom (UK) and United States of America (USA), and entities such as the EU.[26] It has also established Sectoral Dialogue Partnerships with states such as Norway and Switzerland, Development Partnerships with states such as Germany, France and Italy, and institutional partnerships with international organisations such as the Gulf Cooperation Council, the Southern Common Market (MERCOSUR) and the UN. In 1997, spurred to a degree by a financial crash, ASEAN Plus Three was established with China, Japan and South Korea to promote cooperation in these fields and to explore

measures in the case brought by The Gambia against Myanmar on the application of the Convention on the Prevention and Punishment of the Crime of Genocide, (9 Dec. 1948), 78 U.N.T.S. 277, which found that the Rohingya in Myanmar appeared to constitute a 'protected group' under the Convention and that there was a real and imminent risk of irreparable prejudice to their rights, *Application of the Convention on the Prevention and Punishment of the Crime of Genocide (The Gambia v. Myanmar)*, Provisional Measures, I.C.J. Reports 2020, 3.

21. Described as 'flawed democracies', *Democracy Index 2023*, *ibid.*; and 'partly free', Freedom House, 'Freedom in the World 2024: Malaysia', https://freedomhouse.org/country/malaysia/freedom-world/2024, and 'Freedom in the World 2024: Singapore', https://freedomhouse.org/country/singapore/freedom-world/2024.
22. *See* generally CIA, *The World Factbook*, https://www.cia.gov/the-world-factbook/.
23. Harding, 43–44.
24. Report of the Eminent Persons Group on the ASEAN Charter, 13 Jan. 2007, paras 6, 8, https://asean.org/wp-content/uploads/images/archive/19247.pdf (EPG Report). Brunei joined in 1984, Vietnam in 1995, Laos and Myanmar were admitted in 1997, and finally Cambodia joined in 1999.
25. Association of Southeast Asian Nations: Declaration on Formation of the Association, 1331 U.N.T.S. 235.
26. EPG Report, para. 9.

the possibility of economic integration and free trade agreements, which with Australia, India and New Zealand later expanded to ASEAN Plus Six.[27] In keeping with the ASEAN *modus operandi*, these fora lack formal institutions but are based on a flexible framework for multilateral discourse, hopefully leading to agreed responses to transnational problems, akin somewhat to the G20 meetings. To foster regional peace and stability, in 1971 ASEAN adopted the Declaration on the Zone of Peace, Freedom and Neutrality.[28] This was followed by the 1976 Treaty of Amity and Co-operation in Southeast Asia (TAC) and the 1995 Treaty on the Southeast Asia Nuclear Weapon-Free Zone.[29] References to both treaties are made *infra*.

3. Assuring peace and security had been put on a formal footing through the creation of the multilateral ASEAN Regional Forum (ARF), which held its inaugural meeting in 1994, to further dialogue and consultation and to evolve and enhance confidence building, preventive diplomacy and conflict resolution in the region. However, as yet, it does not have the authority to take action directly in conflict situations. ARF reflects the ASEAN approach of intergovernmental cooperation and decision-making by consensus. It operates through the ARF Experts and Eminent Persons group, known as Track One, which meets annually to provide advice and offer suggestions to ARF officials. At an unofficial level, described as second-track, academic institutes and think-tanks provide ARF with subjects for consideration. Membership of ARF numbers twenty-seven states and includes Australia, Bangladesh, Canada, EU, New Zealand, Pakistan, Papua New Guinea, Russia, North Korea, South Korea, Sri Lanka and USA.[30] During the Cold War, ASEAN had sought to steer a middle way and many of its Member States played, and continue to play, an active role in the Non-Aligned Movement and the Group of 77.[31]

4. During this formative phase, which lasted until 1976, ASEAN was described as a flexible body with minimal institutional framework, comporting itself 'in a loose, informal way with few legally binding arrangements and weak institutions'.[32] It was concerned with confidence building and operated on the basis of consensus, known as the 'ASEAN Way'.[33] It has been stated that ASEAN then

27. Malanczuk, paras 74–76; M. Kawai & G. Wignaraja, *ASEAN+3 or ASEAN+6: Which Way Forward?*, ADBI Discussion Paper 77, 2007, 6–7, https://www.adb.org/sites/default/files/publication/156716/adbi-dp77.pdf.
28. Kuala Lumpur Declaration on the Zone of Peace, Freedom and Neutrality (27 Nov. 1971), https://www.icnl.org/wp-content/uploads/Transnational_zone.pdf.
29. Treaty on the Southeast Asia Nuclear Weapons-Free Zone (15 Dec. 1995), I.L.M. 35 (1996): 635.
30. Malanczuk, paras 72–73.
31. *See* generally J.P. Grant & J.C. Barker, *Encyclopaedic Dictionary of International Law* 250, 415–416 (Oxford University Press 3rd ed. 2009).
32. M. Ewing-Chow & L. Bernard, *The ASEAN Charter: The Legalization of ASEAN?*, in *Global Administrative Law: The Casebook* 115, 117 (S. Cassese et al. eds, Institute for International Law and Justice 2012). Another has described ASEAN as 'a mechanism for consolidation of weak states', W.J. Jones, *Universalizing Human Rights The ASEAN Way*, 3 Int'l J. Soc. Sci. 72, 74 (2014). Or in the words of an eminent jurist, a 'limited organisation of a very rudimentary character', D.W. Bowett, *The Law of International Institutions* (Stevens & Sons 2d ed. 1970), 209.
33. ASEAN Charter Art. 20(1). *See* Ewing-Chow & Bernard, 116–117; Seah, 205. The 'ASEAN Way' has been defined as a 'distinctive mode of interaction, marked by informality, consensus, non-adversarial bargaining and a preference for non-legalistic and non-binding approaches to problem

amounted essentially to an 'association for regional cooperation'.[34] Whereas ASEAN possessed attributes of international personality at the time, such as the capacity to conclude treaties, some doubt had been expressed as to whether it satisfied the criteria of international personality fully.[35] It has been observed that ASEAN lacked a supranational decision-making or legislative organ, or one for the enforcement of decisions.[36] Its focus rather was on 'economic integration and "quiet dialogue."'[37]

5. In subsequent years more concrete form was given to the objectives of political and economic cooperation through a series of agreements.[38] Significant in this respect are the TAC and the associated Declaration of ASEAN Concord.[39] The TAC is more than a means for the peaceful settlement of disputes. It embeds the elemental thinking of its Member States, including respect for independence, sovereignty, equality, territorial integrity and national identity, the right of states to be free of external interference, subversion or coercion, non-interference in the internal affairs of states, and the renunciation of the threat or use of force.[40] Additionally, it has

---

solving', A. Acharya, *The Evolution and Limitations of ASEAN Identity*, in *ASEAN@50: Retrospectives and Perspectives on the Making, Substance, Significance and Future of* ASEAN. *Volume 4. Building ASEAN Community: Political-Security and Socio-cultural Reflections* 25, 29 (A. Baviera & L. Maramis eds, Economic Research Institute for ASEAN and East Asia 2017). *See* further Duxbury & Hsein-Li, 122–126. The EPG considered that consensus had served ASEAN well, EPG Report, para. 29.

34. D.A. Desierto, *Universalizing Core Human Rights in the 'New' ASEAN: A Reassessment of Culture and Development Justifications Against the Global Rejection of Impunity*, 1 Göttingen J. Int'l L. 77, 87 (2009).
35. *Reparation for Injuries Suffered in the Service of the United Nations*, Advisory Opinion, I.C.J. Reports 1949, 174. *See* J. Klabbers, *An Introduction to International Institutional Law* 6–12 (Cambridge U. Press, 2d ed. 2009) 6–12; C.H. Lin, *ASEAN Charter: Deeper Regional Integration under International Law?*, 9 Chinese J. Int'l L. 821, 824–826 (2010). One of the objectives of the ASEAN Charter was to remove such doubt and endow it with legal personality, EPG Report, para. 43. However, it has been argued that ASEAN never lacked international personality, S. Chesterman, *Does ASEAN Exist?: The Association of Southeast Asian Nations as an International Legal Person*, 12 *S.Y.B.I.L.* 199 (2008). An organisation's personality may be implied from its constituent instrument and its practice and it therefore seems probable that ASEAN satisfied the test.
36. L.H. Tan, *Will ASEAN Economic Integration Progress Beyond a Free Trade Area?*, 53 I.C.L.Q. 935, 948–949 (2004). The ASEAN Secretariat was only founded in 1976, Agreement on the Establishment of the Association of South East Asian Nations (ASEAN) Secretariat (24 Feb. 1976) 1331 U.N.T.S. 243.
37. Interim Report of the Secretary-General on the Prevention of Armed Conflict, para. 20, UN Doc. A/58/365-S/2003/888 (12 Sep. 2003). According to one commentator, ASEAN's *raison d'être* was political, 'to secure the region's peace, stability, and development', Tan, 935.
38. *See* Sands & Klein, 233–234; Desierto, 87–89. However, even after a decade ASEAN was not considered 'an unqualified success', achieving little in practical terms, J.A. Thomas, *History and International Law in Asia: A Time for Review*, in *Essays in Honour of Wang Tieya* 813, 849 (R.St.J. Macdonald ed., Martinus Nijhoff 1994). However, its progress, even if limited, must be seen in the context of the wide divergences in the political and socio-economic composition and development gap between Member States.
39. Declaration of ASEAN Concord (Bali, 24 Feb. 1976), https://www.icnl.org/research/library/transnational_1976declaration/. The Declaration contains a programme of action as a framework for ASEAN cooperation in the political, economic, social, cultural and security fields.
40. TAC Art. 2.

integration'.[53] It seemed to sanction a radical departure from the traditional positivist statist-orientated way of conducting affairs based on the 'twin pillars' of ASEAN integration, national sovereignty and non-interference in the internal affairs of states, towards a more cooperative, cohesive and coordinated approach.[54] However, the 'constitutionalization' of ASEAN has been described as a false dawn in that the ASEAN Charter institutionalises the power exercised by the Member States which very much remain in control.[55] The basic point needs to be borne in mind that ASEAN is the creation of states which have vested it with certain specific and limited powers and that, like other international organisations, is governed by the principle of speciality.[56]

10. A proper understanding of ASEAN's development must take full account of the significance of the ASEAN Community and is a concrete manifestation of ASEAN's *modus operandi* through 'established practices'.[57] It is based on the aforementioned three pillars, the APSC, the AEC, and the ASCC along with their respective Blueprints covering their sphere of activity: each Community has its own Community Council which coordinates the work of different sectors within its mandate.[58] Each Member State designates a national representative. They meet at least twice a year. In its turn each Community Council is comprised of the relevant Sectoral Ministerial Bodies to undertake its functions.

11. The APSC was envisaged as a means of enhancing peace and security in the region by upholding the principles of democracy, the rule of law and good governance, and promoting and protecting human rights with a view to creating a rules-based community of shared values and norms.[59] However, this does not translate

53. Tan, 949.
54. *Ibid.*, 948; Ewing-Chow & Bernard, 116–117; Duxbury & Hsein-Li, 126–132. On the central nature of the principle of non-interference *see* N. Hitoshi, *Revisiting the Principle of Non-Intervention: A Structural Principle of International Law or a Political Obstacle to Regional Security in Asia?*, 3 Asian J. Int'l L. 25 (2013). This new stance was reinforced by the Bali Declaration on ASEAN Community in a Global Community of Nations Pan of Action (Bali Concord III) (17 Nov. 2011), at: https://www.asean.org/wp-content/uploads/images/2013/other_documents/POA%20of%20Bali%20Concord%20III%20_final_.pdf.
55. J.D. Bagulaya, *ASEAN as* Wayang Kulit*: A Critique of the Constitutional, Extra-Constitutional, and Practical Fetters of ASEAN*, 9 Asian J. Int'l L. 175 (2019).
56. *See Legality of the Threat or Use of Nuclear Weapons*, Advisory Opinion, I.C.J. Reports 1996, 226.
57. ASEAN Charter Art. 11(2)(a).
58. Cha-am Hua Hin Declaration on the Roadmap for an ASEAN Community 2009–2015, 14th ASEAN Summit (1 Mar. 2009), https://asean.org/cha-am-hua-hin-declaration-on-the-roadmap-for-the-asean-community-2009–2015/. For the characteristics and elements of the three pillars, *see* ASEAN, Roadmap for an ASEAN Community 2009–2015, Jakarta: ASEAN Secretariat, April 2009. https://www.asean.org/wp-content/uploads/images/ASEAN_RTK_2014/2_Roadmap_for_ASEAN_Community_20092015.pdf. The Blueprints have since been updated, Kuala Lumpur Declaration on ASEAN 2025: Forging Ahead Together (22 Nov. 2015), in ASEAN 2025: Forging Ahead Together, Jakarta: ASEAN Secretariat, November 2015, 9, https://asean.org/wp-content/uploads/images/2015/November/KL-Declaration/ASEAN%202025%20Forging%20Ahead%20Together%20final.pdf. The importance of the three pillars is evidenced by the fact that they are mentioned in the ASEAN Charter's Preamble.
59. ASEAN Political-Security Community Blueprint, in ASEAN, Roadmap for an ASEAN Community 2009–2015.

into military alliances or a joint foreign policy. Various initiatives and action plans were set out for the implementation of these objectives, including specific sectoral meetings on defence, law and transnational crime.

12. More specifically, ASEAN expressed its support for the notion of comprehensive security, taking account of non-traditional threats posed by transnational crimes such as drug and people trafficking and terrorism. It was reiterated that ASEAN was committed to conflict prevention, preventive diplomacy and confidence building respecting the principles of sovereignty and territorial integrity. ASEAN also reinforced its commitment to conflict resolution and the peaceful settlement of disputes and highlighted the TAC. It expressed its support for post-conflict peace-building, especially boosting ASEAN humanitarian assistance, disaster management and emergency response. The importance of ASEAN Centrality was stressed and the need to promote enhanced links with third states and external partners. It was anticipated that promoting political development would lead to greater 'inter-state solidarity'. Yet in this area ASEAN also faces challenges. This is evident in the political system and governance of the different states set out above, as well as in their relations with third states.

13. The AEC was the most advanced pillar; in 1992, a Common Effective Preferential Tariff (CEPT) Scheme was adopted to reduce tariffs and increase competitiveness. It provided the basis for AFTA. But Bali Concord II had set the AEC as the ambition of regional economic integration and development. The ultimate aim would be greater investment and increased production and exports. Market economies and international trade were central to these goals. However, it was only with the adoption of the Blueprint that the key elements of the AEC were settled on.[60] These are broadly: a single market and production base; a competitive economic region; a region of equitable economic development; and a region fully integrated into the global economy. These ends are to be achieved through, *inter alia*, eliminating tariff and non-tariff barriers, thus enabling the free flow of goods, the free flow of services, the free flow of investment, the freer flow of capital, the free flow of skilled labour, fair competition, intellectual property policy, infrastructure development, and increased participation in global supply networks. Reducing poverty and socio-economic disparities were also essential. However, realising the AEC is arguably ASEAN's greatest challenge. First, economic integration is immeasurably difficult when the economic policies, systems and capacities of the Member States are so wide apart. The economic and development disparity between some of the states, Brunei and Singapore on the one hand, and Laos and Myanmar on the other hand, for instance, are enormous. Consequently, some degree of economic convergence is necessary. Second, progress on tariff and non-tariff barriers has been protracted. Third, reform of legal and regulatory structures has been sluggish in some countries. Despite these difficulties, the attainment of the AEC is a priority.

---

60. ASEAN Economic Community Blueprint, in ASEAN, Roadmap for an ASEAN Community 2009–2015.

14. The ASCC was based on a 'people-orientated and socially responsible' ASEAN Community in order to promote unity and solidarity among the countries and peoples of ASEAN by creating a common identity and promoting the quality of life of its people. The defining elements of the ASCC are human development; social welfare and protection; social justice and rights; environmental sustainability; building an ASEAN identity; and narrowing the Development Gap. These ends are to be achieved through, *inter alia*, better education, promoting decent work, promoting information and communication technology, poverty alleviation, access to healthcare, a social welfare safety net, combating communicable diseases, tackling drug abuse, enhancing the rights and welfare of vulnerable groups such as children and the elderly, addressing global environmental issues such as climate change and transboundary pollution, and promoting and protecting ASEAN cultural heritage. While progress has been made in certain socio-economic areas, it has lagged in others, for instance, pollution and polluting activities although there has been some improvement more recently.[61]

15. While some of the Community goals were translated into reality through the adoption of treaties and declarations the general assessment was that the concrete results of the ASEAN Community 2015 had been disappointing, especially in terms of implementation. In 2011, in accordance with (Bali) Concord III, ASEAN undertook to enhance cooperation at the global level in these fields. In 2015, the ASEAN Community was relaunched as the ASEAN Community Vision 2025,[62] which reaffirms and builds upon the principles and goals enshrined in the ASEAN Charter. It calls for the effective implementation of the ASEAN Charter and the ratification and implementation of ASEAN agreements.

16. Regarding the APSC Community, mention may be made, amongst others, of commitments to upholding international law, respecting the principles of independence, sovereignty, territorial integrity and non-interference, building upon the existing modes of peaceful settlement of disputes, promoting the principles of democracy, instilling a culture of good governance, strengthening the rule of law, promoting and protecting human rights and embedding a culture of tolerance and peace. Significantly, human rights are to be mainstreamed across all three pillars suggesting a higher priority in future. The centrality of ASEAN is to be strengthened, as is cooperation with Dialogue Partners and external parties. Concerning the AEC, a central element is 'equitable and inclusive economic growth … that narrows the development gap'. Poverty eradication and good governance are highlighted. There also are undertakings to achieve a highly integrated and cohesive regional economy which is competitive, innovative and integrated into the global economy. The ASCC goals were reaffirmed, particularly in relation to the rights of women and children.

---

61. *See infra* Part III, Ch. 4.
62. Kuala Lumpur Declaration on ASEAN 2025: Forging Ahead Together (22 Nov. 2015).

17. The ASEAN Community Vision 2025 is the latest manifestation of the fact that ASEAN, like other international organisations, is a dynamic and constantly evolving body prepared to meet the needs and aspirations of its Member States and the challenges of the modern world.

18. What emerges from these Blueprints is that regional integration is premised primarily on economic integration which has clear timetables, as exist in other areas.[63] These, however, are not working to such rigid timetables and there appears to be considerably more flexibility, based more on enhanced cooperation than integration as such. The interesting question that arises is whether its Member States will accept a degree of supranational oversight as ASEAN pursues its agenda of greater economic and political integration, in addition to handling transnational threats more effectively. A statement issued in 2020 suggests that this may be the case. In the 2020 ASEAN Leaders' Vision Statement on a Cohesive and Responsive ASEAN, leaders acknowledge that strengthening the existing bonds of regional solidarity is necessary in order to realise an ASEAN Community that is politically cohesive, economically integrated and socially responsible.[64]

19. Accordingly, the importance of mutual trust and confidence, enhanced dialogue and cooperation in inter-state relations, and a multilateral approach in addressing emerging challenges; contributing to efforts in shaping a more effective multilateral architecture capable of tackling pressing common regional and global issues; and support for a rules-based regional and international order, anchored in international law, is stressed.[65] A particularly interesting development in this regard is the call for practical defence cooperation among ASEAN Member States and between ASEAN and its external partners.[66] It remains to be seen whether the Statement constitutes a pointer to a lasting change of direction for ASEAN in furthering a deeper and closer coordinated relationship or whether the traditional emphasis on a loose association of national sovereigns will prevail.

---

63. *See*, e.g., Master Plan on ASEAN Connectivity (MPAC) 2025, which was adopted at the 17th ASEAN Summit on 28 Oct. 2010, and relaunched in 2016, https://asean.org/wp-content/uploads/2021/08/8_compressed.pdf, to promote intra-ASEAN connectivity and connectivity between the bloc and its partners, towards a smoothly-connected ASEAN community without barriers in five strategic areas: sustainable infrastructure, digital innovation, inter-logistics, optimisation of planning, and movement of people. 'Connectivity' refers to 'the physical (e.g., transport, ICT, and energy), institutional (e.g., trade, investment, and services liberalisation), and people-to-people linkages (e.g., education, culture, and tourism), that are the foundational supportive means to achieving the economic, political-security, and socio-cultural pillars of an integrated ASEAN Community', Vientiane Declaration on the Adoption of the Master Plan on ASEAN Connectivity 2025, in Master Plan on ASEAN Connectivity 2025, Jakarta: ASEAN Secretariat, August 2016, 3, https://asean.org/storage/2016/09/Master-Plan-on-ASEAN-Connectivity-20251.pdf.
64. 2020 ASEAN Leaders' Vision Statement on a Cohesive and Responsive ASEAN: Rising Above Challenges and Sustaining Growth (26 Jun. 2020), at: https://cil.nus.edu.sg/wp-content/uploads/2020/07/2020-VS-Cohesive-ASEAN.pdf.
65. *Ibid.*, para. 5.
66. *Ibid.*, para. 8.

Part II. ASEAN

Chapter 1. The ASEAN Charter: An Overview

20. The ASEAN Charter was adopted on 20 November 2007 and entered into force on 15 December 2008.[67] It provides a legal and institutional framework that transformed the old 'soft' ASEAN into a rule-based organisation and therefore into a 'hard' institution. The ASEAN Charter provides for 'enhanced interaction' across a broad spectrum of collaborative activities in the political, security, socio-cultural, and economic fields. The emphasis has always been to promote and enhance regional integration.[68] As the organisation's constituent document, it enshrines into ASEAN norms, practices, and values, such as the very wide use of consensus, based on what is perceived to be a unique ASEAN Way.[69]

21. The Charter also imposes both legal and political or ideological obligations on its Members with a view, *inter alia*, of promoting the much cherished regional identity.[70] Some of these obligations, of a varied nature, encompassing, for example, peace and security, the economic field, human rights, social and cultural issues, are

67. ASEAN Charter (20 Nov. 2007), 2624 U.N.T.S. 223. Note that, pursuant to the Guidelines on the Use of the Name 'ASEAN', which were adopted at the Sixth Meeting of the ASEAN Coordinating Council (ACC) on 8 Apr. 2010 and agreed upon by the Permanent Representatives Committee on 19 Sep. 2013, the name 'ASEAN' is protected under Art. 6ter of the Paris Convention for the Protection of Industrial Property, adopted in 1883 and revised in Stockholm in 1967, *see* https://asean.org/about-asean/asean-name/.

68. *See* Report of the Eminent Person's Group on the ASEAN Charter, December 2006, at: https://www.asean.org/wp-content/uploads/images/archive/19247.pdf (EPG Report), para. 26; C.H. Lin, *ASEAN Charter: Deeper Regional Integration under International Law?*, 9 Chinese J. Int'l L. 821, 827–829 (2010); S.S.C. Tay, *The ASEAN Charter: Between National Sovereignty and the Region's Constitutional Moment*, 12 S.Y.B.I.L. 151, 156–158, 167 (2008).

69. Jones, 75–77. It has been queried whether the ASEAN Way is compatible with a rules-based organisation, S. Chesterman, *Asia's Ambivalence about International Law and Institutions: Past, Present and Futures*, 27 E.J.I.L. 945, 958 (2016).

70. D.A. Desierto, *Universalizing Core Human Rights in the 'New' ASEAN: A Reassessment of Culture and Development Justifications Against the Global Rejection of Impunity*, 1 Göttingen J. Int'l L. 1 (2009): 77, 287–288; Lin, 829; E.K.B. Tan, *The ASEAN Charter as 'Legs to Go Places': Ideational Norms and Pragmatic Legalism in Community Building in Southeast Asia*, 12 *S.Y.B.I.L.* 171, 177 (2008); EPG Report, paras 28, 57. The ASEAN Charter has been described as containing 'substantive (deep or shallow obligations), structural (binding or non-binding) and review (strong or weak) enforcement elements', D. Seah, *The ASEAN Charter*, 58 I.C.L.Q. 197, 201–202 (2009).

immediate; others set practical and achievable impending goals; others are aspirational social and political desiderata to be realised progressively; others are somewhat vague ambitions.[71] They reflect in part the evolution of the basic values set out in the UN Charter and later instruments and developments that assert the increasing importance of human rights in their widest sense.[72] The ASEAN Charter may be considered a framework treaty in that much of its substantive content is unenumerated, and future enactments are therefore envisaged to give full measure to its aspirations and goals. ASEAN treaties have been adopted on areas such as the settlement of disputes and trafficking in human beings, and various declarations with regard to the protection of the rights and the position of vulnerable groups, including women, children, migrant workers.[73]

22. The ASEAN Charter cannot be labelled an innovative document,[74] at least if compared with the EU's Lisbon Treaty[75] or with the Constitutive Act of the African Union (AU)[76] and the groundbreaking provisions that they contain. The ASEAN Charter is a multifaceted mix of traditional and contemporary values.[77] Despite some non-state, or people-orientated, and progressive neo-Kantian features inspired by the Vienna Declaration on Human Rights,[78] the UN Millennium Declaration and the World Summit Outcome,[79] in other respects, it reads like a typical product of a conservative grouping of states, resistant to legal and institutional developments, united by a common belief in adhering to classical positivist, voluntarist, doctrines of international law. It has been described as a state-centric, sovereignty-based conception of international law, which has institutionalised pre-existing flaws.[80] It adheres to fundamental tenets that may sometimes be difficult to reconcile with the

71. The view has been expressed that the ASEAN Charter commitments to human rights are so generalised that they should be considered merely declaratory, Y. Ginbar, *Human Rights in ASEAN – Setting Sail or Treading Water*, 10 HRLR 504, 512 (2010).
72. *See* Millennium Declaration, UN General Assembly Res. 55/2 (2000).
73. A. Duxbury & T. Hsein-Li, *Can ASEAN Take Human Rights Seriously?* 141–145 (Cambridge U. Press 2019).
74. Tan, 'Legs to Go Places', *supra*.
75. *See* Consolidated Version of the Treaty on European Union and the Treaty on the Functioning of the European Union (13 Dec. 2007) Official Journal of the European Union, C 32, 26.10.2012, p. 47. (TEU and TFEU).
76. Constitutive Act of the African Union (11 Jul. 2000) 2158 U.N.T.S. 3.
77. Tay, 154–158.
78. Vienna Declaration and Programme of Action, adopted by the World Conference on Human Rights 1993, I.L.M. 32 (1993), 1661.
79. World Summit Outcome, UN General Assembly Res. 60/1 (2005).
80. L. Leviter, *The ASEAN Charter: ASEAN Failure or Member Failure?*, 43 N.Y.U. J. I. L. & Pol. 159, 199 (2010). *See* S. Tan, *Not Quite Beyond the 'ASEAN Way': Southeast Asia's Evolution to Rules-Based Management of Intra-ASEAN Differences*, in *ASEAN@50: Retrospectives and Perspectives on the Making, Substance, Significance and Future of ASEAN. Volume 4. Building ASEAN Community: Political-Security and Socio-cultural Reflections* 67, 72–73 (A. Baviera & L. Maramis eds, Economic Research Institute for ASEAN and East Asia 2017). The ASEAN Charter's emphasis on sovereignty has also been highlighted by Seah, 202.

more progressive principles that have evolved in post-Second World War international law involving to some degree the fettering of state sovereignty based on submission to an international rule of law.[81]

23. A putative tension exists between the principle of non-interference in the internal affairs of Member States and those of strengthening democracy and promoting human rights for instance.[82] Asian states, in reaction to their historical experiences with colonialism and engaged in state-building that has sometimes been painful, are warily protective of their sovereignty.[83] In fact, all Member States, with the exception of Thailand, experienced foreign rule and became independent countries only in the post-Second World War period, in fact Brunei gained independence as late as 1984. The ASEAN Charter can thus be likened to a degree to the voided Charter of the Organisation of African Unity.[84] For several years now, a growing disconnect can be evidenced between the very high ideals enshrined in the ASEAN Charter and the realities prevailing in some Member States, especially in the vital areas of human rights and democratic governance.[85] This state of affairs is arguably a source of discontent among the membership, exacerbated by events and developments in ASEAN's vicinity. Regional international organisations, especially those pursuing an agenda of integration, such as ASEAN, should always maintain a high level of sincere cooperation. Disagreements, disputes and the like not only stall the process towards political, economic, etc., integration but could also, if not promptly resolved, reverse the gains achieved. In a global community where regions are in constant competition with each other, ASEAN, being close to powerful states, might not have an opportunity to recover if it were to regress.

24. To that extent, operating by consensus may prove a handicap to its rapid progress. As is very often the case with the constitutive instruments of international organisations, the ASEAN Charter was the product of a compromise between different stakeholders, with the democracies often at odds with the autocracies,[86] and

---

81. A. Cassese, *International Law* 46–68 (Oxford U. Press 2nd ed. 2005). *See Corfu Channel Case (UK v. Albania)*, Merits, I.C.J. Reports 1949, Separate Opinion of Judge Alvarez, 43. A previous UN Secretary-General, Boutros Boutros-Ghali, was moved to comment that the era of absolute sovereignty was over, *Report of the Secretary-General on an Agenda for Peace – Preventative* Diplomacy, Peacemaking and Peacekeeping, 31 I.L.M. (1992): 953, para. 17. *See also* J. H. Jackson, *Sovereignty-Modern: A New Approach to an Outdated Concept*, 97 A.J.I.L. 782, 786–789 (2003).
82. Cassese, 59–60; P. Malanczuk, *Akehurst's Modern Introduction to International Law* 58 (Routledge 7th rev. ed. 1997); Tan, 'Legs to Go Places', 182–185; Tay, 167–168.
83. Seah, 199–200; Tay, 167; Duxbury & Hsein-Li, 66–94.
84. Charter of the Organisation of African Unity (13 Sep. 1963), 479 U.N.T.S. 39. OAU was dissolved in 2001 and replaced by the AU. Some have expressed disappointment at the final version of the ASEAN Charter, M. Caballero-Anthony, *The ASEAN Charter: An Opportunity Missed or One That Cannot Be Missed?*, 27 Southeast Asian Aff. 71, 79–80 (2008).
85. G. Clarke, *The Evolving ASEAN Human Rights System: The ASEAN Human Rights Declaration of 2012*, 11 Northwestern J. Int'l Human Rights 1, 6–9 (2012).
86. *Ibid.*, 7–8, 11–12. The degree to which these values have become rooted in the region has been questioned, V. Muntarbhorn, *Enlarging the Space for the People: Whither Human Rights and Governance in ASEAN*, in *ASEAN@50: Retrospectives and Perspectives on the Making, Substance,*

some of the more radical proposals did not feature in the final document.[87] Disappointment has been expressed because the ASEAN Charter institutionalises the power exercised by the Member States which remain 'masters of the treaty'.[88] It evinces a reluctance to delegate any important sovereign powers to the organisation. But this was always going to be the case while ASEAN remains an intergovernmental, as opposed to a supranational, organisation.

25. However, grounds exist for a more optimistic evaluation. Positive consideration must be given to its incorporation of rules and peoples-based features as a counterweight to its statist aspects.[89] This appears to constitute an acknowledgement that states have a role in securing the needs of individuals who are no longer mere objects of international law.[90] Particularly important in this regard is the Member States' commitment to democratisation, based on respect for human rights, the rule of law and other associated liberal values, and the commitment to economic integration based on a market-driven economy.[91] In this it shares features with the AU Constitutive Act, although eschewing its more radical aspects.[92] But what is particularly interesting about the AU is that it has developed the practical capacity to put these principles into operation, and, as has been argued, an AU legal system has been in the making.[93] Grandiloquent gestures and rhetoric no longer suffice. However, it may have to be accepted that the ASEAN Charter articulates the limits of achievability, bringing together a disparate group of states with very diverse experiences, with differing philosophies and political and legal systems, at different stages of economic and social development.[94]

26. In other words, the ASEAN Charter, as it now stands, has inherent restrictions as to what could be achieved, and this is rather evident by looking at its current stage of progress. On the other hand, membership of ASEAN does *ipso facto* entail compromises, including an abandonment of the notion of absolute sovereignty, which is incompatible with the idea of integration in regional international

---

Significance and Future of ASEAN. Volume 4. Building ASEAN Community: Political-Security and Socio-cultural Reflections 208 (A. Baviera & L. Maramis eds, Economic Research Institute for ASEAN and East Asia 2017).

87. Caballero-Anthony, 74–75; Tan, 'Legs to Go Places', 176–177. The radical proposals not adopted include the ultimate realisation of an ASEAN Union, rejection of unconstitutional and undemocratic changes of government, self-determination, mutual assistance in time of natural disasters, and suspension of membership, EPG Report, paras 23, 31, 60, 61.
88. J.D. Bagulaya, *ASEAN as* Wayang Kulit*: A Critique of the Constitutional, Extra-constitutional, and Practical Fetters of ASEAN*, 9 Asian J. Int'l L. 175 (2019).
89. EPG Report, paras 9, 58; Tay, 168–169. *See also* Cassese, 331.
90. Thus, the individual is considered the 'direct beneficiary of international human rights law and, to that extent, a subject of international law', T. Buergenthal, *International Human Rights in an Historical Perspective*, in *Human Rights: Concept and Standards* 3, 12 (J. Symonides ed. UNESCO/Ashgate 2000).
91. Desierto, 288.
92. K.D. Magliveras & G.J. Naldi, *The African Union (AU)* 139 et seq. (3rd ed. Kluwer Law International 2024).
93. Generally, *see The Emergent African Union Law - Conceptualization, Delimitation, and Application* (O. Amao, M. Olivier & K. Magliveras eds, Oxford University Press 2021).
94. Tan, 'Legs to Go Places', 194–197.

organisations. To work for progress rather than resign itself to stagnation, ASEAN and its Member States must show the necessary political willingness to act in unison and, more importantly, to understand that the welfare of their population depends almost entirely upon them. To expect or to hope that third states or group of states will secure them a better and brighter future is no doubt a fallacy.

27. The ASEAN Charter consists of a preamble, an operative section of fifty-five articles and four annexes, setting forth a series of objectives.[95] Member States are under an unequivocal obligation to uphold the rights and duties contained therein and other obligations of membership, thereby extending its scope to future laws, by adopting legislative or other measures to give effect to them.[96] As is explained in detail later, other Southeast Asian states may apply for membership subject to satisfying a number of criteria.[97] The ASEAN Charter prevails over inconsistent pre-existing ASEAN laws which otherwise continue to bind the whole membership.[98] Provision is made for its amendment at the instigation of a single Member State.[99] Given that the ASEAN Charter does not address the issue of reservations, in accordance with the rules of general international law, Member States may enter reservations on condition that they are accepted by the competent organ, that being the ASEAN Summit.[100]

28. Neither does the ASEAN Charter provide for suspension, expulsion, denunciation or withdrawal. These issues are examined later in this monograph. Suffice to mention here that, where a treaty makes no specific provision for denunciation, the general rule is that the treaty is not subject to denunciation unless: (a) it is established that the parties intended to allow the possibility of denunciation, or (b) a right to do so is implied from the nature of the treaty.[101] Absent these conditions, the presumption is that the treaty cannot be denounced.[102] As regards specifically the withdrawal of Member States from an international organisation, the constitution of which is silent on the matter, the argument has been advanced, based principally on notions of state sovereignty, that a right of withdrawal is either inherent in the constitutive instrument/founding treaty or it should be implied.[103]

29. This latter submission should perhaps be qualified by saying that the multilateral agreements that create international organisations may very well differ from ordinary treaties, which address and regulate a specific issue or matter or situation.

---

95. ASEAN Charter Arts 1–2.
96. ASEAN Charter Art. 5(2).
97. ASEAN Charter Art. 6(2).
98. ASEAN Charter Art. 52. *See* EPG Report, paras 57–60; Desierto, 287.
99. ASEAN Charter Art. 48.
100. Vienna Convention on the Law of Treaties Art. 20(3) (22 May 1969), 1155 U.N.T.S. 331 (VCLT).
101. VCLT Art. 56(1); I. Sinclair, *The Vienna Convention on the Law of Treaties* 186–188 (Manchester U. Press 2nd ed. 1984).
102. I. Brownlie, *Principles of Public International Law* 621 (Oxford U. Press 7th ed. 2008).
103. German Federal Constitutional Court (Bundesverfasssungsgericht), *Brunner and Others v. European Union Treaty* [1994] 1 C.M.L.R 57 (also known as 'German Maastricht Case'). *See* G. Naldi & K. Magliveras, *The Right to Revoke Withdrawal Notices from International Organisations: The Case of Brexit and the European Union*, 28 Maastricht J. Eur. & Comp. L. 30 (2021).

Therefore, a right of withdrawal may not exist if clearly the drafters had not intended it. Even though, to the best of one's knowledge, until today this question has not arisen in ASEAN, in view of the 'sovereignty-based conception' of international law, which is fiercely adhered to in Asia, it seems safe to conclude that a right of withdrawal is presumed. Finally, it should not escape one's attention that states only seldom withdraw from international organisations and even more seldom they are expelled from them. It follows that the practice of international organisations in relation to withdrawing and being expelled is very limited.

30. As the ASEAN institutional structure is discussed more fully below, only a brief summary is provided here. ASEAN operates through several organs,[104] the principal ones being the ASEAN Summit, composed of the Heads of State and Government,[105] the ASEAN Coordinating Council (ACC) composed of the Foreign Ministers,[106] and the Secretary-General / Secretariat.[107] It is clear that, despite its stated integrationist goals, ASEAN operates at an intergovernmental level. Its existing organs do not currently possess supranational powers.[108] It cannot be compared to the EU or even to the AU in this regard.[109]

31. The Summit, which meets twice yearly,[110] is the supreme policy-making body of the Organisation.[111] It is a deliberative body that provides policy guidance and adopts decisions on attaining ASEAN's objectives, on important matters of common interest, and on issues referred to it by other bodies.[112] In addition to exercising administrative authority, the view has been expressed that the Summit thus has executive and legislative functions.[113] It is also the body with responsibility for dealing with emergency situations.[114] Potentially the Summit could assume considerable powers in this context.[115] The Summit appoints the Secretary-General.[116]

---

104. ASEAN Charter, Ch. IV. *See* generally M. Ewing-Chow & L. Bernard, *The ASEAN Charter: The Legalization of ASEAN?*, in *Global Administrative Law: The Casebook* 115, 119–120 (S. Cassese et al. eds, Institute for International Law and Justice 2012); Seah, 202–203; Tan, 'Legs to Go Places', 179–182.
105. ASEAN Charter Art. 7(1).
106. ASEAN Charter Art. 8.
107. ASEAN Charter Art. 11. *See* Tay, 159–160. The Secretariat is based in the Indonesian capital, Jakarta.
108. Lin, 829–832.
109. Case No 6/64 *Costa v. ENEL* [1964] E.C.R. 585, 593; AU Constitutive Act Art. 3(c), (j).
110. ASEAN Charter Art. 7(3)(a). It should be noted that ASEAN's working language is English, ASEAN Charter Art. 34.
111. ASEAN Charter Art. 7(2)(a).
112. ASEAN Charter Art. 7(2)(b).
113. Desierto, 288, 290; Caballero-Anthony, 78.
114. ASEAN Charter Art. 7(2)(d).
115. Desierto, 289–290. Such powers are not unlimited but must be in conformity with the principle of attribution, *see Jurisdiction of the European Commission of the Danube between Galatz and Braila*, Advisory Opinion, PCIJ (ser. B.) No 14, 1927, 64; J. Klabbers, *An Introduction to International Institutional Law* 55–59 (Cambridge U. Press 2nd ed. 2009).
116. ASEAN Charter Art. 11(1).

32. The main responsibilities of the ACC, which also meets twice a year,[117] include preparing the meetings of the ASEAN Summit,[118] coordinating the implementation of agreements and decisions of the ASEAN Summit,[119] and considering the annual report of the Secretary-General on ASEAN's work.[120] It may also be called upon to undertake other tasks or functions by the Summit.[121]

33. The principal responsibility of the Secretary-General, who is ASEAN's Chief Administrative Officer,[122] is to facilitate and monitor progress in the implementation of ASEAN agreements and decisions and submit an annual report on ASEAN's work to the ASEAN Summit.[123] The Secretary-General presents the views of ASEAN and participates in meetings with external parties.[124] The Secretary-General, who must be a national of a Member State, serves a non-renewable term of five years.[125] In a progressive move, consideration must also be given to gender equality in the appointment; so far, there has been no female holding the office.[126] The Secretary-General must remain independent from any government or external party,[127] and Member States must refrain from influencing him/her.[128]

34. The routine work of ASEAN activities is coordinated by the Committee of Permanent Representatives, composed of Permanent Representatives appointed by the Member States with the rank of Ambassador.[129]

35. Interestingly, the ASEAN Charter makes provision for a human rights body but without further elaboration.[130] The ASEAN Intergovernmental Commission on Human Rights (AICHR) was duly founded in October 2009 essentially as a promotional body and is discussed fully below.

36. ASEAN is led by a Chairman, which position rotates annually among the Member State, based on the alphabetical order of the Member States' English names.[131] The Chairman chairs the Summit, the Coordinating Council and other organs.[132] The Chairman's main duties are to promote and enhance the interests and

---

117. ASEAN Charter Art. 8(1).
118. ASEAN Charter Art. 8(2)(a).
119. ASEAN Charter Art. 8(2)(b).
120. ASEAN Charter Art. 8(2)(e).
121. ASEAN Charter Art. 8(2)(h).
122. ASEAN Charter Art. 11(3). It has been suggested that the Secretary-General has limited independence, S. Chesterman, *Asia's Ambivalence About International Law and Institutions: Past, Present and Futures*, 27 E.J.I.L. 945, 958–959 (2016).
123. ASEAN Charter Art. 11(2)(b).
124. ASEAN Charter Art. 11(2)(d).
125. ASEAN Charter Art. 11(1).
126. *Ibid.*
127. ASEAN Charter Art. 11(8)(b).
128. ASEAN Charter Art. 11(9).
129. ASEAN Charter Art. 12.
130. ASEAN Charter Art. 14.
131. ASEAN Charter Art. 31(1).
132. ASEAN Charter Art. 31(2).

well-being of ASEAN, including efforts to build an ASEAN Community through policy initiatives, coordination, consensus and cooperation; to ensure the centrality of ASEAN; to ensure effective and timely responses to urgent issues or crises affecting ASEAN, including providing its good offices and similar arrangements to address immediately these concerns; and to represent ASEAN in strengthening and promoting closer relations with external partners.[133]

37. In relation to decision-making, the general rule is one based on consultation and consensus, reflecting the ASEAN Way, which seeks to avoid confrontation.[134] The possibility of disagreement is acknowledged; however, and consequently, where consensus is not possible, the fall-back position is that the Summit can decide how a decision is to be arrived at,[135] which may well result only in further talks.[136] However, voting does not appear to be ruled out, especially in non-controversial areas.[137] Operating by consensus may be viewed as a recipe for inertia, but the disparate political and socio-economic composition of the Member States can render progress difficult in any case.[138] The important point has been made however, that consensus should not be confused with unanimity; that in allowing states to reach general agreement with no state being singled out and embarrassed as a dissenter is culturally sensitive and thus an appropriate way of proceeding.[139] And majority voting is not necessarily a panacea.[140] As the example of the EU demonstrates, states that have been outvoted may resort to litigation in an attempt to derail the policy adopted.[141] ASEAN policy on this issue is thus considered to have its advantages, particularly as it allows for flexibility.[142]

38. The ASEAN Charter may be interpreted by the ASEAN Secretariat at the request of a Member State.[143] It must be interpreted 'in good faith in accordance with the ordinary meaning to be given to the terms of the Charter in their context and in the light of its object and purpose'.[144] Such interpretation is 'non-binding and non-authoritative'.[145] This role appears to be limited to providing an element of clarification, considering that any *dispute* regarding its interpretation must be settled

133. ASEAN Charter Art. 32.
134. ASEAN Charter Art. 20(1). *See* Duxbury & Hsein-Li, 132–137.
135. ASEAN Charter Art. 20(2).
136. Leviter, 199.
137. EPG Report, *ibid*; Seah, *ibid*.
138. Leviter, 161–162.
139. Tan, 'Legs to Go Places', 189.
140. Tay, 97.
141. *See* generally H. Cullen & A. Charlesworth, *Diplomacy by Other Means: The Use of Legal Basis Litigation as a Political Strategy by the European Parliament and Member States*, 36 Common Mkt. L. Rev. 1423 (1999).
142. Tay, 160.
143. ASEAN Charter Art. 51(1).
144. *See* Rules of Procedure for the Interpretation of the ASEAN Charter, Rule 2(2) (2 Apr. 2012), at: https://asean.org/wp-content/uploads/images/archive/documents/ROP%20for%20Interpretation%20of%20ASEAN%20Charter.pdf. Cf. VCLT Art. 31(1).
145. Rules of Procedure, *ibid*., Rule 2(1). Generally, *see* P. Sookhakich and N. Limsiritong, *Power of ASEAN Secretariat to Interpret the ASEAN Charter*, 58(2) Psychology and Education 1940–1946 (2021).

in accordance with the dispute settlement procedures referred to in Chapter VIII, including good offices, conciliation, mediation and arbitration.[146]

39. An omission from the ASEAN Charter's organisational structure might be that of an assembly representing the peoples of ASEAN, which could take different forms and shapes, e.g., the European Parliament of the EU, the Pan-African Parliament of the AU, the Parliamentary Assembly of the Council of Europe, the Nordic Council of the inter-parliamentary cooperation among the Scandinavian countries, etc. This lack seems to contradict the 'people-orientated' ASEAN. Should ASEAN Member States fear vesting such a parliamentary body with legislative powers, there is no impediment in conferring upon it advisory or consultative ones only[147] and gradually extending its mandate.[148] Finally, although not a formal part of ASEAN, ASEAN does maintain an association with the ASEAN Inter-Parliamentary Assembly (AIPA) which assists in realising ASEAN's goals through inter-parliamentary cooperation.[149]

40. A more conspicuous omission is that of a permanent court of justice. The philosophy of the ASEAN Way may have played a significant part in this. It has been suggested that committing to an ASEAN court would have been premature, especially because the rule of law had yet to become firmly established in some Member States.[150] The associated lack of judicial independence is another factor, while the costs associated with maintaining a permanent court should not be overlooked either.[151] The opportunity to found a standing court was again missed in 2010 with the addition of the Protocol to the ASEAN Charter on Dispute Settlement Mechanisms, which is discussed *infra.*[152] The Protocol, which is applicable to inter-state disputes only, puts in place a formal system to help ASEAN Member States resolve disputes concerning the interpretation or application of the ASEAN Charter. It provides formal techniques for dispute resolution that include good offices, mediation and arbitration. But as ASEAN pursues its goals of greater political and security cooperation and the creation of a single market with a 'free flow of goods, services and investment'[153] the need for a court will surely become apparent. A court with jurisdiction comparable to that of the Court of Justice of the European Union (CJEU) will likely prove necessary. As is the experience with the AU,

146. ASEAN Charter Arts 51(2), 23(1), 25.
147. Cf. Protocol to the Treaty establishing the Establishing the African Economic Community Relating to the Pan-African Parliament (2 Mar. 2001) Art. 11.
148. Cf. Protocol to the Constitutive Act of the African Union relating to the Pan-African Parliament (27 Jun. 2014, not yet in force), at: https://au.int/en/treaties/protocol-constitutive-act-african-union-relating-pan-african-parliament.
149. ASEAN Charter Annex 2.I. According to the Statutes of the ASEAN Inter-Parliamentary Assembly (8th ed., October 2024, at: https://aipasecretariat.org/pages/statutes/), AIPA is the precursor to the ASEAN Inter-Parliamentary Organisation, whose Statutes were signed on 2 Sep. 1977.
150. W. Woon, *Dispute Settlement in ASEAN*, 1 Korean J. Int'l L. 92, 94 (2013).
151. *Ibid.*
152. Protocol to the ASEAN Charter on Dispute Settlement Mechanisms (8 Apr. 2010), https://cil.nus.edu.sg/databasecil/2010-protocol-to-the-asean-charter-on-dispute-settlement-mechanisms/.
153. ASEAN Charter Art. 1(5).

provision could have been made in the ASEAN Charter for a regional court of justice even if it was to be established at some future date.[154] Of course, there is nothing to prevent Member States from adopting an additional protocol in future setting up a court.[155]

41. The preamble to the ASEAN Charter sets out the fundamental ethos of the Organisation and its Member States. Of critical importance is the pledge to enhanced cooperation and integration through building 'an ASEAN Community that is politically cohesive, economically integrated and socially responsible in order to effectively respond to current and future challenges and opportunities'.[156] There are associated commitments to peace, security and stability, sustained economic growth, shared prosperity and social progress, sustainable development.[157] Also noteworthy are adherence to the principles of democracy, the rule of law and good governance, and the protection of human rights and fundamental freedoms, and a people-oriented approach, references to which are made in various other places in this monograph.[158]

42. Significantly, these ideals have not remained at an abstract level but have been enshrined in the operative sections of the Charter. The fundamental values of the Organisation and Member States, its aims, purposes and governing principles, are listed in Articles 1–2 covering its dedicated spheres of activities.[159] Most of the principles constitute an updated version of those enshrined in Article 2 of the UN Charter but with a regional twist to make it more appropriate and relevant. In fact, ASEAN comes within the scope of a regional arrangement or agency relating to international peace and security under Chapter VIII of the UN Charter.[160] Thus, in February 2011 the United Nations Security Council (UNSC) called upon ASEAN to facilitate a resolution to the outbreak of hostilities between Cambodia and Thailand over their disputed border, which led to both countries agreeing to a team of Indonesian observers to monitor the area.[161] The strengthening of 'peace-oriented values' in the region is accomplished by the explicit commitment to the peaceful

---

154. *See* AU Constitutive Act Art. 18; Protocol of the Court of Justice of the African Union (1 Jul. 2001, entered in force 11 Feb. 2009); K. Magliveras & G. Naldi, *The African Court of Justice*, 66 Zeitschrift fuer auslaendisches oeffentiches Recht und Voelkerrecht 187–213 (2006).
155. ASEAN Charter Art. 48 provides for amendments.
156. ASEAN Charter preambular para. 10.
157. ASEAN Charter preambular para. 6.
158. ASEAN Charter preambular paras 7–8.
159. Tay, 156–158.
160. UN Charter Art. 52(1); Memorandum of Understanding Between the Association of Southeast Asian Nations (ASEAN) and the United Nations (UN) on ASEAN-UN Cooperation, Preamble, para. 6 (27 Sep. 2007), https://cil.nus.edu.sg/databasecil/2007-memorandum-of-understanding-between-the-association-of-southeast-asian-nations-and-the-united-nations-on-asean-un-cooperation/. *See* further, ASEAN Secretariat's Information Paper, 'Overview of ASEAN-United Nations Relations', February 2025, at:https://asean.org/wp-content/uploads/2025/02/Overview-ASEAN-UN-Cooperation-as-of-13-February-2025.pdf.
161. UNSC, Press Statement on Cambodia-Thailand Border Situation, UN Press Release SC/10174, 14 Feb. 2011, at: https://press.un.org/en/2011/sc10174.doc.htm). As is explained *infra*, in 2011 a Comprehensive Partnership between ASEAN and the UN was concluded; since then, it has become an important component of the latter's dealings with other regional international organisations.

settlement of disputes between states.[162] Other vital rules include respect for the independence, sovereignty, equality, territorial integrity and national identity of Member States;[163] non-interference in their internal affairs;[164] and abstention from any activity or policy, including the use of its territory, which threatens the sovereignty, territorial integrity or political or economic stability of Member States.[165] These provisions encompass basic tenets of international law referring to the legal equality of states and that of domestic jurisdiction reflected in Article 2(1) and (7) of the UN Charter.[166] In keeping with peremptory rules of international law, aggression and the threat or use of force are renounced.[167]

43. The peaceful settlement of disputes is a principal concern.[168] The latter commitment is supplemented by Chapter VIII of the ASEAN Charter on the Settlement of Disputes which complements existing arrangements.[169] The ASEAN Charter does not entail a commitment to the compulsory settlement of disputes but Member States 'endeavour to resolve peacefully all disputes in a timely manner through dialogue, consultation and negotiation'.[170] The observation has been made that the ASEAN is more concerned with managing disputes rather than resolving them.[171] Various dispute settlement procedures are envisaged in the Charter, including good offices, conciliation and mediation.[172] Disputes concerning specific ASEAN instruments are to be settled in accordance with the system prescribed therein.[173] Disputes which are not concerned with the interpretation or application of any ASEAN instrument are to be resolved according to the Treaty of Amity and Cooperation in

162. ASEAN Charter Arts 1(1), 2(2)(d).
163. ASEAN Charter Art. 2(2)(a).
164. ASEAN Charter Art. 2(2)(e). *See also* ASEAN Charter Art. 2(2)(f) on the right of Member States to exist free from external interference, subversion, and coercion.
165. ASEAN Charter Art. 2 (2)(k). *See also Corfu Channel Case (UK v. Albania)*, Merits, I.C.J. Reports 1949, 4, 35.
166. *See also* Declaration on Friendly Relations and Co-operation among States in Accordance with the Charter of the United Nations, UN General Assembly Res. 2625 (XXV) (1970); Declaration on the Inadmissibility of Intervention in the Internal Affairs of States and the Protection of their Independence and Sovereignty, UN General Assembly Res. 2131 (XX) (1965). These principles have been described as the '*overriding legal standards* that may be regarded as the *constitutional principles* of the international community', Cassese, 48.
167. ASEAN Charter Art. 2(2)(c). *See also* UN Charter Art. 2(4); Declaration on Friendly Relations and Co-operation among States.
168. ASEAN Charter Art. 2(2)(d). *See also* UN Charter Art. 2(3); Manila Declaration on the Peaceful Settlement of Disputes, UN General Assembly Res. 37/10 (1982).
169. Woon, 99.
170. ASEAN Charter Art. 22(1).
171. S. Tan, *Not Quite Beyond the 'ASEAN Way': Southeast Asia's Evolution to Rules-Based Management of Intra-ASEAN Differences*', in *ASEAN@50: Retrospectives and Perspectives on the Making, Substance, Significance and Future of ASEAN. Volume 4. Building ASEAN Community: Political-Security and Socio-cultural Reflections* 67, 71 (A. Baviera & L. Maramis eds, Economic Research Institute for ASEAN and East Asia 2017).
172. ASEAN Charter Art. 23. *See also* ASEAN 2025: Forging Ahead Together: ASEAN Political-Security Community Blueprint 2025, s. II.B.4.3.
173. ASEAN Charter Art. 24(1).

which has consequently declared that democracy fosters the full realisation of human rights.[197] ASEAN itself has recognised this association.[198]

48. These express commitments are especially desirable and reflect similar developments elsewhere.[199] But it does beg the question as to the Member States' interpretation of the principles of democracy which may not correspond to those of Western liberal democracies.[200] To alight on just one example, is the principle of popular sovereignty considered fundamental in the AREAN region and to which extent are constitutional rights protected?[201] While ASEAN apparently has the authority to advance the process of democratisation,[202] examples like the recent elections in Myanmar[203] suggest that it would not accept a right to further democracy by coercive means.[204] Rather ASEAN's culture indicates a reliance on quiet

---

197. *Ibid.,* para. 8.
198. *See* EPG Report, para. 55.
199. *See* Vienna Declaration Part I, para. 8; UN Millennium Declaration paras 24–25; World Summit Outcome paras 11–12. It has been argued that the Vienna Declaration laid the foundations for a democratic global public order, Buergenthal, 18. *See also* TEU Art. 2; AU Constitutive Act Art. 3(g); Protocol of Amendments to the Charter of the Organization of American States (14 Dec. 1992, Protocol of Washington). The members of the Commonwealth, which includes three ASEAN countries (Brunei, Malaysia and Singapore) have reaffirmed their commitment to the core principles of democracy, human rights, the rule of law and good governance amongst others, Charter of the Commonwealth (14 Dec. 2012), https://thecommonwealth.org/sites/default/files/page/documents/CharteroftheCommonwealth.pdf. The view has been expressed that a legal entitlement to democratic rule exists; T.M. Franck, *The Emerging Right to Democratic Governance*, 86 A.J.I.L. 46 (19 92), while absence of democracy in a state constitutes a violation of human rights, Beurgenthal, 55.
200. Seah, 206; Cassese, 395; Y. Khushalani, *Human Rights in Asia and Africa*, 4 H.R.L.J. 403, 405–413 (1983). For a Western viewpoint on the constituent elements of democracy, *see* United Kingdom Foreign and Commonwealth Office (FCO), *Human Rights and Democracy Report 2015*, 5 (all FCO on human rights are available at: https://www.gov.uk/government/collections/human-rights-and-democracy-reports); A. Conte & R. Burchill, *Defining Civil and Political Rights: The Jurisprudence of the United Nations Human Rights Committee* 97–108 (Ashgate 2nd ed. 2009); S. Wheatley, *Democracy in International Law: A European Perspective*, 51 I.C.L.Q. 225 (2002).
201. *See* A. Duxbury & T. Hsein-Li, *Can ASEAN Take Human Rights Seriously?* 216–231 (Cambridge U. Press 2019). This review shows up a pronounce variation between ASEAN Member States.
202. It is argued that a human right to democracy entitles the international community to involve itself with efforts towards democratisation, Buergenthal, 18.
203. By-elections held in Myanmar in 2012 were unofficially monitored by international observers, including from ASEAN, *see* FCO, *Human Rights and Democracy Report 2012,* 131. In 2015, parliamentary elections held in Myanmar, considered to be credible, were also monitored by international observers, *see* FCO, *Human Rights and Democracy Report 2015*, 36–37. But after the November 2020 general election, Myanmar's military staged a coup d'état, seized power, detained senior political leader, and declared a state of emergency, *see* N. Walker, *Myanmar: 2020 parliamentary election* (House of Commons Library, Briefing Paper CBP 9127, 4 Feb. 2021). Independent observers have rejected claims of voter fraud in the 2020 elections, *see* BBC News, *Myanmar election: No evidence fraud in 2020 vote, observers say*, 17 May 2021, https://www.bbc.com/news/world-asia-57144397. The promised for August 2023 general election was postponed by the military regime in power; it cited ongoing violence as reason and justification for extending the state of emergency.
204. The ASEAN Charter lacks an innovative provision such as AU Constitutive Act Art. 4(h), which authorises the AU to intervene in a Member State where atrocities are being perpetrated. There is little prospect of ASEAN following the exceptional precedents of Haiti and Sierra Leone, where the UNSC authorised the use of force to restore democratic rule, *see* UNSC Res. 940 (1994) and Res. 1132 (1997). The former action has been viewed as legitimising an international principle to

suasion. However, democratic values can only be enhanced if ASEAN takes its pertinent pledges seriously. However, given the autocratic nature of most of the regimes in power, lacking popular support or a genuine democratic mandate, this is a large undertaking that ASEAN has so far been unwilling to pursue.

49. For example, Laos and Vietnam are one-party States,[205] while Brunei is an absolute monarchy; the monarch is also vested with the supreme executive authority.[206] In Singapore the same party (People's Action Party) has held national power since independence.[207] Thailand, while a constitutional monarchy, is prone to military coups, 22 since its establishment in 1932, the latest in 2014.[208] Cosmetic commitments to the trappings of democracy, by staging elections which are neither free nor fair do not suffice. Although it has been suggested that one-party systems are compatible with the principles of democracy and can be protective of human rights,[209] this clearly cannot be construed as a rule but has to be verified on a case to case basis.

50. Moreover, a fundamental principle of democracy is that of popular sovereignty; that governments should be based on the consent, and be representative, of the people, who must be free to exercise their democratic rights through participatory politics.[210] As the European Court of Human Rights has stated, 'there can be

---

democracy, F.R. Tesón, *Collective Humanitarian Intervention*, 17 Mich. J. Int'l L. 323, 642 (1996). While, in the past the legality of the use of force to impose or restore democracy has been questioned, ICJ, *Military and Paramilitary Activities in and Against Nicaragua* (*Nicaragua v. United States of America)*, Merits, I.C.J. Reports 1986, 14, 89; O. Schacter, *The Legality of Pro-Democratic Invasion*, 17 A.J.I.L. 645 (1996), one might detect a change of opinion at least in some quarters of the international community, e.g., the Economic Community of West African States (ECOWAS) has on two occasions (the first concerned The Gambia in 2016, the second Niger in August 2023) declared its readiness to use force as a last resort to reinstate democratic normalcy, M. Ronceray, *Can ECOWAS still defend democracy in West Africa after the Niger coup?*, ECDPM Commentary, 11 Sep. 2023, at: https://ecdpm.org/work/can-ecowas-still-defend-democracy-west-africa-after-niger-coup

205. U.S. State Department, Bureau of Democracy, Human Rights, and Labor, *2023 Country Reports on Human Rights Practices*, issued on 22 Apr. 2024, at: https://www.state.gov/reports/2023-country-reports-on-human-rights-practices/; CFO, *Human Rights & Democracy: The 2022 Foreign, Commonwealth & Development Office Report*, issued in July 2023; Freedom House, *Freedom in the World 2024: Laos*, at: https://freedomhouse.org/country/laos/freedom-world/2024; Freedom House, *Freedom in the World 2024: Vietnam*, at: https://freedomhouse.org/country/vietnam/freedom-world/2024.'
206. *See* Brunei Darussalam Constitution of 1959, as revised in 2006, at: https://www.constituteproject.org/constitution/Brunei_2006.
207. U.S. State Department, *2023 Country Reports on Human Rights Practices*, op. cit.; Freedom House, *Freedom in the World 2024: Singapore*, at: https://freedomhouse.org/country/singapore; J. Kurlantzick, *Singapore's Social Contract Is Starting to Fray* (World Politics Review, Briefing, 17 Aug. 2023), at: https://www.worldpoliticsreview.com/singapore-pap-corruption-politics-democracy-lee-hsien-loong/.
208. *See* FCO, *Human Rights and Democracy: The 2014 Foreign & Commonwealth Office Report*, 31.
209. Khushalani, 418–421.
210. UN Secretariat, 'General Comment 25 (the right to participate in public affairs, voting rights and the right of equal access to public service)', adopted by the Human Rights Committee on Civil and Political Rights' in 'Compilation of General Comments and General Recommendations adopted by Human Rights Treaty Bodies', U.N. Doc. HRI/GEN/1/Rev.9 (Vol. 1) (2008).

no democracy without pluralism'; political parties play an essential role in securing the proper functioning of democracy.[211] In order to acquire legitimacy, genuine democratisation must therefore take place.[212] A willingness to embrace the values of democracy must exist and a culture of constitutionalism, pluralism and participatory party politics must be nurtured;[213] a free media must be allowed;[214] civil society must be allocated a role;[215] corruption must be eliminated;[216] the rule of law must be respected.[217]

51. The reaction in the region to the coup in Thailand in 2014 was depressingly predictable; ASEAN remained silent while Myanmar and Vietnam endorsed it.[218] This muted response by ASEAN, the lack of external pressure to restore democracy, is another example of how shallow ASEAN's commitment to democracy may be.[219]

52. Divisions among the Member States as to the coup in Myanmar in 2021 have also been in evidence.[220] While the coup and subsequent events are examined *infra*, suffice to mention here that the first reaction was at an ASEAN Leaders' Meeting in April 2021, at which 'deep concern' at the situation was expressed, a consensus plan

211. *United Communist Party of Turkey and Others v. Turkey,* Appl. No. 133/1996/752/951, Judgment, European Court of Human Rights, 30 Jan. 1998, para. 43, 26 E.H.R.R. 121 (1998).
212. Myanmar's transition to democracy was called into question by the UK Foreign and Commonwealth Office, which described the referendum on the new Constitution held in 2008 as 'flawed' and as having disenfranchised the democratic opposition and ethnic groups, *see* FCO, *Human Rights and Democracy Report 2009*, 89. *See* generally, C.S. Renshaw, *Democratic Transformation and Regional Institutions: The Case of Myanmar and ASEAN*, 32 J. Current Southeast Asian Aff. 29 (2013). The allegations against Myanmar's military regime that it has systemically destroyed (mass murder and sexual violence) the Rohingya minority, which are presently before the ICJ (*Application of the Convention on the Prevention and Punishment of the Crime of Genocide* (*The Gambia v. Myanmar*), lodged on 11 Nov. 2019), might not be unconnected to a 'flawed' Constitution.
213. *See* ASEAN Political-Security Community Blueprint 2025, s. A.2.1.
214. *See* UNSC Res. 2222 (2015) which affirmed a free, independent media as 'one of the essential foundations of a democratic society'.
215. *See* Declaration on the Right and Responsibility to Promote and Protect Universally Protected Human Rights and Fundamental Freedoms, adopted as UNGA Res. 53/144 (9 Dec. 1998). *See* ASEAN Political-Security Community Blueprint 2025, s. B.3.1.vii, B.4.6.ii.
216. *See* General Comment 25; *United Communist Party of Turkey v. Turkey*, para. 44,. *See* ASEAN Political-Security Community Blueprint 2025, s. A.2.3. *See* M. Kirby, *Indicators for the Implementation of Human Rights*, in *Human Rights: Concept and Standards* 325, 337–339 (J. Symonides ed., UNESCO/Ashgate 2000).
217. *See* UN Basic Principles on the Independence of the Judiciary, UN, *Human Rights: A Compilation of International Instruments*, vol. I 410 (United Nations 2002). *See* ASEAN Political-Security Community Blueprint 2025, s. A.2. *See* Kirby, 334–336. The rule of law has been described as a fundamental principle of human rights law, P. Sieghart, *The International Law of Human Rights* 18 (Clarendon Press 1983).
218. *See* BBC News, *Thailand Junta Claims Neighbours' Backing* (5 Jun. 2014), at: https://www.bbc.co.uk/news/world-asia-27694471.
219. Leviter, 194, 197.
220. R. Ebbighausen, *Myanmar Coup: ASEAN Split over the Way Forward*, Deutsche Welle, 29 Mar. 2021, at: https://www.dw.com/en/myanmar-coup-asean-ties/a-57042503.

was agreed (its salient points called for an immediate halt to the violence in Myanmar, for all parties to exercise self-restraint, and for a constructive dialogue leading to a peaceful solution in the interests of the people) but neither a timeframe to resolve the crisis nor the goal of restorating democracy were mentioned.

53. The references to human rights in the ASEAN Charter, albeit in general abstract terms, are nevertheless welcome. As has been pointed out, ASEAN's origins were as a political body and not as a human rights organisation.[221] Notwithstanding, one of ASEAN's essential functions is stated to be to 'promote and protect human rights and fundamental freedoms'.[222] Among the substantive principles which ASEAN and Member States must observe is 'respect for fundamental freedoms, the promotion and protection of human rights and, the promotion of social justice'.[223] The evolution of international law has established that these commitments go beyond a mere statement of lofty ideals but Member States have assumed binding legal obligations.[224] It should be stressed that in human rights discourse the obligation to promote, protect and respect impose a combination of negative and positive duties upon states.[225] The Member States seem to be under a clear duty to secure human rights. As discussed below, ASEAN has adopted a number of discrete treaties and soft law documents on human rights.

54. The commitment to human rights may be considered radical in itself given that Southeast Asian States have traditionally shared the distrust of emerging states that international concern for human rights and democratic governance were mere pretexts for interference in their internal affairs and undermining their sovereignty.[226] Consequently, the existence of an apparent qualification, that 'due regard to the rights and responsibilities of the member states of ASEAN' must be paid,

---

221. Muntarbhorn, 208.
222. ASEAN Charter Art. 1(7). *See* EPG Report, paras 27, 47; ASEAN Political-Security Community Blueprint 2025, s. A.2.5; ASEAN Socio-Cultural Community Blueprint 2025, Sections B.3.
223. ASEAN Charter Art. 2(2)(i).
224. Duxbury & Hsein-Li, 151. In *Legal Consequences for States of the Continued Presence of South Africa in Namibia*, Advisory Opinion, I.C.J. Reports 1971, 16, 57, the ICJ found that the UN Charter had imposed binding obligations on South Africa to promote and respect human rights in relation to Namibia. *See* E. Schwelb, *The International Court of Justice and the Human Rights Clause of the Charter*, 66 A.J.I.L. 337 (1972). This approach has been followed by African regional courts, e.g., Economic Community of West African States (ECOWAS) Community Court of Justice, *Hadjiatou Mani Koraou v. Republic of Niger*, Judgment No. ECW/CCJ/JUD/06/08 (27 Oct. 2008) paras 41–42; and Southern African Development Community (SADC) Tribunal, *Mike Campbell (Pvt.) Ltd. et al. v. The Republic of Zimbabwe*, Judgment, 28 Nov. 2008, 48 *I.L.M.* 534 (2009).
225. M. Nowak, *Civil and Political Rights*, in *Human Rights: Concept and Standards* 69, 72–75 (J. Symonides ed., 2000).
226. For an account of the qualms of Asian countries towards what they perceive as a Western-orientated international law, *see* Donnelly, 131–135; J.A. Thomas, *History and International Law in Asia: A Time for Review*, in *Essays in Honour of Wang Tieya* 813 (R.St.J. Macdonald ed., Martinus Nijhoff 1994). In the 1990s, the Prime Ministers of Malaysia and Singapore in particular were vocal in their support of the virtues of Asian values, C.M. Cerna, *Introductory Note to the Terms of Reference for the Establishment of the ASEAN Intergovernmental Commission on Human Rights (AICOHR)*, 48 *I.L.M.* 1161 (2009).

injects a disturbing note.[227] It could signify a statist bias that allows national law to prevail over international human rights law. But, while states are sovereign, they are not above the law,[228] and, therefore, they must conform to the pertinent rules of international law even if this results in limiting their freedom of action.[229] It is a cardinal benchmark of international human rights law and policy that the international community has a legitimate right to subject a state's behaviour to external scrutiny to ensure its compatibility with international standards; states may not hide behind the cloak of domestic jurisdiction to maltreat their nationals.[230] The application of pressure, either by other states or by international institutions, on states to conform to international human rights standards or to abstain from human rights violations, especially where the violations are gross and systematic, does not constitute illegitimate interference nor does it amount to coercion.[231] The international community as a whole has a rightful interest in upholding human rights.[232] Nevertheless, it must be acknowledged that Asian states have traditionally assumed a conservative stance on this issue, evidently to avoid confrontation.[233] As example one could cite Myanmar's dismissal of Thailand's expression of concern, as ASEAN Chair, at the treatment of then dissident (and now jailed political leader) Aung San Suu Kyi, as tantamount to interference in Myanmar's internal affairs.[234]

55. Indeed, ASEAN's reserved approach to Myanmar's treatment of the Rohingyas is particularly worrisome,[235] and challenges the challenges two of the prevailing concepts, the ASEAN Centrality and the ASEAN Way. The aforementioned Five-Point Consensus (5 PC), which ASEAN leaders adopted in 2021, is still the principal reference document addressing the political crisis in Myanmar, a situation intricately linked to the treatment of the Rohingyas and other population groups in the country. And this despite the fact that the situation has markedly deteriorated and, arguably, there is no viable and sustainable solution in the horizon.

---

227. ASEAN Charter Art. 1(7).
228. Grant and Barker, 563–564; R.L. Bledsoe & B.A. Boczek, *International Law Dictionary* 55 (ABC-Clio 1987).
229. For relevant *obiter dicta* going back one century, *see S.S. Wimbledon (France, Great Britain, Italy, and Japan v. Germany)*, P.C.I.J., Series A, No. 1 (1923) 25; and *Tunis and Morocco Nationality Decrees*, Advisory Opinion, P.C.I.J., Series B, No 4 (1923) 24.
230. Vienna Declaration, Part I, para. 4; United States Court of Appeals for the Second Circuit, *Filartiga v. Peña Irala*, Judgment, 30 Jun. 1980, 630 F.2d 876 (2d Cir. 1980); 19 *I.L.M.* 966, 971 (1980); Buergenthal, 10–12; Cassese, 67; Malanczuk, 220–221.
231. Cassese, 59–60. But *see* Bangkok Declaration, para. 5, that human rights must not be used as an instrument of political pressure.
232. Vienna Declaration, Part I, para. 4; ICJ, *Barcelona Traction, Light and Power Co. (Belgium v. Spain)*, I.C.J. Reports 1970, 3, paras 33–34; ICJ, *East Timor (Portugal v. Australia)* I.C.J. Reports 1995, 89, 102.
233. Tan, 'Legs to Go Places', 185.
234. Cerna, 1162. *See* further, P. Malanczuk, *Regional Protection of Human Rights in the Asia-Pacific Region*, 52 German Y.B.I.L. 107, 115–117 (2009); C.S. Renshaw, *Democratic Transformation and Regional Institutions: The Case of Myanmar and ASEAN*, 32 J. Current Southeast Asian Aff. 29 (2013).
235. Serious violations of human rights have been reported by an International Fact-Finding Mission on Myanmar set up by the UN Human Rights Council, *Detailed findings of the Independent International Fact-Finding Mission on Myanmar*, UN Doc. A/HRC/42/CRP.5 (16 Sep. 2019).

56. The reference to social justice reflects ASEAN's basic attachment to human dignity and its commitment to social progress, social welfare, and development.[236] Clearly, it encompasses second-generation rights, that is, economic, social and cultural rights.[237] The full realisation of such societal goals imposes positive duties that require state intervention and the progressive allocation of resources.[238]

57. Another important ASEAN undertaking, associated with human rights, is the respect for the different cultures, languages and religions in the region.[239] ASEAN's commitment to diversity and social harmony is deep.[240] Tolerance is a rational policy given the diverse ethnic, religious and linguistic composition in Member States.[241] ASEAN must be culturally aware and sensitive and the imposition of homogeny in these areas is therefore to be discouraged.[242] It is important, for instance, that provision is made for the use of minority languages in appropriate circumstances.[243] Sadly, religious minorities continue to encounter discrimination.[244] Relations between different communities in some Member States have not been free from difficulties and it is common knowledge that the Philippines, and Thailand to a much lesser extent,[245] are troubled by long-running insurgencies by Muslim rebels.[246]

---

236. EPG Report, para. 16; ASEAN Socio-Cultural Community Blueprint, Sections II, A-C. Welfare provision is a component part of a liberal democracy, Donnelly, 155.
237. Bangkok Declaration, paras 7–10.
238. UN Secretariat, 'General Comment 12, Adopted by the Committee on Economic Social and Cultural Rights' in 'Compilation of General Comments and General Recommendations adopted by Human Rights Treaty Bodies', U.N. Doc. HRI/GEN/1/Rev.9 (Vol. 1) (2008); A. Eide, *Economic and Social Rights*, in *Human Rights: Concept and Standards* 109, 124–128 (J. Symonides ed., 2000).
239. ASEAN Charter Art. 2(2)(l).
240. ASEAN Charter Art. 1(14). *See also* ASEAN Political-Security Community Blueprint 2025, Sections A.3.
241. *See* World Summit Outcome, para. 14.
242. EPG Report, para. 60.
243. Vienna Declaration, Part I, para. 19; Declaration on the Rights of Persons Belonging to National or Ethnic, Religious or Linguistic Minorities, UNGA Res. 47/135 (1992) Art. 4(3)(4); H. Hannum, *The Rights of Minorities*, in *Human Rights: Concept and Standards* 277, 291–292 (J. Symonides ed. 2000).
244. *See* United States Commission on International Religious Freedom, *Annual Report 2023*, April 2023, at: https://www.uscirf.gov/publication/2023-annual-report; J.L. Neo, *Religious Minorities in Asia: Between the Scylla of Minority Protection and Charybdis of Religious Freedom Rights?* 12 Religions 881 (2021); T.L. Mufford, *A Right for All: Freedom of Religion or Belief in ASEAN* (United States Commission on International Religious Freedom, September 2017).
245. U.S. State Department, *Country Reports on Human Rights Practices for 2009,* at: http://www.state.gov/j/drl/rls/hrrpt/2009/eap/136010.htm. In 2013, Thailand engaged in peace talks with Muslim rebels, Human Rights Watch, *Annual World Report 2014*, 395; BBC News, 'Thailand signs peace talks deal with Muslim rebels' (28 Feb. 2013), at: http://www.bbc.co.uk/news/world-asia-216117 64.
246. U.S. State Department, *Country Reports on Human Rights Practices for 2009, ibid.* However, in 2014 the Philippines government reached agreement with the Moro Islamic Liberation Front on self-rule in parts of the south of the country, pending a comprehensive peace treaty, The Guardian, *Philippines Signs Long-Awaited Peace Deal with Muslim Rebels* (27 Mar. 2014).

58. As has been made obvious from the observations made earlier, Myanmar's treatment of ethnic and religious minorities is reprehensible, to say the least.[247] In 2020, the ICJ granted provisional measures sought by The Gambia ordering Myanmar, *inter alia*, to take all necessary measures to prevent acts of genocide against the Rohingya.[248] Myanmar, which has not complied with the ICJ Order, filed preliminary objections, which were rejected in 2022.[249]

59. Finally, Vietnam is intolerant of religious groups that are not government sanctioned;[250] this is probably justified by the Constitutional provision stipulating that the National Assembly has the duty and power to decide on the State's policies on religions.[251]

60. ASEAN commits itself to upholding the UN Charter and international law,[252] a necessary condition to play a meaningful role in international affairs.[253] Even though the relevant provision in the ASEAN Charter constitutes an affirmation of the primacy of UN Charter obligations in accordance with Article 103 of the UN Charter,[254] it contains a curious qualification in that it explicitly refers to rules of international law accepted by ASEAN States.[255] This may constitute a reference to the traditional positivist conception of international law, with its stress on state

---

247. As far as UN documentation is concerned, *see*, inter alia, UNGA, *Situation of human rights in Myanmar*, UN Doc. A/72/382 (8 Sep. 2017); UNGA, *Situation of human rights of Rohingya Muslims and other minorities in Myanmar - Report of the Secretary-General*, UN Doc. A/78/278 (14 Aug. 2023). *See* further, UNGA Res. 72/248 (24 Dec. 2017), Res. 73/264 (22 Dec. 2018), Res. 74/246 (27 Dec. 2019), Res. 75/238 (31 Dec. 2020), Res. 77/227 (15 Dec. 2022), Res. 78/219 (19 Dec. 2023) and Res. 79/182 (17 Dec. 2024), all titled 'Situation of human rights of Rohingya Muslims and other minorities in Myanmar'. *See* also, Human Rights Council, Res. 46/21, Situation of human rights in Myanmar (24 Mar. 2021); *Situation of human rights in Myanmar since 1 February 2022 - Report of the United Nations High Commissioner for Human Rights*, UN Doc. A/HRC/52/21 (3 Mar. 2023); *Situation of human rights in Myanmar - Report of the United Nations High Commissioner for Human Rights*, UN Doc. A/HRC/54/59 (19 Sep. 2023); *Situation of human rights in Myanmar - Report of the Special Rapporteur on the situation of human rights in Myanmar,* UN Doc. A/HRC/55/65 (14 Mar. 2024). For updated Reports and information, *see* the Special Rapporteur's webpage at: https://www.ohchr.org/en/special-procedures/sr-myanmar.

248. ICJ, *Application of the Convention on the Prevention and Punishment of the Crime of Genocide (The Gambia v. Myanmar)*, Provisional Measures, Order, 23 Jan. 2020, [2020] I.C.J. Reports 3.

249. ICJ, *Application of the Convention on the Prevention and Punishment of the Crime of Genocide (The Gambia v. Myanmar)*, Preliminary Objections, Judgment, 22 Jul. 2022, [2022] I.C.J. Reports 477; G. Naldi & K. Magliveras, *International Court of Justice Dismisses Objections to Its Jurisdiction in the Rohingya Genocide Case*, 38 International Enforcement Law Reporter 304 (2022).

250. United Nations, Human Rights Committee, *Concluding observations on the third periodic report of Viet Nam*, CCPR/C/VNM/CO/3 (29 Aug. 2019), para. 43.

251. Constitution of Vietnam 1992 (revised 2013), Art. 70(5), at: https://www.constituteproject.org/constitution/Socialist_Republic_of_Vietnam_2013.

252. ASEAN Charter Art. 2(2)(j). ASEAN Political-Security Community Blueprint 2025, s. A.1.3.

253. EPG Report, paras 50–53.

254. L.-C. Chen, *An Introduction to Contemporary International Law* 206 (Yale University Press 2d ed. 2000).

255. ASEAN Charter Art. 2(2)(j) proclaims that ASEAN and its Member States are committed to: 'upholding the United Nations Charter and international law, including international humanitarian law, *subscribed to by ASEAN Member States*' (emphasis added).

consent,[256] an argument supported by its 'emphasis on the principles of sovereignty, non-interference and territorial integrity.[257] On the other hand, said provision could allow some measure of deviation from the traditional interpretation of *jus cogens* to accommodate the ASEAN Way, without of course conflicting with it.

61. The reference to international humanitarian law is encouraging. ASEAN States have assumed obligations under the Geneva Conventions 1949 and 1977 Additional Protocols,[258] which are deemed for the most part to be declaratory of customary international law.[259] Conflict in ethnic areas of Myanmar, reference to which has been made above, has raised concerns about violations of international humanitarian law, especially with regard to civilians. But humanitarian law also extends to principles of humanitarian relief assistance in response to natural and human-made disasters.[260] The traditional view is that the legality of the delivery of humanitarian aid is contingent on the consent of the recipient state without which its sovereignty would be violated.[261] But UN practice has established that it can authorise enforcement action on humanitarian grounds, a moral imperative.[262] The regime in Myanmar attracted international condemnation for its callousness towards human suffering. Cyclone Nargis, which struck Myanmar in 2008, gave rise to a humanitarian crisis.[263] International opinion was incensed that the regime refused aid shipments from Western states.[264] Attempts to have the delivery of direct aid authorised by the UN failed but ASEAN did succeed in persuading Myanmar to

256. *See S.S. Lotus (France v. Turkey)* P.C.I.J., Series A, No. 10.
257. ASEAN Charter Art. 2(2)(a). *See* ASEAN Political-Security Community Blueprint 2025, s. A.1.4. *See also* Seah, 199–200.
258. Brunei, Cambodia, Laos and Philippines are parties to all four Geneva Conventions 1949 and Additional Protocols, Indonesia, Malaysia, Myanmar and Thailand are parties to the four Geneva Conventions only, Singapore is a party to the four Geneva Conventions (and 2005 Additional Protocol III on Distinctive Emblems), and Vietnam is a party to the four Geneva Conventions and Additional Protocol I; for updated ratifications' status, *see* https://ihl-databases.icrc.org/ihl.
259. *Military and Paramilitary Activities in and Against Nicaragua* (*Nicaragua v. United States of America*), Judgment, Merits, I.C.J. Reports 1986, 14, 113–114; *Eritrea-Ethiopia Claims Commission*, 135 I.L.R. 519, para. 40.
260. The UNGA has acknowledged that victims of natural disasters are of concern to the international community, *see*, e.g., Res. 43/131, 'Humanitarian assistance to victims of natural disasters and similar emergency situations', 8 Dec. 1988. *See* further Vienna Declaration, Part I, para. 29.
261. ICJ, *Military and Paramilitary Activities in and Against Nicaragua*, Merits, I.C.J. Reports 1986, 14, 243; UNGA Res. 46/182, 'Strengthening of the coordination of humanitarian emergency assistance of the United Nations', 19 Dec. 1991, Annex, para. 3. However, the ICJ has proceeded to express the view that the provision of strictly humanitarian aid limited to the prevention and alleviation of human suffering could not be regarded as unlawful intervention or otherwise contrary to international law, *ibid,* I.C.J. Reports 1986, 242–243. In the influential UN Report of the High-Level Panel on Threats, Challenges and Change, *A More Secure World: Our Shared Responsibility*, UN Doc. A/59/565 (2004), paras 201–202, 231–238, the importance of humanitarian aid and securing access to civilians was stressed.
262. *See*, e.g., UNSC Res. 770 (1992); Res. 794 (1992).
263. Human Rights Watch, *Annual World Report 2009*, 223–224.
264. *Ibid.*

agree to the establishment of a task force to channel international aid.[265] Additionally, the government in Myanmar has been responsible for causing mass human displacement.[266] Although no specific universal treaty protects the internally displaced it is clear that Internally Displaced Persons (IDPs) are not without rights.[267]

62. In 2011, ASEAN reached agreement on founding the ASEAN Co-ordinating Centre for Humanitarian Assistance on Disaster Management.[268] Accordingly, the AHA Centre was established in Jakarta to facilitate cooperation and coordination among the States Parties and relevant international organisations in such circumstances.[269] The AHA Centre operates on the basis that a State will attempt to respond and manage any disasters on its territory, but if it requires assistance from third parties it may turn to it to support its request.[270] The AHA Centre has a number of functions, essentially of an administrative nature.[271] Nevertheless, ASEAN has recognised that its response to these challenges had been found wanting on the whole[272] and in the ASEAN Community Vision 2025 it commits itself to strengthening cooperation on disaster management and emergency response.[273]

63. That no explicit reference is made to international criminal law in the ASEAN Charter[274] may appear surprising in light of the history of the region, specifically the genocidal policies pursued by the Khmer Rouge in Cambodia in the

265. ASEAN Secretariat, *A Humanitarian Call: The ASEAN Response to Cyclone Nargis*, July 2010, at: https://www.humanitarianlibrary.org/sites/default/files/2014/02/a_humanitarian_call.pdf.
266. UNHCR, Global Focus: Myanmar, https://reporting.unhcr.org/operational/operations/myanmar.*See* also, Internal Displacement Monitoring Centre, Myanmar, https://www.internal-displacement.org/countries/myanmar (last updated 26 Aug. 2024). Notwithstanding the acknowledgement of the importance of securing the human rights of refugees, *see* Bangkok Declaration, para. 11, it is disappointing that only Cambodia and the Philippines have ratified the Geneva Convention Relating to the Status of Refugees, 189 U.N.T.S. 137 (28 Jul. 1951) and the Protocol, 606 U.N.T.S. 267 (31 Jan. 1967).
267. On 17 Apr. 1998, the UN Commission on Human Rights adopted a 'soft law' document setting out the humanitarian and human rights standards applicable to IDPs, 'Guiding Principles on Internal Displacement', UN Doc. E/CN.4/1999/79; *see* further, UN Commission on Human Rights, Resolution 1999/47 on Internally Displaced Persons, 27 Apr. 1999.
268. ASEAN Agreement on the Establishment of the ASEAN Co-ordinating Centre for Humanitarian Assistance on Disaster Management (17 Nov. 2011), at: https://agreement.asean.org/media/download/20220330063452.pdf. The Centre had been envisaged in the ASEAN Agreement on Disaster Management and Emergency Response (AADMER), adopted on 26 Jul. 2005, entered into force on 24 Dec. 2009, and in the AADMER Work Programme for 2010 – 2015, at: https://asean.org/wp-content/uploads/2021/09/AADMER-WP-2011.pdf.
269. ASEAN Co-ordinating Centre for Humanitarian Assistance Agreement, Arts 2, 3(1).
270. *Ibid.*, Art. 3(2).
271. *Ibid.*, Art. 4.
272. M. Caballero-Anthony, *From Comprehensive Security to Regional Resilience: Coping with Non-traditional Security Challenges*, in *ASEAN@50: Retrospectives and Perspectives on the Making, Substance, Significance and Future of ASEAN. Volume 4. Building ASEAN Community: Political-Security and Socio-cultural Reflections* 123, 140–141 (A. Baviera & L. Maramis eds, Economic Research Institute for ASEAN and East Asia, 2017).
273. ASEAN Political-Security Community Blueprint, B.3.8.
274. It has been argued that Asian states are largely ambivalent about the principle of universal jurisdiction and that many treaty-based international crimes have yet to be incorporated into domestic

1970s,[275] which eventually led to the establishment of an internationalised or mixed tribunal, the Extraordinary Chambers of the Courts in Cambodia (ECCC), to try the horrific crimes perpetrated by the Khmer Rouge.[276] Regrettably only Cambodia is presently a party to the Rome Statute of the International Criminal Court (ICC).[277]

64. A possible weakness is that it is not clear how adherence to these principles is to be realised. It has also been observed that ASEAN lacks a judicial organ. The Protocol on Dispute Settlement Mechanisms, on which *see infra*, could provide a possible forum. Given its availability to resolve disputes over the interpretation or application of the ASEAN Charter there is no reason to suppose why in light of the Charter's governing principles disputes including but not limited to systematic and gross human rights violations, including the ill-treatment of minorities, such as the Rohingya in Myanmar, and the process of democratisation should not in principle be amenable to the Protocol's methods. Of course, the reality is that such an occurrence seems highly unlikely given the traditional reluctance to submit disputes to third-party adjudication. It is also important to bear in mind that Member States are at liberty under the Charter to submit their legal disputes to the ICJ.[278]

65. An interesting feature of the Charter is the emphasis laid on the relationship with its external partners. The importance of this relationship is underlined by the fact that to 'maintain the centrality and proactive role of ASEAN as the primary driving force in its relations and cooperation with its external partners in a regional architecture' is one of ASEAN's purposes and guiding principles.[279] Accordingly, a whole section of the ASEAN Charter, Chapter XII, is devoted to this issue. ASEAN is therefore dedicated to developing friendly relations and mutually beneficial dialogue, cooperation and partnerships with countries and sub-regional, regional and

---

law, X. Yun, *Asia's Reticence Towards Universal Jurisdiction*, 4 Groningen J. Int'l L. 54 (2016). But *see* Desierto, 85–86 who argues that ASEAN Member States do adhere to the principles of international criminal law.

275. *See* G. Robertson, *Crimes Against Humanity: The Struggle for Global Justice* 297–298 (Penguin 2nd ed. 2002).
276. *See* M.N. Shaw, *International Law* 421–423 (Cambridge U. Press 6th ed. 2008). The ECCC's relationship with the Cambodian Government appeared to be an uneasy one, Human Rights Watch, *Annual World Report 2014*, 317. Generally, *see* K. Magliveras, 'Difficulties and Status of Efforts to Create an International Criminal Court in Cambodia' 3 *Asia-Pacific J. on Human Rights and the Law* 105-135 (2002).
277. Statute of the International Criminal Court 2187 U.N.T.S. 3 (17 Jul. 1998). It has been suggested that Asian states are wary towards the ICC because of its perceived Western set-up, Yun, 65. The broader reasons why Asian states are reluctant to adhere to the Rome Statute include little regard for the law as a guiding principle of society, the problematic state of the criminal justice system, corruption and lack of judicial independence as well as the lack of a common identity, H. Takemura, *The Asian Region and the International Criminal Court*, in *Contemporary Issues in Human Rights Law: Europe and Asia* 107, 109 (Y. Nakanishi ed., Springer Verlag 2017).
278. ASEAN Charter Art. 28.
279. ASEAN Charter Arts 1(15), 2(2)(m). 'Centrality' refers to ASEAN-led foreign policy initiatives, S. Yamakage, *Evolving ASEAN and the Changing Roles of the TAC*, in *ASEAN@50: Retrospectives and Perspectives on the Making, Substance, Significance and Future of ASEAN. Volume 4. Building ASEAN Community: Political-Security and Socio-cultural Reflections* 39, 44 (A. Baviera & L. Maramis eds, Economic Research Institute for ASEAN and East Asia 2017).

Chapter 2. The Institutional Framework

§1. MEMBERSHIP

I. General Observations

68. As has been mentioned, currently, ASEAN comprises ten Member States, which are drawn from the geographical region of Southeast Asia: five are the original ones, and five have acceded at a later stage. Even though, as is later explained, Timor-Leste was in principle admitted as the eleventh member at the 40th and 41st ASEAN Summits (November 2022), its membership has still not been finalised. Presently, it has an observer status which allows it to partake in all ASEAN Meetings (including Summits). Bar Timor-Leste, the last state to be admitted to membership was Cambodia on 30 April 1999 (having been previously an ASEAN guest (1993–1995) and an ASEAN observer (1995–1996)).[294] In reverse chronological order, Brunei joined on 8 January 1984, Vietnam on 28 July 1995, while both Laos and Myanmar/Burma on 23 July 1997. As regards the admission of Burma (even though its name was officially changed in 1989 to Myanmar, Burma is still being used by many states, including the UK), it raised an eyebrow among Western states given its particularly problematic record as regards democracy, the rule of law and human rights. And as explained above, the situation has not improved since admission, and, as of late, it has deteriorated to the point of being accused before the ICJ for genocide. In the event, ASEAN States did not heed the Western concerns and accepted Burma to membership.[295] Arguably, this was meant to show to the complaining states that ASEAN was no longer under their influence, that they could reach sovereign decisions despite the pressure applied, and that the perceived advantages resulting from Burma's accession ranked higher than other considerations.[296] At least the latter contention is open to question because presumably Burma had to gain far more from its membership considering that (a) its accession almost automatically led to international legitimacy as it was allowed to join a *bone fide* international institution and (b) it could have expected that fellow ASEAN countries would be of assistance in fending off the sanctions, which Western states, including the USA, had taken against it from the late 1980s.[297] Thus, one cannot but wonder if Burma were to lodge today an application for membership in ASEAN,

294. On the Cambodia-ASEAN relationship, *see* Cambodian Institute for Cooperation and Peace / Konrad Adenauer Stiftung, *Regional Conference Cambodia and ASEAN: Managing Opportunity and Challenges Beyond 2015*, Phnom Penh, March 2016, at: https://cicp.org.kh/publications/cambodia-and-asean-managing-opportunity-and-challenges-beyond-2015/.
295. For an examination of the membership applications of Burma and Cambodia, *see* K. Moller, *Cambodia and Burma: The ASEAN Way Ends Here*, 38 Asian Survey 1087–1104 (1998).
296. Generally, *see* R. Cribb, *Burma's Entry into ASEAN: Background and Implications*', 22(3) *Asian Perspective* 49–62 (1998).
297. *See* M.F. Martin, *U.S. Sanctions on Burma*, Congressional Research Service, R41336, 19 Oct. 2012, at: https://sgp.fas.org/crs/row/R41336.pdf; M.F. Martin, *U.S. Restrictions on Relations with Burma*, Congressional Research Service, R44570, Updated January 12, 2021, at: https://crsreports.congress.gov/product/pdf/R/R44570/10.

whether the current Member States would be willing to accept it without reservations or whether conditions would be attached. And this because accepting a candidate state with an abysmal record on democracy and human rights cannot but reflect negatively on the whole of ASEAN. And this is especially so since, as explained above, ASEAN strives to portray itself as a rules-based international organisation with a constitutive instrument advocating the observance of all relevant principles, rules and norms.

69. The question of membership was originally addressed in the ASEAN Declaration (the Bangkok Declaration), which was adopted on 8 August 1967 by the founding five states.[298] According to Article Four, ASEAN shall be 'open for participation to all States in the South-East Asian Region subscribing to [its] aims, principles and purposes'. Which are these and which is their content were also laid down in the Bangkok Declaration. They could be summarised as follows. First, to accelerate the region's economic growth, social progress and cultural development. Second, to promote regional peace and stability by adhering to justice, the rule of law as well as the principles enshrined in the UN Charter.[299] Third, to promote collaboration among Member States and to encourage mutual assistance on matters of common interest. Fourth, the provision of mutual assistance among Member States in the educational, professional, technical, and administrative spheres. Fifth, to work together in the areas of agriculture, industry, transportation, and communications, as well as to raise the living standards of their population. Sixth, to promote Southeast Asian studies. Seventh, to cooperate with other relevant international organisations.

II. Admittance and Accession of New Member States: The Primary Role of Consensus in Membership Issues

70. In the ASEAN Charter, the accession of new Member States is regulated in Article 6 thereof. This provision should be considered complementary to the aforementioned provisions of the Bangkok Declaration. Even though Article 6 lays down the criteria, which will have to be met and observed by all applicant states, it leaves the procedural aspects of the accession process to be determined by the ASEAN Coordinating Council. As is later explained, this is organ (it was established pursuant to Article 8 of the ASEAN Charter) that brings together at regular intervals the Foreign Ministers of Member States.[300] The third paragraph of Article 6 stipulates that 'admission shall be decided by consensus by the ASEAN Summit, upon the recommendation of the ASEAN Coordinating Council'. In other international organisations,[301] the accession of new Member States is a matter to be approved by

298. Reproduced in ASEAN Secretariat, *ASEAN Documents Series 1967-1988*, 3d ed., no date.
299. *See* UN Charter Art. 2.
300. The legal basis for the involvement of the Coordinating Council is Art. 8(2)(h) of the Charter: 'The ASEAN Coordinating Council shall ... undertake other tasks provided for in this Charter'.
301. Generally, *see* K. Magliveras, *Membership in International Organisations*, in *Research Handbook on International Organisations* 84 (J. Klabbers & A. Wallendahl eds, Edward Elgar Publishing, 2011).

unanimity (e.g., in the EU)[302] or by qualified majority (e.g., in the UN)[303] or by two-thirds majority (e.g., in the OAS).[304] To decide on accession by consensus should be regarded as a unique feature of ASEAN. It is, of course, in line with Article 20(1) of the Charter, which prescribes that decision-making in the Organisation shall be based on consultation and consensus.[305] Even though consensus is a notion, which has characterised the whole operation of ASEAN ever since it was founded in 1967 and forms part of what has been described as 'the ASEAN Way', the Charter does not offer any definition of it. This is rather strange considering that consensus is also the preferred mode of voting when it comes to amending the Charter.[306] Therefore, it should be accepted that the precise content of the term 'consensus' derives from the way it has been practised by ASEAN organs and Member States over time.[307] It is for this reason that this fundamental norm requires to be constantly evaluated.[308]

71. There has been one particular incident, which has not to do with questions of membership, but as the lack of consensus has caused a rift among Member States, a rift that lasted for a considerable period of time, it is worthwhile to mention it. The facts of the incident can be summarised as follows. When ASEAN Foreign Ministers met in Phnom Penh, Cambodia, in July 2012, they failed to agree on a joint communiqué, which is traditionally issued after the conclusion of each meeting. The cause of the disagreement had nothing to do with the operation of ASEAN, or with the non-fulfilment of obligations, or other institutional matters of contention. It erupted when the Philippines requested that the Foreign Ministers' draft communiqué include a reference to an incident between it and China, which had taken place in the South China Sea in April 2012. Cambodia, invoking its role as ASEAN Chair, refused to do so because it considered it to be a bilateral territorial dispute.[309]

---

302. *See* Art. 49 TEU envisaging that two unanimous approvals are required: the first at the level of Council of Ministers (the principal decision-making organ) in order to commence the accession process and the second at the level of each EU Member State, which is asked to approve the accession agreement according to its domestic constitutional provisions (usually ratification by Parliament followed by promulgation by the Head of State).
303. *See* Art. 4(2) in conjunction with Art. 18(2) of the UN Charter demanding a two-thirds majority of the Member States present and voting.
304. *See* Art. 7 of the OAS Charter.
305. *See* further the Preamble of the ASEAN Charter stipulating that consensus is one of the principles that the *population* of Member States must respect (emphasis added).
306. *See* Art. 48 ASEAN Charter.
307. Generally, *see* A. Collins, *The Subtlety of ASEAN Consensus*, S. Rajaratnam School of International Studies, Commentary No. 222, 22 Nov. 2017, at: https://www.rsis.edu.sg; K.H.R. Villanueva & R.G. Manalo, *ASEAN Consensus: The Intangible Heritage of Southeast Asian Diplomacy, ASEAN@50*, Vol. 4: Building ASEAN Community: Political-Security and Socio-cultural Reflections, August 2017, 88–122, at: http://www.eria.org/ASEAN_at_50_4A.6_Villanueva_final.pdf; and B. Kurus, *The ASEAN Triad: National Interest, Consensus-Seeking, and Economic Co-operation*, 16 Contemp. Southeast Asia 404 (1995).
308. *See* T. Yukawa, *The ASEAN Way as a Symbol: An Analysis of Discourses on the ASEAN Norms*, 31 The Pac. Rev. 298–314 (2018).
309. The incident has become known as the 'Scarborough Shoal Standoff', *see* M. Green et al., *Counter-Coercion Series: Scarborough Shoal Standoff*, Center for Strategic and International Studies, Asia Maritime Transparency Initiative, 22 May 2017, at: https://amti.csis.org/counter-co-scarborough-standoff/.

72. Arguably, this incident was far more than a divergence of opinion on whether a few lines would appear or not in a joint communiqué: it did highlight that Member States' voting patterns may very well be strongly influenced by outside factors, *in casu* the strong economic ties that a certain Member State (Cambodia) had with a third state (China), ties which that Member State was prepared to let overshadow the unity among ASEAN countries.[310] Strictly speaking, at that time the dispute was between the Philippines and China and, therefore, it was not an ASEAN matter per se. On the other hand, it is also true that such joint communiqués often address issues and developments, which are not directly related to ASEAN and its activities but also cover more general matters. Moreover, it does not appear that the Philippines wanted the joint communiqué to record that China was in violation of international law, a statement which could have had consequences important legal consequences as to how the other Member States treated their relations with China.

73. The following year, the Philippines commenced arbitration proceedings against China, which concerned the South China Sea and, in particular, the legality of the so-called Nine-dash line claimed by China; further delays are given later in the monograph. Even though China refused to participate, in October 2015, the Arbitral Tribunal, which was constituted under Annex VII to the UN Convention on the Law of the Sea, declared that it had jurisdiction over the case.[311] 'It unanimously ruled in favour of the Philippines.[312] Malaysia, Thailand and Vietnam were present in the arbitral proceedings through observers; Vietnam, Malaysia and Brunei are also claimant States in the South China Sea. China refused to recognise the validity of the Award. On 14 June 2016, several weeks before the Award was delivered, a Special ASEAN-China Foreign Ministers' Meeting was convened in the Yunnan Province of China. According to the Media Statement, which was circulated by the ASEAN Ministers, the Meeting was held 'in a frank and friendly atmosphere' and 'both sides reaffirmed that the ASEAN-China relations will continue to

---

310. *See* M. del Callar, *PHL Deplores ASEAN Conduct on Issuing Traditional Statement*, *GMA News Online*, 13 Jul. 2012, at: https://www.gmanetwork.com/news/news/nation/265353/phl-deplores-asean-conduct-on-issuing-traditional-statement/story/?related.

311. The South China Sea Arbitration between the Republic of the Philippines and the People's Republic of China, *Award on Jurisdiction and Admissibility*, 29 Oct. 2015, 33 R.I.A.A. 1. Generally, *see* G. Naldi & K. Magliveras, *Dispute Settlement under the UN Convention on the Law of the Sea: Developments on Jurisdiction*, 16 N.Z. Y.B. Int'l L. 207, 212 *et seq.* (2018).

312. PCA, *Philippines v. China*, Case No. 2013–19, Arbitral Award of 12 Jul. 2016, 33 R.I.A.A. 153, at: https://docs.pca-cpa.org/2016/07/PH-CN-20160712-Award.pdf. *See*, *inter alia*, National Institute for South China Sea Studies, *A Legal Critique of the Award of the Arbitral Tribunal in the Matter of the South China Sea Arbitration*, 24 Asian Yearbook of International Law 151-293 (2018); T.J. Schoenbaum, *The South China Sea Arbitration Decision*, 110 AJIL Unbound 290-295 (2016).
Even though it has been argued that the Philippines has promoted a foreign policy of pacifying China and that this policy was driven through ASEAN as well, *see* R.C. De Castro, *The Limits of Intergovernmentalism: The Philippines' Changing Strategy in the South China Sea Dispute and Its Impact on the Association of Southeast Asian Nations (ASEAN)*, 39 J. Current Southeast Asian Aff. 335 (2020), recent events show that the dispute is nowhere near to be resolved and could lead to dangerous tension.

79. The *second condition* is that the applicant state must be recognised by all Member States. While recognition in international law may take many different forms,[323] here it probably means recognition according to the constitutional and domestic legal order of individual Member States. Theoretically speaking, this second condition could potentially obstruct the accession process if a Member State, for its own reasons, does not recognise (officially) the applicant state, even though it might have already established economic and commercial relations with it.[324] While the recognition (or non-recognition for that matter) of states is an exercise of the sovereign powers of the recognising (or not recognising) states, in principle, it is not a matter affecting the question of membership in international organisations. Indeed, there are examples of international organisations whose Member States have not all recognised each other.

80. The classic example is the UN and its Specialised Agencies, where the State of Israel participates alongside Arab and Islamic states even though it has recognised the latter's sovereignty and independence and vice versa. Moreover, States cannot be compelled to recognise a political entity against their wishes.[325] Thus, if they do accept to participate in the same (regional in our case) international organisation together with states which have not been recognised, this should not create any problems, because their membership therein has been premised on this reality. A not very well-known example is the Saharawi Arab Democratic Republic (SADC), the country whose territory covers most of the region of Western Sahara, a former Spanish colony, currently administered (and annexed) by Morocco. SADC has participated as a full Member in the Organisation of African Unity since the mid-1980s and continues its membership in the successor AU, even though its status as an independent state is not recognised by all AU Member States.[326] Another, far more recent, example is the East Mediterranean Gas Forum: it was established in 2020, and both the State of Israel and the State of Palestine are original Member States.[327] Finally, it is of some interest to note that the Court of Appeal of Singapore has held that whether an entity is a state for the purpose of enjoying immunity domestically

323. *See*, *inter alia*, H. Lauterpacht, *Recognition of States in International Law,* 53 Yale L.J. 385–458 (1944); 1 *Oppenheim's International Law* 126 et seq. (R. Jennings & A. Watts, Longman 9th ed. 1992). State recognition is not only a matter of international law but also has an international politics / relations dimension, *see Symposium 'The Politics of International Recognition'*, 5 International Theory 94–176 (2013).

324. As regards the policy of (non) recognition of ASEAN countries towards Taiwan, *see* P.L. Hsieh, *Rethinking non-recognition: Taiwan's new pivot to ASEAN and the one-China policy*, 33 Cambridge Review of International Affairs 204–228 (2020).

325. Cf. the position of Switzerland: there is no obligation under international law for one state to recognise another, even where the criteria for recognition are met, *see* Swiss Federal Department of Foreign Affairs, 'The recognition of states and governments', 27 Nov. 2017..

326. *See* G. Naldi & C. d'Orsi, 'The Sahrawi Arab Democratic Republic: A State That Never Was?' in S. Abidde (ed.), *Palestine, Taiwan, and Western Sahara: Statehood, Sovereignty, and the International System* 201–221 (Lexington Books 2023).

327. *See* G. Naldi & K. Magliveras, *The East Mediterranean Gas Forum: A Regional Institution Struggling in the Mire of Energy Insecurities*, 20 International Organizations Law Review 194–227 (2023).

is 'special and should be treated differently from the general question of whether a state has come into being [as it concerns] not only matters of fact but also matters of policy'.[328]

81. The *third requirement* is that the applicant state must have declared that it agrees to be bound and to abide by the ASEAN Charter, which, however, does not specify what form the solemn declaration should take. For example, should it be a political declaration proclaimed by the applicant state's executive or the form of a legal instrument signed by the Head of State? In practice, this statement was embodied in the so-called Declaration of Admission, which was signed by the existing Member States and deposited with the ASEAN Secretariat. For example, the Declaration of the Admission of Brunei Darussalam, which was signed in Jakarta, Indonesia, on 7 January 1984, stipulated that the Minister for Foreign Affairs of the applicant State solemnly accepted the conditions of membership and agreed to accede to all ASEAN Declarations and Treaties (this took place well before the conclusion of the ASEAN Charter in 2007). The time frame for the accession of Brunei Darussalam to these instruments was not stipulated.

82. However, for those bilateral agreements that Member States have concluded with third states, the accession of a new Member raises the question of the consent of such third state, which must be secured before the validity of these agreements is extended to the new Member.[329] In the case of Cambodia, on the day it acceded to membership (30 April 1999) its Minister for Foreign Affairs signed a (unilateral) Protocol for the Accession of the Kingdom of Cambodia to ASEAN Agreements, which listed all the relevant instruments, and testified to the fact that it would 'immediately observe the commitments and carry out the obligations under the Agreements, and any amendment thereto'.[330] Finally, Cambodia committed to

---

328. *See* Case CA 92/2003, *Civil Aeronautics Administration v. Singapore Airlines Limited*, Appeal Decision of 14 Jan. 2004, [2004] SGCA 3, para. 25, at: https://www.singaporelawwatch.sg/Portals/0/Docs/Judgments/[2004]%20SGCA%203.pdf. The case concerned whether Taiwan is a state recognised by Singapore and, consequently, covered by the State Immunity Act.

329. *See* e.g., the July 1985 Exchange of Letters in relation to the accession of Brunei Darussalam to the Agreement Between the Governments of the Member Countries of ASEAN and the Government of Canada on Economic Cooperation, signed in New York on 25 Sep. 1981, at: https://asean.org/accession-of-brunei-darussalam-to-the-agreement-between-the-governments-of-the-member-countries-of-asean-and-the-government-of-canada-on-economic-cooperation-new-york-9-july-1985/. The Agreement was superseded by the Agreement Between the Governments of the Member Countries of ASEAN and the Government of Canada on Economic Cooperation, signed in Singapore on 28 Jul. 1993, entered into force on 1 Apr. 1994, at: https://cil.nus.edu.sg/wp-content/uploads/2019/02/1993-ASEAN-Canada-Agreement-on-Economic-Cooperation.pdf. It has been complemented by the (non-binding) Joint Declaration Between Canada-ASEAN on Trade and Investment (Jakarta, 2 Oct. 2011), at: https://cil.nus.edu.sg/wp-content/uploads/2019/02/2011-ASEAN-Canada-JD-On-Trade-And-Investment-1.pdf.

330. In the cases of Laos and Myanmar, a second instrument proved to be necessary, *see*, respectively, Protocol for the Accession of the Lao People's Democratic Republic to ASEAN Agreements and Second Protocol for the Accession of the Lao People's Democratic Republic to ASEAN Agreements; and Protocol for the Accession of the Union of Myanmar to ASEAN Agreements and Second Protocol for the Accession of the Union of Myanmar to ASEAN Agreements; all Protocols were signed in the course of 1997.

extend on a reciprocal basis the Most Favoured Nation (MFN) Treatment to the other ASEAN countries.[331] That new Member States assume the obligation to accede to ASEAN treaties and agreements means that they must subsequently implement them and, if necessary, also bring about the required changes in their domestic legal orders. If applicant States have not been adequately preparing for what could be described as 'ASEAN law', or 'ASEAN legal system',[332] the prospect can be daunting.[333]

83. The *fourth condition* is that the applicant state must show its ability and willingness to carry out the obligations flowing from membership in ASEAN. This requirement follows rationally from Article 5(2) of the Charter: it demands that all Member States adopt and implement domestically all necessary measures to comply with it and with the ensuing duties and obligations. The Charter does not explain how elements of ability and willingness would be assessed. Presumably, different tests would have to be applied because an applicant state might objectively be able to comply with its obligations, but the existing Member States could take the opposite view. It should be pointed out that ASEAN has still not resolved the question of monitoring Member States' compliance with their duties and obligations. This is always a very complicated issue for international organisations tantalising the relationship between the organisation and the Member States and also the relationship among Member States[334] but could be addressed with the establishment of a judicial organ. Of these four criteria/conditions/requirements, the first three appear to be objective while the fourth appears to be subjective, in the sense that the opinion of individual Member States on whether the applicant state can or cannot fulfil its duties could differ. Different Member States may employ different criteria, and/or they might project their national interests, their domestic foreign policy priorities, or other considerations as well. Should consensus to accept the membership application cannot be reached, Member States should reject the application, but they could also postpone its consideration (possibly indefinitely).[335] The former would

331. The Agreement, which entered into force on the day it was signed (it was not subject to ratification), provided for Cambodia's accession to 27 ASEAN Agreements, as they had in the meantime been amended, http://agreement.asean.org/media/download/20140119142534.pdf.

332. *Cf.* the Preamble of the ASEAN Charter: 'the Peoples of the Member States … [h]ereby decide to establish, through this Charter, the *legal* … institutional framework for ASEAN' (emphasis added). Note that the Member States themselves have apparently never expressly referred to the existence of an 'ASEAN law'.

333. *See* T. Aye et al., *The Integration of Myanmar's Legal System Into ASEAN*, 2 Singapore J. Int'l & Comp. L. 579–595 (1988).

334. *See* National University of Singapore, Centre for International Law, Integration through Law: *The ASEAN Way in a Comparative Context - The Role of Law and the Rule of Law in Asian Legal Integration / The ASEAN Legal Integration Policy Recommendations*, no date, at: https://cil.nus.edu.sg/wp-content/uploads/2017/07/2.-Research-ASEAN-ASEAN-ITL-Policy-Makers-ASEAN_ITL_Policy_Recommendation.pdf.

335. This has apparently happened with the application lodged by the State of Palestine to be admitted to membership in the United Nations on 23 Sep. 2011, UN Doc. A/66/371–S/2011/592 (2011). Despite the rejection of the UN Security Council's draft resolution recommending Palestine's admission in 2024, it appears that the application still stands; for the events, *see* K. Magliveras, 'The UN General Assembly Upgrades the Position of Palestine but at What Cost and With What

no doubt have very negative consequences for the applicant state's regional standing and should be avoided, unless there is an outright objection to the application. The latter would leave open the possibility that in the future a different constellation of circumstances might allow the required consensus to be reached; in the meantime, the status of 'applicant Member State' could (and should) allow for a constructive dialogue between the aspiring member and the Organisation. These arguments are later examined in more detail by reference to the membership application lodged by Timor-Leste.

84. As it becomes obvious, the ASEAN Charter has avoided the inclusion of membership criteria that could be regarded as politically sensitive. For example, it does not specifically demand that applicant states are run as parliamentary democracies, that they observe democratic norms and the rule of law, that they are committed to the protection and promotion of human rights and fundamental freedoms, and so on. However, there appears to be an inconsistency between the Charter criteria being silent on such demands and the fact that, according to the Charter's Preamble, these are norms which must not only be upheld but also respected and adhered to by the entire membership. Presumably, these norms being applicable to Member States, must be practised in prospective members as well. Additionally, the Charter has included these norms among the principles, which are binding upon both the Organisation and the Member States, when acting in all areas where ASEAN law is pertinent and the ASEAN legal system is appropriate.[336] Finally, as has been mentioned above, Member States must always abide by the fundamental principles that are cited in ASEAN political and legal instruments, irrespective of whether they were adopted / approved before the Charter's entry into force.[337]

85. It follows that Member States must observe, among others, the relevant stipulations of the Kuala Lumpur Declaration on the Establishment of the ASEAN Charter. The Declaration, which was adopted on 12 December 2005, manifested the willingness of the Member States to prepare the transformation of ASEAN into a rules-based international organisation with a proper constitutive instrument taking the form of a legally binding multilateral treaty. In particular, the Kuala Lumpur Declaration stipulates that the legal instrument that later became the ASEAN Charter will, *inter alia*, 'reaffirm principles, goals and ideals contained in ASEAN's milestone agreements', including the promotion of democracy, human rights, transparency and good governance as well as the strengthening of democratic institutions in the Members States.[338] Finally, the aforementioned ASEAN Community Vision 2025 (reproduced in Appendix 3), which is presently being implemented, envisages that ASEAN will develop, *inter alia*, into a community of peoples, all of whom will enjoy human rights and fundamental freedoms.

Consequences?', *International Law Blog*, 20 May 2024, at: https://internationallaw.blog/2024/05/20/the-un-general-assembly-upgrades-the-position-of-palestine-but-at-what-cost-and-with-what-consequences/.

336. *See* Art. 2(2)(h) and (i) of the ASEAN Charter.

337. *Ibid.*, Art. 2(1).

338. *See* para. 4 of the Kuala Lumpur Declaration, at: https://asean.org/asean-charter/kuala-lumpur-declaration/.

86. Given that several important ASEAN instruments clearly refer to the triptych 'democracy – rule of law – human rights', or tetraptych if good governance is also included, the obvious question that arises is why did the ASEAN Charter's drafters not include as a further condition/requirement that applicant states should already apply these norms domestically. To put it otherwise, why does the Charter not make it clear that undemocratic countries[339] not respecting the rule of law and/or being in breach of human rights are not be allowed to submit a membership application? The explanation to be given is that Member States pay only lip service to these norms; therefore, political expediency prevailed and even today they are not willing to change this state of affairs. References have already been made showing that the Southeast Asian region has had and continues to have several totalitarian-–dictatorial regimes in power.

87. This is an important factor, in the sense that, in regional international organisation, and more so in sub-regional organisations, such as ASEAN, existing members would prefer to have states with a similar political system accede. And it would rather be comical for existing totalitarian Member States to pass judgment on the democratic credentials of applicant states. Notwithstanding these considerations, it is of some significance to note that such is the world of international organisations. These could be viewed as self-contained institutions / legal entities, and, therefore, participating states are within their rights to determine which shall be the applicable rules, conditions and procedures on any matter, including accession to membership. Moreover, how participating states apply these rules is rather subjective, and a diverging application could very well lead to double standards and lack of consistency.

88. At the same time, stock should be taken of the aforementioned developments in the Americas, Africa, Europe, the Commonwealth, etc., where regional international organisations have not only promoted but also demanded 'adherence to the triptych / tetraptych 'democracy – rule of law – human rights' / 'good governance' since the late 1980s and early 1990s.[340] Therefore, it would not have been unrealistic to expect that the ASEAN Charter, an instrument negotiated in the 21st century, would have consolidated these norms and would have demanded that applicant states not only subscribe to them but also have in place appropriate domestic legislation and procedures.

89. Once an applicant state has been accepted by the ASEAN Summit, Article 6(4) of the Charter stipulates that it shall be admitted to membership upon signing

---

339. For the different meaning of 'democratic' in inter-state relations, *see* K. Magliveras, 'The Use of the Words 'Democracy/Democratic' in the International Community: Some Reflections', *International Law Blog*, 29 August 2024, at: https://internationallaw.blog/2024/08/29/the-use-of-the-words-democracy-democratic-in-the-international-community-some-reflections/.

340. A period of time that coincided with the end of the so-called Cold War; *see*, generally, K. Magliveras, 'The Role of International Organisations as Promoters, Enforcers and Exporters of Democratic Ideals and the Rule of Law' in European Center for Research and Training of Human Rights and Humanitarian Action (ed.), *Safeguarding Democratic Institutions within a Europe in Crisis: Challenges and Responses*, 85–106 (I. Sideris Publishers, 2021).

an 'Instrument of Accession to the Charter'. Legally speaking, it would appear that new Member States are not required to ratify the Charter. However, as there have been no new members under the ASEAN Charter, it is not known what exactly will happen. A different question is whether the 'Instrument of Accession to the Charter' will have to be ratified by the acceding State and by the Member States or only by the former. Whether the domestic (constitutional) law of the acceding State provides that it must be ratified before it takes effect and the ASEAN Charter binds the new Member State is also a different question. The Charter does not stipulate with whom the 'Instrument of Accession' shall be deposited. However, by analogy to Article 47(3) of the Charter, which provides that the instruments of ratification of the existing Member States 'shall be deposited with the Secretary-General of ASEAN who shall promptly notify all Member States of each deposit', it can safely be assumed that it will also be deposited with the Secretary-General. Indeed, it is customary in international organisations for Secretary-Generals to act as treaty depositor.

90. Finally, reference will be made to the EU's admission and accession process, which for present purposes is comparable to ASEAN. In the EU, the process of admission of new Member States is finalised with the conclusion of an agreement between the existing ones and the applicant State. The purpose of this agreement is not only to set out the conditions of accession but also to make the necessary adjustments to the EU Treaties to allow for the seamless participation of the new Member State. This agreement is subject to ratification by all contracting states (i.e., by all existing Member States and by the applicant); they must follow their respective constitutional requirements.[341] Should a Member State does not approve it, the accession process shall not be concluded and the applicant State shall not gain membership in the EU. Of course, it can also be the case that the applicant itself will not approve the agreement, as it happened with the accession treaties, which were signed with Norway in 1972 and in 1994:[342] neither of them led to Norway acceding to the EU.

IV. The Prospects of an Expanded ASEAN Membership

91. A country that has on numerous occasions expressed the willingness to join ASEAN is Papua New Guinea (PNG), after it gained its independence from Australia in 1975. However, until today, it has not launched an official application and continues to participate as an observer, a status which it has enjoyed since 1976,[343]

---

341. *See* Art. 49 TEU. Generally, *see* C. Hillion, *Accession and Withdrawal in the Law of the European Union*, in *The Oxford Handbook of European Union Law* 126 (D. Chalmers & A. Arnull eds, Oxford U. Press 2015).

342. *See* Act concerning the conditions of accession of the Kingdom of Norway, the Republic of Austria, the Republic of Finland and the Kingdom of Sweden and the adjustments to the Treaties on which the European Union is founded, O.J. C 241, 29.8.1994, p. 9.

343. Generally, *see* K. Hewison, A. Smith & N. Badu, *Papua New Guinea and Membership of ASEAN*, 39 Australian Outlook 171 (1985); L. Hunt, *Papua New Guinea Eyes ASEAN*, The Diplomat, 9

shortly after it acceded to the United Nations (10 October 1975).[344] The reason why Papua New Guinea has not yet applied has principally to do with complications that relate to the ASEAN membership criteria/conditions/requirements that have to be resolved before a membership application is lodged. The first complication is to determine whether Papua New Guinea forms part of the 'Southeast Asian Region', as this term is understood for the purposes of gaining membership to ASEAN. The second complication is whether the country will be able to carry out satisfactorily the obligations and the duties once it has gained membership. The difficulties that Papua New Guinea is expected to experience, should it seek formal accession, can, to an extent, be illustrated by the complications experienced by Timor-Leste (East Timor) in its effort to join ASEAN.

92. Timor-Leste is a former Portuguese colony. During World War II, it was occupied by Japan. Portugal continued exercising colonial authority over it following the Japanese defeat. When East Timor declared its independence from Portugal on 28 November 1975, it was promptly invaded and occupied by Indonesian forces and was incorporated as Indonesian territory in July 1976; it became the province of Timor Timur. It finally became an independent state in May 2002, some three years after the population had opted for independence by exercising its inalienable right to self-determination.[345] In September 2002, it became the 191st UN Member State.[346] The UN was heavily involved in securing Timor-Leste's independence and eventual statehood. Indeed, in 1999, it was the UN that effectively took over the administration of its territory[347] and was instrumental in preparing it to eventually become a sovereign state.[348] The UN involvement ended in late 2012, when the peacekeeping mission, which had been established by the Security Council, completed its mandate.[349]

93. Timor-Leste applied for ASEAN membership in early March 2011, having previously (January 2007) acceded to TAC, whose stipulations it undertook to faithfully perform and carry out.[350] TAC is examined *infra*, but suffice to mention here that it was concluded in February 1976 among the founding ASEAN countries. It

---

Nov. 2011, at: https://thediplomat.com/2011/11/papua-new-guinea-eyes-asean/. PNG is a contracting party to TAC (on which *see infra*) and to its amendments.

344. Pursuant to UNSC Res. 375(1975) of 22 Sep. 1975 and UNGA Res. 3368(XXX) of 10 Oct. 1975.

345. *Cf.* World Conference against Racism, Racial Discrimination, Xenophobia and Related Intolerance, *Durban Declaration*, UN Doc. A/CONF.189/12, 8 Sep. 2001: 'Reaffirming the principles of equal rights and self-determination of peoples … '.

346. UNGA Res. 57/3 of 27 Sep. 2002, *see* UN Press Release, GA/10069, 27 Sep. 2002, at: https://www.un.org/press/en/2002/ga10069.doc.htm.

347. The UN Mission in East Timor, which was established by the UNSC under Res. 1246 (1999) of 11 Jun. 1999, acted as a transitional administration.

348. Generally, *see* M. Benzing, *Midwifing a New State: The United Nations in East Timor*, 9 Max Planck Y.B. United Nations L. 295–372 (2005).

349. *See* UNSC Res. 2037/2012 of 23 Feb. 2012 and UNSC Presidential Statement S/PRST/2012/27 of 19 Dec. 2012, at: https://undocs.org/S/PRST/2012/27.

350. For the Instrument of Accession of 13 January 2007, *see* https://web.archive.org/web/20080623120159/http://www.asean.org/19273.htm.

aims at promoting perpetual peace, everlasting friendship, and close cooperation among them. It was amended on 15 December 1987 (First Protocol) to allow for the accession of states that are located outside the geographical area of Southeast Asia.[351] However, a later amendment (25 July 1998, Second Protocol) restricted accession by demanding that aspiring contracting states have the consent of 'all the States in Southeast Asia'. Accessions during the 2010s included states from different continents: Peru (its application was accepted during the Retreat of ASEAN Foreign Ministers, Chiang Mai, Thailand, on 17 and 18 January 2019),[352] Bahrain, and Germany (November 2019).

94. In the last three years, there has been an explosion in the number of new parties: fourteen states have acceded, including Kuwait, Panama and Serbia (September 2023), a fact reflecting 'the importance and relevance of the TAC in the current regional and global contexts', according to the ASEAN Secretariat.[353] Finally, Luxembourg became the fifty-fifth State to sign TAC on the sidelines of the 44th and 45th ASEAN Summits and Related Summits on 10 October 2024.

95. Timor-Leste, the first new sovereign state of the 21st century, is a country with a population of around 1.3 million and a GDP of around USD 1.6 billion.[354] Its economic situation is precarious with the GBP having fallen in recent years. While not a reason per se for placing insuperable obstacles to join ASEAN, it should be recalled that the last three states which were admitted to membership, namely Laos, Burma and Cambodia, were themselves rather poor countries and have remained so. Thus, it would appear that the economic situation in Timor-Leste has played a negative role ever since the beginning of the accession process.[355] On the other hand, one does understand why regional international organisations (especially ASEAN that has a significant economic dimension) would not be eager to be joined by economically, commercially and financially feeble states.

96. Timor-Leste's road towards being, in principle, admitted to membership in 2022 could be described as follows. During the 51st Foreign Ministers' Meeting (Singapore, August 2018), the ASEAN Sectoral Bodies and Organs were urged to

---

351. The Third Amending Protocol (23 Jul. 2010) extended the right to accession to all regional organisations whose entire membership comprises sovereign states. None has so far acceded.
352. Peru signed the Instrument of Accession on 31 Jul. 2019.
353. *See* ASEAN News, 'Panama, Serbia, Kuwait sign Treaty of Amity and Cooperation in Southeast Asia', 4 Sep. 2023, at: https://asean.org/panama-serbia-kuwait-sign-treaty-of-amity-and-cooperation-in-southeast-asia/.
354. *See* The World Bank, *Timor-Leste Economic Report: From Resources to Results - Transforming Public Spending to High Growth* (Washington, D.C., January 2025), at: http://hdl.handle.net/10986/42806The World Bank, *Timor-Leste Economic Report: Ways to Harvest Prosperity* (Washington, D.C., July 2023), at: http://hdl.handle.net/10986/40269; The World Bank, *Timor-Leste Economic Report: Honoring the Past, Securing the Future* (Washington, D.C, December 2022).
355. *See* K. McGeown, *East Timor Applies to Join ASEAN*, *BBC News*, 4 Mar. 2011, at: https://www.bbc.com/news/world-asia-pacific-12644608.

'continue exploring relevant capacity-building activities for Timor-Leste's participation, in accordance with the elements and procedures outlined by Member States'.[356]

97. From the wording of the Joint Communiqué,' it transpired that there was no consensus among Member States on this matter. Reportedly, Singapore raised objections to its application on economic grounds and also questioned whether Timor-Leste's lack of human resources would not result in being incapable to follow and handle the large number of ASEAN summits and meetings.[357] Myanmar also raised objections; they were of a political nature and concerned the close relationship between the leaders of Timor-Leste and Myanmar's domestic opposition forces led by the Nobel Peace Prize winner Aung San Suu Kyi.[358] At their meeting in the summer of 2019, ASEAN Foreign Ministers noted that arrangements had been made for Fact-Finding Missions (FFM) of the three ASEAN Community pillars to visit Timor-Leste, beginning with the FFM for the Political-Security Community in September 2019.[359] Moreover, capacity-building assistance was to be given to Timor-Leste, which was also encouraged to follow the procedures outlined by Member States.[360] However, the outbreak of Covid 19[361] did not allow preparing and dispatching the FFMs for the ASEAN Economic Community and the ASEAN Socio-Cultural Community pillars, which were necessary for developing a comprehensive assessment of Timor-Leste's application. By August 2021, these FFMs had still not taken place. In the meantime, Timor-Leste was allowed to participate in ASEAN's non-policy-making activities. To that effect, the ASEAN Coordinating Council (ACC) endorsed the 'Guidelines for Timor-Leste's Participation in ASEAN Activities for Capacity Building Purposes' and the accompanying 'Matrices of ASEAN Non-Policy Making Activities for Timor-Leste's Participation for Capacity Building Purposes'.[362] The Government of Timor-Leste appeared to be very satisfied with

---

356. *See* Joint Communiqué, 2 Aug. 2018, para. 73, at: https://asean.org/wp-content/uploads/2018/08/51st-AMM-Joint-Communique-Final.pdf.
357. *See* 'ASEAN to pass on letting East Timor join grouping this year: Kyodo sources', *ABS-CBN News*, 5 Nov. 2017, at: https://news.abs-cbn.com/news/11/05/17/asean-to-pass-on-letting-east-timor-join-grouping-this-year-kyodo-sources.
358. *See* 'East Timor's Accession to ASEAN Treaty Still Resisted 15 Years After Restoration of Independence', *East Timor Law and Justice Bulletin*, 6 Nov. 2017, at: http://www.easttimorlawandjusticebulletin.com/2017/11/east-timors-accession-to-asean-treaty.html.
359. The purpose of these Missions was to identify areas that could turn out to be problematic if Timor-Leste were admitted to membership as well as areas where improvement was required.
360. *See* Joint Communique of the 52nd ASEAN Foreign Ministers' Meeting, Bangkok, 31 Jul. 2019, para. 74.
361. On 30 Jan. 2020, the World Health Organization declared Covid 19 a Public Health Emergency of International Concern (PHEIC) and on 11 Mar. 2020 it characterised it as a pandemic, at: https://www.who.int/europe/emergencies/situations/covid-19.
362. *See* Chairman's Statement of the 36th ASEAN Summit, 'Cohesive and Responsive ASEAN', 26 Jun. 2020, para. 30, at https://asean.org/chairmans-statement-of-the-36th-asean-summit-26-june-2020-cohesive-and-responsive-asean/; Joint Communiqué of the 53rd ASEAN Foreign Ministers' Meeting, 9 Sep. 2020, para. 93, at: https://asean.org/joint-communique-of-the-53rd-asean-foreign-ministers-meeting/; and Joint Communiqué of the 54th ASEAN Foreign Ministers' Meeting, 2 Aug. 2021, para. 88, at: https://asean.org/joint-communique-54-th-asean-foreign-ministers-meeting/.

these developments; it referred to them as 'ASEAN's clear recognition of the positive momentum towards our accession'.[363]

98. It should be noted that capacity-building assistance to Timor-Leste has also been approved by the European Union, through the EU Multiannual Indicative Programme for Timor-Leste 2021–27, which was officially launched in February 2022.[364] The European Commission document on the Programme painted a rather negative picture of the situation in the country. It listed many key challenges facing Timor-Leste, including the following: political instability, limited government capacity, growing corruption, slow economic transformation and diversification, 'lack of regional integration that together with ineffective institutions discourage investment', poor quality infrastructure and connectivity, a persistent high level of poverty, inequality, and low social development.[365] To that extent, linking up with international economic and financial institutions is no doubt the appropriate manner for Timor-Leste to deal with these challenges and problems; on 30 August 2024, Timor-Leste became the 166th member of the World Trade Organization (WTO). Indeed, according to the European Commission document, one of the mutually agreed outcomes of the EU–Timor-Leste dialogue is regional integration, which was explained as follows:

> Better integration of Timor-Leste into the rest of Southeast Asia as well as possible accession to the Association of Southeast Asian Nations (ASEAN) will provide economic opportunities, and bolster Timorese influence. Inclusion of Timor-Leste in a rules-based integration process with close links to the EU has the potential to reduce the risk of it falling under the influence of other players with strategic interests.[366]

The conclusion could be reached that the EU wants to see Timor-Leste become a member of ASEAN, which it regards as a 'rules-based' multilateral institution because otherwise the country would fall into the hands of (unnamed) 'players with strategic interests'.[367]

---

363. *See* Timor-Leste Ministry of Foreign Affairs and Cooperation, *Press Release: Timor-Leste Welcomes the Chairman's Statement of the 36th ASEAN Summit*, 29 Jun. 2020, at: http://timor-leste.gov.tl/?p=24841&lang=en.
364. *See* Government of Timor-Leste, 'Timor-Leste and the European Union sets out joint priority areas for cooperation', 3 Feb. 2022, at: http://timor-leste.gov.tl/?p=30072&n=1&lang=en.
365. European Commission, *Democratic Republic of Timor-Leste Multi-annual Indicative Programme for the period 2021-2027*, C(2021) 9071 final, 14 Dec. 2021, p. 3, at: https://international-partnerships.ec.europa.eu/system/files/2022-01/mip-2021-c2021-9071-timor-leste-annex_en.pdf.
366. *Ibid.*
367. *See* further, European Commission, *Commission Implementing Decision of 29.11.2022 on the financing of the annual action plan in favour of the Democratic Republic of Timor-Leste for 2022*, C(2022) 8902 final, 29 Nov. 2022. One of the Plan's objectives is to support Timor-Leste's economic integration as well as trade in the Southeast Asia region (ASEAN is not expressly mentioned).

May 2024, its attendance rate was at 88.6 per cent).[375] The second was that Timor-Leste was 'encouraged to maintain and promote good relations with all ASEAN Member States, as part of demonstrating its ability and readiness to implement and abide by the ASEAN Charter' (*see* next paragraph).[376] The third was the stipulation in the Roadmap that accession to the ASEAN agreements is part of the process of becoming a member.[377] Two such agreements were mentioned at the Foreign Ministers' Meeting. First, the Southeast Asia Nuclear Weapon-Free Zone (SEANWFZ) Treaty, also known as the Bangkok Treaty: even though the SEANWFZ Commission formally approved its accession in June 2024, the necessary preparations have apparently not yet been concluded. Second, the ASEAN Trade in Goods Agreement (ATIGA), where only its intention to accede was recorded. Finally, in January 2025, ASEAN Foreign Ministers recognised the progress made by Timor-Leste in implementing the 'Roadmap for Full Membership', referred to the adoption of the revised Guidelines for the Implementation of the Observer Status Granted to Timor-Leste, called on the (unnamed) external partners to continue providing capacity building assistance and mentioned the establishment of the Timor-Leste Unit in the ASEAN Secretariat as a means to intensify efforts in facilitating its accession.[378]

101. In the previous edition of this monograph, it was argued that, as Timor-Leste is an aspiring democratic country, whose human rights record is better than that of several Member States, those members having totalitarian / dictatorial regimes in power may very well not look forward to its accession. For example, the relations between Timor-Leste and the military regime in power in Myanmar have turned hostile on account of the latter's abysmal record of human rights. In particular, in late August 2023, Myanmar expelled East Timor's top diplomat in the country, after he had met with the National Unity Government (NUG) of the Republic of the Union of Myanmar, the political movement (and government in exile) that has been established by lawmakers who are associated with Aung San Suu Kyi, the Burmese senior politician and Nobel Peace Prize laureate in 1991.[379] Myanmar's move of diplomatic hostility had, however, been preceded by the statement of the Prime Minister of Timor-Leste that his country would reconsider joining ASEAN if it would not be possible for ASEAN to solve the situation with and conflict in Myanmar. He also said that

---

375. *See* Joint Communiqué of the 57th ASEAN Foreign Ministers' Meeting, Vientiane, 25 Jul. 2024, para. 23, at: https://asean.org/wp-content/uploads/2024/07/Final-Joint-Communique-of-the-57th-AMM.pdf.
376. *Ibid.*
377. *Ibid.*, para. 25. Generally, *see* J. Lin et al., *Timor-Leste in ASEAN: is it ready to join?* (Singapore: ISEAS-Yusof Ishak Institute, Trends in Southeast Asia 1/24, January 2024), at: https://www.iseas.edu.sg/wp-content/uploads/2024/01/TRS1_24.pdf.
378. *See* Press Statement by the Chair of the ASEAN Foreign Ministers' Retreat, 19 Jan. 2025, Langkawi, Malaysia, para. 26.
379. *See* 'Myanmar expels East Timor's diplomat in retaliation for supporting opposition forces', *Associated Press*, 27 Aug. 2023, at: https://apnews.com/. For the NUG, *see* https://www.nugmyanmar.org/en/.

Timor-Leste had firmly adopted democratic ideals and, therefore, could neither accept military dictatorial regimes nor ignore the human rights violations in Myanmar.[380]

V. Competition Between ASEAN and Other Asian Regional Organisations

102. It is worthwhile to examine whether, for those states that are beyond the mere status of ASEAN applicant but whose full membership is still uncompleted (Timor-Leste) or could be described as 'aspiring applicant states' (e.g., PNG) or states that could be regarded as potential candidates (e.g., Australia, Sri Lanka), there might be other international organisations in the wider South Asian region in which they could potentially seek membership. If it were shown that such other organisations exist, one could consider that ASEAN is in competition with them, in the sense that membership in the former could be regarded as a possible and viable alternative to ASEAN.[381] To put it otherwise, if the goal of these states is to accede and participate in South Asian regional organisations and they find it impossible or not appropriate to join ASEAN, membership in some other (broadly comparable) regional organisation/s might be a solution. In this arguably theoretical construction, which aims at showing the dynamics of international organisations in this specific region, any such other organisation could be deemed as a (direct) competitor to ASEAN, which could benefit if the interested states were not to accede to ASEAN. To put it otherwise, the question examined here is to determine whether: (a) countries in the broader South Asian region that are not granted membership in ASEAN or do not accept the membership offered (*see* the Timor-Leste's attitude in relation to how ASEAN deals (or rather fails to deal) with Myanmar) or (b) ASEAN Member States which for whatever reason want to terminate their membership in it and withdraw could accede to other regional international organisations, the latter understood as (actual or potential) competitors of ASEAN.

103. It is submitted that there exist two such regional institutions. The first is the South Asian Association for Regional Cooperation (SAARC); the second is the Bay of Bengal Initiative for Multi-Sectoral Technical and Economic Cooperation (BIMSTEC). What follows is a brief examination of these two organisations, where the common points with ASEAN will be highlighted because, on account of these commonalities, they could be considered to be competitive organisations. SAARC was established on 8 December 1985.[382] The original Member States are Bangladesh, Bhutan, India, Maldives, Nepal, Pakistan, and Sri Lanka. As in the case of ASEAN, SAARC was founded on the principle to respect the norms of sovereign equality,

380. *See* 'Timor-Leste Rethinks its Accession Bid if ASEAN Cannot Handle Myanmar Issue', *Asian News Network*, 7 Aug. 2023, https://asianews.network/timor-leste-rethinks-its-accession-bid-if-asean-cannot-handle-myanmar-issue/.

381. Generally, *see* K. Magliveras, *Legal Aspects of Competition Between International Organizations*, in *Shielding Humanity: Essays in International Law in Honor of Judge Abdul G. Koroma* 242–259 (C. C. Jelloh & O. Elias eds, Brill / Nijhoff 2015).

382. The Charter is available at: https://saarc-sec.org/index.php/about-saarc/saarc-charter.

territorial integrity, political independence, non-interference in the domestic affairs of Member States, and to promote mutual benefit for all participating states.[383] And like ASEAN, SAARC seeks to promote the economic growth, social progress, and cultural development of its membership. SAARC has a long-standing experience in economic cooperation. Starting in 1993 with the Agreement on South Asian Preferential Trading Arrangement (SAPTA),[384] Member States subsequently concluded the South Asian Free Trade Area (SAFTA) Agreement on 6 January 2004, which entered into force on 1 January 2006.[385] This was a necessary step towards the eventual establishment of the South Asian Economic Union (SAEU). The signing of the South Asian Agreement on Trade in Services (SATIS) during the Sixteenth SAARC Summit on 29 April 2010 was another step towards the materialisation of SAEU.[386] SATIS entered into force on 29 November 2012.[387] However, unlike certain ASEAN countries, governments in most SAARC countries appear to subscribe to the basic democratic ideals and principles.[388] This has been possible despite the fact that, like ASEAN countries, they have gone through political instability, domestic strife, and military tensions.[389]

---

383. Generally, *see* N. Haider, *Radical Regional Cooperation: ASEAN and SAARC* (Axis Books 2014); T. Delinic & N. N. Pandey (eds), *SAARC: Towards Meaningful Cooperation* (Centre for South Asian Studies / Konrad Adenauer Stiftung, 2012).
384. It was signed on 11 Apr. 1993 during the 7th SAARC Summit in Dhaka, Bangladesh, entered into force on 7 Dec. 1995.
385. Text at: https://saarc-sec.org/index.php/resources/agreements-conventions/36-agreement-on-south-asian-free-trade-area-safta/file.
386. Generally, *see* S. Kaur, S. Khorana & M. Kaur, *Is There Any Potential in Service Trade of South Asia?* 55 Foreign Trade Review 402–417 (2020). Note also that, like ASEAN, the SARRC has for many years now concluded several treaties and adopted political / declaratory documents especially in the politico-security sector and the social sector addressing pressing problems and presumably seeking uniformity into how Member States dealt with them and regulated them. Suffice to mention the following (available at: https://saarc-sec.org/index.php/resources/agreements-conventions#): the Convention on Suppression of Terrorism (signed on 4 Nov. 1987) and Additional Protocol (6 Jan. 2004); the Convention on Narcotic Drugs and Psychotropic Substances (23 Nov. 1990); the Charter of Democracy (February 2011),which is actually a declaration and rather lacks any legally binding force, at: https://saievac.org/2012/01/23/saarc-charter-of-democracy-2/, *see* also D. Shahi, 'South Asian Association for Regional Cooperation (SAARC)' in *The Democratization of International Institutions - First International Democracy Report* (L. Levi, G. Finizio & N. Vallinoto eds, Routledge 2014); the Agreement on Rapid Response to Natural Disasters (11 Nov. 2011); and the Convention on Combating and Prevention of Trafficking in Women and Children for Prostitution (5 Jan. 2002).
387. Based on these developments as well as on the economic cooperation among ASEAN countries, the argument advanced that there was little intra-regional economic cooperation within South Asia does not seem to be justified, *see* A. Tripathy & A. Paricha, *Regional Cooperation in South Asia*, 15:2 World Affairs: The Journal of International Issues 62–82 (2011).
388. *See* Sixteenth SAARC Summit, *Thimphu Silver Jubilee Declaration 'Towards a Green and Happy South Asia*', Thimphu, Bhutan, 28–29 Apr. 2010, SAARC/SUMMIT.16/15, para. 6: '[L]eaders … appreciate that all the Member States had evolved into multiparty Democracies', text at: https://saarc-sec.org/index.php/resources/summit-declarations/18-sixteenth-saarc-summit-thimphu-2010/file.
389. *See* S.D. Muni, *The New Democratic Wave and Regional Cooperation in South Asia* (International Institute for Democracy and Electoral Assistance, 2009).

104. The SAARC Charter is silent on the question of the admission of new Member States.[390] However, this question was dealt with during the Fourth SAARC Summit (Islamabad, 29–31 December 1988). It endorsed the resolution of the Council of Ministers that any state in the region, which subscribed to the SAARC Charter's objectives and principles, may be admitted as a member by a unanimous decision of the Heads of State or Government.[391] In particular, the admittance of new Member States would be effected through the signing of a Joint Declaration by the existing membership, on the one hand, and the new member, on the other hand, always at the level of Heads of State or Government. During the Thirteenth SAARC Summit (Dhaka, 12–13 November 2005), the application, which had been lodged by Afghanistan, was unanimously accepted, but the Joint Declaration was concluded much later, in April 2007.[392] Afghanistan's application was surrounded by controversy not least because, strictly speaking, it is not located in South Asia. But on this occasion SAARC states overcame the geographical barrier, something which ASEAN States do not appear prepared to do.[393] It is interesting to note that since the treaties adopted under the auspices of SAARC do not envisage accession by third states (there is no such clause in the Charter), a legal machination had to be devised to allow Afghanistan to accede to the SAFTA Agreement. The hurdle was overcome by considering that the Protocol, which allowed Afghanistan to accede to the SAFTA Agreement, was an amendment of the SAFTA Agreement and that it had been reached by consensus.[394]

105. While there is currently no overlapping membership between SAARC and ASEAN,[395] theoretically speaking, an ASEAN Member could withdraw (e.g., on account of very serious disagreements with the other Members that has made its

---

390. Note that only a rather small number of constitutive instruments of international organisations do not contain a clause on the accession of new Member States; the Charter of the Cooperation Council for the Arab States of the Gulf (GCC)(1981, 1288 U.N.T.S. 131) is such an example.
391. *See* Fourth SAARC Summit, *Islamabad Declaration*, 31 Dec. 1988, para. 4, at: https://saarc-sec.org/index.php/resources/summit-declarations/13-fourth-saarc-summit-islambad-1988/file. This is in line with the principle of the law and practice of international organisations that the supreme organ of an international organisation may reach decisions in matters not regulated by the constitutive instrument on the basis of a unanimous vote in which all Member States have participated.
392. *See* Joint Declaration on the Admission of the Islamic Republic of Afghanistan into the South Asian Association for Regional Cooperation (SAARC), New Delhi, 3 Apr. 2007, at: https://saarc-sec.org/index.php/resources/agreements-conventions/39-declaration-on-the-admission-of-the-islamic-republic-of-afghanistan-into-saarc/file.
393. There exist examples of other regional originations where the geographical location of prospective Member States has not been an obstacle. Thus, the Council of Europe started as a Western European organisation but in the 1990s, following the collapse of the USSR, it offered membership to new states not located in what might traditionally be regarded as 'Europe', e.g., to Azerbaijan.
394. The Protocol was signed on 3 Aug. 2008, at: https://saarc-sec.org/index.php/resources/agreements-conventions/42-protocol-of-accession-of-islamic-republic-of-afghanistan-to-safta/file.
395. Reportedly, in May 2008 Myanmar officially wrote to the SAARC Secretariat seeking full membership. But later in the same year, it was decided that Myanmar (as well as Australia) will be associated through the status of observer, *see* Fifteenth SAARC Summit, *Declaration 'Partnership for Growth for Our People'*, Colombo, 2–3 Aug. 2008, para. 40, text at: https://saarc-sec.org/index.php/resources/summit-declarations/9-fifteenth-saarc-summit-colombo-2008/file. Guidelines for cooperation with observers (they also include, China, Iran, Japan, South Korea, USA, and the EU) were approved at the same Summit.

continued participation in ASEAN untenable) and seek to accede to SAARC because they consider it as a regional international organisation that, to use terms and notions from competition law, is active in a 'geographical market' similar to ASEAN, while its operation and activities (in other words, its 'services and the products' it offers to Member States) are also similar to ASEAN.

106. Presently, BIMSTEC, a little-known regional international organisation, which comprises seven states from the South Asia and Southeast Asia regions, namely Bangladesh, India, Myanmar, Sri Lanka, Thailand, Nepal, and Bhutan. It was originally established on 6 June 1997 pursuant to the Declaration on the Establishment of the Bangladesh–India–Sri Lanka–Thailand Economic Cooperation, also known as the Declaration of Bangkok.[396] Through subsequent enlargement, it finally developed to BIMSTEC.[397] The presence of two ASEAN countries among its membership (Myanmar and Thailand) does not appear to have caused any significant problems. Its founding principles are identical to those of SAARC and similar to those of ASEAN. Thus, cooperation within BIMSTEC has been based on respect for sovereign equality, territorial integrity, political independence, non-interference in internal affairs, peaceful co-existence, and mutual benefit. According to the Declaration of Bangkok, pursuing this kind of collaboration is additional to and not a substitute for bilateral, regional or multilateral cooperation. A Framework Agreement on the BIMSTEC Free Trade Area was concluded on 8 February 2004 by all Member States, except Bangladesh which joined it by virtue of the Protocol of 25 June 2004.[398] The BIMSTEC Convention on Cooperation in Combating International Terrorism, Transnational Organized Crime and Illicit Drug Trafficking was concluded in Myanmar on 11 December 2009 and entered into force on 16 March 2021[399] (in comparison, the ASEAN Convention on Counter Terrorism (examined *infra*) was concluded on 13 January 2007, entered into force on 27 May 2011).

107. As was mentioned in the first edition of this monograph, BIMSTEC operated on the basis of the Declaration of Bangkok; in other words, its legal status was similar to that of ASEAN, as it was before the ASEAN Charter's entry into force in 2008. And it was also mentioned that in 2018 the Heads of State and Government resolved to move forward with a Charter so that BIMSTEC would have a legal framework 'delineating roles and responsibilities of different layers of institutional structure and decision-making processes'.[400] It follows that its institutional evolution has been similar to ASEAN's transformation into a rules-based international

396. BIMSTEC documents are available at: https://bimstec.org/others-declarations-and-agreements/.

397. Generally, *see* F. Yahya, *BIMSTEC and Emerging Patterns of Asian Regional and Interregional Cooperation*, 40 Austl. J. Pol. Sci. 391–410 (2005); S.S. Pattanaik, *Transforming Eastern South Asia: Relevance of BIMSTEC*, 42 J. Strategic Analysis 422–429 (2018).

398. *See* J. Sengupta, *BIMSTEC-FTA: A New Hope for Enhanced Regional Trade*, Issue Briefs and Special Reports(New Delhi: Observer Research Foundation, 19 Sep. 2017), https://www.orfonline.org/research/bimstec-fta-new-hope-enhanced-regional-trade/.

399. It was completed by the BIMSTEC Convention on Mutual Legal Assistance in Criminal Matters, signed during the Fifth BIMSTEC Summit on 30 Mar. 2022, https://bimstec.org/agreements-conventions-mous/.

400. *See* Fourth BIMSTEC Summit Declaration, *Towards a Peaceful, Prosperous and Sustainable Bay of Bengal Region*, Kathmandu, 30–31 Aug. 2018, para. 6.

organisation. Finally, the BIMSTEC Charter was signed and adopted during the Fifth BIMSTEC Summit (held virtually in Colombo, Sri Lanka), which as mentioned above was held in March 2022.[401] The Charter, which came into force on 20 May 2024, endows BIMSTEC with international legal personality.

108. According to Article 6 of the Charter, the 'admission of new members' clause sets out the following admission criteria for candidate states: (a) 'territory contiguity' to or primary dependence on the Bay of Bengal and/or any other criterion that might be agreed by the Ministerial Meeting; (b) the obligation to abide by the Charter; (c) the ability and willingness to perform all obligations stemming from membership; and (d) to contribute to the unity and stability of BIMSTEC.[402] Membership applications must also contain a declaration that the applicant state shall fulfil the Charter criteria. That the declaration must be 'made in a formal instrument' presumably means that it must be signed by the Head of State. The question could be asked whether said declaration must have already received the approval of the applicant state's Parliament. However, this is rather a domestic matter and not of concern to BIMSTEC. International organisations operate on the assumption that Member States always comply with all constitutional and other requirements and conditions. Failure to do so may not be invoked as a reason justifying the non-performance of obligations that emanate from membership in an international organisation. Otherwise, Member States would be free to choose which obligations to observe and which to ignore.

Pursuant to Article 6(3)(c) of the Charter, the act of approving admission has been entrusted to the BIMSTEC Summit, which will decide having received the recommendation of the Ministerial Meeting. Whether the latter is a *conditio sine qua non* for the Summit to take a decision on admission is not laid down. However, due to the small number of states participating in BIMSTEC and the fact that its operation is not based on a very stringent legal framework, unlike other international organisations,[403] this is rather a question of minor importance. Once the application has been approved, the new Member State is required to deposit the 'instrument of accession'. No details are given as to the form and content of this instrument. Moreover, it is also not clear if the acceding state must ratify the Charter. However, reference should also be made to Article 30, the clause on legal continuity, which stipulates that all treaties, agreements, declarations and other BIMSTEC documents that were in effect before the Charter's entry into force shall continue to be valid.[404] It follows that the 'instrument of accession' of new Member States should also cover all previous treaties and other legal documents. Even though BIMSTEC acts effectively at a sub-regional level (namely as a sub-regional international organisation for

401. *See* Fifth BIMSTEC Summit Declaration, 30 Mar. 2022, Colombo, Sri Lanka, para. 5. For the text, *see* https://bimstec.org/images/content_page_pdf/1696679710_BIMSTEC%20Charter.pdf.
402. Compare Art. 6 ASEAN Charter.
403. Compare Art. 4 UN Charter.
404. Compare Art. 52 ASEAN Charter.

the Bay of Bengal), there appears to be no reason why, if so resolved by all Member States, it could not open up to other South Asian / Southeast Asian countries as well. As has been argued, the significance of BIMSTEC's role for the wider region has been advancing.[405]

109. Based on the above observations, it transpires that there is room for competition between ASEAN, on the one hand, and SAARC and/or BIMSTEC, on the other hand. These three (sub-regional) international organisations are in different stages of evolution, with ASEAN being by far the most developed, the one with advanced methods of operation, certainly the one with the best connections to countries outside the region and having a very good record of cooperation with other multilateral institutions. But the potential of competition among them should not be underestimated. Generally speaking, the existence of several international organisations in the same (broadly defined) geographical region, founded on common principles and norms, with the same or similar goals and aims and being active in matching areas of activities are the most favourable conditions for competition to take place. The same is true for the broader region of South Asia, where these three regional organisations co-exist and are influenced by each other, and, therefore, it is not unreasonable to expect that there will be a measure of competition among them.

In particular, they could be seen as 'players' that have formed a distinct geographical 'market' of regional international organisations. In this 'market' (we could call it 'the market of South Asian regional organisations'), these 'players' offer similar 'products and services', while potential 'buyers' (i.e., those states that are interested or will be interested in joining them) must meet similar conditions, must assume comparable duties and obligations, and shall enjoy benefits of more or less equal value. In this 'market', ASEAN possesses a dominant position, and, consequently, competition is drawn to its direction. For this reason, it is very difficult for the other two organisations to act as rivals and to contest ASEAN's apparent superiority in the way it operates and in what it has already achieved, However, future conditions and relations in the 'market' could very well change; in the international community, nothing remains the same for long. If, for the purposes of argument, ASEAN would be unable to maintain the position of superiority that it presently holds or, worse, it faces problems that it cannot address promptly and effectively, its Member States would, in theory, have the opportunity to 'migrate' to one of the other two organisations or to any other regional institution that in the meantime might have become a 'player' in the same 'market'. In this scenario, the consequences of a weak ASEAN should be able to be absorbed by the 'market', which will continue to exist and function for the benefit of both 'players' and 'buyers'.

110. Mutatis mutandis, the same should happen if one of the other 'players' were to face insurmountable problems. This could happen, for example, if the 'player' in question failed to keep abreast of the development and advancement of the other 'players' and fell into disuse. In that respect, it should also be noted that the competition that takes place within the 'market' could actually benefit the 'players'

405. *See* N. Agarwala & P. Sahais, *Is the Bay of Bengal Regaining Its Lost Importance?*, 15 J. Indian Ocean Region 336–345 (2019).

because they could start mimicking the 'player/s' that appear to be stronger and more successful. For example, that the institutional evolution of BIMSTEK appears to have followed that of ASEAN and that several provisions in the BIMSTEK Charter resemble the corresponding provisions in the ASEAN Charter is probably not a coincidence, but the outcome of the former being influenced by the latter in the organisational and institutional aspects of cooperation. If this is indeed what has happened, it should be regarded as a favourable outcome of the competition existing in the 'market'.

VI. Withdrawal of Member States: Repudiation of ASEAN Treaties

111. Even though the ASEAN Charter does not contain a withdrawal clause, the example of the EU is of relevance when discussing the possibility that one or more Member States may at some stage express the wish to withdraw from the Organisation. When the EU (as European Economic Community (EEC)) was established in the late 1950s, its founding instrument, the Treaty of Rome, was completely silent on whether Member States had the ability or the right to withdraw. For many decades afterwards, there was a popular belief that, as the Treaty of Rome had been concluded for an unlimited period of time, the original six Member States and the states that acceded at a later stage would be tied to the EEC for as long as it existed. There were also issues of pragmatism: which Member State would wish to leave this regional organisation, which had succeeded in ensuring peace and security, economic prosperity, and a better quality of life for the population of Member States? It could also be pointed out that the UN Charter did (and still does) not feature a withdrawal clause.[406] Therefore, the perception that membership in the EEC was a permanent state of affairs appeared to be a valid one. But the life and evolution of international organisations is mired in politics and the ever-changing priorities and interests of Member States.

112. Thus, in the early 2000s it was decided that a provision permitting withdrawal should be included in the constitutive instrument of (what had by then become) the EU. This decision was made even though everybody seemed to agree that no Member State will ever invoke it, especially since the EU was embarking on the final stages of the world's first-ever multilateral monetary union, and a political union was in the making. It finally culminated in Article 50 of the Treaty on European Union (TEU), the very clause that allowed the United Kingdom to permanently leave the EU on 31 January 2020 (what became known as 'Brexit').[407]

406. The lack of a withdrawal clause in the UN Charter could be explained by the drafters' wish to avoid a repetition of the mass withdrawal of Member States from the League of Nations. With the exception of Indonesia in the mid-1960s, no other Member State has officially declared its intention to withdraw from the UN. Generally, *see* K. Magliveras, *Withdrawal from the League of Nations Revisited*, 10 Dickinson Journal of International Law 25-71 (1991).

407. For an account of the pitfalls of Brexit, *see* G. Naldi & K. Magliveras, *The Right to Revoke Withdrawal Notices from International Organisations: The Case of Brexit and the European Union*, 28 Maastricht J. Eur. & Comp. L. 30-58 (2021).

113. While ASEAN has not reached the intensity of integration that the EU has achieved (ASEAN talks about a *Community* of nations, while the EU is, at least in theory, about a *Union* of nations), that the drafters of the ASEAN Charter did not include any provisions on withdrawal and did not specify the duration of the life of ASEAN leads to obvious questions, whose answers may not be straightforward. If a Member State wanted to part ways with ASEAN, it would not be as easy as making an announcement to that effect or submit a written notice of withdrawal to the Secretary-General and to the other Member States. And this because, legally speaking, the ASEAN Charter is not the treaty which established the international legal person that is ASEAN, even though it is the treaty that endowed it with legal personality pursuant to Article 3 thereof. On the contrary, as stated in its Preamble, the ASEAN Charter is the multilateral instrument through which Member States decided to 'establish … the legal and institutional framework for ASEAN'. A grammatical interpretation of the Preamble rather confirms this submission.

114. It follows that even if a Member State were to repudiate the ASEAN Charter as a multilateral treaty and declare that it is no longer bound by it, this will not necessarily lead to its termination of membership in ASEAN, because, as explained, the Charter is not (again legally speaking) the constitutive instrument of ASEAN. The latter is (and remains so) the 1967 ASEAN (Bangkok) Declaration, where the original five Member States declared that they had established an 'Association for Regional Cooperation among the countries of South-East Asia to be known as the Association of South-East Asian Nations (ASEAN)' to act 'as firm foundation for common action to promote regional cooperation'. As regards the five states which joined it at a later stage, they are deemed to have acceded to the Bangkok Declaration. Therefore, if a Member State, for whatever reason, wanted to leave ASEAN, it would have first to announce the decision to disjoin the contents of the Bangkok Declaration and then find a legal way to repudiate the ASEAN Charter. However, if the other Member States objected to its withdrawal and/or considered it as an illegal act but the Member State in question insisted on parting ways, it would have to resort to other kind of action that would be tantamount to withdrawal. For example, constantly being absent from the meetings of all ASEAN organs, refusing to pay the assessed contributions to the Organisation's budget, refusing to take any domestic legislative and regulatory measures to comply with ASEAN decisions (on these matters, *see* the next chapter) and, generally, adopting a behaviour signifying that it is no longer a Member State and does not want to be treated as such.[408] While one cannot know how the other Member States and the Organisation itself will address this kind of situation, the Member State eager to withdraw would still bear international responsibility for being in breach of its obligations and duties.

115. A further issue that needs to be considered in the case of a purported withdrawal is to determine the fate of participation of such Member State, on the one hand, in the treaties, conventions, agreements and other legal instruments that have

---

408. *Cf.* T. Chalermpalanupap, *No Brexit Repeat in ASEAN. No Country Is Looking to Leave the Southeast Asian Bloc – Yet*, The Diplomat, 28 Jun. 2016, at: https://thediplomat.com/2016/06/no-brexit-repeat-in-asean/.

been concluded with the remaining Member States and/or with third states and, on the other hand, in the ASEAN integration process, especially in the context of the AEC. In the case of the EU, the aforementioned Article 50 TEU dictates that the withdrawing Member concludes an agreement with the rest of the membership. The purpose of this agreement is to decide what their future relationship shall be.[409] Moreover, the withdrawal clauses that are included in the constitutive instruments of other international organisations invariably deal with such issues as, for example, the obligation of the withdrawing Member to settle accounts with the international organisation in question and to pay up any outstanding budgetary contributions before withdrawal takes effect.[410] Thus, if it ever came for an ASEAN Member to wish to withdraw and legal and procedural problems were raised as to how it would be effected, it is important to remember that there exists international practice to ensure an orderly withdrawal process. There is no good reason why a Member State should not leave an international organisation in good terms and not with animosity.

116. To return to the ASEAN treaties that contain a withdrawal clause, two observations should be made. The first is that they do not link the termination of the status of Member State in ASEAN with the continued participation in them. Therefore, it should not be taken for granted that, when a Member State has withdrawn from ASEAN, it will automatically secede from each and every ASEAN legal instrument that it has ratified. Arguably, this is a legal question that was not addressed by the drafters of the ASEAN Charter. It may, however, have to do with the fact that several ASEAN treaties had been concluded before the entry into force of the Charter and, therefore, withdrawal from them would have to follow the relevant clause contained therein. The second observation is that the content of these withdrawal clauses differs considerably. The following examples will illustrate it. First, the ASEAN Convention on Counter Terrorism (ACCT) (2007), which is analysed later in the present monograph: Article XXII stipulates that contracting parties may withdraw at any time once the Convention has entered into force for the party in question and that withdrawal shall take effect 180 days after the receipt of the instrument of withdrawal by the Secretary-General of ASEAN. Second, the Treaty on the Southeast Asia Nuclear-Weapon-Free Zone (also known as Bangkok Treaty), which is mentioned elsewhere in the monograph:[411] Article 22 stipulates that it shall remain in force indefinitely but allows withdrawal only when another contracting party has breached any of the provisions that are essential to the achievement of the objectives of the Treaty; in this case, twelve months' notice must be given.

---

409. See Agreement on the Withdrawal of the United Kingdom of Great Britain and Northern Ireland from the European Union and the European Atomic Energy Community, agreed on 17 Oct. 2019, entered into force on 1 Feb. 2020, O.J., C 384 I, 12.11.2019, p. 1; Political declaration setting out the framework for the future relationship between the European Union and the United Kingdom, adopted on 12 Nov. 2019, O.J. Union, C 384 I, 12.11.2019, p. 178.

410. Generally, *see* Naldi & Magliveras, *The Right to Revoke Withdrawal Notices from International Organisations*, *supra*.

411. It entered into force on 27 Mar. 1997, 1981 U.N.T.S 129; 35 I.L.M. 635 (1996).

§2. Fulfilment, Observance and Compliance with ASEAN Obligations

117. According to the second paragraph of Article 5 of the ASEAN Charter, Member States are obliged to take all measures, including the enactment of appropriate domestic legislation, which are necessary to implement the Charter's provisions in an effective manner. Moreover, Member States are under the general duty to comply with all obligations arising from membership. Given that, pursuant to the first paragraph of Article 5, Member States have equal rights and obligations under the Charter, it follows that the general duty to comply with all membership obligations is attached to each Member State individually. And, at the same time, it becomes a right of each Member State to expect full compliance by any and all other Member States. Thus, even though not expressly mentioned in the Charter, it should be accepted that to observe membership obligations is a duty owed not only to ASEAN, as an international organisation, but also to the entire membership. Indeed, there is a correlation between this duty and this right: it is because a Member State fulfils the duty to observe the membership obligations that it has the right to expect and to demand that the other Member States observe the membership obligations and also that ASEAN performs its own duties, and *vice versa*. This correlation, which invariably applies to international organisations, is perhaps best expressed in Article 2(2) of the UN Charter. It reads: 'All Members, in order to ensure to all of them the rights and benefits resulting from membership, shall fulfill in good faith the obligations assumed by them in accordance with the present Charter.'

118. Very seldom, if ever, the constitutive instruments of international organisations enumerate one by one the membership obligations that must be observed and fulfilled. The ASEAN Charter is no exception to this reality. And while, for example, the UN Charter does set out down in express terms certain fundamental obligations which are attached to all Member States (e.g., the obligation in Article 33 to solve disputes likely to endanger the maintenance of international peace and security through diplomatic, judicial, and other peaceful means), the ASEAN Charter does not. Notwithstanding this submission, it is true to say that Article 2 thereof enumerates the fundamental principles on which ASEAN is founded. As has been explained, these are principles, which are contained in the various declarations, agreements, and conventions that were adopted before the ASEAN Charter came into force. Over the years, they have been reaffirmed by Member States. In their turn, these principles happen to contain several duties and obligations. Suffice to mention the following three: (a) respect for the independence, sovereignty, equality, territorial integrity, and national identity of all Member States; (b) renunciation of aggression as well as of the threat of or the use of force;[412] and (c) non-interference in the internal affairs of the other Member States.

412. *See* Art. 52(1) UN Charter, which stipulates that it does not preclude the existence of regional arrangements or agencies to deal with matters concerning the maintenance of international (and by necessary implication) regional peace and security, subject to the *provisio* that such arrangements and agencies must act in compliance with the UN purposes and principles.

119. These duties and obligations and the underlying rules and norms are not only to be found in the legal system that over the years has been created through the various acts and activities pursued by ASEAN; as explained above, one could refer to this legal system as 'ASEAN law'. On the contrary, they are rather a manifestation of peremptory rules of public international law imposing the responsibility upon all states to always comply with them and never to breach them. Thus, if for the sake of argument these principles and the ensuing obligations had not been enumerated in Article 2 of the ASEAN Charter, they would have anyway been binding upon all Member States on account of the following two reasons: (a) that ASEAN members participate in other international organisations as well (and principally in the United Nations),[413] and (b) that they are contracting parties in relevant multilateral agreements and treaties setting out such principles and imposing such obligations. As regards those duties and obligations that are specific to ASEAN and its Member States, arguably Article 2 envisages the following two: (a) the shared commitment and the collective responsibility to promote regional peace, security and prosperity, and (b) the enhanced consultations on matters which seriously affect ASEAN's common interests.

120. Moreover, the ASEAN Charter contains the following obligations, some of which are of a procedural nature. They will be briefly examined in the order appearing in the Charter. First, Article 7(3)(a), pursuant to which Summit Meetings shall be held twice annually and shall be hosted by the Member State holding the ASEAN Chairmanship. From the same paragraph derives the duty of the heads of state or government of all Member States to participate in all Summit meetings. No doubt, this is a necessary duty given that consensus is the principal mode of decision-making. However, this is a duty that cannot be easily legally enforced. Second, Article 8(1), which lays down the duty of the Member States' foreign ministers to participate in all meetings of the Coordinating Council. Again, this is a difficult to enforce duty. Third, Article 22, which obliges Member States to endeavour to resolve all disputes peacefully and in a timely manner by using dialogue, consultations, and negotiations. Fourth, Article 30(2), which stipulates that the operational budget of the ASEAN Secretariat shall be covered by all Member States through equal annual contributions. They must be promptly remitted to the Organisation. Fifth, Article 33, which obliges Member States to adhere to existing diplomatic protocol and practices when carrying out any endeavours relating to ASEAN and its activities. Sixth, Article 41(4), which concerns the conduct of Member States in the area of ASEAN external relations. In particular, on the basis of the principles of unity and solidarity, they must coordinate their policies, while developing common positions and pursuing joint actions. Arguably, this duty is under the unwritten *provisio* that such common positions do not run contrary to vital national interests. And if this were the case, the requirement that all decisions are reached by consensus should allow for taking into account any Member State's serious concerns and reservations.

---

413. *See ibid.*, Art. 2.

121. Finally, the aforementioned Article 5 of the ASEAN Charter does not expressly refer to the so-called principle of sincere cooperation, which has been included in the constitutive instruments of only few international organisations. The prime example is the EU: Article 4(3) TEU stipulates that the EU and its Member States must, in full mutual respect, assist each other in carrying out their respective tasks; that the Member States must take all measures to ensure that their Treaty obligations are fulfilled and to observe any and all decisions which are issued by the EU; and that Member States must refrain from acting in a way which could endanger the attainment of its objectives.[414] If ASEAN were to develop into a genuine community of nations, the principle of sincere cooperation should be enshrined in an evolving ASEAN legal system and become a norm of ASEAN law.

I. The Question of the Implementation of and Compliance with ASEAN Obligations from the Perspective of the Domestic (Constitutional) Law of Member States

122. The duty of all Member States to implement, to comply with and not to breach the obligations emanating from the ASEAN Charter could also be addressed from the point of view of their domestic legal systems. To ensure that the entire membership fully applies and gives the maximum effect domestically to the various duties and obligations assumed under the ASEAN Charter[415] – and indeed under any other ratified agreement or treaty – the Member States' legal systems (and primarily the Constitution as the hierarchically superior law) should contain rules as to how these duties and obligations are incorporated therein and how they are observed. Member States should also determine the associated question of whether the provisions of international agreements and treaties, in our case the provisions of the ASEAN Charter, take precedence over domestic laws and whether, in the case of a conflict, the Charter provisions prevail, thus rendering domestic legislation inapplicable. Notwithstanding the importance of the answer to this question – domestic law supersedes ratified international agreements or the latter rank higher than domestic law – it is true that there are not many Constitutions which expressly address it.[416] Indeed, this is a delicate and complicated question, not least because it also relates to the question of state sovereignty. And, as regards specifically the participation of states in international organisations, it has to do with the extent of the powers and competencies that states are prepared to transfer to them. In the case

414. Generally, *see* M. Klamert, *The Principle of Loyalty in EU Law* (Oxford U. Press 2014). Compare CJEU, Case C-660/13, *Council of the European Union v. European Commission*, Judgment (Grand Chamber), 28 Jul. 2016, ECLI:EU:C:2016:616.

415. For the question of the obligations assumed by Member States in international organisations, *see* Magliveras, 'Membership in International Organisations' in Research Handbook on International Organisations, *supra*, 90 et seq.

416. *See* S. Lee ed., *Encyclopedia of Public International Law in Asia* (Brill / Nijhoff 2021). Generally, *see* V.S. Vereshchet, *New Constitutions and the Old Problem of the Relationship between International Law and National Law*, 7 Eur. J. Int'l L. 29–41 (1996); S.A. Riesenfeld & F.M. Abbott (eds), *Parliamentary Participation in the Making and Operation of Treaties: A Comparative Study* (Martinus Nijhoff Publishers 1994).

of international organisations that aim at the integration of Member States, the transfer of many and significant sovereign powers is a *sine ne qua non* for their operation. These organisations are collectively known as REIOs (regional economic integration organisations) and invariably operate having the European Union as the prototype. The EU is presently the most integrated and advanced REIO. Indeed, it has moved beyond economic integration to monetary integration featuring a common current (the euro) and a common central bank (the European Central Bank – ECB). Even though ASEAN is not yet a proper REIO, there is no doubt that this is the direction that for several years has been pursued by its Member States.

123. The overview of the relevant provisions in the constitutions of the ASEAN Member States, which is undertaken in the following paragraphs, reveals that few of them actually contain clauses on the implementation of obligations flowing from being contracting parties to treaties establishing international organisation as well as from membership therein.[417] The question of the primacy of international law rules, including ratified treaties, over domestic law is invariably not addressed. However, in some cases there is ordinary domestic legislation which deals with this question. It should also be noted that the text of these Constitutions is regularly amended and that their codified text, which includes the latest amendments, may not always be available in English. However, it is the present authors' belief that the sources relied upon in this overview are up-to-date.[418]

124. In the Constitution of the Kingdom of Cambodia (1993),[419] Article 8(2) thereof stipulates that the King, the Head of State for life, shall be the guarantor of international treaties. In accordance with Article 26, the King shall sign and ratify international treaties and conventions after a vote of approval by the National Assembly and the Senate. This provision should be read together with Article 90, which stipulates that the National Assembly shall adopt or repeal treaties and international conventions.[420] As regards specifically the question of the treaties' validity in the domestic legal system, the only relevant provision is Article 31. It provides

417. It is true that the exact legal position of each Member State will depend on whether it is a monist or a dualist country. However, within the confines of the present monograph, it is not possible to elaborate further on this issue. Suffice to mention that, as is later explained, in certain ASEAN Member States there are elements of both systems.

418. The reader may wish to also consult the reports submitted for the project 'The ASEAN Legal Order: The Legal Regimes of ASEAN and that of its Member States', which was carried out by the Centre for International Law, National University of Singapore, at: https://cil.nus.edu.sg/research/asean-law-and-policy/asean-integration-through-law-project/general-architecture/the-asean-legal-order-the-legal-regimes-of-asean-and-that-of-its-member-states/, as well as the reports in ASEAN Law Association, *Legal System in ASEAN*, at: https://www.aseanlawassociation.org/legal-system-in-asean/. *See* further, S. Chesterman, H. Owada and B. Saul (eds), *The Oxford Handbook of International Law in Asia and the Pacific* (Oxford: Oxford University Press 2019).

419. It was adopted by the Constitutional Assembly on 21 Sep. 1993. An English translation, which includes the March 1999 amendments and was published in 2017, is available at the Government's website, *see* https://pressocm.gov.kh/en/archives/9539.

420. Generally, *see* M. Bora, *The 1993 Cambodian Constitution and International Law: A Normative Perspective*, in *Cambodian Constitutional Law* 69–85 (H. Peng, K. Phallack & J. Menzel eds, Konrad-Adenauer-Stiftung 2016), at: https://constitutions.albasio.eu/wp-content/uploads/2019/02/Cambodian-Constitutional-Law.pdf.

that Cambodia recognises and respects human rights, as enshrined in the UN Charter, in the Universal Declaration of Human Rights (UDHR) of 1948, as well as in all international conventions relating to human rights, women's rights, and children's rights.[421]

125. But even this limited in scope provision is subject to Article 55, which reads: 'Any treaty and agreement incompatible with the independence, sovereignty, territorial integrity, neutrality and national unity of the Kingdom of Cambodia shall be abrogated.' Thus, one has to presume that Cambodia treats the ASEAN Charter, and the treaties concluded under its auspices, and generally its membership in the Organisation, as not being incompatible with its sovereignty. Finally, a decision rendered by the Constitutional Council, an organ resembling the French *Conseil d'état*, in 2007 confirmed that the laws of the country include the international conventions that have been accepted by Cambodia.[422]

126. In the case of the Republic of Indonesia, the Constitution appears to be far more adept to the country's participation in international organisations,[423] especially in multilateral institutions like ASEAN in which membership invariably entails consequences not only for the Member States but also for the population. Thus, Article 11(2) thereof stipulates that when the President concludes international agreements, which will produce an extensive and fundamental impact on the lives of the people or will result in a financial burden for the state, and/or will require amendments to existing legislation or the enactment of new legislation, the President is obliged to obtain the approval of the House of Representatives. But as regards specifically the domestic impact of ratified treaties, the Constitution only provides in the third paragraph of Article 11 that: 'Further provisions regarding international agreements shall be regulated by law', leaving this important matter into the hands of the ordinary legislator.[424] The relevant legislation is Law No.

421. As regards the ASEAN Human Rights Declaration (2012) (reproduced in Appendix 2 and analysed *infra*), it is presumably a question of interpretation whether it comes within the ambit of Art. 31, as it is neither a treaty nor a convention. Since the UDHR is recognised and respected therein, presumably the 2012 Declaration, which was approved by all ASEAN Member States, should enjoy the same (or comparable) legal status in the Cambodian legal system. However, only an express reference in the Constitution would have ensured equal legal status with the other human rights instruments which are expressly mentioned.
422. *See* Constitutional Council of Cambodia, *Royal Message of His Majesty Preah Bath Samdech Preah Boromneath Norodom Sihamoni, King of Cambodia, requesting the Constitutional Council to review the constitutionality of the Article 8 of the Law on the Aggravating Circumstances of Felonies*, Decision No. 092/003/2007 CC.D of 10 Jul. 2007, at: https://www.ccc.gov.kh/detail_info_en.php?_txtID=453.
423. The text of the Constitution of 1945 (rumoured to have been the shortest Constitution in the world at the time), as amended in 1999, in 2000, in 2001, and in 2002 under the Fourth Amendment, is available as certified translation at: http://www.humanrights.asia/indonesian-constitution-1945-consolidated/#section-24, and as unofficial translation at: https://jdih.bapeten.go.id/unggah/dokumen/peraturan/116-full.pdf.
424. Generally, *see* I. Palguna & A. Wardana, *Pragmatic Monism: The Practice of the Indonesian Constitutional Court in Engaging with International Law*, Asian Journal of International Law, published online January 2024, doi:10.1017/S2044251323000723; S. Butt, *The Position of International Law within the Indonesian Legal System*, 28 Emory Int'l L. Rev. 1–28 (2014).

24/2000 concerning international accords, which was adopted on 23 October 2000. The Law deals mostly with the procedural aspects of the signing and ratification of international agreements and not with the effect of approved treaties in the domestic legal system.[425]

127. There has been some litigation before domestic courts of justice concerning the content of Law No. 24/2000, on the meaning of ratification of treaties in the Indonesian legal system and, specifically, on the ASEAN Charter. Thus, in Decision No. 33/PUU/IX/2011 of 26 February 2013, the Constitutional Court held that it had the authority to examine the ASEAN Charter because, as a legal document, it formed an inseparable part of Law 24/2000, whose legality the Constitutional Court had the authority to investigate. In other words, the Constitutional Court could test its legality because, under Indonesian law, the ASEAN Charter was a law (i.e., an instrument of legislation). The present case, which had to do with the legality of the ASEAN Charter, was, in reality, an application for the judicial review of Law No. 38/2008, by virtue of which Indonesia had ratified the ASEAN Charter. According to the petitioners, the ASEAN Charter runs contrary to the Constitution because it, *inter alia*, refers to the creation of a free trade area,[426] which could result in many workers losing their jobs. It followed, the petitioners reasoned, that this eventuality contravened Article 27(2) of the Constitution (it reads: 'Each citizen shall be entitled to an occupation and an existence proper for a human being'). Therefore, by ratifying the ASEAN Charter, the Indonesian State must be regarded as not having protected the rights of citizens as it was obliged to do.

128. The Constitution of the Federation of Malaysia, a former British colony and for this reason a predominantly dualist country,[427] expressly refers to the incorporation of the decisions of international organisations into the domestic legal system. However, it makes no provision as to the legal status of such implementing legislation. Moreover, it is silent on whether it shall supersede national legislation that might be in conflict with the acts adopted by an international organisation.[428] In particular, Article 74 in conjunction with Article 76(1)(a) of the Federal Constitution stipulate that Parliament shall make laws with respect to matters pertaining to giving effect to any treaty, agreement or convention between the Federation of Malaysia and any other state, or any decision of an international organisation in which the

425. Generally, *see* E. Pratomo & R. B. Riyanto, *The Legal Status of Treaty/International Agreement and Ratification in the Indonesian Practice Within the Framework of the Development of the National Legal System*, 21(2) J. Legal, Ethical & Reg. Issues (2018) at: https://www.abacademies.org/articles/The-legal-status-of-treaty-international-agreement-and-ratification-in-the-indonesian-practice-within-the-framework-of-the-development-of-the-national-legal-system-1544-0044-21-2-180.pdf.

426. The relevant provision is Art. 1(5) of the ASEAN Charter, which actually talks about 'facilitat[ing] movement of business persons, professionals, talents and labour'.

427. *See* further, J. L. Neo, *Incorporating Human Rights: Mitigated Dualism and Interpretation in Malaysian Courts*, 18 Asian Y.B. Int'l L. 1–37 (2012); F. S. Shuaib, *The Status of International Law in the Malaysian Municipal Legal System: Creeping Monism in Legal Discourse?*, 16 Int'l Islamic U. Malaysia L.J. 181 (2008).

428. The Federal Constitution, including amendments up to September 2019, is available at: https://lom.agc.gov.my/federal-constitution.php.

Federation participates as a Member State.[429] The constitution is silent as to the primacy of international law as well as the law emanating from international organisations in which Malaysia participates as a Member State over domestic law.

129. The Constitution of the Philippines[430] has very few provisions of relevance. In particular, section 21 of Article VII thereof stipulates that no treaty and no international agreement shall be valid and effective unless at least two-thirds of all members of the Senate have concurred.[431] Moreover, under section 5 of Article VIII, the Supreme Court is competent to rule on all cases where the constitutionality or validity of any treaty, international agreement or executive agreement concluded by the Philippines is questioned. Even though the Constitution does not specifically say so, the Supreme Court is presumably entitled to review the legality of the domestic legislation that was promulgated to give effect to the acts (including resolutions) of the international organisations in which it participates.

130. Reference will be made to the judgment of the Supreme Court of the Philippines in *Tañada v. Angara*, which was handed down in 1997 because it strongly implied that international law takes precedence over national law. In particular, the Supreme Court held that 'By their inherent nature, treaties really limit or restrict the absoluteness of sovereignty … treaties have been used to record agreements between States concerning such widely diverse matters as … the establishment of international organizations … [t]he sovereignty of a state therefore cannot in fact and in reality be considered absolute.'[432] Furthermore, in *Bayan v. Zamora* delivered in 2000, the Supreme Court held that 'As an integral part of the community of nations, we are responsible to assure that our government, Constitution and laws will carry out our international obligation.'[433]

131. The text of the Constitution of the Socialist Republic of Vietnam, which was approved in 1992 and was revised on 28 November 2013,[434] reveals that it was

---

429. Presumably, this provision covers, for example, the mandatory decisions adopted by the UN Security Council under the authority of Chapter VII of the UN Charter in conjunction with Art. 25 thereof. *See* further, Art. 169 of the Constitution on the validity of the treaties and decisions of international organisations that were in force before the Merdeka (Independence) Day from the British Empire, namely 31 Aug. 1957.

430. The Constitution, as ratified on 2 Feb. 1987, is available at: https://www.officialgazette.gov.ph/constitutions/1987-constitution/.

431. *See* further, UN General Assembly, Sixth Committee, 71st session, Item 84 - The Rule of Law at the National and International Levels, 5–6 Oct. 2016, Statement of the Philippines, at: https://www.un.org/en/ga/sixth/71/pdfs/statements/rule_of_law/philippines.pdf; and R. C. Pangalangan, *Philippine Materials in International Law* 157–242 (Brill / Nijhoff 2021).

432. Cited by R. J. Casis, *Dualism and the Incongruence Between Objective International Law and the Philippine Practice of International Law*, 17 Philippine Yearbook of International Law 41, 47–48 (2020).

433. *Ibid.*, p. 48.

434. Available at: http://constitutionnet.org/sites/default/files/tranlation_of_vietnams_new_constitution_enuk_2.pdf.

probably drafted to cater for the country's participation in international organisations and multilateral institutions, including ASEAN.[435] This argument is adduced from a combined reading of Article 12 and Article 70(14) thereof. The former provision sets out the role of Vietnam in the world community. According to this provision, Vietnam 'seeks multilateral and diversified relations and actively seeks international integration and cooperation … [Vietnam] conforms to the … international treaties in which [it] is a member; [Vietnam is] a friend, reliable partner and responsible member in the international community for the sake of national interests … '.

132. According to the latter provision, the National Assembly has the power to decide, among other areas, on the fundamental policies in its external relations and its membership 'in important international and regional organisations'. There is no doubt that ASEAN is included in the ambit of such regional organisations. Furthermore, pursuant to Article 98(5), the Prime Minister is empowered (a) to decide on the commencement of negotiations for international treaties, (b) to direct the negotiations, (c) to conclude international treaties, and (d) to organise the implementation of international treaties in which Vietnam has become a contracting party. Finally, Article 50 stipulates that Vietnam strives to build an independent and self-reliant economy, which promotes international integration and cooperation. Again, the reference to ASEAN, and specifically to the AEC, is rather obvious.

133. In addition to these Constitutional provisions, in April 2016 specific legislation was passed to regulate all aspects of the participation of Vietnam in international agreements, the Law on Treaties.[436] Article 4 thereof stipulates that a treaty shall be concluded in the name of the State, *inter alia*, when it concerns the founding of, accession to or withdrawal from an international organisation or a regional organisation, and this affects national fundamental policies on foreign relations, national defence, security, socio-economic development, as well as financial and monetary issues.

134. In the Constitution of Negara Brunei Darussalam,[437] the only relevant provision is Article 42(1) thereof, which prohibits members of the Legislative from introducing or proposing Bills or amendments to any Bill, which would appear to the Head of State (referred to as 'His Majesty the Sultan and Yang Di-Pertuan') to be inconsistent with any obligations imposed upon him by virtue of a treaty or an agreement with a third state. The Constitution does not contain any other provisions

---

435. Generally, *see* L. Ah Nguyen, H. Duy Phan & J. Freeman, 'International and ASEAN Law in the ASEAN 10 National Jurisdictions: The Reception of International Law in the Legal System of Vietnam', in: *ASEAN Integration Through Law: The ASEAN Way in a Comparative Context Plenary on Rule of Law in the ASEAN Community*, at: https://cil.nus.edu.sg/wp-content/uploads/2016/08/SD_ES-ASEAN-10-Vietnam-study.pdf.
436. Law No. 108/2016/QH13, promulgated on 9 Apr. 2016, English translation at: http://vbpl.vn/TW/Pages/vbpqen-toanvan.aspx?ItemID=11039. It replaced the Law on Conclusion, Accession to and Implementation of Treaties, No. 41/2005/QH11, promulgated in 2005.
437. The Constitution was adopted in 1959. For the revised edition of 2011, *see* https://www.agc.gov.bn/AGC%20Images/LOB/cons_doc/constitution_i.pdf.

on the conclusion, ratification, etc., of treaties and on the country's participation in international organisations, presumably because the Sultan is the sole holder of all state power without any limitations in its exercise. Thus, in the case of ASEAN, since (presumably) the Sultan has himself accepted the obligations flowing from membership therein, they cannot be compromised by the adoption of subsequent domestic legislation, unless of course the Sultan decides otherwise. It should, however, be noted that the case of Brunei Darussalam is rather unique because nowadays there are only few states in the world where the head of state controls virtually all powers and all prerogatives. In such a political system, one would not expect that questions, such as the primacy of international law or the decisions of international organisations over domestic law, would be regulated.

135. In the Constitution of the Lao People's Democratic Republic (Lao PDR),[438] Article 12 thereof, a rather generally drafted clause, provides that the country pursues a foreign policy, whose principal characteristics are friendship and cooperation, while it seeks to promote good relations with all other states. However, the provision that is more relevant to its participation in ASEAN is Article 20. It reads: '[Lao] implements open policies on economic cooperation with foreign countries in different ways, on a multilateral basis and in different forms, on the basis of respect for each other's independence, sovereignty, equality and mutual benefit.' Furthermore, Article 53(18) stipulates that the National Assembly has the right, on the recommendation of the Prime Minister, to decide on the ratification of or on the revocation of or on the withdrawal from treaties and agreements that have been concluded with third states. However, under Article 70(12), it is the government's prerogative to make, enter into, interpret and implement the treaties and international agreements to which Lao has become a party. The Constitution does not indicate which is the legal status of the provisions of ratified treaties within the domestic legal system. However, according to the Ordinances of the President of Lao PDR on Establishment and Member Participating and the Implementation of International Conventions, approved international treaties shall take precedence over domestic law in cases of inconsistency, with the exception of the Constitution, this being the supreme law of the land.[439]

136. The Constitution of the Kingdom of Thailand, which was adopted in 2017,[440] is one of the few Constitutions under review which contains provisions that are appropriate to ensure the country's participation in international organisations and, by necessary implication, in ASEAN as well. In particular, according to section 178(1)–(2) thereof, it is the King's royal prerogative to conclude treaties with third states as well as with international organisations. Hoverer, if a treaty requires

438. It was promulgated on 6 May 2003 and revised in 2015; for an unofficial English translation, *see* https://www.constituteproject.org/constitution/Laos_2015.

439. The Ordinances were published in the Lao Official Gazette of 28 May 2014, *see* further 'Southeast Asian Region Countries Law', University of Melbourne Library, online, at: https://unimelb.libguides.com/c.php?g=930183&p=6721984.

440. For an unofficial English translation, *see* https://cdc.parliament.go.th/draftconstitution2/download/article/article_20180829093502.pdf. Note that Thailand's first Constitution was promulgated in 1932 and until today there have been some twenty Constitutions.

the enactment of domestic legislation for its implementation and/or might have a significant effect on Thailand's economy, society, trade or investments, it must be approved by the National Assembly as well.[441] The third paragraph of section 178 defines these treaties as those pertaining to free trade, to a customs union, to the authorisation of utilising natural resources or to surrendering sovereign rights over natural resources. Importantly, the Constitution prescribes that the population should be involved in these instances. This is laid down in section 178(4) in the following terms: 'There shall also be a law prescribing procedures for the public to participate in the expression of opinions and to obtain necessary remedy from the effects of conclusion of a treaty under paragraph three [of Section 178].' The Constitution of Thailand is also silent on the legal position of ratified treaties domestically and whether they take precedence over conflicting provisions of domestic law.[442]

137. The Constitution of the Republic of Singapore, which was enacted on 22 December 1965, has been considerably amended since then.[443] The relevant provisions are contained within Part III thereof, which is titled 'Protection of the Sovereignty of the Republic of Singapore', and in particular Article 7 concerning the 'Participation in co-operative international schemes which are beneficial to Singapore'. The connection between the country's participation in multinational institutions and the protection of its sovereignty could be described as follows: pursuant to Article 6 of the Constitution, any surrender or transfer, wholly or in part, of sovereignty in any manner whatsoever is strictly prohibited unless it is approved by not less than two-thirds of the total number of votes cast at a national referendum. In that respect, pursuant to Article 7(a), the participation of Singapore in multilateral institutions is regarded as an acceptable exception to Article 6. It follows that no referendum is required when Singapore participates or cooperates or contributes 'towards, any scheme, venture, project, enterprise or undertaking of whatsoever nature, in conjunction or in concert with any other sovereign state or with any Federation, Confederation, country or countries …, where such scheme, venture, project, enterprise or undertaking confers, has the effect of conferring or is intended to confer, on Singapore … any economic, financial, industrial, social, cultural, educational or other benefit of any kind or is, or appears to be, advantageous in any way to Singapore'. The same stipulation is, *mutatis mutandis*, applicable, under Article 7(b), which concerns entering into treaties with other sovereign states, etc., provided that such treaties have been concluded for the mutual or collective security or for any other purpose whatsoever, and provided that they are beneficial or advantageous to Singapore in any way.

---

441. *See also* s. 66 of the Constitution stipulating that the State should cooperate with international organisations.

442. *See* further, K. Umpai, *Judicial Decision and Rethinking the Constitutional Principles Concerning Treaty Making Power and Process of Thailand,* 4 Brawijaya L.J. 1–28 (2017), at: https://lawjournal.ub.ac.id/index.php/law/article/view/68.

443. For the current version of the Constitution, which incorporates all amendments up to and including 1 Dec. 2021 (it came into operation on 31 Dec. 2021), *see* https://sso.agc.gov.sg/Act/CONS1963#pr7-.

138. The Constitution is silent on the interface between international law and the domestic legal system. However, it should be mentioned that, as Singapore was a Crown colony of the United Kingdom, it has retained the dualist system as regards the validity of ratified treaties domestically. This was confirmed by the High Court in *Public Prosecutor v. Tan Cheng Yew and another appeal*. The High Court held that: 'It is trite law that Singapore follows a dualist position … Singapore's international law obligations do not give rise to individual rights and obligations in the domestic context unless and until transposed into domestic law by legislation.'[444] A few years later, the Court of Appeal confirmed it.[445] According to the Court of Appeal, the issue *in casu* was whether peremptory norms of international law are automatically incorporated into the law of Singapore and take precedence over domestic legislation in the event there is an inconsistency between them.[446]

139. Finally, the Constitution of the Republic of the Union of Myanmar was approved by a referendum held in May 2008.[447] The legality of the referendum was much disputed.[448] The relevant provision is Article 108 of the Constitution. It stipulates that the Union Assembly, the Pyidaungsu Hluttaw,[449] shall, on the one hand, determine matters relating to ratifying, annulling and revoking international, regional or bilateral treaties, which have been submitted by the President, and, on the other hand, may confer upon the President the authority to conclude, annul and revoke any such treaty without its approval. It would appear that this is a rather self-defeating clause because it allows the President to create international obligations for the State without any scrutiny by the Assembly. The essence of this clause is reflected in the powers that the President holds. In particular, under Article 209 of the Constitution, the President shall enter into, ratify, annul or revoke international, regional or bilateral treaties, which either require the approval of the Pyidaungsu Hluttaw or do not require such approval. As is explained elsewhere in this monograph, Myanmar is a country that for several years now has been ruled by a military regime, while throughout its history, with only brief exceptions, it has been controlled by the armed forces. This is evidently reflected in the Constitutional provisions allocating one-fourth of the seats in Parliament to be occupied by serving

---

444. Magistrate's Appeals No. 97 of 2011/01 and 97 of 2011/02, Judgment of 30 Nov. 2012, [2012] SGHC 241; [2013] 1 SLR 1095, para. 56, at: https://www.elitigation.sg/gd/s/2012_SGHC_241.
445. Criminal Appeal No. 11 of 2013, *Yong Vui Kong v. Public Prosecutor*, Judgment of 4 Mar. 2015, [2015] SGCA 11, paras 28 et seq., at: https://www.singaporelawwatch.sg/Portals/0/Docs/Judgments/[2015]%20SGCA%2011.pdf, reproduced in (2016) 55 I.L.M. 307–338; (2011) 143 *International Law Reports* 374–425. *See* further, Y. McDermott, *Yong Vui Kong v. Public Prosecutor and the Mandatory Death Penalty for Drug Offences in Singapore: A Dead End for Constitutional Challenge?*, 1 International Journal on Human Rights and Drug Policy 35–52 (2010).
446. *Ibid.*
447. Translation by the Ministry of Information, September 2009, at: http://www.burmalibrary.org/docs5/Myanmar_Constitution-2008-en.pdf.
448. *See* M. F. Martin, *Burma's 2010 Elections: Implications of the New Constitution and Election Laws*, Congressional Research Service, R41218, 29 Apr. 2010, at: https://fas.org/sgp/crs/row/R41218.pdf.
449. The Pyidaungsu Hluttaw is made up of two chambers, the Amyotha Hluttaw (the House of Nationalities) and the Pyithu Hluttaw (the House of Representatives).

army officers. The latter are also solely entitled to become Ministers of Home Affairs and of Defence as well as to be appointed to one of the two positions of Vice President.

II. Dealing with Recalcitrant Member States

140. That not all Member States fulfil all their duties and obligations at all times is a reality in all international organisations. However, not all international organisations react in the same manner against (what in effect are) recalcitrant Member States. By examining the constitutive instruments, one could argue that international organisations could be divided into the following three categories: (1) those that have elaborate provisions and stipulate which punitive measures (sanctions) will be ordered against them, including the suspension of membership rights and, ultimately, expulsion from the organisation;[450] (2) those that have only a general framework of action, which may not always contain a punitive element but may envisage other (e.g., diplomatic) means to resolve the situation; and (3) those that do not regulate the reaction to infractions committed by Member States; in other words, it is a case of omission. Presumably, the third category indicates the unwillingness of Member States to allow the international organisation concerned to address and handle transgressions committed by themselves. This should be considered as a deliberate choice of the membership, a choice that could be overturned at a later stage (the example of the European Community / European Union).[451]

141. As regards ASEAN, it rather falls within the ambit of the second category.[452] Thus, Article 5(3) of the Charter provides that, in the case of its serious breach or non-compliance with its provisions, 'the matter shall be referred to Article 20 [of the Charter]'. Regrettably, there is no indication in the Charter what constitutes 'serious breach or noncompliance'. Clearly, this wording could have several interpretations, as different states would probably view the intensity of the same infraction/s differently. Moreover, it is submitted that Article 5(3) suffers from bad draftsmanship because, strictly speaking, it is not the question of the serious breach or non-compliance, which 'shall be referred to Article 20' but it is that Article 20 shall be applied in such instances. It will be recalled that Article 20, which forms part of Chapter VII of the Charter, is the clause enshrining the basic principle that

450. Generally, *see* K. Magliveras, *Exclusion from Participation in International Organisations: The Law and Practice Behind Member States' Expulsion and Suspension of Membership* (Kluwer Law International, 1999).

451. Generally, *see* K. Magliveras & G. Naldi, *The Question of Recalcitrant Member States in the Context of the European Union* 3 Evrigenis Yearbook of International and European Law 205–238 (2021).

452. It should be noted that this sub-chapter is not concerned with instances where the non-compliance of ASEAN Member States with their obligations has been the object of an arbitral award or has been otherwise settled and the recalcitrant Member State has not followed the award or the settlement.

decision-making in ASEAN is founded on the principles of consultation and consensus and that, only if consensus cannot be achieved, the Summit, as the highest-ranking organ, has the discretion to determine what specific decision-making mode will be applied.

142. Given the very specific content of Article 20 of the Charter, it is rather strange that the question of a serious breach of or non-compliance with membership obligations was included therein and was not treated separately, as indeed it is the case with the constitutive instruments of a very large number of international organisations. Notwithstanding this observation and taking into account the need for the constitutive instruments to be drafted with a measure of precision when addressing membership issues, one would have expected Article 20 to have laid down ASEAN's response to infractions allegedly committed by Member States. However, the fifth paragraph of Article 20 simply provides that 'the matter shall be referred to the ASEAN Summit for decision'. Therefore, Article 20 should be read together with Article 7(2)(e), which is the provision allowing the Summit to decide on the matters referred to it under, *inter alia*, Chapter VII of the Charter.[453]

143. Several issues of interpretation arise from these provisions. Before examining them, it should be noted that: (a) to the best of one's knowledge, there is no actual practice on Article 20 and (b) as argued above, the present monograph takes the view that there exists an ASEAN legal system and, therefore, ASEAN law should be complied with. The first is who is going to determine the existence of instances of serious breach or non-compliance. The use of the word 'shall' in Article 20(5) would suggest that whoever is responsible for referring infractions to the Summit is obligated to do so, and there is no discretion not to address a situation of non-compliance. The second issue is to delineate which infractions constitute 'serious breaches' and whether the word 'serious' covers persistent violations as well[454] or whether a single violation would be enough to trigger referral to the Summit. The third issue is whether the Summit is under a duty to discuss the referred infraction and to act accordingly or whether, for political reasons or reasons of expedience or any other reason, it could avoid discussing the situation. The fourth issue is whether once the Summit has discussed the situation and has taken the view that one or more infractions have been committed for which there were no mitigating factors, it could leave the matter there without taking any action. To be inactive should not be an option and, moreover, to maintain the problem-free operation of ASEAN should be a top priority. Therefore, it is important that the Summit's response is regulated in the Charter and not be left to its discretion. The fifth issue concerns the kind of measures that the Summit will be allowed to take, when it has recorded the infraction and is determined to deal with it. Finally, the sixth issue concerns the question of enforcement should the recalcitrant Member States fail to rectify the breach or fail to comply with the measures or the orders issued by the Summit. Here, the question

453. Generally, *see* S. Chesterman, *From Community to Compliance? The Evolution of Monitoring Obligations in ASEAN* (Cambridge University Press, 2015).

454. Cf. Art. 5 UN Charter: 'A Member of the United Nations which has *persistently* violated the Principles contained in the present Charter ... ' (emphasis added).

of enforcement should be varied, according to whether there is a deliberate failure or there are objective obstacles that need to be first overcome (e.g., amending the national legislation) or there are vital national interests at stake. Notwithstanding this variation, it is important to understand that even national interests should give way to ensure what is best for the international organisation.

144. Article 51(1) of the ASEAN Charter deals with the issue of interpretation. It stipulates that any requests for interpretation lodged by a Member State will be dealt with by the Secretariat, pursuant to the Rules of Procedure for the Interpretation of the ASEAN Charter.[455] It has been argued that these Rules of Procedure 'extend the ASEAN Summit's control over the organization [they] serve as extra-constitutional fetters of ASEAN … outside the text of the Charter'.[456] It should be counter-argued that: (a) these Rules are in line with the soft law approach that has characterised ASEAN since its beginning; (b) in such a closely knitted regional organisation as ASEAN, it is to be expected that the organ, in which the heads of state participate, will exercise control over its whole operation and functioning; and (c) international organisations have always adopted instruments or mechanisms that are outside the regime of the founding treaty / constitutive instrument.[457] These instruments, which should be regarded as *de facto* amendments of the founding treaty / constitutive instrument, do not raise any questions of legality, if they have been adopted by the entire membership (unanimous decision) and/or by the competent organ and no Member State has raised any objections. The Rules of Procedure for the Interpretation of the ASEAN Charter appear to fulfil these conditions.

145. Interestingly enough, Rule 1(2) of the Rules of Procedure extends their ambit to requests that have been made by any ASEAN organ to the Secretariat seeking clarification or information relating to matters within the scope of the requesting organ's terms of reference and activities. Under Rule 3, requests for interpretation should be neither vague nor abstract. On the contrary, they should contain, as a minimum, the specific Charter provision/s to be interpreted and the precise question/s to be answered by the Secretariat. The procedure to be followed is laid down in Rule 4. In particular, the maximum period of time required to render

---

455. Rules of Procedure for the Interpretation of the ASEAN Charter, adopted by the Coordinating Council, Phnom Penh, Cambodia, 2 Apr. 2012, at: https://asean.org/wp-content/uploads/images/archive/documents/ROP%20for%20Interpretation%20of%20ASEAN%20Charter.pdf. Generally, *see* N. Limsiritong, *How to Apply Protocol to the ASEAN Charter on Dispute Settlement Mechanisms 2010 in Case of ASEAN Charter Interpretation*, 1:1 Asian Political Science Review 8 (2017).

456. *See* J. D. Bagulaya, *ASEAN as Wayang Kulit: A Critique of the Constitutional, Extra-constitutional, and Practical Fetters of ASEAN*, 9 Asian Journal of International Law 275–297 (2019).

457. A typical example are the UN peacekeeping missions, a creation of practice by the UN Security Council primarily under Chapter VII of the Charter. Apparently, UN Member States have not questioned the legality of the establishment of such missions as well as their mandate. Given not only the many decades of non-opposition but also the continued willingness of states to implement UNSC resolutions establishing peacekeeping and peace enforcement mission, one could argue that are now akin to international customary law.

an interpretation is calculated at 112 days, which are broken down as follows: fifteen days for the Secretariat to acknowledge receipt of the request, seven days to communicate the request to the Member States, sixty days for comments and observations to be made by any interested Member State/s, and thirty days for the Secretariat to prepare the text of the interpretation. The number of days should be understood as calendar days and not as working days.

146. In accordance with Rule 2(1) of the Rules of Procedure, the interpretation to be given by the Secretariat shall be neither binding nor authoritative in nature. Moreover, it may not be invoked as representing the views of the Member States and/or of the Organisation. It follows that these interpretations should be regarded as only an expression of the Secretariat's opinion. Nevertheless, they do carry some weight. Arguably, those that requested them may not ignore them and/or act in the exact opposite way, for otherwise this would defy the whole purpose of having this institutional mechanism in place. However, this argument raises the question of what will happen if the Member State that filed the request and/or any other Member State having a legitimate interest in the interpretation given are not satisfied with its content. In such instances and depending on how serious the disagreement is, they should be able to resort to the mechanism for the settlement of disputes under Chapter VIII of the ASEAN Charter, which is analysed later.

147. To return to the lack of direct references in the ASEAN Charter on the possibility of the Summit taking measures of a punitive nature against Member States, which have violated and/or have not observed their obligations, two observations should be made. The first is that, when the Charter was in the stage of negotiations and the first drafts appeared, apparently there had been clauses on compliance with obligations, including a system of monitoring as well as a range of punitive measures in the event of Charter breaches and violations. But at subsequent stages, they were dropped,[458] which clearly suggests that Member States preferred to leave these matters unregulated. The second observation is that the Summit is not authorised to order sanctions, even in those cases where not only serious but also very serious breaches and other instances of non-compliance with membership duties and obligations have been recorded. Reference should also be made to the Report of the Eminent Persons Group on the ASEAN Charter (EPG Report), which was published in December 2006. Its purpose was to make recommendations on the ASEAN's institutional architecture and similar matters to be included in the Charter, which at the time was at the drafting stage.[459] The EPG Report did suggest that specific sanctions be contained to rectify the consequences of serious breaches and cases of non-compliance.

458. *See* M. E. Manyin, M. J. Garcia & W. M. Morrison, *U.S. Accession to the Association of Southeast Asian Nations' Treaty of Amity and Cooperation (TAC)*, Congressional Research Service, R40583, 13 Jul. 2009, 7, at: https://fas.org/sgp/crs/row/R40583.pdf.

459. *See* T. Koh, R. G. Manalo & W. Woon (eds), *The Making of the ASEAN Charter* 121–122 (World Scientific 2009).

According to the EPG Report:

> The ASEAN Charter should seek to preserve and strengthen the ASEAN membership, cohesion and unity. ASEAN Leaders should take appropriate measures to help Member States fully comply with ASEAN's objectives, principles, and commitments under the Charter and important ASEAN agreements. At the same time, the Charter should also include provisions for measures to redress non-compliance and serious breaches. Such measures may include, among others, the temporary suspension of rights and privileges of membership, such as withholding the right to participate in ASEAN activities, and to chair ASEAN bodies and their meetings.[460]

The EPG Report proposed that the ASEAN Council[461] should be allowed to consider taking any measure, including but not limited to the suspension of rights and privileges when any Member State had seriously violated the objectives, the principles, and the commitments laid down in ASEAN declarations, agreements, concords, and treaties as well as in its norms and values. These measures (clearly of a punitive nature even though not so stated in the EPG Report) would have been ordered upon the proposal of the Member States concerned and following the recommendation of the ASEAN Foreign Ministers. That the initiative for setting in motion this (effectively sanctioning) procedure did not rest with ASEAN and its organs but with the Member States themselves had, arguably, the following problem: it did not guarantee that the Organisation would be able to address and counteract infractions, if, for political, diplomatic or other reasons, no Member State would be willing to initiate it. According to the EPG Report, decisions on the temporary suspension of the rights and privileges of membership had to be taken by unanimity and with the compulsory abstention of the recalcitrant Member State/s.[462] Finally, the exercise of these rights and privileges were to be restored by the ASEAN Council upon the recommendation of ASEAN Foreign Ministers based on the progress made by the recalcitrant Member State/s.[463]

148. That the Eminent Persons Report made specific recommendations, but the Member States finally rejected them *in toto*, could be interpreted as their aversion towards allowing ASEAN to address instances of (even grave) non-compliance by applying its rules and regulations, which, in the present circumstances, constitute duties and obligations for the whole membership. Plainly, Member States were (and seemingly still are) unwilling to equip ASEAN with the necessary armoury to address such instances in an effective manner and to limit the damage that it could suffer as a result. However, it will be submitted that the ASEAN Summit not only

---

460. *See* EPG Report, para. 31 at p. 17, at: https://www.asean.org/wp-content/uploads/images/archive/19247.pdf.
461. This was to be the highest-ranking, supreme policy-making organ in ASEAN, pursuant to the structure proposed in the EPG Report. In the ASEAN Charter, as finally adopted, it is the ASEAN Summit.
462. *See* EPG Report, 41.
463. *Ibid.*, 31.

could but also should be in the position to order an array of measures, not least because it should be regarded as having a duty to protect the best interests of ASEAN.

149. This argument is principally based on the theory of the implied powers of international organisations.[464] If this theory were employed to the present circumstances, the principal organ/s (i.e., the organ/s in which the entire membership is represented without exceptions, which has/have been endowed with the most significant powers and which has/have been authorised to take the most important decisions) should be able to act when the international organisation in question is confronted with the violation of obligations by one or more of the Member States, the founding treaty / constitutive instrument is silent and imminent harm might be done to the international organisation.[465] It follows that, even though the question of non-compliance is not addressed in the ASEAN Charter, appropriate action must be taken, not least in order to protect it. This action does not necessarily have to involve measures of a punitive nature (invariably referred to as 'sanctions'). However, it is the application of the latter that are usually considered necessary and appropriate to bring about the expected results, namely the termination of the infraction/s.

150. Thus, the ASEAN Summit might be able to adopt, depending on the situation at hand and provided that there is consensus among the participating Member States (the recalcitrant state/s should obviously be excluded from the deliberations), all or some of the following four types of measures. It should be emphasised that their (legal) rationale is not necessarily to 'punish' the recalcitrant Member State/s, given that the ASEAN Charter does not envisage such 'punishment'. Based on the arguments made above, their justification could very well be the goal to protect the Organisation, its operation, its activities, and its organs as well as to induce the recalcitrant states to return to normalcy as soon as possible, thus mitigating the damage to the Organisation and to the rest of the membership. The first type involves the ASEAN Summit reprimanding the states in question severely for their wrongful

464. Generally, *see* K. Skubiszewski, *Implied Powers of International Organizations*, in *International Law at a Time of Perplexity. Essays in Honour of Shabtai Rosenne* 855 (Y. Dinstein ed., Martinus Nijhoff 1989); Magliveras, *Exclusion from Participation in International Organisations: The Law and Practice Behind Member States' Expulsion and Suspension of Membership*, 254 et seq.

465. The doctrine of implied powers has been discussed and analysed in the jurisprudence of international courts of justice over many years, *see*, *inter alia*, Permanent Court of International Justice (PCIJ), *Competence of the ILO to Regulate Incidentally the Personal Work of the Employer*, Advisory Opinion of 23 Jul. 1926, Series B, No. 13, p. 18; PCIJ, *Jurisdiction of the European Commission of the Danube between Galatz and Braila*, Advisory Opinion of 8 Dec. 1927, Series B, No. 14, pp. 64 et seq.; PCIJ, *Interpretation of the Greco-Turkish Agreement of 1 December 1926*, Advisory Opinion of 28 Aug. 1928, Series B, No. 16, p. 18; ICJ, *Reparations for Injuries Suffered in the Service of the United Nations*, Advisory Opinion of 11 Apr. 1949, 1949 ICJ Reports 182; ICJ, *Effect of Awards of Compensation made by the U.N. Administrative Tribunal*, Advisory Opinion of 13 Jul. 13, 1954 ICJ Reports 47; ICJ, *Certain Expenses of the United Nations (Article 17, paragraph 2, of the Charter)*, Advisory Opinion of 20 Jul. 1962, 1962 ICJ Reports 151; ICJ, *Legality of the Use by a State of Nuclear Weapons in Armed Conflict (Request by the World Health Organization)*, Advisory Opinion of 8 Jul. 1996, 1996 I.C.J. Reports 66.

and offending behaviour. Moreover, it could adopt a 'name and shame' strategy targeting the reputation of the states concerned in the expectation that such bad publicity will result in compliance with the ASEAN rules and norms.[466] However, this is not likely to happen in the current constellation within ASEAN. Second, it could order them to cease the infraction immediately, to observe their duties and obligations and to make a solemn declaration not to repeat it. Third, it could order measures of a punitive nature against them, in other words, inflict sanctions of a diplomatic, political, economic, or other nature. The principle of proportionality will have to be applied: the most severe sanctions will be ordered when the breach of the Charter is deliberate and has led to serious problems in ASEAN's operation. Fourth, which could be tied up to the third, the Summit could order them to make good any damage arising from the serious breach caused to ASEAN itself and/or to any other Member State/s.

151. The legal construction to allow the Summit to take corrective and/or punitive action and measures against recalcitrant Member States is not without problems. One might agree with the reasons for which the Soviet international law jurist Grigory Tunkin rejected the theory of implied powers. According to him, it 'implies a refusal to respect international treaties and its practical application would lead to chaos in international relations and aggravation of international tensions'.[467] On the other hand, one cannot easily discard the fact that the ASEAN Charter does not envisage that the Summit may take action when there is enough evidence to conclude that a Member State's unwillingness to retract its recalcitrant behaviour is deliberate and wants to cause harm to ASEAN and threaten its continued operation. In contrast, the constitutive instruments of other regional international organisations, which were (like the ASEAN Charter) negotiated and concluded in the early twenty-first century, expressly allow them to take measures against recalcitrant Member States. Examples include the EU[468] and the AU.[469]

---

466. The issue of 'shaming' in multilateral institutions has both an international law and an international relation perspective. Generally, *see* R. Brewster, 'Reputation in International Relations and International Law Theory, in *Interdisciplinary Perspectives on International Law and International Relations* (J. L. Dunoff & M. A. Pollack eds, Cambridge University Press 2013) 524–543; A. Carnegie & A. Carson, *The Spotlight's Harsh Glare: Rethinking Publicity and International Order*, 72 International Organization (2015) 627–657; G. W. Downs & M. A. Jones, *Reputation, Compliance, and International Law*, 31 The Journal of Legal Studies (2002) 95–114; J. DeMeritt, *International Organizations and Government Killing: Does Naming and Shaming Save Lives?*, 38 International Interactions (2012) 597–621; *The Politics of Leverage in International Relations: Name, Shame, and Sanction* (R.H. Friman ed., Palgrave Macmillan 2015); and S. Mohamed, *Shame in the Security Council*, 90 Washington University Law Review (2013) 1191–1254.

467. G. Tunkin, *International Law in the International System*, 147 Recueil des Cours de l'Académie de Droit International 187 (1975-IV).

468. *See* TEU Art. 7.

469. *See* AU Constitutive Act, Arts 23 and 30. For discussion, *see* K. Magliveras, 'The Multiple Sanctioning Regimes in the African Union: Analysis and Synthesis' in, *The Emergent African Union Law: Conceptualization, Delimitation, and Application* (F. Amao, M. Olivier & K. Magliveras (eds), Oxford University Press, 2021), 359-377.

152. Another consideration that could justify applying the theory of implied powers is the fact that ASEAN has set very demanding goals which the membership has presumably a duty to achieve. These include the creation of a single market where goods, services and investments will circulate freely, and where the interstate movement of labour will be facilitated. In any regional multinational institution, whose principal goal is the economic integration of participating states, namely the so-called REIOs (regional economic integration organisations), the accomplishment of these goals invariably demands that all Member States, without exception, comply fully and promptly with all the relevant rules, norms, procedures and, generally, the law generated by the REIO in question. Therefore, the existence of a sanctioning regime could also operate as deterrence to those participating states which may consider flouting their obligations. However, as it is the apparent wish of the ASEAN membership not to adopt measures of a punitive nature, at the end of the day, this should be accepted and respected. Presumably, at any given moment in the future, Member States could amend the ASEAN Charter and introduce a mechanism for dealing (at least) with any cases of serious breaches and instances of grave non-compliance. It is instructive to recall that is, *mutatis mutandis*, how the EU came to deal with a 'clear risk of a serious breach' of human dignity, freedom, democracy, equality, the rule of law and human rights culminating to the aforementioned Article 7 TEU. Given that the amendment procedure, which is laid down in Article 48 of the ASEAN Charter, is also subject to the overarching principle of consensus, it follows that the future process to insert new clauses on its infringement will have to meet with the Member States' overall approval and that none of them will raise unsurpassable objections, a rather tall order to be achieved.

III. Are There Any Other Avenues Open to Deal with Recalcitrant Member States? The Question of Expelling Member States from ASEAN

153. Clearly, it was not the intention of Member States to include in the ASEAN Charter specific procedures and processes to allow the Organisation to address 'serious breach and noncompliance'. Indeed, commentators have taken opposing views on the necessity of having in place a sanctioning regime to address Charter infractions: one commentator claims that it is imperative,[470] while another sides with the argument that political pressure and constructive engagement are adequate responses and that, anyway, sanctions are a controversial issue for ASEAN.[471] Based on the above analysis, it is submitted that to have in place a mechanism for dealing with recalcitrant Member States, which could involve punitive action as well, could be beneficial for ASEAN in the long run. Therefore, the argument will

470. *See* R. Sumka, *ASEAN Beyond 2015: The Imperatives for Further Institutional Changes*, Centre for Strategic and International Studies, ERIA Discussion Paper Series, January 2014, at: https://www.eria.org/ERIA-DP-2014-01.pdf.

471. *See* Singapore Institute of International Affairs, *Reviewing the ASEAN Charter: An Opportunity to Reform ASEAN Processes*, Policy Brief, September 2014, at: http://www.siiaonline.org/wp-content/uploads/2016/10/2014-10-Policy-Brief-Reviewing-the-ASEAN-Charter-An-Opportunity-to-Reform-ASEAN-Processes.pdf.

be advanced that there might be other possibilities, which could be employed to deal with instances of Charter violations, cases of (deliberate) non-compliance with obligations, etc.

154. The first possibility is based on Article 7(2)(d) of the ASEAN Charter. It stipulates that the Summit has the duty to address emergency situations affecting the Organisation by taking appropriate actions. While this provision does not explain what would constitute 'appropriate actions', its wording suggests that the Summit may also act on its own initiative. For the purposes of the submission made here, this procedure could be used only if the serious breach or non-compliance committed by one or more Member States has led to a situation of extreme gravity within ASEAN. Article 7(2)(d) should be read in conjunction with Article 7(3)(b), which allows the holding of special or *ad hoc* Summit meetings to be chaired by the Member State holding the ASEAN Chairmanship at that moment.

155. Unlike the constitutive instruments of other international organisations, Article 7(3)(b) does not lay down the parameters for holding such (effectively extraordinary) meetings and, significantly, does not distinguish between special and *ad hoc* meetings. However, common sense would suggest the following distinction: special meetings concern the deliberation of serious problems, which have been encountered in an area of ASEAN activities and threaten vital interests, whereas *ad hoc* meetings are held to deliberate, for example, the behaviour of Member States, which has resulted in serious Charter violations (e.g., failing to comply with obligations). Furthermore, Article 7(3)(b) is silent on the minimum number of Member States required to call for such a meeting, thus leaving open the question whether a single Member State may propose it. Considering that consensus is the principal mode for the operation of ASEAN, it could be argued with some persuasion that even one state, acting on its own, should be able to propose the holding of an *ad hoc* Summit session, provided that there is no (official) opposition registered by the other Member States. The state holding the ASEAN Chairmanship should be deemed obligated to organise it and prepare the agenda. Until today, Article 7(2)(d) has not been invoked and, therefore, there is no recorded practice.

156. The second possibility would be for the Secretary-General to refer instances of serious breach or non-compliance to the Summit. This submission is based on Article 11(2)(b) of the Charter, which stipulates that the Secretary-General shall 'facilitate and monitor progress in the implementation of ASEAN agreements and decisions and submit an annual report on the work of ASEAN to the ASEAN Summit'. Importantly, this provision does not expressly refer to the implementation of the Charter, but a broad interpretation of the term 'ASEAN agreements' would not doubt cover the Charter as well. Admittedly, this suggestion is not without problems. For example, the content of the annual reports, which the Secretary-General has submitted to the Summit so far, reveals that their content is a mere record of

ASEAN events, activities and actions taken.[472] Notwithstanding these comments, at the end of the day it could be a question of how proactive a Secretary-General wants (or is allowed) to be. Given that the term of the office of Secretary-General is not renewable, a proactive one would not have to fear that he or she will not be re-elected because he recorded cases of Member States' serious infractions. Moreover, since Article 11(8)(c) of the ASEAN Charter clearly provides that the Secretary-General is responsible only to ASEAN, arguably to record such infractions in the annual reports might be regarded as a duty owed to the Organisation.

157. The latter argument is reinforced by the fact that ASEAN lacks a procedure for registering infractions and for requesting that allegedly recalcitrant Member States justify their behaviour. Such a procedure has always existed in the European Community / European Union and has been one of its main innovations in international institutional law. In particular, the European Commission, in its capacity as guardian of the EU Founding Treaties, acting either on its own initiative or on information received on possible breaches of or non-compliance with EU law, is empowered to send letters of formal notice to the Member State/s concerned and to demand further information. Effectively, the European Commission is asking Member States to defend that domestic legislation that is deemed to run contrary to EU law and offers them a last chance to comply with it. This is the first stage of the so-called infringement procedure. If the allegedly recalcitrant states do not offer adequate justifications and/or do not amend domestic law, the European Commission may refer the matter to the EU Court of Justice and ask it to record the infraction. If the CJEU confirms it, the Member States concerned are under a strict duty to take promptly all required measures to comply with the relevant provisions of EU law.[473] This infringement procedure is characterised by openness in the sense that anyone has

472. *See* ASEAN Annual Report 2024, 'ASEAN: Enhancing Connectivity and Resilience', ASEAN Secretariat, December 2024; at: https://asean.org/wp-content/uploads/2024/12/ASEAN-AR-2024_e-pub_web.pdf; ASEAN Annual Report 2022–2023 'ASEAN Matters: Epicentrum of Growth', ASEAN Secretariat, Jakarta, July 2023, at: https://asean.org/wp-content/uploads/2023/07/NEW-FINAL-ASEAN-Annual-Report-2022-2023.pdf; ASEAN Annual Report 2021–2022 'Addressing Challenges Together', ASEAN Secretariat, July 2022, at: https://asean.org/book/annual-report-2021-2022-addressing-challenges-together/; ASEAN Annual Report 2020–2021 'We Care, We Prepare, We Prosper', ASEAN Secretariat, July 2021, at: https://asean.org/book/asean-annual-report-2020-2021/; ASEAN Annual Report 2019–2020 'ASEAN 2020: Cohesive and Responsive', ASEAN Secretariat, July 2020, at: https://asean.org/book/asean-annual-report-2019-2020/; ASEAN Annual Report 2018–2019 'Advancing Partnership for Sustainability', ASEAN Secretariat, July 2019, at: https://asean.org/book/asean-annual-report-2018-2019-advancing-partnership-for-sustainability/; ASEAN Annual Report 2017–2018' 'A Resilient and Innovative ASEAN Community', ASEAN Secretariat, July 2018, at: https://asean.org/wp-content/uploads/2018/08/ASEAN-Annual-Report-2017-2018.pdf; and ASEAN Annual Report 2016–2017 'Partnering for Change, Engaging the World', ASEAN Secretariat, July 2017, at: https://asean.org/wp-content/uploads/2017/08/ASEAN-ANNUAL-REPORT-2016-2017-7-Aug1.pdf.

473. *See* TFEU Art. 258. It should be noted that the claim of breach or non-compliance may also be advanced by another Member State, *see ibid.*, Art. 259. However, for reasons of political expedience, Member States avoid accusing fellow Member States, invariably leaving to the European Commission, effectively the EU Secretariat, the task of commencing the infringement procedure.

access to the relevant proceedings.[474] The European Commission publishes annual reports on monitoring the application of EU law, which make interesting reading for the population of Member States because they can read the recorded instances and cases of infraction.[475] Even though it is obvious that the present institutional structure and evolution of ASEAN cannot support this mechanism for recording and confirming infractions by Member States, the argument made here is that such practices and solutions do exist in other regional international organisations and that in the future ASEAN might draw inspiration from them.

158. A final question to be asked is whether the ASEAN can cause the expulsion of recalcitrant Member States for having committed grave violations of the Charter. This question is not necessarily connected to the ASEAN having (or not having) in place a sanctioning regime. Indeed, ordering punitive measures against a Member State, which has violated its obligations (*e.g.*, to suspend its membership in the organisation or to temporarily cancel its voting rights in the organs of the organisation), is not necessarily a precondition for a decision to expel it.[476] Expulsion is invariably seen as the ultimate 'punishment' that an international organisation can inflict on recalcitrant Member States. But, depending on the circumstances, an international organisation may have to expel a Member State, if this is the only way to be protected from an unruly state, constantly causing problems and undermining its proper functioning.

159. The aforementioned EPG Report addressed the question of whether measures to redress non-compliance and serious breaches should include the expulsion of Member States. The recommendation was that ordinarily Member States should not be expelled: 'unless otherwise decided by the ASEAN Council [now, the ASEAN Summit] in exceptional circumstances, there shall be no recourse to expulsion of membership'.[477] Indeed, the ASEAN Charter, as already explained, does not contemplate expulsion as a possibility, and therefore it lacks a weapon to confront any Member State that has consistently failed to comply with and/or has breached its duties and obligations. Seen from another perspective, this approach is in line with the doctrine of (absolute) state sovereignty to which most Member States subscribe. It is also consistent with the idea that states participate in ASEAN as of right and that nobody has the power to disrupt and interfere with this right, let alone to cancel it. In conclusion, ASEAN Member States should be deemed to have the right

474. An online search of European Commission decisions on infringements of EU law by Member State or by policy area is available at: http://ec.europa.eu/atwork/applying-eu-law/infringements-proceedings/infringement_decisions/?lang_code=en.

475. The Reports from the year 1983 until the year 2024 (*see* COM(2024) 358 final, 25 Jul. 2024) are available at: https://ec.europa.eu/info/publications/annual-reports-monitoring-application-eu-law_en.

476. Compare Arts 5 and 6 UN Charter. It is, however, a precondition in the Council of Europe, *see* Arts 7 and 8 of the Statute, which was adopted in 1949 and has never been amended, 87 U.N.T.S. 103; *see* K. Magliveras, *Legal and Procedural Issues Arising from the Expulsion of the Russian Federation from the Council of Europe*, 23:1 International and Comparative Law Review (Special Issue on International Law and the Russian Invasion of Ukraine) 95–116 (2023).

477. *See* EPG Report, para. 32 at p. 17.

to decide, by a unanimous vote taken in the context of the Organisation's highest-ranking organ, to expel a recalcitrant member, if, on the one hand, this is for its benefit and proper functioning and, on the other hand, for the Member States to protect their own membership rights, privileges and benefits.

A. *Events in Myanmar in 2021, the Stance of ASEAN and the Question of Myanmar's Continued Membership*

160. The question of the consequences on the membership of a state that (deliberately) violates the principles, norms and ideals of the ASEAN Charter can be examined by taking as prime example the military *coup d'état* in Myanmar in February 2021 (the events that took place are mentioned in other parts of the present monograph). The large-scale violence against the population that followed, especially the ruling military regime's use of force against the Rohingya people, which, in terms of international law, should be considered as a religious minority, has arguably shown that the ASEAN Charter was not drafted to address such situations. The situation that has developed in Myanmar has been treated quite differently by commentators. In particular, an academic report has referred to the compelling prospects of suspending and/or expelling Myanmar from ASEAN but without actually explaining how it could be brought about.[478] Another academic article has claimed that the February 2021 events did not amount to a serious breach of the ASEAN Charter. In particular, it has argued that the aforementioned Article 5(3) of the Charter could not have been activated to address this situation on account of three reasons: (1) the Charter does not contain a definition of what constitutes a serious breach of and non-compliance with its provisions; (2) while the ultimately competent organ to deal with serious breaches and non-compliance is the Summit under Article 20(4) of the Charter (*see* also *infra*), the effect of the latter is to pass on the responsibility of interpretation to the Secretariat (under Article 51(2) of the Charter and Rule 2(1) of the Rules of Procedure mentioned *supra*), whose role in this matter is rather limited; and (3) under the aforementioned Article 20(1) of the Charter, the decision-making method for applying Article 5(3) is consultation and consensus, 'which is based on politic compromise way more than legal binding way'.[479]

Even though these arguments are valid, and the ensuing problems were highlighted *supra*, what should be emphasised is that when the founding treaty / constitutive instrument of an international organisation (in our case, the ASEAN Charter) does not regulate a specific matter, this does not mean that the competent

478. *See* The University of Queensland Asia Pacific Centre for the Responsibility to Protect School of Political Science and International Studies, *ASEAN and the Myanmar Humanitarian Crisis: Overcoming Challenges and Identifying Pathways*, April 2023, p. 1, at: https://r2pasiapacific.org/files/9923/2023_ASEAN_Myanmar_Humanitarian_Crisis.pdf.

479. *See* N. Limsiritong & P. Sookhakich, *Is there a Serious Breach of ASEAN Charter?: A Case Study of the Myanmar Military Coup 2021 Violence Against Civilians*, 10:1 International Journal of Crime, Law and Social Issues (2023) 1–8, at: https://doi.org/10.14456/ijclsi.2023.1.

organ/s may not take any action to address it. When serious breach and non-compliance have taken place, threatening the welfare of the international organisation in question, what is of paramount importance – and what is the duty of the membership – is to take all necessary and proportionate measures and ensure that it will continue to function and deliver.

As regards specifically the *coup d'etat* in Myanmar in 2021, it could be argued that it was a domestic affair, and that ASEAN may not engage with matters that fall within the internal sphere of Member States. This is a point of view that has some merit but probably reflects an outdated point of view of the relationship between international organisations and their Member States. On the contrary, this is a relationship that is always evolving: increasingly international organisations become involved with political developments that take place in the territory of Member States. This happens especially in those cases where such developments are regarded as breaching and/or as being non-compliant with the (written or customary) commitments / duties / obligations that the allegedly recalcitrant member owes to the international organisation concerned or to the international community at large. Therefore, political developments in a Member State that result in the violation of the very values on which an international organisation is founded, not to speak of the peremptory rules of international law, cannot be left unanswered simply because the founding treaty or the constitutive instrument does not regulate it. There is, of course, the obvious exception that the other Member States will declare that they are not willing to take any action or take no action by omitting to carry out the relevant provisions in the constitutive instrument of the international organisation in question.

161. Moreover, two things should be taken into consideration. The first is, and it has explained *supra*, that the Preamble of the ASEAN Charter extols that Member States adhere to the principles of democracy, the rule of law, good governance, respect for and protection of human rights and fundamental freedoms. The second is that in the present phase of its evolution, ASEAN has the role of a building stone towards the creation of the ASEAN Community, the next step in the evolutionary process of integration in the region of Southeast Asia. Member States have willingly, and presumably without any outside pressure, assumed these principles, have agreed to follow this process of evolution and have concurred in fulfilling and not violating all obligations, duties, limitations, and restrictions that flow from the constitutional instruments of ASEAN. It follows that when the constitutive instrument (the ASEAN Charter) is silent and does not regulate specific situations, this silence may not be used as a justification for not acting against recalcitrant Member States, which have knowingly acted against the international organisation's rules and norms (in effect, what constitute the legal system of ASEAN or the ASEAN law, as has been argued *supra*). If in the domestic legal systems of Member States impunity goes against the rule of law, the same should apply to international organisations when Member States flout its law and are left 'unpunished'.

162. The ASEAN Leaders' Meeting which took place in April 2021 at the offices of the ASEAN Secretariat reaffirmed the principle of multilateral cooperation, which is anchored in international law and aims at achieving peace, security, stability, and prosperity in the region and beyond.[480] This was an interesting development because what was also discussed was the situation in Myanmar following the 1 February 2021 *coup d'etat* as well as the escalation of violence that followed it and led to the death of many hundreds of people (the events are explained elsewhere in the monograph). According to the Chairman's Statement, 'as an ASEAN family', ASEAN Leaders had a close discussion on this matter, expressed their deep concern and 'acknowledged ASEAN's positive and constructive role in facilitating a peaceful solution in the interest of the people of Myanmar and their livelihoods' These discussions were held with Myanmar's military regime being present. They culminated in the so-called Five-Point Consensus (also referred to as '5 PC'), the text of which was attached to the Chairman's Statement, presumably to give it a measure of authority and be regarded as a binding decision.[481]

The five points that were agreed upon were the following: (1) there must be an immediate cessation of violence in Myanmar, and all parties must exercise utmost restraint; (2) a constructive dialogue must start among all parties to seek a peaceful solution in the interests of the population; (3) mediation in this dialogue shall be facilitated by a special envoy of the ASEAN Chair, with the assistance of the Secretary-General; (4) ASEAN shall provide humanitarian assistance to Myanmar through the ASEAN Coordinating Centre for Humanitarian Assistance on disaster management (AHA Centre);[482] and (5) the special envoy and a delegation (on which no details were given) shall visit Myanmar and meet with all parties concerned.[483] As it becomes obvious, the 'Five-Point Consensus' was not concerned with the situation in the Rakhine State, where violent clashes between the local population and the military have been ongoing since October 2016. Moreover, ASEAN leaders were no doubt aware of the Report, which had been submitted in January 2020 to the government of Myanmar by a panel appointed by it (the Independent Commission of Enquiry – ICOE) to investigate alleged abuses in the Rakhine State. However, the Chairman's Statement only 'underscored the importance of efforts to addressing the root causes of the situation in Rakhine State'.[484] The ICOE Report, reference to which has been made *supra*, concluded that war crimes and abuses had taken place, but there was no evidence that the military tried to commit genocide of the Rohingyas.

---

480. *See* Chairman's Statement on the ASEAN Leaders' Meeting, 24 Apr. 2021, para. 3, at: https://asean.org/wp-content/uploads/Chairmans-Statement-on-ALM-Five-Point-Consensus-24-April-2021-FINAL-a-1.pdf.
481. *Ibid.*
482. The AHA Centre is an intergovernmental organisation, which was established by the Member States to facilitate cooperation and coordination of disaster management among them; *see* the Agreement on the Establishment of the ASEAN Coordinating Centre for Humanitarian Assistance on disaster management, which was signed by ASEAN Foreign Ministers on 17 Nov. 2011, at: https://agreement.asean.org/media/download/20220330063452.pdf.
483. Chairman's Statement, 24 Apr. 2021, para. 8.
484. *Ibid.*, para. 9. On the report, *see* N. Lynn Aung, 'Myanmar panel finds war crimes committed in Rakhine but no genocidal intent', *The Myanmar Times*, 20 Jan. 2020, at: https://web.archive.org/web/20200711054458/https://www.mmtimes.com/news/myanmar-panel-finds-war-crimes-committed-rakhine-no-genocidal-intent.html-0

163. Arguably, the 'Five-Point Consensus' is a mild form of interference in the domestic affairs of Myanmar. Even though, prima facie, it goes against the ASEAN Charter's principle of not interfering, it could be justified because the value of Member States' multilateral cooperation to attain peace and stability in the region, as affirmed in the Chairman's Statement of April 2021, obviously ranks much higher. A *coup d' état* cannot be condoned in an ASEAN Member State unless there are unique and exceptional circumstances, if, e.g., the country's independence or existence was at stake. This was not the case with the coup of February 2021. Moreover, events in Myanmar had by then become a serious problem for ASEAN and the region beyond. Therefore, this form of interference, which was not in any way punitive and did not even attempt to remove the ruling military regime from power, was within the powers of the Summit. Whether it was meaningful and appropriate under the circumstances, these are of course different questions. Basically, all the 5PC did was to request that Myanmar's ruling military regime participate in a constructive dialogue with the other political forces in the country and accept the mediation of ASEAN. As the 5PC was reached by consensus, it could be argued with certainty that the representative of Myanmar also agreed to its content. Interestingly enough, the wording of the 'Five-Point Consensus' did not indicate that the dialogue between the political forces should aim at restoring democracy, the rule of law and the other principles that, as has been explained above, are considered cornerstones of the ASEAN Charter.

164. Myanmar's military regime in power was not forthcoming in implementing the 'Five-Point Consensus', while the situation in the country deteriorated. Therefore, Myanmar was no longer only a problem but also an embarrassment for ASEAN and for the whole region considering that ASEAN's lofty principles were at best ignored, at worst breached. In October 2021, an emergency ASEAN Foreign Ministers' Meeting (AMM) was held to discuss preparations for the 38th and 39th ASEAN Summits due to be held in Brunei at the end of the same month. The Statement issued after the Meeting recorded that no consensus had been reached for a political representative from Myanmar to attend to it. There were also competing claims as to who should participate, effectively who should be recognised as the official representative of the Republic of the Union of Myanmar. According to the Statement, despite extensive discussions, there was no consensus reached for a political representative from Myanmar to attend the upcoming Summits. Finally, 'to allow Myanmar the space to restore its internal affairs and return to normalcy', the Meeting, 'while noting the reservations from the Myanmar representative', resolved that a non-political representative from Myanmar should be invited.[485] Later on, Singapore justified this pronouncement by saying that it was 'a difficult but necessary decision to uphold ASEAN's credibility given the unsatisfactory and highly limited progress' in the implementation of the 'Five-Point Consensus'.[486] However, it will be argued that the effect has been an indirect amendment of Article 7(1) of

485. *See* Statement of the Chair of the ASEAN Foreign Ministers' Meeting, 15 Oct. 2021, at: https://www.burmalibrary.org/en/statement-of-the-chair-of-the-asean-foreign-ministers-meeting.

486. Singapore also urged Myanmar's military authorities to cooperate with the ASEAN Special Envoy, *see* Ministry of Foreign Affairs of Singapore, 'MFA Spokesperson's Comments in Response to

the ASEAN Summit, which stipulates that the Summit comprises the Heads of State or Government of (all) Member States. Thus, it was probably political expediency and the avoidance of reaching difficult determinations as to the consequences of the *coup d'etat* in the continued participation of the *de facto* government of Myanmar in ASEAN organs and activities that excused this decision. However, from a legal point of view and given that presently it is still applied, a precedence has been created and the ability of ASEAN to operate as a rules-based Organisation could (and should) be questioned.

Based on the decision of the emergency AMM, when Brunei sent out invitations for the October 2021 Summits, the invitation addressed to Myanmar was specifically for a 'non-political representative' to partake, effectively barring the military regime and *de facto* government of Myanmar from attending as the lawful representative of the country. The military government decided not to have a representative attending and, therefore, not to participate in the Summit. Arguably, this was contrary to Myanmar's ASEAN Charter obligations because it is the duty of all Member States to participate in all Summits. Furthermore, Brunei's move resulted in effectively having the State of Myanmar excluded from the Summit, even though the aim was to prevent the military leaders from attending it. And at the same time, to show to the international community that ASEAN no longer condoned such behaviour by a Member State. The (deliberate) non-participation of Myanmar was not recorded in the Chairman's Statement, which was issued by Brunei after the Summit. In particular, instead of starting with the usual words 'We, the Heads of State/Government of ASEAN Member States', it read: 'We, the Association of Southeast Asian Nations (ASEAN), gathered for the 38th and 39th ASEAN Summits on 26 October 2021 under the Chairmanship of Brunei Darussalam … .'[487] Strictly legally speaking and based on the arguments put forward in the previous paragraph, this was untrue: even though there was only one Member State not attending, there was no 'ASEAN'.

165. The Chairman's Statement dealt with developments in Myanmar twice: (a) in the section dealing with the ASEAN Socio-Cultural Community and (b) in the section concerning 'Regional and International Issues'. In the former, it covered events in the Rakhine State and in the latter, the consequences of the *coup d'état* as well as the implementation of the 'Five-Point Consensus'. It follows that ASEAN leaders continued to regard them as separate items on the Summits' agenda, which made sense from a political and diplomatic point of view. However, the two issues were and are still related because the events in Rakhine State and the treatment of Rohingyas as well as the *coup d'état* are primarily the making of the military regime that is in power and exercises effective control of the largest part of the territory of Myanmar. ASEAN leaders reaffirmed the support for a more visible and enhanced ASEAN role to support Myanmar by providing humanitarian assistance, facilitating

Media Queries on the Emergency ASEAN Foreign Ministers' Meeting on 15 October 2021', 16 Oct. 2021, at: https://www.mfa.gov.sg/Newsroom/Press-Statements-Transcripts-and-Photos/2021/10/20211016-ASEAN-FM-Meeting.

487. *See* Chairman's Statement of the 38th and 39th ASEAN Summits, 28 Oct. 2021 (by videoconference), para. 1, at: https://asean.org/chairmans-statement-of-the-38th-and-39th-asean-summits/.

the repatriation process of exiled Rohingyas, and promoting sustainable development in Rakhine State. They insisted that the voluntary return of displaced persons must be undertaken in a safe, secure, and dignified manner and in accordance with the terms of the bilateral agreement between Myanmar and Bangladesh on repatriation.[488] They also praised the efforts of the Secretary-General as regards the implementation of the recommendations of the Preliminary Needs Assessment (PNA), the 'contribution from ASEAN Member States and some external partners in supporting ASEAN activities', and looked forward to the conduct of the Comprehensive Needs Assessment (CNA) when conditions would allow it.[489] It follows that the treatment of Rohingyas and the situation in Rakhine State was dealt with in a formal and bureaucratic manner, while the questions of the responsibility and liability of those who had forced the local population to emigrate were not touched upon. And so was also the question of the military regime's obligation to offer compensation / restitution to the victims and their families.

166. As regards the 'Five-Point Consensus', even though the Summit 'called on Myanmar to fulfil its commitment' to carry it out, the military regime in power was not expressly mentioned, but the rather vague wording 'all parties concerned in Myanmar' was used.[490] The Summit, by respecting the principle of non-interference, reaffirmed the adherence to the rule of law, good governance, the principles of democracy and constitutional government as well as the need to strike an appropriate balance to the application of ASEAN principles on the situation in Myanmar. Moreover, the Summit reaffirmed the decision reached by the Emergency ASEAN Foreign Ministers' Meeting on 15 October 2021. Presumably, in order to dispel any conclusions regarding Myanmar's membership status, it 'reiterated that Myanmar remains a member of the ASEAN family and recognised that Myanmar needs both time and political space to deal with its many and complex challenges'.[491] While the Statement did not explain which these challenges were, arguably there was a feeling that the situation in Myanmar could derail progress in the Organisation. And this could very well explain why the Statement went on to say '[e]xpressed the view that Myanmar's national preoccupation should not affect ASEAN Community building process and decision making'.[492]

167. The 40th and 41st Summits were held in Cambodia in November 2022. ASEAN leaders attended the event in person. In the period that had lapsed since the 38th and 39th Summits, the question of Myanmar had been reviewed by the ASEAN

488. Even though no further details were given, the reference was probably to the Arrangement on Return of Displaced Persons from Rakhine State between the Government of Myanmar and the Government of Bangladesh, which was signed on 23 Nov. 2017, at: https://reliefweb.int/report/bangladesh/bangladesh-and-myanmar-conclude-arrangement-return-displaced-persons-rakhine-state. Note that the two countries signed another Agreement on 15 Jan. 2018, reportedly under the influence exerted by China, to repatriate some 645,000 refugees to the state of Rakhine over a two-year period. The Agreement concerned those Myanmar nationals who had fled Rakhine state during the violence of 2016 and 2017.
489. Chairman's Statement of the 38th and 39th ASEAN Summits, para. 85.
490. *Ibid.*, para. 101.
491. *Ibid.*, para. 102.
492. *Ibid.*

Foreign Ministers' Meeting (AMM). In particular, the AMM held in August 2022 reiterated that the Organisation continued to support Myanmar's efforts to bring peace, stability, the rule of law, to promote harmony and reconciliation among the various communities, including in Rakhine State, and recorded its deep disappointment by the limited progress and the lack of commitment of 'the Nay Pyi Taw authorities' (a euphemism for the military regime in power in Myanmar) to the complete implementation of the 'Five-Point Consensus'.[493] Both at the 55th AMM and at the Special ASEAN Foreign Ministers' Meeting, which was held in late October 2022 specifically to deliberate the execution of the 'Five-Point Consensus' and put forward pertinent recommendations to the 40th and 41st ASEAN Summits, a non-political representative from Myanmar was invited but with no positive response.[494] It follows that deliberately the military regime ruling Myanmar was staying away from the ASEAN principal organs. It is submitted that this behaviour amounted to self-imposed exclusion from the Organisation, a state of affairs somewhat resembling temporary secession. Obviously, there were important institutional consequences for ASEAN, which probably explain why the Special AMM in October 2022, on the one hand, referred to 'the need to resume Myanmar's full and normal engagements with ASEAN' and, on the other hand, 'unanimously agreed that decision-making in ASEAN shall be based on consultation and consensus, while the fundamental principles stipulated in the ASEAN Charter shall guide ASEAN's collective efforts to address the situation in Myanmar'.[495]

168. There is no doubt that the situation in Myanmar constituted a new chapter in the relationship between ASEAN and Member States, and the way to handle it was not envisaged in the Charter. At the same time, as there has been no official determination that Myanmar is in breach of its obligations, legally speaking, it is very difficult to be treated as a recalcitrant Member State and have drastic measures taken against it to comply with its obligations. During the 40th and 41st ASEAN Summits, the question of Rakhine State was again discussed.[496] The only development was that the MOU between the Government of Myanmar, the Office of the United Nations High Commissioner for Refugees (UNHCR), and the United Nations Development Programme (UNDP) for the voluntary, safe, dignified and sustainable repatriation of Rohingya refugees from Bangladesh was extended to March 2023.[497] As regards the political crisis in the country, the important role played by the United Nations (the Special Envoy of the UN Secretary-General on

493. *See* Joint Communiqué of the 55th ASEAN Foreign Ministers' Meeting, 3 Aug. 2022, paras 96 and 117.

494. *See* Statement of the Chair of the Special ASEAN Foreign Ministers' Meeting, 27 Oct. 2022, ASEAN Secretariat, Jakarta, at: https://reliefweb.int/report/myanmar/statement-chair-special-asean-foreign-ministers-meeting-27-october-2022-asean-secretariat-jakarta.

495. *Ibid.*

496. *See* Chairman's Statement of the 40th and 41st ASEAN Summits, Phnom Penh, Cambodia, 11 Nov. 2022, paras 87–88, at: https://asean.org/wp-content/uploads/2022/11/01-Chairmans-Statement-of-the-40th-and-41st-ASEAN-Summits-rev.pdf.

497. It was originally signed on 6 Jun. 2018, *see* https://reliefweb.int/report/myanmar/government-myanmar-and-united-nations-agencies-sign-mou-assistance-repatriation.

Myanmar[498] visited the country in August 2022[499]) and by other (unnamed) 'external partners in facilitating a peaceful solution in Myanmar' was recorded.[500]

The 40th and 41st Summits also considered the implementation of the 'Five-Point Consensus', but, somehow, it did not form part of the formal deliberations. The outcome was the 'ASEAN Leaders' Review and Decision on the Implementation of the Five-Point Consensus'.[501] Even though it was endorsed by the Summit,[502] it was not attached to the Chairman's Statement. Finally, reference should be made to the ASEAN Leaders' Statement on the 55th Anniversary of ASEAN adopted by the Summit. What is relevant to the present discussion is that the text of the Statement did not begin with 'We the heads of state and government of ASEAN Member States … ' but with 'We, the Association of Southeast Asian Nations (ASEAN), namely [the official names of the Member States including Myanmar] gathered in Phnom Penh, Kingdom of Cambodia, on the occasion of the 55th Anniversary of ASEAN … '. This indicated that a representative of Myanmar attended the event. And this representative was no doubt from the ruling military regime.

169. From an institutional point of view, that the ASEAN Summit does not issue separate decisions or resolutions but what has been decided is recorded in the form of 'Chairman's Statements' could be problematic, especially when the binding nature of what was decided needs to be ascertained. And to put it into context, does the 'ASEAN Leaders' Review and Decision' bind all Member States, including Myanmar, which was not in attendance? Thus, should it be regarded as a political text, a declaration of intent so to speak, or is it akin to a legal instrument which requires to be fully observed? If the latter is the case, and if it had not adhered to, should this be a cause for attributing responsibility to the Member States concerned? As regards the 'Five-Point Consensus', it was obvious from the Statements issued after the aforementioned Summits and the AMMs that it has been treated as a decision that had to be implemented by its addresses, principally the political entities in and the military regime of Myanmar. And this is because, according to ASEAN leaders, the 5PC constituted the solution to the political crisis in Myanmar agreed by all other ASEAN States. However, there is another way of looking at it: the situation in Myanmar constitutes a (very serious) problem that concerns ASEAN (i.e., an international organisation) and a specific Member State, and the former has the authority to resolve it.

---

498. The appointment of a special envoy on Myanmar was envisaged in UNGA Res. 72/248, 'Situation of human rights in Myanmar', 24 Dec. 2017, para. 10.
499. *See* UNSG, 'Statement by the Secretary-General's Special Envoy on Myanmar, Noeleen Heyzer', 17 Aug. 2022, at: https://www.un.org/sg/en/content/sg/note-correspondents/2022-08-17/note-correspondents-statement-the-secretary-general%E2%80%99s-special-envoy-myanmar-noeleen-heyzer.
500. Chairman's Statement of the 40th and 41st ASEAN Summits, para. 105.
501. Text at: https://asean.org/wp-content/uploads/2022/11/06-ASEAN-Leaders-Review-and-Decision-on-the-Implementation-of-the-Five-Point-Consensus_fin.pdf.
502. Chairman's Statement of the 40th and 41st ASEAN Summits, para. 106.

170. Comparing these two documents, the 'ASEAN Leaders' Review and Decision' was not only drafted in a far more legalistic form than the 'Five-Point Consensus', but importantly the word 'decision' in the title suggested that it should be treated as a (proper) Summit resolution. More specifically, it invokes Articles 7 and 20 of the ASEAN Charter: Article 7 lays down the functions and powers of ASEAN Summits. Article 20 provides for the basic principles of consultation and consensus in ASEAN decision-making as well as for the duty to refer instances of serious breach of the Charter or non-compliance with its provisions to the ASEAN Summit for decision (Article 20(4)). It is not clear whether the 'ASEAN Leaders' Review and Decision' is the very decision envisaged in the fourth paragraph of Article 20, in other words, whether it is the action that the Summit has taken to address a serious breach of the Charter perpetrated by Myanmar's military government.

To elaborate further on this, the 'ASEAN Leaders' Review and Decision' refers to the growing violence in Myanmar as a major concern affecting not only Myanmar but also ASEAN's Community building efforts, and, for this reason, ASEAN is committed to assisting Myanmar in finding a peaceful and durable solution to the crisis. Moreover, this wording justifies the argument made above, namely that the prohibition of interfering in the domestic affairs of a Member State does not apply when the situation at hand has negative consequences for the Organisation and its proper functioning. The text also made it clear that the 'Five-Point Consensus' was still valid; therefore, the Myanmar Armed Forces had to 'comply with its commitments to the ASEAN Leaders'.[503] The consequences of non-compliance were apparently not discussed.

171. The pressing issue of Myanmar's participation in the Organisation was also addressed. The 'ASEAN Leaders' Review and Decision' resolved to maintain the demand for Myanmar's non-political representation to attend the ASEAN Summits and the AMMs. As far as the meetings of the other organs are concerned, the Coordinating Council was tasked with reviewing the question of representation, if and when required. However, considering that both the AMM and the Coordinating Council comprise foreign ministers, it is rather interesting that in the case of the former it was the Summit that decided on representation, while in the case of the latter it was left to the Coordinating Council's discretion. Finally, it was reaffirmed that the Summit is the supreme decision-making body, that it will make the final decision on whether the 'Five-Point Consensus' has been implemented, and that it will find a solution in case consensus cannot be achieved.[504] ASEAN leaders appear to have treated the 'Five-Point Consensus' as a blueprint for ending the decades-long political strife in Myanmar. However, even if it were to be implemented in full by the military regime in power and the other domestic political actors, it would only lead to a dialogue between the parties to the conflict. Clearly, the way the Summit has handled this matter shows that ASEAN lacks the skills, the expertise and the resolution to deal promptly and effectively with situations that involve loss of

503. ASEAN Leaders' Review and Decision on the Implementation of the Five-Point Consensus, paras 5 and 6.
504. *Ibid.*, paras 9 and 10.

life, grave violations of human rights and negation of basic democratic ideals. Unable to take a proactive role, ASEAN is rather a mere reviewer of events and not a creator of sustainable solutions.

172. The 42nd ASEAN Summit held in May 2023 reiterated the 'unified position that the Five-Point Consensus remains [the] main reference' and that the 'ASEAN Leaders' Review and Decision' stands.[505] The only new element was that the peaceful and durable solution to be found in the situation in Myanmar (always with the direct engagement of the ASEAN Chair) should be 'Myanmar-owned and Myanmar-led'.[506] Apparently, this was an attempt to legitimise the process by keeping it as close as possible to the principle of non-interference. Equally, the AMM that took place in July 2023 had nothing of substance to add.[507] Two months later, the 43rd ASEAN Summit was held. Myanmar again did not participate, as the ASEAN Chair's request that a non-political representative be sent was not complied with. It could be argued that Myanmar's military government follows the so-called policy of the empty chair. This is a well-known way for Member States to show to the international organisation in which they participate that they disagree with certain activities or actions, that they object to the direction the organisation has taken, and so on.[508]

173. At the 43rd Summit, the nine participating states declared their readiness to strengthen ASEAN and make it robust and agile, to equip it with strengthened capacity and institutional effectiveness to address challenges and remain relevant for its people and the region.[509] Arguably, the very positive picture painted for the Organisation's future was in contradistinction with the apparent inability to deal resolutely with events in one of its Member States, arguably constituting the largest challenge that it presently faces. The Summit strongly condemned the continued escalation of violence, the population's prolonged suffering, the ongoing humanitarian crisis, the destruction of public facilities, all of which had 'adverse impacts

505. *See* Chairman's Statement of the 42nd ASEAN Summit, Labuan Bajo, Indonesia, 10–11 May 2023, para. 125, at: https://asean.org/wp-content/uploads/2023/05/FINAL-Chairmans-Statement-42nd-ASEAN-Summit-1.pdf.

506. *Ibid.*

507. *See* Joint Communiqué of the 56th ASEAN Foreign Ministers' Meeting, Jakarta, Indonesia, 11–12 Jul. 2023, paras 142 et seq., at: https://asean.org/wp-content/uploads/2023/07/The-56th-AMM-Joint-Communique.pdf.

508. This policy does not lead to the withdrawal of the Member State in question, which must continue to fulfil all its obligations to the international organisation. For a relatively recent example, in April 2018, the governments of Argentina, Brazil, Chile, Colombia, Paraguay and Peru announced their temporary suspension of their participation in the Union of South American Nations, *see* N. Comini & J. A. Sanahuja, 'The New Right governments' empty chair strategy at UNASUR', *Open Democracy*, 7 May 2018, at: https://www.opendemocracy.net/en/democraciaabierta/new-right-governments-empty-chair-strategy-at-/.

509. *See* Chairman's Statement of the 43rd ASEAN Summit, Jakarta, Indonesia, 5 Sep. 2023, para. 2, at: https://asean.org/wp-content/uploads/2023/09/CHAIRMAN-STATEMENT-OF-THE-43RD-ASEAN-SUMMIT-FIN-2.pdf. Note that on 5 Nov. 2023 and at the invitation of the Minister for Foreign Affairs of Indonesia another AMM was held, which discussed the situation in Myanmar but nothing substantial emerged from it.

on regional stability'.[510] The fact that ASEAN Leaders recognised that the situation in Myanmar had disrupted regional stability was of significance because it meant that it was no longer a domestic matter. And while the Statement did not refer to a disruption of peace and security (this would have possibly required them to notify the UN Security Council and bring the situation before it under the relevant provisions of the UN Charter),[511] it is submitted that their insistence on keeping the 'Five-Point Consensus' as the 'main reference to address the political crisis in Myanmar' was an obsolete policy.

Finally, the 43rd Summit endorsed another document, the 'ASEAN Leaders' Review and Decision on the Implementation of the Five-Point Consensus'. It should be made clear that this is not the document that had been adopted during the aforementioned 40th and 41st ASEAN Summits but the outcome of another review of the situation in Myanmar that had taken place on the sidelines of the 43rd Summit. Given the policy of the 'empty chair' pursued by Myanmar, the statement made in the new 'ASEAN Leaders' Review and Decision' that Myanmar 'remains an integral part of ASEAN'[512] arguably gave out the wrong message. While Myanmar's membership remained intact and was not affected, by staying away from the Summits and other high-level meetings and, consequently by not participating in the decision-making processes, showed a deliberate behaviour not to be an active Member State.

The 43rd Summit resolved that, in order to 'ensure sustainability of ASEAN's on-going efforts and other relevant approaches', a troika may be formed as an informal consultation mechanism consisting of the current, previous, and incoming Chairs of ASEAN, always working in line with the 'Five-Point Consensus'.[513] Furthermore, it was decided to continue demanding Myanmar's non-political representation at Summits and AMMs and to task the ASEAN Coordinating Council to review this decision when there was concrete progress in the implementation of the 5PC.[514] The question could be asked why are both the Coordinating Council and the AMM involved in reviewing developments in the situation in Myanmar. Considering that, as explained, both consist of the foreign ministers of Member States, effectively, it is the same group of persons deliberating the same situation.

The new 'ASEAN Leaders' Review and Decision' also resolved (without giving any reasons or citing any legal basis) that the ASEAN Chairmanship for the year 2026 shall be assumed by the Philippines and that in the following years the Chairmanship rotation shall continue based on the alphabetical order, until a different decision is made. What this means in practice is that Myanmar will not assume the Chairmanship for the year 2026 (the Philippines ought to have assume the ASEAN

510. *Ibid.*, para. 160.
511. Compare Art. 35(1) UN Charter.
512. ASEAN Leaders' Review and Decision on the Implementation of the Five-Point Consensus, Jakarta, Indonesia, 5 Sep. 2023, at: https://asean.org/wp-content/uploads/2023/09/01.FINAL-ASEAN-LEADERS-REVIEW-AND-DECISION-ON-THE-IMPLEMENTATION-OF-THE-5PC-1.pdf.
513. *Ibid.*, para. 13. In reality, the engagement of ASEAN Chairs in the situation in Myanmar has been through the Special Envoy of the ASEAN Chair on Myanmar.
514. *Ibid.*, para. 14.

Chair in 2027).[515] However, holding the Chair is an administrative duty, and the relevant provision in the ASEAN Charter (Article 31) does not lay down any exceptions to the rule that it rotates annually on the basis of the alphabetical order of the Member States' English names. Arguably, this decision lacks any legal authority. At the same time, if it were to be regarded as a measure of a punitive nature, it seriously questions Myanmar's membership status.

It is also notable that this decision was not included in the Chairman's Statement of the 43rd ASEAN Summit. Therefore, the question arises as to why ASEAN leaders were so eager to deal with a future event at such an early stage. There does not appear to be any satisfactory answer other than that they wanted to warn Myanmar's military regime that it will not be allowed to act as Chair and perform the functions associated with it. Given that one of these functions is to strengthen and promote closer relations between the Organisation and external partners,[516] effectively the state holding the Chair acts as ASEAN's ambassador to the world at large. It follows that Member States did not want to have as collective 'ambassador' a state that has been accused of genocide before the ICJ (Case of *The Gambia v. Myanmar*, *see supra*). However, logical as this decision might be, from a legal point of view, it must be justified how a Member State, which is otherwise in good standing (its membership has not been suspended), is prevented from assuming a role within the Organisation to which it is entitled. Moreover, until the time of writing, the other Member States have avoided reaching a crucial determination regarding which is the legitimate government of Myanmar and whether the present military regime should be treated as the sole representative of the State of Myanmar. The conclusion is that ASEAN, as a regional international organisation that wants to operate a Political-Security Community, is (to say the least) ill-equipped to deal with unconstitutional overthrows of government, *coups d'etat* and other breaches of the democratic ideals to which the Charter subscribes.[517] And ASEAN cannot overlook the possibility that in the future there might be similar situations in other Member States. Therefore, tackling promptly, efficiently and effectively the situation in Myanmar should also be regarded as an investment for the future.

174. Finally, the new 'ASEAN Leaders' Review and Decision' recorded that Member States resolved to enhance cooperation not only among them but also between the Organisation and the neighbouring countries of Myanmar (which include India, China and Thailand) so as to address the consequences of the crisis in the country, which included an increase of trafficking in narcotics and in trafficking in human beings (THB).[518] This is additional proof that ASEAN has (officially) accepted that the situation had gone well beyond being a domestic affair and had

515. ASEAN Leaders' Review and Decision on the Implementation of the Five-Point Consensus, 5 Sep. 2023, para. 15.
516. Art. 32(d) ASEAN Charter.
517. The African Union is an excellent example of a regional organisation that is equipped both institutionally and procedurally to deal with such situations, *see* specifically the functions and the powers of the African Peace and Security Council; K. Magliveras & G. Naldi, *The African Union* (3rd ed., Wolters Kluwer 2024), 221 et seq.
518. ASEAN Leaders' Review and Decision on the Implementation of the Five-Point Consensus, 5 Sep. 2023, para. 18.

become a regional problem. But there is another dimension which the ASEAN Leaders might not have thought of. More specifically, the international community regards both trafficking in narcotics and THB as transnational crimes, and it has adopted multilateral treaties that compel all contracting parties to arrest the alleged perpetrators, to prosecute them, to put them on trial and to impose harsh criminal penalties if found guilty. Moreover, THB is very closely associated with slavery, the slave trade and the grave violation of several human rights and fundamental freedoms. Therefore, additional obligations are placed on the ASEAN States and neighbouring states. It goes beyond the scope of this monograph to examine if these obligations are performed.

175. Another question which can also not be avoided is the engagement of the UN Security Council in this situation. So far, it has not been substantial. More specifically, Resolution 2669(2022), which was adopted on 21 December 2022, demanded an immediate end to all forms of violence throughout Myanmar. It also requested that, by 15 March 2023, the UN Secretary-General or his Special Envoy,[519] in coordination with the ASEAN Special Envoy, report orally on UN support for the implementation of the 'Five-Point Consensus'.[520] Since then, the only action at the UNSC level has been the holding of so-called Arria-formula meetings.[521]

Reference will be made to the following two meetings. The first took place on 19 May 2023. The purpose was to discuss the worsening humanitarian situation in Myanmar and to consider what the international community can do to address it and to mitigate the associated risks to international peace and security.[522] The second 'Arria-formula meeting' took place on 29 May 2024. It was convened again by the United Kingdom, while the invitees were the UNSC members, all ASEAN Member States as well as the bordering countries. The purpose was to highlight the effects of the ongoing conflict in Myanmar on children, youth and the future generations.[523]

519. At the time, the Special Envoy was Noeleen Heyzer from Singapore, whose contract ended on 12 Jun. 2023. The vacant post was filed on 5 Apr. 2024 when Julie Bishop from Australia was appointed, *see* https://www.un.org/sg/en/content/sg/personnel-appointments/2024-04-05/ms-julie-bishop-of-australia-special-envoy-myanmar.

520. Previously, UNSC Presidential Statement, S/PRST/2021/5 of 10 Mar. 2021, had expressed support for the democratic process in Myanmar, condemned the violence in the country, and emphasised the need to pursue dialogue and reconciliation.

521. Named after Ambassador Diego Arria of Venezuela, who initiated the practice in 1992, these are very informal and confidential gatherings of UNSC members at the invitation of one or more of them. The idea is for the members to exchange views on a particular topic, without following any procedural protocol and without keeping any minutes.

522. The meeting was convened by the United Kingdom; the Concept Paper is available at: https://admin.aplusforpeace.ch/sites/default/files/2023-05/Myanmar%20Arria%20Concept%20Note%20-%2019%20May%202023.pdf.

523. Generally, *see* United Nations Office for the Coordination of Humanitarian Affairs (OCHA), *Myanmar Humanitarian Update No. 38*, 24 May 2024, at: https://reliefweb.int/report/myanmar/myanmar-humanitarian-update-no-38-24-may-2024; UNICEF Myanmar, Humanitarian Situation Report No. 3/2024, 23 May 2024, at: https://www.unicef.org/myanmar/reports/unicef-myanmar-humanitarian-situation-report-no-3.

This group of the population was seen as 'as agents of change and participants in a peaceful, genuine, and inclusive process towards a sustainable political resolution'.[524] At the time, its serious plight and its precarious condition were confirmed by different UN sources.[525] Briefly, since then, the Security Council has discussed the situation in Myanmar under the agenda item 'Any Other Business' on 3 July 2024, in closed consultations on 19 September 2024, as a private meeting of UNSC members on 20 November 2024 and again in closed consultations on 30 January 2025.

It should be mentioned that UNSC members are also informed of developments regarding the situation in Myanmar through the open briefings of the UN Assistant Secretary-General for the Middle East, Asia and the Pacific. However, these briefings (and the same applies to 'Arria-formula meetings') are not ordinary UNSC meetings where decisions may be taken pursuant to the provisions of Chapter VI or Chapter VII of the UN Charter. That the UNSC has taken no action in relation to the situation in Myanmar was lamented by South Korea during the briefing that took place in April 2024.[526] However, it transpires that at least two UNSC members, both permanent members, do not regard that the situation is presently apt for UNSC action. More specifically, according to the Russian Federation, 'Myanmar does not pose a threat to international security', but it is the Western delegations that attempt to politicise the Myanmar dossier, while China stated that the conflict in Rakhine State is Myanmar's internal affair.[527] In contradistinction, the US representative submitted that the military regime had disregarded Resolution 2669(2022) and the 'Five-Point Consensus' and that this state of affairs heightened the need for UNSC measures to safeguard peace, prosperity, and security in Myanmar and in the region.[528] The US representative did not explain what these measures might be or what they would entail.

---

524. *See* the UK Concept Note prepared for the Meeting at: https://www.securitycouncilreport.org/un-documents/document/arria-formula-concept-note-arria-formula-meeting-on-myanmar.php. Note that a video of the meeting is available online at: https://webtv.un.org/en/asset/k1y/k1you6ou6c.

525. *See* United Nations Office for the Coordination of Humanitarian Affairs (OCHA), *Myanmar Humanitarian Update No. 38*, 24 May 2024, at: https://reliefweb.int/report/myanmar/myanmar-humanitarian-update-no-38-24-may-2024; UNICEF Myanmar, Humanitarian Situation Report No. 3/2024, 23 May 2024, at: https://www.unicef.org/myanmar/reports/unicef-myanmar-humanitarian-situation-report-no-3; and United Nations, *Children and armed conflict: report of the Secretary-General*, UN Doc. A/77/895-S/2023/363 (5 Jun 2023). For the latest report, *see* United Nations, *Children and armed conflict: report of the Secretary-General*, UN Doc. A/78/842-S/2024/384 (3 Jun. 2024).

526. *See* the statement by the representative of South Korea: 'Regrettably, there is currently no UN Special Envoy, no UN Resident Coordinator, and no regular meetings or a reporting mechanism of the Security Council. The scale of the Myanmar crisis requires more than domestic, bilateral or regional efforts', in United Nations, 'As Crisis in Myanmar Worsens, Security Council Must Take Resolute Action to End Violence by Country's Military, Address Humanitarian Situation, Speakers Urge', UN Doc. SC/15652, 4 Apr. 2024, at: https://press.un.org/en/2024/sc15652.doc.htm.

527. *Ibid.*

528. *See* United States Mission to the United Nations, 'Remarks at a UN Security Council Briefing on Myanmar', 4 Apr. 2024, at: https://usun.usmission.gov/remarks-at-a-un-security-council-briefing-on-myanmar/.

176. With the 'Five-Point Consensus' more than three years old and clearly unworkable, ASEAN Foreign Ministers met in July 2024.[529] As has been the standard practice in these meetings, the situation of Myanmar was essentially discussed as two different items on the agenda. The first dealt with the political aspects: Foreign Ministers reaffirmed the continued support for Myanmar's efforts to bring peace, stability, the rule of law, promote harmony and reconciliation among the countries' various communities, as well as ensure sustainable and equitable development in Rakhine State.[530] It is not very clear what the Foreign Ministers meant when they referred to 'Myanmar's efforts to bring peace [illegible]'; surely they could not have meant the military regime in power. The second dealt with the humanitarian aspects, where, interestingly enough, there was no mention of the UN's role but only a very general comment appreciating the contributions made by (unnamed) 'external partners'.[531] The Foreign Ministers reiterated that the resolution of the situation must be Myanmar-owned and Myanmar-led in order to ensure peace, security and stability in the region. The same was repeated in January 2025 when a Meeting of ASEAN Foreign Ministers was told by a low-level official from the Ministry of Foreign Affairs of Myanmar, who acted as the representative of Myanmar, that the military regime is planning a general election in 2025. First peace and then elections is what the other Foreign Ministers told Myanmar's representative. At the same meeting. Malaysia, which is the ASEAN Chair for 2025, announced the appointment of former Malaysian diplomat Othman Hashim as special envoy on the crisis in Myanmar.[532]

While this is undoubtedly a noble and important goal, it is submitted that presently there does not exist one 'Myanmar' in the sense that the country is in a situation which is not very dissimilar to a civil war. Therefore, a status quo appears to have emerged, whereby ASEAN avoids reaching crucial determinations, including the following: which party/entity/group is the lawful representative of Myanmar in its international relations and specifically in relation to its ASEAN membership; which rights and powers (if any) does ASEAN have to intervene in Myanmar in a resolute manner; and whether the question of the accountability for the alleged crimes that have been committed and continue to be perpetrated in Myanmar is within ASEAN's purview. On the contrary, ASEAN continues the policy of not accepting any representatives from the ruling military regime at its Summits but apparently accepting them at lower-level meetings and during celebratory events while insisting on perpetuating the clearly inadequate and inappropriate under the prevailing circumstances 5PC.

---

529. Note that another Foreign Ministers Meeting, which took place in January 2024 (it was the event that commenced the Laos ASEAN Chairmanship for the year 2024), *inter alia*, reviewed the situation in Myanmar but nothing worth of note came out of it, *see* Press Statement by the Chair of the ASEAN Foreign Ministers' Retreat, 29 Jan. 2024, Luang Prabang, Lao PDR, para. 22, at: https://asean.org/wp-content/uploads/2024/01/Press-Statement-by-the-Chair-of-the-AMM-Retreat-29-Jan-2024.-Final.pdf.
530. *See* Joint Communiqué of the 57th ASEAN Foreign Ministers' Meeting, Vientiane, 25 Jul. 2024, para. 123, at: https://asean.org/wp-content/uploads/2024/07/Final-Joint-Communique-of-the-57th-AMM.pdf.
531. *Ibid.*, para. 159.
532. See 'ASEAN tells Myanmar military rulers peace should be priority, not election', *Al Jazeera*, 19 January 2025, at: https://www.aljazeera.com/news/2025/1/19/asean-tells-myanmar-military-rulers-peace-should-be-priority-not-election

Chapter 3. The Institutional Architecture of ASEAN

§1. General Observations

177. On the whole, ASEAN subscribes to the traditional institutional architecture of international organisations, which envisages the following three organs. The first is composed of the representatives of all Member States meeting at the highest level (i.e., at the level of heads of state or government). It is responsible for taking all major decisions and determines the future direction of the international organisation. The second, hierarchically inferior to the first, is of an executive nature, where all or some of the Member States are represented at the level of foreign (and other) ministers; if only some Member States participate in it, they are usually elected by the first organ for a certain period of time or on a rotational manner. The third is the Secretariat, which comprises the personnel of the international organisation and is headed by the Secretary-General, who is usually elected by the first organ. Various names have been given to the first two organs: respectively, Assembly, General Assembly, General Council, General Conference, Board of Governors; and Council, Council of Ministers, Executive Council, Board of Directors.

178. The first organ is always the one endowed with the most important functions and powers. However, given that it is composed of the representatives of the Member States at the highest level, it is often practically impossible to operate at very frequent intervals, let alone to undertake the day-to-day running of the organisation. In the case of ASEAN, this organ is the Summit. The second organ comprises the ministers of foreign affairs or other ministers (usually having the portfolio of the matter/s appearing on the agenda, e.g., ministers of the economy, health ministers, and so on) of all or most of the Member States or their representatives. Its role is to execute and, if required, to take measures to implement the decisions reached by the first organ, hence its executive nature. It meets at regular intervals and even more often at the level of permanent representatives. In the case of ASEAN, there are actually two organs performing these tasks: the ASEAN Foreign Ministerial Meetings (AMM), which were established by the ASEAN (Bangkok) Declaration of 1967, and the ASEAN Coordinating Council, which is envisaged in Article 8 of the ASEAN Charter. Finally, the third organ comprises the human resources of the international organisation; almost always they must have the nationality of one of the Member States. In the case of ASEAN, it is the Secretariat. Its tasks include to prepare the meetings of the other organs, to draft reports and other documents, and, generally, to ensure the smooth operation of the Organisation.

179. Furthermore, depending on the nature, the goals, and the specific activities of each international organisation, as well as the degree of transfer of specific powers and competencies from the Member States to it, the institutional architecture may include other organs as well, for example a legal/judicial organ or a disputes settlement organ, or a parliamentary organ or an organ dealing with social and health issues, economic matters, etc. This is, however, not the case with ASEAN.

Very often, the founding treaties / constitutive instrument of international organisations envisage the creation of subsidiary organs or confer to the principal organ the right to establish other organs (commissions, committees, etc.), as these are each time deemed appropriate. The ASEAN Charter makes provision for subsidiary organs. Finally, the Member States themselves may create new, additional, organs either by amending/revising the constitutive instrument or by concluding multilateral conventions among them for this specific purpose. This has not yet happened in ASEAN.

§2. The ASEAN Summit

180. According to Article 7 of the ASEAN Charter, the Summit, which comprises the Heads of State or Government of all Member States, has the following roles, functions, and powers. *First*, it is the 'supreme policy-making body of ASEAN'. *Second*, it has the power to deliberate and adopt decisions on important matters concerning the fulfilment of the Organisation's objectives but also matters of significant interest to Member States. Moreover, it discusses all issues that might have been referred to it by other organs, these being the ASEAN Coordinating Council, the ASEAN Community Councils, and the ASEAN Sectoral Ministerial Bodies. *Third*, it is empowered to instruct the Ministers comprising each of the three ASEAN Community Councils to organise ad hoc meetings, and to address important issues concerning ASEAN horizontally. *Fourth*, it is authorised to deal with emergency situations, which affect the Organisation, and to take 'appropriate actions'. *Fifth*, it has the power to reach decisions on the matters referred to it under Chapter VII and under Chapter VIII of the Charter.

In particular, Chapter VII (Articles 20–21) deals with decision-making. The relevant provision is Article 20(4): as mentioned above, it stipulates that instances of serious breach of or non-compliance with the Charter shall be referred to the Summit for decision. Chapter VIII (Articles 22–28) deals with the settlement of disputes among Member States. This is analysed in Part III of the present monograph. Suffice to mention here that, under Article 26, if, despite the application of all modes of dispute settlement envisaged in Chapter VIII, a disagreement remained unresolved, it shall be referred to the Summit for its decision. *Sixth*, it has the power to authorise the establishment and the dissolution of the Sectoral Ministerial Bodies as well as of other ASEAN institutions. Finally, upon the recommendation by a Foreign Ministers Meeting and subject to the further particulars that are laid down in Article 11 of the Charter, the Summit is empowered to approve the appointment of the Secretary-General. He or she has the rank and status of a Minister and serves 'with the confidence and at the pleasure of the Heads of State or Government'. Over and above these roles, functions and powers, the Summit is also the competent organ to decide on the admission of new Member States pursuant to Article 6(3) of the Charter. A detailed examination of the admission process has been made above.

181. Regarding the mode of operation of Summits, it is based on meetings, which are ordinarily convened twice annually. They are hosted by the Member State that holds the rotating ASEAN Chairmanship. Invariably, Summits are held under a different each time theme, which has to do with the overall operation of ASEAN and some grand idea that it seeks to promote. Thus, the 36th Summit, which took place in Ha Noi, Vietnam, in June 2020 amidst the COVID-19 pandemic, had the appropriate title 'Cohesive and Responsive ASEAN'.[533] Given that the Chairmanship rotates annually, this practically means that two successive Summit meetings are usually held in the territory of the same Member State (they take place in its capital city or at some resort). Thus, in the course of 2023, the 42nd and 43rd Summits took place in Jakarta, Indonesia, respectively, on 4–7 September 2023 and on 9–11 May 2023. They were convened with the theme 'ASEAN Matters: Epicentrum of Growth'. Member States often choose a logo for the ASEAN Chairmanship which has some form of symbolism. For the year 2023 (Indonesian Chairmanship), the logo depicted images of the sky, mountains, the earth, oceans, and the Maleo bird and visualised the sky that embraces the globe, and particularly the countries of the region. The symbolism was that the sky is the umbrella that covers the globe. In November 2023, Laos announced the theme and logo for its Chairmanship for the year 2024. The theme chosen was 'ASEAN: Enhancing Connectivity and Resilience', and the logo reflected the challenges and the opportunities that the region has faced over the past decades, namely economic difficulties, climate change, natural disasters, and security issues. As regards the logo, it has the four colours of the ASEAN flag (blue, white, red and yellow) and has been designed in a circle, which is a combination of the letter C (for Connectivity) and the letter R (for Resilience) and symbolises the globe as well as ASEAN's relationships with partners around the world.

182. So far, there have been three instances where two Summits were held simultaneously. The first instance was the 28th and 29th Summits which took place on 6 and 7 September 2016, in Vientiane, the capital of Lao, under the theme 'Turning Vision into Reality for a Dynamic ASEAN Community'.[534] The second instance was the 38th and 39th Summits, which were held via videoconference on 26 October 2021 under the Chairmanship of Brunei Darussalam and featuring the theme 'We Care, We Prepare, We Prosper'.[535] The third instance was the 40th and 41st Summits, which were held in Phnom Penh, Cambodia, on 11 November 2022 featuring the theme 'ASEAN A.C.T.: Addressing Challenges Together'.[536] Summit meetings may be convened whenever it is necessary and would take the form of special or ad hoc meetings to be chaired by the Member State holding at the time the ASEAN Chairmanship and at the venues to be agreed upon by the membership.[537]

533. *See* Chairman's Statement of the 36th ASEAN Summit, 26 Jun. 2020, at: https://asean.org/asean2020/wp-content/uploads/2021/03/13.-Chairman-Statement-of-the-36th-ASEAN-Summit-FINAL.pdf.
534. *See* Chairman's Statement of the 28th and 29th ASEAN Summits, at: https://asean.org/chairmans-statement-of-the-28th-and-29th-asean-summits/.
535. *See* Chairman's Statement of the 38th and 39th ASEAN Summits, at: https://asean.org/wp-content/uploads/2021/10/FINAL-Chairmans-Statement-of-the-38th-and-39th-ASEAN-Summits-26-Oct....pdf.
536. *See* Chairman's Statement of the 40th and 41st ASEAN Summits, at: https://asean.org/wp-content/uploads/2022/11/01-Chairmans-Statement-of-the-40th-and-41st-ASEAN-Summits-rev.pdf.
537. *See* ASEAN Charter Art. 7(3).

Until today, there has only been one Special Summit held in April 2020 through videoconference, but this was held under extraordinary circumstances, namely the outbreak of the COVID-19 pandemic. Therefore, it is not possible to draw any conclusions on the role that Special Summits may play.[538]

183. Despite the continuing pandemic, in April 2021, Member States met in person at the ASEAN Secretariat in Jakarta, Indonesia. However, this was not regarded as a Summit Meeting but as an 'ASEAN Leaders' Meeting'. Chaired by Brunei Darussalam, the holder of the Chairmanship for the year 2021, it was convened to advance ASEAN Community building, to hasten recovery from the pandemic, to strengthen ASEAN's external relations and to address pressing issues of common interest to all ASEAN Member States.[539] Even though it was not referred to as Special Summit, its extraordinary character is rather obvious, especially if one takes into consideration that the 'ordinary' Summit Meetings for the year 2021 (38th and 39th Summits) were held, as explained, via videoconference in October 2021.

184. Unlike other international organisations where the decision-making organs adopt decisions or resolutions that are numbered and their text is published in an official publication accessible by anyone (this is characteristic of REIOs, e.g., in the EU all legislative acts and other documents of importance appear in the *Official Journal*), in the case of the ASEAN Summit what has been discussed and what has been resolved during the meetings is recorded only in the so-called Chairman's Statements. The text invariably starts with an overview of what the meeting has achieved. Thereafter, the text chronicles the outcome of the deliberations (sometimes referred to as 'key deliverables') for each of the ASEAN Community Pillars, i.e., the three Communities which make up the Organisation, namely the Political-Security Community, the Economic Community, and the Socio-Cultural Community. The text of Chairman's Statements concludes with recording developments in the field of external relations, referencing other regional and international issues and, generally, matters of particular concern to the Member States.

185. To give an illustration of the contents of 'Chairman's Statements', reference will be made to those circulated after the conclusion of the 33rd and the 32nd Summit Meetings. Both sessions took place in Singapore, respectively, on 13 November 2018 and on 28 April 2018. The Chairman's Statement of the 33rd Summit gave the following overview of the discussions held:

> We reviewed ASEAN's progress in building a resilient and innovative Community, and deepening links with the rest of the world. We also exchanged

538. *See* Declaration of the Special ASEAN Summit on Coronavirus Disease 2019 (COVID-19), 14 Apr. 2020, at: https://asean.org/wp-content/uploads/2021/09/FINAL-Declaration-of-the-Special-ASEAN-Summit-on-COVID-19.pdf.

539. *See* Chairman's Statement on the ASEAN Leaders' Meeting, 24 Apr. 2021 and Five-Point Consensus, 24 Apr. 2021, at: https://asean.org/chairmans-statement-on-the-asean-leaders-meeting-24-april-2021-and-five-point-consensus/.

views on recent global and regional developments and discussed how to take ASEAN forward at a time of rapid change.[540]

Regarding the Political-Security Community, the Summit did not actually reach any decisions but commented upon developments that had taken place since the 32nd Summit. In particular, Member States: (a) welcomed the ASEAN Plan of Action to Prevent and Counter the Rise of Radicalisation and Violent Extremism 2018–2025, which had been adopted by the 12th ASEAN Ministerial Meeting on Transnational Crime (AMMTC) in Nay Pyi Taw, Myanmar, in October 2018 (it emphasised the need to promote the cooperation among Member States in tackling the growing challenge of transnational crime);[541] (b) acknowledged the achievement of further progress in defence cooperation among Member States as well as with the so-called Plus Countries, namely India, Australia, Japan, New Zealand, China, South Korea, Russia, and the USA, as well as the continued commitment of the defence sector to maintaining regional peace and security; and (c) looked forward to the full operationalisation of the ASEAN Militaries Ready Group on Humanitarian Assistance and Disaster Relief (AMRG on HADR). The creation of this entity has been founded on the very features characterising ASEAN: respect for sovereignty and territorial integrity, consensus-based decision-making, participation of Member States on the basis of a flexible, voluntary, and non-binding nature, and at a pace comfortable to all.

186. Moreover, the 33rd Summit repeated the pledge to preserve Southeast Asia as a zone free of nuclear weapons and weapons of mass destruction (WMD). This objective is laid down in the Treaty on the Southeast Asia Nuclear Weapons-Free Zone (SEANWFZ Treaty, also known as Bangkok Treaty), a reference to which has already been made.[542] The pledge is also envisaged in the ASEAN Charter, where it features as the third of the ASEAN Purposes enumerated in Article 1 thereof. To that extent, the Summit emphasised the need to fully and effectively implement the

540. *See* Chairman's Statement of the 33rd ASEAN Summit, 14 Nov. 2018, at: https://asean.org/chairmans-statement-of-the-33rd-asean-summit/.

541. The mandate for the Action Plan originated from the Manila Declaration to Counter the Rise of Radicalisation and Violent Extremism, which had been approved by the previous session of the AMMTC on 20 Sep. 2017, at: https://asean.org/manila-declaration-to-counter-the-rise-of-radicalisation-and-violent-extremism/.

542. It was opened for signature on 15 Dec. 1995, entered into force on 27 Mar. 1997 (1996) 35 I.L.M. 635. All Member States are currently contracting parties. Note that the Treaty was accompanied by a Protocol, which was concluded on the same day, text at: https://asean.org/protocol-to-the-treaty-on-the-southeast-asia-nuclear-weapon-free-zone/. It stipulates that each contracting party undertakes to respect it, to abstain from contributing to any act which would constitute a violation of its provisions, and not to use or threaten to use nuclear weapons against another contracting party or within the SEANWF Zone). The last Member State to ratify the Protocol was the Philippines on 21 Jun. 2001. Those third States possessing nuclear weapons (they are named as the five permanent UN Security Council members) may, if they so wish, become contracting parties to the Protocol; none has signed it so far. Generally, *see* E.A. Cornellier, *In the Zone: Why the United States Should Sign the Protocol to the Southeast Asia Nuclear-Weapon-Free Zone*, 12 Pac. Rim L. & Pol'y J. Ass'n 233–261 (2003).

SEANWFZ Treaty, taking into account the relevant Plan of Action.[543] Finally, the Summit affirmed the aspiration for a drug-free region, as envisaged in the ASEAN Statement Against Legalisation of Controlled Drugs;[544] The competent body is the ASEAN Senior Officials on Drug Matters (ASOD).[545]

187. As regards the Economic Community, the 33rd Summit noted the progress achieved in realising the five economic thrusts, which had been identified for implementation in the course of 2018. In particular, these were: (a) to promote innovation and e-commerce; (b) to improve trade facilitation; (c) to deepen integration in the services sector and in the investment sector; (d) to cultivate a conducive regulatory environment; and (e) to promote the external relations of ASEAN. Moreover, the Summit highlighted the continuing efforts to achieve the targets set for renewable energy, which were prognosed to reach 23% in the region's total energy mix by 2025. To achieve this goal, ASEAN and the International Renewable Energy Agency (IRENA) concluded in Singapore a Memorandum of Understanding (MoU) and an accompanied Action Plan on 30 October 2018.[546]

188. As far as the Socio-Cultural Community is concerned, the Summit decided to deepen the sense of ASEAN identity, awareness, connectedness and belonging, and to come up with innovative ways to equip the population of the region with skills and capabilities. The main purpose is to allow ASEAN to continue being a vibrant, inclusive and dynamic place to live and work. The Summit also referred to the development of the ASEAN Regional Guidelines and Procedures to Address the

---

543. *See* Plan of Action to Strengthen the Implementation of the SEANWFZ Treaty (2018–2022), adopted on 4 Aug. 2017. It has since been succeeded by the Plan of Action for the years 2023 to 2027, which was adopted by the SEANWFZ Commission on 2 Aug. 2022, at: https://asean.org/wp-content/uploads/2022/12/Plan-of-Action-to-Strengthen-the-Implementation-of-the-Treaty-on-the-Southeast-Asia-Nuclear-Weapon-Free-Zone-2023-2027.pdf.
544. The Statement was adopted by the Sixth ASEAN Ministerial Meeting on Drug Matters (AMMD), which was held in Ha Noi, Vietnam, on 18 Oct. 2018, *see* Chairman's Statement, at: https://asean.org/speechandstatement/chairmans-statement-of-the-sixth-asean-ministerial-meeting-on-drug-matters-6th-ammd/. At the time, the guiding instruments were: (a) the ASEAN Work Plan on Securing Communities Against Illicit Drugs 2016–2025, adopted by the Fifth AMMD held in Singapore on 19–20 Oct. 2016; and (b) the ASEAN Cooperation Plan to Tackle Illicit Drug Production and Trafficking in the Golden Triangle 2017–2019 (it was continued by the ASEAN Cooperation Plan 2020–2022). Generally, *see* R. Emmers, *International Regime-Building in ASEAN: Cooperation Against the Illicit Trafficking and Abuse of Drugs*, 29 Contemp. Southeast Asia 506–525 (2007).
545. For its last meeting, *see* Eighth ASEAN Ministerial Meeting on Drug Matters (8th AMMD), Chairman's Statement, 11 Aug. 2023, Vientiane, Lao PDR, at: https://asean.org/wp-content/uploads/2023/08/ADOPTED_8th-AMMD-Chairmans_Statement.pdf. *See* further, the yearly Drug Monitoring Reports published by the ASEAN Narcotics Cooperation Center; for the year 2022, *see*, *ASEAN Drug Monitoring Report 2022*, Bangkok, 2023, https://asean.org/wp-content/uploads/2023/11/Drug-Monitoring-Report-2022.pdf.
546. Text at: https://cil.nus.edu.sg/wp-content/uploads/2019/10/2018%20MOU%20between%20ASEAN%20and%20IRENA.pdf. IRENA is an intergovernmental organisation headquartered in Abu Dhabi, which supports states wishing to make a transition to sustainable energy. Its Statute was signed in Bonn, Germany, on 26 Jan. 2009, https://www.irena.org/officialdocuments. Only few ASEAN States are among the currently 161 Member States.

Needs of Victims of Trafficking in Persons, Especially Women and Children.[547] These Guidelines, which were officially launched in April 2019 with assistance from the US Administration,[548] supplement the provisions of the ASEAN Convention Against Trafficking in Persons, Especially Women and Children (ACTIP). As explained elsewhere in the monograph, the Convention was approved during the 27th ASEAN Summit (2015) and, following ratification by the required six Member States, it entered into force in March 2017.

189. Finally, the Summit dealt with the humanitarian situation in Myanmar's Rakhine State, which was characterised as 'a matter of concern', obviously an understatement given the severity of the situation. The reference was to the still ongoing conflict in the northern part of Myanmar, where the Rakhine State is located, which has taken the form of sectarian violence between the Rohingya Muslim community and the Rakhine Buddhist community coupled with a military crackdown on Rohingya civilians by the state security forces. It has been estimated that, in the second half of 2017, between 655,000 and 700,000 Rohingya people fled to neighbouring Bangladesh to avoid ethnic and religious persecution.[549] At the time, a United Nations Report had recorded that Myanmar's military had put into effect a 'systematic process' of forcing hundreds of thousands of Rohingyas to leave the country,[550] while the UNGA had expressed its deep concern at the situation and had called upon the Myanmar authorities to cease its military operations.[551] Member States could not have foreseen how the events would have escalated and how, as already mentioned, Myanmar would be accused before the ICJ to have orchestrated genocide against the Rohingyas.[552] However, these considerations cannot hide the fact that the way this extremely important matter was handled from the beginning has revealed the limitations in the Summit handling complicated issues that take place within the territory of Member States, especially grave breaches of human rights but also other matters that may involve State sovereignty. In the

547. *See* further, ASEAN Plan of Action Against Trafficking in Persons, Especially Women and Children, endorsed in Kuala Lumpur, Malaysia, on 29 Sep. 2015, at: https://cil.nus.edu.sg/wp-content/uploads/2019/02/2015-ASEAN-TIP-POA.pdf.

548. *See* U.S. Mission to ASEAN, *Launch of the ACWC Regional Guidelines and Procedures to Address the Needs of Victims of Trafficking in Persons (TIP) and Practitioners' Workshop*, Press Release, 4 Apr. 2019, at: https://asean.usmission.gov/.

549. *See* further, M. Zarni & N. Brinham, *Waves of Genocidal Terror against Rohingyas by Myanmar and the Resultant Exodus Since 1978* (Middle East Institute 14 Nov. 2017), at: https://www.mei.edu/publications/waves-genocidal-terror-against-rohingyas-myanmar-and-resultant-exodus-1978.

550. *See* UN Office of the High Commissioner for Human Rights, *Mission report of OHCHR rapid response mission to Cox's Bazar, Bangladesh, 13–24 September 2017*, 11 Oct. 2017, at: https://www.ohchr.org/Documents/Countries/MM/CXBMissionSummaryFindingsOctober2017.pdf. *See also* UN General Assembly, *Report of the Special Rapporteur on the situation of human rights in Myanmar*, UN Doc. A/72/382, 8 Sep. 2017.

551. *See* UNGA Res. 72/248 of 24 Dec. 2017. *See* further Res. 73/264 of 22 Dec. 2018 and Res. 74/246 of 27 Dec. 2019.

552. *See* ICJ, *Application of the Convention on the Prevention and Punishment of the Crime of Genocide (The Gambia v. Myanmar)*, pending.

present case, since a third Member State is involved, namely Bangladesh, the Summit should have taken a more proactive role.[553] However, ASEAN lacks the dimension of what could be referred to as a 'common foreign policy'. In the event, the Summit only noted that the Joint Working Group created between Myanmar and Bangladesh had agreed to commence the repatriation of verified displaced persons from Rakhine State to Myanmar, estimated at 1.2 million people.[554] By March 2025, the number of Rohingya refugees living in Bangladesh does not appear to have been reduced; their needs in nutrition, in shelter, in healthcare, etc. is partly financed by the EU.

190. As regards the 32nd ASEAN Summit (April 2018), the Chairman's Statement started by referring to developments pertaining to the Political-Security Community.[555] It, *inter alia*: (a) recorded the adoption of the ASEAN Leaders' Statement on Cybersecurity Cooperation, which aimed at addressing 'the growing urgency and sophistication of transboundary cyber threats';[556] (b) welcomed the Joint Statement by the Defence Ministers on Countering Terrorism in ASEAN, which had been issued on 8 February 2018,[557] while recording the need for enhanced regional cooperation in countering terrorism and preventing violent extremism;[558] and (c) reported progress on the draft Guidelines on Consular Assistance by ASEAN Member States Missions in Third Countries to Nationals of Other ASEAN Member States were discussed. Finally, the Guidelines were adopted by the Twelfth ASEAN Ministerial Meeting on Transnational Crime (AMMTC) on 31 October 2018 and endorsed during the 33rd ASEAN Summit).[559] Finally, the Statement welcomed the fact that the text of the Model ASEAN Extradition Treaty had been finalised in March 2018. It was subsequently endorsed by the Tenth ASEAN Law Ministers Meeting (ALAWMM) on 12 October 2018.[560]

---

553. *See* European Commission, 'EU boosts humanitarian aid in Bangladesh, Myanmar and for the Rohingya refugee crisis', 3 March 2025, at: https://ec.europa.eu/commission/presscorner/detail/en/ip_25_639.
554. As the repatriation process of Rohingyas was stalled, it was reported that in September 2019 a new Joint Working Group was formed, this time under the mediation of China. Representatives from the two involved countries met for the fifth time on 15 Jun. 2022, but the matter has still not been resolved; *see* S.S. Nath, 'Is Rohingya Repatriation Finally Moving Forward?', *The Diplomat*, 18 May 2023, at: https://thediplomat.com/2023/05/is-rohingya-repatriation-finally-moving-forward/.
555. Available at: https://asean.org/wp-content/uploads/2018/04/Chairmans-Statement-of-the-32nd-ASEAN-Summit.pdf.
556. Text at: https://asean.org/wp-content/uploads/2018/04/ASEAN-Leaders-Statement-on-Cybersecurity-Cooperation.pdf.
557. According to the Statement, terrorism 'is a severe threat to ASEAN's progress, prosperity, and very way of life', at: https://asean.org/wp-content/uploads/2018/02/ADMM-Joint-Statement-on-Counter-Terrorism_Final.pdf.
558. Note that external actors are also involved, e.g., the EU-ASEAN Work Plan to Combat Terrorism and Transnational Crime (2018–2020), followed by the ASEAN-EU Work Plan to Combat Terrorism and Transnational Crime (2022–2024); generally, *see* Plan of Action to Implement the ASEAN-EU Strategic Partnership (2023–2027), AFM-EU/2022/01/POA, August 2022, point 1.3, at: https://asean.org/plan-of-action-to-implement-the-asean-eu-strategic-partnership-2023-2027/.
559. Text at: https://asean.org/wp-content/uploads/2024/03/04.-Guidelines-on-Consular-Assistance-ADOPTED-by-12th-AMMTC-on-31-October-2018.pdf.
560. Text at: https://asean.org/wp-content/uploads/2021/01/ASEAN-Extradition-Treaty-by-10th-ALAWMM.pdf.

191. As far as the Economic Community is concerned, the Summit noted the significant progress made in the negotiations for the conclusion of the ASEAN Trade in Services Agreement (ATISA). Even though ATISA was originally adopted at the sidelines of the ASEAN Economic Ministers Meeting (AEM), which was held on 29 August 2018, and approved at a later meeting in the course of 2019,[561] it was finally signed by all Member States in October 2020. The Summit also approved the Fourth Protocol amending the ASEAN Comprehensive Investment Agreement (ACIA).[562] It also noted the meeting of the Finance Ministers and Central Bank Governors, which had taken place in April 2018, and the 'continued commitment towards financial integration by focusing on initiatives to sustain growth, boost resilience, and foster innovation'. Finally, the progress made in concluding the negotiations for an ASEAN Agreement on Electronic Commerce was recorded. The Agreement was subsequently approved on 12 November 2018 during the next (33rd) Summit and was signed in Hanoi on 22 January 2019.[563]

192. As regards the Socio-Cultural Community, the Summit recalled the signing of the ASEAN Consensus on the Protection and Promotion of the Rights of Migrant Workers[564] and looked forward to the adoption of its Action Plan at the forthcoming ASEAN Labour Ministers' Meeting. The latter was meant to be held in August 2018 but actually took place in November 2018.[565] Moreover, it discussed the promotion

---

561. *See* T.S. Yean, *ASEAN Trade in Services Agreement (ATISA): Advancing Services Liberalization for ASEAN?* (Yusof Ishak Institute, Perspective 2019:54, Singapore, July 2019).
562. *See* Joint Media Statement, 51st ASEAN Economic Ministers' (AEM) Meeting, 6 Sep. 2019, Bangkok, Thailand, para. 26, at: https://asean.org/the-51st-asean-economic-ministers-aem-meeting/.
563. Text at: http://agreement.asean.org/media/download/20190306035048.pdf. The Agreement, which requires ratification by all Member States, is an interesting example of ASEAN treaty law-making in an area which has developed very differently among them. The Chairman's Statement of the 38th and 39th ASEAN Summits issued on 26 Oct. 2021, para. 52, recorded the Agreement's ratification as well as the launch of the Work Plan on implementation 2021–2025, which promotes a harmonised approach for the whole membership while aligning their domestic laws and regulations with international best practices.
564. This quite elaborate instrument, signed during the 31st ASEAN Summit (Manila, the Philippines) on 14 Nov. 2017, and published by the ASEAN Secretariat in March 2018, at: https://asean.org/book/asean-consensus-on-the-protection-and-promotion-of-the-rights-of-migrant-workers-2/, is not an international law agreement but is akin to a political declaration, even though it lays down obligations for both the sending and the receiving ASEAN countries. Reportedly, the Philippines favoured a 'morally binding' agreement, but Indonesia insisted on a 'legally binding' agreement; despite the instrument's title, whether consensus actually worked is highly questionable, *see* T.K.S. Koh, 'Manila's Parting Gift: ASEAN's Next Steps on Labor Migration: A Small Step Forward on Migrant Labor Rights in ASEAN', *The Diplomat*, 22 Nov. 2017. Its purpose is to reinforce the commitments laid down in the ASEAN Declaration on the Protection and Promotion of the Rights of Migrant Workers, adopted during the 12th ASEAN Summit on 13 Jan. 2007. Generally, *see* M. Olivier, *Social Protection for Migrant Workers in ASEAN: Developments, Challenges, and Prospects* (International Labour Organization 2018), at: https://www.social-protection.org/gimi/RessourcePDF.action?id=55654.
565. *See* Action Plan (2018–2025) to Implement the ASEAN Consensus on the Protection and Promotion of the Rights of Migrant Workers. For the contribution of civil society organisations, *see Regional Civil Society Recommendations on the Implementation of the 2017 ASEAN Consensus on the Protection and Promotion of the Rights of Migrant Workers*, 21 Feb. 2018, at: https://www.spf.org/global-image/units/upfiles/51288-1-20181115134749_b5becfa7509c10.pdf.

of complementarities between the ASEAN Community Vision 2025, which had been adopted at the 27th Summit (Kuala Lumpur, Malaysia, 18–22 November 2015),[566] and the United Nations 2030 Agenda for Sustainable Development.[567] The latter was approved in New York in September 2015[568] as the next phase to the Post-2015 Development Agenda, a UN-led process which lasted from 2012 until 2015 and defined the global development framework to succeed the so-called Millennium Development Goals.

193. What follows is an overview of developments during most ASEAN Summits, which have been held since 1976, when the first one was held. The overview refers to policy documents, treaties and other notable instruments approved, adopted or signed during ASEAN Summits as well as other important events and developments. Several of these documents and affairs are examined and analysed elsewhere in the present monograph. The overview should not be understood as a complete record; it principally aims at offering to the reader a comprehensive idea of the range and ambit of ASEAN activities, actions and endeavours. All in all, it could be seen as a legal history of ASEAN as a regional international organisation as well as of ASEAN institutions. Moreover, given that the present monograph argues that a certain ASEAN law, an ASEAN legal system, has emerged over the many decades of ASEAN's existence, this brief legal history serves to support this contention.

194. For present purposes, ASEAN Summits are chronologically divided into two categories. The first category covers those which were held before their operation was institutionalised in 1992, namely when it was resolved that Summits should not be held at random intervals but every three years. The second category covers those which have taken place from 1992 onwards and until the present time.

195. At the First Summit (Bali, Indonesia, February 1976), ASEAN leaders adopted the Treaty of Amity and Cooperation (TAC) to promote the goals of perpetual peace, an everlasting friendship and cooperation among the people of Southeast Asia, to raise their strength and solidarity and to bring about a closer relationship.[569] So far, TAC has been amended three times. The purpose of the first

566. The central theme of Vision 2025 is the development of a stable and resilient ASEAN characterised by its enhanced capacity to respond effectively to challenges and its ability to become an outward-looking region within the global community of nations. Generally, *see* X. Li & L. Tianyi, 'ASEAN Community Vision 2025 with the Belt and Road Initiative', in *Routledge Handbook of the Belt and Road* 439 (C. Fang & P. Nolan eds, Routledge 2019). Note that the Vision 2025 has been restated, *see ASEAN Leaders' Vision Statement on a Cohesive and Responsive ASEAN: Rising Above Challenges and Sustaining Growth*, Ha Noi, 26 Jun. 2020, at: https://asean.org/asean-leaders-vision-statement-on-a-cohesive-and-responsive-asean-rising-above-challenges-and-sustaining-growth/.

567. *See* United Nations Economic and Social Commission for Asia and the Pacific, *Complementarities between the ASEAN Community Vision 2025 and the United Nations 2030 Agenda for Sustainable Development: A Framework for Action*, November 2017, at: https://www.unescap.org/sites/default/files/publications/UN%20ASEAN%20Complementarities%20Report_Final_PRINT.pdf.

568. *See* UNGA Res. 70/1, 'Transforming our world: the 2030 Agenda for Sustainable Development', 25 Sep. 2015.

569. Adopted on 24 Feb. 1976, entered into force on 15 Jul. 1976, 1025 U.N.T.S. 319.

amendment was to allow the accession of other Southeast Asian states.[570] The purpose of the second amendment was to expand the possibility of accession to non-Southeast Asian states.[571] The purpose of the third amendment was to expand even more the possibility of accession by adding 'regional organisations whose members are only sovereign States subject to the consent of all the States in Southeast Asia'.[572] ASEAN leaders also adopted the Declaration of ASEAN Concord (the so-called Bali Concord I), a programme of action in multiple spheres of activity (political, economic, social, cultural, information, and security) whose purpose was to serve as the framework for their collective future cooperation.[573] It should be noted that the accord to cooperate in the economic field was very important because it altered the direction that ASEAN had taken until then, namely to be regarded and act as a political regional institution. Thus, the Declaration of ASEAN Concord expressly regarded economic cooperation as one of the prerequisites to bring about the goal of achieving political stability in the region. On 24 February 1977, the Agreement on ASEAN Preferential Trading Arrangements (PTA) was signed.[574] It was the precursor to a Free Trade Area (FTA), itself a priority area for Member States, as it had already been agreed upon during the First Summit.

196. The 2nd Summit (Kuala Lumpur, Malaysia, August 1977) was marked by the first meeting between the ASEAN States and Japan at the level of Heads of State or Government.[575] The 3rd Summit took place in Manila, the Philippines, in December 1987. It has been suggested that the choice of Manila as a Summit venue was driven by a desire of the other Member States to show their backing to the new regime in the Philippines, which had come into power after years of domestic political instability.[576] Member States approved the Manila Declaration, a policy instrument which envisaged, *inter alia*, further measures to promote the so-called functional cooperation. In ASEAN jargon, this term is understood to mean the use of education, institutional linkages, and improved flow of information to 'inculcate in the people the common socioeconomic values and heritage [of ASEAN], and promote mutual understanding of the culture, traditions and ways of life of their

---

570. Under the Protocol of 15 Dec. 1987, which was signed in Manila.
571. Under the Protocol of 25 Jul. 1998, which was signed in Manila. Generally, *see* D. Seah, *The Treaty of Amity and Cooperation in Southeast Asia: The Issue of Non-Intervention and Its Accession by Australia and the USA*, 11 Chinese J. Int'l L. 785–822 (2012). The Instrument of Accession of the People's Republic of China was concluded in Bali, Indonesia, on 18 Oct. 2003.
572. Under the Protocol of 23 Jul. 2010, which was signed in Ha Noi, Vietnam. The EU has also acceded, *see* Council Decision 2012/308/CFSP of 26 Apr. 2012 on the accession of the European Union to the Treaty of Amity and Cooperation in Southeast Asia, O.J. L 154, 15 Jun. 2012, p. 1.
573. Text at: https://cil.nus.edu.sg/databasecil/1976-declaration-of-asean-concord/.
574. At: https://cil.nus.edu.sg/databasecil/1977-agreement-on-the-asean-preferential-trading-arrangements/ *See* J. Devan, *The ASEAN Preferential Trading Arrangement: Some Problems, Ex ante Results, and a Multipronged Approach to Future Intra-ASEAN Trade Development*, 4 ASEAN Econ. Bull. 197–212 (1987).
575. *See* H. H. Indorf, *The Kuala Lumpur Summit: A Second for ASEAN*, Southeast Asian Affairs 35–44 (1978).
576. *See* D. Albert, *Staying the Course: From a Southeast Asian Community to an ASEAN Community*, in *An Evolving Asian: Vison and Reality* 36–55, 48 (J. Menon & C. Lee eds, Asian Development Bank September 2019).

nations'.[577] Finally, during the 3rd Summit, Member States committed themselves to strengthening intra-ASEAN economic cooperation to maximise the realisation of the region's potential in trade and development.

197. At the 4th Summit (Singapore, January 1992), the Singapore Declaration was signed. It was principally a roadmap for the following four activity areas.[578] *First*, to secure regional peace and prosperity through a higher plane of political and economic cooperation. *Second*, to safeguard ASEAN collective interests in response to the powerful economic groupings that were being formed among developed countries. *Third*, to seek ways to engage Member States in new areas of cooperation in security matters. *Fourth*, to forge closer relations with the Indochinese countries (a decision which later led to the accession of these countries to ASEAN). Moreover, the 4th Summit adopted the Framework Agreement on Enhancing ASEAN Economic Cooperation, which concerned the areas of trade, industry, minerals and energy, finance and banking, food, agriculture and forestry, transportation, and communications.[579] Additionally, ASEAN leaders acknowledged that subregional arrangements among Member States, or between Member States and non-ASEAN States, could complement the overall economic cooperation in their region. They also signed the Agreement on the Common Effective Preferential Tariff Scheme for the ASEAN Free Trade Area,[580] a move signifying that the deeper economic cooperation among the Member States had not only become a focal point but had also taken the form of an irreversible process.[581] Finally, it was resolved to henceforth hold Summits every three years, thus ending their randomness.

198. The 5th Summit (Bangkok, Thailand, December 1995) adopted the Bangkok Declaration, another milestone document in the history of the Organisation. ASEAN leaders agreed to promote, among others, the following goals.[582] *First*, to elevate the so-called functional cooperation to an even higher level to bring shared prosperity to the population of all participating states. *Second*, to promote greater economic integration by building on the existing economic cooperation activities but also by initiating cooperation in new areas. *Third*, to undertake measures to further strengthen their national and regional resilience in the political economic, social, cultural, and humanitarian fields. *Fourth*, to ensure that ASEAN remains an outward-looking regional organisation and that it deepens its external relations with partners, especially taking into account the globally interdependent world which was developing. A final agreed goal was to further institutionalise the operation of

577. Text at: https://asean.org/speechandstatement/3rd-asean-summit-manila-14-15-december-1987/. A selection of the documents adopted has appeared in 27 I.L.M. 596 (1988).
578. Reproduced in 31 I.L.M. 498 (1992). For ASEAN materials until 2003, *see* also S. Siddique & S. Kumar, *The 2nd ASEAN Reader* (Institute of Southeast Asian Studies Publishing 2003).
579. Reproduced in 31 I.L.M. 506 (1992).
580. Reproduced in 31 I.L.M. 513 (1992).
581. *See* R. Severino, *Southeast Asia in Search of an ASEAN Community: Insights from the Former ASEAN Secretary-General* 222 (Institute of Southeast Asian Studies / Asian Development Bank 2006).
582. Bangkok Summit Declaration, 14–15 Dec. 1995, at: https://asean.org/speechandstatement/5th-asean-summit-bangkok-14-15-december-1995/.

Summits by holding informal meetings every year. However, it proved to be a rather short-lived goal: in the period between 1996 and 2000, four Informal Summits were held: in Jakarta (November 1996), in Kuala Lumpur (December 1997), in Manila (November 1999), and in Singapore (November 2000). Apparently, none has been held ever since. During the 5th Summit, the aforementioned Treaty on the Southeast Asia Nuclear Weapon-Free Zone and the Protocol to Amend the Framework Agreement on Enhancing ASEAN Economic Cooperation of 1992 were also signed.[583] The latter legal instrument had to do with new accessions to ASEAN (Vietnam had joined in July 1995). It stipulated that acceding states to the Framework Agreement will do so on the basis of the terms and conditions agreed between them and the existing ASEAN membership.

199. The Second (out of the four) Informal Summit was held in Kuala Lumpur, Malaysia, on 15 December 1997 at a very difficult time for the region on account of the outbreak of the East Asian financial crisis earlier in the summer of the same year.[584] During the 30th ASEAN Ministerial Meeting, held in Subang Jaya, Malaysia, on 25 July 1997, ASEAN Foreign Ministers had expressed their serious concern and had called for further intensification of ASEAN's cooperation to safeguard and promote its interests. In Kuala Lumpur, ASEAN leaders responded by adopting the so-called ASEAN Vision 2020,[585] which regarded the Organisation as 'a concert of Southeast Asian nations, outward-looking, living in peace, stability and prosperity, bonded together in partnership in dynamic development and in a community of caring societies'.[586]

200. The 6th Summit (Hanoi, Vietnam, December 1998) was organised under the theme 'Unity and Cooperation for an ASEAN of Peace, Stability and Equitable Development'. ASEAN Leaders approved the Hanoi Declaration and the Hanoi Plan of Action as part of the implementation of ASEAN Vision 2020.[587] They also agreed on a number of actions, which were referred to as 'bold measures' and whose purpose was to further strengthen their economic, political and security cooperation. Finally, they approved Cambodia's application for membership, a decision recorded in the second paragraph of the Hanoi Declaration in rather simple terms: 'We have decided to admit the Kingdom of Cambodia as the tenth member of ASEAN.'[588]

583. At: https://asean.org/5th-asean-summit/.
584. For this and other challenges that ASEAN had faced at that time, *see* J. Funston, *ASEAN: Out of Its Depth?*, 20(1) Contemp. Southeast Asia 22–37 (1998).
585. *See* Press Statement of the 2nd ASEAN Informal Meeting of Heads of State/Government of the Member States of ASEAN, Kuala Lumpur, Malaysia, 15 Dec. 1997, at: https://asean.org/press-statement-of-the-2nd-asean-informal-meeting-of-heads-of-state-government-of-the-member-states-of-asean-kuala-lumpur-malaysia-15-december-1997/.
586. Text at: https://www.icnl.org/wp-content/uploads/Transnational_vision.pdf.
587. Reproduced in *ASEAN into the Next Millennium: ASEAN Vision 2020, Hanoi Plan of Action*, Jakarta: ASEAN Secretariat, 1999.
588. *See* Ha Noi Declaration of 1998, 16 Dec. 1998, at: https://asean.org/ha-noi-declaration-of-1998-16-december-1998/.

201. During the 7th Summit (Bandar Seri Begawan, Brunei, November 2001), ASEAN leaders endorsed the Mid-Term Review of the Hanoi Plan of Action and identified new priority areas for their cooperation. These included information and communications technology as well as human capacity building. They also adopted the ASEAN Declaration on Joint Action to Counter Terrorism[589] as well as a Declaration on Human Immunodeficiency Virus (HIV) /Acquired Immunodeficiency Syndrome (AIDS). At the 8th Summit (Phnom Penh, Cambodia, November 2002), discussions among Member States were dominated, on the one hand, by the task of materialising the goal of integrating further their region and, on the other hand, by the fight against terrorism.[590] They also signed the ASEAN Tourism Agreement.[591]

202. The highlight of the 9th Summit (Bali, Indonesia, October 2003) was the adoption of a very important document in ASEAN's evolutionary process, the Declaration of ASEAN Concord II.[592] This document, also known as 'Bali Concord II', elaborated on the themes of ASEAN Vision 2020 and set concrete milestones, including the establishment of an ASEAN Community by 2020. This ASEAN Community was devised to address the close collaboration of Member States in the following three areas: political and security cooperation, economic cooperation, and socio-cultural cooperation. In time, they became the three pillars of the ASEAN Community. The 10th Summit (Vientiane, Laos, November 2004) centred on building up the institutions of the ASEAN Community. To that effect, ASEAN leaders adopted the Vientiane Action Programme (VAP) 2004–2010,[593] the instrument succeeding the aforementioned Hanoi Plan of Action. It is rather important to note that VAP was devised with an inherent mechanism for monitoring and evaluating the activities undertaken. According to the text of VAP, this mechanism was an attempt to fulfil the principles of transparency and accountability as it 'was deemed necessary to ensure that targets are achieved, timely corrective measures are undertaken if needed, and that initiatives and activities remain consistent with the stated goals of the VAP and are responsive to emerging issues and priorities'.[594] The necessary financial resources to support the implementation of VAP were to be secured through the ASEAN Development Fund (ADF). The latter was established by ASEAN Foreign Ministers on 26 July 2005,[595] as the successor to the ASEAN

589. At: https://asean.org/wp-content/uploads/2012/05/2001-ASEAN-Declaration-on-Joint-Action-to-Counter-Terrorism.pdf. Generally, *see* H. Nasu, R. McLaughlin, D. R. Rothwell & S. S. Tan, *The Legal Authority of ASEAN as a Security Institution*, 78 et seq. (Cambridge U. Press 2019).

590. Generally, *see* G. Rose & D. Nestorovska, *Towards an ASEAN Counter-Terrorism Treaty*, 9 Singapore Y.B. Int'l L. 157–189 (2005).

591. Text at: https://www.mofa.go.jp/region/asia-paci/asean/pmv0211/tourism.html. Generally, *see* N. Mistilis & L. Dwyer, *A Model of ASEAN Collaboration in Tourism*, 38 Annals of Tourism Res. 882–899 (2011).

592. At: https://asean.org/speechandstatement/declaration-of-asean-concord-ii-bali-concord-ii/.

593. Reproduced in *ASEAN Documents Series 2004*, Jakarta: ASEAN Secretariat, January 2005, p. 20. Generally, *see* M. Davies, *Explaining the Vientiane Action Programme: ASEAN and the Institutionalisation of Human Rights*, 26 The Pac. Rev. 385–406 (2013).

594. Vientiane Action Programme, Part 5.3.

595. Agreement on the Establishment of the ASEAN Development Fund, done at Vientiane, Lao on 26 Jul. 2005, at: http://agreement.asean.org/media/download/20140422144316.pdf. Its entry into force

Fund, which had been created eleven years earlier.[596] The existence of other bilateral development funds, where ASEAN is at the receiving end of funding, should be noted. Thus, the Japan–ASEAN Integration Fund, which began its operation in March 2006, implemented the pledge made by Japan during the 9th Japan–ASEAN Summit in December 2005 to assist in bringing about the open, dynamic, and resilient ASEAN Community. This was a reference to the Community envisaged in the Declaration of ASEAN Concord II. It is of some importance to observe that the financial assistance extended by Japan to ASEAN countries goes back to 1999, when the Japan-ASEAN Solidarity Fund was created to assist them in recovering from the 1997 Asian financial crisis.[597]

203. The 11th Summit (Kuala Lumpur, Malaysia, December 2005) saw the beginning of the process of moving from ASEAN, an international institution with a loose institutional basis and structure, to ASEAN, a rules-based international organisation with a legally binding constitutive instrument and endowing it with specific organs and powers while creating duties and obligations that Member States must observe and fulfil. Thus, the theme of the 11th Summit, 'One Vision, One Identity, One Community' reflected this evolutionary process because it was no longer to be the various Member States acting individually within ASEAN but the Member States acting as one. This process was envisaged in the Kuala Lumpur Declaration on the Establishment of the ASEAN, in which ASEAN leaders declared their commitment to conclude the ASEAN Charter, which 'will serve as a legal and institutional framework of ASEAN to support the realisation of its goals and objectives'.[598]

204. Following the conclusion of the 11th Summit, the inaugural East Asia Summit (EAS) took place on 14 December 2005.[599] The idea behind the holding of an East Asia Summit[600] was to promote ties among the so-called ASEAN Plus Three

---

required only the signature by Member States. Its duration has not been laid down, and it will operate until the Agreement is terminated by the decision of ASEAN Foreign Ministers. The Terms of Reference of the ASEAN Development Fund came into force simultaneously with the Agreement, text at: https://asean.org/wp-content/uploads/images/archive/ADF-TOR.pdf.

596. Agreement for the Establishment of a Fund for ASEAN, signed by the Foreign Ministers on 23 Jul. 1994, entered into force on the same day, at: http://agreement.asean.org/media/download/20131230231809.pdf. When the Agreement was terminated on 26 Jul. 2005, all its funds were transferred to the ASEAN Development Fund. Note that the 1994 Agreement had superseded the Agreement for the Establishment of a Fund for ASEAN Rules Governing the Control, Disbursement and Accounting of the Fund for the ASEAN, done at Cameron Highlands, Malaysia, 17 Dec. 1969, entered into force on the same day.

597. Generally, *see* H. Sato, *How Can ASEAN and Japan Mutually Benefit from ASEAN Economic Integration* (Regional Office for Asia and the Pacific October 2014), at: https://www.ilo.org/wcmsp5/groups/public/---asia/---ro-bangkok/documents/publication/wcms_314225.pdf.

598. Reproduced in *ASEAN Documents Series 2005*, Jakarta: ASEAN Secretariat, April 2006, 7.

599. For the documents adopted, *see East Asia Summit (EAS) Documents Series 2005-2014*, Jakarta: ASEAN Secretariat, May 2015.

600. *See* A. Berkofsky, *The East Asia Summit (EAS) – Really Towards an East Asian Community (EAC)?*, 4 Asia-Pacific J. EU Stud. 95–104 (2006).

group of countries,[601] which later was expanded and formed the so-called ASEAN Plus Six group of countries.[602] The membership in these two regional groupings comprised, respectively, on the one hand, the ASEAN Member States and, on the other hand, China, Japan, and South Korea (the 'Plus Three'); later on, India, Australia, and New Zealand were added (becoming the 'Plus Six'). As is indicated elsewhere in this monograph, several topics and issues, which have been of concern to ASEAN leaders, have also been discussed in the course of EAS meetings. It should be noted that accession to the aforementioned TAC is a *conditio sine qua non* for states to participate in East Asia Summits. It is also of some interest to explain that the inaugural EAS was not the only occasion that ASEAN States had the opportunity to meet and deliberate with these third countries; on the contrary, they did so during other meetings, always at a summit level and bilateral in nature. In particular, during the two days leading to the inaugural EAS, the following meetings took place: on 12 December 2005, the 9th ASEAN Plus Three Summit as well as the 9th ASEAN-China Summit; and on 13 December 2005, the 9th ASEAN-Japan Summit, the 4th ASEAN-India Summit, and the 9th ASEAN-Republic of Korea Summit. Finally, it was also on 13 December 2005 that the First ASEAN-Russian Federation Summit was held. The Russian Federation is now a member of EAS and so is the USA.

205. Over the years, EAS has been transformed into a self-standing multilateral institution featuring regular meetings at different levels of seniority. Thus, while the eighteen Heads of State still meet at the same time that the ASEAN Summit takes place (usually in November / December of each year), there is also an annual EAS Foreign Ministers Meeting, while a number of EAS Senior Officials' Meetings are held throughout the year to implement and promote what has been agreed at the level of EAS Leaders. Moreover, since 2014, there has also been an annual EAS Economic Ministers' Meeting, which is complemented by the annual gatherings of the EAS Environment, Energy, and Education Ministers. Finally, at the level of *fonctionnaires*, there is a dedicated EAS Unit within the ASEAN Secretariat (located in Jakarta, Indonesia). It is also there that the ambassadors from EAS countries prepare future meetings and discuss fresh developments at a diplomatic level. The 10th EAS Foreign Ministers' Meeting took place on 9 September 2020[603] and, with the exception of discussing how to respond to and recover from the COVID-19 pandemic, the other topics were almost the same as the agenda of the 14th EAS, which had been held on 4 November 2019, namely, maritime security and the South

601. *See* Y. Hidetaka, *Political Leadership, Informality, and Regional Integration in East Asia: The Evolution of ASEAN Plus Three*, 4 Eur. J. East Asian Stud. 205–232 (2005); A.D. Ba, *Regionalism's Multiple Negotiations. ASEAN in East Asia*, 22 Cambridge Rev. Int'l Aff. 345–367 (2009).

602. *See* R. Stubbs, *ASEAN Plus Three: Emerging East Asian Regionalism?*, 42 Asian Surv. 440–455 (2002); S. Suzuki, *East Asian Cooperation Through Conference Diplomacy: Institutional Aspects of the ASEAN Plus Three (APT) Framework*, APEC Study Center / Institute of Developing Economies, Working Paper Series 03/04 – No. 7, Chiba, Japan, March 2004, at: https://www.kita.net/biz/trade_import/upfiles/east_asian_cooperation_through_conference_diplomacy220.pdf.

603. *See* Chairman's Statement of the 10th East Asia Summit Foreign Ministers' Meeting, 9 Sep. 2020, Vietnam (via videoconference), at: https://www.mofa.go.jp/mofaj/files/100093522.pdf.

China Sea, the Korean Peninsula, the situation in the Rakhine State, and counter terrorism.[604] Thereafter, the Eleventh EAS Foreign Ministers' Meeting was held via videoconference in August 2021,[605] the Twelfth meeting in August 2022,[606] the Thirteenth Meeting in July 2023 (it lasted for 120 minutes),[607] and the Fourteenth Meeting in July 2024.[608]

206. The latter Meeting described EAS 'as the premier Leaders-led forum for dialogue and cooperation on broad strategic, political, and economic issues of common interest and concern with the aim of promoting peace, stability and economic prosperity in East Asia in line with the EAS fundamental documents and based on the established principles, objectives and modalities of the EAS'.[609] And later on, when discussing the strengthening of EAS' institutional capacity, it was agreed that 'the prevailing geopolitical dynamics make it imperative that the EAS platform is fully utilised as it was envisioned, a platform for dialogue on broad strategic, political, and economic issues, with ASEAN as the driving force'.[610] The 15th EAS Foreign Ministers' Meeting is to be held in Malaysia in 2025.

207. The 12th ASEAN Summit was originally to be held in Cebu, the Philippines, in December 2006. However, due to the very adverse weather conditions prevailing at the time in the area, it was decided to postpone it, and it finally took place in the same city in January 2007. It was a rather fruitful meeting. Leaders evaluated the process of transforming ASEAN, adopted the Cebu Declaration on the Acceleration of the Establishment of an ASEAN Community by 2015[611] and endorsed the Cebu Declaration on the Blueprint of the ASEAN Charter. The purpose of the latter document was twofold. First, to celebrate the 'crowning achievement of 40 years of ASEAN' which has enabled it to meet future challenges and opportunities. Second, to act 'as a firm foundation in achieving one ASEAN Community by providing an enhanced institutional framework as well as conferring a legal personality to ASEAN'.[612] The other document of note signed during the 12th Summit was the ASEAN Declaration on the Protection and Promotion of the Rights of Migrant

604. *See* Chairman's Statement of the 14th East Asia Summit, Bangkok / Nonthaburi, 4 Nov. 2019, https://www.mofa.go.jp/files/000535021.pdf.'
605. *See* Chairman's Statement of the 11th East Asia Summit (EAS) Foreign Ministers' Meeting via videoconference, 4 Aug. 2021, at: https://www.mofa.go.jp/files/100220788.pdf.
606. *See* Chairman's Statement of the 12th East Asia Summit (EAS) Foreign Ministers' Meeting, Phnom Penh, Cambodia, 5 Aug. 2022, at: https://asean.org/chairmans-statement-of-the-12th-east-asia-summit-eas-foreign-ministers-meeting/.
607. *See* Chairman's Statement of the 13th East Asia Summit (EAS) Foreign Ministers' Meeting, Jakarta, Indonesia, 14 Jul. 2023, at: https://www.mofa.go.jp/files/100531753.pdf.
608. *See* Chairman's Statement of the 14th East Asia Summit (EAS) Foreign Ministers' Meeting, Vientiane, Lao PDR, 27 Jul. 2024, at: https://asean.org/chairmans-statement-of-the-14th-east-asia-summit-foreign-ministers-meeting/.
609. *Ibid.*, para. 2.
610. *Ibid.*, para. 40.
611. For all documents adopted during the Summit, *see* https://asean.org/speechandstatement/12th-asean-summit-cebu-philippines-9-15-january-2007/.
612. *Ibid.*

Workers (discussed later).[613] It is rather interesting that, even though intra-ASEAN migration has always accounted for a very large percentage of the region's total international migrant force,[614] it was presumably not possible for ASEAN leaders to concur to a multilateral treaty and, instead, they only issued a political document.

208. As regards the United Nations yardstick for the regulation of transnational migration for economic purposes, namely the International Convention on the Protection of the Rights of All Migrant Workers and Members of their Families,[615] it has been ratified by two ASEAN countries, the Philippines on 5 July 1995 (it signed it on 15 November 1993) and by Indonesia on 31 May 2012 (it signed it on 22 September 2004), Cambodia signed it on 27 September 2004 but has not ratified it, and aspirant Member State Timor Leste acceded to it on 30 January 2004. As regards the International Labour Organisation (ILO), its most recent Convention in the area of transnational migration, namely the Domestic Workers Convention,[616] at the time of writing was only ratified by the Philippines on 5 September 2012 (it was the second ILO Member State ever to ratify it); no other ASEAN country has currently signed it. As regards the other recent ILO Convention relating to migration, namely the Violence and Harassment Convention, it was signed only by the Philippines on 20 February 2024 (the Convention entered into force for the Philippines on 20 February 2025).[617] Finally, the 12th Summit adopted the ASEAN Convention on Counter Terrorism, which entered into force on 27 May 2011.[618]

613. See ASEAN Declaration on the Protection of Migrant Workers and Family Members in Crisis Situations and its Guidelines, Jakarta: ASEAN Secretariat, October 2023, at: https://asean.org/wp-content/uploads/2023/11/ASEAN_Declaration_on_the_Protection_of_Migrant_Workers_Family_Members-in-Crisis-Situation-and-its-Guidelines.pdf.

614. According to recent data, there are in total 9.7 million international migrants living in ASEAN's net destination countries (Brunei Darussalam, Malaysia, Singapore and Thailand), of which 7.1 million are 'intra-ASEAN migrants', namely immigrants coming from origin countries that are part of the ASEAN region. This was a significant increase in 'intra-ASEAN migrants' considering that in 1990 there were 3.2 million and in 2019 there were 6.9 million (all figures are estimates), such immigrants coming from the net-origin countries (Cambodia, Indonesia, Lao PDR, Myanmar, the Philippines and Vietnam), *see* International Labour Organization / Australian Government Department of Foreign Affairs / Trade and Global Affairs Canada, *Triangle in ASEAN Programme Quarterly Briefing Note*, October–December 2023, 6.

615. The Convention, one of the so-called core UN treaties for the protection of human rights, was opened for signature in New York on 18 Dec. 1990 pursuant to UNGA Res. 45/158, entered into force on 1 Jul. 2003, 2220 U.N.T.S. 3.

616. Convention concerning Decent Work for Domestic Workers, C 189, adopted on 16 Jun. 2011 by the 100th Session of the International Labour Conference (ILO Convention No. 189), entered into force on 5 Sep. 2013.

617. Convention concerning the elimination of violence and harassment in the world of work, C190, adopted on 21 Jun. 2019 by the 108th International Labour Conference session (ILO Convention No. 190), entered into force on 25 Jun. 2021.

618. 3200 U.N.T.S. I-54629, at: https://asean.org/wp-content/uploads/2012/05/ACCT.pdf. Generally, *see* A. R. Ahmad, *The ASEAN Convention on Counter-Terrorism 2007*, 14 Asia-Pacific J. Hum. Rts. & L. 93–147 (2013); H. Nasu, R. Laughlin, D. R. Rothwell, S. S. Tan, *The Legal Authority of ASEAN as a Security Institution* 78–111 (Cambridge University Press 2019).

209. The process of transforming ASEAN into a rules-based international organisation was successfully concluded during the 13th ASEAN Summit (Singapore, November 2007) when all Member States signed the ASEAN Charter as well as the Declaration on the ASEAN Economic Community Blueprint.[619] It was the 40th anniversary of ASEAN. A new era had begun for ASEAN, and the goal of regional integration was redefined.[620] During the 13th Summit, whose theme was 'Energy, Environment, Climate Change and Sustainable Development', ASEAN leaders also adopted the Declaration on Environmental Sustainability.[621] On 21 November 2007 and in the context of the 3rd East Asia Summit, the ASEAN Plus Six signed the Singapore Declaration on the Environment.[622] At the 14th ASEAN Summit (Cha-am and Hua Hin, Thailand, February/March 2009 and Pattaya, Thailand, April 2009),[623] ASEAN leaders signed a Declaration promoting the creation of an ASEAN Community[624] and also adopted a number of documents of strategic importance to further the development of ASEAN.

210. During the 15th ASEAN Summit (Cha-Am Hua Hin, Thailand, October 2009), two important documents were adopted concerning the operation of entities active in the area of protecting and promoting human rights and fundamental freedoms. The first document was the Cha-am Hua Hin Declaration on the Inauguration of the ASEAN Intergovernmental Commission on Human Rights (AICHR).[625] It cited Article 14 of the ASEAN Charter as the legal basis for creating the AICHR; interestingly enough, Article 14 does refer to the establishment of an ASEAN human rights body without, however, indicating which will be its principal features. The Declaration was rather a self-congratulatory document applauding the inauguration of the AICHR and the entry into force of its Terms of Reference (TOR) (*see also* discussion *infra*). The second document was the Terms of Reference of the

619. Text at: https://asean.org/?static_post=declaration-on-the-asean-economic-community-blueprint. *See* H. Soesastro, *Implementing the ASEAN Economic Community (AEC) Blueprint*, in *Deepening Economic Integration – The ASEAN Economic Community and Beyond* 47–59 (H. Soesastro ed., ERIA Research Project Report 2007-1-2, IDE-JETRO 2008), at: http://www.eria.org/uploads/media/Research-Project-Report/RPR_FY2007_1-2_Chapter_3.pdf.

620. Generally, *see* S. Narine, *Forty Years of ASEAN: A Historical Review*, 21 The Pac. Rev. 411–429 (2008).

621. At: https://asean.org/asean-declaration-on-environmental-sustainability/. *See* K. Kheng-Lian (ed.), *ASEAN Environmental Law Policy and Governance – Selected Documents* (Vol. I, World Scientific 2009).

622. Text at: https://www.mofa.go.jp/region/asia-paci/eas/dec0711.pdf.

623. That the 14th Summit was split into two parts is explained as follows: originally the Summit was scheduled to be held in December 2008 but, due to the political crisis that had swept Thailand at the time, it was decided to move it into the following year. The April 2009 meeting was aborted due to problems which had been created by protesters at the venue of the Summit, *see* T. Fuller, *Thailand Cancels Summit After Protests* (The New York Times, 11 Apr. 2009), at: https://www.nytimes.com/2009/04/12/world/asia/12thai.html.

624. Cha-am Hua Hin Declaration on the Roadmap for an ASEAN Community (2009–2015), 1 Mar. 2009, at: https://asean.org/cha-am-hua-hin-declaration-on-the-roadmap-for-the-asean-community-2009-2015/.

625. At: https://aichr.org/wp-content/uploads/2020/02/Cha-am-Hua-Hin-Declaration-AICHR.pdf.

ASEAN Commission for the Promotion and Protection of the Rights of Women and Children (ACWC),[626] which was inaugurated in the following (16th) ASEAN Summit.

211. Finally, the 15th Summit adopted the Agreement on the Privileges and Immunities of the Association of Southeast Asian Nations.[627] The Agreement, whose legal basis is Articles 17, 18 and 19 of the ASEAN Charter, accords to ASEAN those privileges and immunities in the territories of Member States that are necessary to fulfil its various purposes and tasks. The Agreement was also necessary for two other reasons: (a) to allow the Secretary-General and other ASEAN staff to exercise their functions in an independent fashion, and (b) to allow the Member States' Permanent Representatives to ASEAN and other officials to carry out their tasks as required. It should be noted that two prior instruments of relevance, namely the Agreement between the Government of the Republic of Indonesia and ASEAN Relating to the Privileges and Immunities of the ASEAN Secretariat (1979) and the Agreement on the Use and Maintenance of the Premises of the ASEAN Secretariat (1981) were replaced by the Agreement Between the Government of the Republic of Indonesia and ASEAN on Hosting and Granting Privileges and Immunities to the ASEAN Secretariat (2012).[628]

212. The 16th ASEAN Summit (Hanoi, Vietnam, April 2010) was held under the theme 'Towards the ASEAN Community: from Vision to Action'. Deliberations centred on ASEAN's foreign relations and its strengthening ties with partner states and other international institutions. Leaders 'appreciated the valuable support and financial assistance accorded to ASEAN by its external partners'.[629] During the Summit, Foreign Ministers signed the Protocol to the ASEAN Charter on Dispute Settlement Mechanisms (discussed at length *infra*).[630] This move also signified the determination to transform ASEAN into a rules-based organisation where the implementation of the Charter is facilitated.[631]

213. At the following two ASEAN Summits, namely the 17th Summit (Ha Noi, Vietnam, October 2010) and the 18th Summit (Jakarta, Indonesia, May 2011), leaders concentrated on developing human resources in the region, on the protection of women and children, on consolidating relations among the membership, and on promoting its position in the global community. The latter endeavour was also the subject matter of the 6th EAS (Bali, Indonesia, November 2011) and was reflected in

626. At: https://www.asean.org/wp-content/uploads/images/archive/documents/TOR-ACWC.pdf.

627. Adopted on 25 Oct. 2009, entered into force on 20 Apr. 2017, at: https://www.asean.org/wp-content/uploads/images/archive/15thsummit/Agreement-on-Privileges-and-Immunities.pdf.

628. Concluded in Phnom Penh, Cambodia, on 2 Apr. 2012, at: http://agreement.asean.org/media/download/20140416010338.pdf.

629. *See* Chairman's Statement of the 16th ASEAN Summit, Ha Noi, 9 Apr. 2010, para. 40, at: https://asean.org/speechandstatement/16th-asean-summit-ha-noi-8-9-april-2010/.

630. Generally, *see* H. D. Phan, *Towards A Rules-Based ASEAN: The Protocol to the ASEAN Charter on Dispute Settlement Mechanisms*, 5 Arb. L. Rev. 254–276 (2013).

631. *See* Statement of the ASEAN Chair on the Signing of the Protocol to the ASEAN Charter on Dispute Settlement Mechanisms by the Foreign Ministers of ASEAN, Ha Noi, Vietnam, 8 Apr. 2010.

the title of the Statement delivered by the Summit Chairman: *ASEAN Community in a Global Community of Nations*.[632] Among the other documents approved during these two Summits, suffice to mention the following three. *First*, the Rules for Reference of Unresolved Disputes to the ASEAN Summit, which were adopted on 27 October 2010 and were incorporated as Annex 5 to the Protocol on Dispute Settlement Mechanisms (discussed *infra*).[633] *Second*, the Joint Statement on the Establishment of the ASEAN Institute for Peace and Reconciliation (ASEAN-IPR).[634] *Third*, the Joint Statement in Enhancing Cooperation against Trafficking in Persons in Southeast Asia,[635] which called on the competent ASEAN Ministers to accelerate their efforts and conclude the treaty fighting human trafficking. This proved possible much later, on 1 November 2015, when the ASEAN Convention against Trafficking in Persons, Especially Women and Children (ACTIP) was signed.[636] It entered into force on 8 March 2017 (discussed *infra*).

214. During the 19th ASEAN Summit (Bali, Indonesia, November 2011), ASEAN leaders adopted several documents on themes similar to previous sessions, including the Bali Declaration on ASEAN Community in a Global Community of Nations (also known as 'Bali Concord III'),[637] the Agreement of the Establishment of the ASEAN Coordinating Centre for Humanitarian Assistance on Disaster Management, and the ASEAN Declaration on Unity in Diversity: Toward Strengthening the ASEAN Community.[638] The documents approved during the 20th ASEAN Summit (Phnom Penh, Cambodia, April 2012) concerned the continued efforts to construct even closer ties among Member States: the Phnom Penh Agenda on ASEAN

---

632. Text at: https://www.mofa.go.jp/region/asia-paci/eas/pdfs/state111119.pdf.
633. *See* Instrument of Incorporation of the Rules for Reference of Unresolved Disputes to the ASEAN Summit to the Protocol to the ASEAN Charter on Dispute Settlement Mechanisms, 27 Oct. 2010, at: https://www.asean.org/wp-content/uploads/images/archive/documents/Instrument%20of%20Incorporation%20of%20Rules%20for%20Reference%20of%20Unresolved%20Disputes.pdf.
634. At: https://asean.org/wp-content/uploads/2021/09/Joint_Statement_IPR.pdf. The Terms of Reference of ASEAN-IPR were adopted by the 45th ASEAN Foreign Ministers Meeting in July 2012. It was officially launched by ASEAN leaders at the sidelines of the 21st Summit on 18 Nov. 2012.
635. Adopted on 8 May 2011, *see* ASEAN Document Series on Transnational Crime: Terrorism and Violent Extremism; Drugs; Cybercrime; and Trafficking in Persons (Jakarta: The ASEAN Secretariat, December 2017), p. 3.
636. U.N.T.S. I-54455, text at: https://www.asean.org/wp-content/uploads/2015/12/ACTIP.pdf. For an early assessment of the Convention, *see* R. Yusran, *The ASEAN Convention Against Trafficking in Persons: A Preliminary Assessment*, 8 Asian J. Int'l L. 258–292 (2018). *See also*, Liberty Asia, *ASEAN & ACTIP: Using a Regional Legal Framework to Fight a Global Crime*, September 2017, at: https://globalinitiative.net/asean-actip-using-a-regional-legal-framework-to-fight-a-global-crime/. For comparison with the relevant instrument adopted under the auspices of the Council of Europe, *see* M. Jovanovic, *Comparison of Anti-Trafficking Legal Regimes and Actions in the Council of Europe and ASEAN: Realities, Frameworks and Possibilities for Collaboration*, Secretariat of the Council of Europe Convention on Action against Trafficking in Human Beings, May 2018, at: https://rm.coe.int/coe-asean-study-thb/16808c1b91.
637. A Plan of Action to implement the Bali Concord III for the period between 2013 and 2017 was also approved at the Summit, at: https://www.asean.org/wp-content/uploads/images/2013/other_documents/POA%20of%20Bali%20Concord%20III%20_final_.pdf.
638. All available in *ASEAN Documents Series 2011* (Jakarta: ASEAN Secretariat, August 2012).

Community Building[639] and the Phnom Penh Declaration on 'ASEAN: One Community, One Destiny'.[640] Belatedly, it will be argued, ASEAN leaders also dealt with the acute problem of narcotics and adopted the Declaration on Drug-Free ASEAN 2015, which was rather short on recommending meaningful measures.[641]

215. The 21st Summit (Phnom Penh, Cambodia, November 2012) was held under the theme 'One Community, One Destiny'. There were two developments of note. Following earlier positive developments in the area of economic cooperation, the first was the decision of ASEAN leaders to instigate the AEC on 31 December 2015.[642] The second was the adoption of the ASEAN Human Rights Declaration (AHRD), a non-legally binding instrument which is discussed *infra* and whose importance lies in the fact that for the first time the rather vague references to human rights in the ASEAN Charter became more concrete.[643] However, the fact that leaders were not apparently prepared to adopt a regional treaty for the protection and promotion of human rights and fundamental freedoms should not go unnoticed. Finally, the Summit urged Member States to expedite the ratification of the ASEAN Framework Agreement for Visa Exemption (for ASEAN Nationals), which was signed in Kuala Lumpur on 25 July 2006;[644] apparently it has still not entered into force. Its coming into force will be an important step towards promoting not only interregional tourism but also the process of the unhindered movement of people between Member States.[645]

216. At the 22nd ASEAN Summit (Bandar Seri Begawan, Brunei Darussalam, April 2013), which was held under the theme 'Our People, Our Future Together', ASEAN leaders agreed to press on with the promotion of the AEC Blueprint and to realise the goal of establishing the ASEAN Community before the end of 2015. They also reached consensus on starting negotiations on the Regional Comprehensive Economic Partnership (RCEP), which had been scheduled to take place in May

---

639. Text at: https://cil.nus.edu.sg/wp-content/uploads/formidable/18/2012-Phnom-Penh-Agenda-for-ASEAN-Community-Building.pdf.
640. At: https://cil.nus.edu.sg/wp-content/uploads/formidable/18/2012-Phnom-Penh-Declaration-on-ASEAN.pdf.
641. *See* also, Chairman's Statement of the 20th ASEAN Summit, Phnom Penh, 3–4 Apr. 2012, para. 53 at: https://asean.org/speechandstatement/20th-asean-summit-phnom-penh-cambodia-03-04-april-2012/.
642. *See* Chairman's Statement of the 21st ASEAN Summit, Phnom Penh, 18 Nov. 2012, para. 9, at: https://www.asean.org/wp-content/uploads/images/documents/Chairman%E2%80%99s%20Statement%20of%20the%2021st%20ASEAN%20Summit.pdf.
643. *See* Phnom Penh Statement on the Adoption of the ASEAN Human Rights Declaration (AHRD), 18 Nov. 2012, at: https://asean.org/phnom-penh-statement-on-the-adoption-of-the-asean-human-rights-declaration-ahrd/. The Statement reaffirmed the ASEAN leaders' commitment to ensure that the AHRD's implementation will be in accordance with the UN Charter, the UDHR, the Vienna Declaration and Programme of Action, and other international human rights instruments to which Member States were parties.
644. Text at: http://agreement.asean.org/media/download/20160831072909.pdf.
645. *See* also, ASEAN Plan of Action for Cooperation on Immigration Matters adopted in 2000 and Declaration on the Guidelines on Consular Assistance by ASEAN Member States' Missions in Third Countries to Nationals of Other ASEAN Member States adopted in November 2018.

2013 in Brunei Darussalam.[646] Finally, it was resolved to promote their cooperation in the context of the ASEAN Agreement on Transboundary Haze Pollution (AATHP), which had been concluded in Kuala Lumpur, Malaysia, on 10 June 2002,[647] and is discussed *infra*. It should be noted that for the purpose of implementing AATHP, the ASEAN Transboundary Haze Pollution Control Fund (Haze Fund) has been established.[648]

217. During the 23rd ASEAN Summit (Bandar Seri Begawan, Brunei Darussalam, October 2013), the efforts to promote the building up of the ASEAN Community and to formulate a post-2015 ASEAN Vision continued. The Bandar Seri Begawan Declaration on the ASEAN Community's Post-2015 Vision contained the guidelines.[649] The following two ASEAN Summits, namely the 24th Summit (Nay Pyi Taw, Myanmar, May 2014) and the 25th Summit (Nay Pyi Taw, Myanmar, November 2014), focused again on the formation of the ASEAN Community and on the post-2015 Vision, as evidenced by the Declarations adopted at the end of each session.[650] Among the documents that ASEAN leaders approved during the 26th ASEAN Summit (Kuala Lumpur and Langkawi, Malaysia, April 2015), the following three should be mentioned. *First*, the Kuala Lumpur Declaration on a

---

646. *See* Chairman's Statement of the 22nd ASEAN Summit, 'Our People, Our Future Together', Bandar Seri Begawan, 24–25 Apr. 2013, para. 30, at: https://asean.org/chairmans-statement-of-the-22nd-asean-summit-our-people-our-future-together/.
647. Text at: https://asean.org/wp-content/uploads/2021/01/ASEANAgreementonTransboundaryHazePollution-1.pdf; *see* P. Charusombat, *ASEAN Cooperation on Transboundary Haze Pollution: The Perspective of Institutional Incremental Change*, 2022(2) Journal of Environmental Information Science 1-12. Previous ASEAN documents on the protection of the environment included the *Kuala Lumpur Accord on Environment and Development*, which was adopted on 19 Jun. 1990, the *ASEAN Co-operation Plan on Transboundary Pollution* of 1995, and the *Regional Haze Action Plan* of 1997. Generally, *see* D. Heilmann, *After Indonesia's Ratification: The ASEAN Agreement on Transboundary Haze Pollution and Its Effectiveness as a Regional Environmental Governance Tool*, 34 J. Current Southeast Asian Aff. 95–121 (2015); H. Varkkey, *Regional Cooperation, Patronage and the ASEAN Agreement on Transboundary Haze Pollution*, 14(1) Int'l Envtl. Agreements: Pol., L. & Econ. 65–81 (2014); L. Nurhidayah, S. Alam & Z. Lipman, *The Influence of International Law upon ASEAN Approaches in Addressing Transboundary Haze Pollution in Southeast Asia*, 37 Contemp. Southeast Asia 183–210 (2015).
648. Further, *see* Roadmap on ASEAN Cooperation towards Transboundary Haze Pollution Control with Means of Implementation (2016-2020), and Second Roadmap on ASEAN Cooperation towards Transboundary Haze Pollution Control with Means of Implementation (2023-2030), which was adopted during the 18th Meeting of the Conference of the Parties to ASEAN Agreement on Transboundary Haze Pollution (COP-18) in August 2023. Generally, *see* L. Mai, 'Extinguishing a Point of Contention: Examining Transboundary Haze in Southeast Asia', Center for Strategic and International Studies, 17 Nov. 2023, at: https://www.csis.org/blogs/new-perspectives-asia/extinguishing-point-contention-examining-transboundary-haze-southeast.
649. Text at: https://cil.nus.edu.sg/wp-content/uploads/2017/07/2013-Bandar-Seri-Begawan-Declaration-on-the-ASEAN-Community%E2%80%99s-Post-2015-Vision.pdf.
650. *See Nay Pyi Taw Declaration on Realisation of the ASEAN Community*, adopted on 11 May 2014, and *Nay Pyi Taw Declaration on the ASEAN Community's Post-2015 Vision*, adopted on 12 Nov. 2014, at: https://cil.nus.edu.sg/databasecil/2014-nay-pyi-taw-declaration-on-the-asean-communitys-post-2015-vision/.

People-Oriented, People-Centered ASEAN, which was the first-ever official document to refer to a 'people-oriented ASEAN'.[651] *Second*, the Langkawi Declaration on the Global Movement of Moderates, which built upon the ASEAN Concept Paper on the Global Movement of Moderates adopted during the 20th Summit and which as an initiative promotes a culture of peace complementing other relevant projects, such as the United Nations Alliance of Civilisations.[652] *Third*, the Declaration on Institutionalizing the Resilience of ASEAN and its Communities and People to Disasters and Climate Change.[653]

218. The goal that ASEAN countries have been working so hard on, namely the establishment of the ASEAN Community, was proclaimed that it will take place on 31 December 2015 at the 27th ASEAN Summit (Kuala Lumpur, Malaysia, November 2015). It was followed by a Declaration mapping the evolution of ASEAN over the next ten years.[654] The following four documents were appended: the ASEAN Community Vision 2025; the ASEAN Political-Security Community Blueprint 2025; the ASEAN Economic Community Blueprint 2025; and the ASEAN Socio-Cultural Community Blueprint 2025.[655] According to Vision 2025, the ASEAN Community will not only be a people-oriented and people-centred institution but will also become an institution respecting rules and norms and will be made up of a community of peoples, all of whom will enjoy human rights and fundamental freedoms.

219. Thus, what was actually achieved at the 27th ASEAN Summit was, on the one hand, that ASEAN was proclaimed a Community, which strives to be 'politically cohesive, economically integrated, and socially responsible' international organisation, and, on the other hand, the elaboration of a plan setting out its evolution to 2025, which more or less coincides with the goals and aspirations of the ASEAN Community. This plan, admittedly, was not based on any new, groundbreaking, themes but rather carried on the traditional ASEAN ideas, namely consolidation, integration, and stronger cohesiveness among the membership. Notwithstanding this argument, the aspirations of the original ASEAN membership in 1967 were to a very large extent materialised in a region and in a world which, in the meantime, had changed fundamentally.

220. A detailed account of the 32nd ASEAN Summit (Singapore, April 2018) and of the 33rd ASEAN Summit (Singapore, November 2018) has already been given *supra*. The 34th ASEAN Summit was held in Bangkok in June 2019 under

651. Text at: https://asean.org/wp-content/uploads/2012/05/26th-KUALA-LUMPUR-DECLARATION-ON-A-PEOPLE-ORIENTED-PEOPLE-CENTRED-ASEAN-Final.pdf.
652. At: https://asean.org/wp-content/uploads/2012/05/LANGKAWI-DECLARATION-ON-THE-GLOBAL-MOVEMENT-OF-MODERATES-Final.pdf.
653. At: https://asean.org/wp-content/uploads/2012/05/26th-DECLARATION-ON-INSTITUTIONALISING-Final.pdf.
654. *See Kuala Lumpur Declaration on ASEAN 2025: Forging Ahead Together*, 22 Nov. 2015, at: https://asean.org/kuala-lumpur-declaration-on-asean-2025-forging-ahead-together/. *See* also *ASEANFocus, Special Issue on ASEAN 2025: Forging Ahead Together*, Issue 1/ 2016, January 2016, at: https://www.iseas.edu.sg.
655. Reproduced in *ASEAN 2025 – Forging Ahead Together* (Jakarta: ASEAN Secretariat, May 2016).

the theme 'Advancing Partnership for Sustainability'.[656] It discussed the Plan of Action to Strengthen the Implementation of the SEANWFZ Treaty (2018–2022),[657] commended the development of the Work Plan of the ASEAN Plan of Action to Prevent and Counter the Rise of Radicalisation and Violent Extremism 2018–2025, and also indicated that ASEAN leaders would be interested in concluding an ASEAN Extradition Treaty; it has still not been concluded.[658] Moreover, in the area of responding to disasters effectively and uniformly, i.e., having a single ASEAN response, they discussed the operationalisation of the ASEAN Militaries Ready Group on Humanitarian Assistance and Disaster Relief (AMRG on HADR).

221. Finally, reference should be made to the ongoing situation in Myanmar, and the actions of the ruling military regime in the Rakhine State since the mid-2010s, which have precipitated the mass displacement of people, mostly Muslims, into neighbouring Bangladesh. The military government of Myanmar had established an Independent Commission of Enquiry (ICOE) to investigate the events that have taken place during and after August 2017, especially their consequences as regards the mass displacement of the local population. The aim was to bring accountability and to come up with recommendations on what had to be done to ensure sustainable peace and development in the Rakhine State. The Summit said that it expected that the ICOE 'would seek accountability by carrying out an independent and impartial investigation into alleged human rights violations and related issues'.[659]

222. According to the United Nations fact-finding mission on Myanmar, which was set up by the Human Rights Council in its Resolution 34/22,[660] ICOE failed to meet the standards of an impartial and independent human rights investigation.[661] ICOE submitted its final Report to the government of Myanmar on 20 January

656. *See* Chairman's Statement of the 34th ASEAN Summit, Bangkok, 23 Jun. 2019, 'Advancing Partnership for Sustainability', at: https://asean.org/chairmans-statement-of-the-34th-asean-summit/.
657. It had been adopted in Manila, the Philippines, on 4 Aug. 2017, at: https://cil.nus.edu.sg/wp-content/uploads/2020/08/PoA-SEANWFZ-2018-2022.pdf.
658. In February 2025, the 12th ASEAN Senior Law Officials Meeting Working Group on the ASEAN Extradition Treaty Meeting was held. It completed the seventh reading of the draft text; however, more compromise is required to make the draft Treaty acceptable to all members.
659. *See* Chairman's Statement of the 34th ASEAN Summit, para. 43.
660. UNGA Res. 34/22, 'Situation of human rights in Myanmar', adopted on 24 Mar. 2017, decided to dispatch urgently an independent international fact-finding mission (IIFFM) to Myanmar. The members of IIFFM were appointed by the President of the Human Rights Council, a subsidiary UNGA organ, and their mandate was to establish the facts and circumstances of the alleged human rights violations and abuses by the country's military regime and security forces, in particular in the Rakhine State.
661. *See* UN Human Rights Council, *Report of the independent international fact-finding mission on Myanmar*, UN Doc. A/HRC/39/64, 12 Sep. 2018, para. 96 at p. 18. The mandate of IIFFMM ended in September 2019, when it handed over its evidence to the Independent Investigative Mechanism for Myanmar (IIMM), which had been established by the Human Rights Council Res. 39/2 of 27 Sep. 2018. UNGA welcomed the creation of IIMM in Res. 73/264, 'Situation of human rights in Myanmar', adopted on 22 Dec. 2018. IIMM is still active, *see* UNGA, *Situation of human rights of Rohingya Muslims and other minorities in Myanmar - Report of the Secretary-General*, UN Doc. A/78/278, 14 Aug. 2023; and UN Human Rights Council, *Situation of human rights of Rohingya Muslims and other minorities in Myanmar* - Report of the United Nations High Commissioner for Human Rights, UN Doc. A/HRC/56/23 (18 Jun. 2024).

2020.[662] In December 2023, the UN General Assembly adopted a very lengthy (sixteen pages) Resolution regarding the situation in Myanmar.[663] The Resolution, *inter alia*, praised ASEAN's 'important role in facilitating a peaceful solution to the crisis in Myanmar in the interests of the people of Myanmar .... to address the root causes of the crisis and displacement so that affected communities can rebuild their lives after their return to Myanmar', welcomed the ASEAN Leaders' decision to maintain the Five-Point Consensus on Myanmar (reference to which was made *infra*) as the main reference to address the political crisis in Myanmar and expressed the view that it should be implemented in its entirety.[664] Resolution 78/219 called upon the Myanmar military regime to release the ICOE Report in full because, despite its limitations, it acknowledged that war crimes as well as serious human rights had been committed by multiple actors and that there were reasonable grounds to believe that members of Myanmar security forces were involved. The follow-up UNGA Resolution adopted in December 2024 was even lengthier (eighteen pages). It is regretted that the full ICOE Report remains unpublished.[665]

223. The 35th ASEAN Summit also took place in Bangkok in November 2019. The theme was the same with the previous Summit.[666] Leaders discussed, *inter alia*, developments in the various sub-regional schemes, which have been initiated and run by groups of Member States,[667] including the following:

a. the Ayeyawady–Chao Phraya–Mekong Economic Cooperation Strategy (ACMECS);[668] (b) the Indonesia–Malaysia–Thailand Growth Triangle (IMT-GT);[669]
b. the Brunei Darussalam–Indonesia–Malaysia–Philippines East ASEAN Growth Area (BIMP-EAGA);[670]

---

662. For the Report's Executive Summary, *see* https://reliefweb.int/report/myanmar/executive-summary-independent-commission-enquiry-icoe.
663. UNGA Res. 78/219, 'Situation of human rights of Rohingya Muslims and other minorities in Myanmar' adopted on 19 Dec. 2023.
664. The Security Council has also mentioned ASEAN's central role in finding a peaceful solution in the situation in Myanmar and has made specific reference to the Five-Point Consensus, *see* the aforementioned UNSC Res. 2669 (2022), 21 Dec. 2022, para. 5.
665. UNGA Res. 79/182, 'Situation of human rights of Rohingya Muslims and other minorities in Myanmar', 17 December 2024.
666. *See* Chairman's Statement of the 35th ASEAN Summit, Bangkok/Nonthaburi, 3 Nov. 2019, 'Advancing Partnership for Sustainability', at: https://asean.org/speechandstatement/chairmans-statement-of-the-35th-asean-summit/.
667. Generally, *see* K. Klecha-Tylec, *The Theoretical and Practical Dimensions of Regionalism in East Asia* (Palgrave Macmillan 2017).
668. *See* ACMECS Plan of Action 2016–2018, adopted by the ACMECS Leaders at the 6th ACMECS Summit, Nay Pyi Taw, Myanmar, 23 Jun. 2015. Generally, *see* C. na Thalang & A. Patchimnan, 'Rethinking ACMECS amidst Changing Regionalism in Southeast Asia' (Heinrich-Böll-Stiftung, 27 May 2023), at: https://th.boell.org/en/2023/05/27/rethinking-acmecs-regionalism-southeast-asia.
669. *See* 'IMT-GT VISION 2036', Malaysia: Centre for IMT-GT Subregional Cooperation, April 2017, at: https://imtgt.org/vision-2036/.
670. *See* 'BIMP-EAGA Vision 2025', 2017, at: https://bimp-eaga.asia/sites/default/files/publications/bimp-eaga-vision-2025.pdf.

c. the Cambodia–Laos–Myanmar–Vietnam (CLMV group) cooperation;[671]
d. the Cambodia–Laos–Vietnam (CLV) Development Triangle Area;[672] and
e. the Singapore–Johor–Riau Growth Triangle (SIJORI Growth Triangle).[673]

224. The closer coordination between ASEAN and these cooperation frameworks, several of which were created well before the signing of the ASEAN Charter, is meant to narrow the development gap among Member States.[674] However, as they progress, they are bound to enter into competition with each other and, should they progress at different speeds, it could be rather difficult for the same Member State (e.g., Cambodia) to participate in all relevant schemes. To put it otherwise, the existence of some five sub-regional groupings within a region (ASEAN) where only ten states participate might not be workable in the long term. It should be noted that Africa is another region where several sub-regional groupings with overlapping membership exist (they are collectively known as 'African Regional Economic Communities' (RECs)) alongside a continental international organisation, the African Union. However, what is different is that AU has a membership of fifty-five states, and there are eight (recognised) RECs, which include the Southern Africa Development Community (SADC), the East Africa Community (EAC), and the Common Market of Eastern and Southern Africa (COMESA). These RECs are referred to as 'building blocks' and assist the AU in its activities as well as to achieve its goals, while the AU coordinates and harmonises policies between them.[675]

671. Initiated by Vietnam, the CLMV mechanism was established in August 2010. *See* Twelfth CLMV Economic Ministers' Meeting, 24 Aug. 2020, Videoconference, Joint Media Statement, https://asean.org/joint-media-statement-of-the-twelfth-clmv-economic-ministers-meeting/; United Nations Economic and Social Commission for Asia and the Pacific, *Trade integration within ASEAN: The role of non-tariff measures for Cambodia, the Lao People's Democratic Republic, Myanmar and Viet Nam*, ST/ESCAP/2793, 2017, at: https://www.unescap.org/sites/default/d8files/Full_Trade_Integration_within_ASEAN_The_role_of_NTMs_for_CLMV_0.pdf. Note that on 16 Sep. 2022 the CLMV Action Plan for the 2023–2024 period was approved at the Fourteenth CLMV Economic Ministers' Meeting (CLMV-EMM 14), which took place in the framework of the Fifty-Fourth ASEAN Economic Ministers' Meeting (AEM-54). *See* further, L. Cuyvers, *The 'ASEAN Way' and ASEAN's development gap with Cambodia, Laos, Myanmar and Vietnam: a critical view*, 25 Asia Pacific Business Review 683-704 (2019).
672. It was established in the late 1980s and created by a MOU signed on 17 Dec. 1994. *See* V. Chheang, *The Cambodia-Laos-Vietnam Development Triangle Area* (SEAS-Yusof Ishak Institute June 2018), at: https://www.iseas.edu.sg; X. Xiaodong, *The SIJORI Growth Triangle: Progress, Problems and Prospect*, 3(1) J. of Maritime Studies and National Integration 1-13 (2019), at: https://doi.org/10.14710/jmsni.v3i1.4473. Note that the XI Summit, held by videoconference on 9 Dec. 2020, resolved to strengthen cooperation within the CLV area.
673. *See* J. Revilla Diez, M. Breul & J. Moneke, *The SIJORI Growth Triangle*, 36 J. Southeast Asian Econ. (Special Issue: ASEAN: Towards Economic Convergence) 71–90 (2019).
674. *See* further, ASEAN Leaders' Vision Statement on a Cohesive and Responsive ASEAN: *Rising Above Challenges and Sustaining Growth*, Ha Noi, 26 Jun. 2020, para. 19, which refers to Member States promoting equitable development across the ASEAN Community by aligning sub-regional growth in these areas with the comprehensive development of ASEAN.
675. *See* Art. 3(m) of the AU Constitutive Act; K. Magliveras & G. Naldi, *The African Union (AU)* (3rd ed., Wolters Kluwer, 2024), 224-225.

225. As has been mentioned *supra*, a Special ASEAN Summit via videoconference took place on 14 April 2020. It was presided by the Prime Minister of Vietnam in his capacity as ASEAN Chair. The purpose was to discuss and decide on how the Organisation should address and cope with the COVID 19 pandemic. There was no Chairman's Statement circulated after the Special Summit, but a Declaration was issued, which should be regarded as having the same legal value.[676] The previous relevant document had been the Chairman's Statement on ASEAN Collective Response to the Outbreak of Coronavirus Disease 2019; it had been issued exactly two months earlier by the Prime Minister of Vietnam.[677] The Declaration portrayed ASEAN as a kind and compassionate international organisation where the first priority is the well-being of the Member States and the welfare of their population, the catchword being a 'Cohesive and Responsive ASEAN'. In particular, ASEAN leaders reaffirmed their determination and commitment to remain united and to act jointly to control the spread of the disease while mitigating its adverse impact on the livelihood of their people, their societies and their economies. To that end, they 'called for further enhancement of a *caring and sharing ASEAN Community* where ASEAN Member States help each other' (emphasis added).[678] This involved where collective action is taken, where policies to minimise the economic and social impact of the pandemic are coordinated and where maintaining socio-economic stability is safeguarded.[679] As regards the Member States' economic and commercial stability, their Economic Ministers were tasked to explore how, in accordance with the rights and obligations under the WTO agreements, with the ASEAN Trade in Goods Agreement (ATIGA) and with the rules of international law, the supply chain connectivity will be preserved so that the trade in essential goods, food and medical products will continue uninterrupted, no unnecessary restrictions on their flow will be placed, and the air and land routes as well as the seaports will remain open.[680]

226. The 36th ASEAN Summit was scheduled to be held in Da Nang, Vietnam, but was postponed due to the COVID-19 pandemic. It finally took place via videoconferencing from Ha Noi, Vietnam, in June 2020 under the theme 'Cohesive and

676. *See* Declaration of the Special ASEAN Summit on Coronavirus Disease 2019 (COVID-19), 14 Apr. 2020, at: https://asean.org/wp-content/uploads/2021/09/FINAL-Declaration-of-the-Special-ASEAN-Summit-on-COVID-19.pdf.

677. At: https://asean.org/chairmans-statement-on-asean-collective-response-to-the-outbreak-of-coronavirus-disease-2019/. Note that the Statement was circulated to the World Trade Organization (WTO) at the request of the delegation of Vietnam, Doc. WT/GC/210, 1 May 2020.

678. Declaration of the Special ASEAN Summit on Coronavirus Disease 2019, para. 8.

679. *Ibid.*, para. 9(iv). *See* further, Memorandum of Understanding (MOU) on the Implementation of Non-Tariff Measures on Essential Goods under the Ha Noi Plan of Action on Strengthening ASEAN Economic Cooperation and Supply Chain Connectivity in Response to the COVID-19 Pandemic, signed on 13 Nov. 2020, at: https://asean.org/wp-content/uploads/2021/09/5.-MOU-on-NTMs-on-Essential-Goods-for-upload.pdf. The validity of the MOU, which expressly states that it does not create any rights or legal obligations under international law and will not be subject to any dispute settlement mechanism, has been extended to 30 Nov. 2024.

680. *Ibid.*, para. 9(vi). As mentioned *supra*, ATIGA was signed in Feb. 2009, entered into force in May 2010.

Responsive ASEAN'.[681] The Summit approved a Plan of Action elaborating the Organisation's response to the pandemic.[682] It implemented the Declaration of the Special ASEAN Summit on the Coronavirus Disease, which had been adopted by the Special Summit on 14 April 2020, and the ASEAN Economic Ministers' Statement on Strengthening ASEAN's Economic Resilience in Response to the Outbreak of COVID-19, which had been issued on 10 March 2020. The Plan of Action was meant to be a temporary arrangement to maintain the connectivity supply chain for the duration of the pandemic, in other words to identify and address disruptions in the trade of food, medicines and medical supplies as well as any of other essential products. It is rather interesting that, as ASEAN States participate in the global regulation of trade and are themselves involved in regional economic integration, the Plan of Action clearly stipulated that it will be implemented pursuant, respectively, to the rights and obligations of the General Agreement on Tariffs and Trade (GATT) 1994, to the AEC Blueprint 2025, to the ASEAN Trade in Goods Agreement (ATIGA), and to other relevant Agreements.

227. Finally, ASEAN Leaders adopted the Vision Statement on a Cohesive and Responsive ASEAN. The purpose was to seize the opportunities and to respond effectively to the challenges facing the Organisation (these were stated in the document 'ASEAN Community Vision 2025'); to maintain ASEAN's unity and centrality; and to enhance its capacity to harness the opportunities brought about by digital transformation; and the Fourth Industrial Revolution (4IR).[683] The Vision Statement is effectively a roadmap on how the goal of an ASEAN Community will be achieved. It is divided into two parts, which are titled, respectively, 'A Cohesive ASEAN Community That Is United, Peaceful, Integrated and Resilient' and 'A Responsive ASEAN Community in a Transforming and Uncertain World'. Even though there are no decisive elements distinguishing the international organisation called ASEAN from the ASEAN Community, the latter should be understood as the international institution with which the populations of the Member States should develop a close sense of belonging. More specifically, the ASEAN Community is invested in fostering an ASEAN identity among the people by raising awareness of ASEAN's cultural heritage and their shared values and, at the same time, by employing common symbols as much as possible.

To that extent, all Member States are asked to display the ASEAN Flag,[684] to use the ASEAN Anthem during functions, and to have so-called ASEAN Lanes inside

---

681. *See* Chairman's Statement of the 36th ASEAN Summit, 27 Jun. 2020, 'Cohesive and Responsive ASEAN', at: https://asean.org/chairmans-statement-of-the-36th-asean-summit-26-june-2020-cohesive-and-responsive-asean/.
682. *See Hanoi Plan of Action on Strengthening ASEAN Economic Cooperation and Supply Chain Connectivity in Response to the COVID-19 Pandemic*, 26 Jun. 2020, at: https://cil.nus.edu.sg/wp-content/uploads/2020/07/2020-Hanoi-PoA.pdf.
683. *See* ASEAN Leaders' Vision Statement on a Cohesive and Responsive ASEAN: *Rising Above Challenges and Sustaining Growth*, Ha Noi, 26 Jun. 2020, at: https://asean.org/wp-content/uploads/2020/06/Final-ASEAN-Leaders-Vision-Statement-on-a-Cohesive-and-Responsive-ASEAN-final.pdf.
684. This practice is already observed in the EU: the national flags of Member States are always displayed together with the EU flag. However, in the EU, the notion of an 'EU citizenship' has been developed over many years now.

the international airports located in the Member States.[685] Throughout the Vision Statement, it becomes obvious that the concern of ASEAN leaders is to connect existing programmes and activities to Community Vision 2025. To give an example, the aforementioned ASEAN Agreement on Disaster Management and Emergency Response, which had already entered into force for more than a decade, was now to be implemented by 'a people-centred, people-oriented, sustainable, and networked approach by 2025'.[686] Finally, the Vision Statement referred to the need to strengthen the Organisation's institutional capacity by promoting the efficient operation of its organs, by improving work processes, and by continuing to assess the Charter as regards ASEAN structures as well as the application of the rules and procedures that govern ASEAN activities.[687]

228. The 37th ASEAN Summit, the second to take place in the course of 2020, took place in Ha Noi under the Chairmanship of the Socialist Republic of Vietnam in November 2020 (it was the last Summit that a representative of the Myanmar's ruling military government participated). ASEAN leaders acknowledged the stable progress in achieving economic integration, expressed the opinion that the Organisation had an enhanced capacity to adapt to changing regional and global dynamics and were gratified by its achievements in contributing to the global cause for peace, stability and sustainable development.[688] For yet another time, the same rhetoric was repeated: an affirmation of their shared commitment to maintaining and promoting peace, security, and stability in the region, as well as to the peaceful resolution of disputes, including full respect for legal and diplomatic processes, without resorting to the threat or use of force but adhering to the universal principles of international law, including the UN Convention on the Law of the Sea.[689] No doubt, the latter was a subtle, yet direct, reference to the confrontation with China pertaining to the South China Sea and the understanding that China was against the principles of the law of the sea. Moreover, a lot of emphasis was placed on developing an ASEAN Identity,[690] which as explained above is very closely connected to the project of an ASEAN Community.

At the 37th Summit, it was also resolved to develop a Post-2025 vision for the ASEAN Community,[691] even though at the time it was unknown if the goals for 2025 would have been achieved in full. In particular, Member States mandated the ASEAN Coordinating Council, the organ comprising of the foreign ministers, to supervise the Vision's formation as well as to devise a roadmap and to elaborate the core elements of the Vision; thereafter, a High-Level Task Force was agreed to be

685. Leaders' Vision Statement on a Cohesive and Responsive ASEAN, para. 19.
686. *Ibid.*, para. 44.
687. *Ibid.*, para. 26.
688. *See* Chairman's Statement of the 37th ASEAN Summit 'Cohesive and Responsive', Ha Noi, 12 Nov. 2020, para. 2, at: https://asean.org/wp-content/uploads/43-Chairmans-Statement-of-37th-ASEAN-Summit-FINAL.pdf.
689. *Ibid.*, para. 9.
690. *Ibid.*, paras 29–-30.
691. *Ibid.*, para. 27. To that end, the Ha Noi Declaration on the ASEAN Community's Post-2025 Vision was issued during the Summit, at: https://asean.org/ha-noi-declaration-on-the-asean-communitys-post-2025-vision/.

established to plan a post-2025 vision and prepare the attendant documents.[692] Finally, the Vietnam chairmanship pressed ahead with the task of updating and revising the ASEAN Charter, a task also addressed at the 30th ASEAN Summit.[693] Following deliberations at the 53rd Foreign Ministers' Meeting,[694] the 37th Summit asked the Secretariat to complete a so-called Scoping Report reviewing the Charter's implementation as regards the operation of ASEAN organs as well as the application of the rules and procedures that govern its daily activities.[695] Reportedly, a draft Scoping Report was actually produced and identified many provisions of the ASEAN Charter for revision, including those on the admission of new members (Article 6), on the ASEAN Secretary-General and Secretariat (Article 11), on budget and finances (Article 30) and on the conduct of external relations (Articles 41–46).[696] But a final Report has apparently never been published and the task of revising the Charter has never been set off the ground. Thus, ASEAN joins several other international organisations whose constitutive instrument has never been revised to adapt to developments and new realities, including the UN Charter and the Statute of the Council of Europe.

229. The 38th and 39th ASEAN Summits were held on the same day in late October 2021 by means of videoconference due to the COVID 19 pandemic. The Chairmanship was held by Brunei Darussalam and the theme was 'We Care, We Prepare, We Prosper'. ASEAN leaders adopted the Terms of Reference for the High-Level Task Force (HLTF) on the ASEAN Community's Post-2025 Vision (HLTF-ACV) and Roadmap. The composition of HLTF was resolved to be eminent persons and high-level representatives to be nominated by Member States and to be chaired by one of them (the so-called permanent shepherd) together with the current year's ASEAN Chair. Malaysia was chosen to be the 'permanent shepherd'.[697] Thus, the 16th Meeting of the HLTF-ACV was held on 31 July 2024 under the chairmanship of Malaysia and Laos and deliberated the ASEAN Community Vision 2045 and the Strategic Plans of the three Community Pillars and ASEAN Connectivity, which are expected to be adopted sometime in 2025. The 38th and 39th ASEAN Summits also adopted the Bandar Seri Begawan Declaration on the Strategic and Holistic Initiative to Link ASEAN Responses to Emergencies and Disasters (ASEAN

---

692. *Ibid.*

693. *See* Chairman's Statement 30th ASEAN Summit 'Partnering for Change, Engaging the World', Manila, 29 Apr. 2017, para. 13, at: https://asean.org/wp-content/uploads/2017/04/Chairs-Statement-of-30th-ASEAN-Summit_FINAL.pdf. Note that the work of a High-Level Task Force on 'Strengthening the ASEAN Secretariat and Reviewing the ASEAN Organs', which was established at the 25th ASEAN Summit, did not bear any fruits.

694. *See* Joint Communiqué of the 53rd ASEAN Foreign Ministers' Meeting, 9 Sep. 2020, para. 5, https://asean.org/wp-content/uploads/2021/03/12.-FINAL-Joint-Communique-of-the-53rd-AMM.pdf.

695. Chairman's Statement of the 37th ASEAN Summit, para. 28.

696. *See* S. Seah, 'A Review of the ASEAN Charter: In the Fullness of Time' (ISEAS – Yusof Ishak Institute, 18 Sep. 2020), at: https://www.iseas.edu.sg/media/commentaries/a-review-of-the-asean-charter-in-the-fullness-of-time/.

697. *See* Chairman's Statement of the 38th and 39th ASEAN Summits, 26 Oct. 2021 via videoconference, para. 5, at: https://asean.org/wp-content/uploads/2021/10/FINAL-Chairmans-Statement-of-the-38th-and-39th-ASEAN-Summits-26-Oct....pdf.

SHIELD).[698] It was described as 'a strategic, holistic, cross-sectoral and coordinated approach across the three ASEAN Community Pillars'.[699] Its aim is to ensure that the Organisation is able to put up a collective, rapid and effective response that will mitigate the effects of the emergencies and disasters that have already affected or might affect the ASEAN region and offer an advanced protection of both the society and the economy. Furthermore, the ASEAN Leaders' Declaration on Upholding Multilateralism was adopted. It is another political document where the Organisation is depicted as a rules-based regional institution whose architecture, founded on the principles of the UN Charter and on international law, is able to deal with important and tenacious common regional and global issues.[700] A considerable part of the Chairman's Statement was dedicated to how (successfully) the Organisation responded to the COVID-19 pandemic.[701]

The 38th and 39th ASEAN Summits also deliberated the question of ASEAN integration, a particularly difficult and sensitive project given the significant development gap that exists among Member States and their hugely varying degree of competitiveness. Arguably, it is in reality a division between older and newer members, which will become even more acute once Timor-Leste joins as the eleventh Member State. The instrument presently implemented to deal with these issues is the Initiative for ASEAN Integration Work Plan IV (2021–2025), which had been adopted by the 37th Summit.[702] What is rather interesting is that its successful implementation has been hinged on the 'continued engagement with ASEAN Partners and other external parties'. This and similar statements are to be found in several ASEAN documents and rather show the Organisation's continued reliance upon third states and international institutions.[703] Moreover, the combined Summit reviewed developments as regards the Treaty of Amity and Cooperation in Southeast Asia. TAC, which is discussed elsewhere in this monograph, was referred to as 'the key code of conduct in governing inter-state relations in the region and a foundation for maintaining regional peace and stability'.

This statement appears to reflect the present state of affairs, considering that an increasing number of states from outside the region are willing to accede to it, including Qatar, the United Arab Emirates, the Netherlands, the Hellenic Republic, the Kingdom of Denmark, and the Sultanate of Oman.[704] As explained later, as a region, ASEAN does not yet have a human rights system that is based on a human rights treaty and an oversight mechanism, as is the case with Europe, Africa, the

698. Text at: https://asean.org/wp-content/uploads/2021/10/2.-BSB-Declaration-on-ASEAN-SHIELD.pdf.
699. Chairman's Statement of the 38th and 39th ASEAN Summits, para. 8.
700. *Ibid.*, para. 9, at: https://asean.org/wp-content/uploads/2021/10/3.-FINAL-ASEAN-Leaders-Declaration-on-Upholding-Multilateralism.pdf.
701. *Ibid.*, paras 19-28.
702. It was launched at the Fourth ASEAN Informal Summit (Singapore, 2000). *See* Initiative for ASEAN Integration (IAI) Work Plan IV (2021-2025), Jakarta: ASEAN Secretariat, November 2020, at: https://asean.org/wp-content/uploads/IAI-workplan-IV.pdf.
703. *See* Chairman's Statement of the 38th and 39th ASEAN Summits, para. 29.
704. *Ibid.*, para. 37. These states acceded to TAC in August 2022. Ukraine acceded in November 2022. For a list of ratifications and accessions, *see* https://cil.nus.edu.sg/databasecil/1976-treaty-of-amity-and-cooperation-in-southeast-asia-3/.

Americas and partly the Arab world. The current regime comprises a political document, the ASEAN Human Rights Declaration (AHRD) and, at an institutional level, the ASEAN Intergovernmental Commission on Human Rights (AICHR). The merged Summit 'noted with appreciation' recent AICHR activities (they included advocating, among others, for human rights due diligence in the private sector, for environmental rights, and for the right to health), the convening of the ASEAN Human Rights Dialogue 2021,[705] and the conclusion of the Regional Dialogue on Self-Assessment of AICHR Progress After 10 Years, which had been conducted in between July and September 2021.[706]

230. The 40th and 41st Summits were also held as a double Summit, which was held with the physical presence of ASEAN leaders in Phnom Penh, Cambodia, in November 2022. The double Summit marked fifty-five years of ASEAN's existence. While it was not that important an anniversary, a celebratory Statement was issued, which basically repeated the goals of the Organisation and enumerated which projects and plans were underway and which would be adopted in the future to attain the same.[707] According to the Chairman's Statement, ASEAN leaders reaffirmed their commitment to advance the so-called ASEAN Centrality. The latter is the primary driving force behind the 'substantive dialogue and cooperation with our external partners, particularly in the context of all ASEAN-led mechanisms in building an ASEAN Community'.[708] As indicated above, while the mechanisms for bringing about the goals of an ASEAN Community are 'ASEAN-led', the Organisation appears to be dependent, perhaps too much so, on external partners. Suffice it to mention the Master Plan on ASEAN Connectivity (MPAC) 2025,[709] one of the major projects presently implemented by the Organisation.[710]

As regards the ASEAN Political-Security Community, the Summit reviewed developments in several societal problems and challenges, which are often associated with the commission of international crimes; they are tackled by several ASEAN Sectoral Bodies, headed by the ASEAN Ministerial Meeting on Transnational Crime (AMMTC).[711] From the topics, issues and developments that were discussed and the actions taken, suffice to mention the following:

---

705. Previously, the Dialogue had been held in 2013 and 2014; and since then, in 2022. At the 43rd ASEAN Summit (Sep. 2023), it was agreed to institutionalise the Dialogue and to turn it into a regular ASEAN activity, *see* ASEAN Leaders' Declaration on the ASEAN Human Rights Dialogue, 5 Sep. 2023, at: https://asean.org/asean-leaders-declaration-on-the-asean-human-rights-dialogue/.
706. *See* Chairman's Statement of the 38th and 39th ASEAN Summits, para. 40.
707. *See* ASEAN Leaders' Statement on the 55th Anniversary of ASEAN, 11 Nov. 2022, at: https://asean.org/wp-content/uploads/2022/11/03-ASEAN-Leaders-Statement-on-the-55th-Anniversary-of-ASEAN_.pdf. It is reproduced as Appendix 4 to this monograph.
708. *See* Chairman's Statement of the 40th and 41st ASEAN Summits, Phnom Penh, Cambodia, 11 Nov. 2022, para. 14, at: https://asean.org/wp-content/uploads/2022/11/01-Chairmans-Statement-of-the-40th-and-41st-ASEAN-Summits-2.pdf.
709. It was adopted on 6 Sep. 2016, at: https://asean.org/wp-content/uploads/2018/01/47.-December-2017-MPAC2025-2nd-Reprint-.pdf.
710. Chairman's Statement of the 40th and 41st ASEAN Summits, para. 26.
711. *Ibid.*, paras 29 et seq.

a. the implementation of the Bohol Trafficking in Persons (TIP) Work Plan 2017–2020,[712] the adoption of its Final Review Report,[713] and the work towards finalisation of the successor ASEAN Multi-Final Sectoral Work Plan Against Trafficking in Persons 2022–2027;[714]
b. the carrying out of the Work Plan of the ASEAN Plan of Action to Prevent and Counter the Rise of Radicalisation and Violent Extremism 2019–2025;[715]
c. the updated ASEAN Cybersecurity Cooperation Strategy 2021–2025;[716]
d. as regards combatting illicit drugs in the region, where the emphasis is on cross-sectoral and cross pillar coordination as well as on achieving a drugs-free region, review of the aforementioned Mid-Term Review of the ASEAN Work Plan on Securing Communities Against Illicit Drugs 2016–2025 and of the ASEAN Cooperation Plan to Tackle Illicit Drug Production and Trafficking in the Golden Triangle 2020–2022;
e. examination of developments on the ASEAN Extradition Treaty (AET) that is still negotiated; and[717]
f. recording the inaugural meeting of the ASEAN Ministers/ Attorneys General Meeting of the Central Authorities on Mutual Legal Assistance in Criminal Matters (AMAG-MLAT). The latter are the national authorities responsible for the effective carrying out of the ASEAN Treaty on Mutual Legal Assistance (MLAT) in Criminal Matters, which was adopted on 29 November 2004. Two

---

712. It was adopted in November 2017 to carry out the provisions of the 2015 ASEAN Convention and Plan of Action against Trafficking in Persons, Especially Women and Children, at: https://asean.org/wp-content/uploads/2021/01/Final-Version-of-Bohol-TIP-Work-Plan-2017-2020_13Nov2017.pdf.

713. Review of the Bohol Trafficking in Persons Work Plan 2017-2020, Final Report, adopted *ad referendum*, 5 Jul. 2022, at: https://asean.org/wp-content/uploads/2022/09/Adopted-Final-Review-Report-of-Bohol-TIP-Work-Plan-2017-2020.pdf.

714. It was finally adopted by the 17th AMMTC on 21 Aug. 2023, also known as 'Bohol TIP Work Plan 2.0', at: https://cil.nus.edu.sg/wp-content/uploads/2024/03/2023-2028-ASEAN-WP-TIP.pdf.

715. The so-called Bali Work Plan, text at: https://asean.org/wp-content/uploads/2012/05/Bali-PCRVE-Work-Plan-2019-2025_asof11Dec2019.pdf, which was adopted by the 13th AMMTC, *see* Joint Statement Thirteenth ASEAN Ministerial Meeting on Transnational Crime (13TH AMMTC), Bangkok, Thailand, 27 Nov. 2019, para. 5, at: https://asean.org/wp-content/uploads/2022/02/Adopted-Joint-Statement-of-the-13th-AMMTC-Bangkok-Thailand-27-November-2019.pdf.

716. Adopted by the 2nd ASEAN Digital Ministers' Meeting (ADGMIN), 27 to 28 Jan. 2022, at: https://cil.nus.edu.sg/wp-content/uploads/2023/08/2021-2025-ASEAN-Cybersercurity-Cooperation-Strategy.pdf. Generally, *see* K. Lin Tay, *ASEAN Cyber-security Cooperation: Towards a Regional Emergency-response Framework* (The International Institute for Strategic Studies, June 2023), at: https://www.iiss.org/globalassets/media-library---content--migration/files/research-papers/2023/06/asean-cyber-security-cooperation.pdf; M.B. Manantan (ed.), *Advancing Cyber Resiliency and Capacity in Southeast Asia* (Cyber ASEAN / Pacific Forum International, March 2024), at: https://cyberasean.pacforum.org/report.

717. The Sixth Meeting of ASEAN Senior Law Officials Meeting (ASLOM) Working Group on ASEAN Extradition Treaty, which has been tasked with drafting the treaty, was held in September 2023. The Twelfth ASEAN Law Ministers' Meeting (ALAWMM), held on 25 Jan. 2024 via videoconference, hosted and chaired by Myanmar, simply referred to the 'development of an ASEAN Extradition Treaty', *see* the Joint Communique, at: https://asean.org/wp-content/uploads/2024/01/Adopted-Joint-Communique-of-the-12th-ALAWMM-25-January-2024.pdf. AET should not be confused with the Model ASEAN Extradition Treaty, which was adopted on 12 Oct. 2018 by the Tenth ALAWMM Meeting, at: https://asean.org/wp-content/uploads/2021/01/ASEAN-Extradition-Treaty-by-10th-ALAWMM.pdf. It is not known if any ASEAN members have already concluded a treaty based on the Model Treaty.

things should be noted about this Treaty. First, the rather strangely worded clause on entry into force (Article 31(1)): it does not say that the Treaty itself will come into force; on the contrary, 'the Treaty shall enter into force for each Party ratifying, accepting, approving or acceding to it on the date of the deposit of its instrument of ratification, acceptance, approval or accession its party on the day that it will deposit its instrument of ratification/ acceptance/ approval'.[718] Second, the MLAT was elevated to an 'ASEAN Treaty' and the AMAG-MLAT was elevated to an ASEAN Sectoral Body under the ASEAN Political-Security Community (Annex 1 of the ASEAN Charter) at the Sixth Meeting of the Attorneys-General/Ministers of Justice and Minister of Law that took place in April 2019.[719]

231. The 42nd ASEAN Summit took place on 10–11 May 2023 under the Chairmanship of Indonesia (the theme was 'ASEAN Matters: Epicentrum of Growth') and was 'convened in accordance with the ASEAN Charter'.[720] This wording, which was also to be found in the Chairman's Statement of the 40th and 41st Summits, probably had to do with the non-participation of a representative of Myanmar on account of the *coup d'état* that had happened in the country in 2021 (the events are explained elsewhere in the monograph). However, considering that Article 7(1) of the ASEAN Charter stipulates that the ASEAN Summit *shall* comprise the Heads of State or Government of the Member States (emphasis added), it will be submitted that in case neither the head of state nor the head of government from a single Member State is present, the Summit is not lawfully composed. To put it otherwise, even though not expressly stated in the Charter, the quorum for the Summit to meet, to deliberate and to take decisions necessitates that all ten Member States are in attendance, barring any situations where objectively one or more representatives are unable to be physically present.[721] It follows that since no representative from Myanmar was deliberately present, this constituted an anomaly. This state of affairs was also discussed *supra*. But it should be noted that the ASEAN Summit has not adopted Rules of Procedure (the Charter is silent on this), which could have dealt with the consequences of Member States not attending its sessions, depending on whether they deliberately obtained (i.e., on their own volition) or were for other reasons presented.

232. As regards developments in the area of economic cooperation, the 42nd Summit was encouraged by the region's continued growth momentum (an expected increase of 4.7% for 2023 and 5.0% for 2024) 'propelled by strong domestic consumption, net exports, and accelerated recovery in services'. Leaders were determined to make Southeast Asia the centre of regional economic growth and an engine for global growth 'through robust cooperation by ensuring that ASEAN

718. All Member States became contracting between April 2005 and January 2013, *see* https://agreement.asean.org/agreement/detail/56.html.
719. *See* Chairman's Statement of the 34th ASEAN Summit, 23 Jun. 2019, para. 12.
720. *See* Chairman's Statement of the 42nd ASEAN Summit, Labuan Bajo, Indonesia, 10–11 May 2023, para. 1, at: https://asean.org/wp-content/uploads/2023/05/FINAL-Chairmans-Statement-42nd-ASEAN-Summit-1.pdf.
721. However, even in such a situation, it should be possible to join the Summit by teleconference.

remains relevant, competitive, forward-looking, resilient, and responsive'.[722] Moreover, ASEAN's digital transformation and the agenda for a digital economy integration were reviewed in the context of the implementation of the Bandar Seri Begawan Roadmap.[723] One of the principal goals is to conclude an ASEAN Digital Economy Framework Agreement (DEFA).[724] The conclusions of a study towards the commencement of negotiations were endorsed at the 55th AEM Meeting in the summer of August 2023, while on 31 October 2023, a document titled 'Study on the ASEAN Digital Economy Framework Agreement' was published. According to the latter documents, which makes quite interesting reading not least because it was prepared by a non-ASEAN private company (Boston Consulting Group) and supported by a non-ASEAN country (the Australian government through the Australia for ASEAN Futures Economic and Connectivity),[725] Member States were to begin negotiations in December 2023 and conclude them by the end of 2025. This was in line with the decision taken by ASEAN leaders when they gathered on 5 September 2023 on the occasion of the 43rd ASEAN Summit.[726] If successfully concluded, the implementation of DEFA will assist in creating the so-called ASEAN Digital Economic Community 2045.[727] It is expected to lead to very substantial financial benefits, calculated at 2 trillion USD by the year 2030.[728]

§3. The ASEAN Coordinating Council

233. In accordance with Article 8 of the ASEAN Charter, a Coordinating Council is established comprising the Foreign Ministers of all Member States. It meets at

722. Chairman's Statement of the 42nd ASEAN Summit, paras 52 and 53.
723. *Ibid.*, para. 60; *see* The Bandar Seri Begawan Roadmap: An ASEAN Digital Transformation Agenda to Accelerate ASEAN's Economic Recovery and Digital Economy Integration, which was adopted on 9 Sep. 2021 by the 53rd AEM Meeting and endorsed at the 20th ASEAN Economic Community Council (AECC) meeting on 18 Oct. 2021, at: https://asean.org/wp-content/uploads/2021/10/Bandar-Seri-Begawan-Roadmap-on-ASEAN-Digital-Transformation-Agenda_Endorsed.pdf.
724. *See* 55th ASEAN AEM Meeting, Semarang, Indonesia, Joint Media Statement, 19 Aug. 2023, paras 33 – 34, at: https://asean.org/wp-content/uploads/2023/08/AEM-55-JMS_19-Aug.pdf. *See* further, Framework for Negotiating ASEAN Digital Economy Framework Agreement, endorsed by the 23rd ASEAN Economic Community Council meeting on 3 Sep. 2023, at: https://asean.org/wp-content/uploads/2023/09/Framework-for-Negotiating-DEFA_ENDORSED_23rd-AECC-for-uploading.pdf.
725. Text at: https://asean.org/wp-content/uploads/2023/10/ASEAN-Digital-Economy-Framework-Agreement-Public-Summary_Final-published-version-1.pdf.
726. *See* Leaders' Statement on the Development of the ASEAN Digital Economy Framework Agreement (DEFA), at: https://asean.org/wp-content/uploads/2023/09/Leaders-Statement-DIGITAL-ECONOMY-FRAMEWORK-AGREEMENT.pdf. It should be noted that Myanmar was present at this meeting.
727. *See* M. Sefrina, *Understanding the ASEAN Digital Economy Framework Agreement: A Means to Support ASEAN Integration* (Economic Research Institute for ASEAN and East Asia Policy Brief No. 2023-01, April 2023), at: https://www.eria.org/uploads/media/policy-brief/FY2023/Understanding-the-ASEAN-Digital-Economy-Framework-Agreement.pdf.
728. *See* I. K. Rohman, K. N. Gunawan & A. Johanes, *The ASEAN Digital Economy Framework Agreement: Uniting or Dividing?* (RSIS Commentary No. 044, 3 Apr. 2024), at: https://www.rsis.edu.sg/wp-content/uploads/2024/04/CO24044.pdf.

least twice a year, and its work is supported by competent senior officials from the Member States. There is no indication in the Charter how the obligation to convene 'at least twice a year' is to be understood. Arguably, any meetings, which are held following the second meeting during the same year should not be considered as 'special or ad hoc meetings', as in the case of the ASEAN Summit, but as ordinary meetings.

234. The mandate of the Coordinating Council is laid down in the second paragraph of Article 8. In particular, it has the duty to prepare the meetings of the ASEAN Summit; to coordinate the implementation of the agreements and decisions, which have been adopted during the ASEAN Summits; to coordinate with the ASEAN Community Councils for the purpose of promoting policy coherence, efficiency and cooperation; to forward the reports of the ASEAN Community Councils to the ASEAN Summit; to discuss the annual reports prepared by the Secretary-General on the work of the Organisation; to consider the Secretary-General reports on the functions and operations of the ASEAN Secretariat and other relevant bodies; and to approve the appointment and the termination of the office of Deputy Secretaries-General, pursuant to the recommendations of the Secretary-General. On the whole, its mandate is akin to the role and the functions carried out by the executive organs of international organisations.

Being effectively the executive organ of ASEAN, the Coordinating Council is also mandated to undertake any other tasks, which are provided for in the ASEAN Charter, and/or any functions which may have been assigned to it by the Summit. To offer an illustration of the latter, reference will be made to Article 6(1) of the ASEAN Charter. This, as will be recalled, is the provision setting out the criteria to be fulfilled by the states which have applied to join ASEAN. It also stipulates that the procedural aspects of the accession process will be determined by the Coordinating Council. The crucial role that this organ plays in the accession process is confirmed by the third paragraph of Article 6, which authorises the Coordinating Council to recommend to the ASEAN Summit which applicant states should be admitted to membership. Furthermore, in accordance with Article 7(2)(b), the Coordinating Council is entitled to refer to the Summit any issue that it deems important, and the latter must not only deliberate it but also take decisions on it. Finally, under Article 7(2)(c), the Coordinating Council must adopt the Rules of Procedure for *the ad hoc* inter-Ministerial meetings, which are held in the context of the ASEAN Community Councils as per the instructions which have been given by the Summit.

235. The Coordinating Council has also an important role to play in the area of the external relations of ASEAN and, in particular, as regards the relations it pursues with third IGOs and other international institutions. In particular, Article 45 of the ASEAN Charter stipulates that, while 'ASEAN may seek an appropriate status with the United Nations system as well as with other sub-regional, regional, international organisations and institutions', it is the Coordinating Council which shall decide on the Organisation's participation in other sub-regional, regional, and international organisations.

236. To give an indication of the range of issues that are deliberated in a typical meeting of the Coordinating Council, reference will be made to the topics covered during the 32nd Coordinating Council Meeting and ASEAN Foreign Ministers Retreat, which was held in Jakarta in February 2023.[729] They were the following: the priorities of ASEAN for the year 2023; the further development of ASEAN Institutions; developments in the area of human rights; the continued commitment to the Southeast Asia Nuclear Weapon-Free Zone; developments in the ASEAN Political-Security Community Cooperation, in the ASEAN Economic Community Cooperation and in the ASEAN Socio-Cultural Community Cooperation; developments in the ASEAN Outlook on the Indo-Pacific;[730] developments in trade partnerships with third states; the question of sustainable development; developments in two principal projects, the ASEAN Connectivity and the ASEAN Centrality; the membership application of Timor-Leste; reaffirming the universally recognised principles of international law, including the 1982 United Nations Convention on the Law of the Sea (UNCLOS); the developing situation in the South China Sea as it affects Member States; developments in the Korean Peninsula and in Myanmar; the question of religious tolerance; and, finally, developments in TAC.

729. *See* Press Statement by the Chair of the 32nd ASEAN Coordinating Council (ACC) Meeting and ASEAN Foreign Ministers' Retreat, Jakarta, 3–4 Feb. 2023, at: https://asean.org/wp-content/uploads/2023/02/CHAIRs-PRESS-STATEMENT-32nd-ACC-AMM-RETREAT.pdf.

730. The Outlook is a mechanism guiding ASEAN's engagement in the Asia-Pacific and Indian Ocean regions; *see* the Concept Note on the ASEAN Roadmap for Promoting ASEAN Outlook on the Indo-Pacific, and J. Lin, *Advancing the ASEAN Outlook on the Indo-Pacific Beyond Indonesia's Chairmanship* (Yusof Ishak Institute Perspective, Issue 2024/9, 2 Feb. 2024) at: https://www.iseas.edu.sg/wp-content/uploads/2024/01/ISEAS_Perspective_2024_9.pdf.

Part III. Activities

Chapter 1. Settlement of Disputes

237. The peaceful settlement of disputes has assumed a more prominent role in ASEAN as it transforms itself into a rules-based organisation and embarks on institution-building processes. This development gains added significance in light of the existence of long-standing territorial and boundary disputes between ASEAN Member States, such as that regarding the Temple of Preah Vihear complex on the Cambodian/Thai border which the ICJ had awarded to Cambodia in 1962,[731] and maritime boundary disputes, particularly in relation to competing claims to the Paracel and Spratly Islands, among others, in the South China Sea, which also include China.[732] The generalisation that Asian States have customarily regarded formal legal dispute resolution procedures with some wariness seems to have some foundation.[733] The ethos that found expression in the maxim of the 'ASEAN Way' emphasised informality, consensus and non-interference and sought to avoid the

731. *Temple of Preah Vihear (Cambodia v. Thailand)*, Merits, I.C.J. Reports 1962, 6. Serious border clashes broke out between Cambodia and Thailand in 2010/11, leading Cambodia to request from the ICJ, *inter alia*, the urgent indication of provisional measures of protection, ICJ Press Release No. 2011/14, 28 Apr. 2011. The ICJ duly ordered both parties to withdraw their military forces from the disputed area and refrain from armed activities therein, *Request for Interpretation of the Judgment of 15 June 1962 in the case concerning the Temple of Preah Vihear (Cambodia v. Thailand)*, Provisional Measures, I.C.J. Reports 2011, 537. In November 2013, the ICJ reaffirmed that Cambodia had sovereignty over Preah Vihear, *Request for Interpretation of the Judgment of 15 June 1962 in the case concerning the Temple of Preah Vihear (Cambodia v. Thailand)*, Judgment, I.C.J. Reports 2013, 281. In February 2011, the UN Security Council called upon ASEAN to facilitate a resolution to the dispute between the two countries, UNSC 'Security Council Press Statement on Cambodia-Thailand Border Situation' (14 Feb. 2011), Press Release SC/10174, which led to both countries agreeing to a team of Indonesian observers to monitor the area, 'Thailand and Cambodia reach deal on temple border' (*BBC News*, 21 Dec. 2011), https://www.bbc.co.uk/news/world-asia-pacific-16294309. However, further agreement between the two parties did not prove possible, *Request for Interpretation of the Judgment of 15 June 1962 in the case concerning the Temple of Preah Vihear (Cambodia v. Thailand)*, Provisional Measures, I.C.J. Reports 2011, 537, 550–551.

732. *See* C.-H. Park, *The South China Sea Disputes: Who Owns the Islands and the Natural Resources*, 5 Ocean Dev. & Int'l L.J. 33 (1978); J.I. Charney, *Central East Asian Maritime Boundaries and the Law of the Sea*, 89 A.J.I.L. 724 (1995). In 2016, an arbitral tribunal, while it did not rule on the sovereignty over islands or delimit maritime boundaries, rejected China's claims to maritime entitlements in the South China Sea, *South China Sea Arbitration (Philippines v. China)*, Award, 33 R.I.A.A. 153 (2015-16).

733. T. Koh, *International Law and the Peaceful Resolution of Disputes: Asian Perspectives, Contributions, and Challenges*, 1 Asian J.I.L. 57, 59 (2011); S. Chesterman, *Asia's Ambivalence About International Law and Institutions: Past, Present and Futures*, 27 E.J.I.L. 945, 962–965 (2016).

adversarial and confrontational conditions associated with formal legal adjudication.[734] Rather, resort to ad hoc diplomatic or political arrangements which did not constrain states unduly was traditionally the preferred mode of dispute settlement.[735] This policy has entailed 'a combination of discussion, consultation and formal talks'.[736] These methods may be said to have the advantage of flexibility and compromise and allow for 'a carefully negotiated settlement'.[737] However, in recent years such guardedness has been set aside and recourse to international tribunals has become a viable option.[738] In 2010, Asean Member States adopted in Hanoi the Protocol to the ASEAN Charter on Dispute Settlement Mechanisms, a salient development in that Organisation's progress towards promoting peace and security and conflict prevention and management.[739] The Protocol puts in place a formal system to facilitate the resolution of disputes among ASEAN Member States concerning the interpretation or application of the ASEAN Charter.[740] This development, which was envisaged by the ASEAN Charter,[741] was necessitated by the need to enhance ASEAN's dispute resolution capacity and to establish an operational structure for the more effective management and resolution of disputes.[742] ASEAN thus joined

734. D. Seah, *The ASEAN Charter*, 58 I.C.L.Q. 197, 198–199 (2009); M. Ewing-Chow & L. Bernard, *The ASEAN Charter: The Legalization of ASEAN?*, in *Global Administrative Law: The Casebook* 115, 116 (S. Cassese et al. eds, Institute for International Law & Justice 2012). *See* further B. Loke, *The 'ASEAN Way': Towards Regional Order and Security Cooperation*, 30 Melb. J. Pol. 8 (2005).
735. Ewing-Chow & Bernard *ibid.*; Koh, 57–58. Fifteen territorial disputes were settled by negotiation between ASEAN Member States in the period 1969–1997, R. Amer, *The Association of Southeast Asian Nations and the Management of Territorial Disputes*, 9 Boundary & Sec. Bull. 81, 81–82 (1999).
736. Amer, 84.
737. A. Aust, *Handbook of International Law* 7 397 (Cambridge U. Press 2 ed. 2010); *Handbook on the Peaceful Settlement of Disputes Between States* paras 22–23 (United Nations 1992) (*Handbook*).
738. These include the following: ICJ, *Sovereignty over Pulau Litigan and Pulau Sipadan* (*Indonesia/Malaysia*), Judgment, 17 Dec. 2002, I.C.J. Reports 2002, 625; ICJ, *Sovereignty over Pedra Branca/Pulau Batu Puteh, Middle Rocks and South Ledge* (*Malaysia/Singapore*), Judgment, 23 May 2008, I.C.J. Reports 2008, 12; *Request for Interpretation of the Judgment of 15 June 1962 in the case concerning the Temple of Preah Vihear (Cambodia v. Thailand) (Cambodia v. Thailand)*, Judgment, I.C.J. Reports 2013, and international arbitration, *Land Reclamation by Singapore In and Around the Straits of Johore (Malaysia v. Singapore)*, 27 R.I.A.A. 133 (2008). *See* Chesterman, 961–962.
739. Protocol to the ASEAN Charter on Dispute Settlement Mechanisms (8 Apr. 2010). The Protocol entered into force on 28 Jul. 2017, at: http://agreement.asean.org/media/download/20200128121018.pdf.
740. ASEAN Charter (20 Nov. 2007), 2624 U.N.T.S. 223. The Protocol applies also to other ASEAN instruments which do not specifically provide for dispute settlement mechanisms.
741. Ewing-Chow & Bernard, 118.
742. Report of the Eminent Persons Group on the ASEAN Charter, para. 64 (EPG) (13 Jan. 2007), https://asean.org/wp-content/uploads/images/archive/19247.pdf. The existing ASEAN conflict management structure was deemed deficient, Amer, 85. Resort to regional dispute settlement mechanisms is encouraged by the UN Charter Art. 33(1), UN General Assembly Res. 2625 (XXV) 1970 Declaration on Friendly Relations and Co-operation among States in Accordance with the Charter of the United Nations, and UN General Assembly Res. 37/590 (1982) Manila Declaration on the Peaceful Settlement of Disputes, Part I, para. 6 (Manila Declaration).

the ranks of those multilateral institution-based systems of inter-state dispute settlement.[743] The willingness shown by Asean Member States, heretofore jealous guardians of their sovereignty, to undertake a prior commitment to dispute settlement mechanisms can be deemed significant. However, as will be seen, it cannot be said to set up a truly comprehensive regime of dispute settlement.

§1. Treaty of Amity and Co-operation in Southeast Asia

238. Prior to the adoption of the ASEAN Charter in 2007 ASEAN made no provision for institutional or formal means of dispute settlement until the adoption of the TAC in 1976.[744] The Declaration of ASEAN Concord had that very year committed Member States to 'rely exclusively on peaceful processes in the settlement of intra-regional differences'[745] and the TAC reiterated that pledge by declaring the settlement of disputes by peaceful means a 'fundamental principle'.[746] The TAC provides for consensual and 'diplomatic', that is, non-judicial, modes for the peaceful resolution of disputes between State parties[747] as opposed to third-party legal

743. Cf. Revised General Act for the Pacific Settlement of International Disputes (28 Apr. 1949) 71 U.N.T.S. 101 (General Act), American Treaty on Pacific Settlement (Pact of Bogotá) (30 Apr. 1948) 30 U.N.T.S. 449, European Convention for the Peaceful Settlement of Disputes (29 Apr. 1957) 320 U.N.T.S. 423. All have either attracted few parties or remain underutilised.

744. Treaty of Amity and Co-operation in Southeast Asia, signed 24 Feb. 1976, entered into force on 21 Jun. 1976, 1025 U.N.T.S. 297. TAC has been ratified by all Member States. Under the Manila Protocol Amending the Treaty of Amity and Co-operation in Southeast Asia, signed 15 Dec. 1987, entered into force 2 Jul. 1988, http://agreement.asean.org/media/download/20131231005052.pdf, non-ASEAN States, the 'dialogue partners', can accede to it. States such as Australia, Canada, China, France, Germany, India, United Kingdom and USA have done so, as well as the EU. More recent parties include Argentina, Chile, Colombia, Denmark, Egypt, Greece, Iran, Kuwait, Morocco, Netherlands, Norway, Peru, Saudi Arabia, South Africa, Spain and Ukraine. For the full list of parties *see* https://cil.nus.edu.sg/databasecil/1976-treaty-of-amity-and-cooperation-in-southeast-asia-3/. *See* further Second Protocol Amending the Treaty of Amity and Co-operation in Southeast Asia Art. 1, signed 25 Jul. 1998, entered into force 17 Jul. 2000, http://agreement.asean.org/media/download/20140117142023.pdf. The Third Protocol Amending the Treaty of Amity and Co-operation in Southeast Asia, signed 3 Jul. 2010, entered into force 8 Jun. 2012, permits accession by regional organisations composed of sovereign states, such as the EU, http://agreement.asean.org/media/download/20140117144104.pdf. *See* S. Yamakage, *Evolving ASEAN and the Changing Roles of the TAC*, in *ASEAN@50: Retrospectives and Perspective son the Making, Substance, Significance and Future of ASEAN. Volume 4. Building ASEAN Community: Political-Security and Socio-cultural Reflections* 39, 43 (A. Baviera & L. Maramis eds, Economic Research Institute for ASEAN and East Asia 2017). It should also be observed that ASEAN has concluded bilateral agreements on dispute settlement with third states, e.g., Agreement on Dispute Settlement Mechanism under the Framework Agreement on Comprehensive Economic Cooperation between the Association of Southeast Asian Nations and the Republic of India (13 Aug. 2009), https://asean.org/wp-content/uploads/images/2012/Economic/AEM/document/22679.pdf.

745. Amer, 85–86. *See* Declaration of ASEAN Concord, http://cil.nus.edu.sg/1976/1976-declaration-of-asean-concord-signed-on-24-february-1976-in-bali-indonesia-by-the-heads-of-stategovernment/.

746. TAC Art. 2(d).

747. Rule of Procedure 6(2) of the High Council, http://yamakage-ken.com/citrus/projects/ASEAN/ASEAN/AS20010723E%20Rules%20of%20Procedure%20Treaty%20of%20Amity%20.htm. An arbitral tribunal has expressed the view that the TAC does not provide a 'binding mechanism' but functions as a facilitator enabling the parties to a dispute to agree on the means of settlement, *South China Sea Arbitration (Philippines v. China)*, Award, 33 R.I.A.A. 153 (2015-16), para. 159.

adjudication.[748] It is appropriate for disputes in the political and security field[749] which are not concerned with the interpretation or application of any ASEAN instrument.[750] Given the scope of the ASEAN Charter the TAC may now have lesser relevance insofar as intra-ASEAN disputes are concerned but may play a useful role with regard to disputes with dialogue partners.[751] Nevertheless, ASEAN Member States remain committed to its principles.[752] A standing body exists in the form of the High Council, consisting of representatives from the ASEAN Member States and, if relevant, from non-ASEAN States directly involved in the dispute.[753] Decisions are taken by consensus.[754] First and foremost, disputes should be settled between the parties through 'friendly negotiations'.[755] Failing this, the High Council is meant to 'take cognizance of the dispute' and accordingly recommend 'appropriate means of settlement such as good offices, mediation, inquiry or conciliation', that is, the traditional diplomatic methods for the resolution of inter-state disputes.[756] The High Council may offer its good offices or, if the parties agree, it may constitute itself into a committee of mediation, enquiry or conciliation.[757] However, the High Council's role is considerably limited by the fact the parties must agree to its involvement.[758] Resort to other procedures, as set out in Article 33(1) of the UN Charter, which includes judicial settlement, taking in, of course, the ICJ, is permitted, although this is clearly considered a last resort.[759] The lack of any express provision for judicial settlement has been described as one of the TAC's 'glaring weaknesses'.[760] It should be noted that the High Council has yet to become operational.[761]

§2. Manila Protocol on Enhanced Dispute Settlement Procedure

239. Disputes relating to economic and trade agreements are governed by a separate dispute settlement procedure. The aspiration to develop economic cooperation and integration and trade liberalisation led ASEAN to adopt the Framework

748. Amer, 86–87; Ewing-Chow & Bernard, 121–122; W. Woon, *Dispute Settlement in ASEAN*, 1 Korean J. Int'l & Comp. L. 92, 96 (2013).
749. Disputes 'likely to disturb regional peace and harmony', TAC Art. 13.
750. ASEAN Charter Art. 24(2).
751. Yamakage, 46.
752. ASEAN 2025: Forging Ahead Together: ASEAN Political-Security Community Blueprint 2025, s. A.1.7.
753. TAC Art. 14 (as amended by the First Protocol).
754. Rule of Procedure 19 of the High Council.
755. TAC Art. 13.
756. *Ibid.*, Art. 15. *See* J.G. Merrills, *International Dispute Settlement* 27–87 (Cambridge U. Press 3rd ed. 1998).
757. TAC Art. 15.
758. *Ibid.*, Art. 16; Rules of Procedures 8–9 of the High Council. *See* Amer, 88–89; Woon, *ibid.*
759. TAC Art. 17.
760. Woon, *ibid.*, who observes that neither is any express reference made to arbitration.
761. Its Rules of Procedure were adopted only in 2001, Amer, 88. One reason for this may be that third states, 'dialogue partners', have the status of observers at meetings of the High Council and that ASEAN States are reluctant to air their differences in public, Woon, 97.

Agreement on Enhancing ASEAN Economic Cooperation in 1992.[762] The Agreement contains an imprecise dispute settlement clause which necessitated the drafting of more structured procedures.[763] The prevailing instrument is the Manila Protocol on Enhanced Dispute Settlement Procedure, adopted in 2019,[764] a revised version of the Vientiane Protocol on Enhanced Dispute Settlement Procedure 2004.[765] The Manila Protocol is designed to address flaws and omissions in the Vientiane Protocol[766] but does not supersede it *in toto*. The Manila Protocol applies to disputes brought under it, whereas disputes brought under the Vientiane Protocol continue to be governed by it in principle.[767] However, the Vientiane Protocol has never been invoked and is therefore effectively terminated. The Manila Protocol removes any ambiguity as to whether future economic agreements are subject to ASEAN dispute settlement mechanisms.[768] Economic agreements can therefore be updated by the Secretariat in consultation with and endorsed by the Senior Economic Officials Meeting (SEOM).[769]

240. Recourse to the Manila Protocol is optional and resort may be made to other fora.[770] This can include good offices, conciliation or mediation.[771] In general, disputes should be 'settled amicably' through consultations between the disputing states.[772] Consultations under the Manila Protocol are distinct from, and without prejudice to, consultations under covered agreements.[773] Solutions emanating from consultations must be consistent with the covered agreements and must not nullify or impair benefits in favour of any Member State under those agreements.[774] Should the Member State to which the request for consultations is made not reply within a certain time frame or the consultations fail to settle the dispute within sixty days, the complaining party may request the SEOM to establish a panel to examine the

---

762. Framework Agreement on Enhancing ASEAN Economic Cooperation (28 Jan. 1992), I.L.M. 31 (1992), 506 (Agreement).
763. *Ibid.*, Art. 9.
764. ASEAN Protocol on Enhanced Dispute Settlement (20 Dec. 2019) Art. 1(1), http://agreement.asean.org/media/download/20200128120825.pdf. The Manila Protocol entered into force on 20 Jun. 2022. For comment *see* E.W. Sim, *ASEAN Further Enhances Its Dispute Settlement Mechanism*, 7 Indonesian J. Int'l & Comp. L. 279 (2020).
765. Vientiane Protocol on Enhanced Dispute Settlement (29 Nov 2004), 2624 U.N.T.S. 177. The Vientiane Protocol governed disputes relating to economic and trade agreements, *see* ASEAN Charter Art. 24(3). The Vientiane Protocol superseded the Protocol on Dispute Settlement Mechanism (20 Nov. 1996), Art. 21(2).
766. Sim, 280–283.
767. Manila Protocol Art. 27(3). The Manila Protocol applies also to agreements listed in Appendix I, the 'covered agreements', Art. 1.
768. Manila Protocol Art. 1.
769. *Ibid.*, Art. 26(2)(a). The SEOM is the body that administers the Manila Protocol and, in general, the consultation and dispute settlement provisions of the covered agreements, *ibid.*, Art. 2(1).
770. Manila Protocol Art. 1(3). *See* ASEAN 2025: Forging Ahead Together: ASEAN Economic Community Blueprint 2025, s. III.A.82.iv.
771. Manila Protocol Art. 4.
772. *Ibid.*, Art. 3(1).
773. *Ibid.*
774. *Ibid.*, Art. 3(7). *See* Sim, 284.

matter.[775] Under the Manila Protocol, panels can address all claims on which a finding is necessary to ensure an effective resolution rather than the covered agreements only under the Vientiane Protocol.[776] A panel, after objectively assessing the dispute, examining the facts of the case and the applicability of and conformity with the relevant provisions of the Agreement or any covered agreements, submits a report to the SEOM containing its findings and recommendations.[777] The parties to the dispute may appeal the panel reports to the Appellate Body[778] on points of law and legal interpretation only.[779] The Appellate Body's report is adopted by the SEOM, unless it decides by consensus not to do so, and must be accepted unconditionally by the parties.[780] The reports adopted by the SEOM are binding on the parties to the dispute which must comply with them;[781] the SEOM supervises compliance.[782] Failure to comply may result in the imposition of temporary sanctions[783] which itself can lead to this issue being submitted to arbitration.[784] Significantly, provision is made for recourse to arbitration should the parties agree.[785] These nearly identical features in the Vientiane Protocol were described as having 'clear similarities to the dispute settlement procedure of the World Trade Organization'[786] and that depiction seems just as apt in the case of the Manila Protocol.

241. Special provision is made for Least-Developed Member States. Accordingly, Member States must 'exercise due restraint' in resorting to the Manila Protocol and seeking reparation from a Least-Developed Member State.[787] Should a satisfactory solution prove elusive in such a dispute the Chair of the SEOM may offer his or her good offices, conciliation or mediation.[788] Prima facie such special treatment does not appear compatible with the principle of sovereign equality of states but may be explicable on the basis of the economic and legal underdevelopment of some states.

775. Manila Protocol Art. 6(1), although the SEOM may decide against by consensus. A single panel may be established where more than one Member State make a complaint about the same matter, *ibid.*, Art. 12(1). On the composition of the panels, *see ibid.*, Art. 8.
776. Manila Protocol Art. 7(2).
777. Manila Protocol Art. 9. The interests of other Member States under a covered agreement must be taken into account, while those of third parties, i.e., those with 'a substantial interest' in the dispute, have a right to be heard before the panel and submit written opinions, *ibid.*, Art. 13(1), (2). The rights of third parties in the proceedings have been expanded under the Manila Protocol, *ibid.*, Art. 13(4).
778. Manila Protocol Art. 14(1). On the composition of the Appellate Body, *see ibid.*, 14(1)-(3).
779. *Ibid.*, Art. 14(6). Third parties do not have a right of appeal but those with 'a substantial interest' may be heard before the Appellate Body and submit written opinions, *ibid.*, Art. 14(4).
780. *Ibid.*, Art. 14(13). The Appellate Body is generally expected to issue its report within sixty days, *ibid.*, Art. 14(5).
781. *Ibid.*, Art. 17(1).
782. *Ibid.*, Art. 17(6).
783. *Ibid.*, Art. 18(1).
784. *Ibid.*, Art. 18(7).
785. *Ibid.*, Art. 19.
786. Woon, 99.
787. Manila Protocol Art. 23(1).
788. *Ibid.*, Art. 23(2).

242. The timeframe for the issuance of the reports of the panel and the Appellate Body under the Manila Protocol has been increased. The panel now has six months in which to submit its report and a further three months in exceptional cases,[789] whereas the Appellate Body may request extra time but no more than a further thirty days.[790] The SEOM is also given extra time to consider the panel report.[791] Furthermore, the parties may request extra time to comply with a finding.[792] Nevertheless, the Manila Protocol sets a maximum timeframe of nine months from the establishment of the panel to the date the SEOM considers the final report or twelve months if the report is appealed.[793] However, as a general rule, timeframes may be modified by the parties.[794]

243. The Manila Protocol effects certain institutional changes. The role of the SEOM has been expanded.[795] The provisions on the composition of panels are now integrated into the text of the treaty rather than in an appendix.[796] Members of panels and the Appellate Body and arbitrators are now subject to rules of conduct.[797] In addition, working procedures are set out for the panels and appellate review.[798] Interestingly, the Secretariat is authorised to provide legal advice and assistance in an impartial manner to a Member State if requested.[799]

§3. Dispute Settlement under the ASEAN Charter

244. The recommendation by the EPG that the ASEAN institutional framework be extended to encompass dispute settlement mechanisms, including binding adjudication, proved persuasive.[800] Accordingly, the peaceful settlement of disputes, as set out in Article 2(2)(d) of the ASEAN Charter, is one of ASEAN's foundational principles. This basic pledge is supplemented and expanded upon by Chapter VIII of the ASEAN Charter on the Settlement of Disputes which contains a commitment in general terms to the establishment and maintenance of institutional dispute settlement mechanisms.[801] It is important to note that the ASEAN Charter does not impose an obligation on Member States to the compulsory settlement of disputes, but in keeping with their obligations under general international law Member States 'endeavour to resolve peacefully all disputes in a timely manner through dialogue, consultation and negotiation'.[802] The Member States still retain their autonomy

789. *Ibid.*, Art. 10(2).
790. *Ibid.*, Art. 14(5).
791. *Ibid.*, Art. 11(2).
792. *Ibid.*, Art. 17(2).
793. *Ibid.*, Art. 21(1).
794. *Ibid.*, Art. 21(2).
795. Sim, passim.
796. Manila Protocol Art. 8.
797. *Ibid.*, Art. 5, Appendix II.
798. *Ibid.*, Appendices III, IV.
799. *Ibid.*, Art. 22(4).
800. EPG Report para. 64.
801. ASEAN Charter Arts 22(2), 25. *See* Ewing-Chow & Bernard, 123–125.
802. ASEAN Charter Art. 22(1).

therefore, but the ASEAN Charter could be said to play the role of a 'facilitator'. Various dispute settlement methods are envisaged in the ASEAN Charter, including good offices, conciliation and mediation, without a framework being specified.[803] The ASEAN Charter mechanism does not replace, but is supplemental to, existing arrangements.[804] In fact, it could even be described as residual. This is because disputes relating to specific ASEAN instruments are to be settled in accordance with the system specified therein.[805] Where this is not the case, disputes are to be settled peacefully in accordance with the TAC, which remains an option.[806] The renewed outbreak of violence in 2010/11 between Cambodia and Thailand over their border dispute engaged the procedures both in the ASEAN Charter and the TAC and resulted in an ASEAN-negotiated interim resolution. Disputes concerning treaties of an economic nature are to be settled in accordance with the Vientiane Protocol unless specifically provided for otherwise.[807] With regard to disputes concerning the interpretation or application of the ASEAN Charter[808] or other ASEAN instruments, where not otherwise specifically provided, appropriate dispute settlement mechanisms may be established, including arbitration.[809] The inclusion of arbitration appears to have been a compromise between the competing visions of the advocates of the ASEAN Way and supporters of rules-based standing institutions.[810] However, there seemed to be a general acceptance that an ASEAN court would be a premature step.[811] The Protocol to the ASEAN Charter on Dispute Settlement Mechanisms was thus signed in 2010 with the purpose of making these mechanisms available.[812] Recourse to other procedures is not excluded as the modes available under Article 33(1) of the UN Charter are explicitly permitted.[813] Disputes

803. *Ibid.*, Arts 23, 25. *Also* TAC Art. 15. Inquiry is not specifically mentioned in the ASEAN Charter but could come within the scope of the conciliation procedure, *Handbook*, para. 140. Conciliation and mediation have been picked out as suitable modalities for dispute settlement in Asia, Koh, 57–58. An example of mediation is that envisaged by the Five-Point Consensus on Myanmar, *see* the aforementioned Chairman's Statement on the ASEAN Leaders' Meeting, 24 Apr. 2021.
804. Woon, *ibid.* However, it should be noted that, in the case of any inconsistency between the rights and obligations of Member States under prior ASEAN treaties and the ASEAN Charter, the latter prevails, ASEAN Charter Art. 52(2). *See* Vienna Convention on the Law of Treaties Art. 30 (22 May 1969), 1155 U.N.T.S. 331 (VCLT).
805. ASEAN Charter Art. 24(1). An example is the Agreement on Transboundary Haze Pollution (10 Jun. 2002), https://asean.org/wp-content/uploads/2021/01/ASEANAgreementonTransboundaryHazePollution-1.pdf, which provides that disputes are to be settled amicably by consultation or negotiation, Art. 27.
806. ASEAN Charter Art. 24(2).
807. ASEAN Charter Art. 24(3).
808. *Ibid.*, Art. 51(2). This phrase is capable of having an alternate or cumulative meaning, M.O. Hudson, *The Permanent Court of International Justice 1920-1942* 640–641 (MacMillan 1943).
809. ASEAN Charter Art. 25.
810. Woon, 99–100; H.D. Phan, *Towards A Rules-Based ASEAN: The Protocol to The ASEAN Charter on Dispute Settlement Mechanisms*, 5 Y.B. Arb. & Mediation 254, 257–258 (2013).
811. Woon, 99.
812. 'ASEAN signs protocol mechanisms to settle disputes' ', https://en.vietnamplus.vn/asean-signs-protocol-on-mechanisms-to-settle-disputes/18184.vnp.
813. ASEAN Charter Art. 28. *See also* TAC Art. 17.

which remain unresolved are submitted to the ASEAN Summit for decision,[814] a procedure described as 'highly unsatisfactory' due to the leading role played by consensus.[815]

245. Compliance with the outcome of a dispute settlement mechanism, either an arbitral award or settlement agreement, is monitored by ASEAN's Secretary-General.[816] In the event of non-compliance, an affected Member State may refer the matter to the ASEAN Summit for decision,[817] thus endowing it with '*quasi-judicial* oversight'.[818] Such recourse to a third authority is not an unusual feature.[819] In April 2012, Rules for Reference of Non-Compliance to the ASEAN Summit were adopted in order to provide guidelines as to the procedures to be applied in instances of non-compliance.[820] The Rules for Reference provide yet another example of ASEAN's 'quiet diplomacy'. Before a case of non-compliance can be submitted to the ASEAN Summit, the ASEAN Coordinating Council[821] must seek to facilitate discussions between the disputants with a view to securing compliance.[822] Only where such intervention fails to secure an outcome is the matter to be referred to the ASEAN Summit by the ASEAN Coordinating Council along with its recommendations.[823] While ASEAN's lack of formal punitive powers may be considered a failure in this context, nevertheless the adoption of disciplinary measures cannot be excluded.

§4. The Protocol to the ASEAN Charter on Dispute Settlement Mechanisms

246. The ASEAN Charter undertakes a general commitment to the establishment and maintenance of institutional dispute settlement mechanisms; an institutionalised system providing specific dispute resolution methods had to await the Protocol to the ASEAN Charter on Dispute Settlement Mechanisms 2010 (Protocol).[824] The Protocol reaffirms the central directive that it applies to disputes concerning the interpretation

814. ASEAN Charter Art. 26. *See further* Rules for Reference of Unresolved Disputes to the ASEAN Summit, https://www.asean.org/wp-content/uploads/images/archive/documents/Rules%20of%20Reference%20of%20Unresolved%20Disputes%20to%20the%20ASEAN%20Summit.pdf.
815. E.K.B. Tan, *The ASEAN Charter as 'Legs to Go Places': Ideational Norms and Pragmatic Legalism in Community Building in Southeast Asia*, 12 S.Y.B.I.L. 171, 186 (2008).
816. ASEAN Charter Art. 27(1).
817. *Ibid.*, Art. 27(2). *See also ibid.*, Art. 20(4).
818. D.A. Desierto, *ASEAN's Constitutionalization of International Law: Challenges to Evolution under the New ASEAN Charter*, 49 Colum. J. Transnat'l L. 268, 290 (2010–2011).
819. Cf. European Convention for the Peaceful Settlement of Disputes Art. 39(2); Pact of Bogotá Art. L.
820. Rules for Reference of Non-Compliance to the ASEAN Summit to the Protocol to the ASEAN Charter on Dispute Settlement Mechanisms, at: http://agreement.asean.org/media/download/20160316010200.pdf.
821. Comprised of ASEAN Foreign Ministers, ASEAN Charter Art. 8.
822. Rules for Reference 3(a).
823. *Ibid.*, Rule 5.
824. Protocol to the ASEAN Charter on Dispute Settlement Mechanisms, adopted 8 Apr. 2010, entered into force 28 Jul. 2017, at: http://agreement.asean.org/media/download/20200128121018.pdf.

or application of the ASEAN Charter,[825] other ASEAN instruments which expressly state that the Protocol, or part thereof, applies[826] or other ASEAN instruments unless specific means of dispute settlement are already provided for.[827] Again States parties are urged to make every effort to reach a mutually agreed solution to their dispute.[828] The term 'dispute' is not defined either in the ASEAN Charter or in the Protocol, but the fact that Article 22(1) of the ASEAN Charter refers to 'all disputes' points towards legal and political differences arising over the ASEAN Charter coming within the Protocol's ambit.[829] Whilst arbitration may constitute the most suitable procedure for handling legal disputes, there is nothing in the ASEAN Charter or the Protocol to suggest that arbitration is restricted to legal disputes.[830] There is no reason to suppose why in light of the ASEAN Charter's governing principles disputes including but not limited to territorial and boundary issues, such as in the South China Sea, the use of force, systematic and gross human rights violations, including the ill-treatment of minorities, such as the Rohingya in Myanmar,[831] or the process of democratisation, should not in principle be amenable to the Protocol's methods.

247. Only States parties may have recourse to the Protocol and, like other similar treaties, parties commit themselves in advance to the possibility of submitting certain categories of dispute to the settlement modes set out therein.[832] However, submission of a dispute to any of the available procedures rests on consent. This is because in each specific instance the respondent state must agree to the dispute

---

According to Woon, 101, the Protocol is modelled on the Vientiane Protocol. *See* generally, Phan; G.J. Naldi, *The ASEAN Protocol on Dispute Settlement Mechanisms: An Appraisal*, 5 J. Int'l Disp. Res. 105 (2014).

825. Protocol Art. 2(1)(a). *See* ASEAN Charter Art. 25.
826. Protocol Art. 2(1)(c).
827. *Ibid.*, Art. 2(1)(b). However, parties to a dispute may mutually agree that the Protocol shall apply, *ibid.*, Art. 2(2).
828. *Ibid.*, Art. 3(2).
829. Many disputes have legal and political dimensions which are intertwined, Merrills, 155–159. International law defines a legal dispute as 'a disagreement on a point of law or fact, a conflict of legal views or of interests', *Mavrommatis Palestine Concessions (Greece v. Great Britain)*, Jurisdiction, P.C.I.J., Series A, No. 2, 11 (1924). A contemporary formulation has it that a dispute exists where States 'hold clearly opposite views concerning the question of the performance or non-performance of certain international obligations', *Application of the International Convention on the Elimination of All Forms of Racial Discrimination (Georgia v. Russia),* Preliminary Objections, I.C.J. Reports 2011, 70, 115.
830. Hague Convention for the Pacific Settlement of International Disputes Art. 38 (18 Oct. 1907), http://www.pca-cpa.org/showpage.asp?pag_id=1187.
831. This is evidenced by the fact that proceedings have been instituted against Myanmar at the ICJ, *Application Instituting Proceedings and Request for Provisional Measures* (*Republic of The Gambia v. Republic of the Union of Myanmar*) (11 Nov. 2019), I.C.J. Press Release No. 2019/47 (11 Nov. 2019).
832. The Protocol was subject to ratification by all the Member States to enter into force, Protocol Art. 19(2). The Protocol does not address accession by new Member States. Given the import of the Protocol and the fact that it can become operational only with its unanimous acceptance by Member States it is submitted that membership of ASEAN should be conditional on the simultaneous ratification of the Protocol.

being submitted to the procedure in question.[833] However, there appears to be a notable exception to this general rule. The use of mandatory terms, the verb 'direct' and the noun 'direction', in Articles 9(1) and 10(1) of the Protocol suggests that in a very specific, limited circumstance, the ASEAN Coordinating Council can ultimately compel the recalcitrant party to submit to one of the methods contemplated under the Protocol. Naturally, by ratifying the Protocol all the States parties will have consented in advance to this possibility. The Protocol is applicable to interstate disputes only, concerning the state as a direct party and consequently does not provide for so-called mixed arbitrations.[834] There appears to be no obstacle in principle to ASEAN Member States inserting a compromissory clause in bilateral treaties referring certain categories of dispute arising thereunder to the Protocol dispute resolution procedures, subject naturally to the provisos already mentioned. It is interesting to note that whereas the dialogue partners and other non-ASEAN States and regional organisations can participate in the TAC, no comparable privilege has been extended to them in the Protocol. A dispute between an ASEAN State and a dialogue partner would appear to be amenable to the TAC resolution procedures.[835] The Protocol is to be interpreted in accordance with the customary rules of treaty interpretation of public international law;[836] no mention is made of the Vienna Convention on the Law of Treaties (VCLT), possibly on the grounds that to date only five of the ASEAN States have become parties to the VCLT.[837] However, many of the rules of treaty interpretation listed in the VCLT have been held additionally to be rules of customary law and thus binding *erga omnes*.[838]

248. The Protocol is silent on the question of reservations but given the nature of the treaty it could be argued that reservations are precluded because to allow them would undermine the very object and purpose of the treaty.[839] This is especially true if a reservation were aimed at excluding any particular mode of settlement envisaged under the Protocol or another signatory. In any case, it could be argued that, given that the submission of disputes is in many instances dependent on consent, reservations appear superfluous. Nevertheless, it is not beyond doubt that subject matter reservations, relating to human rights perhaps, are prohibited. This is an issue that may not be clarified until it arises.

833. This position reflects the fundamental principle that no state can, without its consent, be compelled to submit its disputes to any kind of pacific settlement, *Eastern Carelia*, Advisory Opinion, P.C.I.J., Series B, No. 5, 7 (1923); *East Timor (Portugal v. Australia)*, I.C.J. Reports 1995, 89, para. 26.

834. State entities also appear to be excluded, H. Fox, *States and the Undertaking to Arbitrate*, 37 I.C.L.Q. 1, 3 (1988).

835. Manila Protocol Art. 2.

836. Protocol Art. 3(1).

837. Laos, Malaysia, Myanmar, Philippines, and Vietnam. But *see* Phan, 255, who observes that all the ASEAN States have applied the VCLT at some time or another.

838. *See* e.g., *Territorial Dispute (Libya v. Chad)*, Judgment, I.C.J. Reports 1994, 6, para. 4; *Kasikili/Sedudu Island (Botswana v. Namibia)*, Judgment, I.C.J. Reports 1999, 1045, para. 18; *Sovereignty over Pulau Litigan and Pulau Sipadan (Indonesia v. Malaysia)*, Judgment, I.C.J. Reports 2002, 625, para. 37.

839. A. Peters, *International Dispute Settlement: A Network of Cooperational Duties*, 14 E.J.I.L. 1, 20–21 (2003). It should be observed that other comparable treaties permit reservations only on limited grounds, General Act Art. 39; European Convention for the Peaceful Settlement of Disputes Art. 35.

249. Neither does the Protocol provide for denunciation. Although other dispute settlement treaties permit denunciation,[840] the fact that the Protocol requires all Member States to become parties suggests that denunciation is not sanctioned.[841] However, the Protocol does allow for the possibility of amendment at the instigation of a Member State.[842]

250. The Protocol provides for formal techniques for dispute resolution which range from the traditional diplomatic, or political, processes, that is, consultation, to good offices, mediation and conciliation, to the quasi-judicial, arbitration.[843] The general rule is that the former procedures cannot result in the imposition of binding decisions and are but advisory, while the latter does.[844] What tends to distinguish one political process from another is the degree of third-party involvement, which is incremental the more formal it becomes. It is interesting to note that, unlike the TAC, inquiry, or fact-finding, is not specifically mentioned in the Protocol.[845] Neither does the Protocol make provision for a court of justice. However, given that arbitration is an available option, this omission may not presently amount to a fatal flaw. Nonetheless, the lack of a permanent court may need to be revisited in future in light of ASEAN's evolution towards deeper integration. The paramount consideration is that, at all times, parties to a dispute are encouraged to endeavour to reach a 'mutually agreed solution'.[846]

I. Consultation

251. The Protocol provides for the parties to a dispute to seek to resolve their differences through direct bilateral negotiation in a procedure known in this instance as consultation.[847] Consultation is little different to negotiation[848] and is usually regarded as 'the first step' in every dispute.[849] The Protocol adopts the position that recourse to consultation is discretionary and other modes are available alternatives.

840. Hague Convention Art. 96; European Convention for the Peaceful Settlement of Disputes Art. 40; General Act Art. 45(3); Pact of Bogotá Art. LVI.
841. VCLT Art. 56(1); I. Brownlie, *Principles of Public International Law* 621 (Oxford University Press 7th ed. 2008).
842. ASEAN Charter Art. 21.
843. Cf. UN Charter Art. 33(1); Manila Declaration, Part I, para. 5.
844. Hague Convention Art. 6.
845. Cf. Hague Convention Arts 9–36.
846. Protocol Art. 3(2).
847. *Ibid.*, Art. 5.
848. *Handbook*, para. 24. Negotiation is described as a 'diplomatic procedure in which representatives of states, in direct personal contact or through correspondence, engage in discussing matters of mutual concern and attempt to resolve disputes', R.L. Bledsoe & B.A. Boczek, *International Law Dictionary* 302 (ABC-Clio 1987). The flexible nature of negotiation is highlighted by the Manila Declaration, Part I para. 10. *See also Handbook*, para. 22. It is considered 'the principal means of handling all international disputes', Merrills, 2. Its importance was stressed by the ICJ in *North Sea Continental Shelf (Germany/ Denmark; Germany/Netherlands)*, Judgment, I.C.J. Reports 1969, 3, 48.
849. Aust, 431–432.

States in essence have a range of options from which to choose, and engaging in consultations is not a prerequisite for submitting to other modes.[850]

252. Unilateral references are possible under the consultation procedure. While the other modes under the Protocol are formally dependent on the respondent's consent to happen in practice the responding party will have difficulty evading having the matter submitted to one mode of settlement or another once a complaining party invokes the procedure and requests consultation. Consequently, if the request for consultation is not met, and the respondent must give meaningful consideration to the request and provide adequate opportunity for consultation,[851] or if the consultation fails to settle the dispute, the complainant can request the dispute be submitted to arbitration.[852] If the respondent does not agree to the establishment of an arbitration tribunal the complainant can refer the dispute to the ASEAN Coordinating Council[853] which may instruct the parties to resolve their dispute through good offices, mediation, conciliation, or arbitration.[854] As mentioned earlier, this seems the only instance under the Protocol when a state may be compelled to submit to a settlement procedure, and it may take the view that it may be more convenient to negotiate sooner rather than later. If the ASEAN Coordinating Council cannot decide how the dispute is to be resolved any party may refer the dispute to the ASEAN Summit under Article 26 of the ASEAN Charter.[855]

253. The Protocol requires that the consultation be conducted within specified timeframes.[856] Once the complainant requests consultation, the respondent must reply within thirty days and enter into consultation within sixty days. The consultation must be completed within ninety days or other mutually agreed period.[857] Failure to meet any of these directives can result in the complainant requesting the dispute be submitted to arbitration.[858] These deadlines should ensure that the procedure is not unduly and calculatingly prolonged.

254. The fact that the respondent is obliged to give 'meaningful consideration' to a request and provide 'adequate opportunity' for consultation strongly suggests that the Protocol implicitly reflects the responsibility under general international law that states must conduct all their negotiations sincerely and in good faith.[859]

---

850. *Land and Maritime Boundary between Cameroon and Nigeria (Cameroon v. Nigeria)*, Preliminary Objections, I.C.J. Reports 1998, 275, 303; Hudson, 413–416; Peters, 14–15.
851. Protocol Art. 5(1).
852. *Ibid.*, Art. 8(1).
853. *Ibid.*, Art. 8(4).
854. *Ibid.*, Art. 9(1).
855. *Ibid.*, Art. 9(4).
856. In general, such timeframes are dependent on the circumstances, *Handbook*, para. 50.
857. Protocol Art. 5(3).
858. *Ibid.*, Art. 8(1).
859. *North Sea Continental Shelf (Germany/Denmark; Germany/ Netherlands)*, Judgment, I.C.J. Reports 1969, 3, 47; *Legality of the Threat or Use of Nuclear Weapons*, Advisory Opinion, I.C.J. Reports 1996, 226, 264; *South China Sea Arbitration (Republic of the Philippines v. People's Republic of China)*, Award, 33 R.I.A.A. 153 (2015-16), paras 1171–1172; Manila Declaration Pt I, para. 10; *Handbook*, paras 54–58.

II. Good Offices, Mediation and Conciliation

255. Provision is made for third-party involvement to facilitate resolution of disputes through the means of good offices, mediation, or conciliation. Thus, the parties to a dispute *may agree* at any time to good offices, mediation, or conciliation, which may begin or terminate at any time.[860] Recourse to these modes is not conditional upon the breakdown of consultations. It should be noted that unilateral recourse to these methods is not possible but is dependent on consent by both parties.[861] Third party initiatives are not possible under the Protocol

256. The persons volunteering their good offices, mediation or conciliation share a primary function in common, that of assisting and facilitating the parties to the dispute to reach an amicable settlement.[862] Another shared characteristic is that said persons are required to act in an 'independent, neutral and impartial manner'.[863] Said persons may be ASEAN's Chairman or Secretary-General.[864] In the alternative, the person providing good offices must be a 'suitable person'.[865] The single mediator[866] must be agreed upon by the parties and may be chosen from the list of arbitrators maintained by ASEAN's Secretary-General.[867] This is similarly the case with the appointment of the conciliator.[868]

257. The procedures involved in good offices, mediation or conciliation are set out in the Rules annexed to the Protocol. In light of the relatively informal nature of the techniques of good offices and mediation, which can take a variety of differing forms of negotiation that can overlap,[869] the Rules of necessity say little in relation to good offices in the way of specifics but seem intended to allow for flexibility. Consequently, the provider of good offices may proceed in any manner considered appropriate, 'taking into account the circumstances of the case and the wishes' of the parties.[870] The Rules are more prescriptive in relation to mediation which renders this particular method more formal. The mediator's role is stated to be to help

---

860. Protocol Art. 6(1).
861. *Handbook*, paras 101, 129.
862. Protocol Art. 7(1).
863. *Ibid.* Annex 1, Rule 2; Annex 2, Rule 2; Annex 3, Rule 4(1). *See* further Merrills, 33–34.
864. Protocol Art. 6(2). *See also* ASEAN Charter Art. 23(2). It should be noted that the UN Secretary-General has often played an important role in this regard, *Handbook*, paras 112–15.
865. Protocol Annex 1, Rule 1(1).
866. *Ibid.*, Annex 2, Rule 1.
867. *Ibid.*
868. *Ibid.*, Annex 3, Rule 1(1).
869. It is difficult to make rigid distinctions between the different techniques of dispute settlement; it is often a matter of degree in some measure dependent on the parent agreement or governing treaty, *Handbook*, paras 102–103. Good offices describes a situation 'whereby a third party acting with the consent of the disputing states serves as a friendly intermediary in an effort to induce them to negotiate between themselves without necessarily offering … substantive suggestions of settlement', Bledsoe and Boczek, 290. Mediation has been defined as a situation whereby a third party seeks 'to reconcile the claims of the contending parties and to advance his own proposals aimed at a mutually acceptable compromise solution', *Handbook*, para. 123. What both share in common is the 'character of advice', Hague Convention Art. 6. *See* generally, Merrills, 27–43.
870. Protocol Annex 1, Rule 3.

'facilitate communication and negotiation' between the parties.[871] To this end, the mediator acts as a 'channel of communication' between them; he or she may invite the parties to meet with him or her or may communicate with them orally or in writing, either together or with each of them separately.[872] It is unclear whether the mediator's function is limited to attempting to reconcile the parties' positions or whether he or she may be expected to take a proactive role. This is because according to the Rules the parties may determine how the mediation will be conducted.[873] Given that one of the roles of the good offices provider and the mediator is to 'assist' the parties there does not appear to be any bar in principle to him or her making substantive suggestions aimed at resolving the dispute. The Protocol is, however, silent on this issue, but it is standard international practice.[874] But the fact that the conciliator is expressly authorised to make proposals for a settlement under the Rules suggests that such a facility may lie beyond their remit.[875]

258. The Rules regarding conciliation are considerably more detailed which is to be expected given its more formal nature while still allowing for flexibility.[876] Conciliation has been defined as 'a kind of institutionalised negotiation … to encourage and structure the parties' dialogue, while providing them with whatever assistance may be necessary to bring it to a successful conclusion'.[877] Its purpose has been described broadly as, 'to investigate the dispute and to suggest the terms of a possible settlement',[878] but the particulars will vary from case to case. The directives of the Protocol share this basic goal. The conciliator has wide discretionary powers as to how to conduct proceedings, taking into account the circumstances of the case, including previous practices between the parties, the wishes of the parties, and their rights and obligations.[879] Nevertheless, it is clear that considerable scope exists for adaptation to the specifics of each particular case. The process is initiated with the parties submitting a brief written statement describing the general nature of the dispute and the points in question.[880] However, oral statements may also be taken.[881] The conciliator may communicate or meet with the parties either

871. *Ibid.*, Annex 2, Rule 2. *See* generally, *Handbook*, para. 130; Merrills, 35–39. According to Hague Convention Art. 4, the aim is to reconcile the opposing claims and appease the feelings between the disputants.
872. Protocol Annex 2, Rule 4.
873. *Ibid.*, Rule 5. Failing agreement between the parties the mediator can decide how the mediation will be conducted.
874. *Handbook*, para. 123.
875. Protocol Annex 3, Rule 4(3).
876. *See* generally Merrills, 62–87. They bear a close similarity to the PCA Optional Conciliation Rules, effective 1 Jul. 1996, at: https://docs.pca-cpa.org/2016/01/Permanent-Court-of-Arbitration-Optional-Conciliation-Rules.pdf.
877. Merrills, 70. According to the PCA, the conciliator 'assists' the parties in reaching a settlement, PCA Optional Conciliation Rules Art. 7(1).
878. Merrills, 70. Conciliation is said to combine elements of enquiry and mediation, *Handbook*, para. 140.
879. Protocol Annex 3, Rule 4(2), 6.
880. Protocol Annex 3, Rule 2(1). The conciliator may request further written statements, documentation or information, *ibid.*, Rule 2(2)–(3).
881. *Ibid.*, Rule 6.

jointly or separately.[882] It is only in the context of conciliation that the parties are under a stated obligation to cooperate with the conciliator in good faith; in fact, this is the only express reference to good faith in the entire Protocol.[883]

259. There is only one conciliator unless the parties agree that there are to be two or three who may be chosen from the list of arbitrators maintained by ASEAN's Secretary-General.[884] Where there is but one conciliator, the parties should agree on this person; where there are two, each party appoints one conciliator; where there are three, each party appoints one conciliator and should agree on the third.[885] However, the Rules are silent on how to proceed where the parties cannot reach agreement. It may be that ASEAN's Secretary-General or the ASEAN Coordinating Council should then have the responsibility of finding a mutually acceptable person or the ASEAN Summit may even need to impose someone on the parties. The PCA makes provision for such a possibility.[886] Conciliators are expected to act jointly wherever possible,[887] in keeping with ASEAN's emphasis on consensus, but the possibility of acting by majority appears possible.[888]

260. The conciliator may make proposals for a settlement of the dispute, which need not be in writing nor reasoned, at any time.[889] The parties may also submit their own suggested solutions,[890] which are purely advisory. If the conciliator believes that an acceptable solution is possible he or she should submit the terms to the parties for their observations; these terms may then be redrawn in light of the parties' comments.[891] If agreement is reached the parties will draft and sign a settlement agreement, with or without the conciliator's input.[892]

261. While any solution proposed as a result of good offices, mediation or conciliation is not binding upon the parties a settlement agreement that emerges therefrom concluded between the parties is binding.[893] This is a salient feature of the Protocol in keeping with the PCA Optional Conciliation Rules.[894] It constitutes a departure from the traditional position of these modes of dispute settlement that they do not impose a solution on the parties.[895] A settlement agreement, freely arrived at

882. *Ibid.*, Rule 5.
883. *Ibid.*, Rule 8.
884. *Ibid.*, Rule 1(1). Generally, the appointment of a number of conciliators is envisaged, *Handbook*, para. 150. *See*, e.g., General Act Art. 4(1).
885. Protocol Annex 3, Rule 1(3).
886. PCA Optional Conciliation Rules Art. 4(2)(b), (3)(b). *See also*, e.g., General Act Art. 6.
887. Protocol Annex 3, Rule 1(2).
888. Cf. General Act Art. 12.
889. Protocol Annex 3, Rule 4(3).
890. *Ibid.*, Rule 9.
891. *Ibid.*, Rule 10(1).
892. *Ibid.*, Rule 10(2).
893. Protocol Arts 7(3), 16(1). That all settlement agreements should be implemented by states in good faith is emphasised by the Manila Declaration Pt I, para. 11.
894. Cf. PCA Optional Conciliation Rules Art. 13(3).
895. Merrills, 31, 62. *See*, e.g., Pact of Bogotá Art. XXVIII.

and expressly accepted by the parties, is quite another matter. As a written binding document[896] it would appear to satisfy the definition of a treaty under international law.[897]

III. Arbitration

262. Arbitration has been defined as 'the settlement of differences between States by judges of their own choice and on the basis of respect for law. Recourse to arbitration implies an engagement to submit in good faith to the award'.[898] The Protocol reflects these basic characteristics. It bears similarities with the PCA Arbitration Rules but there are also important differences.[899] Freedom of choice is thus the exception rather than the rule. Unlike recourse to ad hoc arbitration the parties to the Protocol do not have absolute autonomy in a number of areas. These include the tribunal's composition, competences, governing procedure and the applicable law.[900] In some cases no deviation is allowed, for example, regarding the composition of the tribunal, or the language of arbitration, which is English,[901] but in some limited instances the parties do have some latitude to dictate the procedure. This is the case, for example, with regard to third-party participation. The parties may agree on the place of arbitration, if not, the arbitration is to be held at the ASEAN Secretariat in Jakarta.[902]

263. The function of the arbitral tribunal (tribunal) is declared to be to examine the facts of the case before it and decide it in light of the ASEAN Charter and relevant ASEAN instruments relied upon by the parties.[903] However, the applicable law is not limited thereto but extends to public international law as well as to other rules of law.[904] A tribunal will decide a case *ex aequo et bono* should the parties so agree.[905] The latter inclusion is of significance because it has been held that without

896. Protocol Art. 7(2)–(3).
897. *See* VCLT Art. 2(1)(a); Aust, 52–55.
898. Hague Convention 1907 Art. 37; *Article 3, Paragraph 2, of the Treaty of Lausanne (Frontier between Turkey and Iraq)*, Advisory Opinion, P.C.I.J., Series B, Nos 12, 26; *Maritime Delimitation and Territorial Questions between Qatar-Bahrain (Qatar v. Bahrain)*, Judgment, I.C.J. Reports 2001, 40. *See* generally *Handbook*, paras 168–95; Merrills, ch. 5.
899. PCA Arbitration Rules 2012, https://pca-cpa.org/wp-content/uploads/sites/175/2015/11/PCA-Arbitration-Rules-2012.pdf.
900. *See* Merrills, 92–102.
901. Protocol Annex 4, Rule 13(1). ASEAN's working language is English, ASEAN Charter Art. 34. Cf. PCA Arbitration Rules Art. 19(1) which allows the parties or, failing which, the tribunal, to determine the language or languages to be used in the proceedings.
902. Protocol Annex 4, Rule 12(1).
903. Protocol Art. 12.
904. *Ibid.*, Art. 14(1)–(2). *See* generally Merrills, 100–102. The application of public international law appears to be the default position where no applicable law is specified, *Handbook*, paras 181–82; PCA Arbitration Rules Art. 35(1)(a).
905. Protocol Art. 14(2). Cf. General Act Art. 28.

explicit authorisation a tribunal cannot decide a case on this basis.[906] The fact that the parties are not free to specify the applicable law distinguishes the Protocol from one of the main features of arbitration.[907]

264. In keeping with general practice,[908] the tribunal consists of three arbitrators,[909] one appointed by each party,[910] and the third by mutual agreement.[911] It is the latter who acts as the chair of the tribunal.[912] Where a party fails to appoint an arbitrator within the specified time limit the other party can request the ASEAN Secretary General to appoint the arbitrator, who must do so after consulting the defaulting party.[913] If the parties fail to agree on the third arbitrator either party may request the ASEAN Coordinating Council to appoint such person, which it must do.[914] The problem of so-called truncated tribunals does not thus arise in the ASEAN system.[915]

265. The arbitrators are chosen from a list drawn up and maintained by the ASEAN Secretary-General.[916] Each Member State can make ten nominations.[917] While no mention is made of the PCA there is no reason why recourse should not be had to this facility as the Protocol does not require that all arbitrators be Member State nationals, although it is preferred that arbitrators have expertise in the law relating to the ASEAN Charter and associated instruments.[918] However, the chair of the tribunal will usually be a national of a Member State unless 'exceptional circumstances' dictate otherwise.[919] Naturally the chair of the tribunal cannot be a national of a disputing party.[920]

266. Justifiably the arbitrators must additionally have expertise and experience in law, or dispute resolution under international law.[921] They must be persons of good character[922] and be wholly independent of, nor associated with nor take direction

906. *Maritime Boundary Delimitation (Guinea v. Guinea-Bissau)*, 25 I.L.M. (1986), 251, para. 88; PCA Arbitration Rules Art. 35(2). *See* further Merrills, 102–105.
907. Bledsoe & Boczek, 280; Merrills, 99–102. Cf. PCA Arbitration Rules Art. 35(1). *See* further *Handbook*, para. 181.
908. *Handbook*, para. 178. *See* generally Merrills, 92–93.
909. Protocol Annex 4, Rule 1(1). Cf. PCA Arbitration Rules Art. 7(1).
910. Protocol Annex 4, Rule 1(2). Cf. PCA Arbitration Rules Art. 9(1).
911. Protocol Annex 4, Rule 1(4)(a). PCA Arbitration Rules Art. 9(1) provides that the third arbitrator is chosen by the other arbitrators.
912. Protocol Annex 4, Rule 1(4)(c). *See* PCA Arbitration Rules Art. 9(1).
913. Protocol Annex 4, Rule 1(3). Recourse to a third party as an appointing authority is again common practice, *Handbook*, para. 178.
914. Protocol Annex 4, Rule 1(4)(b).
915. Merrills, 93–94; Peters, 24–25.
916. Protocol Annex 4, Rule 5(1).
917. *Ibid.*
918. Protocol Art. 11(2)(a).
919. Protocol Annex 4, Rule 1(4)(d).
920. Protocol Art. 11(3).
921. *Ibid.*
922. *Ibid.*, Art. 11(2)(b).

from, any party.[923] In order to avoid conflict of interest an arbitrator must not have had any previous involvement with the matter.[924] However, the Protocol goes further in seeking to avoid any semblance of partiality and requires arbitrators to disclose to the parties any 'information which may give rise to justifiable doubts as to their independence and impartiality'.[925]

267. Doubts on this score may give rise to a challenge to the arbitrator.[926] If a challenge is made within the specified timeframe various possibilities arise. First, that the other party may accept the challenge and/or the arbitrator may choose to step down. Such actions would be without prejudice.[927] Second, that the challenge is rejected by the other party and/or the arbitrator may refuse to withdraw.[928] In that case, should the matter relate to arbitrators appointed by the parties, the decision is made by the ASEAN Secretary-General, but if it concerns the third arbitrator, the decision is taken by the ASEAN Coordinating Council.[929] If a challenge is sustained, a substitute arbitrator must be appointed.[930]

268. Arbitrators may be replaced by a substitute arbitrator as a result of death or resignation.[931] However, the tribunal may refuse to accept a resignation unless it is convinced that 'sufficient reasons' exist.[932] In the case of incapacity, or where an arbitrator fails to participate in the arbitration, the tribunal, unless the parties agree otherwise, has the discretion, in light of all available circumstances, of continuing with the case or declaring the office vacant.[933] If the chair is replaced all hearings must be repeated.[934]

---

923. *Ibid.*, Art. 11(2)(c). *See Mauritius v. United Kingdom (Reasoned Decision on Challenge)* 1 Dec. 2011 para. 135, https://pcacases.com/web/sendAttach/1792; PCA No. 2012-04, *Arbitration between the Republic of Croatia and the Republic of Slovenia*, Partial Award, 30 Jun. 2016, para. 175, https://pcacases.com/web/sendAttach/1787.
924. Protocol Art. 11(2)(d).
925. *Ibid.*, Art. 11(2)(e), Annex 4, Rule 2(1). *See* PCA Arbitration Rules Art. 11. *See* further *Mauritius v. United Kingdom*, para. 136, https://pcacases.com/web/sendAttach/1792.
926. Protocol Annex 4, Rule 2(2). The appointing Party can only challenge the arbitrator once the appointment has been made, *ibid.*, Rule 2(3). Reasons for the challenge must be provided, *ibid.* Annex 4, Rule 2(5). *See* PCA Arbitration Rules Arts 10(1), 12(1)–(2), 13(2); *Mauritius v. United Kingdom*, para. 151. *See* also, *Croatia v. Slovenia Arbitration*; PCA Case No. 2019-28, *Dispute Concerning the Detention of Ukrainian Naval Vessels and Servicemen* (*Ukraine v. Russian Federation*), *Decision on Challenges*, 6 Mar. 2024, https://pcacases.com/web/sendAttach/52784.
927. Protocol Annex 4, Rule 2(6). *See* PCA Arbitration Rules Art. 13(4).
928. Protocol Annex 4, Rule 2(7).
929. *Ibid.*, Rule 2(7)(a)-(b), in both instances in consultation with the ASEAN Committee of Permanent Representatives. Cf. PCA Arbitration Rules Art. 13(4).
930. Protocol Annex 4, Rule 2(8).
931. *Ibid.*, Rule 3(1). Cf. PCA Arbitration Rules Art. 14(1) which does not specify a reason for the replacement.
932. Protocol Annex 4, Rule 3(1).
933. *Ibid.*, Rule 3(2)-(3).
934. *Ibid.*, Rule 4. However, if another arbitrator is replaced the tribunal has the discretion whether or not to repeat the hearings, *ibid.* Cf. PCA Arbitration Rules Art. 15.

269. The Protocol determines a number of procedural matters, but the tribunal is given the discretion to adopt further procedures where required.[935] This power is important because the Protocol does not provide an exhaustive set of rules to govern possible eventualities and various gaps exist.

270. Since arbitration may be *ante hoc* and compulsory in certain circumstances the Protocol addresses the possibility of a challenge to the tribunal's jurisdiction. It states that the tribunal has the power to rule on objections to its jurisdiction.[936] This authority reflects an established principle of international law, namely, 'the inherent power of a tribunal to interpret the text establishing its jurisdiction' (*Kompetenz-–Kompetenz*).[937] The Protocol allows for the objections to be joined to the merits but as the exception;[938] usually the tribunal will be expected to rule initially on the question of jurisdiction before proceeding to consider the case on the merits.

271. The failure of a party to appear before the tribunal or to defend its case does not block the proceedings. The other party may therefore request the tribunal to continue with the case and make its award.[939] While no further points are specified the application of the principle of non-frustration is a constructive step. It remains to be seen whether the tribunal will adopt the practice whereby a tribunal will consider legal arguments that the absent party may have submitted in support of its case had it appeared.[940]

272. As has been indicated, recourse to arbitration is possible in two circumstances, either by mutual consent or where directed by the ASEAN Coordinating Council following the failure of consultation.[941] This latter element, as has been

935. Protocol Annex 4, Rule 8(1). *See* further *Handbook*, para. 180. PCA Arbitration Rules Art. 17(1) provides the tribunal with a wide measure of discretion.
936. Protocol Annex 4, Rule 16(1). *See* PCA Arbitration Rules Art. 23(1).
937. *Nottebohm (Liechtenstein v. Guatemala)*, Preliminary Objection, I.C.J. Reports 1953, 111, 119; *Croatia v. Slovenia Arbitration*, paras 148-157.
938. Protocol Annex 4, Rule 16(3). Cf. PCA Arbitration Rules Art. 23(3) which allows the tribunal to rule on an objection at any stage of the proceedings. *See*, e.g., PCA Case No. 2011-03, *Mauritius v. United Kingdom Procedural Order No. 2 (Application to Bifurcate Proceedings)*, 15 Jan. 2013, https://pcacases.com/web/sendAttach/1795.
939. Protocol Annex 4, Rule 15. Cf. PCA Arbitration Rules Art. 30(2) with the added rider that the non-appearing party had no 'sufficient cause'. *See Arctic Sunrise (Netherlands v. Russia)*, Provisional Measures, International Tribunal for the Law of the Sea, I.L.M. 53 (2014), 607, paras 48–52; *Arctic Sunrise Arbitration (Netherlands v. Russia)*, Award on Merits, 32 R.I.A.A. 205 (2015), para. 10; *South China Sea Arbitration (Philippines v. China)*, Jurisdiction and Admissibility, 33 R.I.A.A. 1 (2015) paras 11, 114; *Detention of Three Ukrainian Naval Vessels (Ukraine v. Russia)*, Provisional Measures, International Tribunal for the Law of the Sea, I.L.M. 58 (2019), 1150, para. 123. Generally, *see* G. Naldi & K. Magliveras, *Dispute Settlement under the UN Convention on the Law of the Sea: Developments on Jurisdiction*, 16 N.Z. Y.B. Int'l L. 207 (2018).
940. *See*, e.g., *Fisheries Jurisdiction (United Kingdom v. Iceland)*, Judgment, I.C.J. Reports 1974, 3; *US Diplomatic and Consular Staff in Tehran (United States v. Iran)*, Judgment, I.C.J. Reports 1980, 3; *Arctic Sunrise Arbitration (Netherlands v. Russia)*, Award on Merits, 32 R.I.A.A. 205 (2015), para. 19; *South China Sea Arbitration (Philippines v. China)*, Jurisdiction and Admissibility, 33 R.I.A.A. 1 (2015), paras 12, 14–15.
941. Protocol Arts 8(4), 9(1).

mentioned, is an atypical feature of the Protocol. The possibility of a dispute involving more than two parties is envisaged and in such a situation the procedures apply *mutatis mutandis.*[942] An exception relates to the number of arbitrators which is subject to an ad hoc agreement between all the parties.[943] The likely scenario is that each party will be entitled to appoint an arbitrator, although care should be taken to avoid an even number in order to preclude the possibility of a tie when voting on a decision, unless the chair of the tribunal is given the casting vote.[944]

273. Where arbitration results from the consultation procedure[945] the Protocol allows a Member State with a 'substantial interest' in the case to declare its interest as a third party.[946] The third party has the opportunity to be heard by the tribunal and make submissions to it.[947] Although the Protocol is not free from ambiguity on the point whether the third party can intervene as of right the better view seems to be that it is for the tribunal to decide whether the third party is allowed to join the case.[948] This follows from the fact that, first, a state may be deemed not to have a 'substantial interest', and second, that absent anything to the contrary, the tribunal has 'the right to decide as to its own jurisdiction and has the power to interpret for this purpose the instruments which govern that jurisdiction'.[949] It remains to be seen what degree of interest would be required but if the tribunal chose to be guided by the practice of other tribunals it should be observed that ICJ practice under Article 62 of its Statute demonstrates that it has applied a very strict test.[950] For example, if the tribunal were asked to delimit a maritime boundary between Malaysia and Brunei in the South China Sea such a case would be of profound interest to other claimants, such as the Philippines and Vietnam, and it is highly probable that they would have little difficulty establishing a 'substantial interest'. By way of contrast, under some treaties intervention is permitted when the interpretation of a treaty to which states other than the disputants are parties.[951] It is unlikely that such a broad view would be admissible under the Protocol.

274. If a third party is allowed to participate the parties to the dispute may provide it with additional rights or impose conditions but the tribunal can do so only

942. *Ibid.*, Annex 4, Rule 6(1).
943. *Ibid.*
944. Protocol Annex 4, Rule 14.
945. Protocol Arts 8(3), 9.
946. *Ibid.*, Art. 13(1). Cf. General Act Art. 36(1); PCA Arbitration Rules Art. 17(5).
947. Protocol Art. 13(2).
948. Cf. European Convention Art. 33(2); General Act Art. 36(2).
949. *Nottebohm (Liechtenstein v. Guatemala)*, Preliminary Objection, I.C.J. Reports 1953, 111, 119.
950. *See* C. Chinkin, *Third Party Intervention Before the International Court of Justice*, 80 A.J.I.L. 495 (1986); *Land, Island and Maritime Frontier Dispute (El Salvador v. Honduras)*, Application by Nicaragua to Intervene, I.C.J. Reports 1990, 92; *Sovereignty over Pulau Litigan and Pulau Sipadan (Indonesia v. Malaysia)*, Application by Philippines to Intervene, I.C.J. Reports 2001, 575. Under the European Convention Art. 33(1), a third state must have 'legitimate interests' which suggests a less strict standard.
951. Hague Convention Art. 84; ICJ Statute Art. 63.

with the parties' consent.[952] Curiously, the Protocol does not explicitly state that the third party is also bound by the award.[953] However, this is likely to be so since the awards are binding on the *parties*.[954]

275. The Protocol is silent on the question of intervention by non-Member States. Since the Protocol is open to ASEAN Member States only there is no reason to believe that the legal interests of a third state that could be affected by the decision would necessarily be protected. Under the PCA Arbitration Rules intervention is subject to the intervenor being a party to the arbitration agreement.[955] For instance, China has competing claims in the South China Sea and its vital national interest could very well be affected by an arbitral decision between, for example, Vietnam and the Philippines. Precedent suggests that the tribunal would be within its rights to decline to determine any question that involved a state that was not a party to the arbitration.[956]

276. It is open to the parties to the dispute to reach a settlement at any time before the award is made.[957] If for any other reason continuation of the proceedings becomes 'unnecessary or impossible' the tribunal may seek to terminate the proceedings.[958] This may refer to the effect of the principles of force majeure or *rebus sic stantibus* for instance. However, a party is given the opportunity to raise 'justifiable grounds' for objecting to this step.[959] No guidance is provided as to what reasons may amount to 'justifiable grounds' but it follows that in such an event the tribunal will have to hear legal argument on this point and may well be persuaded to rescind its order.

277. Many questions of procedure are not addressed by the Protocol, one significant omission being interim, or provisional, measures of protection.[960] However, the tribunal is given the discretion to adopt further procedures[961] and this is one important power that it may feel the need to adopt. Questions relating to evidence or the role of experts are other areas wholly unaddressed by the Protocol.[962]

278. In general the Protocol's provisions concerning awards are in keeping with established international standards.[963] Thus, decisions must be taken by a majority, with the chair having the casting vote,[964] must be in writing[965] and confined to the

952. Protocol Annex 4, Rule 7.
953. Cf. Hague Convention *ibid.*
954. Protocol Arts 15(1), 16(1).
955. PCA Arbitration Rules Art. 17(5).
956. *Delimitation of Maritime Area between Canada and the French Republic (St Pierre et Miquelon) (Canada v. France)*, I.L.M. 31 (1992), 1149, para. 79.
957. Protocol Annex 4, Rule 10(1). Cf. PCA Arbitration Rules Art. 36(1).
958. Protocol Annex 4, Rule 10(2). Cf. PCA Arbitration Rules Art. 36(2).
959. Protocol Annex 4, Rule 10(2).
960. Cf. PCA Arbitration Rules Art. 26.
961. Protocol Annex 4, Rule 8(1).
962. *See Handbook*, para. 186. Cf. PCA Arbitration Rules Arts 27, 28(2), 29.
963. *See Handbook*, paras 192–193.
964. Protocol Annex 4, Rule 14. Cf. PCA Arbitration Rules Art. 33(1).

subject matter of the dispute,[966] must be reasoned,[967] and separate and dissenting opinions may be attached.[968] There is no requirement that the award be read in open court but confidentially is not an uncommon practice in arbitration.[969] Indeed, the Protocol is silent on whether the decision will be made public.

279. Crucially, the tribunal's awards are stated to be binding and must be complied with by the parties to the case.[970] Should a party fail to abide by an award the other party could invoke the ASEAN Rules for Reference of Non-Compliance. Unlike most inter-state, or international, arbitrations the Protocol therefore imposes submission to a third authority.[971] The possibility of repudiation of the award by a party would thus appear to be covered. The award is also final[972] and therefore cannot be appealed.[973] The Protocol does not in fact make express provision for the validity of an award to be challenged.[974] No provision is made for the possibility of the revision of awards in the light of new facts, for which no general power exists.[975] Nor does it address the possibility that a tribunal may be asked to interpret its rulings.[976] As a general rule challenges are permissible on grounds of, *inter alia,* manifest error of law or fact, or an error relating to an essential procedural requirement. Usually these procedures must be the 'subject of an express grant',[977] but absent that the dispute should be submitted to the tribunal that rendered the ruling.[978] It is therefore a matter of speculation as to how such a grievance might be resolved but recourse to diplomacy is a possible scenario. Neither is specific provision made for the correction of clerical or similar errors.[979] However, this seems to be an inherent power.[980]

---

965. Protocol Annex 4, Rule 17(1). Cf. PCA Arbitration Rules Art. 34(2).
966. Protocol Annex 4, Protocol Annex 4, Rule 17(1). This raises the principle of excès de pouvoir, *see Arbitral Award of 31 July 1989 (Guinea-Bissau v. Senegal)*, Judgment, I.C.J. Reports 1991, 53, paras 37–41.
967. Protocol Art. 12, Annex 4, Rule 17(1). Cf. PCA Arbitration Rules Art. 34(3). *See Arbitral Award of 31 July 1989 (Guinea-Bissau v. Senegal)*, I.C.J. Reports 1991, 53, paras 42–43.
968. Protocol Annex 4, Rule 17(2).
969. M. Shaw, *International Law* 1055 (Cambridge U. Press 6th ed. 2008). However, the Hague Convention stipulates that the awards be given in public, Hague Convention Art. 80. Cf. PCA Arbitration Rules Art. 34(5) which states that the award *may* be made public.
970. Protocol Arts 15(1), 16(1). Such a provision is stated to be 'usual', Fox, 8. *See* further *Handbook*, para. 192. Cf. Hague Convention Art. 84; PCA Arbitration Rules Art. 34(2).
971. Fox, *ibid.*
972. Protocol Art. 15(1). Cf. PCA Arbitration Rules Art. 34(2). The Hague Convention employs the expression, 'puts an end to the dispute definitively', Hague Convention Art. 81.
973. Hague Convention *ibid. See* further *Arbitral Award Made by the King of Spain on 23 November 1906 (Honduras v. Nicaragua)*, Judgment, 18 Nov. 1960, I.C.J. Reports 1960, 192, 214; *Arbitral Award of 31 July 1989 (Guinea-Bissau v. Senegal)*, Judgment, 12 Nov. 1991, I.C.J. Reports 1991, 53, 62.
974. *See* generally *Arbitral Award of 31 July 1989*, *ibid*; Merrills, 108–11; Shaw, 1053–54.
975. Merrills, 107. Cf. Hague Convention Art. 83.
976. *Handbook*, para. 194. Cf. Hague Convention Art. 82; PCA Arbitration Rules Art. 37.
977. Merrills, 105.
978. *Handbook*, para. 195.
979. *Handbook*, para. 194. Cf. PCA Arbitration Rules Art. 38.
980. Merrills, 108.

280. The Protocol makes it explicit that the tribunal's awards do not 'add to or diminish the rights and obligations' in the ASEAN Charter and other ASEAN legal instruments.[981] This seems to embody the principle that an award has no binding force except between the parties but it is capable of being understood as an attempt to fetter the tribunal from contributing to the gradual development of the law through its interpretation and application of these treaties. Such a standpoint is unlikely to prosper; judicial pronouncements, including those of arbitral tribunals, tend to develop the law and acquire a persuasive status.[982]

281. The tribunal has no express mandate under the Protocol on its own motion to order remedies or consequential measures requiring states to take certain positive steps, or that compensation or damages be paid for breach of an obligation by the losing party. The default position under the Protocol seems to be that an award constitutes just satisfaction in itself. Whether the tribunal may be authorised to make a determination on reparations at the request of the parties remains to be seen. There appears to be no valid reason why in principle the tribunal should not be able to do so if the parties agree to this in the *compromis*.[983]

282. Although the ASEAN Way contemplates that disputes should generally be 'settled amicably' through direct negotiations between Member States, an approach confirmed in the TAC, that casual informal style does not seem appropriate for every dispute, particularly given ASEAN's evolution. The ASEAN Charter undertakes an important commitment towards the peaceful settlement of disputes. In the Protocol, ASEAN has proclaimed its readiness to adopt a more concrete approach to dispute settlement by putting in place mechanisms to enable Member States resolve their future disputes. As is to be expected in contemporary international law, the autonomy of states in approving consensual arrangements for the submission of disputes to resolution becomes subject to some constraints. These do not appear unduly burdensome or restrictive. The mechanisms envisaged by the Protocol are, however, of the traditional type instantly recognisable to the international lawyer. They are, in one sense, reactive. In that respect the Protocol is not innovative. It does not have the capacity for deterrent mechanisms that might obviate the need to resort to complex dispute settlement processes *post hoc*. Neither is it designed to be preventative and proactive; it does not put in place an institutional framework for the peaceful prevention of disputes and conflicts, with the emphasis on anticipatory, confidence-building and preventive measures. Of course, it could be rightly argued that this was never the role envisaged for the Protocol which is designed to address but one dimension of dispute settlement.

283. In having a standing system in place much of the preparatory work relating to the establishment of an arbitral tribunal, often difficult, protracted and expensive,

981. Protocol Art. 15(2).
982. *See*, e.g., *Island of Palmas Case (US v. Netherlands)*, 2 R.I.A.A. 829 (1928); *Naulilaa Case (Portugal v. Germany)*, 2 R.I.A.A. 1012 (1928); *Clipperton Island Case (France v. Mexico)*, 2 R.I.A.A. 1105 (1931); *Trail Smelter Arbitration (US v. Canada)*, 3 R.I.A.A. 1905 (1941).
983. *See Rainbow Warrior (New Zealand v. France)*, 20 R.I.A.A. 2151 (1990).

is avoided. The risk of repudiation of an award is diminished. The Protocol does have limitations though. It does not provide a comprehensive system of dispute settlement. It is restricted in its scope to the interpretation or application of the ASEAN Charter. It does not establish a court. A number of procedural issues are left unaddressed. However, it is more specific in the procedures to be followed for each method than comparable treaties. And if it encourages states to submit their disputes to some form of settlement it must be viewed in a positive light.

284. Previous attempts by ASEAN to put in place dispute settlement mechanisms proved disappointing. They remain unused or underutilised. A preference for bilateral case by case basis remains. In fact, it is disappointing, though not surprising, that the dispute settlement clauses in some post-ASEAN Charter treaties refer exclusively to consultation or negotiation.[984] But the Protocol is now in force and therefore provides grounds for optimism. ASEAN's determination to accelerate and strengthen the establishment of an ASEAN Community in the near future suggests that the Protocol will have a full part to play in ASEAN's future. However, it appears that to date it has not been called into use.

984. *See* ASEAN Agreement on the Establishment of the ASEAN Co-ordinating Centre for Humanitarian Assistance on Disaster Management Art. 15 (17 Nov. 2011), https://agreement.asean.org/media/download/20220330063452.pdf. Other treaties refer to 'other peaceful means for the settlement of disputes as agreed between the Parties', e.g., ASEAN Convention Against Trafficking in Persons, Especially Women and Children Art. 27 (21 Nov. 2015), http://agreement.asean.org/media/download/20160303122945.pdf, which could therefore include arbitration.

Chapter 2. Human Rights

§1. ASEAN and Human Rights

285. The Asia-Pacific region is one of the few significant geo-political communities lacking a comprehensive human rights system, a regional human rights treaty with associated oversight machinery, well into the twenty-first century. Notwithstanding recurring calls for a rights-based approach to policy-making,[985] Asian governments consistently showed a marked reluctance to pay heed to human rights, the emphasis habitually placed on the doctrines of state sovereignty and economic development in particular.[986] Accordingly under the Bangkok Declaration adopted in 1993, Asian States, while acknowledging the possibility of establishing regional arrangements for the promotion and protection of human rights in Asia, called for human rights to be construed in their national and regional settings and laid stress on the principles of sovereignty and non-interference in the internal affairs of states.[987] Nonetheless, from the late 1990s ASEAN began to follow a human rights-based path,[988] as evidenced by the adoption in the early 2000s of a number of declarations with a human rights theme such as the ASEAN Declaration on the Protection of the Rights of Migrant Workers in 2007.[989] However, as ASEAN embarked on its transition towards a rules-based, integrated organisation engaged in legal and political reform, human rights assumed a higher, more structured, priority.[990] In 2005, ASEAN proclaimed that the ASEAN Charter would contain human rights commitments.[991] The EPG, the body tasked with drawing up key recommendations for inclusion in the ASEAN Charter, proposed that respect for human

985. *See* V. Muntarbhorn, *Asia, Human Rights and the New Millennium: Time for a Regional Human Rights Charter?*, 8 Transnat'l L. & Contemp. Probs. 407 (1998).

986. K. Engle, *Culture and Human Rights: The Asian Values Debate in Context*, 32 N.Y. U. J. Int'l L. & Pol. 291, 318–319 (2000); S.R. Harris, *Asian Human Rights: Forming a Regional Covenant*, 1 Asian-Pacific L. & Pol. J. 1, 11–13 (2000); S.S.C. Tay, *The ASEAN Charter: Between National Sovereignty and the Region's Constitutional Moment*, 12 S.Y.B.I.L. 151, 167 (2008); L.-A. Thio, *Implementing Human Rights in ASEAN Countries: Promises to Keep and Miles to Go Before I Sleep*, 2 Yale Hum. Rts. & Dev. L.J. 1, 49–57 (1999). According to one distinguished jurist such responses were based on 'the need to justify authoritarianism and occasional repression', Y. Ghai, *Human Rights and Governance: The Asia Debate*, 15 A.Y.B.I.L. 1, 6 (1994).

987. The Regional Meeting for Asia of the World Conference on Human Rights, Bangkok, Thailand, 29 Mar.–2 Apr. 1993, *Bangkok Declaration*, *Human Rights Law Journal* 14 (1993): 370. This position reflected the 'ASEAN Way'. *See* Engle, 316–324; P. Malanczuk, *Regional Protection of Human Rights in the Asia-Pacific Region*, 52 German Y.B.I.L. 107, 111–112 (2009).

988. H.-L. Tan, *The ASEAN Human Rights Body: Incorporating Forgotten Promises for Policy Coherence and Efficacy*, 12 S.Y.B.I.L. 239, 248–249 (2008).

989. ASEAN Declaration on the Protection and Promotion of the Rights of Migrant Workers (13 Jan. 2007), at: https://cil.nus.edu.sg/wp-content/uploads/2019/12/2007-ASEAN-Decl-Rights-Migrant-Wkrs.pdf.

990. Report of the Eminent Persons Group on the ASEAN Charter paras 23, 27 (2006) (EPG), https://www.asean.org/wp-content/uploads/images/archive/19247.pdf, [hereinafter '*EPG*'].

991. Kuala Lumpur Declaration on the Establishment of the ASEAN Charter, 11th ASEAN Summit (12 Dec. 2005), http://www.asean.org/news/item/kuala-lumpur-declaration-on-the-establishment-of-the-asean-charter-kuala-lumpur-12-december-2005.

rights form a key aspect of the ASEAN Charter, which would have the effect of buttressing ASEAN's peace and stability.[992] Under the ASEAN Charter, the promotion and protection of human rights is stipulated as one of ASEAN's purposes[993] and Asean commits itself to respect, promote and protect human rights and fundamental freedoms, as well as adhering to the principles of democracy, the rule of law and good governance.[994] The commitment to these rights and principles was reiterated in the APSC Blueprint.[995] Under Article 14(1) of the ASEAN Charter, ASEAN had undertaken to establish a human rights body. Accordingly, in October 2009, the AICHR was brought into being.[996] At the same time, a sectoral body, the ACWC was founded.[997] While the AICHR remains a work in progress arguably its major achievement to date has been the drafting of a human rights declaration.[998] ASEAN's adoption of the AHRD in 2012 was a landmark development.[999]

§2. The Human Rights Record of ASEAN States

286. Given ASEAN's stated commitment to human rights and democracy it is interesting to enquire into the strength of these values in ASEAN Member States. As has already been observed in Part I above, few of these states can be classified as fully functioning liberal participatory democracies. They swing between guided, or directed, democracies to authoritarian or repressive regimes.[1000]

287. According to the Economist Intelligence Unit, *Democracy Index 2023*, Laos and Vietnam are one-party, authoritarian states.[1001] A decade of democratisation in Myanmar (Burma) came to a violent end in February 2021 when the military

---

992. EPG Report, paras 3, 12, 23, 27, 55.
993. ASEAN Charter (20 Nov. 2007), 2624 U.N.T.S. 223, Art. 1(7).
994. ASEAN Charter Art. 2(2)(h–i). This commitment is also set out in the Preamble. *See* C.H. Lin, *ASEAN Charter: Deeper Regional Integration under International Law?*, 9 Chinese J. Int'l L. 821, 828 (2010).
995. ASEAN Political-Security Community Blueprint, in ASEAN, *Roadmap for an ASEAN Community 2009-2015*, para. 7.
996. Cha-am Hua Hin Declaration on the Intergovernmental Commission on Human Rights, 15th ASEAN Summit (23 Oct. 2009), https://www.asean.org/wp-content/uploads/images/archive/15thsummit/Declaration-AICHR.pdf (Cha-am Hua Hin Declaration). On the role of the AICHR, *see infra* paras 268 et seq.
997. *See infra* paras 276 et seq.
998. The AICHR was given the responsibility for developing a normative framework in the form of a human rights declaration. *See* C.M. Cerna, *Introductory Note to the Terms of Reference for the Establishment of the ASEAN Intergovernmental Commission on Human Rights (AICOHR)*, 48 I.L.M. 1161, 1162 (2009); G. Clarke, *The Evolving ASEAN Human Rights System: The ASEAN Human Rights Declaration of 2012*, 11 N.w. J. Int'l Hum. Rts. 1, 15–19 (2012).
999. *Phnom Penh Statement on the Adoption of the ASEAN Human Rights Declaration (AHRD)* (19 Nov. 2012), https://asean.org/phnom-penh-statement-on-the-adoption-of-the-asean-human-rights-declaration-ahrd/.
1000. *See* generally A. Duxbury & T. Hsein-Li, *Can ASEAN Take Human Rights Seriously?* 66–90 (Cambridge U. Press 2019).
1001. The human rights record of both States is problematic, with many basic rights 'severely restricted', *see* U.S. State Department, *2023 Country Reports on Human Rights Practices: Laos*, https://www.state.gov/reports/2023-country-reports-on-human-rights-practices/laos/; U.S. State

retook power in a coup d'état, leading to mass human rights abuses, and the imposition of an authoritarian regime.[1002] The treatment of the Rohingya Muslim minority, an attempt at ethnic cleansing, is particularly problematic.[1003] Brunei, an absolute monarchy, is a virtual personal fiefdom, with emergency powers in place that give the Sultan sweeping authority, and civil and political rights are severely curtailed.[1004] However, the introduction in 2014 and 2019 of strict Sharia laws, including death by stoning, the severing of limbs and flogging, has given rise to considerable concern[1005] and has been rightly criticised by the UN as incompatible with international human rights standards.[1006] Cambodia is a new democracy but is effectively a one-party state which has descended into authoritarianism.[1007] Recent years have witnessed a deterioration in securing human rights.[1008] National elections held in 2023 were deemed deeply flawed.[1009] Cambodia is in a curious position; the genocidal policies pursued by the Khmer Rouge in the 1970s,[1010] the toppling of the regime by Vietnam and disagreement over the legitimate government of Cambodia eventually led to UN oversight. The UN Transitional Authority in Cambodia

---

Department, *2023 Country Reports on Human Rights Practices: Vietnam*, https://www.state.gov/reports/2023-country-reports-on-human-rights-practices/vietnam/.

1002. FCDO, *Human Rights and Democracy: the 2021 Foreign, Commonwealth & Development Office Report*, 56–57. The UN Security Council was very critical of this event, UN Security Council Res. 2669 (2022).

1003. U.S. State Department, *Country Reports on Human Rights Practices for 2017*, https://www.state.gov/reports/2017-country-reports-on-human-rights-practices/burma/. The UN General Assembly continues to express its deep concern and to condemn the continued violence and abuses of human rights against the Rohingyas, UN General Assembly Res. 79/182. In November 2019, Gambia instituted proceedings against Myanmar before the International Court of Justice claiming that the maltreatment of the Rohingya community constituted genocidal acts in breach of the Convention on the Prevention and Punishment of the Crime of Genocide (9 Dec. 1948) 78 U.N.T.S. 277, to which both states are parties, ICJ Press Release No. 2019/47 (11 Nov. 2019). The ICJ granted The Gambia the provisional measures, ordering Myanmar, *inter alia*, to take all necessary measures to prevent acts of genocide against the Rohingya, *Application of the Convention on the Prevention and Punishment of the Crime of Genocide (The Gambia v. Myanmar), Provisional Measures* I.C.J. Reports 2020, 3.

1004. U.S. State Department, *2023 Country Reports on Human Rights Practices: Brunei*, https://www.state.gov/reports/2023-country-reports-on-human-rights-practices/brunei/.

1005. U.S. State Department, *Country Reports on Human Rights Practices for 2014*, https://www.state.gov/j/drl/rls/hrrpt/2014humanrightsreport/index.htm#wrapper; EU Annual Report on Human Rights and Democracy in the World 2023 Country Updates, 179–180, https://www.eeas.europa.eu/sites/default/files/documents/2024/2023%20EU%20country%20updates%20on%20human%20rights%20and%20democracy_2.pdf.

1006. *UN concerned at broad application of death penalty in Brunei's revised penal code*, UN News Centre, 11 Apr. 2014, https://news.un.org/en/story/2014/04/465902; *Bachelet urges Brunei to stop entry into force of 'draconian' new penal code*, UN News Centre, 1 Apr. 2019, https://www.ohchr.org/en/press-releases/2019/04/bachelet-urges-brunei-stop-entry-force-draconian-new-penal-code?LangID=E&NewsID=24432.

1007. U.S. State Department, *2023 Country Reports on Human Rights Practices: Cambodia*, https://www.state.gov/reports/2023-country-reports-on-human-rights-practices/cambodia/.

1008. EU Annual Report on Human Rights and Democracy in the World 2023 Country Updates, 181–182, https://www.eeas.europa.eu/sites/default/files/documents/2024/2023%20EU%20country%20updates%20on%20human%20rights%20and%20democracy_2.pdf.

1009. *Ibid.*, 181.

1010. *See* G. Robertson, *Crimes Against Humanity: The Struggle for Global Justice* 297–298 (Penguin 2nd ed. 2002).

assumed state and administrative functions from 1992–1993 while a comprehensive political settlement was realised.[1011] Additionally, with UN assistance, to the establishment of an internationalised or mixed tribunal, the ECCC, to try the horrific crimes perpetrated by the Khmer Rouge.[1012] Malaysia is a federal constitutional monarchy with a parliamentary system of government although listed as a flawed democracy by the Economist Intelligence Unit, *Democracy Index 2023*. While the government generally respects human rights and progress has been made, some problems persist relating, in particular, to arbitrary arrests and detention under the country's draconian internal security laws, and the impartiality and independence of the judiciary.[1013] Also described as a flawed democracy by the Economist Intelligence Unit, *Democracy Index 2023*, Singapore is a parliamentary republic but opposition parties face many obstacles. The government have broad powers to limit the rights of individuals.[1014] Although flawed in some respects, Indonesia is a multiparty democracy 'with free and fair elections, a pluralistic media landscape and a vibrant civil society'.[1015] In general, it respects human rights and upholds civil liberties although there are some areas of concern.[1016] The Philippines is also a multiparty constitutional democracy, but problems persist, including endemic corruption, arbitrary and unlawful killings, and arbitrary arrests and detentions.[1017] The election of a new President in 2022 has seen improvements in human rights.[1018] There is also an enduring insurgency in parts of the country.[1019] Thailand is a constitutional monarchy but may deserve the description of a flawed democracy 'Thailand has experienced pronounced political unrest for a number of years since the constitutional government was overthrown by the military in 2006.[1020] Civilian rule was nominally restored in 2019, but the elections held that year were not

---

1011. UN Security Council Res. 745 (1992).
1012. *See* M. Shaw, *International Law* 308–309 (Cambridge U. Press 8th ed. 2017). The ECCC's relationship with the Cambodian Government appears to be an uneasy one, P. Lobba & N. Pons, *Rethinking the Legacy of the ECCC: Selectivity, Accountability, Ownership*, 18 J. Int'l Crim. Just. 599 (2020).
1013. U.S. State Department, *2023 Country Reports on Human Rights Practices: Malaysia*, https://www.state.gov/reports/2023-country-reports-on-human-rights-practices/malaysia/.
1014. U.S. State Department, *2023 Country Reports on Human Rights Practices: Singapore*, https://www.state.gov/reports/2023-country-reports-on-human-rights-practices/singapore/.
1015. EU Annual Report on Human Rights and Democracy in the World 2023 Country Updates, 192, https://www.eeas.europa.eu/sites/default/files/documents/2024/2023%20EU%20country%20updates%20on%20human%20rights%20and%20democracy_2.pdf.
1016. U.S. State Department, *2023 Country Reports on Human Rights Practices*, https://www.state.gov/reports/2023-country-reports-on-human-rights-practices/indonesia/.
1017. U.S. State Department, *2023 Country Reports on Human Rights Practices: Philippines*, https://www.state.gov/reports/2023-country-reports-on-human-rights-practices/philippines/.
1018. EU Annual Report on Human Rights and Democracy in the World 2023 Country Updates, 213–214, https://www.eeas.europa.eu/sites/default/files/documents/2024/2023%20EU%20country%20updates%20on%20human%20rights%20and%20democracy_2.pdf.
1019. U.S. State Department, *2023 Country Reports on Human Rights Practices: Philippines*, https://www.state.gov/reports/2023-country-reports-on-human-rights-practices/philippines/.
1020. European Parliamentary Research Service, *Thailand: from coup to crisis*, https://www.europarl.europa.eu/RegData/etudes/ATAG/2020/659330/EPRS_ATA(2020)659330_EN.pdf.

deemed free.[1021] Elections held in 2023 were considered free and fair, but opposition politicians and political parties faced severe obstacles through the courts and the human rights situation remains challenging.[1022] Holding these states to account at the international level is problematical due to the simple fact that most of these regimes refuse to assume legally binding obligations or subject themselves to too much international oversight.[1023] Only the Philippines has a commendable record in this regard, although these achievements had come under assault from the Duterte regime.[1024] The table below, X indicating ratification, S signature and W withdrawal, suggests little enthusiasm for the cause of international human rights.[1025]

1021. Freedom House, *Freedom in the World 2020: Thailand*, https://freedomhouse.org/country/thailand/freedom-world/2020.

1022. U.S. State Department, *2023 Country Reports on Human Rights Practices: Thailand*, https://www.state.gov/reports/2023-country-reports-on-human-rights-practices/thailand/. *See* Constitutional Court Ruling No. 5/2563 (2020) which resulted in the dissolution of the Future Forward Party on the disputed ground of unlawful receipt of donations.

1023. *See* Clarke, 8–9. On ASEAN States' UN periodic reviews of their National Reports, *see* A. Duxbury & T. Hsein-Li, *Can ASEAN Take Human Rights Seriously?* 17–60 (Cambridge U. Press 2019).

1024. On 17 Mar. 2019, the Philippines' withdrawal from the Rome Statute became effective. This step appears to have been occasioned by the decision of the ICC's Prosecutor to open a preliminary examination on the Government's 'war on drugs' campaign which allegedly involve extrajudicial killings, ICC Press Release ICC-CPI-20180320-PR1371, 'ICC Statement on The Philippines' notice of withdrawal: State participation in Rome Statute system essential to international rule of law' (20 Mar. 2018) https://www.icc-cpi.int/Pages/item.aspx?name=pr1371. However, on 11 Mar. 2025 former President Duterte was arrested by the local authorities and transferred to the ICC to stand trial for the crime against humanity of murder under the Rome Statute Art. 7(1)(a) committed in the Philippines. In the arrest warrant issued on 7 March 2025, Pre-Trial Chamber I held that it had jurisdiction over the case against Duterte as the alleged crimes occurred during the period when the Philippines was a State Party to the Rome Statute, *Situation in the Republic of the Philippines*, Warrant of Arrest for Mr Rodrigo Roa Duterte, ICC-01/21, P.-T. Ch. I, 7 Mar. 2025.

1025. *See* Duxbury & Hsein-Li, 249–255.

	ICESCR[1026]	ICESCR-OP[1027]	ICCPR[1028]	ICCPR–OP 1[1029]	ICCPR-OP2[1030]	ICERD[1031]	CEDAW[1032]	OP- CEDAW[1033]	CRC[1034]	CAT[1035]	OP-CAT[1036]	CPED[1037]	ICMW[1038]	CRPD[1039]	OP-CRPD[1040]	ICC[1041]
Brunei							X		X	S				X		
Cambodia	X		X	S		X	X	X	X	X	X		S	X	S	X
Indonesia	X		X			X	X	X	X	X		S	X		X	

1026. International Covenant on Economic, Social and Cultural Rights (16 Dec. 1966), 993 U.N.T.S. 3 (ICESCR).
1027. Optional Protocol to the International Covenant on Economic, Social and Cultural Rights (10 Dec. 2008), 2922 U.N.T.S. 29 (ICESCR-OP).
1028. International Covenant on Civil and Political Rights (16 Dec. 1966), 999 U.N.T.S. 171 (ICCPR).
1029. Optional Protocol to the International Covenant on Civil and Political Rights (16 Dec. 1966), 999 U.N.T.S. 171 (ICCPR–OP 1).
1030. Second Optional Protocol to the International Covenant on Civil and Political Rights Aiming at the Abolition of the Death Penalty (15 Dec. 1989), 1642 U.N.T.S. 414 (ICCPR–OP 2).
1031. International Convention on the Elimination of All Forms of Racial Discrimination (21 Dec. 1965), 660 U.N.T.S. 195 (ICERD).
1032. Convention on the Elimination of All Forms of Discrimination Against Women (18 Dec. 1979), 1249 U.N.T.S. 13 (CEDAW).
1033. Optional Protocol to the Convention on the Elimination of All Forms of Discrimination Against Women (10 Dec. 1999), 2131 U.N.T.S. 83 (OP-CEDAW).
1034. Convention on the Rights of the Child (20 Nov. 1989), 1577 U.N.T.S. 3 (CRC).
1035. Convention Against Torture and Other Cruel, Inhuman or Degrading Treatment or Punishment (10 Dec. 1984), 1465 U.N.T.S. 85 (CAT).
1036. Optional Protocol to the Convention Against Torture and Other Cruel, Inhuman or Degrading Treatment or Punishment (10 Dec. 1984), 2375 U.N.T.S. 237 (OP-CAT).
1037. International Convention for the Protection of All Persons from Enforced Disappearance (20 Dec. 2006), 2716 U.N.T.S. 3 (CCPED).
1038. International Convention on the Protection of the Rights of All Migrant Workers and Members of Their Families (18 Dec. 1990), 2220 U.N.T.S. 3 (ICMW).
1039. Convention on the Rights of Persons with Disabilities (12 Dec. 2006), 2515 U.N.T.S. 3 (CRPD).
1040. Optional Protocol to the Convention on the Rights of Persons with Disabilities (12 Dec. 2006), 2518 U.N.T.S. 283 (OP-CRPD).
1041. Statute of the International Criminal Court (17 Jul. 1998), 2187 U.N.T.S. 3.

	ICESCR[1026]	ICESCR-OP[1027]	ICCPR[1028]	ICCPR–OP 1[1029]	ICCPR-OP2[1030]	ICERD[1031]	CEDAW[1032]	OP- CEDAW[1033]	CRC[1034]	CAT[1035]	OP-CAT[1036]	CPED[1037]	ICMW[1038]	CRPD[1039]	OP-CRPD[1040]	ICC[1041]
Laos	X		X			X	X		X	X		X		X		
Malaysia							X		X					X		
Myanmar	X						X		X					X		
Philippines	X		X	X	X	X	X	X	X	X	X		X	X		W
Singapore						X	X		X					X		
Thailand	X		X			X	X	X	X	X		X		X		S
Vietnam	X		X			X	X		X	X				X		

It should also be noted that the Convention on the Prevention and Punishment of the Crime of Genocide has been ratified by Cambodia, Laos, Malaysia, Myanmar, the Philippines, Singapore and Vietnam.[1042] Obviously, there is considerable scope for ASEAN countries to improve their reputation by acceding to these universal treaties.[1043]

§3. THE ASEAN HUMAN RIGHTS DECLARATION

288. On 19 November 2012, ASEAN leaders adopted the AHRD.[1044] Its underlying theme is that, through mutual cooperation and with the assistance of competent entities, Member States have expressed their common interest in respecting human rights in accordance with their broad pledges under the ASEAN Charter.

289. It should immediately be understood that the AHRD is an instrument of a political nature; it is not, and should not be construed, as being a legal text entailing binding obligations for Member States nor is it a treaty-based regime. Rather, it is a proclamation, 'soft law', a hortatory text setting common standard taking the legal form of a recommendation, which, however, demands a certain level of acquiescence. To put it into the context of similar universal and regional instruments, it is comparable *strictu sensu* to the UDHR 1948,[1045] the American Declaration of the Rights and Duties of Man 1948[1046] or the Cairo Declaration on Human Rights in Islam 1990.[1047] The AHRD's Preamble does in fact contain a commitment, *inter alia*, to the UDHR and the aforementioned Vienna Declaration on Human Rights and Programme of Action (1993). It therefore lacks any protective machinery.

1042. Convention for the Prevention and Punishment of the Crime of Genocide (9 Dec. 1948), 78 U.N.T.S. 277.

1043. The implementation of their treaty obligations in domestic law seems problematic, Duxbury & Hsein-Li, 255–262.

1044. At: https://asean.org/asean-human-rights-declaration/; https://www.refworld.org/docid/50c9fea82.html. *See* generally Clarke; Duxbury & Hsein-Li; G.J. Naldi & K.D. Magliveras, *The ASEAN Human Rights Declaration*, 3 Int'l Hum. Rts. L. Rev. 183 (2014); C.S. Renshaw, *The ASEAN Human Rights Declaration 2012*, 13 HRLR 557 (2013); J. Dupouey, *Les droits de l'homme au sein de l'ASEAN, un régime protecteur en construction*, 14 Rev. des droits de l'homme 1 (2018).

1045. *Human Rights: A Compilation of International Instruments, Vol. I (First Part): Universal Instruments* 1 (United Nations 2002).

1046. *Human Rights: A Compilation of International Instruments, Vol. II: Regional Instruments* 5 (United Nations 1997).

1047. *Ibid.*, 478. Note that in November 2020, the Foreign Ministers of the Organisation of Islamic Cooperation during their 47th Session approved a new Cairo Declaration on Human Rights, English translation at: http://oic-iphrc.org/ckfinder/userfiles/files/FINAL%20OHRD%20CLEAN%20%20VERSION%2024_12_2020.pdf. The new Declaration marks a huge departure from the 1990 Declaration, in essence it is an altogether different instrument, emanating from, arguably, a far more pro-Western attitude on fundamental freedoms. It has been said that it 'affirms compatibility of Islamic values with universal human rights to meet evolving demographic, social and cultural realities without compromising on Islamic teachings and values', *see Summary Report of the 17th Regular Session of the OIC Independent Permanent Human Rights Commission held ONLINE from 28 to 31 March 2021*, Jeddah, 31 Mar. 2021, 1, https://oic-iphrc.org/pdf/En/Sessions%20Documents/Summary%20Report%20of%20the%2017th%20Regular%20Session%20of%20the%20OIC%20IPHRC_EV_adopted%20(1).pdf. It remains to be seen if the 2020

Human rights treaty regimes, with monitoring bodies, are hence generally considered to offer a better level of protection compared to instruments of a declaratory nature, the effectiveness of which depends largely on the good faith of states to abide by the stated principles.

290. The decision of ASEAN Member States to conclude their first-ever general human rights instrument in the form of a declaration and not a treaty is explicable by the ASEAN Way.[1048] It is not necessarily a negative development in itself, provided that Member States are prepared to match pledges with concrete action. At the same time, Member States addressed the concern of those commentators, who had claimed that the lack in the ASEAN Charter of any references to universally accepted human rights standards '[left] a lot of room ... . to interpret the contents of human rights in a way that fits with their interests'.[1049] This attitude sends out the signal that the Member States' stance on human rights is a qualified one.

291. It must also be stressed that it is a well-known occurrence in international law for hortatory documents to evolve and acquire normative status. Such is the case with the UDHR and the American Declaration of the Rights of Man which are widely considered authoritative interpretations of the human rights provisions of the UN Charter[1050] and the Charter of the Organization of American States respectively,[1051] and the EU Charter of Fundamental Rights, initially concluded as a political declaration in December 2000.[1052]

Declaration (a legally non-binding instrument) will have any appreciable effect in the domestic legislation and national policies of those ASEAN Member States having a predominantly Muslim population.

1048. Duxbury & Hsein-Li, 281–282.

1049. H.D. Phan, *A Blueprint for a Southeast Asian Court of Human Rights*, 10 Asian-Pacific L. & Pol'y J. 384 (2009); Duxbury & Hsein-Li, 279–281.

1050. *Accordance with International Law of the Unilateral Declaration of Independence in Respect of Kosovo*, Advisory Opinion, I.C.J. Reports 2010, 403, 523, paras 202–204 (Separate Opinion of Judge Cançado-Trindade); I. Brownlie, *Basic Documents in International Law* 255 (Oxford U. Press 4th ed. 1995); A.H. Robertson & J.G. Merrills, *Human Rights in the World* 29 (Manchester U. Press 4th ed. 1996); B. Simma & P. Alston, *The Source of Human Rights Law: Custom, Jus Cogens, and General Principles*, 12 A.Y.B.I.L. 82, 84, 93 (1992). It has additionally been argued that the UDHR has become, or reflects, customary international law, *Legal Consequences for States of the Continued Presence of South Africa in Namibia Case*, Advisory Opinion, I.C.J. Reports 1971, 16, 76 (Separate Opinion of Judge Ammoun).

1051. *Interpretation of the American Declaration of the Rights and Duties of Man Within the Framework of Art. 64 of the American Convention on Human Rights*, Advisory Opinion, Inter-American Court of Human Rights, OC-10/89, Series A, No. 10 (1989), paras 43–45.

1052. Charter of Fundamental Rights of the European Union, OJ 2000 C 364/01. *See*, e.g., Case C-173/99 *BECTU v. Secretary of State for Trade & Industry* [2001] E.C.R. I – 4881, ECLI:EU:C:2001:356 (especially the Opinion of Advocate General Tizzano); Case C-540/03 *European Parliament v. Council of the European Union (Family Reunification)* [2006] E.C.R. I – 5769, ECLI:EU:C:2006:429; Case C-275/06 *Productores de Música de España Promusciae v. Telefonica de España SAU* [2008] E.C.R. I – 271, ECLI:EU:C:2008:54. *See* generally, G. de Búrca, *After the EU Charter of Fundamental Rights: The Court of Justice as a Human Rights Adjudicator?*, 20 Maastricht J. Eur. & Comp. L. 169 (2013).

292. Moreover, such a declaratory instrument may at any given moment acquire a legally binding nature by being incorporated into the constitutive instrument of the organisation which adopted it. The prime example is the aforementioned EU Charter on Fundamental Rights, which in 2010 was given legally binding force by being incorporated in the constitutive instruments through Article 6(1) of the Consolidated Version of the TEU.[1053] The EU Charter provides a powerful precedent for 'soft law' instruments to become 'hard law'. Indeed, it has been suggested that this example could be followed by ASEAN, which could transform the AHRD into a treaty at some stage in the future.[1054]

293. That ASEAN Member States opted for a declaration could also be viewed from another perspective. In particular, many of the rights contained in the AHRD already form part of customary and peremptory norms of international law and, for this reason, are binding on all states.[1055] While the document itself may be non-binding many of the rights set out therein are *a priori*. At the very least, the AHRD lays down agreed international standards against which Member States' laws, regulations and practices can be assessed and even held accountable. However, were it to fall below international standards, the states in question would be under moral and political pressure at least to address and remedy the situation. It could also be the case that a third Member State might be prepared to raise the issue of divergence from the standards imposed by the AHRD. Such confrontation could, theoretically speaking, become a dispute between two or more Member States concerning the AHRD's interpretation or application. In these circumstances, the disagreement might be submitted to the dispute resolution methods laid down in the Protocol on Dispute Settlement Mechanisms, which covers all written instruments adopted by Member States giving rise to respective rights and obligations in accordance with international law.[1056] In such an eventuality, the possibility that the rights envisaged in the AHRD are applied cannot be ruled out.

294. The AHRD reflects the contemporary trend of incorporating all three generations of human rights. This is no coincidence: Asian states have been instrumental in calling for parity to be given to second and third-generation rights, arguing that the totality of rights cannot be dissociated from each other and from the promotion of social justice.[1057] This strong belief is manifested in Article 7 of the AHRD: 'All human rights are universal, indivisible, interdependent and interrelated. All human rights and fundamental freedoms in this Declaration must be

---

1053. The Charter as a legally binding instrument is published in OJ C 326, 26.10.2012, 391.

1054. Renshaw, 558; Duxbury & Hsein-Li, 286–287.

1055. *See* L. Henkin, R.C. Pugh, O. Schachter & H. Smit, *International Law: Cases and Materials* 996–1000 (West Publishing Co. 2nd ed. 1987).

1056. Protocol to the ASEAN Charter on Dispute Settlement Mechanisms, 8 Apr. 2010, http://cil.nus.edu.sg/2010/2010-protocol-to-the-asean-charter-on-dispute-settlement-mechanisms/. If the AHRD were not regarded as an 'instrument' for the purpose of applying the Protocol, Art. 2(2) thereof stipulates that the parties to a dispute could mutually agree that its terms shall nevertheless apply.

1057. Bangkok Declaration 1993, paras 7, 10. *See* generally J.J. Shestack, *The Philosophical Foundations of Human Rights*, in *Human Rights: Concepts and Standards* 31, 46–52 (J. Symonides ed., Ashgate & UNESCO 2000).

treated in a fair and equal manner, on the same footing and with the same emphasis.' The AHRD is thus inspired partly by the Asian philosophy of rights, which places greater emphasis on the nexus between the individual and the wider community, and focuses on the collective rather than the Western classical theory of human rights, characterised by individualism.[1058]

295. The AHRD does not seem to address the basic questions which Western legal and political theory has raised against the extension of human rights to second and third-generation rights. It is not necessary to enter here into a discussion on the legal nature of such 'rights', only to observe that they have found expression in instruments such as the International Covenant on Economic, Social and Cultural Rights (ICESCR),[1059] or the African Charter on Human and Peoples' Rights,[1060] that their precise status is a matter of controversy, and that developing states generally tend to favour them.[1061]

296. The AHRD addresses the question of cultural variation or relativism. Thus, according to Article 7, 'the realisation of human rights must be considered in the regional and national context bearing in mind different political, economic, legal, social, cultural, historical and religious backgrounds'.[1062] As has been accepted, human diversity may sometimes necessitate that rights be influenced, interpreted and applied in a culturally sensitive way permitting 'justifiable modifications'.[1063] The very content of human rights does not impose a straightjacket that insists on absolute uniformity. However, cultural relativism should be applied with caution for it could be used as a pretext for undermining their universality.[1064] It follows that, on the one hand, states cannot be released from complying with universal and elementary human rights standards[1065] and, on the other hand, harmful social and cultural practices, including forms of punishment, should be eliminated.[1066] In a

1058. D.A. Bell, *The East Asian Challenge to Human Rights: Reflections on an East West Dialogue*, 18 Hum. Rts. Q. 641 (1996). It should not be overlooked that the influential Vienna Declaration also calls for parity between the different generations of rights.

1059. *See* M. Ssenyonjo, *Economic, Social and Cultural Rights*, in *International Human Rights Law. Six Decades after the UDHR and Beyond* 49, 81 (M.A. Baderin & M. Ssenyonjo eds, Ashgate 2010).

1060. African Charter on Human and Peoples' Rights (17 Jun. 1981) 1520 U.N.T.S. 217 (African Charter).

1061. Committee on Social, Economic and Cultural Rights, The Nature of States Parties' Obligations, General Comment 3, 14 Dec. 1990, UN Doc. HRI/GEN/1/Rev.6, 58; P. Sieghart, *The International Law of Human Rights* 367–368 (Oxford University Press 1984). Cf. UN General Assembly Res. 53/144, Declaration on the Right and Responsibility of Individuals, Groups and Organs of Society to Promote and Protect Universally Recognized Human Rights and Fundamental Freedoms Annex, Art. 7, suggesting that human rights are ever evolving, that third-generation rights have a clear foundation and, therefore, their existence cannot be disputed.

1062. Reflecting the 1993 Bangkok Declaration para. 8.

1063. Vienna Declaration, Part I, para. 5, and endorsed by UN General Assembly Res. 48/121.

1064. *See* generally, J. Donnelly, *Universal Human Rights in Theory and Practice* 57 et seq. (Cornell U. Press 2nd ed. 2003). *See* further W.J. Jones, *Universalizing Human Rights the ASEAN Way*, 3 Int'l J. Soc. Sci. 72, 78–83 (2014).

1065. Shestack, 58–61.

1066. Corporal punishment, caning, can be imposed as a sentence in Singapore under the Criminal Procedure Code 2010.

similar fashion Article 9 proclaims that 'the principles of impartiality, objectivity, non-selectivity, non-discrimination, non-confrontation and avoidance of double standards and politicisation, should always be upheld [*vis-à-vis* rights protected under the AHRD]'. This provision is likely a manifestation of the developing states' preoccupation that Western countries are selective, if not hypocritical, when applying and enforcing international law.[1067]

297. Occasionally, the AHRD makes use of the so-called clawback clauses, i.e., provisions making the rights guaranteed subject to domestic law, or at the discretion of national authorities.[1068] Article 27(2), on the freedom of association, is probably the most egregious example. It states, *inter alia*, 'Every person has the right to form trade unions and join the trade union of his or her choice … *in accordance with national laws and regulations*' (emphasis added). The obvious risk with such clauses is that they may negate the very rights and freedoms they purport to protect.[1069] UN experts have criticised the AHRD on this ground because '[i]f the recognition of human rights is qualified with provisions such as "in accordance with national law", this could be used by Governments as a justification to go below international standards'.[1070] But the AHRD counter-balances the possible negative effects of 'clawback' clauses with a safeguard clause in Article 40 to the effect that no state, group or person can invoke them to perform acts aimed at the destruction of its rights and freedoms and/or the international human rights instruments ratified by Member States.

298. The rights and freedoms recognised by the AHRD are set out in thirty-eight articles under the following five broad categories: general principles; civil and political rights; economic, social and cultural rights; the right to development; and the right to peace. The latter two form part of the third-generation (peoples' or collective) rights. The AHRD has benefited from the evolutionary process of international human rights law and has taken it into account. However, there exist other examples where the rights and freedoms are expressed in general terms; future enactments may therefore be necessary to give them full measure. The specific rights included in the AHRD are in many instances phrased in similar, but updated, fashion to those enshrined in the UDHR and the two UN International Covenants of 1966.

1067. *See* 1993 Bangkok Declaration para. 7.

1068. R. Higgins, *Derogations under Human Rights Treaties*, 48 B.Y.B.I.L. 281 (1976–1977); E.M. Hafner-Burton, L.R. Helfer & C.J. Fariss, *Emergency and Escape: Explaining Derogations from Human Rights Treaties*, 65 Int'l Org. 673 (2011).

1069. Note that while the African Charter makes extensive use of 'clawback' clauses, the African Commission has held that the applicable standard is that of international human rights, *see* K. Magliveras & G. Naldi, *The African Union: History, Institutions and Activities* 242–245 (Kluwer Law International 2018).

1070. 'ASEAN Human Rights Declaration Should Maintain International Standards', An Open Letter from the Coordination Committee of the Special Procedures of the Human Rights Council on the draft ASEAN Human Rights Declaration, no date, www.ohchr.org/Documents/HRBodies/SP/LetterASEAN_Nov2012.doc.

I. The General Principles of the AHRD

299. This first category of protected freedoms contains a set of basic beliefs seeking to influence the way the AHRD should be considered. Accordingly, Article 1 proclaims the fundamental ethos underlying the corpus of human rights, namely that all persons are born free and equal in dignity and privileges. It also lists certain substantive rights, such as the equal right of all persons to the rights and freedoms guaranteed in the AHRD (Article 2); the right to recognition as a person as well as the right to equality before the law (Article 3); and the right to effective and enforceable remedies (Article 5). Taking account of the stated Asian position,[1071] as well as the evolution of human rights law, Article 4 states explicitly that the rights of women, children, the elderly, persons with disabilities, migrant workers, and vulnerable and marginalised groups form an inalienable, integral and indivisible part of fundamental freedoms. Interestingly enough, Article 4 makes no mention of refugees and asylum seekers. However, in light of Article 16, which guarantees the right to seek and receive asylum, these groups should also enjoy a measure of protection.[1072]

300. Article 2 of the AHRD guarantees that every person is entitled to the rights and freedoms set out therein without distinction on 'race, gender, age, language, religion, political or other opinion, national or social origin, economic status, birth, disability or other status'. Clearly, the reference to 'every person' requires states to protect all persons within their jurisdiction, nationals and non-nationals alike. This is a fundamental principle: contracting parties to human rights treaties are under an obligation to secure to everyone within their jurisdiction the rights and freedoms defined therein, and to provide an effective remedy before a national authority for everyone whose rights are violated.[1073] As is true of corresponding provisions in other such instruments, Article 2 does not lay down a general proscription of discrimination but only prohibits unfairness as it affects the enjoyment of AHRD rights and as such complements the subsequent substantive provisions.[1074] Article 2 ought to be read together with Article 9 stipulating that the principle of non-discrimination should always be upheld. The use of 'should' rather than 'must' suggests that it is an advisory rather than mandatory provision. Regrettably, the drafters chose not to include a general non-discrimination clause such as Article 26 of the

1071. 1993 Bangkok Declaration para. 11.

1072. It is clearly established that human rights law extends to refugees and asylum seekers, *see,* e.g., *M.S.S. v. Belgium and Greece*, Appl. No. 30696/09, Judgment, European Court of Human Rights 21 Jan. 2011, para. 251 (2011) 53 E.H.R.R. 2. It is claimed that on the whole Asian States offer sanctuary to refugees and asylum seekers, S. Moretti, *Keeping Up Appearances: State Sovereignty and the Protection of Refugees in Southeast Asia*, 17 Eur. J. East Asian Stud. 3 (2018). For a pessimistic assessment, *see* B. Dewansyah & I. Handayani, *Reconciling Refugee Protection and Sovereignty in ASEAN Member States*, 12 Central Eur. J. Int'l & Sec. Stud. 473 (2018).

1073. J.G. Merrills & A.H. Robertson, *Human Rights in Europe* 25–28 (Manchester U. Press 4th ed. 1993); A. Conte & R. Burchill, *Defining Civil and Political Rights: The Jurisprudence of the United Nations Human Rights Committee* 5–6 (Ashgate 2nd ed. 2009).

1074. Merrills & Robertson, 199.

International Covenant on Civil and Political Rights (ICCPR).[1075] They may have acted on a combination of fear of assuming significant commitments and the influence of cultural relativism. However, it should be noted that in the European Convention of Human Rights (ECHR), a general prohibition of non-discrimination was introduced only in 2000.[1076]

301. Notwithstanding this criticism, Article 2 does have positive, progressive aspects. First, while not comprehensive in scope, the term 'other status' indicates that the enumeration of the grounds is neither closed nor exhaustive.[1077] Second, the addition of the grounds of age and disability.[1078] Third, the substitution of the term 'gender' for the term 'sex', the former having a broader scope than the latter. But there is no express reference to equality between men and women, although this could be implied, and no mention of sexual orientation.[1079] Finally, the absence of the ground based on property is troublesome. It could be offset by the inclusion of 'economic status', which as a notion depends on one's wealth, and by the recognition of the right to property in Article 17.

302. Equally positive is the provision of Article 5 guaranteeing the right to effective and enforceable remedies, to be determined by courts or other competent authorities, for acts violating the rights granted by the national constitution or legislation. Since the scope is not limited to 'domestic' authorities, a broad interpretation would lead to additional remedies on the international plane, while the reference to legislation could also be interpreted as extending to international human rights law as well.[1080]

303. A salient feature is Article 6: it imposes a general duty of responsibilities upon the individual to 'other individuals, the community and the society where one lives'. The need to balance rights and responsibilities reflects traditional East Asian

---

1075. International Covenant on Civil and Political Rights (16 Dec. 1966) 999 U.N.T.S. 171 (ICCPR).
1076. Under Protocol No. 12 to the ECHR (4 Nov. 2000) CETS No. 177.
1077. Conte & Burchill, 307–309. In African Court of Human and Peoples' Rights, *African Commission on Human and Peoples' Rights v. Kenya*, App. No. 006/2012, Judgment of 26 May 2017, para. 138, the Court held that African Charter Art. 2 encompasses other types of discrimination not foreseen when the African Charter was adopted. For an expansive list of grounds, cf. EU Charter of Fundamental Rights Art. 21(1), and the Inter-American Convention Against All Forms of Discrimination and Intolerance (5 Jun. 2013) Art. 1(1).
1078. In 2006, the UN adopted a Convention on the Rights of Persons with Disabilities (6 Dec. 2006), 2515 U.N.T.S. 3. The Organisation of American States has adopted the Inter-American Convention on the Elimination of All Forms of Discrimination Against Persons with Disabilities (8 Jun. 1999), the Inter-American Convention on Protecting the Human Rights of Older Persons (15 Jun. 2015), I.L.M. 55 (2016): 989. The AU has adopted a Protocol on the Rights of Older Persons (31 Jan. 2016) and a Protocol on the Rights of Persons with Disabilities in Africa (29 Jan. 2018).
1079. Cf. Consolidated Version of the TFEU Art. 10 (13 Dec. 2007) 2010 OJ C 83/01 (TFEU). Sexual orientation comes within the scope of the European Convention for the Protection of Human Rights and Fundamental Freedoms (4 Nov. 1950) (as amended), 213 U.N.T.S. 222 (ECHR), D.J. Harris, M. O'Boyle, C. Warbrick & E. Bates, *Law of the European Convention on Human Rights* 595–599 (Oxford University Press 2nd ed. 2009). *See also* Conte & Burchill, 301–302.
1080. Cf. Art. 13 ECHR; Harris, O'Boyle, Warbrick, 558–560.

values, namely the emphasis on 'harmony and deference within a group'.[1081] On the other hand, it is difficult to reconcile with the individualistic approach of Western liberal democratic thought, although the AHRD is not unique in this respect; other international instruments recognise that individuals have responsibilities, implied or otherwise, towards their social environment.[1082] Arguably, the vague and generalised wording in Article 6 could adversely affect the enjoyment of rights. UN experts have criticised the AHRD because it 'creates much greater scope for Governments to place arbitrary, disproportionate and unnecessary restrictions on human rights'.[1083] By definition, civic-type duties of good neighbourliness are of a general nature presumably placing a moral rather than a legal obligation upon the individual. But they could also refer to the fulfilment of legal obligations such as paying taxes. Therefore, it is difficult to provide definitive answers to such questions as to whether they should be considered enforceable and whether individuals deemed to have failed in their duties would be answerable under municipal law. But in a declaratory instrument such as the AHRD one would not expect these issues to be addressed.

304. Article 8 of the AHRD stipulates that rights can be subject to limitations and justifiable interferences. These should not be open ended exceptions but 'determined by law' to secure the human rights of others in 'the general welfare of the peoples in a democratic society'. Moreover, they must be justified by objective grounds, e.g., national security, public order, public morality, and public health. However, international human rights law is more demanding than Article 8, since it additionally requests that restrictions must be necessary in a democratic society (this appears to be a higher threshold than 'the general welfare' test of the AHRD), non-arbitrary and proportionate.[1084] The seemingly limitless scope of Article 8, which can apply to *all* rights and freedoms without distinction, is arguably incompatible with international human rights law which contain rights-specific limitation provisions.[1085] Thus, the AHRD should have proclaimed that such rights as the freedom from torture and ill-treatment, the freedom from slavery and the prohibition of forced labour are absolute and cannot be restricted in any circumstances, including times of national emergencies.[1086] UN experts have rightly expressed concern because 'of the risk of these terms being used as a pretext by Governments to place arbitrary, disproportionate and unnecessary restrictions on human rights'.[1087]

1081. J. Donnelly, *International Human Rights* 131 (Westview 2nd ed. 1997).
1082. *See* e.g., UDHR Art. 29(1); ECHR Arts 10(2), 11(2), and 17; American Convention on Human Rights Art. 32(1) (22 Nov. 1969), 1144 U.N.T.S. 123 (ACHR). The African Charter is notable for incorporating a list of explicit duties owed by the individual, *see* K.D. Magliveras & G.J. Naldi, *The African Union (AU)* 245–246 (Kluwer Law International 2nd ed. 2018).
1083. *See also* Jones, 78.
1084. Harris, O'Boyle & Warbrick, 349–359; Sieghart, 94–98.
1085. Conte & Burchill, 53–54. However, this provision of the AHRD is similar to UDHR Art. 29.
1086. Conte & Burchill, 40–42; Harris, O'Boyle & Warbrick, 638–639.
1087. *See* n. 647.

II. Civil and Political Rights

305. The civil and political rights, in summary, are: right to life (Article 11); right to personal liberty and security (Article 12); freedom from servitude or slavery, including human trafficking (Article 13); freedom from torture or cruel, inhuman or degrading treatment or punishment (Article 14); right to freedom of movement and residence (Article 15); right to seek and receive asylum (Article 16); right to property (Article 17); right to a nationality (Article 18); right to marry and found a family (Article 19); right to a fair trial by an independent and impartial tribunal (including the right to a defence, presumption of innocence, prohibition of retrospective criminal laws, and the principle *of ne bis in idem*) (Article 20); right to privacy, family, home or correspondence (Article 21); freedom of thought, conscience and religion (Article 22); freedom of opinion and expression (Article 23); freedom of peaceful assembly (Article 24); and, finally, political rights, including the right to vote (Article 25).

306. The wording of the second sentence of Article 11 ('No person shall be deprived of life save in accordance with law') denotes that the death penalty is not only accepted but that the AHRD is not even abolitionist in outlook.[1088] This is not surprising because many ASEAN States regard it as a matter of national policy falling exclusively within their domestic jurisdiction.[1089] Not one ASEAN State has acceded to the ICCPR Second Optional Protocol. The only undertaking is against the arbitrary deprivation of life which requires that procedural guarantees be observed. The inclusion of a specific guarantee against abduction in Article 12 takes account of developments in international human rights law extending the definition of cruel, inhuman or degrading treatment and the right to liberty and security to encompass enforced disappearances.[1090]

307. The prohibition on slavery in any form contained in Article 13 has been brought into line with contemporary developments to include human smuggling and trafficking in persons,[1091] including trafficking in human organs. However, it seems

1088. ACHR Art. 4(3).

1089. M. Davies, *The ASEAN Synthesis: Human Rights, Non-Intervention and the ASEAN Human Rights Declaration*, 14(2) Geo. J. Int'l Aff. 27 (2013). Singapore and Thailand, for instance, carried out a number of executions in 2019, Human Rights Watch, *World Report 2019*, 516, 580. UN human rights agencies have expressed concerns about the revised penal code in Brunei Darussalam which stipulates the death penalty for numerous offences, UN News, 'UN agencies urge Brunei to repeal new "extreme and unjustified" penal code' (4 Apr. 2019), https://news.un.org/en/story/2019/04/1036121.

1090. *Velasquez Rodriguez v. Honduras*, Merits, Inter-American Court of Human Rights, Series C, No. 4 (1988); International Convention for the Protection of All Persons from Enforced Disappearance (20 Dec. 2006), 2175 U.N.T.S. 3.

1091. *See* Protocol to Prevent, Suppress and Punish Trafficking in Persons, Especially Women and Children, supplementing the UN Convention against Transnational Organised Crime (15 Nov. 2000) 2237 U.N.T.S. 319. *See* below on the ASEAN Convention Against Trafficking in Persons Particularly Women and Children. For the situation in individual ASEAN countries, *see* U.S. Department of State, *Trafficking in Persons Report 2020*, 20th ed., June 2020 https://www.state.gov/reports/2020-trafficking-in-persons-report/, and *Trafficking in Persons Report 2021*, June 2021, https://www.state.gov/reports/2021-trafficking-in-persons-report/.

regrettable that, unlike the ICCPR, an express prohibition on forced labour has been omitted,[1092] especially when the figures from the International Labour Organization show that the Asia-Pacific region accounts for a large number of forced labourers.[1093]

308. The right under Article 16 to seek and receive asylum is worthy of note since general international law does not oblige states to admit refuge seekers and grant asylum.[1094] As has been argued, 'the grant of *asylum*...is conferred by states in their discretion. Aliens have no "right" of asylum, it is merely the right of the state to grant it'.[1095] Unlike Article 14(1) UDHR, Article 16 is qualified and without prejudice to state sovereignty as it is subject to the receiving state's legislation and applicable international agreements. While it is encouraging that the AHRD explicitly acknowledges this right, ultimately Article 16 confers no additional safeguards (it omits the principle of *non-refoulement*)[1096] but simply constitutes a reaffirmation of the current position that individuals have a right to *request* asylum.

309. The right to family life in Article 19 includes the right to dissolve a marriage,[1097] which, however, is subject to the qualification 'as prescribed by law' and, therefore, open to different regulations by domestic law. Notwithstanding that grounds for divorce and other formal requirements vary from state to state, the fact that the traditional interpretation of Islamic law, which is followed in many ASEAN countries, seems to confer on women a status inferior to men,[1098] the implication of Article 19 is disturbing. While no minimum age for lawful marriage is specified, the fact that 'free and full consent' must be given suggests that child marriage is not sanctioned. This would appear to be also true of forced marriage. Finally, the right to privacy, family, home or correspondence contained in Article 21 has been updated to include personal data.[1099]

1092. Cf. Art. 8(3)(a) ICCPR.

1093. International Labour Office and Walk Free Foundation, *Global Estimates of Modern Slavery: Forced Labour and Forced Marriage*, Geneva, 2017, https://www.ilo.org/global/publications/books/WCMS_575479/lang--en/index.htm.

1094. G.S. Goodwin-Gill, *International Law and the Movement of Persons Between States* 138 (Oxford U. Press 1978). According to the European Court of Human Rights, 'States have the right, as a matter of well-established international law ... to control the entry, residence and expulsion of aliens', *see*, *Abdulaziz, Cabales and Balkandali v. United Kingdom*, Appl. Nos 9214/80; 9473/81; 9474/81, Judgment, 28 May 1985 (1985) 7 E.H.R.R. 471, para. 67; *Saadi v. Italy*, Appl. No. 37201/06, Judgment, 28 Feb. 2008 (2009) 49 E.H.R.R. 30, para. 124; *Hirsi Jamaa v. Italy*, Appl. No. 37201/06, Judgment, 23 Feb. 2012, para. 113.

1095. A. Aust, *Handbook of International Law* 170 (Cambridge U. Press 2 ed. 2010).

1096. According to the United Nations High Commission for Refugees, *non-refoulement* is a rule of customary international law and a human right, quoted in the aforementioned case *M.S.S. v. Belgium and Greece* (2011) 53 E.H.R.R. 2, para. 56. ASEAN would appear to uphold this principle, Moretti, 9–12.

1097. Cf. UDHR Art. 16(1); ICCPR Art. 23(4). No right to a divorce exists under the ECHR, *Johnston v. Ireland*, Appl. No. 9697/82, Judgment, European Court of Human Rights, 18 Dec. 1986 (1987) 9 E.H.R.R. 203.

1098. N.J. DeLong-Bas, *Women, Islam, and the Twenty-First Century*, Focus On, *Oxford Islamic Studies Online*, http://www.oxfordislamicstudies.com/Public/focus/essay1107_women.html.

1099. Harris, O'Boyle & Warbrick, 368–370. *See also* TFEU Art. 16(1); EU Charter of Fundamental Rights Art. 8.

310. The freedom of religion in Article 22 also invites attention. While the right to hold religious beliefs may be absolute,[1100] the AHRD is silent on the attendant freedom to change religion,[1101] an issue of concern given that in Islam, a dominant faith in the region, apostasy attracts harsh penalties.[1102] Article 22 proceeds to call for the elimination of all forms of intolerance, discrimination and incitement of hatred based on religion and beliefs.[1103] This builds upon the commitment to tolerance in the ASEAN Charter but could also reflect the concern by Muslim countries towards Islamophobia and the defamation of religion.[1104]

311. The affirmation of the principles of democracy and constitutional government in the ASEAN Charter is manifested in Article 25 of the AHRD, which provides that every citizen has the right of political participation, including the right to a free vote in genuine periodic elections.[1105] As is true with other regional human rights instruments, such stipulations contradict the existing state of affairs in those Member States which have authoritarian and dictatorial regimes in power. To that extent, there is a good measure of pretence in these instruments. Even though it is true that Article 25 does not explicitly guarantee multiparty politics, the divergence between the reality and what the AHRD purports to protect should be a cause for concern. As Article 25 has been worded, there appear to be no external restraints on those Member States which may prevent the formation of political parties or dissolve existing parties. In these circumstances any external restraints will have to come from the regimes created by the multilateral human rights treaties to which individual Member States participate and, of course, from the ASEAN Charter itself.

312. A notable absence from the list of civil and political rights is the freedom of association, although Article 27(2) does guarantee the right to form and join trade unions. However, the freedom of association has a wider ambit: it not only includes the right to protest but goes further to endow individuals with the freedom to create

1100. Office of the UN High Commissioner for Human Rights, General Comment 22, *The Right to Freedom of Thought, Conscience and Religion*, UN Doc. CCPR/C/21/Rev.1/Add. 4, 30 Jul. 1993, para. 3.

1101. *Ibid.*, para. 5.

1102. B. Tibi, *The European Tradition of Human Rights and the Culture of Islam*, in *Human Rights in Africa: Cross-Cultural Perspectives* 104 (A.A. An-Nai'm & F.M. Deng eds, Brookings Institution Press 1990). *See* UN News, 'UN agencies urge Brunei to repeal new "extreme and unjustified" penal code' (4 Apr. 2019), https://news.un.org/en/story/2019/04/1036121.

1103. Cf. ICCPR Art. 20.

1104. *See*, e.g., Organisation of Islamic Cooperation, Resolutions on Legal Affairs adopted by the 38th Session of the Council of Foreign Ministers, Resolution No. 1/38-LEG on the Follow-up and Coordination of Work on Human Rights, para. 8, I.L.M. 50 (2011) 1152. In 2022 the UN General Assembly adopted Resolution 76/254 sponsored by the OIC designating 15 March as the International Day to Combat Islamophobia.

1105. Cf. ICCPR Art. 25, described as 'the core of democratic government based on the consent of the people', Office of the UN High Commissioner for Human Rights, General Comment 25, *The Right to Participate in Public Affairs, Voting Rights and the Right of Equal Access to Public Service*, UN Doc. CCPR/C/21/Rev.1/Add.7, 12 Jul. 1996, para. 1. *See* generally, R. Burchill, *Regional Integration and the Promotion and Protection of Democracy in Asia: Lessons from ASEAN*, 13 Asian Y.B. Int'l L. 135 (2007).

and join, without state interference, political parties, professional bodies and any other organised group through which legitimate interests can be pursued. In its absence therefore, ASEAN countries are under no obvious legal restriction to abstain from interfering with their free formation. This could have a negative impact on participatory democracy.

III. Economic, Social and Cultural Rights

313. The relevant section in the AHRD commences with the affirmation in Article 26 that Member States subscribe to the rights as set out in the UDHR. While it is a fundamental AHRD tenet that all human rights are indivisible and interdependent, it is clear from Article 33 that their immediate application is not regarded as a feasible proposition. Thus, for the time being Member States should ensure that minimum essential levels are satisfied leaving full realisation to an undefined future time, dependent on available resources and international assistance and cooperation. Moreover, Article 34 makes it clear that non-nationals may be excluded from benefiting from certain economic and social rights. Presumably, the drafters had in mind migrant workers in particular. Notwithstanding that states have a sovereign right to determine how to deal with non-nationals, they are under a number of obligations, namely to uphold the principle of non-discrimination and to ensure that any restrictions imposed, such as qualification periods, are reasonable and proportionate.[1106]

314. The following economic, social and cultural rights are recognised: right to work (including just, decent and favourable conditions of work) (Article 27(1)); right to form and join trade unions (Article 27(2)); protection of children and young persons from economic and social exploitation (Article 27(3)); right to an adequate standard of living, including adequate and affordable food, clothing, housing; medical care and social services; safe drinking water and sanitation; and a safe, clean and sustainable environment (Article 28); right to the highest attainable standard of physical, mental and reproductive health, to basic and affordable healthcare services, and to access medical facilities (Article 29(1)); right to social security (Article 30(1)); special protection for mothers and children (Article 30(2)–(3)); right to education, primary education being compulsory and free, secondary education available and accessible to all, higher education equally accessible to all on the basis of merit (Article 31); and the right to take part in cultural life, to enjoy the arts and the benefits of scientific progress and to protection of the moral and material interests resulting from scientific, literary or artistic productions (Article 32).

315. The right to work contained in Article 27(1) merits particular attention for a number of reasons. First, it has been restrictively drafted because the right 'to enjoy just, decent and favourable conditions of work' does not necessarily cover a working environment which is both safe and healthy. Labour conditions in the

1106. Office of the UN High Commissioner for Human Rights, General Comment No. 23, *The Rights of Minorities*, UN Doc. CCPR/C/21/Rev.1/Add. 5, 8 Apr. 1994.

region means there is limited access to social protection schemes.[1107] Second, the right to free choice of employment should have been envisaged as a further prohibition of forced labour. Third, no right to equal pay for equal work is specifically listed. While discrimination on the basis of sex is prohibited, it is regrettable that combating gender discrimination in the workplace, one of the main areas where it manifests, is not mentioned. Fourth, there is no explicit mention of 'just and favourable remuneration' or 'fair wages'.[1108] And finally, the right to rest and leisure has been omitted.[1109] While such a right is probably implied, it should be recalled that these arc considered distinct rights in the UDHR.[1110]

316. Article 27(3) on the protection of children also invites attention since the AHRD neither defines a child or young person nor specifies an age of majority.[1111] This may be an acknowledgement that the age of majority varies between Member States. However, this lack of uniformity becomes problematic for the setting of a minimum age for admission to employment, which is left to the Member States.[1112] A positive feature of Article 27(3) is that child labour, if harmful, is punishable by law.[1113] Although the protection of children and young persons from sexual exploitation is not made explicit it appears to be covered given that work harmful to, *inter alia*, their morals is specified.[1114] It is deeply regrettable that the AHRD is silent on

1107. International Labour Organization, *World Employment and Social Outlook: Trends 2024*, 49, https://www.ilo.org/sites/default/files/wcmsp5/groups/public/%40dgreports/%40inst/documents/publication/wcms_908142.pdf. *See generally* M. Olivier, *Social Protection for Migrant Workers in ASEAN: Developments, Challenges, and Prospects* (International Labour Organization 2018), https://www.ilo.org/wcmsp5/groups/public/---asia/---ro-bangkok/documents/publication/wcms_655176.pdf. Note that the right to health also encompasses occupational health, cf. UN Human Rights Council, *Report of the Special Rapporteur on the right of everyone to the enjoyment of the highest attainable standard of physical and mental health, Anand Grover*, UN Doc. A/HRC/20/15, 10 Apr. 2012.

1108. Cf. UDHR Art. 23.

1109. Cf. ICESCR Art. 7(d).

1110. Cf. UDHR Art. 24.

1111. This appears to be eighteen, UN Convention on the Rights of the Child Art. 1 (20 Nov. 1989), 1577 U.N.T.S. 3 (CRC), ratified by all ASEAN Member States.

1112. Although this is in keeping with CRC, Art. 32(2)(a). *See* further, ILO Convention No. 138 concerning Minimum Age for Admission to Employment 1015 U.N.T.S. 297 (26 Jun. 1973), ratified by most ASEAN Member States.

1113. CRC Art. 32(1). Child labour appears to be a problem in Thailand, *see* U.S. Department of Labor, Bureau of International Labor Affairs, *Child Labor and Forced Labor Reports: Thailand*, 2019, https://www.dol.gov/agencies/ilab/resources/reports/child-labor/thailand.

1114. CRC Art. 34; ILO Convention No. 182 on the Worst Forms of Child Labour Art. 3(b), (d) (17 Jun. 1999) I.L.M. 38 (1999): 1207; and Optional Protocol to the Convention on the Rights of the Child on the Sale of Children, Child Prostitution and Child Pornography (25 May 2000) 2171 U.N.T.S. 227. The sexual exploitation of children is a problem particularly in the Mekong region (Thailand, Cambodia, Laos, and Vietnam), as evidenced by the project *Childhood*, implemented during the period 2010–2014 by the UN Office on Drugs and Crime, *see* https://www.unodc.org/documents/evaluation/Independent_Project_Evaluations/2014/XSPT33_Independent_Project_Evaluation_Report_June_2014.pdf.

the phenomenon of the participation and recruitment of children in armed conflicts, which is deeply offensive to basic notions of humanity.[1115]

317. The constituent elements that comprise a standard of living include, pursuant to Article 28(e), safe drinking water and sanitation. The right to water, which has been described as 'indispensable for leading a life in human dignity',[1116] has also found recognition in UN General Assembly resolutions[1117] and the UN Human Rights Council.[1118] The domestic legislation of some ASEAN countries envisages that the state must guarantee individual access and availability of water for everyone residing within the territory[1119] but in other states the position is more restrictive. Thus, in an apparent attempt to prevent exportation of a precious resource, Article 12 of the Constitution of the Philippines 1987 provides that water belongs to the state and that disposition or utilisation shall be limited to its citizens.[1120]

318. Another significant inclusion is the right to a safe, clean and sustainable environment guaranteed in Article 28(f). A clean and safe environment is closely intertwined with, *inter alia*, the right to water and the right to health and its inclusion in this provision is supportive of that view.[1121] In relation to the right to health, the commitment in Article 29(2) to address the diverse problems experienced by people suffering from communicable diseases, including HIV/AIDS, is noteworthy.[1122]

IV. Collective Rights

319. The inclusion of rights variously described as collective rights, peoples' rights, group rights or third-generation rights in the AHRD constitutes a key, but no

---

1115. ILO Convention No. 182 Art. 3(a); Optional Protocol to the Convention on the Rights of the Child on the Involvement of Children in Armed Conflict (25 May 2000), 2173 U.N.T.S. 222. The Statute establishing the International Criminal Court Art. 8(2)(b)(xxvi) (17 Jul. 1998), 2187 U.N.T.S. 3, depicts such activity as a 'war crime'.

1116. UN Economic and Social Council, General Comment No. 15, *The Right to Water*, UN Doc. E/C.12/2002/11, 20 Jan. 2003, para. 1. *See* UDHR Art. 25(1); ICESCR Art. 12.

1117. UNGA Res. 64/292, The human right to water and sanitation, 3 Aug. 2010.

1118. *See, inter alia*, Resolution A/HRC/24/L.31, The human right to safe drinking water and sanitation, 23 Sep. 2013; and *Progressive realization of the human rights to water and sanitation: Report of the Special Rapporteur on the human rights to safe drinking water and sanitation*, UN Doc. A/HRC/45/10, 8 Jul. 2020.

1119. *See, inter alia*, Art. 5 of Law No. 7/2004 Water Resources Law of Indonesia, reproduced in *Law, Environment and Development Journal* 2 (2006): 118, http://www.lead-journal.org/content/06118.pdf.

1120. At: www.gov.ph/constitutions/the-1987-constitution-of-the-republic-of-the-philippines/.

1121. UN ECOSOC, General Comment No. 14, *The Right to the Highest Attainable Standard of Health*, UN Doc. E/C.12/2000/4, 11 Aug. 2000, para. 11; General Comment No. 15, The Right to Water (Arts. 11 and 12 of the Covenant), E/C.12/2002/11. 20 Jan. 2003, para. 8. *See* further, UNGARes. 37/7, World Charter for Nature, 28 Oct. 1982.

1122. General Comment No. 14, para. 16. *See also* UNGA Res. S-26/2, Declaration of Commitment on HIV/AIDS, 27 Jun. 2001; UNGA Res. 60/262, Political Declaration on HIV/AIDS, 15 Jun. 2006; and UNGA Res. 65/277, Political Declaration on HIV and AIDS: Intensifying Our Efforts to Eliminate HIV and AIDS, 10 Jun. 2011.

longer distinctive, feature. In reality, the AHRD limits itself essentially to two such rights, the right to development and the right to peace. While the right of self-determination was not included, presumably on account of a reluctance to provide encouragement to separatists,[1123] the commitment to democracy should make references to the internal dimension of self-determination redundant. Moreover, the right to a healthy, clean, and sustainable environment was not inserted as a self-standing right but only as one of the constituent elements of Article 28, which purports to guarantee to everyone an adequate standard of living. This is regrettable and retrogressive but also problematic given that Article 1(9) of the ASEAN Charter does list the protection of the environment as one of its goals.

320. Article 35 of the AHRD enshrines the right to development, composed of interrelated economic, social, cultural and political strands but otherwise largely undefined; it is described as 'an inalienable human right',[1124] a contentious assertion.[1125] Nevertheless, the AHRD is simply reaffirming the Vienna Declaration's stance on this issue.[1126] Intriguingly, no mention is made of the associated concept of permanent sovereignty over natural resources as well as of the rights of peoples to dispose of their natural wealth for their own ends and to equal enjoyment of the common heritage of humankind. This could suggest that autocratic regimes currently in power are reluctant to lose control over vital economic resources. However, the lack of development may not be invoked as a justification for the violation of internationally recognised human rights.[1127] By making a direct connection between economic development and human rights, the AHRD acknowledges that a human rights culture is indispensable in fostering economic growth.[1128]

321. Member States ought to secure the exercise of the right to development, both individually and collectively. Article 36 of the AHRD encourages them to adopt domestic development programmes aiming at poverty alleviation and the progressive narrowing of the development gap within ASEAN. But Article 37 also recognises that such development can only take place when a favourable and equitable economic order exists both at a national and international level. While it is true that a negative global economic climate compromises development (especially in countries such as those in ASEAN), arguably prudent states should amass wealth during times of global or domestic economic growth and use it to weather negative economic conditions without having to sacrifice development.

1123. Note that some ASEAN countries, including Myanmar and the Philippines, have problems with separatists, *see US State Department Country Reports on Human Rights Practices 2009*, www.state.gov/j/drl/rls/hrrpt/2009.

1124. *See* UNGA Res. 41/128, United Nations Declaration on the Right to Development, 4 Dec. 1986.

1125. S. Marks, *The Human Right to Development: Between Rhetoric and Reality*, 17 Harv. Hum. Rts. J. 137 (2004).

1126. Vienna Declaration and Programme of Action, Part I, paras 10, 72.

1127. UN ECOSOC, General Comment No. 12, *The Right to Adequate Food*, UN Doc. E/C.12/1999/5, 12 May 1999, para. 5.

1128. Cf. UNGA Res. 60/1, 2005 World Summit Outcome, para. 9, 24 Oct. 2005, where Member States recognised that development, peace and security and human rights are interlinked and mutually reinforcing.

322. The only other collective right accepted by the AHRD is the right to peace in Article 38. While it refers to peace within an ASEAN framework of security and stability, curiously no reference is made to the relevant UN law and principles on friendly relations. However, numerous references have been made to these in other contexts and it may therefore be considered superfluous. Moreover, Article 38 envisages duties for the Member States both at domestic and regional levels. Thus, they must ensure that the populations enjoy peace, security and stability, and between them they must promote friendship and cooperation and bring harmony to the region. It has been seen that these are priority areas for ASEAN.

323. Another noteworthy omission is any explicit safeguard for the rights of members of minorities.[1129] While Article 2(2)(l) of the ASEAN Charter upholds respect for the different cultures, languages and religions in the region, this has not translated into the protection of minority rights per se. The guarantees are provided to individuals; the fact they may belong to a minority is incidental. While, as has been explained, the AHRD contains guarantees on non-discrimination and equal protection before the law, such rights are not considered as sufficient in themselves because they are not distinct and specific to persons belonging to a separate religious, ethnic, or cultural community.[1130] While it is true that regional human rights texts are silent on the issue of minorities,[1131] in the twenty-first century, minorities should be explicitly acknowledged.

324. Neither does the AHRD make any overt mention of indigenous or tribal peoples, although they should come within the scope of vulnerable and marginalised groups.[1132] Native title to land is a contested issue but the right to property is recognised by Article 17. There is ample international jurisprudence that indigenous peoples have a right both to the land they traditionally inhabit and to its natural resources. The example of the Inter-American Court of Human Rights (IACHR) stands out.[1133]

1129. A. Meijknecht & B.S. de Vries, *Is There a Place for Minorities' and Indigenous Peoples' Rights Within ASEAN?: Asian Values, ASEAN Values and the Protection of Southeast Asian Minorities and Indigenous Peoples'*, 17 Int'l J. Minority & Group Rts. 75 (2010).
1130. General Comment 23, paras 4, 5.1. *See* ICCPR Art. 27.
1131. Cf. TEU Art. 2; EU Charter of Fundamental Freedoms Art. 21.
1132. Indigenous peoples can be found mainly in Malaysia, Myanmar, Philippines and Thailand but the question of indigenous identity is controversial in Asia, *see* R.H. Barnes, *Introduction*, in *Indigenous Peoples of Asia* 3 (R.H. Barnes, A. Gray & B. Kingsbury eds, Association for Asian Studies 1995). It would seem that indigenous peoples in ASEAN States tend to be discriminated against and marginalised, *see* Asia Indigenous Peoples Pact, *Indigenous Peoples and ASEAN Integration*, December 2015, https://aippnet.org/indigenous-peoples-and-asean-integration/. It is claimed that ethnic minority voters were suppressed in Myanmar's 2020 general election, *see* R. Ratcliffe 'Myanmar minorities, including Rohingya, excluded from voting in election' *The Guardian*, 6 Nov. 2020, https://www.theguardian.com/world/2020/nov/06/myanmar-minorities-rohingya-excluded-voting-election-poll-aung-san-suu-kyi-rights.
1133. There are numerous decisions of the Inter-American Court of Human Rights, e.g., *Case of the Xucuru Indigenous Peoples and its members v. Brazil*, Preliminary Objections, Merits, Reparations, and Costs, Judgment of 5 Feb. 2018, Series C No. 346. In 1990, the Inter-American Commission on Human Rights created the Office of the Special Rapporteur on the Rights of Indigenous

325. Its flaws notwithstanding, the AHRD must be considered as a positive, if tentative, first step. It may in time lead to a human rights treaty proper. For the present it sets a standard agreed upon by the ASEAN Member States themselves so that objections about Western 'influences' will no longer seem valid. Acceptance of these standards is therefore a litmus test for ASEAN.

§4. Other ASEAN Declarations on Human Rights

326. Whilst the AHRD is a significant achievement, it is not in fact the first declaration on a human rights theme adopted by ASEAN. In fact, ASEAN has demonstrated a marked preference in the field of human rights for proceeding on the basis of non-binding instruments rather than treaties.[1134] Before the advent of the AHRD, ASEAN had adopted a number of declarations for the protection of specific groups regarded as vulnerable. Women and children have been a priority area. The Declaration on the Commitments for Children seeks to protect, *inter alia*, the homeless and disadvantaged, and those at risk of violence, drugs, HIV/AIDS, and human trafficking.[1135] Under the Declaration on the Protection of Children from All Forms of Online Exploitation and Abuse, ASEAN commits itself to protecting children from all such forms of exploitation and abuse, in particular by promoting, developing, and implementing comprehensive national legal frameworks in each ASEAN Member State and working towards improving child protection standards and policies on online exploitation and abuse across ASEAN Member States; enhancing law enforcement, judicial and legal professional capabilities; encouraging the establishment of national specialised units with the remit to lead, support and coordinate investigations; increasing effectiveness of rights-based and gender-responsive child protection and support services and social welfare programmes; and promoting national education programmes and school curricula to raise awareness of sexual and other forms of exploitation of to empower children, young people, parents, communities and others.[1136] In accordance with the Joint Statement on Reaffirmation of Commitment to Advancing the Rights of the Child, ASEAN commits itself,

---

Peoples, http://www.oas.org/en/iachr/indigenous/mandate/composition.asp. The rights of indigenous peoples in Africa have also been recognised, African Commission on Human and Peoples' Rights, *Centre for Minority Rights Development (Kenya) and Minority Rights Group International on behalf of Endorois Welfare Council v. Kenya*, Communication No. 276/2003 (2009) AHRLR 75.

1134. Duxbury & Hsein-Li, 145.

1135. Declaration on the Commitments for Children in ASEAN (Singapore, 2 Aug. 2001), https://bice.org/app/uploads/2014/10/declaration_on_the_commitments_for_children_in_asean.pdf.

1136. Declaration on the Protection of Children from All Forms of Online Exploitation and Abuse in ASEAN (Bangkok, 2 Nov. 2019), https://asean.org/wp-content/uploads/2019/11/3-Declaration-on-the-Protection-of-Children-from-all-Forms-of-Online-Exploitation-and-Abuse-in-ASEAN.pdf. It should be observed that, apart from Singapore, all the other ASEAN States have ratified or acceded to the Optional Protocol to the Convention on the Rights of the Child on the sale of children, child prostitution and child pornography (25 May 2000), 2171 U.N.T.S. 227.

inter alia, to achieving gender equality and empowerment of children, to strengthening child rights legal frameworks, to strengthening national policies and programmes relating to health, nutrition, education, water, sanitation and hygiene, child protection and social work and protection, and to increasing social investment to lift children out of poverty.[1137]

327. In 2004, ASEAN adopted two declarations with direct relevance to women's rights, the Declaration on the Elimination of Violence Against Women[1138] and the Declaration Against Trafficking in Persons, specifically Trafficking of Women and Children.[1139] Under the former Declaration, ASEAN Member States commit to a detailed programme, *inter alia*, to eliminate violence against women by changing societal attitudes and behaviour, to take appropriate action against offenders, to eliminate discrimination against women and to adopt suitable legislation and other measures.

328. In 2013 a follow-up document was adopted, the Declaration on the Elimination of Violence against Women and Children.[1140] As is apparent from its title this Declaration addresses violence against women and children, including women and children with disabilities, women and children living with and affected by HIV/AIDS, women and children of ethnic and/or indigenous groups, and migrant women and children, in the one document, enumerating particular forms of violence in both the private and public spheres, including domestic violence, sexual exploitation, cyber pornography, bullying and discrimination. The Declaration directs ASEAN Member States to take all appropriate measures to promote and protect human rights and to change social and cultural behaviour in order to eliminate prejudices based on preconceptions of the superiority/inferiority of the sexes and stereotyped views of their roles. The Declaration proceeds to recognise the important role that civil society can play in preventing and responding to these social ills and calls on the Commission on the Promotion and Protection of the Rights of Women and Children (ACWC) to promote the implementation of the Declaration. The Ha Noi Declaration on the Enhancement of Welfare and Development of ASEAN Women and Children was a further attempt to promote and protect the rights of women and

1137. Joint Statement on Reaffirmation of Commitment to Advancing the Rights of the Child in ASEAN (Bangkok, 2 Nov. 2019), https://asean.org/joint-statement-on-reaffirmation-of-commitment-to-advancing-the-rights-of-the-child-in-asean/.

1138. Declaration on the Elimination of Violence Against Women in the ASEAN Region (Jakarta, 30 Jun. 2004), https://asean.org/declaration-on-the-elimination-of-violence-against-women-in-the-asean-region-30-june-2004-jakarta-indonesia/. The importance of the role of women and the necessity of meeting their needs and aspirations had been acknowledged by the Declaration on the Advancement of Women in the ASEAN Region (Bangkok, 5 Jul. 1988), https://asean.org/declaration-of-the-advancement-of-women-in-the-asean-region-bangkok-thailand-5-july-1988-2/.

1139. Declaration against Trafficking in Persons, Particularly Trafficking of Women and Children (Vientiane, 29 Nov. 2004), https://asean.org/wp-content/uploads/2012/05/ASEAN-Declaration-against-Trafficking-in-Persons-Particularly-Women-and-Children-TPPWC.pdf.

1140. Declaration on the Elimination of Violence against Women and Elimination of Violence against Children (9 Oct. 2013), https://asean.org/wp-content/uploads/2021/08/Declaration-on-the-Elimination-of-Violence-Against-WC.pdf.

children.[1141] The Ha Noi Declaration accentuates the importance of the family as the basic unit of society and calls for maternal health and reproductive rights. ASEAN Member States undertake to provide basic social services and other basic necessities such as housing, safe drinking water, sanitation and educational facilities. The Hanoi Declaration calls on ASEAN Member States to enhance the effective participation of women in decision-making and leadership and to promote gender equality and women's participation in the labour market.

329. The declarations on women which seek to bridge the 'gender gap' reflect developments in international human rights law but only up to a point. They do not deal with women's rights in a comprehensive manner but are somewhat limited in scope.[1142] This observation seems to be true also with respect to children's rights. There is ample scope for ASEAN to extend the substantive range of the existing rights of these vulnerable groups. And it needs to be borne in mind that these declarations are not legally binding texts.

330. The ASEAN Declaration on the Rights of Migrant Workers (ADMW) of 2007 sets out the obligations of the countries of origin and the countries of destination, which undertake, *inter alia*, to take notice of the fundamental rights and dignity of migrant workers; to provide employment protection as well as decent wages, working and living conditions; to secure access to justice and social welfare services; to promote fair employment; and to take concrete measures to deal with human trafficking. It also calls for an ASEAN treaty on this subject.[1143] The end result was not a treaty, which did not prove possible due to lack of agreement, but another non-binding document, the ASEAN Consensus on the Rights of Migrant Workers (Consensus) of 2017.[1144] Notwithstanding the fact that the Consensus is a hortatory document, the ASEAN Member States nevertheless were careful to underline that determining migration policy relating to migrant workers, including controlling entry into and departure from their territory and under which conditions migrant workers may stay, remained a sovereign decision.[1145]

1141. Ha Noi Declaration on the Enhancement of Welfare and Development of ASEAN Women and Children (28 Oct. 2010), https://asean.org/ha-noi-declaration-on-the-enhancement-of-welfare-and-development-of-asean-women-and-children/.

1142. The standard setter in this instance is the Council of Europe Convention on Preventing and Combating Violence against Women and Domestic Violence (Istanbul Convention) (11 May 2011) C.E.T.S. 210, described as 'a potentially powerful tool in the elimination of violence against women', L. Grans, *The Istanbul Convention and the Positive Obligation to Prevent Violence*, 18 HRLR 133, 136 (2018).

1143. ASEAN Declaration on the Protection and Promotion of the Rights of Migrant Workers (13 Jan. 2007), https://asean.org/asean-declaration-on-the-protection-and-promotion-of-the-rights-of-migrant-workers/.

1144. ASEAN Consensus on the Protection and Promotion of the Rights of Migrant Workers (14 Nov. 2017), https://asean.org/wp-content/uploads/2018/03/3.-March-2018-ASEAN-Consensus-on-the-Protection-and-Promotion-of-the-Rights-of-Migrant-Workers.pdf.

1145. Consensus Preamble. This position reflects a basic principle of international law, Human Rights Committee, General Comment No. 15, The position of aliens under the Covenant, UN Doc. HRI/GEN/1/Rev.3 (1997) para. 5; *Saadi v. Italy* [GC], Appl. no. 37201/06, Judgment, European Court of Human Rights, para. 124; *Hirsi Jamaa and Others v. Italy* [GC], Judgment, European Court of Human Rights, Appl. no. 27765/09, para. 113 (23 Feb. 2012).

331. The Consensus, partially inspired by the specific need to protect the fundamental rights of migrant workers and their families, was adopted pursuant to the ADMW and, taking account of the 'shared and balanced responsibilities' and the 'legitimate concerns' of the Receiving and Sending Member States, and acknowledging the need to adopt suitable migration policies on migrant workers, aims to establish a framework for cooperation on migrant workers in the ASEAN region.[1146] Consistent with the Consensus, ASEAN Member States recognise that migrant workers have fundamental rights under applicable international and regional treaties which ASEAN Member States are parties to, and commit themselves to protect the rights of migrant workers, particularly women, in accordance with the obligations of ASEAN Member States under appropriate international instruments to which they are parties.[1147] In view that few ASEAN countries are parties to such treaties the extent and substance of the commitments undertaken is subject to question. In addition, the commitment to upholding the fundamental rights of migrant workers is subject to the laws and policies of the Receiving States.[1148] Such rights are therefore made conditional and potentially meaningless. Another deficiency is that the Consensus only covers documented migrant workers and those who become undocumented through no fault of their own.[1149] This is contrary to the CMW which applies to all migrant workers, documented or undocumented.[1150]

332. In view of the fact that children are an especially vulnerable group, in 2019, ASEAN adopted the Declaration on the Rights of Children in the Context of Migration.[1151] Thereunder, ASEAN Member States reiterated that the best interests of the child is a primary consideration in all relevant policies and practices in the context of migration; acknowledged the need to strengthen national systems in the ASEAN region to enhance their accessibility for children affected by migration, and the need to enhance the identification, referral and protection of, and assistance to all such children, to ensure that national systems address the rights and needs of children in the context of migration; called upon ASEAN Member States to recognise that children in the context of migration are particularly vulnerable and to cooperate and build partnerships with relevant stakeholders to address and prevent violence, abuse, exploitation; resolved to provide access to basic services such as health and psychosocial support services for children in the context of migration; and agreed that in

1146. Consensus Preamble.
1147. Consensus Art. 1(c), (e).
1148. Consensus Art. 1(d).
1149. Consensus Art. 2.
1150. *See also* the decision of the Inter-American Court of Human Rights that, 'Due process of law is a right that must be ensured to all persons, irrespective of their migratory status', *Juridical Condition and Rights of Undocumented Migrants*, Advisory Opinion, Inter-American Court of Human Rights, 17 Sep. 2003, OC-18/03, Series A No.18, para. 121.
1151. ASEAN Declaration on the Rights of Children in the Context of Migration (Bangkok, 2 Nov. 2019), https://asean.org/wp-content/uploads/2019/11/4-ASEAN-Declaration-on-the-Rights-of-Children-in-the-Context-of-Migration.pdf.

order to promote the best interests of the child, States should develop effective procedures and alternatives to child immigration detention to reduce its impact, and ensure that, where possible, children are kept together with their families in a non-custodial and safe environment.

§5. ASEAN Convention Against Trafficking in Persons

333. As mentioned, ASEAN had adopted a Declaration against Trafficking in Persons,[1152] which sought to establish a regional network to prevent and combat trafficking in persons. Thus, the Declaration, *inter alia*, urged ASEAN Member States to take measures to protect the integrity of their passports, identity documents and other official documents from fraud; to tighten controls at borders and adopt appropriate legislation; and to distinguish victims of trafficking from perpetrators, safeguard the human rights of victims and identify the countries of origin as well as their nationalities. However, the Declaration has since been overtaken by a treaty, the Convention Against Trafficking in Persons.[1153]

334. Trafficking in persons in one form or another has long preoccupied the international community.[1154] However, it was only in 2000 that a specific universal treaty was adopted, the UN Protocol against Trafficking in Persons.[1155] The Council of Europe had also taken steps to deal with this phenomenon.[1156] Human trafficking in Southeast Asia has been a long-standing problem which concentrates mainly on sexual exploitation and forced labour.[1157] While human trafficking in this part of the world is undeniably a problem of considerable magnitude, hard and fast figures on the number of victims are hard to come by.[1158] ASEAN had taken a number of initiatives to combat human trafficking based on soft law documents and the ACTP

1152. ASEAN Declaration against Trafficking in Persons, specifically Trafficking of Women and Children (Vientiane, 29 Nov. 2004), https://asean.org/wp-content/uploads/2012/05/ASEAN-Declaration-against-Trafficking-in-Persons-Particularly-Women-and-Children-TPPWC.pdf.

1153. ASEAN Convention Against Trafficking in Persons, specifically Trafficking of Women and Children (Kuala Lumpur, 21 Nov. 2015), https://asean.org/wp-content/uploads/2015/12/ACTIP.pdf (ACTP). The ACTP entered into force on 8 Mar. 2017. *See* generally R. Yusran, *The ASEAN Convention Against Trafficking in Persons: A Preliminary Assessment*, 8 Asian J. Int'l L. 258 (2018).

1154. *See*, e.g., Convention to Suppress the Slave Trade and Slavery (25 Sep. 1926) 60 L.N.T.S. 253, which has only been acceded to by the Philippines (1955).

1155. Protocol to Prevent, Suppress and Punish Trafficking in Persons, Especially Women and Children, supplementing the United Nations Convention against Transnational Organised Crime (adopted 15 Nov. 2000) 2237 U.N.T.S. 319 (Palermo Protocol). All ASEAN States have ratified or acceded to this treaty.

1156. European Convention on Action against Trafficking in Human Beings (16 May 2005) C.E.T.S. No. 197. It is generally agreed that this Convention is the most sophisticated of its type, M. Jovanovic, *Comparison of Anti-Trafficking Legal Regimes and Actions in the Council of Europe and ASEAN: Realities, Frameworks and Possibilities for Collaboration* 11 (Council of Europe 2018).

1157. Jovanovic, 16–19; Yusran, 259, 263; S. Yazid & I. Septiyana, *The Prospect of ASEAN Migration Governance*, 9 J. Indonesian Soc. Sci. & Human. 95, 101–102 (2019); C. Renshaw, *Human Trafficking in Southeast Asia: Uncovering the Dynamics of State Commitment and Compliance*, 37 Mich. J. Int'l L. 611, 630 (2016).

1158. Jovanovic, 15; Yusran, 259, 262.

was only adopted in 2015.[1159] The reasons why a treaty was considered necessary in a departure from the customary approach were based on notions of security, tackling transnational crime, law-enforcement and enhanced regional cooperation.[1160]

335. The ACTP's objectives are based on the so-called 4Ps, prevention, protection, prosecution and partnership, that is, to prevent and combat trafficking in persons, especially against women and children, to protect and assist victims of trafficking, to ensure just and effective punishment of traffickers, and to promote cooperation among the parties.[1161] The emphasis on women and children has been criticised as being 'outdated' on the ground that men form a not insignificant number of victims, particular in relation to forced labour.[1162] However, the ACTP contains a non-discrimination clause which implies that it applies regardless of sex, nationality, etc.[1163] Nevertheless, in relation to the protection of victims of trafficking, the ACTP requires that account be taken of their age, gender and the special needs of children which could arguably be justified on the basis of their particular vulnerability.[1164] It is important to note that the ACTP calls for 'full respect' for the victims' human rights[1165] which has led to it being described as having a human rights dimension.[1166] Like the Palermo Protocol, the ACTP's scope is limited to cross-border trafficking only and does not address trafficking internally which remains a matter for domestic law.[1167] States Parties must not transgress the sovereign rights of other parties, for example, by exercising jurisdiction extraterritorially.[1168]

336. In terms of prevention, States Parties are under an obligation to establish comprehensive policies and programmes to prevent and combat trafficking and to protect victims of trafficking in persons from revictimisation.[1169] They must therefore 'endeavour' to undertake measures such as research, information and mass media campaigns and social and economic initiatives to prevent and combat trafficking, a weak undertaking.[1170] However, more robustly, they must take or strengthen measures, including through bilateral or multilateral cooperation, to address the root causes of trafficking.[1171]

337. States Parties are encouraged to cooperate in order to prevent trafficking in persons,[1172] which includes strengthening regional cooperation in the investigation

1159. Jovanovic, 22–23; Yusran, 268–271.
1160. Yazid & Septiyana, 102; Renshaw, 645–650.
1161. ACTP Art. 1(1). Cf. Palermo Protocol Art. 2.
1162. Jovanovic, 29; Yusran, 264–267.
1163. Yusran, 273.
1164. ACTP Art. 14(12).
1165. ACTP Art. 1(1)(b).
1166. Yusran, *ibid.*
1167. ACTP Art. 3. Cf. Palermo Protocol Art. 4.
1168. ACTP Art. 4.
1169. ACTP Art. 11(1).
1170. ACTP Art. 11(2).
1171. ACTP Arts 11(4), (5), 12(b), (c). *See* Yusran, 279.
1172. ACTP Art. 12.

and prosecution of trafficking.[1173] They are therefore urged to discourage the demand that leads to exploitation and trafficking, which includes allowing legal migration.[1174]

338. The ACTP adopts the Palermo Protocol's definition of trafficking in its entirety.[1175] Whereas the Palermo Protocol does not provide a definition of 'victim', the ACTP's definition of 'victim' is virtually identical to that of the European Convention against Trafficking.[1176] And while its substantive measures on victim protection are deemed to be weaker than the European Convention against Trafficking they are nevertheless considered an improvement on the Palermo Protocol.[1177] Parties are under an obligation to 'endeavour' to provide for the physical safety of victims of trafficking while they are within their territory.[1178] They must 'consider', on humanitarian and compassionate grounds, adopting measures to permit victims of trafficking to remain in their territory, temporarily or permanently.[1179] They must provide care and support to identified victims of trafficking, such as appropriate housing, medical assistance and employment and educational opportunities.[1180] Finally, victims of trafficking should have the 'possibility' of obtaining compensation for damage suffered[1181] rather than a guarantee.[1182]

339. Victim identification is a key element in protecting victims' rights and in pursuing criminal action against traffickers.[1183] States Parties are therefore required to adopt national guidelines and procedures for the proper identification of victims of trafficking.[1184] They must also respect and recognise the identification of victims of trafficking made by the receiving party.[1185] While the privacy and identity of victims of trafficking should be protected, in 'appropriate cases and to the extent possible under its domestic laws',[1186] such safeguard is undermined by the obligation on the receiving party to notify the sending party of the identification unless the victim objects.[1187] Of course, this presupposes that the victim is in a position to make an informed choice.[1188]

1173. ACTP Art. 12(d).
1174. ACTP Art. 12(a), (e).
1175. ACTP Art. 2(a)–(c). Cf. Palermo Protocol Art. 3.
1176. A victim is defined as 'any natural person who is subject to an act of trafficking in persons as defined in this convention', ACTP Art. 2(e). Cf. European Convention against Trafficking Art. 4(e).
1177. Jovanovic, 32–33; Yusran, 277.
1178. ACTP Art. 14(5).
1179. ACTP Art. 14(4).
1180. ACTP Art. 14(10).
1181. ACTP Art. 14(13).
1182. Yusran, 281.
1183. Cf. European Convention against Trafficking Art. 10.
1184. ACTP Art. 14(1).
1185. ACTP Art. 14(2).
1186. ACTP Art. 14(6).
1187. ACTP Art. 14(3), (6).
1188. Jovanovic, 32.

340. An important provision of the ACTP is Article 14(7) which requires parties to 'consider' not holding victims of trafficking criminally or administratively liable for unlawful acts committed by them, if such acts are directly related to the acts of trafficking. However, this guarantee is not as solid as it may appear at first sight and on closer examination is actually considerably weak. First, it simply compels parties to 'consider' non-liability rather than imposing an obligation. Second, the recommendation, for that it was it truly is, is subject to the parties' domestic laws, rules, regulations and policies. And third, it applies 'in appropriate cases' only. In fact, an awkward party could cynically refuse to absolve victims of trafficking of criminality by invoking the disclaimers in the provision. Identified victims of trafficking should not be held unreasonably in detention or in prison, prior to, during, or after civil, criminal, or administrative proceedings for trafficking in persons.[1189] Naturally, this begs the question of what is 'unreasonable'.[1190]

341. The repatriation and return of victims are governed by Article 15.[1191] This provision requires the party of which a victim of trafficking is a national or has the right of permanent residence to facilitate and accept, with due regard for the safety of that person, the return of that person without undue or unreasonable delay. It has been pointed out that the ACTP does not refer to the return being voluntary.[1192] Unlike the European Convention against Trafficking, the ACTP does not mention the principle of *non-refoulement.*[1193]

342. With regard to prosecution, the ACTP requires parties to criminalise the intentional trafficking in persons.[1194] Furthermore, they should ensure that any person who perpetrates or supports trafficking in persons is brought to justice.[1195] The ACTP does not specify any particular punishment for offenders except that it must be 'just and effective'.[1196] However, it does list a number of aggravating circumstances that should attract higher penalties, such as serious injury or death of the victim or another person, where the victim is a vulnerable person such as a child or if offender has previous convictions for the same or similar offences.[1197] Criminalisation extends to attempts, participating as an accomplice or organising or directing other persons to traffic in persons. Whereas the ACTP does not stipulate liability for legal persons and entities,[1198] it does demand the criminalisation of participation in an organised criminal group.[1199] Moreover, it further requires the criminalisation of the laundering of proceeds of crime,[1200] the criminalisation of corruption,[1201] and

1189. ACTP Art. 14(8).
1190. *See* Jovanovic, 33.
1191. *Ibid.*; Yusran, 282.
1192. Jovanovic, *ibid.*
1193. *Ibid.*, 32. Cf. European Convention against Trafficking Art. 40(4).
1194. ACTP Art 5(1).
1195. ACTP Art. 12(h).
1196. ACTP Art. 1(1)(a).
1197. ACTP Art. 5(3).
1198. Cf. European Convention against Trafficking Art. 22.
1199. ACTP Art. 6.
1200. ACTP Art. 7.
1201. ACTP Art. 8.

the criminalisation of the obstruction of justice.[1202] Parties must therefore take steps to detect, deter and punish corruption, money laundering, participation in organised criminal groups and obstruction of justice contributing to trafficking in persons.[1203] All these go beyond the requirements of the Palermo Protocol and the European Convention against Trafficking.

343. Regarding law enforcement, the initiative lies with the States Parties. Accordingly, the offences established under the ACTP and associated legal issues are reserved to the parties' domestic laws, and such offences shall be prosecuted and punished in accordance with those laws.[1204] More specifically, parties should adopt a long statute of limitations period in which to commence proceedings for any offence covered by the ACTP and a longer period where the alleged offender has evaded the administration of justice.[1205] States Parties must ensure that their legal systems are capable of dealing with trafficking cases.[1206] Furthermore, the integrity of the criminal justice process must be preserved, especially through protecting victims and witnesses from intimidation and harassment and punishing the perpetrators of such acts.[1207]

344. In order to deal effectively with trafficking, the ACTP requires States Parties to put in place measures, stricter than under the European Convention against Trafficking, to allow confiscation and seizure of proceeds of crime and property derived from trafficking offences.[1208] In order to stay one step ahead of offenders who may attempt to hide their ill-gotten gains the ACTP requires States Parties to adopt measures to make possible their identification, tracing, freezing or seizure.[1209] Offenders may be required to demonstrate the lawful origin of alleged proceeds of crime or other property.[1210] Banking secrecy must not be invoked to prevent courts or other competent authorities from ordering that bank, financial or commercial records be made available or seized.[1211]

345. States Parties are under an obligation to cooperate in this field. Consequently, a party that receives a request from another party having jurisdiction over an offence for confiscation of proceeds of crime or property must submit it to the competent authorities to obtain a confiscation order and to implement it if granted,

1202. ACTP Art. 9.
1203. ACTP Art. 16(2).
1204. ACTP Art. 16(9).
1205. ACTP Art. 16(8).
1206. ACTP Art. 16(3).
1207. ACTP Art. 16(7).
1208. ACTP Art. 17(1). It is immaterial whether the proceeds of crime and property are 'intermingled' with legitimate assets, *ibid.* Art. 17(4), (5).
1209. ACTP Art. 17(2).
1210. ACTP Art. 17(7).
1211. ACTP Art. 17(6).

or take measures to identify, trace and freeze or seize proceeds of crime or property.[1212] Confiscated proceeds of crime or property are to be disposed of in accordance with the laws of the confiscating state.[1213]

346. States Parties are required to establish jurisdiction over the offences covered by the ACTP.[1214] Jurisdiction is based primarily on the territoriality principle[1215] but may additionally be based on the nationality principle and the passive personality principle.[1216]

347. The ACTP makes provision for extradition.[1217] Trafficking is deemed an extraditable offence in any existing or future extradition treaty between parties.[1218] Where no extradition treaty exists between two parties to the ACTP, the ACTP itself can be considered the legal basis for extradition.[1219] The ACTP also enshrines the *aut dedere aut judicare* principle.[1220]

348. In order to combat the transnational aspects of trafficking, the ACTP requires States Parties to 'afford one another the widest measure of mutual legal assistance in criminal investigations or criminal proceedings'.[1221] They must act in accordance with the ASEAN Treaty on Mutual Legal Assistance in Criminal Matters (AMLAT).[1222]

349. The ACTP obliges States Parties to offer victims of trafficking the possibility of obtaining compensation for damage suffered.[1223] Confiscated proceeds of crime or property can be used for the purposes of compensation and assistance to these victims.[1224]

350. Assessments of the ACTP are mixed, with both positive and negative features. The most praiseworthy aspect of the ACTP seems to be the provisions on partnership, whereas on prevention it is deemed not to constitute an improvement on

1212. ACTP Art. 21(1)(a), (2).
1213. ACTP Art. 22(1).
1214. ACTP Art. 10(1).
1215. *Ibid.*
1216. ACTP Art. 10(2).
1217. ACTP Art. 19.
1218. ACTP Art. 19(1).
1219. ACTP Art. 19(2).
1220. ACTP Art. 19(4).
1221. ACTP Art. 18(1).
1222. ACCT Art. 12(2). *See* Treaty on Mutual Legal Assistance in Criminal Matters (29 Nov. 2004), http://agreement.asean.org/media/download/20160901074559.pdf. The Treaty enters into force for each Party ratifying or acceding to it on the date of its ratification or accession, Art. 31(1).
1223. ACTP Art. 14(13).
1224. ACTP Art. 22(2).

other treaties, on prosecution it contains advantages and disadvantages, and on protection it is considered somewhat disappointing.[1225] Furthermore, the lack of a compliance mechanism is viewed as a considerable failure.[1226] Nevertheless, in the final analysis, the ACTP must be considered as making an important contribution to the fight against a modern form of slavery and exploitation.

§6. ASEAN Intergovernmental Commission on Human Rights

351. The ASEAN Declaration on Human Rights (AHRD) being a soft law instrument has no supervisory mechanism, let alone any enforcement machinery. This begs the question as to who might be able to play a role in securing that its rights and freedoms are protected and promoted. For the time being, the obvious candidate is the ASEAN Intergovernmental Commission on Human Rights (AICHR), which as has been explained, preceded the AHDR. However, it is a consultative body having no powers of enforcement: it is not a court or a tribunal and has no quasi-judicial functions.

352. The AICHR could be said to be the first concrete manifestation of the ASEAN Charter's commitment to the promotion and protection of human rights.[1227] The ASEAN Charter makes provision for the establishment of a human rights body[1228] and its all-important TOR (AICHR) was adopted in July 2009.[1229] Accordingly, in October 2009 Asean brought into being a new regional organ on human rights, the AICHR.[1230] With the ASEAN human rights system is in its infancy the establishment of the AICHR was hailed as a 'historic milestone'.[1231] The

1225. Jovanovic, 40–41.
1226. Yusran, 292.
1227. ASEAN Charter Art. 1(7).
1228. ASEAN Charter Art. 14(2). The Roadmap for an ASEAN Community (2009–2015) 2009, also called for the establishment of an ASEAN commission on the promotion and protection of the rights of women and children, ASEAN Political-Security Community Blueprint, s. II A1 5 vii, https://www.asean.org/wp-content/uploads/images/archive/5187-18.pdf.
1229. 42nd ASEAN Foreign Ministers Meeting, Thailand (20 Jul. 2009), 48 I.L.M. 1161 (2009).
1230. Cha-am Hua Hin Declaration on the Intergovernmental Commission on Human Rights, 15th ASEAN Summit, Cha-am Hua Hin, Thailand (23 Oct. 2009), https://asean.org/wp-content/uploads/2021/09/Declaration-AICHR.pdf. *See* C.M. Cerna, *Introductory Note to the Terms of Reference for the Establishment of the ASEAN International Commission on Human Rights (AICOHR)*, 48 I.L.M. 1161 (2009). For analysis, *see* A. Duxbury & T. Hsein-Li, *Can ASEAN Take Human Rights Seriously?* 171–203 (Cambridge U. Press 2019); D. Basham-Jones, *ASEAN's Intergovernmental Commission on Human Rights: A Pale Shadow of What It Could Have Been*, 13 Asia-Pacific J. Hum. Rts. & L. 1 (2012); A. Durbach, C. Renshaw & A. Byrnes, *'A Tongue But No Teeth?': The Emergence of a Regional Human Rights Mechanism in the Asia Pacific Region*, 31 Sydney L. Rev. 211 (2009); G.J. Naldi, *The ASEAN Intergovernmental Commission on Human Rights: A 'Damp Squib'?*, 22(2) Sri Lanka J. Int'l L. 1 (2010); H.D. Phan, *Promotional Versus Protective Design: The Case of the ASEAN Intergovernmental Commission on Human Rights*, 23 Int'l J. Hum. Rts. 915 (2019); Y. Wahyuningrum, *The ASEAN Intergovernmental Commission on Human Rights: Origins, Evolution and the Way Forward* (IDEA International 2014).
1231. Cha-am Hua Hin Declaration, para. 4.

AICHR, described as the 'overarching human rights institution in ASEAN',[1232] is designated an intergovernmental body which is an integral part of the ASEAN institutional structure.[1233] It consequently consists of the ASEAN Member States,[1234] each of which appoints a Representative to the AICHR who is accountable to the appointing Government.[1235] This situation raises questions about the independence of the Representatives.[1236] While Representatives are under a general obligation to act impartially in the discharge of their duties,[1237] and their ability to act as their conscience dictates may be constrained by the knowledge that their tenure of office may be terminated by their Government at any time.[1238] This in turn raises questions about government influence over the work of the AICHR and its ability to hold States to account.[1239] Despite these real concerns it would appear that this disquiet may have been overdone and that the Representatives are doing a worthy job.[1240] Representatives must have some familiarity, or 'competence', in human rights.[1241] In a progressive move, consideration must be given to ensuring gender equality within the AICHR.[1242] They serve a three-year term and may be re-appointed for a second term.[1243] The Chair of the AICHR rotates annually which is the Representative of the Member State holding the ASEAN chairmanship for that year.[1244] The AICHR holds two regular meetings a year, but additional meetings can be held if required.[1245] The AICHR submits an annual report and other reports, as required to the ASEAN Foreign Minister's Meeting.[1246]

353. Decision-making in the AICHR is based on 'consultation and consensus in accordance with Article 20 of the ASEAN Charter', reflecting the so-called ASEAN Way.[1247] This would suggest that the AICHR cannot act without all ten Representatives being in agreement, but the provision in question does not actually stipulate that decisions *shall be adopted by consensus*, although it may amount to the same

---

1232. AICHR TOR Art. 6.8.
1233. AICHR TOR Art. 3. *See also* ASEAN Charter Art. 14(1). The AICHR has been established under the ASEAN Political-Security Community Blueprint. It thus suffers from the perception of being a 'state-centric' body, Duxbury & Hsein-Li, 174.
1234. AICHR TOR Art. 5.1.
1235. AICHR TOR Art. 5.2.
1236. Naldi, 23; Phan, 920.
1237. AICHR TOR Art. 5.7.
1238. AICHR TOR Art. 5.6 states, *inter alia*, that 'the appointing Government may decide, at its discretion, to replace its Representative.'
1239. H. Bui, *The ASEAN Human Rights System: A Critical Analysis*, 11 Asian J. Comp. L. 111, 129–131 (2016).
1240. Duxbury & Hsein-Li, 194–197.
1241. AICHR TOR Art. 5.3.
1242. *Ibid.*
1243. AICHR TOR Art. 5.5.
1244. AICHR TOR Art. 5.9.
1245. AICHR TOR Arts 6.2, 6.4, 6.5.
1246. AICHR TOR Art. 6.6.
1247. AICHR TOR Art. 6.1.

thing in practice, since the ASEAN Charter allows for the possibility of disagreement.[1248] Proceeding on the basis of unanimity on every topic is a recipe for stasis.[1249]

354. The AICHR is described as 'a consultative body',[1250] and consequently its mandate and functions, as set out in a number of guidelines set out in the AICHR TOR, appear modest.[1251] An essential function of the AICHR is to promote and protect human rights in ASEAN, responsive to Asian needs.[1252] This remit must be exercised 'within the regional context, bearing in mind national and regional peculiarities and mutual respect for different historical, cultural and religious backgrounds'.[1253] This could be understood as an assertion of legitimate cultural variety, but, negatively, it could be interpreted as a reference to the concept of cultural relativism to which many Asian states adhere.[1254] It will achieve the promotion of human rights through standard-setting, first and foremost, by developing strategies for their promotion and protection complementing the building of the ASEAN community.[1255] Its promotional mandate includes raising public awareness of human rights through education, research, and dissemination of information.[1256] It will additionally develop common approaches and positions on human rights matters of interest to ASEAN.[1257] The AICHR will promote the full implementation of ASEAN human rights instruments[1258] as well as capacity building for the effective implementation of international human rights treaty obligations assumed by ASEAN Member States as well as ASEAN human rights instruments.[1259] Furthermore, it will encourage ASEAN Member States to consider acceding to and ratifying international human rights instruments.[1260] There is much that ASEAN Member States can do in this regard. The AICHR can prepare studies on thematic issues of human rights[1261] and has adopted a couple of such reports, such as on women and natural disasters.[1262] However, civil society organisations (CSOs) have complained

1248. ASEAN Charter Art. 20(2) states, 'Where consensus cannot be achieved, the ASEAN Summit may decide how a specific decision can be made'.
1249. Phan, 921.
1250. AICHR TOR Art. 3.
1251. AICHR TOR Art. 4.
1252. AICHR TOR Arts 1.1, 1.4.
1253. AICHR TOR Art. 1.4.
1254. J. Donnelly, *International Human Rights* 131–35 (Westview 2nd ed. 1997). *See* Bangkok Declaration para. 8; Vienna Declaration and Programme of Action, I.L.M. 32 (1993) 1661, I, para. 5.
1255. AICHR TOR Art. 4.1.
1256. AICHR TOR Art. 4.3.
1257. AICHR TOR Art. 4.11.
1258. AICHR TOR Art. 4.6.
1259. AICHR TOR Art. 4.4.
1260. AICHR TOR Art. 4.5.
1261. AICHR TOR Art. 4.12.
1262. *The ASEAN Intergovernmental Commission on Human Rights (AICHR) Annual Report 2018*, https://aichr.org/aichr-annual-report-2018/.

about a lack of transparency and accountability by the AICHR in carrying out its thematic studies.[1263] The AICHR is also expected to maintain contacts with other ASEAN bodies, including CSOs.[1264]

355. Following a hesitant start, the AICHR is now engaged in a number of activities, such as enhancing its educational and informative role, organising workshops, including training workshops, and liaising with dialogue partners such as the EU and states such as Australia.[1265] With regard to CSOs, in 2015 the AICHR adopted a set of Guidelines on the AICHR's Relations with Civil Society Organisations, which, *inter alia*, call for consultations or dialogue between the AICHR and CSOs.[1266] However, in an extraordinary open letter in 2018 a number of Asian CSOs complained, *inter alia*, about the AICHR's lack of any significant engagement and involvement with CSOs.[1267]

356. There are aspects of the AICHR's role which could assist in developing procedures of a supervisory nature. In particular, as mentioned above, it can prepare thematic studies and can obtain information from Member States on the promotion and protection of human rights.[1268] If the AICHR were prepared to use these powers creatively, it could establish thematic procedures setting up working groups and special rapporteurs, appointing country-specific reporters and adopting relevant resolutions. In cases of alleged violations of fundamental freedoms, it could have the ability to investigate them by appointing special rapporteurs or by sending fact-finding missions. The AICHR could create a reporting system requiring Member States to submit periodic reports on the steps taken to give effect to human rights. Finally, it could even assume responsibilities to examine gross violations of human rights comparable to those taken up by UN organs under Resolution 1235 (XLII) 1967 and Resolution 1503 (XLVIII), which were adopted by the United Nations Economic and Social Council (ECOSOC), respectively in 1967 and in 1970.[1269] These suggestions are neither new nor radical but refer to well-established practices of international and regional human rights entities, which have interpreted their TOR broadly and have developed over time specific procedures to deal with different issues.

1263. *Joint Submission to the ASEAN Intergovernmental Commission on Human Rights: Civil Society Organizations request meaningful engagement*, https://www.forum-asia.org/uploads/wp/2018/08/Joint-Submission-CSOs-to-demand-meaningful-engagement-with-AICHR-V02-8-August-2018-FINAL.pdf.

1264. AICHR TOR Art. 4.8.

1265. *See*, e.g., *The ASEAN Intergovernmental Commission on Human Rights (AICHR) Annual Report 2018*; Duxbury & Hsein-Li, 192–193.

1266. Guidelines on the AICHR's Relations with Civil Society Organisations (11 Feb. 2015), https://aichr.org/wp-content/uploads/2018/12/Guidelines_On_The_AICHRS_Relations_With__CSOs.pdf.

1267. *Joint Submission to the ASEAN Intergovernmental Commission on Human Rights: Civil Society Organizations request meaningful engagement.*

1268. AICHR TOR Art. 4.10. Although there does not appear to be an obligation on States to provide such information, Phan, 920.

1269. *See* T. Buergenthal, D. Shelton, D. Stewart & C. Vasquez, *International Human Rights in a Nutshell* 156–158 (West Group 5th ed. 2017).

357. The loudest criticism of the AICHR is its lack of any enforcement or compliance capacity.[1270] CSOs have consistently called for the AICHR's protective mandate to be strengthened.[1271] While its mandate does not contain any express authorisation for entertaining individual complaints, its broad mandate (the protection of human rights and fundamental freedoms of ASEAN peoples)[1272] could arguably be interpreted as sanctioning the development of some form of control machinery. Thus, it has been given 'overall responsibility for the promotion and *protection* of human rights in ASEAN' (emphasis added), while it is directed to 'uphold' international human rights standards.[1273] In the language of human rights discourse, 'the protection of human rights' necessitates certain outcomes.[1274] The African Commission on Human and Peoples' Rights spelled out what this requirement entailed for States: 'Protection generally entails the creation and maintenance of an atmosphere or framework by an effective interplay of laws and regulations so that individuals will be able to freely realize their rights and freedoms.'[1275] The example of the African Commission is in fact instructive because doubts had initially been harboured as to whether it had the competence to receive individual complaints, but this practice quickly became an established facet of the African Commission's functions.[1276] Development along such lines would not thus constitute an abnormal occurrence. Additional support for such an occurrence could be found in the doctrines of implied powers and/or inherent powers.[1277]

358. However, persuasive counter arguments can be found in the fundamental beliefs of ASEAN Member States and in the AICHR TOR. First and foremost, the AICHR must conduct itself in accordance with ASEAN's fundamental principles embodied in Article 2 of the ASEAN Charter, including respect for the independence, sovereignty, equality, territorial integrity and national identity of ASEAN Member States, non-interference in the internal affairs of Member States, and recognition that the primary responsibility for promoting and protecting human rights rests with the Member States.[1278] These provisions stress a basic tenet of international law, that of domestic jurisdiction reflected in Article 2(7) of the UN Charter,

1270. Basham-Jones, 12; Bui, 131–133; Doyle, 73–74; Naldi, 22; Phan, 920; Vanoverbeke & Reiterer, 188.
1271. *Joint Submission to the ASEAN Intergovernmental Commission on Human Rights: Civil Society Organizations request meaningful engagement*. CSOs have accused the AICHR of remaining 'passive even in the face of major human rights crises in the region', *ibid.*
1272. AICHR TOR Art. 1.1.
1273. AICHR TOR Arts 6.8 & 1.6.
1274. UN Office of the High Commissioner for Human Rights, General Comment No. 31, *Nature of the General Legal Obligation Imposed on States Parties to the Covenant*, UN Doc. CCPR/C/21/Rev.1/Add.13 (26 May 2004).
1275. *Social and Economic Rights Action Center v. Nigeria*, Communication No. 155/96, 15th Activity Report 2001–2002, para. 46.
1276. G.J. Naldi, *The Role of The African Union and Regionalism in Human Rights*, in *The African Charter on Human and Peoples' Rights* 20, 35 (M. Evans & R. Murray eds, Cambridge U. Press 2nd ed. 2008).
1277. J. Klabbers, *An Introduction to International Institutional Law* 59–69 (Cambridge U. Press 2nd ed. 2009).
1278. AICHR TOR Arts 2.1(a), (b), 2.3.

but which appears to ignore the development of the law of human rights, which prevails over notions of sovereignty and domestic jurisdiction and which imposes an element of international scrutiny. The AICHR is additionally mandated with pursuing 'a constructive and non-confrontational approach'.[1279] This is in keeping with the Asian view that disputes should be resolved by negotiation, conciliation and consensus rather than other methods which may be perceived as provocative or hostile. Consequently, the AICHR is expected to play a loose, facilitative role rather than a quasi-judicial one. Second, it is meant to adopt 'an evolutionary approach' to the development of ASEAN human rights norms and standards.[1280] This instructs a gradual and measured position which seems to be the prevailing outlook. The lack of any specific authorisation constitutes a significant hurdle; the AICHR seems reluctant to take radical steps on its own volition not least because it could be accused of acting *ultra vires*. Equally, if the AICHR were to consider establishing subsidiary bodies with a human rights mandate, comparable to the UN Sub-Commission on Promotion and Protection of Human Rights, it would have to overcome the hurdle of Article 7(2)(f) of the ASEAN Charter stipulating that the creation of such bodies is reserved to the ASEAN Summit. Although the AICHR continues to maintain that it has no mandate to examine individual cases, it will accept letters of complaint from the public *via* the ASEAN Secretariat which will take note of the complaint and forward it to the AICHR Chair for consideration at an AICHR meeting.[1281] Disappointingly, the AICHR has yet to respond publicly to any complaint.

§7. ASEAN Commission on the Promotion and Protection of the Rights of Women and Children

359. While the AICHR may be considered the all-purpose human rights mechanism other so-called Sectoral or Thematic Bodies have been established. One such is the Commission on the Promotion and Protection of the Rights of Women and Children (ACWC), which was inaugurated in April 2010 and is described as a consultative intergovernmental body integrated in the ASEAN organisational structure.[1282] The ACWC's mandate and functions are similar but more explicit than those of the AICHR with an obvious focus on women and children's rights.

1279. AICHR TOR Art. 2.4.

1280. AICHR TOR Art. 2.5. An ASEAN functionary wrote in 2008 that, 'The [AICHR] will represent a new learning process for all the ASEAN Member States … Undoubtedly the process will develop gradually. More important work can be done when the comfort level among the Member States in human rights cooperation rises, and when capability of the [AICHR] increases. This will take time', Termsak Chalempalanupap, *Promoting and Protecting Human Rights in ASEAN*, December 2008, 5, at: https://www.asean.org/wp-content/uploads/images/archive/HLP-OtherDoc-2.pdf.

1281. ASEAN Secretariat, *AICHR: What You Need to Know* 26 (ASEAN Secretariat 2d ed. June 2014), at: https://aichr.org/wp-content/uploads/2018/10/AICHR_Booklet_2nd_Edition_1.pdf. *See* Duxbury & Hsein-Li, 198–199.

1282. ACWC Terms of Reference (ACWC TOR) Art. 4, https://www.asean.org/wp-content/uploads/images/2012/Social_cultural/ACW/TOR-ACWC.pdf. The ACWC adopted Rules of Procedure in 2016, at: https://acwc.asean.org/wp-content/uploads/2016/10/Rules-of-Procedure-of-ACWC_

360. The ACWC's composition is also similar to that of the AICHR. It consists of the ASEAN Member States,[1283] each of which appoints two representatives to the ACWC, due regard being given to gender equality,[1284] one on women's rights and one on children's rights.[1285] This allows for greater expertise; indeed, representatives must have 'competence' in the relevant fields.[1286] Unlike the AICHR, the selection process for representatives must be transparent, open, participatory and inclusive.[1287] Representatives must act impartially in the discharge of their duties,[1288] and in a positive difference with the AICHR, there is no stated requirement for representatives to be accountable to the appointing Government.[1289] However, questions about the degree of independence of the representatives remain as their Governments' capacity to replace them at any time has been retained.[1290] Representatives serve for three years and may be re-appointed for a further term.[1291] The Chair of the ACWC serves a term of three years, and the Chair is rotated among ASEAN Member States on an alphabetical basis.[1292] The ACWC holds two regular meetings a year, but additional meetings can be held if necessary.[1293] Unsurprisingly, decision-making is based on 'consultation and consensus in accordance with the ASEAN Charter'.[1294] The ACWC submits an annual report and other reports to the ASEAN Minister's Meeting on Social Welfare and Development.[1295]

361. The ACWC's role includes promoting and protecting the human rights and fundamental freedoms of women and children in ASEAN, taking account of responsive the 'different historical, political, socio-cultural, religious and economic context in the region and the balances between rights and responsibilities',[1296] promoting the well-being, development, empowerment and participation of women and children in the ASEAN Community building process,[1297] enhancing regional and international cooperation to complement national and international efforts on

---

FINAL.pdf. The establishment of the ACWC had been envisaged by the 2004–2010 Ventiane Action Programme (29 Nov. 2004) para. 1.1.4.7., https://cil.nus.edu.sg/wp-content/uploads/formidable/18/2004-2010-Vientiane-Action-Programme.pdf, but was been established under the ASEAN Socio-Cultural Community Blueprint. For analysis, *see* A. Pisanò, *Towards an ASEAN Human Rights Mechanism: The ASEAN Commission on the Promotion and Protection of the Rights of Women and Children*, 20 Int'l J. Hum. Rts. 321 (2016); A. Pisanò, *The ASEAN Commission on the Promotion and Protection of the Rights of Women and Children*, in *International Human Rights of Women* 155–171 (N. Reilly ed., Springer 2019).

1283. ACWC TOR Art. 6.1.
1284. ACWC TOR Art. 6.3.
1285. ACWC TOR Art. 6.2.
1286. ACWC TOR Art. 6.3.
1287. ACWC TOR Art. 6.4.
1288. ACWC TOR Art. 6.9.
1289. AICHR TOR Art. 5.2.
1290. ACWC TOR Art. 6.8.
1291. ACWC TOR Art. 6.5.
1292. ACWC TOR Art. 6.11.
1293. ACWC TOR Arts 7.2, 7.4.
1294. ACWC TOR Art. 7.1. However, Rule of Procedure 2.6 does refer to Art. 20 ASEAN Charter.
1295. ACWC TOR Art. 7.5.
1296. ACWC TOR Art. 2.1.
1297. ACWC TOR Art. 2.3.

the promotion and protection of the rights of women and children,[1298] and upholding human rights as set down in CEDAW, CRC, international humanitarian law, and other international human rights instruments and regional declarations to which ASEAN Member States are parties.[1299] This feature has been highlighted as providing ACWC with a firmer foundation.[1300] As all ASEAN Member States are parties to CEDAW and CRC, standard-setting does not come within the ACWC's remit. The ACWC has thus been described as having two principal roles, namely, acting as a 'bridge' between the international human rights system and ASEAN Member States and supporting the latter's policies relating to women and children.[1301]

362. The ACWC is guided by a set of principles similar to those of the AICHR. It must thus abide by the principles of ASEAN as set out in Article 2 of the ASEAN Charter,[1302] an obvious reference to the doctrines of sovereignty and non-interference in the internal affairs of Member States, and it must recognise the primary responsibility of Member States in promoting and protecting the human rights women and children.[1303] The ACWC is instructed to pursue 'a constructive, non-confrontational and cooperative approach',[1304] including with ASEAN States, academia and civil society,[1305] and, in keeping with the ASEAN outlook, to adopt 'an evolutionary approach' to the realisation of the rights of women and children in ASEAN.[1306] While the ACWC is directed to respect human rights, especially relating to women and children, in keeping with the governing principles of CEDAW and CRC,[1307] it must complement, rather than duplicate, the function of the CEDAW and CRC Committees.[1308]

363. The ACWC's mandate and functions include promoting the implementation of international and ASEAN instruments on the rights of women and children,[1309] developing policies, programmes and strategies,[1310] promoting public awareness and education on the rights of women and children,[1311] campaigning on behalf of women and children, especially the vulnerable and marginalised, and encouraging ASEAN Member States to improve their situation,[1312] assisting ASEAN Member States in the preparation of their CEDAW and CRC periodic

1298. ACWC TOR Art. 2.4.
1299. ACWC TOR Art. 2.5.
1300. Duxbury & Hsein-Li, 205; Y. Ginbar, *Human Rights in ASEAN: Setting Sail or Treading Water?*, 10 HRLR 504, 515–516 (2010).
1301. Pisanò, 333.
1302. ACWC TOR Art. 3.1.
1303. ACWC TOR Art. 3.5.
1304. ACWC TOR Art. 3.6.
1305. ACWC TOR Art. 3.9.
1306. ACWC TOR Art. 3.8.
1307. ACWC TOR Art. 3.2.
1308. ACWC TOR Art. 3.4.
1309. ACWC TOR Art. 5.1.
1310. ACWC TOR Art. 5.2.
1311. ACWC TOR Art. 5.3.
1312. ACWC TOR Art. 5.4.

reports,[1313] and assisting them in the implementation of the Concluding Observations of the CEDAW and CRC Committees,[1314] encouraging ASEAN Member States to undertake periodic reviews of national legislation, policies and practices relating to the rights of women and children,[1315] and encouraging ASEAN Member States to accede or ratify international treaties relating to the rights of women and children.[1316]

364. In 2012, the ACWC adopted a five-year plan of action with a particular focus on the elimination of violence against women and children, trafficking in women and children, women and children and AIDS and HIV, the rights of women and children with disabilities, child protection systems, the participation of women in political life, amongst others. The plan of action was described as being mostly about the promotion of rights.[1317] Nevertheless, the ACWC drafted the ASEAN Declaration on the Elimination of Violence against Women and Children, which was adopted in 2013.

365. The assessment of a CSO, Forum-ASIA, on the work of the ACWC is somewhat subdued. It attributes its institutional failings on a lack of funding and resources, a low-profile visibility and lack of institutional support. It specifically criticises the ACWC for its silence in the face of the persecution of the Rohingya in Myanmar.[1318]Recommendations for the enhancement of its institutional capacities include establishing a complaint mechanism, monitoring ASEAN Member States compliance with their human rights obligations, advancing its engagement with CSOs, and engaging with national human rights institutions.[1319]

366. Arguably, there is an issue of duplication of efforts, which was discussed during the AICHR's Twelfth Meeting (May 2013),[1320] but no concrete action has yet been taken. Given that at its Fourteenth Meeting (February 2014) the AICHR resolved to review its TOR,[1321] an excellent opportunity arises to strengthen its mandate, consolidate its functions and possibly assume a supervisory role as suggested in the previous paragraphs. The ASEAN foreign ministers, who will have to

---

1313. ACWC TOR Art. 5.6.
1314. ACWC TOR Art. 5.7.
1315. ACWC TOR Art. 5.10.
1316. ACWC TOR Art. 5.13.
1317. At: https://aichr.org/wp-content/uploads/2018/10/AICHR_Five-Year_Work_Plan_2012-2015.pdf. *See* Pisanò, 337.
1318. Forum-ASIA, *Reasonable Doubt: The Journey Within: A Report on the Annual Performance of the AEAN Human Rights Mechanisms in 2017*, October 2018, 28, https://www.forum-asia.org/uploads/wp/2018/11/ASEAN-Human-Rights-Institution-Performance-Report-2017-Final-2-1.pdf.
1319. *Ibid.*, 28–29.
1320. *See* www.asean.org/news/asean-secretariat-news/item/twelfth-meeting-of-the-asean-intergovernmental-commission-on-human-rights.
1321. *See* https://aichr.org/news/14th-meeting-of-the-asean-intergovernmental-commission-on-human-rights/.

approve any changes, should press towards in this direction to brush off suggestions that the AICHR was created to shield their countries' human rights record from international scrutiny.[1322]

§8. ASEAN Committee on the Implementation of the ASEAN Declaration on the Protection and Promotion of the Rights of Migrant Workers

367. The ASEAN Committee on the Implementation of the ASEAN Declaration on the Protection and Promotion of the Rights of Migrant Workers (ACMW) was formally established in September 2008 following the adoption of the ADMW in 2007.[1323] The ACMW, which meets once a year, is composed of a representative from each of the ASEAN Member States and the ASEAN Secretariat. It reports to the Senior Labour Officials Meeting. It must operate, more so than the other ASEAN human rights bodies, subject to the laws and policies of the ASEAN Member States. The ACMW's functions include implementing the objectives of the ADMW; facilitating the sharing of best practices in the ASEAN region relating to migrant workers; promoting bilateral and regional cooperation on matters concerning the rights of migrant workers; and work with international organisations, sending and receiving countries and other countries to support, assist and implement ASEAN's policies in this area.[1324] It has been described as having the narrowest remit of the ASEAN human rights bodies.[1325] In common with the other human rights bodies it does not have investigative powers or a mandate to handle individual complaints.

368. Under its first Work Plan adopted in 2008 the ACMW prioritised four topics: enhancing the protection and promotion of the rights of migrant workers against exploitation and mistreatment; strengthening labour migration governance in ASEAN countries; combating human trafficking; and developing an ASEAN instrument on the rights of migrant workers (the Consensus of 2017 discussed above).[1326] Under its second Work Plan adopted in 2016, the ACMW's focus is on strengthening social protection systems and reducing the incidence of workers in vulnerable situations, including forced labour.[1327]

1322. N. Lynn Aung, *Review of ASEAN Human Rights Mechanism Begins*, Myanmar Times (13 Feb. 2014), at: www.mmtimes.com/index.php/national-news/9559-review-of-asean-human-rights-mechanism-begins.html.

1323. ASEAN Committee on the Implementation of the ASEAN Declaration on the Protection and Promotion of the Rights of Migrant Workers – Work Plan, 2008, https://asean.org/wp-content/uploads/images/archive/23062.pdf. The ACMW was set up under the ASEAN Political-Security Community Blueprint.

1324. Statement of the Establishment of the ASEAN Committee on the Implementation of the ASEAN Declaration on the Protection and Promotion of the Rights of Migrant Workers, 13 Jul. 2007, https://www.ilo.org/dyn/migpractice/docs/117/Declaration.pdf.

1325. Duxbury & Hsein-Li, 207.

1326. *See* n. 490.

1327. ASEAN Committee on the Implementation of the ASEAN Declaration on the Protection and Promotion of the Rights of Migrant Workers – Work Plan 2016–2020, at: https://www.aseanrokfund.

369. Of all the ASEAN human rights bodies, the ACMW is the one most shrouded in opaqueness; it operates with a relative lack of transparency and openness, and a lack of formal engagement with CSOs. It is also disadvantaged by a very insubstantial mandate, further handicapped by the express direction to defer to the Member States. But the ACMW should encourage ASEAN Member States to accede to international instruments such as the International Convention on the Protection of the Rights of Migrant Workers (only Indonesia and the Philippines are parties) and relevant ILO Conventions.[1328]

com/resources/asean-committee-on-the-implementation-of-the-asean-declaration-the-protection-and-promotion-of-the-rights-of-migrant-workers-acmw-work-plan-2016-2020.

1328. Information on participation by ASEAN Member States in ILO Conventions is available at its website, https://www.ilo.org/dyn/normlex/en/f?p=1000:11001:4474922897863::::P11001_COUNTRY_SORT:2#Asia%20and%20the%20Pacific. All ASEAN Member States are parties to the Convention concerning Forced or Compulsory Labour (No. 29) (28 Jun. 1930) 39 U.N.T.S. 55.

Chapter 3. Terrorism

370. Terrorism has been described as 'one of the most serious threats to international peace and security in the twenty-first century' and as a 'threat to all states and to all humanity'.[1329] Southeast Asia has not escaped the blight of international terrorism, with the tourist playground of Bali in Indonesia bearing the brunt of a number of atrocities by jihadist groups.[1330] Additionally, it is common knowledge that the Philippines and Thailand, to a much lesser extent,[1331] have fought home-grown terrorist groups in long running insurgencies by Muslim rebels.[1332] ASEAN had initially treated terrorism as a transnational crime, and Member States responded with law-enforcement measures, but a lack of suitable legal mechanisms and deficient law-enforcement capacity meant that these measures were hardly adequate.[1333] In 2001, ASEAN adopted the Declaration on Joint Action to Counter Terrorism designed to boost law-enforcement measures and regional capacity to deal with terrorism but which has also been interpreted as a rejection of the Bush Administration's 'War on Terror' approach.[1334] However, in light of the above and other acts of violence, ASEAN acknowledged that terrorism, in whatever manifestation, posed a threat to international peace and security and undermined ASEAN's progress, prosperity and stability,[1335] and agreed at a conference held in Cebu, the Philippines in 2007 to adopt a Convention on Counter Terrorism (ACCT).[1336]

§1. The ASEAN Convention on Counter Terrorism

371. The purpose of the ACCT is to provide a framework for regional cooperation to tackle terrorism and to extend cooperation among the parties' relevant authorities in countering terrorism.[1337] It is important to note that the ACCT's preamble rejects any notion of linking terrorism with any religion, civilisation or ethnic group. It addresses apprehension from Muslim States and populations, a dominant religion in parts of Southeast Asia, that the 'war on terror' amounted to a disguised war on Islam.[1338] The ACCT does not itself attempt a definition of 'terrorism' or 'terrorist act', in fact a comprehensive definition has thus far eluded the

1329. UN Security Council Res. 1377 (2001).
1330. T.S. Hafidz, *A Long Row to Hoe: A Critical Assessment of ASEAN Cooperation on Counter-Terrorism*, 11 Kyoto Rev. Southeast Asia (2009), at: https://kyotoreview.org/issue.11/a-long-row-to-hoe-a-critical-assessment-of-asean-cooperation-on-counter-terrorism/.
1331. *See supra* n. 942.
1332. *Ibid.*
1333. A. Ahmad, *The ASEAN Convention on Counter Terrorism 2007*, 14 Asia-Pacific J. Hum. Rts. & L. 93, 95 (2013); S.S. Tan & H. Nasu, *ASEAN and the Development of Counter Terrorism Law and Policy in Southeast Asia*, 39 U. New S. Wales L.J. 1219, 1222–1226 (2016).
1334. At: https://2001-2009.state.gov/s/ct/rls/other/65902.htm. *See* Hafidz; Tan & Nasu, 1223–1224.
1335. ASEAN Convention on Counter Terrorism (13 Jan. 2007), 3200 U.N.T.S., Preamble.
1336. The ACCT entered into force on 27 May 2011. The sluggish response by ASEAN and its Member States has been criticised, Tan & Nasu, 1220–1221; M. Borelli, *ASEAN Counter-Terrorism Weaknesses*, 9 Counter Terrorist Trends & Analyses 14, 15 (2017).
1337. ACCT Art. 1.
1338. Ahmad, 102.

international community, but denotes an 'offence' by reference to a long list of pre-existing international treaties on terrorism.[1339] This approach has the merit of evading getting mired in discussions as to definitions when prompt agreement may have been deemed necessary, and a number of reasons have been put forward for this approach, ranging from a lack of expertise in the area, the need for a unified approach, the fact that other regional treaties have adopted this policy, to the need to ensure that as many types of terrorist act came within the scope of the ACCT.[1340] A negative aspect, however, probably due to an exaggerated respect for sovereignty, is that a Party which is not a party to any of the listed treaties may choose to exclude the application of those treaties, thereby limiting the scope of an 'offence'.[1341] Furthermore, it seems regrettable that it did not prove possible to update the definition of terrorism to include, for instance, ecological crimes, in the sense of wilful and severe damage to the natural environment, or cyber terrorism.[1342] However, in order to neutralise the effects of the latter omission, in 2017 ASEAN adopted the Declaration to Prevent and Combat Cybercrime. It commits Member States to cooperate in preventing and combating cybercrime by, *inter alia*, encouraging them to consider acceding to existing regional and international instruments in combating cybercrime, to develop national plans of actions to address cybercrimes, to strengthen their capacities to address cybercrime, and to strengthen cooperation among ASEAN countries and bodies, between ASEAN Member States and its Dialogue Partners, as well as regional and international agencies and organisations.[1343] While the ACCT does make reference to 'terrorism in all its forms and manifestations',[1344] a seemingly catch-all phrase, its effectiveness is nullified by the fact that the offences for the purposes of the ACCT are those as defined in the treaties listed exclusively. A person engaged in cyber terrorism would not therefore be committing an offence under the ACCT. Of course, in theory it would be possible to amend the ACCT and add to the list of treaties.[1345]

1339. ACCT Art. 2(1). These include the International Convention against the Taking of Hostages (17 Dec. 1979) 1316 U.N.T.S. 205, the International Convention for the Suppression of Terrorist Bombings (25 Nov. 1997), 2149 U.N.T.S. 256, the International Convention for the Suppression of the Financing of Terrorism (9 Dec. 1999), 2179 U.N.T.S. 197, the UN Convention for the Suppression of Acts of Nuclear Terrorism (13 Apr. 2003), 44 I.L.M. 815 (2005), the International Maritime Organisation Convention for the Suppression of Unlawful Acts Against the Safety of Maritime Navigation (10 Mar. 1988) 1678 U.N.T.S. 201, and the Protocol to the Convention for the Suppression of Unlawful Acts Against the Safety of Maritime Navigation (14 Oct. 2005), IMO Doc. LEG/CONF. 15/21.

1340. Ahmad, 104–105. A definition suitable for adoption by ASEAN had been previously proposed, *see* G. Rose & D. Nestorovska, *Towards an ASEAN Counter-Terrorism Treaty*, 9 SYBIL 157, 159–160 (2005).

1341. ACCT Art. 2(2).

1342. *See* UN Security Council Res. 2341 (2017). The view has been expressed that ASEAN States may be vulnerable to cyber-attacks, Borelli, 19–20.

1343. ASEAN Declaration to Prevent and Combat Cybercrime (13 Nov. 2017), https://asean.org/wp-content/uploads/2017/11/ASEAN-Declaration-to-Combat-Cybercrime.pdf.

1344. ACCT Art. 1. UN Security Council Res. 1269 (1999) and Res. 1566 (2004) state that acts of terrorism are unjustifiable regardless of motivation.

1345. ACCT Art. 21(4).

372. Another omission concerns the fact the ACCT does not address the question of state-sponsored terrorism, which has assumed greater significance in recent years as a consequence of '9/11' and the threat posed by jihadist groups. ASEAN's deference to sovereignty and non-interference is given as the reason for this, probably short-sighted, stance.[1346]

373. The ACCT adopts the principle of *aut dedere aut judicare*. States are hence bound to arrest and prosecute or extradite perpetrators of terrorist acts.[1347] Terrorist acts as designated in the ACCT must become an extraditable offence within all extradition treaties.[1348] It is made plain that for the purposes of extradition, terrorist acts cannot be justified as politically motivated, and a request for extradition cannot be rejected on such grounds.[1349] Where no extradition treaty exists between Parties, the ACCT itself may be considered as the legal basis for extradition.[1350] This provision minimises the risk of an alleged offender evading justice. Jurisdiction is established on various grounds,[1351] principally where the act is committed in the territory of the state[1352] or on board a ship or aircraft registered there.[1353] It also extends to offences committed by stateless persons in the territory of the state.[1354] However, jurisdiction is additionally provided for on the basis of the nationality, or active personality, principle,[1355] the passive personality principle[1356] and the protective principle.[1357] It is asserted that provision is made for universal jurisdiction where an alleged offender is in the territory of a state but chooses not to extradite him/her.[1358]

374. Parties to the ACCT are under an obligation to give assistance with investigations or criminal proceedings regarding terrorist offences.[1359] This extends to mutual legal assistance if the parties are parties to the AMLAT.[1360] The AMLAT predates the ACCT which explains why the ACCT does not enter into detail on the subject. Assistance under the former treaty extends to extraterritorial investigations (commission rogatoire). The parties therefore undertake to assist in, *inter alia*, the

---

1346. Ahmad, 104.
1347. ACCT Arts 7(3), 13(1). An ASEAN Extradition Treaty has been mooted but has not yet materialised.
1348. ACCT Art. 13(2).
1349. ACCT Art. 14.
1350. ACCT Art. 13(3).
1351. *See* Ahmad, 140–141.
1352. ACCT Art. 7(1)(a).
1353. ACCT Art. 7(1)(b).
1354. ACCT Art. 7(2)(d).
1355. ACCT Art. 7(1)(c).
1356. ACCT Art. 7(2)(a).
1357. ACCT Art. 7(2)(b), (c).
1358. ACCT Art. 7(3). *See* Ahmad, 141–142.
1359. ACCT Art. 12(1).
1360. ACCT Art. 12(2). *See* Treaty on Mutual Legal Assistance in Criminal Matters (29 Nov. 2004), *supra*, para. 265. The Treaty enters into force for each Party ratifying or acceding to it on the date of its ratification or accession, Art. 31(1); all Member States have done so.

taking of evidence or voluntary statements,[1361] the execution of searches and seizures,[1362] the serving of judicial documents,[1363] the collection of documents,[1364] and the location and identification of witnesses and suspects.[1365] A significant problem could exist potentially vis-à-vis the ACCT in that the AMLAT does not apply to the arrest or detention of any person with a view to his/her extradition.[1366]

375. The AMLAT contains a number of safeguards. It incorporates the double criminality principle which should only present a problem if the Requested Party has failed to criminalise one or more of the offences listed in the ACCT and constitutes the offence for which the person is sought by the Requesting Party.[1367] Assistance may be refused where substantial grounds exist for believing that the request was made for the purpose of investigating or prosecuting a person on account of race, religion, sex, ethnic origin, nationality or political opinions,[1368] or if the provision of the assistance could endanger a person, whether within or without the territory of the Requested Party.[1369] Or indeed if the request for assistance relates to an offence of a political nature.[1370] However, it has been stressed above that terrorism does not qualify as a political offence under the ACCT. Furthermore, the AMLAT specifies that an offence within the scope of any international convention to which both the Requesting and Requested Parties are parties to, for example, the International Convention against the Taking of Hostages, and which imposes on the parties an obligation to extradite or prosecute a person accused of the commission of that offence, does not constitute an offence of a political nature.[1371]

376. Assistance may also be refused if the request and the execution of a request would affect the sovereignty, security, public order, public interest or essential interests of the requested state,[1372] the Requesting Party fails to undertake that the item requested for will not be used for a matter other than the criminal matter in respect of which the request was made,[1373] the provision of assistance could prejudice a criminal matter in the Requested Party,[1374] or could be contrary to the laws of the Requested Party.[1375]

377. It is a credo of liberal democratic societies that the fight against terrorism should not undermine its values and should therefore be fought in conformity with

1361. AMLAT Art. 1(2)(a).
1362. AMLAT Arts 1(2)(d), 18.
1363. AMLAT Art. 1(2)(c).
1364. AMLAT Arts 1(2)(f), 13.
1365. AMLAT Art. 1(2)(j).
1366. AMLAT Art. 2(1)(a).
1367. AMLAT Art. 3(1)(e).
1368. AMLAT Art. 3(1)(c).
1369. AMLAT Art. 3(2)(b).
1370. AMLAT Art. 3(1)(a).
1371. AMLAT Art. 3(3)(c).
1372. AMLAT Art. 3(1)(f).
1373. AMLAT Art. 3(1)(h).
1374. AMLAT Art. 3(1)(j).
1375. AMLAT Art. 3(1)(k).

the principles of democracy and international human rights.[1376] The ACCT reflects this fundamental position, with the preamble reaffirming the commitment to 'human rights, fair treatment, the rule of law, and due process'. Persons in custody or who stand accused are guaranteed fair treatment, including all rights extant under international law, including international human rights.[1377] Although the expression 'fair treatment' is not defined, it should be taken to refer to elementary standards of a fair trial. And although there is no express mention of a prohibition on torture, inhuman and degrading treatment its proscription should be obvious under the terms of the provision. The reference to international law may also secure rights such as consular access where parties are parties to the Vienna Convention on Consular Relations.[1378]

378. An innovative feature of the ACCT is its commitment to rehabilitation, in that states should share best practices on rehabilitative programmes, including social reintegration.[1379] These initiatives seek to address the root causes of terrorism and aim to prevent radicalisation and recidivism.[1380]

379. The ACCT Protocol omits an important element in the fight against terrorism, that of the confiscation, freezing, and seizure of funds and assets.[1381] This seems surprising in light of the fact that the ACCT seeks to prevent and suppress the financing of terrorism.[1382] However, this omission is mitigated, but not eliminated, by the AMLAT which authorises the Requested Party to freeze, seize, forfeit or confiscate property derived from the commission of an offence and instrumentalities of crime.[1383]

380. A curious feature of the ACCT is the explicit emphasis given to the principles of sovereignty, territorial integrity and non-interference.[1384] As mentioned on many previous occasions, this is explicable in the context of ASEAN values but it still seems unusual to see them figure so prominently.

381. It should be observed that the ASEAN Charter, which postdates the ACCT, makes no express reference to terrorism.[1385] It is not immediately apparent why no mention is made of this particular subject in the ASEAN Charter,[1386] but security is an important element of the ASEAN project, and the ASEAN Charter refers to the

1376. *See*, e.g., UN Security Council Res. 1456 (2003) and Res. 2178 (2014). *See* generally, T. Bingham, *The Rule of Law* 133–159 (Penguin 2011).
1377. ACCT Art. 8(1).
1378. Vienna Convention on Consular Relations (22 Apr. 1963), 596 U.N.T.S. 261.
1379. ACCT Art. 11.
1380. Ahmad, 138–140.
1381. *See* UN Security Council Res. 1373 (2001).
1382. ACCT Art. 6(1)(b).
1383. AMLAT Art. 22(1).
1384. ACCT Arts 3, 4.
1385. ASEAN Charter (20 Nov. 2007), 2624 U.N.T.S. 223.
1386. Although mention is made of it in the Constitutive Act of the African Union Art. 4(o) (26 May 2001), 2158 U.N.T.S. 3.

importance of security a number of times,[1387] including responding to all forms of threats and transnational crimes.[1388] Clearly terrorism comes within the scope of these provisions.

§2. Comprehensive Plan of Action on Counter Terrorism

382. Since 1999 ASEAN has adopted a series of plans of action recommending practical measures designed to have in place the legal and resource capacities to combat terrorism effectively.[1389] Significant for present purposes are those that followed the ACCT, the ASEAN Comprehensive Plan of Action on Counter Terrorism 2009[1390] and 2017,[1391] the latter an updated version, which are designed to supplement and fill out the ACCT with a detailed programme of recommendations. The objective of the Plan of Action is 'to counter, prevent and suppress terrorism, [and] terrorist organisations ... to disrupt their support networks and impede their plan of terror acts, and to bring them to justice'[1392] and to address its root causes.[1393]

383. The Plan of Action stresses that the primary responsibility for dealing with terrorism rests with the ASEAN Member States and that it aims to complement national efforts by, *inter alia*, strengthening the national capabilities of ASEAN Member States through sharing best practice, exchange of knowledge, expertise, technology and information, enhancing cooperation by establishing effective mechanisms among law-enforcement agencies and authorities, and promoting international cooperation.[1394] The latter could take the form of adhering to relevant UNSC resolutions and international instruments on terrorism,[1395] and implementing regional instruments on terrorism.[1396] The importance of establishing appropriate jurisdiction by putting into practice the *aut dedere aut judicare* principle as set out in the ACCT is highlighted.[1397] The Plan of Action also calls for the setting up of institutionalised mechanisms for the exchange of information and intelligence on the surveillance and tracking of suspected terrorists with a view to prevention.[1398] The Plan of Action calls on ASEAN Member States to legislate in areas such as financing of terrorism and money laundering,[1399] and criminalise the trafficking in firearms and control firearms and explosives.[1400]

1387. ASEAN Charter Art. 1(1)(2).
1388. ASEAN Charter Art. 1(8).
1389. Tan & Nasu, 1222–1226.
1390. *Ibid.*, 1227.
1391. ASEAN Comprehensive Plan of Action on Counter Terrorism (2017), *supra* para. 299 (Plan of Action).
1392. Plan of Action para. 1.1.
1393. *Ibid.*, paras 1.2, 5.
1394. *Ibid.* para. 2.
1395. *Ibid.* para. 3.
1396. *Ibid.* para. 4.
1397. *Ibid.* para. 4.1.
1398. *Ibid.* para. 10.
1399. *Ibid.* para. 12.1.
1400. *Ibid.* para. 14.

384. The ACCT and the AMLAT together set out the governing framework for combating terrorism, supplemented by the Plan of Action. Viewed in isolation these documents provide a workable basis for taking effective action against terrorism, but it is apparent from the Plan of Action that much still needs to be done by the ASEAN Member States. At a practical level, action appears necessary at a legislative level in order to ensure that proper laws are in place to make certain that those accused of terrorist charges can face justice, law-enforcement agencies need to have the proper means in terms of human, technological and funding resources, and the political will must exist to enable effective cooperation to take place amongst the different Member States. Without proper resources and reservations between Member States, the fight against terrorism is immeasurably more difficult.

Chapter 4. Environment

385. Southeast Asia has not escaped the affliction of environmental degradation. The threats are common knowledge and include pollution, deforestation, land degradation and the spoliation of natural resources, poaching and trade in endangered species,[1401] amongst others. These threats, some transboundary, call for collective and separate action, and the ASEAN Charter contains a commitment, albeit decidedly limited, to the promotion of 'sustainable development so as to ensure the protection of the region's environment'.[1402] This is the sole reference to the environment in the ASEAN Charter and seems to be an indication of its ranking in the organisation's priorities. Environmental protection per se, or conservation, does not appear to be a major concern except in the context of sustainable development. This attitude appears to be reflected in the AHRD which enshrines the right to a safe, clean and sustainable environment.[1403] Naturally, much depends on how this guarantee is interpreted but a dynamic construction should bring within its scope without straining the terms of the provision protection of the environment from, *inter alia*, pollution and polluting activities. This conclusion is based additionally on ASEAN's commitment to respond effectively to transboundary challenges, which pollution undoubtedly is.[1404] It is in this specific area in fact that ASEAN has taken action.

§1. The ASEAN Agreement on Transboundary Haze Pollution

386. In 2002, ASEAN adopted the Agreement on Transboundary Haze Pollution (Agreement).[1405] The basic objective of the Agreement is 'to prevent and monitor transboundary haze pollution as a result of land and/or forest fires which should be mitigated, through concerted national efforts and intensified regional and international co-operation'.[1406] The Agreement was a direct response to the crisis in atmospheric pollution that afflicted Southeast Asia in the late 1990s caused by land

1401. In 2019, ASEAN acknowledged the challenge posed by the illegal trade in wildlife and emphasised the importance of enhanced cooperation to tackle poaching and trafficking. It therefore committed itself, *inter alia*, to increased demand reduction and law-enforcement measures, Chiang Mai Statement of ASEAN Ministers Responsible for CITES and Wildlife Enforcement on Illegal Wildlife Trade, 22 Mar. 2019, https://asean.org/wp-content/uploads/2019/06/Chiang-Mai-Statement-of-ASEAN-Ministers-Responsible-for-CITES.pdf.

1402. ASEAN Charter Art. 1(9). ASEAN had acknowledged environmental concerns in the 1980s when it adopted the Agreement on the Conservation of Nature and Natural Resources (9 Jul. 1985) but the Agreement remains unratified to this day, https://environment.asean.org/agreement-on-the-conservation-of-nature-and-natural-resources/.

1403. Article 28(f).

1404. ASEAN Charter Art. 1(8).

1405. ASEAN Agreement on Transboundary Haze Pollution (10 Jun. 2002), https://asean.org/wp-content/uploads/2021/01/ASEANAgreementonTransboundaryHazePollution-1.pdf. It entered into force on 25 Nov. 2003. Indonesia was the last state to ratify, in 2015.

1406. Article 2. Transboundary haze pollution has been defined as 'haze pollution whose physical origin is situated wholly or in part within the area under the national jurisdiction of one Member State and which is transported into the area under the jurisdiction of another Member State', Agreement Art. 1(13).

clearing, largely illegal, for palm oil plantations, principally in Indonesia.[1407] Haze pollution was not in fact a new problem but one that had been ongoing since the 1980s, but it was not until the next decade that ASEAN began to address the matter in a determined manner through a series of cooperative initiatives.[1408] Particularly significant in this regard was the Regional Haze Action Plan 1997.[1409] Its objectives were to prevent land and forest fires through better management policies and enforcement; to establish operational mechanisms to monitor land and forest fires; and to strengthen regional land and forest fire-fighting capabilities. However, these collaborative efforts were not legally binding and their achievements were modest,[1410] so that certain states, those that suffered badly from transboundary pollution, were of the view that only a treaty which imposed binding legal obligations could effect radical change.

387. As has been observed, the Agreement was adopted in 2002 and entered into force the following year. It is the first regional treaty of its type. The general obligations assumed by States Parties include cooperating in developing and implementing measures to prevent and monitor transboundary haze pollution as a result of land and/or forest fires, the control of sources of fires, including by the identification of fires, development of monitoring, assessment and early warning systems, exchange of information and technology, and the provision of mutual assistance,[1411] and the prompt response to a request for relevant information or consultations sought by a state or states that are or may be affected by transboundary haze pollution, with a view to minimising the consequences of the transboundary haze pollution, when the transboundary haze pollution originates from within their territories.[1412] It incorporates key principles of international environmental law, although not that of the 'polluter pays'.[1413] Thus States Parties 'have, in accordance with the Charter of the United Nations and the principles of international law, the sovereign right to exploit their own resources pursuant to their own environmental and developmental policies, and the responsibility to ensure that activities within their jurisdiction or control do not cause damage to the environment and harm to

1407. D. Heilmann, *After Indonesia's Ratification: The ASEAN Agreement on Transboundary Haze Pollution and Its Effectiveness As a Regional Environmental Governance Tool*, 34 J. Current Southeast Asian Aff. 95 at 98–100 (2015); F.A. Ghani, N.I.N. Redzuan, N.F.M. Nasir & M. Salamat, *Review on ASEAN Agreement on Transboundary Haze Pollution Agreement 2002: Problems and Solutions*, 1 J. Human., Language, Culture & Bus. 153, 154 (2017); R. Mushkat, *Creating Regional Environmental Governance Regimes: Implications of Southeast Asian Responses to Transboundary Haze Pollution*, 4 Wash. & Lee J. Energy, Climate & Env't 103, 141–143 (2012). Haze pollution has been defined as 'smoke resulting from land and/or forest fire which causes deleterious effects of such a nature as to endanger human health, harm living resources and ecosystems and material property and impair or interfere with amenities and other legitimate uses of the environment', Agreement Art. 1(6).

1408. Heilmann, 101–102; Mushkat, 143.

1409. Available at: https://cil.nus.edu.sg/wp-content/uploads/2017/07/1997-Regional-Haze-Action-Plan-1.pdf. Heilmann, 101–102; Mushkat, 143–144.

1410. Mushkat, 144.

1411. Agreement Art. 4(1).

1412. Agreement Art. 4(2).

1413. Heilmann, 105.

human health of other States or of areas beyond the limits of national jurisdiction'.[1414] This provision reproduces Principle 21 of the Stockholm Declaration[1415] which reflects in part the no-harm principle first laid down in the *Trail Smelter Arbitration* that states are under an obligation not to cause transboundary damage.[1416]

388. However, it is noteworthy that this objective is to be pursued in the overall context of the right of states to exploit their natural resources subject to the principle of sustainable development. This obligation is reinforced by the commitment to the ecologically sound and sustainable management and use of their natural resources.[1417] The ability of states to ravage the natural environment is somewhat constrained.

389. The Agreement incorporates a version of the precautionary principle or approach, *in casu* 'precautionary measures'.[1418] Curiously, insofar as the anticipation, prevention and monitoring of transboundary haze pollution are concerned, the parties are merely counselled to take precautionary measures ('should take'), whereas where threats of serious or irreversible damage from transboundary haze pollution exist, even without full scientific certainty, the parties are obliged to take precautionary measures ('shall be taken').

390. Specific obligations are undertaken by States Parties in relation to monitoring, prevention and response. Consequently, parties must ('take appropriate measures') monitor fire-prone areas, all land and forest fires, the environmental conditions conducive to such land and forest fires, and haze pollution arising from such land and forest fires.[1419] In the event of fires, parties must take immediate

1414. Agreement Art. 3(1).
1415. Stockholm Declaration on the Human Environment, 11 I.L.M. 1416 (1972).
1416. *Trail Smelter (United States v. Canada),* 3 R.I.A.A. 133 (1938) 1905. This principle has been reiterated by further international jurisprudence, *see Lake Lanoux (France v. Spain)*, 12 R.I.A.A. 281 (1957); *Legality of the Threat or Use by a State of Nuclear Weapons*, Advisory Opinion, I.C.J. Reports 1996, 226, para. 29, and international declarations, *see* Rio Declaration on Environment and Development, 31 I.L.M. 874 (1992) (Principle 2).
1417. Agreement Art. 3(4).
1418. Agreement Art. 3(3). *See* further, Rio Declaration on Environment and Development (Principle 15). The ICJ seems to regard the precautionary principle as having persuasive authority as an emergent norm of international law, *Gabcíkovo-Nagymaros Project Case (Hungary /Slovakia)*, Judgment, I.C.J. Reports 1997, 7, paras 112–113; *Pulp Mills on the River Uruguay (Argentina v. Uruguay)*, Judgment, I.C.J. Reports 2010, 14, para. 164. *See also* the Dissenting Opinions of Judges Weeramantry and Koroma in *Request for an Examination of the Situation in Accordance with paragraph 63 of the Court's Judgment in the 1974 Nuclear Tests Case (New Zealand v. France)*, I.C.J. Reports 1995, 288, 342–344, and 368 respectively. A distinction has been drawn between the precautionary approach and the precautionary principle, the former seeming to possess the advantage of flexibility, *see* the Separate Opinions of Judges Laing and Treves in *Southern Bluefin Tuna Cases* (*New Zealand v. Japan*; *Australia v. Japan*), Provisional Measures, International Tribunal for the Law of the Sea, 38 I.L.M. 1624, 1641–1642, 1645 (1999), respectively. The 'precautionary approach' may now form part of customary law, *Responsibilities and Obligations of States Sponsoring Persons and Entities with respect to Activities in the Area*, Advisory Opinion, I.T.L.O.S. Reports 2011, 10, para. 135.
1419. Agreement Art. 7(1).

action to control or to put them out.[1420] Regarding prevention parties must, *inter alia*, develop and implement legislative and other regulatory measures to promote zero burning policy, identify and monitor areas prone to occurrence of land and forest fires, strengthen local fire management and fire-fighting capability and coordination, and ensure that legislative, administrative and/or other relevant measures are taken to control open burning and to prevent land clearing using fire.[1421] Parties must be in a state of preparedness, with strategies and response plans in place.[1422]

391. Should a party require assistance as a result of land or forest fires or haze pollution arising within its territory, it may request assistance from any other party or even from other States or international organisations.[1423] However, it is made clear that assistance can only be provided at the request of and with the consent of the requesting party, or, when offered by another party, with the consent of the receiving party.[1424] The traditional view posits that the legality of the delivery of assistance of a humanitarian nature is contingent on the consent of the recipient state, without which its sovereignty would be violated.[1425]

392. A treaty of this nature necessitates an institutional framework. The governing body is the Conference of the Parties which supervises the implementation of the Agreement and can take such action as is necessary to ensure its effective implementation.[1426] It is supported by a Secretariat, in fact, the ASEAN Secretariat.[1427] However, of greater practical significance is the ASEAN Co-ordinating Centre for Transboundary Haze Pollution Control, mandated with facilitating cooperation and coordination among the parties in managing the impact of land and/or forest fires and haze pollution.[1428] It works on the basis that the national authority will act first to combat the fires, but it may request the ASEAN Centre's assistance if an emergency situation is declared.[1429] The ASEAN Centre's functions as set out in Annex to the Agreement and include maintaining regular contact with the respective National Monitoring Centres regarding data relating to land and /or forest fire, and air quality and levels of pollution; consolidating, analysing and processing such data; facilitating coordination among the parties, other states and relevant organisations in taking effective measures to mitigate the impact of land and/or forest fires or haze pollution; establishing and maintaining contact with prospective donor states and organisations for mobilising financial and other resources required for the

1420. Agreement Art. 7(3).
1421. Agreement Art. 9.
1422. Agreement Arts 10(1), 11.
1423. Agreement Art. 12(1).
1424. Agreement Art. 12(2).
1425. Only the provision of strictly humanitarian aid limited to the prevention and alleviation of human suffering may not be regarded as unlawful intervention or otherwise contrary to international law, *Military and Paramilitary Activities in and against Nicaragua* (*Nicaragua v. United States*), 1986 I.C.J. Reports, 14, paras 242–243.
1426. Agreement Art. 18.
1427. Agreement Art. 19.
1428. Agreement Art. 5(1).
1429. Agreement Art. 5(2).

prevention and mitigation of land and/or forest fires or haze pollution and preparedness of the parties, including fire-fighting capabilities; and responding to requests for or offer of assistance in the event of land and/or forest fires or haze pollution by transmitting promptly such requests to other states and organisations, and coordinating such assistance if asked for by the requesting party or offered by the assisting party.

393. Although the Agreement has been praised for bringing forth a legal regime,[1430] its weak points must be acknowledged. Although many aspects of the Agreement are to be welcomed, cooperation and coordination initiatives, information sharing, assistance, public education and awareness-building campaigns, etc., they are not in themselves sufficient. The root causes of haze pollution, such as deforestation, logging, land clearing, both legal and illegal must be tackled robustly and replaced with sustainable development policies. To do otherwise simply means mitigating the damage caused which one day will become irreversible. Enforcement of treaty obligations is weak and is dependent in essence on political/diplomatic suasion.[1431] Accordingly, disputes between parties are to be settled amicably by consultation or negotiation in the usual ASEAN manner.[1432] No express provision is made for the imposition of sanctions on transgressors though it is possible that the Conference of the Parties could apply pressure against a recalcitrant State. A major practical drawback was the fact that the worst culprit in causing haze pollution, Indonesia, only ratified the Agreement in 2014. And the sad fact remains that haze pollution is still a problem. As is often the case, one of the root causes is an apparent lack of will to confront the crisis.

§2. ASEAN Action on Marine Debris

394. Another transboundary problem that requires urgent attention from ASEAN is that of pollution caused by marine debris, including plastics.[1433] Marine plastic pollution impacts negatively across a variety of areas, including the environment, marine ecosystems, food security, human health and the economy.[1434] Until recently this menace does not appear to have been a priority area for ASEAN Member States individually which seem to have taken little concrete action to curtail the generation of waste.[1435] The health of the oceans has, by contrast, been a matter of concern for the United Nations for a considerable time. In 2012, the UN General Assembly acknowledged, *inter alia*, the threat posed by marine pollution and the importance of the conservation and sustainable use of the oceans' resources for sustainable

1430. *See* Mushkat, 144.
1431. Ghani et al., 158; Heilmann, 108–111.
1432. Agreement Art. 27.
1433. Y. Lyons, T. Su & M.L. Neo, *A Review of Research on Marine Plastics in Southeast Asia: Who Does What?* (2019), https://www.gov.uk/government/publications/a-review-of-research-on-marine-plastics-in-sea-who-does-what.
1434. *Ibid.*, 11.
1435. *Ibid.*, 15–37.

development.[1436] Moreover, in 2017 the UN General Assembly adopted another resolution which, *inter alia*, called on States to achieve significant reductions in marine debris by 2025.[1437] Arguably more significant is the 2030 Agenda for Sustainable Development which sets a number of Sustainable Development Goals, including preventing and reducing marine pollution.[1438] ASEAN has accordingly awoken to this danger.[1439] In 2019, ASEAN consequently adopted the Framework of Action on Marine Debris (Framework).[1440] As its designation implies, the Framework is not a treaty nor a soft law document but a comprehensive strategy for concerted action. It therefore calls for concerted efforts, activities and strategies across a number of priority areas, which are: Policy Support and Planning; Research, Innovation and Capacity Building; Public Awareness, Education and Outreach; and Private Sector Engagement. More specifically, the actions and activities call for, *inter alia*, mainstreaming marine debris policy measures in ASEAN's agenda and developing combat strategies, developing regional action plans, encouraging the implementation of relevant international laws relating to waste management by ASEAN Member States, enhancing scientific knowledge and transferring technology, information sharing, promoting behaviour change, and encouraging the private sector to use alternative materials in packaging and increase recycling and waste recovery.

395. The Framework does not define marine debris, but it is evident from the document that it has a wide scope, taking in sea and land-based pollution, and specifically ship-generated waste, hazardous waste, fishing nets and other waste from fishing vessels, and plastics, among others. National laws and ASEAN agreements would need to reflect these categories.

396. The adoption of the Framework was welcomed by ASEAN in the Bangkok Declaration on Combating Marine Debris.[1441] ASEAN Member States thereby resolve to prevent and significantly reduce marine debris by, *inter alia*, strengthening action at the national level, through national laws and regulations, as well as through collaborative action among ASEAN Member States, as well as enhancing regional and international cooperation. The adoption of the ASEAN Framework of Action on Marine Debris followed.[1442] It puts forward the phased implementation of a systematic and integrated response to guide regional action in addressing the issue of marine plastic pollution in ASEAN over the years 2021-2025.

1436. UN General Assembly Res. 66/288 (2012).
1437. UN General Assembly Res. 72/73 (2017) para. 187.
1438. UN General Assembly Res. 70/1 (2015) Goal 14.1.
1439. Lyons, Su & Neo, 38–45. *See* ASEAN Regional Action Plan for Combating Marine Debris in the ASEAN Member States (2021-2025) 2-3, https://asean.org/wp-content/uploads/2021/05/FINAL_210524-ASEAN-Regional-Action-Plan_Ready-to-Publish_v2.pdf.
1440. ASEAN Framework of Action on Marine Debris, https://asean.org/wp-content/uploads/2021/01/3.-ASEAN-Framework-of-Action-on-Marine-Debris-FINAL.pdf.
1441. Bangkok Declaration on Combating Marine Debris in the ASEAN Region, adopted in Bangkok, Thailand (22 Jun. 2019), https://cil.nus.edu.sg/databasecil/2019-bangkok-declaration-on-combating-marine-debris-in-the-asean-region/.
1442. ASEAN Regional Action Plan for Combating Marine Debris in the ASEAN Member States (2021-2025), https://asean.org/wp-content/uploads/2021/05/FINAL_210524-ASEAN-Regional-Action-Plan_Ready-to-Publish_v2.pdf.

397. Marine debris and pollution pose a pressing danger to all the oceans, but it is not the only threat they face, which includes overfishing. Nevertheless, it is encouraging that ASEAN has awoken to the need for urgent action in this area. The nature of the problem highlights the necessity for regional cooperative action. But international organisations can be slow to act; for a variety of reasons intractable states can play a spoiling role. It can only be hoped that ASEAN acts promptly.

Part IV. ASEAN External Relations

Chapter 1. Introduction: The So-Called External Parties

398. ASEAN has always been very eager to establish relations with third states, regions, international organisations and multilateral institutions. This has been reciprocal. Thus, the ASEAN Meeting of Foreign Ministers, which took place in July 2019, reported that there was a growing interest from states and regional international organisations outside the ASEAN region to engage and to collaborate, and that ninety-two foreign ambassadors had been accredited to ASEAN.[1443] However, on 26 July 2024, there were sixty-one accredited ambassadors to ASEAN.[1444]

399. A good example of ASEAN opening up to other regional international organisations is the Meeting between the Foreign Ministers of ASEAN and of the Gulf Cooperation Council (GCC), which took place in New York, on the sidelines of the 74th Ordinary Session of the UN General Assembly on 28 September 2019.[1445] During the Meeting, it was, *inter alia*, agreed to press ahead with an early conclusion of the ASEAN–GCC Framework of Cooperation for 2020–2024. By taking into account the progress made in the implementation of the previous ASEAN-GCC Two-Year Action Plan (2010–2012), its purpose was to elaborate on the joint activities to be undertaken in areas of mutual interest covering a very broad spectrum: trade and investment, smart cities, countering terrorism and violent extremism, Islamic finance, equitable development, infrastructure and connectivity, agriculture, food security, public health, education and training, cultural exchanges, etc.[1446] Presently, the ASEAN–GCC Framework of Cooperation 2024–2028 is being

1443. *See* Joint Communique of the 52nd ASEAN Foreign Ministers' Meeting, Bangkok, 31 Jul. 2019, para. 66, at https://asean.org/joint-communique-of-the-52nd-asean-foreign-ministers-meeting/. For the accreditation of non-ASEAN Member States and intergovernmental organisations, *see* Art. 46 of the Charter.

1444. *See* https://asean.org/our-communities/asean-political-security-community/outward-looking-community/external-relations/.

1445. For a history of ASEAN-GCC relations, *see* S. Niu, *The Economic and Trade Cooperation Between ASEAN and the Gulf Cooperation Council*, 4(4) J. Middle Eastern & Islamic Stud. (in Asia) 82–101 (2010); G. Burton, *Connectivity Between the Gulf Cooperation Council and Asia*, Bussola Institute, Research Paper no. 5, February 2020, at: https://www.bussolainstitute.org/research/connectivity-between-the-gulf-cooperation-council-and-asia.

1446. *See* The Association of Southeast Asian Nations – Cooperation Council for the Arab States of the Gulf (ASEAN-GCC) Foreign Ministers' Meeting, *Co-Chairs' Press Statement*, New York, 28 Sep. 2019, at: https://asean.org/wp-content/uploads/2021/09/FINAL-Co-Chairs-Press-Statement-for-the-ASEAN-GCC-Foreign-Ministers-Mee....pdf.

implemented.[1447] The closer links between the two regional international organisations led the King of Saudi Arabia to invite the Leaders of GCC and ASEAN to a Summit which took place in Saudi Arabia on 20 October 2023.[1448] The Second ASEAN-GCC Summit will be held in May 2025. Commentators have questioned the wisdom of the invitation that Malaysia (holder of the ASEAN Chair for 2025) has extended to China to attend the Summit, arguing that it probably has to do more with Malaysia's own interests and goals.[1449] To that extent, it should be noted that the relations between ASEAN and GCC do not prevent individual ASEAN members from negotiating bilateral Agreements with the GCC (e.g., Indonesia, *see infra*). It follows that relationships develop at different levels.

400. Article 44 of the ASEAN Charter refers to the so-called external parties. Even though a definition of this term is not given, it could safely be assumed that 'external parties' includes both state actors (third states whether from the region of South-Southeast Asia or beyond it) and international organisations (whether global or regional in scope) as well as non-state actors (e.g., international Non-governmental Organisations (NGOs), namely NGOs having their seat or headquarters in one state but being active in several states).[1450] In particular, the first paragraph of Article 44 stipulates that, in the context of carrying out its external relations, the Meeting of Foreign Ministers has the power and the discretion to confer upon external parties 'the formal status of Dialogue Partner,[1451] Sectoral Dialogue Partner,[1452] Development Partner,[1453] Special Observer,[1454] Guest' or any other status to be established in the future.[1455] It should be noted that, even if the

1447. At: https://asean.org/asean-gulf-cooperation-council-framework-of-cooperation-2024-2028/. Generally, *see* King Faisal Center for Research and Islamic Studies, *The GCC-ASEAN Summit: Charting Regional Interests and Future Challenges*, January 2024.

1448. *See* Summit of the Association of Southeast Asian Nations (ASEAN) and the Gulf Cooperation Council (GCC), *Joint Statement*, Riyadh, 20 Oct. 2023, at: https://asean.org/wp-content/uploads/2023/10/FINAL-ASEAN-GCC-Summit-JS.pdf.

1449. See Sharon Seah, 'ASEAN should hope for the best but prepare for the worst in 2025', *East Asia Forum*, 20 Jan. 2025, at: https://eastasiaforum.org/2025/01/20/asean-should-hope-for-the-best-but-prepare-for-the-worst-in-2025/.

1450. Generally, *see* K. Magliveras, *The Transnational Regulation of NGOs: Revisiting the Council of Europe Convention on Recognition of the Legal Personality of International Non-Governmental Organisations*, The Jean Monet Papers on Political Economy 07/2013, University of the Peloponnese, December 2013, at: https://www.uop.gr/images/files/magliveras.pdf.

1451. Presently, these are Australia, Canada, China, European Union, India, Japan, Korea, New Zealand, Russian Federation, United Kingdom, and USA.

1452. Presently, these are Brazil, Morocco, Norway, Pakistan, South Africa, Switzerland, Turkey, and United Arab Emirates.

1453. Presently, these are Chile, France, Germany, Italy, the Netherlands and Peru.

1454. It would appear that this is the same as the status of Observer, which had existed before the ASEAN Charter. Papua New Guinea was given Observer status in 1976, while in 1992 it was conferred the status of 'Special observer', *see Joint Communique of the 25th ASEAN Ministerial Meeting*, Manila, the Philippines, 22 Jul. 1992, para. 8. Note States were given observer status before applying officially for ASEAN membership. Timor-Leste, as explained above, became an observer in November 2022.

1455. *See* further, ASEAN Community Vision 2025, the ASEAN Political-Security Community Blueprint 2025, section C.2. The status of 'Strategic Partner' falls into the category of 'other status to be established in the future' and, in terms of hierarchy, it stands higher compared to the 'Dialogue

Meeting of Foreign Ministers does, for whatever reason, not grant this formal status, the second paragraph of Article 44 makes it a quite straightforward process to have 'external partners' follow developments in ASEAN, as they may be invited to participate in meetings or in cooperative activities pursuant to the relevant stipulations of the Rules of Procedure.

401. Presently, ASEAN maintains partnerships with several regional international organisations and multilateral institutions, primarily from Asia and South America, including the following: the Community of Latin American and Caribbean States (CELAC), the Economic Cooperation Organisation (ECO), the Eurasian Economic Union (EAEU), the GCC, the Indian Ocean Rim Association (IORA), the Pacific Alliance (PA), the Pacific Islands Forum (PIF), the Shanghai Cooperation Organisation (SCO), the Southern Common Market (MERCOSUR), and the aforementioned South Asian Association for Regional Cooperation (SAARC).

402. As already indicated, the status of 'Dialogue Partner' has been extended to countries which belong to the so-called G-8 / G-7 and G-20 groups of states. Regular high-level meetings between the ASEAN Member States and the Dialogue Partners have taken place for many years now. Thus, in the course of 2018 and 2019, the following meetings were, among others, convened:[1456] (a) the 25th Anniversary of ASEAN-India Dialogue Relations,[1457] which builds on the Framework Agreement on Comprehensive Economic Cooperation Between the Republic of India and the Association of Southeast Asian Nations, concluded in Bali on 8 October 2003 and continues very dynamically;[1458] (b) the 21st ASEAN-China Summit;[1459] (c) the

Partner' status. Presently only with Australia, China, India, Japan, South Korea and USA has a 'Comprehensive Strategic Partnership' been established.

1456. *See* ASEAN Annual Report 2018–2019, *Advancing Partnership for Sustainability*, Jakarta: ASEAN Secretariat, July 2019, 11 et seq.

1457. It was held on 25 Jan. 2018 under the theme of 'Shared Values, Common Destiny', *see* Delhi Declaration of the ASEAN-India Commemorative Summit to mark the 25th Anniversary of ASEAN-India Dialogue Relations. Several bilateral agreements have also been concluded. However, the long-awaited negotiations for the ASEAN–India Air Transport Agreement have still not commenced, while the text of the ASEAN–India Maritime Transport Agreement was finalised after considerable delay, *see* 'ASEAN, India reaffirm comprehensive strategic partnership', 19 Mar. 2024, at: https://asean.org/24th-meeting-of-asean-india-joint-cooperation-committee-convenes/.

1458. Cf. the article published by Indian Prime Minister Shri Narendra Modi on 25 Jan. 2018, at: https://www.indiplomacy.com/2018/01/25/delhi-declaration-of-the-asean-india-commemorative-summit-to-mark-the-25th-anniversary-of-asean-india-dialogue-relations/. *See* further, Plan of Action to Implement the ASEAN-India Partnership for Peace, Progress and Shared Prosperity (2016–2020), which was carried on by the namesake Plan of Action covering the years 2021–2025, at: https://asean.org/wp-content/uploads/2020/09/ASEAN-India-POA-2021-2025-Final.pdf; 'Overview: Asean-India Comprehensive Strategic Partnership', June 2024, at: https://asean.org/wp-content/uploads/2024/06/Overview-ASEAN-India-as-of-June-2024-cl.pdf

1459. It was held in Singapore on 14 Nov. 2018, *see* Chairman's Statement of the 21st ASEAN-China Summit to Commemorate the 15th Anniversary of ASEAN-China Strategic Partnership, at: https://asean.org/chairmans-statement-of-the-21st-asean-china-summit-to-commemorate-the-15th-anniversary-of-asean-china-strategic-partnership-2/. The 27th ASEAN-China Summit was held on 10 October 2024, *see* the Chairman's Statement at: https://asean.org/chairmans-statement-of-the-27th-asean-china-summit/.

21st ASEAN-Japan Summit;[1460] (d) the 20th ASEAN-Republic of Korea Summit;[1461] (e) the 3rd ASEAN-Russia Summit;[1462] (f) the 6th ASEAN-U.S. Summit;[1463] and (g) the 22nd ASEAN-EU Ministerial Meeting.[1464] Moreover, during the same period, the so-called Informal Breakfast Summits were held with two Strategic Partners, namely India and Australia.

403. As regards Australia, the ASEAN-Australia Special Summit, held in Sydney on 17–18 March 2018, was a major breakthrough in bilateral relations, cemented the strategic partnership between them and culminated in the Sydney Declaration that laid down the objectives for future cooperation.[1465] The ASEAN Meeting of Foreign Ministers in July 2019 expressed its willingness to adopt the Plan of Action to Implement the ASEAN-Australia Strategic Partnership (2020–2024) in the context of the 45th Anniversary of the ASEAN-Australia Dialogue Relations.[1466] The Action Plan, which was adopted in August 2019 and was

1460. It was held in Singapore on 14 Nov. 2018 to commemorate the 45th anniversary of ASEAN-Japan friendship and cooperation, *see* Chairman's Statement of the 21st ASEAN-Japan Summit, at: https://asean.org/chairmans-statement-of-the-21st-asean-japan-summit/. The 27th ASEAN-Japan Summit was held on 10 October 2024, *see* the Chairman's Statement at: https://asean.org/chairmans-statement-of-the-27th-asean-japan-summit/.

1461. It was held in Singapore on 14 Nov. 2018, *see* Chairman's Statement of the 20th ASEAN-Republic of Korea Summit, at: https://asean.org/speechandstatement/chairmans-statement-of-the-20th-asean-republic-of-korea-summit/. The 25th ASEAN-Republic of Korea Summit commemorating the 35th Anniversary of Dialogue Relations was held on 10 October 2024, *see* the Chairman's Statement at: https://asean.org/wp-content/uploads/2024/10/2.-Final-Chairmans-Statement-of-the-25th-ASEAN-ROK-Summit-1.pdf.

1462. It was held in Singapore on 14 Nov. 2018, *see* Chairman's Statement of the 3rd ASEAN-Russia Summit, at: https://asean.org/chairmans-statement-of-the-3rd-asean-russia-summit/. The 4th ASEAN-Russia Summit commemorating the 30th Anniversary of bilateral relations was held via videoconference on 28 October 2021, see the Joint Statement at: https://asean.org/wp-content/uploads/2021/11/82.-Joint-Statement-of-the-4th-ASEAN-Russia-Summit-Final.pdf.

1463. It was held in Singapore on 15 Nov. 2018, *see* Chairman's Statement of the 6th ASEAN-United States Summit, at: https://asean.org/chairmans-statement-of-the-6th-asean-united-states-summit/. The 12th ASEAN-US Summit was held on 11 October 2024, *see* the Chairman's Statement at: https://asean.org/wp-content/uploads/2024/10/8.-Final-Chairmans-Statement-of-the-12th-ASEAN-U.S.-Summit.pdf

1464. It was held on 21 Jan. 2019 in Brussels, *see* the Joint Statement, at: https://www.consilium.europa.eu/en/press/press-releases/2019/01/21/joint-statement-of-the-22nd-eu-asean-ministerial-meeting/. The 24th EU-ASEAN ministerial meeting was held in Brussels on 2 Feb 2024, see Joint Ministerial Statement, at: https://www.consilium.europa.eu/media/69944/st06074-en24.pdf. Note that a score of other entities has also been tasked with promoting EU-ASEAN cooperation: the ASEAN Post-Ministerial Conference with the EU; the EU-ASEAN Trade Commissioner Consultations; the EU-ASEAN Senior Officials' Meeting; the EU-ASEAN Senior Economic Officials' Meeting; and the EU-ASEAN Joint Cooperation Committee. Finally, sectoral meetings between ASEAN and the EU have taken place at regular intervals, among them the EU-ASEAN Information and Communication Technologies Dialogue; the EU-ASEAN Science, Technology and Innovation Dialogue; the EU-ASEAN High Level Transport Dialogue; the EU-ASEAN High Level Dialogue on Environment and Climate Change; and the EU-ASEAN Policy Dialogue on Human Rights.

1465. *See* Joint Statement of the ASEAN-Australia Special Summit: The Sydney Declaration, 18 Mar. 2018, at: https://asean.org/joint-statement-of-the-asean-australia-special-summit-the-sydney-declaration/.

1466. *See* Joint Communique of the 52nd ASEAN Foreign Ministers' Meeting, *supra*, para. 67.

approved in September 2020,[1467] is part of the strong history of bilateral cooperation that goes back to the mid-1970s. It is structured on the basis of the three pillars of ASEAN activities, namely Political and Security Cooperation, Economic Cooperation, and Socio-Cultural Cooperation. The 2019 Action Plan covered an impressively large number of areas, and importantly involved the private sector as well. Suffice to mention the following areas of bilateral cooperation: Non-Traditional Security and Counterterrorism; Information Communications Technology and Digital Integration; Energy; Agriculture and Forestry; Disaster Management and Humanitarian Assistance; Social Inclusion and Gender; Climate Change Adaptation and Mitigation; and Cybersecurity.

404. A successor Action Plan was concluded in July 2024 to cover the period from 2025 to 2029.[1468] Overall, it follows the structure as well as the fields of cooperation of the previous Action Plan. It should be noted that the various actions are described in quite general terms. For example, in the area of immigration, the Action Plan mentions that it will support the implementation of the aforementioned ASEAN Consensus on the Protection and Promotion of the Rights of Migrant Workers (ACMW) and encourage further cooperation under 'relevant ASEAN Declaration and frameworks', including the ASEAN Declaration on Portability of Social Security Benefits for Migrant Workers in ASEAN,[1469] and the ASEAN Declaration on Placement and Protection of Migrant Fishers.[1470]

405. Relations between ASEAN and Australia are indeed close, not least because Australia appears to have been playing with the idea of applying for ASEAN membership.[1471] A Report, which was submitted to the Australian Parliament on the occasion of a summit meeting held between Australia and ASEAN Member States in Sydney in March 2018, suggested that ASEAN would be unwilling to accept it to membership. It was also pointed out that, if it were to join the Organisation, Australia would have to refrain from criticising fellow ASEAN countries on their human rights record and accommodate any position that ASEAN might opt to promote on democracy, and irrespective of how unpalatable it might

---

1467. The text of the Action Plan, which succeeds the previous one (2015–2019), is available at: https://asean.org/wp-content/uploads/2021/09/ASEAN-Australia-POA-2020-2024-FINAL.pdf.
1468. Plan of Action to Implement the ASEAN-Australia Comprehensive Strategic Partnership (2025-2029), at: https://asean.org/wp-content/uploads/2024/07/Adopted-ASEAN-Australia-POA-2025-2029.pdf.
1469. It was adopted at the 40th and 41st ASEAN Summits on 11 Nov. 2022 and will serve as a roadmap of regional actions until 2030, at: https://asean.org/asean-declaration-on-portability-of-social-security-benefits-for-migrant-workers-in-asean/.
1470. It was adopted during the 42nd ASEAN Summit on 10 May 2023, at: https://asean.org/wp-content/uploads/2023/05/10-ASEAN-Declaration-on-Protection-and-Promotion-of-the-Rights-of-Migrant-Fishers_adopted-1.pdf.
1471. Generally, *see* G. Dobell, *Australia as an ASEAN Community Partner* (Australian Strategic Policy Institute 20 Feb. 2018), at: https://www.aspi.org.au/report/australia-asean-community-partner. The Report recommended that New Zealand joined ASEAN alongside Australia. On New Zealand-ASEAN relations, *see* M. McKinnon, *New Zealand and ASEAN: A History* (Asia New Zealand Foundation 2016).

be to Australia and its population.[1472] It follows that, for different reasons, neither ASEAN nor Australia might be willing to proceed with the latter's membership. ASEAN States might look suspiciously at the economic strength of Australia and its rule of law and democratic credentials.[1473]

406. Interestingly enough, while the 2018 Sydney Declaration confirmed that they had several ideals and values in common (e.g., peace, the rule of law, human rights, good governance, respect, trust, tolerance, social responsibility and diversity), democracy was not among them. However, the 2019 Action Plan included the exchange of best practices in promoting democracy and democratic institutions among the joint actions to be pursued. Bilateral cooperation was promoted in the area of peace and security. Thus, a Joint Declaration on counter terrorism was signed in March 2018, expressing grave concerns about North Korea's nuclear and ballistic missile programmes.

In September 2020, the two sides decided to hold an annual ASEAN-Australia Summit, starting from the following year. However, this did not happen, and it was only on 4–6 March 2024 that a Special Summit was held in Melbourne, Australia, as the high-level meeting to commemorate the 50th anniversary of bilateral Dialogue Relations.[1474] Two documents emanated from the Summit, the ASEAN-Australia Leaders' Vision Statement – Partners for peace and prosperity[1475] and The Melbourne Declaration – A partnership for the future. Neither document contains any hints on any future possibility that Australia might seek some kind of membership in ASEAN. However, the content of the documents reveals that both sides believe that they form part of a specific region; e.g., they resolved 'to promote economic integration in the region'.[1476]

1472. *See* F. Frost, *The ASEAN-Australia Special Summit, Sydney, March 2018: Issues and Implications*, Parliamentary Library, Research Paper Series, 2017–18, 1 Mar. 2018, p. 15, at: http://parlinfo.aph.gov.au/parlInfo/download/library/prspub/5819952/upload_binary/5819952.pdf; G. Dobell, *ASEAN and Australia Go to the Summit*, 72 Austl. J. Int'l Aff. 314–321 (2018).

1473. For other considerations, *see* L.A.M. Adducul, *The Challenges to Australia's ASEAN Membership*, *CIRSS Commentaries*, Vol. V, No. 10 (June 2018), at: https://www.fsi.gov.ph/the-challenges-to-australias-asean-membership/.

1474. The meeting was also attended by Timor-Leste, as it has done with most meetings held with third States and international organisations. For analysis of the issues addressed by the Special Summit from an Australian point of view, *see* V. Lam, 'The 2024 ASEAN-Australia Special Summit', Parliament of Australia, Research Paper Series 2023–24, 28 Feb. 2024, at: https://parlinfo.aph.gov.au/parlInfo/download/library/prspub/9622713/upload_binary/9622713.pdf.

1475. At: https://www.pm.gov.au/media/asean-australia-leaders-vision-statement-partners-peace-and-prosperity.

1476. *See* The Melbourne Declaration, para. 27, at: https://www.pm.gov.au/media/melbourne-declaration-partnership-future.

Chapter 2. The Conclusion of ASEAN International Agreements

407. The seventh paragraph of Article 41 of the ASEAN Charter endows it with a very generally worded power to enter into agreements with third states as well as with sub-regional, regional and international organisations and institutions. This power is based on Article 3 thereof, which expressly confers legal personality on ASEAN and characterises it as an IGO.[1477] This provision does not stipulate which will be the subject matter of these international agreements or which ASEAN activities they may concern. Therefore, it could be concluded that they may cover any of the pursuits that are promoted by the three pillars of the ASEAN Community. On 17 November 2011, the Rules of Procedure for Conclusion of International Agreements by ASEAN were adopted.[1478] What is meant by 'international agreements' is explained in Rule 2: 'any written agreement, regardless of its particular designation, governed by international law which creates rights and obligations for ASEAN as a distinct entity from its Member States'. It follows that a MoU could very well be considered an international agreement if it meets these conditions.[1479] However, whether it will be legally binding and create mutual legal obligations depends on the wording of the MoU (e.g., the MoU between the Islamic Development Bank Group and the ASEAN Secretariat signed on 16 September 2008) or on an express provision stipulating that it is a mere record of understanding (e.g., Article 3 of the ASEAN – World Tourism Organization (UNWTO) concluded on 22 January 2008).

408. The scope of the Rules of Procedure is given in Rule 1. The procedure for the conclusion of two categories of international agreements is laid down. The first is those agreements signed in ASEAN's capacity as an IGO and in the conduct of its external relations pursuant to the aforementioned Article 41(7) of the Charter. The second is those international agreements, which are concluded by all ASEAN Member States collectively, but create duties and obligations at the level of individual Member States.

409. In a nutshell, pursuant to Rules 3 et seq., the procedure is as follows. The proposal to commence negotiations will be coordinated with the Committee of Permanent Representatives by the relevant ASEAN Sectoral Ministerial Body. The latter will also decide on the proposal and will appoint the ASEAN representatives who will participate in the negotiations. The basis for the negotiations will be the common position, which Member States shall reach pursuant to Article 41(4) of the

1477. *See* H.D. Phan, *The Association of Southeast Asian Nations: International Legal Personality and Its Treaty-Making Power*, 13 Int'l Organisations L. Rev. 273–307 (2016); M Cremona *et al*, *ASEAN's External Agreements: Law, Practice and the Quest for Collective Action* (Cambridge University Press, 2015).

1478. Available at: https://cil.nus.edu.sg/databasecil/2011-rules-of-procedure-for-conclusion-of-international-agreements-by-asean/. Generally, *see* Z. Chen, *ASEAN and Its Problematic Treaty-Making Practice: Can International Organizations Conclude Treaties 'on Behalf of' Their Member States?*, 4 Asian J. Int'l L. 391–419 (2014).

1479. *See,* e.g., Memorandum of Understanding between the Association of Southeast Asian Nations and the Asian Development Bank (2012); Memorandum of Understanding between the Association of Southeast Asian Nations and the International Telecommunication Union (2015)

ASEAN Charter. Representatives are obliged to adhere to the adopted common position. When the negotiations have been completed, the representatives are allowed to initialise the draft text of the international agreement, which, however, does not bind ASEAN: it only finalises the form and content of the negotiated text. More specifically, as far as ASEAN is concerned, the initialised draft text must be further endorsed pursuant to Rule 7. In practice, the ASEAN Sectoral Ministerial Body, in consultation with the Committee of Permanent Representatives, will endorse the draft agreement, which will be submitted to the (following) ASEAN Foreign Ministers meeting for its consideration.

410. Under Rule 8, the consent of ASEAN to be bound by an international agreement is conveyed by the signature or an act of formal confirmation, depending on the specific clauses of the agreement in question. In other words, it will depend on whether the agreement envisages that it will enter into force upon signature[1480] or whether it will require to be ratified / approved by all or some of the signatory parties. Who the person to sign the international agreement on behalf of ASEAN will be laid down in Rule 5: the Foreign Ministers Meeting may appoint either the Secretary-General or any other person. Finally, according to Rule 10, this procedure will also apply, *mutatis mutandis*, to the amendment, suspension, and termination of international agreements to which ASEAN is a contracting party.

1480. For example, Art. VII of the Agreement of Co-operation Between ASEAN and United Nations Educational, Scientific and Cultural Organization (UNESCO), signed on 12 Sep. 1998. The Agreement was superseded and replaced on 17 Dec. 2013, when the Framework Agreement for Cooperation between ASEAN and UNESCO was concluded. The Framework Agreement, under Art. 21, became effective for a period of five years from the date of signature and may be extended for further periods of five years, by mutual written consent between the contracting parties and based on a joint review.

Chapter 3. ASEAN United Nations Relations

411. Pursuant to Article 45(1) of the ASEAN Charter, 'ASEAN may seek an appropriate status with the United Nations system'. However, the foundation of a dedicated relationship between ASEAN and the Organisation of the United Nations precedes the conclusion of the ASEAN Charter. Indeed, the first (bilateral) Summit took place in 2000.[1481] Its agenda featured the questions of peace and security, the development of human resources, and South-South cooperation. The 2nd (bilateral) Summit was held at the UN Headquarters in New York on 13 September 2005.[1482] It concentrated on how to broaden collaboration between the two Organisations and, specifically, how the relevant UN Agencies (which together form the so-called United Nations Asia-Pacific Regional Coordination Mechanism) could be involved in promoting those development issues that are important for the ASEAN region. These topics included poverty eradication, prevention and control of infectious diseases, trade and investment, as well as peace and security. The possibility of ASEAN seeking an observer status in the UN General Assembly was also discussed. The next two years proved to be of significance because bilateral relations were intensified with (a) ASEAN being granted observer status in the General Assembly[1483] and (b) the signing of a MoU on ASEAN–UN Cooperation on 27 September 2007, which envisaged regular discussions on topics of strategic importance.[1484]

412. But despite the MoU, relations between the UN and ASEAN were still not institutionalised.[1485] This was achieved at the Fourth (bilateral) Summit,[1486] which was convened in Bali, Indonesia, in November 2011 and resulted in what was described as a 'comprehensive partnership'. Following the Joint Declaration adopted at Bali,[1487] during the Eighth Summit, which was held in Vientiane, Laos, in September 2016, a five-year Plan of Action was adopted, which ended in

1481. It was held in Bangkok on 13 Feb. 2000 at the sidelines of the Tenth Session of the UN Conference on Trade and Development.
1482. Note that in the intervening years the UN General Assembly had called for strengthening the UN's cooperation with ASEAN, *see* Res. 57/35, 'Cooperation between the United Nations and the Association of South-East Asian Nations' of 21 Nov. 2002 and Res. 59/05 of 22 Oct. 2004 having the same title.
1483. *See* UNGA Res. 61/46, 'Cooperation between the United Nations and the Association of Southeast Asian Nations' of 4 Dec. 2006.
1484. At: https://asean.org/wp-content/uploads/2017/12/2007-Memorandum-of-Understanding-between-ASEAN-and-the-UN-on-ASEAN-UN-Cooperation.pdf.
1485. For bilateral relations until 2010, *see* UN Economic and Social Commission for Asia and the Pacific, *Striving Together: ASEAN & the UN*, UN Doc. ST/ESCAP/2585, 2010; Henry Dunant Centre for Humanitarian Dialogue, *New Directions in the Relationship between ASEAN and the UN*, Briefing Paper, January 2009, at: https://www.files.ethz.ch/isn/97029/ASEAN_Feb2009.pdf.
1486. Note that the Third (bilateral) Summit took place in Hanoi, Vietnam, on 29 Oct. 2010 and resulted, *inter alia*, in the Joint Declaration on ASEAN-UN Collaboration in Disaster Management. The outcome of the Summit was reflected in a Co-Chairs' Statement.
1487. *See* Joint Declaration on Comprehensive Partnership Between ASEAN and the United Nations, and Annex, 19 Nov. 2011.

2020.[1488] The Plan of Action resulted in a number of projects, including the ASEAN–UN Joint Strategic Plan on Disaster Management 2016–2020[1489] and the ASEAN–UN Environment and Climate Change Action Plan 2016–2020.[1490] The former instrument was presented to the World Humanitarian Summit (Istanbul, May 2016) as an example of best practices on disaster management emanating from the cooperation between the UN and regional international organisations.

413. The Tenth UN–ASEAN Summit was held in Bangkok, Thailand, on 3 November 2019 under the general theme 'Advancing Partnership for Sustainability'.[1491] The two sides discussed the development of a new Plan of Action to cover the period 2021–2025 and to build upon the success of the then current Plan, where over 90% of the action lines had been addressed by the end of 2019. Moreover, the Summit referred to cooperation in the area of promotion and protection of human rights in the ASEAN region, increasing engagements between the AICHR and the UN (for this purpose, so-called Interface Meetings have been organised). As the Summit coincided with the thirtieth anniversary of the adoption of the UN Convention on the Rights of the Child (CRC), which has been ratified by all ASEAN Member States but subject to several reservations,[1492] the Summit welcomed the adoption of the following three ASEAN documents: (a) the Joint Statement on Reaffirmation of Commitment to Advancing the Rights of the Child in ASEAN;[1493] (b) the ASEAN Declaration on the Rights of Children in the context of Migration;[1494] and (c) the Declaration on the Protection of Children from All Forms of Online Exploitation and Abuse in ASEAN.[1495] All three documents had been proclaimed the previous day (2 November 2019) during the 35th ASEAN Summit.[1496] Finally, the Tenth Summit reviewed the progress made in several joint Programmes of Action. These included the ASEAN–UN Joint Strategic Plan of Action on Disaster Management (2016–2020), the ASEAN–UN Environment and Climate Change Action

1488. *See* Plan of Action to Implement the Joint Declaration on Comprehensive Partnership between ASEAN and the United Nations (2016–2020).

1489. Text at: https://asean.org/book/asean-un-joint-strategic-plan-of-action-on-disaster-management-2016-2020/. *See* further, Center for Excellence in Disaster Management & Humanitarian Assistance, *ASEAN Disaster Management Reference Handbook*, March 2019, at: https://reliefweb.int/sites/reliefweb.int/files/resources/2019%20ASEAN%20DM%20Handbook.pdf.

1490. *See* B. Boer, *International Environmental Law*, in *The Oxford Handbook of International Law in Asia and the Pacific* 170, 182 (S. Chesterman, H. Owada & B. Saoul eds, Oxford U. Press 2019).

1491. *See* Chairman's Statement of the 10th ASEAN-United Nations Summit, Bangkok / Nonthaburi, 3 Nov. 2019, at: https://asean.org/chairmans-statement-of-the-10th-asean-united-nations-summit/.

1492. The reservations are available at: https://treaties.un.org/Pages/ViewDetails.aspx?src=TREATY&mtdsg_no=IV-11&chapter=4&clang=_en#11. Generally, *see* S. Linton, *ASEAN States, Their Reservations to Human Rights Treaties and the Proposed ASEAN Commission on Women and Children*, 30 Hum. Rts. Q. 436–493 (2008).

1493. At: https://asean.org/joint-statement-on-reaffirmation-of-commitment-to-advancing-the-rights-of-the-child-in-asean/.

1494. At: https://asean.org/asean-declaration-on-the-rights-of-children-in-the-context-of-migration/.

1495. At: https://asean.org/declaration-on-the-protection-of-children-from-all-forms-of-online-exploitation-and-abuse-in-asean/.

1496. *See* Chairman's Statement of the 35th ASEAN Summit, 'Advancing Partnership for Sustainability', Bangkok / Nonthaburi, 3 Nov. 2019, at: https://asean.org/wp-content/uploads/2021/03/97.pdf.

Plan (2016–2020), and the ASEAN–Food and Agriculture Organization (FAO) Cooperation on Agriculture and Forestry (2019–2024).

414. The Eleventh Summit was held via videoconference on 15 November 2020. Its noteworthy achievement was that ASEAN leaders and the UN Secretary-General concluded the new Plan of Action covering the period 2021–2025.[1497] Since then, the Twelfth Summit was held in Cambodia in November 2022,[1498] and the Thirteenth Summit in Indonesia in September 2023.[1499] At the latter Summit, the UN Secretary-General remarked, *inter alia*, that 'ASEAN's convening power, commitment to dialogue, and experience in conflict prevention are crucial pillars of stability … I commend ASEAN for your vital role in building bridges of understanding all over the world … I am grateful for your steadfast support for multilateral solutions and your contribution of over 5000 peacekeepers from ASEAN countries … ASEAN is uniquely positioned to be a leader of an energy transition that is global, sustainable, just, inclusive, and equitable.'[1500] The most recent Summit was held in October 2024. It underscored the significance of the bilateral Comprehensive Partnership in addressing global challenges and reaffirmed a shared commitment to uphold multilateralism, the rule of law and a rules-based international order as the tools to address the increasingly complex global challenges.[1501]

As has been indicated above, for many years now the UN General Assembly has adopted resolutions on UN with ASEAN. The format of these resolutions, which seem to be adopted every two years, is that the UNGA takes note of the Report of the UNSG on the UN's cooperation with regional international organisations (including ASEAN) and reviews the developments that have taken place both within ASEAN and in the UN–ASEAN relationship since its previous resolution.[1502] In

---

1497. *See* Plan of Action to Implement the Joint Declaration on Comprehensive Partnership between ASEAN and the United Nations (2021–2025), at: https://asean.org/wp-content/uploads/2020/10/ASEAN-UN-POA-2021-2025-final.pdf. *See* also, Chairman's Statement of the 11th ASEAN-United Nations Summit, Vietnam, 15 Nov. 2020, at: https://asean.org/chairmans-statement-of-the-11th-asean-united-nations-summit/.

1498. *See* Chairman's Statement of the 12th ASEAN-United Nations Summit, Phnom Penh, Cambodia, 11 Nov. 2022, at: https://asean.org/wp-content/uploads/2022/11/7.-Final-CS-12th-ASEAN-UN-Summit.pdf.

1499. *See* Chairman's Statement of the 13th ASEAN-United Nations Summit, Jakarta, Indonesia, 7 Sep. 2023, at: https://asean.org/wp-content/uploads/2023/09/Chairmans-Statement-of-13th-ASEAN-UN-Summit_Final.pdf.

1500. *See* United Nations, 'Secretary-General's remarks at the ASEAN-UN Summit', 7 Sep. 2023, at: https://www.un.org/sg/en/content/sg/statement/2023-09-07/secretary-generals-remarks-the-asean-un-summit.

1501. *See* Chairman's Statement of the 14th ASEAN-United Nations Summit, Vientiane, Lao PDR, 11 Oct. 2024, at: https://asean.org/chairmans-statement-of-the-14th-asean-united-nations-summit/.

1502. *See*, *inter alia*, UNGA Res. 77/12, 'Cooperation between the United Nations and the Association of Southeast Asian Nations' of 21 Nov. 2022, which cited UNSG Report UN Doc. A/77/277 – S/2022/606 (8 Aug. 2022), paras 36–47; Res. 75/15, 'Cooperation between the United Nations and the Association of Southeast Asian Nations' of 23 Nov. 2020, which cited UNSG Report UN Doc. A/75/345 – S/2020/898. (11 Sep. 2020), and Res. 73/259 of 20 Dec. 2018, 'Cooperation between the United Nations and the Association of Southeast Asian Nations', which cited UNSG Report A/73/328 – S/2018/592 (17 Aug. 2018).

August 2024, the UNSG delivered its Report on cooperation with regional organisations,[1503] but the UNGA during its current (79th) ordinary session has not adopted a resolution on cooperation with ASEAN.

415. As is the case with the other bilateral partnerships that the UN holds with third international organisations, there is a process of evaluating their implementation. In the instance of ASEAN, this task is carried out by a meeting between the ASEAN Foreign Ministers, the UN Secretary-General and the UNGA President; this meeting has also been designated as the primary policy level mechanism. Presently, the UN maintains a Liaison Officer in Jakarta; its creation had been agreed during the Fifth ASEAN–UN Summit.[1504] Finally, ASEAN became the first-ever regional international organisation to be commemored in an UNGA resolution: on 19 July 2017, Resolution 71/317, which was adopted without a vote, commemorated the fiftieth anniversary of the establishment of ASEAN.[1505]

1503. See UNSG Report A/79/302 - S/2024/600 (8 August 2024), at: https://digitallibrary.un.org/record/4061951?ln=fr&v=pdf.

1504. It was held in Bandar Seri Begawan, Brunei Darussalam, on 10 Oct. 2013. Note that the next two Summits took place, respectively, in Nay Pyi Taw, Myanmar, on 12 Nov. 2014, and in Kuala Lumpur, Malaysia, on 22 Nov. 2015.

1505. Text at: https://documents.un.org/doc/undoc/gen/n17/222/27/pdf/n1722227.pdf.

Chapter 4. ASEAN: Pacific Alliance Relations

416. While the desire of ASEAN to maintain close institutional ties with the United Nations is quite understandable, especially given the considerable know-how that the latter has acquired over several decades in many an area of activity where ASEAN is also active (including the Millennium Development Goals (MDGs) and, the successor, Sustainable Development Goals (SDGs)), what might not be so clear is the policy of ASEAN to maintain close relations with other regional and sub-regional international organisations, which operate in other continents. To that extent, suffice to mention relations with the Pacific Alliance, a Latin American sub-regional integration institution. Its creation was agreed in April 2011, its constitutive instrument was signed in June 2012;[1506] presently, there are four participating states (Chile, Colombia, Mexico and Peru). Very soon after the establishment of the Pacific Alliance, and at the initiative of ASEAN, firm bilateral relations were forged and regular meetings have been held; for example, in September 2019 and on the sidelines of the UN General Assembly's annual ordinary session in New York, the 6th ASEAN-Pacific Alliance Ministerial Meeting took place.[1507] The coordinatorship of the bilateral relations is rotated alphabetically among ASEAN Member States on a one-year basis; Singapore is the coordinator for 2025.[1508]

417. In 2016, the ASEAN–Pacific Alliance Framework for Cooperation was concluded. It led to the successfully completed Work Plan that run from 2017 until 2019 and was extended to December 2020. A follow-up Work Plan to cover the years 2021 to 2025 has been agreed. It extends bilateral cooperation to the following areas: economic cooperation; education and people-to-people contacts; science, technology, innovation, smart cities and connectivity; environment and sustainable development; and cooperation on post-pandemic recovery due to COVID-19.[1509] Finally, notwithstanding the bilateral relations, individual ASEAN Member States have developed their own relationship with the Pacific Alliance. In particular, Indonesia, Singapore (since 2013), Thailand, and the Philippines have been granted the status of Observer State, while Singapore has upgraded its status and became the

1506. *See* Acuerdo Marco de la Allianza del Pacifico (Framework Agreement of the Pacific Alliance), at: https://alianzapacifico.net/en/documents-and-studies/. An Additional Amending Protocol was signed in February 2014 (it entered into force in May 2016), and a second Amending Protocol was concluded on 1 Jul. 2016.

1507. *See* Co-chairs' Press Release 6th ASEAN-Pacific Alliance Ministerial Meeting, 28 Sep. 2019, at: https://alianzapacifico.net/en/co-chairs-press-release-6th-asean-pacific-alliance-ministerial-meeting/.

1508. See ASEAN Secretariat Information Paper, 'Overview of ASEAN-Pacific Alliance Relations', 23 January 2025, at: https://asean.org/wp-content/uploads/2025/01/Overview-of-ASEAN-Pacific-Alliance-Relations-as-of-23-January-2025.pdf.

1509. Text at: https://alianzapacifico.net/wp-content/uploads/2021/11/Final-Draft-ASEAN-Pacific-Alliance-WP-2021-2025.pdf.

first associate member on 26 January 2022,[1510] having signed a Free Trade Agreement with the Trade Ministers of Chile, Colombia, Mexico and Peru on the same day.[1511]

1510. *See* Joint Declaration Between the Pacific Alliance and Singapore, 26 Jan. 2022, at: https://alianzapacifico.net/instrumentos-declaraciones-conjuntas/.
1511. Text at: https://alianzapacifico.net/en/instruments-alcaps/.

Chapter 5. The South China Sea Dispute

418. The territorial and maritime dispute in the South China Sea involves China and four ASEAN Member States, namely Brunei, Malaysia, the Philippines and Vietnam (Taiwan also has claims but is not a member of ASEAN, whereas Indonesia is a claimant in the region but is presently not a party to the dispute).[1512] The dispute concerns claims to sovereignty of overlapping maritime zones and over several small islands and reefs, in particular the Paracel and Spratly Islands.[1513] The region has significant natural resources in fisheries, natural gas and oil. Furthermore, strategic shipping lanes criss-cross the region. While the origins of the disputes are historically long-standing, in the 1940s China published its 'nine-dash line' map reiterating its claim to sovereignty over a large section of the South China Sea,[1514] it was only in more recent times that the disputes have come to the fore. In 1974 and in 1988, China and Vietnam clashed over the disputed islands and reefs, while in 1994 incidents occurred between China and the Philippines. Very strong disagreements have escalated as China has resorted to building infrastructures, including military ones, on the Paracels and Spratlys and the Chinese Navy makes its presence in the area more and more prominent.[1515] China's actions have met with international condemnation with the USA conducting freedom of navigation operations in the South China Sea.

419. In 2013, as has been mentioned *infra*, the Philippines brought a case against China before an arbitral tribunal established according to Annex VII of the UN Convention on the Law of the Sea (UNCLOS)[1516] concerning maritime rights and entitlements in their disputed part of the South China Sea. Although the Tribunal sought to avoid ruling on questions of territorial sovereignty in light of both its lack

1512. Indonesian Note Verbale No. 126/POL-703/V/20 to UN Secretary-General (26 May 2020), at: https://www.un.org/Depts/los/clcs_new/submissions_files/mys_12_12_2019/2020_05_26_IDN_NV_UN_001_English.pdf.

1513. The legal literature on the competing claims in the South China Sea is vast. *See*, e.g., J. Huang & A. Billo, *Territorial Disputes in the South China Sea* (Palgrave Macmillan 2015); C.-H. Park, *The South China Sea Disputes: Who Owns the Islands and the Natural Resources*, 5 Ocean Dev. & Int'l L.J. 33 (1978); J.I. Charney, *Central East Asian Maritime Boundaries and the Law of the Sea*, 89 A.J.I.L. 724 (1995); F. Dupuy & P.-M. Dupuy, *A Legal Analysis of China's Historic Rights Claim in the South China Sea*, 107 A.J.I.L. 124 (2013); R. Beckman, *The UN Convention on the Law of the Sea and the Maritime Disputes in the South China Sea*, 107 A.J.I.L. 142 (2013); Chinese Society of International Law, *The South China Sea Awards: A Critical Study*, 17 Chinese J. Int'l L. 207 (2018); Md. M. Hasan & H. Jian, *Spratly Islands Dispute in the South China Sea: Potential Solutions*, 12 J. East Asia & Int'l L. 145-168 (2019); L. Langer, *The South China Sea as a Challenge to International Law and to International Legal Scholarship*, 36 Berkeley J. Int'l L. 362 (2018).

1514. The 'nine-dash line' refers to the dashed lines marked on Chinese maps, *see* Zhiguo Gao & Bing Bing Jia, *The Nine-Dash Line in the South China Sea: History, Status, and Implications*, 107 A.J.I.L. 98 (2013).

1515. *See* generally, Y.-H. Chen, *South China Sea Tension on Fire: China's Recent Moves on Building Artificial Islands in Troubled Waters and Their Implications on Maritime Law*, 1 Mar. Safety & Sec. L.J. (2015) 1.

1516. UN Convention on the Law of the Sea (10 Dec. 1982), 1833 U.N.T.S. 3 (UNCLOS).

of jurisdiction under UNCLOS and of China's Declaration when it ratified UNCLOS excluding such questions from the UNCLOS dispute settlement procedures, arguably the final decision undermined China's claims.[1517] In May 2020, Indonesia issued a *note verbale* to the UN reaffirming that its legal understanding of UNCLOS had been upheld by the Tribunal and rejecting China's claims.[1518] A few months later Australia issued a similar *note verbale*,[1519] as did France, Germany and the United Kingdom in a joint *note verbale*.[1520] However, it is not the intention of this section to analyse the competing legal case of the claimants but solely to consider ASEAN's role in the dispute.

420. ASEAN's role has been largely characterised by its discreet efforts to maintain peace and security in the South China Sea by maintaining and promoting dialogue with China.[1521] This low-key approach was and continues to be necessary because ASEAN Member States have differing interests in the matter,[1522] an approach that has been described as one of 'neutrality'.[1523] The situation is further complicated by the fact that China's preference is for bilateral rather than regional negotiations on the grounds that the dispute is not with ASEAN but with certain States that happen to be members of ASEAN.[1524] Nevertheless, since the early 1990s, ASEAN has pursued a more proactive role, playing the role of mediator and seeking to prevent hostilities from breaking out in the region. It has placed reliance on the ARF, a multilateral round-table for official discussions on peace and security issues,[1525] to further discussions with China on the matter.[1526] ASEAN issued its first significant statement on the disputes in 1992, the ASEAN (Manila) Declaration

1517. *South China Sea Arbitration (Republic of the Philippines v. People's Republic of China)* PCA Case No. 2013/19 (12 Jul. 2016). *See* generally, L. Reed & K. Wong, *Marine Entitlements in the South China Sea: The Arbitration Between the Philippines and China,* 110 A.J.I.L. 746-760 (2016).
1518. Indonesian Note Verbale No. 126/POL-703/V/20 (26 May 2020), at: https://www.un.org/Depts/los/clcs_new/submissions_files/mys_12_12_2019/2020_05_26_IDN_NV_UN_001_English.pdf.
1519. Australian Note Verbale No. 20/026 (23 Jul. 2020), at: https://www.un.org/depts/los/clcs_new/submissions_files/mys_12_12_2019/2020_07_23_AUS_NV_UN_001_OLA-2020-00373.pdf.
1520. UK Note Verbale No. 162/20 (16 Sep. 2020), https://www.un.org/depts/los/clcs_new/submissions_files/mys_12_12_2019/2020_09_16_GBR_NV_UN_001.pdf.
1521. *See* generally, M. York, *ASEAN's Ambiguous Role in Resolving South China Sea Disputes*, 12 Indonesian J. Int'l L. 286 (2015).
1522. *See, e.g.*, Khmer Times, *Cambodia Stays Neutral in South China Sea Dispute* (26 Jun. 2020), https://www.khmertimeskh.com/738181/cambodia-stays-neutral-in-south-china-sea-dispute/.
1523. L.K. Heng, *ASEAN's Position on the South China Sea and Implications for Regional Peace and Security*, in *Territorial Disputes in the South China Sea* 69, 70–71 (J. Huang & A. Billo eds, Palgrave Macmillan 2015).
1524. A. Gerstl, *The South China Sea Dispute: A Shift to a More Proactive Role in ASEAN's Discourse and Policies Since 2012?*, in *Unresolved Border, Land and Maritime Disputes in Southeast Asia. Bi- and Multilateral Conflict Resolution Approaches and ASEAN's Centrality* 183, 184 (A. Gerstl & M. Strašáková eds, Brill 2016); D. Scott, *Conflict Irresolution in the South China Sea*, 52 Asian Survey 1019-1042 (2012); K-C. Lin & A.V. Gerstl, *Maritime Security in the Asia-Pacific: China and the Emerging Order in the East and South China Seas* 20 (Chatham House 2015).
1525. *See* e.g., Chairman's Statement of the 3rd Meeting of the ASEAN Regional Forum, Jakarta, 23 Jul. 1996.
1526. R. Cruz De Castro, *The ASEAN Regional Forum in the Face of Great-Power Competition in the South China Sea: The Limits of ASEAN's Approach in Addressing 21st-Century Maritime Security Issues*, in *Security Architectures Under Threat: The Status of Multilateral Fora* (Konrad-Adenauer-Stiftung 2017), 31–46.

on the South China Sea.[1527] The Declaration stressed the necessity to resolve the dispute by peaceful means eschewing the use of force. Moreover, it called upon the parties to exercise restraint in order to create a positive climate for the eventual resolution of all disputes in the region.

421. In 2002, ASEAN and China jointly agreed to the Declaration on Conduct (DOC) of Parties in the South China Sea,[1528] which ASEAN had endorsed as early as 1996.[1529] The DOC, which is a political rather than a legally binding agreement,[1530] enshrines a collective commitment to the peaceful resolution of disputes in conformity with international law and particularly UNCLOS, a number of voluntary cooperative activities and a reaffirmation to trust and confidence-building measures. For some, the DOC was a disappointment.[1531] In 2004, ASEAN and China agreed on an action plan, a series of guidelines, to implement the DOC,[1532] which after tortuous negotiations was only adopted in 2011.[1533] However, the Guidelines are, in fact, thin fare. They provide, *inter alia*, that the DOC should be implemented gradually, that the decision to implement measures or activities of the DOC should be based on consensus, that participation in activities or projects should be on a voluntary basis, and that the initial activities to be undertaken under the DOC should be confidence-building measures.

422. ASEAN, however, struggled to reach agreement on the Code of Conduct (COC).[1534] In 2012, Indonesian diplomacy resulted in the adoption of ASEAN's Six-Point Principles on the South China Sea. It reaffirmed ASEAN's commitment to the full implementation of the DOC in the South China Sea; the Guidelines; the early conclusion of a regional COC in the South China Sea; the full respect of the universally recognised principles of international law, including UNCLOS; the continued exercise of self-restraint and non-use of force by all parties; and the peaceful resolution of disputes.[1535]

1527. ASEAN Declaration on the South China Sea, 22 Jul. 1992, at: https://cil.nus.edu.sg/wp-content/uploads/2017/07/1992-ASEAN-Declaration-on-the-South-China-Sea.pdf.
1528. Declaration on Conduct of Parties in the South China Sea, Phnom Penh, 4 Nov. 2002, at: https://cil.nus.edu.sg/databasecil/2002-declaration-on-the-conduct-of-parties-in-the-south-china-sea/.
1529. Joint Communiqué of the 29th ASEAN Ministerial Meeting, Jakarta, 20–21 Jul. 1996.
1530. *South China Sea Arbitration ('*PCA Case No. 2013/19, *supra*, para. 213.
1531. M. Li, *Managing Security in the South China Sea: From DOC to COC*, 15 Kyoto Rev. of Southeast Asia (2014), at: https://kyotoreview.org/issue-15/managing-security-in-the-south-china-sea-from-doc-to-coc/.
1532. Plan of Action to Implement the Joint Declaration on the ASEAN-China Strategic Partnership for Peace and Prosperity, Vientiane, 29 Nov. 2004.
1533. Guidelines for the Implementation of the DOC, at: https://www.asean.org/wp-content/uploads/images/archive/documents/20185-DOC.pdf. *See* C.A. Thayer, *ASEAN's Code of Conduct in the South China Sea: A Litmus Test for Community Building?*, 10 Asia-Pacific J. 1, 2 (2012).
1534. Thayer, 4–15.
1535. Statement of the ASEAN Foreign Ministers, Phnom Penh, Cambodia, 20 Jul. 2012, 'ASEAN's Six-Point Principles on the South China Sea', at: https://www.asean.org/wp-content/uploads/images/AFMs%20Statement%20on%206%20Principles%20on%20SCS.pdf. *See* Thayer, 16.

423. However, it was only in 2018 that a draft COC was agreed between ASEAN and China.[1536] The draft COC was considered flawed because, *inter alia*, its status as a legally binding document was uncertain, its geographical scope was vague and the applicability of international law was also unclear.[1537] Nevertheless, the hope was that the COC would be agreed within three years.[1538] However, with negotiations on the COC still ongoing, in June 2020, ASEAN leaders, perhaps due to the diplomacy of the then chair Vietnam, appear to have taken a more robust position on the South China Sea dispute. In particular they declared that 'UNCLOS is the basis for determining maritime entitlements, sovereign rights, jurisdiction and legitimate interests over maritime zones, and … UNCLOS sets out the legal framework within which all activities in the oceans and seas must be carried out.'[1539]

424. Until the time of writing, the COC had not been agreed upon by the two sides, even though it would appear that consistent efforts had been made to finalise it. In particular, on 13 July 2023 agreement was reached among them on new guidelines to accelerate negotiations and to conclude COC,[1540] which is meant to be a legally binding instrument.[1541] Impetus was given by Indonesia, which at the time was holding the ASEAN Chairmanship. This and other developments *vis-à-vis* the China South Sea debacle were included in the Chairman's Statement that reflected on the outcome of the meetings between ASEAN and China in the context of the ministerial deliberations that ASEAN had with third states in mid-July 2024. Even the subtle diplomatic language in which such statements are written could not hide the fact that the situation has been in constant deterioration. Thus, the ministers from (unnamed) ASEAN Member States spoke about serious incidents in the South China Sea, putting the safety of persons at risk, damage to the marine environment, an erosion of trust and confidence and tensions that could undermine peace, security, and stability in the region. According to the Chairman's Statement, ASEAN countries ought to exercise self-restraint in the conduct of activities that would otherwise complicate or escalate disputes and affect peace and stability, should avoid

1536. *See* Joint Communique of the 51st ASEAN Foreign Ministers' Meeting, Singapore, 2 Aug. 2018, para. 73, at: https://asean.org/wp-content/uploads/2018/08/51st-AMM-Joint-Communique-Final.pdf.

1537. *See* C. Thayer, *A Closer Look at the ASEAN-China Single Draft South China Sea Code of Conduct*, The Diplomat, 3 Aug. 2018, at: https://thediplomat.com/2018/08/a-closer-look-at-the-asean-china-single-draft-south-china-sea-code-of-conduct/.

1538. The Strait Times, *ASEAN and China Should Aim to Conclude Talks on Maritime Code of Conduct in 3 Years: PM Lee*, 14 Nov. 2018, at: https://www.straitstimes.com.

1539. Chairman's Statement of the 36th ASEAN Summit, 26 Jun. 2020 (via Videoconference), para. 65, at: https://cil.nus.edu.sg/databasecil/2020-chairmans-statement-of-the-36th-asean-summit/. *See* Asia Times, *ASEAN Finally Pushes Back on China's Sea Claims*, 30 Jun. 2020, at: https://asiatimes.com/2020/06/asean-finally-pushes-back-on-chinas-sea-claims/.

1540. *See* The ASEAN Post Ministerial Conference (PMC) 10+1 Sessions with the Dialogue Partners and Trilateral Meetings, Jakarta, Indonesia, 13–14 Jul. 2023, Chairman's Statement, paras 14–15, at: https://asean.org/wp-content/uploads/2023/07/FINAL-Chairmans-Statement-PMC-101-with-DPs-and-Trilateral-.pdf.

1541. The full title is 'Guidelines for Accelerating the Early Conclusion of an Effective and Substantive Code of Conduct in the South China Sea'. The document does not appear to have been made public.

actions that may further complicate the situation, and should undertake confidence-building and preventive measures to promoting trust and confidence amongst the two sides.[1542] Finally, the Guidelines were adopted during the 26th ASEAN-China Summit, which was held on 6 September 2023.[1543] And on 26 October 2023, the 21st ASEAN-China Senior Officials Meeting on the Declaration on the Conduct of Parties in the South China Sea (SOM on DOC), which was held in Beijing, announced the commencement of the third reading of the Single Draft COC Negotiating Text (SDNT). At the time of writing, the negotiations have been ongoing.[1544]

425. The South China Sea Dispute is not going to be resolved any time soon. However, it is important to understand (and this has to do with how ASEAN, as a regional international organisation, conducts and pursues its foreign affairs) that, despite the very dispute, the ASEAN-China comprehensive strategic partnership is not only (at least directly) affected but also has consistently been promoted with vigour. Suffice it to mention the Joint Statement on Mutually Beneficial Cooperation on the ASEAN Outlook on the Indo-Pacific (adopted during the aforementioned 26th ASEAN-China Summit),[1545] where references to maritime cooperation between ASEAN and China are made without, however, any mention of the dispute.

426. And a deeper engagement with China is gaining traction: on 19 June 2024, the ASEAN-China Future Relations Forum was convened at ASEAN headquarters. Co-hosted by the Mission of China to ASEAN and the Permanent Mission of Myanmar to ASEAN, and supported by the ASEAN Secretariat,[1546] the Forum praised the rapid advancement of the ASEAN-China comprehensive strategic partnership, noting that it had resulted in tangible contributions to regional peace, stability and development. Finally, participants at the Forum expressed the belief that the two sides should uphold true multilateralism and open regionalism, while the bilateral partnership should be further enhanced by strengthening cooperation in such areas as trade and investment, connectivity, green transformation, cybersecurity, and combating transnational crime.

1542. ASEAN Post Ministerial Conference 10+1 Sessions with the Dialogue Partners and Trilateral Meetings, Jakarta, Indonesia, 13 – 14 Jul. 2023, Chairman's Statement.

1543. *See* Chairman's Statement of the 26th ASEAN-China Summit, Jakarta, Indonesia, 6 Sep. 2023, para. 36, at: https://asean.org/wp-content/uploads/2023/09/FINAL-Chairmans-Statement-of-the-26th-ASEAN-China-Summit.pdf.

1544. See C. Thayer, 'The State of the South China Sea: Coercion at Sea, Slow Progress on a Code of Conduct', *The Diplomat*, 27 January 2025, at: https://thediplomat.com/2025/01/the-state-of-the-south-china-sea-coercion-at-sea-slow-progress-on-a-code-of-conduct/.

1545. Text at: https://asean.org/wp-content/uploads/2023/09/Final-ASEAN-China-Joint-Statement-on-Mutually-Beneficial-Cooperation-on-the-ASEAN-Outlook-on-the-Indo-Pacific.pdf.

1546. See the remarks made by the ASEAN Secretary General at the opening of the Forum, at: https://asean.org/wp-content/uploads/2024/06/Remarks-by-SG-Dr.-Kao-at-ASEAN-China-Future-Relations-Forum_As-Delivered.pdf.

427. It has been argued that the South China Sea dispute acts as an impediment to ASEAN solidarity and to the process of community building.[1547] Correct as this argument might be, what should be clarified is that ASEAN, as a regional international organisation, is (legally and politically) separate from its ten Member States and their problems, disputes, confrontations, etc., with third states. Even though the South China Sea dispute is, as has been shown, of concern to ASEAN and there are serious attempts to adopt measures to alleviate it, it is not a bilateral ASEAN–China problem. It is a problem between, on the one hand, several individual Asian states and, on the other hand, China. And while their joint membership in ASEAN is one of the closest links among this group of states, if not the closest, they all participate in other international organisations as well, notably the United Nations. Therefore, the South China Sea dispute could be seen as much a problem for ASEAN as it is for the UN, which actually should be more concerned given that China is a fellow Member State.

1547. *See* M. Chakraborty, 'ASEAN's Tryst with Community-Building: Towards Comprehensive Dispute Settlement' in M. Lim *et al* (eds), *ASEAN's Critical Assessment and Practical Reforms* (Cambodia: Konrad-Adenauer-Stiftung & Asian Vision Institute 2023) 22–35, 23.

Part V. ASEAN Economic Community

Chapter 1. Introduction: The Position of the AEC in the Structure of the ASEAN Charter – The AEC Council

428. Long before ASEAN became a rules-based international regional organisation through the entry into force of the ASEAN Charter in 2008, Member States had decided to establish the so-called ASEAN Community. During the 9th ASEAN Summit, which was held in Bali, Indonesia, in 2003, they resolved to create an integrative entity to consist of the following three pillars: the APSC; the AEC; and the ASCC.[1548] Arguably, it was a very bold movement by a regional institution with no significant experience in integration. The ASEAN Community promised to bring about the integration of the Member States in many and diverse areas, a goal which, at the time, had not been attempted even by the prototype of regional institutions, namely the EU. The principal considerations for creating the ASEAN Community were (a) the need to consolidate what has already been achieved and to avoid any regression; and (b) to secure a better future for their population. These goals demanded the further promotion of their close cooperation across different areas.[1549]

429. Given the determination of Member States to create an ASEAN Community comprising these three broad pillars (and the Roadmap that had been agreed), one would have expected that the ASEAN Charter, signed four years later, would have made extensive references to it. Indeed, it was only reasonable to assume that the ASEAN Charter would have also been the founding (or constitutive) instrument of the three-pillar ASEAN Community. However, the only references are to be found in the Preamble of the Charter. According to it, Member States, on the one hand, were convinced that the existing bonds of regional solidarity were adequate to realise a politically cohesive, economically integrated and socially responsible ASEAN Community and, on the other hand, committed themselves to deepen community building through enhanced regional cooperation, in particular by establishing an ASEAN Community, as specifically provided for in Bali Concord II.

1548. *See* I. Karuppana, *The ASEAN Community and ASEAN Charter: Toward a New ASEAN*, J. Dipl. & Foreign Rel. 49 (2005).

1549. *See Declaration of ASEAN Concord II* (Bali Concord II), 7 Oct. 2003. *See* further the Recommendations of the High Level Task Force on ASEAN Economic Integration, which were adopted on the same day, at: https://asean.org/recommendations-of-the-high-level-task-force-on-asean-economic-integration/.

430. It follows that, from a legal point of view, the ASEAN Economic Community (AEC) is separated from the Charter. Moreover, Article 1 of the Charter, the provision setting out the purposes of ASEAN, refers to the ASEAN Community only in the context of how the development of human resources through cooperation in education and life-long learning will strengthen it. This could be interpreted as a reference to only the ASEAN Socio-Cultural Community (ASCC). At the same time, even though Article 1 of the Charter mentions the creation of a single market – it describes it as stable, prosperous, highly competitive and economically integrated market – it does not mention the AEC at all. Finally, Article 1 does not stipulate that the single market shall be realised through the AEC or that the AEC will become the vehicle for the free movement of goods, services, investment, and so on.

431. However, when Chapter IV of the Charter lays down the institutional architecture of ASEAN, it provides for the operation for one Council for each of the three pillars of the ASEAN Community. Thus, according to Article 9 of the Charter, which is titled 'ASEAN Community Councils', there shall, *inter alia*, be an AEC Council, which shall have under its purview the relevant Sectoral Ministerial Bodies and shall comprise the national representation that each Member State has designated.[1550] Pursuant to the fourth paragraph of Article 9, the mandate of each of the three ASEAN Community Councils shall be: (a) to ensure that the relevant decisions of the ASEAN Summit are implemented and executed; (b) to coordinate the work of the different sectors under its purview but also matters which cut across the other two Community Councils; and (c) to submit pertinent reports and recommendations to the ASEAN Summit. Finally, Article 9 stipulates that the ASEAN Community Councils shall meet at least twice every year and be chaired by the appropriate Minister coming from the Member State that holds the ASEAN Chairmanship. There is no mention of the voting rules when taking decisions. Therefore, it should be assumed that they shall be taken by consensus, reflecting Article 20 of the Charter, the provision, which, as explained *supra*, states that the basic ASEAN principles of decision-making are consultations and consensus. However, since Article 21(1) of the Charter stipulates that each ASEAN Community Council must set its own rules of procedure, the AEC Rules of Procedure might take a different direction in decision-making. The example of the EU shows that an economic integration project demands strict rules in voting.

1550. It follows that it is up to each Member State to determine the composition of its delegation; the other Member States cannot object to it. For example, the representative of Thailand is at the level of Deputy Prime Minister, *see List of AEC Ministers as of October 2016*, at: https://asean.org/wp-content/uploads/2012/05/List-of-AEC-Council-Ministers_Details_Oct-2016_Public.pdf.

Chapter 2. From Free Trade among Member States to the AEC

432. Since the early 1990s, Member States have been involved in cooperation in the economic sphere. More specifically, the Agreement establishing the ASEAN Free Trade Area (AFTA) was signed in Singapore on 28 January 1992.[1551] It was followed by a Facilitation Agreement six years later.[1552] Interestingly enough, the early 1990s were a busy time for economic integration in all regions as well. As regards Europe, 1992 was a pivotal year in the development of the EEC (now the EU), as it marked the final year of the enterprise to complete the so-called European Single Market, also known as 'Internal Market', this being the FTA that was created pursuant to the Treaty establishing the European Economic Community (1957).[1553] In the African continent, the Treaty Establishing the African Economic Community was concluded the following year.[1554] Finally, in the region of Latin America, only in the first four years of the 1990s, there were three free trade zones established or reactivated, namely the Andean Pact, the Central American Common Market, and MERCOSUR.[1555]

433. The drive towards economic integration in the ASEAN region gained momentum with the conclusion of three other key treaties: the ASEAN Framework Agreement on Services (AFAS),[1556] the ASEAN Trade in Goods Agreement (ATIGA),[1557] and the ASEAN Comprehensive Investment Agreement (ACIA).[1558] So far, AFAS has gone through ten so-called Packages. In particular, during Packages 1–7, which lasted from 1995–2009, the participation of foreign equity in the registered capital of a company was not to exceed forty-nine per cent thereof. This effectively meant that the controlling percentage of the registered capital remained in the hands of domestic investors. The exact opposite, i.e., that the control over

1551. Two treaties were actually signed: the Agreement on the Common Effective Preferential Tariff Scheme for the ASEAN Free Trade Area, and the Framework Agreement on Enhancing ASEAN Economic Cooperation, at: https://agreement.asean.org/media/download/20140119154919.pdf; both became effective upon conclusion, no ratification was required.

1552. *See* ASEAN Framework Agreement on the Facilitation of Goods in Transit, signed in Hanoi, Vietnam, on 16 Dec. 1998, at: https://agreement.asean.org/media/download/20140119122917.pdf; it was subject to ratification or acceptance by all signatory parties.

1553. *See* the Single European Act of 1986, a multilateral treaty concluded by the then EEC Member States (it entered into force on 1 Jul. 1987). Its objectives included the establishment of an 'internal market', which was defined as 'an area without internal frontiers in which the free movement of goods, persons, services and capital is ensured'.

1554. Signed on 3 Jun. 1991, entered into force on 12 May 1994. *See* G. Naldi & K. Magliveras, *The African Economic Community: Emancipation for African States or Yet Another Glorious Failure?*, 24 N.C. J. Int'l L. & Com. Reg. 601–631 (1999).

1555. *See* R. Devlin & R. French-Davis, *Towards an Evaluation of Regional Integration in Latin America in the 1990s* (Inter-American Development Bank Integration / Institute for the Integration of Latin America and the Caribbean, Working Paper 2, December 1998), at: https://publications.iadb.org/en/publication/towards-evaluation-regional-integration-latin-america-1990s.

1556. Signed in Bangkok, Thailand, on 15 Dec. 1995, entered into force on 12 Aug. 1998, at: http://investasean.asean.org/files/upload/Doc%2008%20-%20AFAS.pdf.

1557. Signed in Cha-am, Thailand, on 26 Feb. 2009, entered into force on 17 May 2010, at: http://investasean.asean.org/files/upload/Doc%2002%20-%20ATIGA.pdf.

1558. Signed in Cha-am, Thailand, on 26 Feb. 2009, entered into force on 29 Mar. 2012, at: http://investasean.asean.org/files/upload/Doc%2005%20-%20ACIA.pdf.

companies could also be held by foreign investors, was the goal of the next three Packages. However, this was to be achieved progressively and differed from services sector to services sector. Thus, during the duration of Package 8 (2010–2015), foreign equity participation could not exceed 70% of the registered capital in the sectors of health, telecommunications and tourism, was restricted to 51% in some 80 services subsectors but it was completely eliminated in another 128 services subsectors.[1559] As regards Package 9 (2016–2018), the sector of logistics was added to the sectors with a maximum 70% foreign participation in the registered capital, while restrictions were abolished in some 100 other services subsectors.[1560] Finally, Package 10, which was agreed in 2018, calls for the removal of restrictions in a total of 128 services subsectors.[1561]

434. The aim of adopting ACIA was to replace the existing regulatory framework on investments, namely the Framework Agreement on the ASEAN Investment Area (AIA)[1562] and the ASEAN Agreement for the Promotion and Protection of Investments.[1563] That the regulatory framework was not only revised but overhauled was consistent with the requirements of an economic integration project but also with the fact that, in order to attract more inward investment to the ASEAN region, improved features and norms had to be introduced, comparable to international best practices.[1564]

435. To return to the promises pledged in Bali Concord II (2003), the AEC ought to have been operative by 2020 and lead to 'a stable, prosperous and highly competitive ASEAN economic region in which there is a free flow of goods, services, investment and a freer flow of capital, equitable economic development and reduced poverty and socio-economic disparities'.[1565] Projects towards regional economic integration are very often delayed, deadlines are not met, and milestones are missed. Indeed, this has happened with the EEC, while the African Economic Community

---

1559. *See* Protocol to Implement the Eighth Package of Commitments under the ASEAN Framework Agreement on Services, done in Hanoi, Vietnam, 28 Oct. 2010, at: https://asean.org/protocol-to-implement-the-eighth-package-of-commitments-under-the-asean-framework-agreement-on-services/.

1560. *See* Protocol to Implement the Ninth Package of Commitments under the ASEAN Framework Agreement on Services, done in Makati City, the Philippines, 27 Nov. 2015, at: https://asean.org/wp-content/uploads/2021/09/AFAS-9-Protocol-FINAL.pdf.

1561. *See* Protocol to Implement the Tenth Package of Commitments under the ASEAN Framework Agreement on Services, done in Singapore, 11 Nov. 2018, at: https://asean.org/wp-content/uploads/2021/09/AFAS-Tenth-Package-2018.pdf. *See* also D. Neo, P. Sauvé & I. Streho, *Services Trade in ASEAN – The Road Taken and the Journey Ahead* (Cambridge U. Press 2019).

1562. Signed in Makati City, the Philippines, on 7 Oct. 1998, at: http://agreement.asean.org/media/download/20140119040024.pdf.

1563. Signed in Manila, Philippines, on 15 Dec. 1987, entered into force on 2 Aug. 1988, at: https://investmentpolicy.unctad.org/international-investment-agreements/treaty-files/5554/download. It was terminated on 29 Mar. 2012.

1564. Generally, *see* L. Hsu *et al.*, *Improving Connectivity Between ASEAN's Legal Systems to Address Commercial Issues* (Interim Report, School of Law, Singapore Management University, August 2017), 23 et seq., at: https://core.ac.uk/download/pdf/132698413.pdf.

1565. Bali Concord II, *supra*, operative para. B(1).

was effectively abandoned in the late 1990s and was only picked up again in the late 2010s as a trade liberalisation project.[1566]

436. Notwithstanding the experience from other regional economic integration projects, ASEAN leaders decided to bring forward the completion of the AEC to 2015. In particular, at the AEM Meeting, which was held in Kuala Lumpur, Malaysia, in August 2006, it was agreed to develop a single and coherent blueprint to advance the AEC.[1567] It identified the key elements of the AEC and set out clear targets and step-by-step deadlines for the implementation of the required measures by 2015, while maintaining a degree of pre-agreed flexibility. This was meant to take into account and cater for the interests of all Member States a sensible measure given that the status of their economies differs considerably.[1568]

437. During the 12th ASEAN Summit (2007), ASEAN leaders affirmed their strong commitment to bring forward the launch of the ASEAN Community and to have it in operation by 2015. As regards specifically the AEC, the goal was to transform ASEAN into a region with free movement of goods, services, investment, and skilled labour and with unhindered flow of capital.[1569] This pledge was articulated in the Cebu Declaration on the Acceleration of the Establishment of an ASEAN Community by 2015, which acknowledged that there were different levels of development within ASEAN. This called for flexibility to accomplish the region's more integrated and interconnected future, which, in turn, should have been able to address the growing number of regional challenges.[1570] The interdependence of the ASEAN economies within the region was already a reality.

438. At the following (13th) ASEAN Summit, which was held in Singapore on 20 November 2007, ASEAN leaders approved the ASEAN Economic Community

1566. *See* K. Magliveras & G. Naldi, *The African Union (AU)* (3rd ed., Wolters Kluwer 2024), 120–121.
1567. *See Joint Media Statement of the Thirty-Eight ASEAN Economic Ministers' (AEM) Meeting*, Kuala Lumpur, 22 Aug. 2006, para. 9, at: https://asean.org/speechandstatement/joint-media-statement-of-the-thirty-eight-asean-economic-ministers-aem-meeting-kuala-lumpur-22-august-2006/. Generally, *see* P. Rana, *Economic Integration in East Asia: Trends, Prospects, and a Possible Roadmap* Asian Development Bank Working Paper Series on Regional Economic Integration No. 2, July 2006).
1568. Note that Art. I(3) of the Framework Agreement on Enhancing ASEAN Economic Cooperation, *supra*, stipulated that, in the implementation of the economic arrangements envisaged therein, two or more Member States may proceed first, if other Member States were not ready to implement these arrangements. *See* also the discussion of the 'ASEAN Minus X formula' *infra*, and Art. 21(2) of the ASEAN Charter.
1569. *See Chairperson's Statement of the 12th ASEAN Summit, H.E. the President Gloria Macapagal-Arroyo*, Cebu, Philippines, 13 Jan. 2007, at: https://asean.org/speechandstatement/12th-asean-summit-cebu-philippines-9-15-january-2007/.
1570. It was adopted during the 12th ASEAN Summit in Cebu, the Philippines, 13 Jan. 2007, at: https://asean.org/cebu-declaration-on-the-acceleration-of-the-establishment-of-an-asean-community-by-2015/.

Blueprint, which has become known as 'AEC Blueprint 2015'.[1571] Even though it was at best a soft law document, the text of the Declaration leaves no doubt that all Member States had assumed the obligation to give full effect to it: 'each ASEAN Member Country shall abide by [the AEC Blueprint] and implement the AEC by 2015'.[1572]

439. The AEC Blueprint 2015 comprised four pillars, whose successful completion would have allowed ASEAN to become (a) a single market and production base; (b) a highly competitive economic region; (c) a region of equitable economic development; and (d) a region fully integrated into the global economy. These four AEC characteristics or pillars are interrelated and mutually reinforcing. They can be summarised as follows. The first pillar sought to achieve a single market, characterised by the so-called four freedoms, namely the free flow (movement) of goods, of services, of labour, and the 'freer flow' of capital.[1573] At a global level, these four freedoms were first articulated in the Treaty establishing the European Economic Community (1957).[1574] Their achievement is the first significant milestone in the road towards any economic integration project. The EU paradigm shows that, even if they are achieved and the envisaged single market is in full operation, there will always be a need for further regulation, to better protect the end users of these four freedoms, namely consumers, professionals, businesses, etc. While it might appear to be an end in itself, it is a process that seemingly never ends. As noted by the European Commission in 2012, it is always possible to develop further the single market and to exploit its untapped potential as an engine for growth and increased welfare.[1575] Finally, regional economic integration projects should be aligned to technological and similar developments; for example, in the EU ideas were put forward for a strategy towards a digital single market,[1576] which led to the Digital Decade Policy Programme 2030.[1577]

1571. *See Declaration on the ASEAN Economic Community Blueprint*, reproduced in ASEAN Economic Community Blueprint, Jakarta: ASEAN Secretariat, January 2008, at: https://asean.org/declaration-on-the-asean-economic-community-blueprint/.
1572. *Ibid.*, operative para. 1.
1573. That the flow of capital from one Member State to the other was to be 'freer' rather than 'free', as was the case with goods, services, and labour, indicates that certain Member States wanted to prevent capital flight as this would have caused significant problems in maintaining adequate foreign currency reserves, *see* the ASEAN Economic Community Blueprint at para. 32: 'The liberalisation of capital movements is to be guided by the following principles: a) Ensuring an orderly capital account liberalisation consistent with member countries' national agenda and readiness of the economy … .'
1574. For their current formulation in EU law, *see* Arts 4(2)(a), 26, 27, 114 and 115 TFEU.
1575. *See* Communication from the Commission to the European Parliament, the Council, the European Economic and Social Committee and the Committee of the Regions, *Single Market Act II: Together for new growth*, COM(2012) 573 final, 3 Oct. 2012.
1576. *See* Communication from the Commission to the European Parliament, the Council, the European Economic and Social Committee and the Committee of the Regions, *Upgrading the Single Market: more opportunities for people and business*, COM(2015) 550 final, 28 Oct. 2015.
1577. *See* European Commission, *Report on the State of the Digital Decade*, 2024, at: https://digital-strategy.ec.europa.eu/en/policies/2024-state-digital-decade-package.

440. The second pillar aimed at creating an economic environment, which would be conducive to business, and which would support innovation. Achieving this goal is very demanding: ASEAN Member States must abandon national measures and national policies and subscribe to common, uniform, principles, and norms. The latter cover many and diverse sectors, including agriculture, financial services, competition policy, intellectual property rights, and consumer protection.

441. The objective of the third pillar was to achieve sustainable and balanced growth and development through equitable advancement. This pillar reflected the fact that not all ASEAN Member States were (and are still not) at the same level of economic development. Even though when the AEC became operative in 2015, ASEAN was considered to be the seventh largest economy in the world in terms of gross domestic product (in 2019, it was calculated to have become the fifth largest with a total GDP reaching three trillion USD),[1578] there are significant deviations in the economic power of Member States. Indeed, the ASEAN membership features one of the richest countries in the words (in terms of GDP per capita), namely Singapore (USD 84,734 in 2023), and two of the poorest (outside Africa) countries, namely Myanmar (USD 1,233 in 2023) and Cambodia (USD 2,430 in 2023).[1579] That the states involved in a process of economic integration happen to be at different levels of economic empowerment is not necessarily a problem. However, economic inequality could become a problem if, for example, it is used to promote a domestic political agenda or if the poorer countries press for the adoption of wealth redistribution policies or demand for concessions during negotiations at the objection of the wealthier states.

442. Finally, the fourth pillar aimed at realising a much stronger position for ASEAN in the global economy, which is characterised by interdependent markets and globalised industries. This meant that ASEAN businesses have to compete not only regionally (outside ASEAN) but also internationally and become a segment of the global supply chain, while ensuring that ASEAN as a region continues to be attractive for foreign investment. Given the inequality of the Member States' economies, a comprehensive package of technical assistance had to be developed for the less developed among them to upgrade their industrial capability and productivity.

443. Taking into consideration that the timetable for launching the AEC was shortened by five years, time was of essence in securing its launch by the end of 2015. For this reason, the AEC Blueprint 2015 contained detailed provisions on implementation and on streamlining the decision-making process. In particular, it recommended, *inter alia*, the following measures: (a) the promotion of transparency; (b) the ratification of the relevant ASEAN legal instruments within six months of signing; (c) the use of consensus as the decision-making rule at the level of economic bodies and, where consensus cannot be reached, to consider other options,

---

1578. *See ASEAN Integration Report 2019*, Jakarta: ASEAN Secretariat, October 2019, xiv, at: https://asean.org/book/asean-integration-report-2019/.

1579. All data are taken from the World Bank website, at: https://data.worldbank.org/indicator.

always with the objective to expedite the process; and (d) making use of the aforementioned 'ASEAN Minus X formula' in an effort to accelerate the implementation of the agreed initiatives.

444. This formula is laid down in Article 21(2) ASEAN Charter, which reads: '[i]n the implementation of economic commitments, a formula for flexible participation, including the *ASEAN Minus X* formula, may be applied where there is a consensus to do so'. To a very large extent, this was a reaffirmation of the aforementioned Article I(3) of the Framework Agreement on Enhancing ASEAN Economic Cooperation (1992), i.e., that two or more ASEAN Member States may move ahead in economic liberalisation provided that the remaining states will follow at a later stage. It has been argued that 'ASEAN may explore the potential of ASEAN Minus X as an alternative mode of decision-making, especially in the field of economic cooperation'.[1580] It is not unknown to have different decision-making methods in regional international organisations depending on the area/sector to be regulated. However, in a process of regional economic integration, where hundreds of legal instruments may have to be adopted and which, over time, are invariably amended, revised, or replaced, to have two or three categories of membership, depending on how fast they proceed with economic liberalisation, appear to be neither sensible nor manageable.

445. At the 14th ASEAN Summit, which took place in Cha-am, Thailand, in 2009, ASEAN leaders adopted the namesake Declaration on the Roadmap for an ASEAN Community 2009–2015. Effectively, they bundled together the Blueprint for the ASEAN Economic Community and the Blueprints for the ASEAN Political-Security Community and the ASEAN Socio-Cultural Community with the Initiative for ASEAN integration to create the Roadmap for an ASEAN Community.[1581] There appears to be no good reason why a new superstructure had to be created. However, it is submitted that ASEAN leaders are accustomed to adopting new instruments, which simply reaffirm what has already been agreed. In the following years, the target for completing the ASEAN Community by 2015, including of course the AEC, was re-confirmed in the following two documents. First, the Phnom Penh Agenda for ASEAN Community Building, which was adopted during the 20th ASEAN Summit in Phnom Penh, Cambodia, on 3 April 2012.[1582] Second, the Nay Pyi Taw Declaration on Realisation of the ASEAN Community by 2015, which was adopted during the 24th ASEAN Summit in the eponymous city in Myanmar on 11 May 2014.[1583]

1580. *See* U. Aimsiranun, *Comparative Study on the Legal Framework on General Differentiated Integration Mechanisms in the European Union, APEC, and ASEAN* (Working Paper 1107, Tokyo: Asian Development Bank Institute, April 2020), 14, at: https://www.adb.org/publications/comparative-study-differentiated-integration-mechanisms-eu-apec-asean.
1581. *See Roadmap for an ASEAN Community 2009-2015*, Jakarta: ASEAN Secretariat, April 2009.
1582. Text at: https://cil.nus.edu.sg/wp-content/uploads/formidable/18/2012-Phnom-Penh-Agenda-for-ASEAN-Community-Building.pdf.
1583. At: https://asean.org/wp-content/uploads/2012/05/24th-NPT-Declaration.pdf.

Chapter 3. The Establishment of the AEC and the Economic Community Blueprint 2025

446. On 31 December 2015, the ASEAN Community was formally established. It came one month after ASEAN leaders had adopted, during the 27th ASEAN Summit (Kuala Lumpur, Malaysia, 22 November 2015), the namesake Declaration on the Establishment of the ASEAN Community.[1584] But ASEAN leaders did not stop there: they also agreed as to how their Organisation should be shaped during the next decade. And they did so by embracing a new milestone, the so-called ASEAN 2025.[1585] In particular, they adopted the ASEAN Community Vision 2025, one Blueprint for each of the three ASEAN Communities. The latter together with the Kuala Lumpur Declaration on ASEAN 2025 constitute the currently running project 'ASEAN 2025: Forging Ahead Together', which is the successor to the Roadmap for an ASEAN Community (2009–2015).

447. According to the ASEAN Economic Community Blueprint 2025, by 2025 the following targets/goals ought to have been achieved.[1586] *First*, the creation of a deeply integrated and highly cohesive ASEAN economy. The level of integration must be such to support sustained high economic growth, but there must also be flexibility to address any global economic shocks and the ensuing volatility. *Second*, the economic growth to be achieved should be more equitable and inclusive. This is necessary to narrow the development gap in the ASEAN region, to reduce poverty significantly, and to sustain the rising middle class. *Third*, the promotion of the growth in productivity by means of innovation, technological development, and the advancement of human resources. A more specific goal is to move ASEAN into the global value chains (GVCs), which are characterised by industries using advanced technology and knowledge-intensive manufacturing and services. *Fourth*, the promotion of the principles of good governance and transparency as well as the creation of responsive regulatory regimes where the private sector, community-based organisations, and other stakeholders shall have an active engagement. *Fifth*, the advancement of what is called 'ASEAN connectivity' with emphasis on the facilitation of capital movements as well as the movement of skilled labour (in effect the immigration of skilled workers from Member State to Member State).[1587] *Sixth*, the creation of a more dynamic and resilient ASEAN, especially by means of strong national and regional mechanisms, able to respond effectively to future food

1584. Reproduced in *ASEAN Documents Series 2015*, Jakarta: ASEAN Secretariat, October 2016, 70, text at: https://asean.org/kuala-lumpur-declaration-on-the-establishment-of-the-asean-community/.

1585. *See* 27th ASEAN Summit, *Kuala Lumpur Declaration on ASEAN 2025: Forging Ahead Together*, 22 Nov. 2015, reproduced in *ibid.*, 72.

1586. *See ASEAN Economic Community Blueprint 2025*, Jakarta: ASEAN Secretariat, November 2015, at: https://asean.org/asean-economic-community-blueprint-2025/.

1587. *See* further, *Vientiane Declaration on the Adoption of the Master Plan on ASEAN Connectivity 2025*, adopted in Vientiane, Laos, on 6 Sep. 2016, at: https://connectivity.asean.org/resource/vientiane-declaration-on-the-adoption-of-the-master-plan-on-asean-connectivity-2025/, reproduced in *ASEAN Documents Series 2016*, Jakarta, ASEAN Secretariat, October 2017, 22.

and energy security issues, natural disasters,[1588] economic shocks, and other trade-related issues. *Seventh*, the incorporation of a sustainable growth agenda in ASEAN activities, which will be characterised by green technology and green energy. *Eighth*, the promotion of the prompt resolution of economic disputes, especially by making increased use of the ASEAN Protocol on Enhanced Dispute Settlement Mechanism (*see supra*). *Ninth*, the reinforcement of ASEAN's significance in the emerging regional economic architecture by maintaining its role as the epicentre and facilitator of economic integration in the whole of the East Asian region (on which, see, e.g., the Regional Comprehensive Economic Partnership *infra*). *Tenth*, the elaboration of a policy of adopting common positions, which should increase the position and augment the bargaining power of ASEAN in global economic fora.

§1. The Structure of the AEC

448. As has been explained above, pursuant to Article 9(2) of the ASEAN Treaty, the AEC Council, like the other two ASEAN Community Councils, has under its purview the so-called Sectoral Ministerial Bodies. This is a generic term to describe a whole array of organs, entities and bodies dedicated to moving forward the AEC agenda, as it is each time determined by ASEAN leaders. Sectoral Ministerial Bodies should be considered as secondary organs to the extent that their establishment as well as their dissolution is authorised by the ASEAN Summit, as stipulated in Article 7(2)(f) of the ASEAN Charter. They are chaired, where appropriate, by the annually rotating ASEAN Chairmanship.[1589] They have the power to address issues and matters to the ASEAN Summit, which is obliged to deliberate them and reach decisions.[1590] Article 10(1) of the Charter lays down which are the four principal duties of the Sectoral Ministerial Bodies. *First*, to function in accordance with the mandate given when they were established. *Second*, to implement the agreements and the decisions of the ASEAN Summit under their respective purview. *Third*, to bolster cooperation among the membership so as to support the ultimate aim of ASEAN integration. *Fourth*, to submit reports and recommendations to the respective Community Councils.

449. Under the second paragraph of Article 10 of the ASEAN Charter, each of the Sectoral Ministerial Bodies may create subsidiary entities to assist them when undertaking its functions. Which these entities are appears in Annex 1 of the Charter.

1588. *See* further, *Declaration on Institutionalising the Resilience of ASEAN and Its Communities and Peoples to Disasters and Climate Change*, adopted in Kuala Lumpur, Malaysia, on 27 Apr. 2015, at: https://asean.org/wp-content/uploads/2012/05/26th-DECLARATION-ON-INSTITUTIONALISING-Final.pdf, reproduced in *ASEAN Documents Series 2015*, 3; and *ASEAN Declaration on One ASEAN One Response: ASEAN Responding to Disasters as One in the Region and Outside the Region*, adopted in Vientiane, Laos, on 6 Sep. 2016, at: https://asean.org/asean-declaration-on-one-asean-one-response-asean-responding-to-disasters-as-one-in-the-region-and-outside-the-region/, reproduced in *ASEAN Documents Series 2016*, 5.

1589. *See* ASEAN Charter Art. 31(2)(d).

1590. *Ibid.*, Art. 7(2)(b).

The Secretary-General is empowered to update this Annex following the recommendation of the Committee of Permanent Representatives and without having recourse to the Charter provisions concerning amendment. Presently, the Sectoral Ministerial Bodies within the purview of the AEC are the following:[1591]

1. The ASEAN Economic Ministers Meeting (AEM), with subsidiary organs the High Level Task Force on ASEAN Economic Integration (HLTF-EI), the Senior Economic Officials Meeting (SEOM), and the ASEAN Community Statistical System (ACSS) Committee.
2. The ASEAN Free Trade Area (AFTA) Council.
3. The ASEAN Investment Area (AIA) Council.
4. The ASEAN Finance Ministers Meeting (AFMM), with subsidiary organs the ASEAN Finance Deputies Meeting (AFDM), and the ASEAN Directors-General of Customs Meeting (CustomsDG).
5. The ASEAN Central Bank Governors Meeting (ACGM), with subsidiary organs the ASEAN Central Bank Deputies Meeting (ACDM), and the ASEAN Senior Level Committee (SLC) on Financial Integration.
6. The ASEAN Finance Ministers and Central Bank Governors Meeting (AFMGM), with subsidiary organ the ASEAN Finance and Central Bank Deputies Meeting (AFCDM).
7. The ASEAN Ministers Meeting on Agriculture and Forestry (AMAF), with subsidiary organs the Senior Officials Meeting of the ASEAN Ministers on Agriculture and Forestry (SOM-AMAF), and the ASEAN Senior Officials on Forestry (ASOF).
8. The ASEAN Ministers on Energy Meeting (AMEM), with subsidiary organ the Senior Officials Meeting on Energy (SOME).
9. The ASEAN Ministerial Meeting on Minerals (AMMin), with subsidiary organ the ASEAN Senior Officials Meeting on Minerals (ASOMM)
10. The ASEAN Ministerial Meeting on Science, Technology and Innovation (AMMSTI), with subsidiary organ the Committee on Science, Technology and Innovation (COSTI).
11. The ASEAN Digital Ministers Meeting (ADGMIN), with subsidiary organs the ASEAN Digital Senior Officials Meeting (ADGSOM), and the ASEAN Telecommunications Regulators' Council (ATRC).
12. The ASEAN Transport Ministers Meeting (ATM), with subsidiary organ the Senior Transport Officials Meeting (STOM).
13. The Meeting of the ASEAN Tourism Ministers (M-ATM), with subsidiary organ the Meeting of the ASEAN National Tourism Organisations (ASEAN NTOs).
14. The ASEAN Mekong Basin Development Cooperation (AMBDC), with subsidiary organs the ASEAN Mekong Basin Development Cooperation Steering Committee (AMBDC SC) and the High Level Finance Committee (HLFC).
15. The ASEAN Centre for Energy.
16. The ASEAN-Japan Centre in Tokyo.

1591. *See ibid.*, Annex 1, updated on 30 October 2023 pursuant to Article 10 (2) ASEAN Charter, at: https://asean.org/who-we-work-with/asean-sectoral-ministerial-bodies/.

§2. Law-Making in the AEC: The Question of the Requirements for the Entry into Force of ASEAN Economic Treaties

450. Law-making in the AEC is quite complex and perplexed. It differs from the way REIOs produce rules and regulations. There, the various integration goals are invariably set out in the respective constitutive instrument, which has established them. At the same time, the competent organs follow a specific type of law-making, which produces secondary legislation (in the EU they take the form of 'regulations' and 'directives').[1592] However, ASEAN has followed a markedly different path.[1593] The reason is, of course, that Member States resolved to move towards economic integration and to establish the AEC years before ASEAN had acquired a proper constitutive instrument (it will be recalled that the ASEAN Charter was signed in 2007). Thus, in the years before 2008 when the Charter came into force, there was no institutional legal basis for adopting binding decisions pertaining to economic cooperation among Member States, which would have led to integration. This meant that Member States had to resort to multilateral treaties as the legal instrument to implement their cooperation and to promote the goal of economic integration. To put it otherwise, since the AEC was effectively established before the ASEAN Charter was concluded, the latter could not have become its constitutive instrument. In effect, and from a strict legal point of view, the AEC (and indeed the other two Communities as well) should be understood as being outside the formal institutional framework of the Charter. And this even though, as has been explained, the Charter does create organs whose mandate is to carry out the necessary cooperation and integration, as intended by the AEC and the other two Community Councils. It has been calculated that by December 2020, ASEAN countries had signed 240 legal instruments.[1594]

451. Arguably, this is a complicated state of affairs. Thus, it is quite unlike the road followed by the EEC. There, the goal of economic integration was laid down expressly in the constitutive instrument (the Treaty of Rome Establishing the European Economic Community (1957), as amended), which had envisaged that the integration project would be carried out through specific secondary legislation. But the ASEAN Charter does nothing of the sort; indeed, it has not been drafted as the constitutive instrument of a REIO would have been drafted. Therefore, relying on multilateral treaties to adopt the required measures and procedures has been the only way to implement the integration project.[1595] Finally, it should be noted in relation

1592. The constitutive instrument of the REIO is the primary legislation.

1593. Note that ASEAN countries have adopted the Medical Device Directive. However, this is not akin to an EU directive but it is a proper treaty: its full title is 'ASEAN Agreement on Medical Device Directive', signed on 21 Nov. 2014, entered into force on 1 Jan. 2015, at: https://agreement.asean.org/media/download/20141204115621.pdf, reproduced in *ASEAN Medical Device Directive*, Jakarta: ASEAN Secretariat, September 2015.

1594. *See* Y. Fukunaga, *Use of Legal Instruments in the ASEAN Economic Community building*, 10 J. Contemp. East Asia Stud. 65–82 (2021).

1595. Generally, *see* M. Plummer, *The ASEAN Economic Community and the European Experience*, ADB Working Paper Series on Regional Economic Integration No. 1, Asian Development Bank, July 2006.

to the European Community that when it could not have regulated certain matters affecting the integration process by means of secondary legislation, it had also to resort to the negotiation and conclusion of treaties. Suffice to mention the Brussels Convention on Jurisdiction and the Enforcement of Judgments in Civil and Commercial Matters (1968). Several decades later, and as the European Community had in the meantime evolved institutionally and was no longer only about economic integration, this Convention was replaced with secondary legislation, namely Regulation 44/2001.[1596] Of course, there is an important difference in regulating economic cooperation and integration on the one hand with specially concluded treaties and on the other hand with secondary legislation issued by an international organisation in question: while all Member States are (automatically) bound by the latter, to be bound by the former invariably requires that they ratify/accept the relevant treaties. Finally, it is usually easier and more straightforward to amend/revise secondary legislation than treaties.

452. It is not possible to enumerate all the treaties of an economic nature that ASEAN Member States have concluded over the years (they are probably well over 100 in total, including Protocols and Memoranda of Understanding).[1597] Even though they form part of what has been described above as ASEAN law, or ASEAN legal system, it is only possible to refer to a handful of them, which, however, will give a broad sample of the areas and fields that they regulate in the AEC. A very important difference between secondary legislation adopted by an international organisation and the treaties adopted by the Member States of an international organisation for pursuing economic integration is that the validity of the former could start as soon as they were approved by the competent organ/s. On the contrary, for treaties to come into force and become operative, they ordinarily have to be ratified, according to domestic constitutional rules, by the number of signatory parties that is laid down in their text.[1598] It follows that the exact time at which each and every treaty will enter into force can never be prognosed, it could even many years. Invariably, it depends on how few or how many ratifications are required to enter into force.

453. However, in the context of economic integration projects, there are very important factors. The first is time. A future step may not be possible to be implemented, if a previous step has not been achieved. Thus, prompt ratification and the entry into force of treaties at the earliest possible time are of paramount importance. The second is uniformity in regulation, in other words that the same rules are applied and are followed by all participating states with no exceptions. Both these factors are present in several ASEAN treaties, which stipulate, on the one hand, that they shall enter into force after all Member States have deposited their instruments

1596. Council Regulation 44/2001 of 22 Dec. 2000 on jurisdiction and the recognition and enforcement of judgments in civil and commercial matters, O.J. L 12, 16.1.2001, p. 1.

1597. Some of these treaties are reproduced in L. Riccardi and Riccardi, *Invest in ASEAN Countries: Analysis and Treaties* (Springer, 2020).

1598. For details on the position of treaties in the legal systems of ASEAN countries, *see supra,* paras 83 et seq.

of ratification with the Secretary-General and, on the other hand, that the process of ratification must not take more than a pre-determined period of time.

454. For example, the ASEAN Agreement on the Movement of Natural Persons provides that the maximum period envisaged for ratification is 180 days from the day it was signed.[1599] While the use of 'shall' in the wording of such clauses denotes that Member States assume the obligation to ratify them promptly, practice shows that it is an obligation not always fulfilled. Thus, in the case of the Agreement on the Movement of Natural Persons, no Member State had notified its ratification instrument within the 180-day period (Malaysia was the first to do so on 17 June 2013). In the event, the Agreement came into force three years later when the Philippines submitted its ratification instrument on 14 June 2016. Another example is the ASEAN Agreement on Customs (2012); it also envisaged ratification within a 180-day period, which, however, was not observed as it took another two years to be ratified by all Member States and enter into force.[1600]

455. But there are other treaties falling into the ambit of the AEC that have a different entry into force clause. In particular, they provide for entry into force without previous ratification by all Member States, in which case they will only be applicable to those Member States which have submitted their instruments of ratification. Two examples will be given. The first example is the ASEAN Multilateral Agreement on the Full Liberalisation of Passenger Air Services:[1601] Article 19(3) stipulates that it shall enter into force on the date of the third instrument of ratification's deposit and shall become effective only among the contracting parties which have ratified it. There is no doubt that this kind of provision ensures that the treaty in question will come into force relatively soon or at least sooner than if ratification by all Member States had been required. Given that ASEAN agreements are effectively multilateral treaties, three is the smallest number of required ratifications for

---

1599. *See* Art. 16(1) of the Agreement, signed in Phnom Penh, Cambodia, on 19 Nov. 2012, entered into force on 14 Jun. 2016, at: https://investasean.asean.org/files/upload/ASEANMNPMainText.pdf. Generally, *see* Y. Fukunaga & H. Ishido, *Values and Limitations of the ASEAN Agreement on the Movement of Natural Persons* (ERIA Discussion Paper Series, ERIA-DP-2015-20, March 2015), at: https://www.eria.org/ERIA-DP-2015-20.pdf. Note that in order to promote the unhindered circulation of skilled workforce within the region, ASEAN has adopted agreements for the mutual recognition of professional skills and diplomas. So far, these instruments (called 'ASEAN Mutual Recognition Arrangements') have been adopted on Accountancy Services in 2014, on Medical Practitioners in 2009, on Dental Practitioners in 2009, on Nursing Services in 2006, on Engineering Services in 2005, on Architectural Services in 2007, on Mutual Recognition of Surveying Qualifications in 2007, and on Tourism Professionals in 2013; the texts are available at: https://investasean.asean.org/asean-free-trade-area-agreements/view/757/newsid/868/asean-mutual-reco
gnition-arrangements.html. *See* further, *Guidelines for the Development of Mutual Recognition Arrangements*, Jakarta: ASEAN Secretariat, September 2014.

1600. *See* Art. 63(1) of the Agreement on Customs, signed in Phnom Penh, Cambodia, on 30 Mar. 2012, entered into force on 7 Nov. 2014, at: http://agreement.asean.org/media/download/20140117163238.pdf. The Agreement terminated the operation of the predecessor ASEAN Agreement on Customs, which had been concluded in Phuket, Thailand, on 1 Mar. 1997.

1601. The Agreement was signed on 12 Nov. 2010, entered into force on 30 Jun. 2011, at: https://asean.org/wp-content/uploads/images/archive/transport/Agreement-101112.pdf.

entry into force (if the requirement was for only two ratifications and one of the contracting parties decided to withdraw from it or to repudiate it, the treaty would have been terminated, considering that there can be no treaty with only one contracting party and regardless of how many the signatory parties there are). Notwithstanding the advantage of a potentially quicker entry into force, as was explained above, regional projects of economic integration demand a high level of uniformity among participating States. The question, therefore, to be asked is this: are ASEAN interests and goals better met when air services are liberalised between three or four Member States or when liberalisation becomes the norm for all members? Another matter that should be very briefly touched upon are the possible complications when supplementary instruments are adopted in the context of a treaty that is not in force for all Member States. Regarding the Liberalisation of Air Passenger Services Agreement, two Protocols were signed on the very day it was concluded,[1602] a third one was concluded on 13 October 2017, and a fourth one on 9 November 2018.[1603]

456. The second example is Article 22 of the ASEAN Agreement on Medical Device Directive, which has been mentioned above. It stipulates that it shall be subject to ratification by Member States in accordance with their internal domestic requirements, but it does not provide expressly the required period of time for ratification. On the contrary, this derives indirectly from the second paragraph of Article 22, which reads: '[the Agreement] shall enter into force on 1 January 2015 and shall be in force only among the Member States that have ratified … it'. The obvious questions arising from this arrangement are: (a) what would happen if no Member State had approved it by the stipulated date; and (b) considering that this Agreement was adopted as part of the ASEAN FTA, which would be the consequences if one or more Member States failed to approve it or if they approved it with considerable delay (e.g., the Philippines deposited its instrument of ratification on 4 March 2021).

457. As regards the first question, no Member State had ratified it by 1 January 2015 (Singapore deposited its ratification instrument in November 2015 and Lao in December 2015) but apparently this caused no problems. As regards the second question, it could lead to a state of confusion, especially for those who would like to take advantage of the benefits of an FTA. More specifically, it is not conducive to consistency and uniformity, two important elements that characterise regional economic integration projects. The situation becomes more complicated for two reasons. First, because as has been explained, ASEAN has had to rely on the conclusion of several treaties to adopt the norms, rules and procedures of the AEC, which effectively could be described as AEC law. Second, because, objectively, the drafters of such agreements are not able to know when (and if) they will actually become

1602. Namely, Protocol 1 on Unlimited Third and Fourth Freedom Traffic Rights Between Any ASEAN Cities, and Protocol 2 on Unlimited Third and Fourth Freedom Traffic Rights Between Any ASEAN Cities, both signed on 12 Nov. 2010.

1603. Generally, *see* J. Woon Lee, 'ASEAN Air Transport Integration and Liberalization: A Slow but Practical Model' in P. L. Hsieh & B. Mercurio B (eds), *ASEAN Law in the New Regional Economic Order: Global Trends and Shifting Paradigms* (Cambridge: Cambridge University Press 2019), 186–206.

operative. This has led to situations where one ASEAN Agreement does mention another ASEAN Agreement even though the latter has not yet been signed! Suffice to mention the ASEAN Agreement on Electronic Commerce, which was signed in January 2019. Article 4(1) thereof stipulates that it is not the Agreement's purpose to derogate from the existing rights and obligations of a Member State under any other relevant Agreement to which it is a party.[1604] Article 4(1) includes into the ambit of the 'relevant Agreements' the ASEAN Trade in Services Agreement (ATISA) and stipulates that it shall be deemed to be a relevant ASEAN agreement regardless of its entry into force. However, it was only in September 2019 that ASEAN Economic Ministers welcomed the conclusion of ATISA and, while they had expected that it would have signed by the end of 2019,[1605] it was even further delayed. Finally, it was signed by the entire membership in Manila, the Philippines, on 7 October 2020.[1606]

1604. Signed in Ha Noi, Vietnam, on 22 Jan. 2019, entered into force on 2 Dec. 2021, at: http://agreement.asean.org/media/download/20190306035048.pdf. The Agreement required ratification by all Member States to enter into force, *see* Art. 19(1).

1605. *See* 51st ASEAN Economic Ministers' (AEM) Meeting, 6 Sep. 2019, Bangkok, Thailand, Joint Media Statement, para. 22, at: https://asean.org/the-51st-asean-economic-ministers-aem-meeting/.

1606. Text at: http://agreement.asean.org/media/download/20201111041414.pdf.

Chapter 4. FTAs Between the Member States of ASEAN and Third States

458. ASEAN Member States have not only been trying to set up their own FTA but have also been active in establishing FTAs with other states in Asia and in Oceana.[1607] The latter states have reciprocated in these efforts. So far, ASEAN has had six FTA partners (in alphabetical order): Australia, China, India, Japan, New Zealand, and South Korea. These FTAs are in different stages of evolution. Reference will be made to the FTA with South Korea as well as to the FTA with Australia and New Zealand.

§1. The FTA with South Korea

459. In December 2005, a Framework Agreement on Comprehensive Economic Cooperation was signed between ASEAN Member States and South Korea.[1608] This legal instrument is considered to be the ASEAN-Korea Free Trade Agreement (AKFTA). The following year, the Agreement on Trade in Goods under the Framework Agreement (AKTIG) was concluded during the 4th Consultations between the ASEAN Economic Ministers and the Minister for Trade of Korea; it became operative in June 2007.[1609] Later on, two additional treaties were concluded under the Framework Agreement/AKFTA. The first was the Agreement on Trade in Services, which was signed on 21 November 2007 and entered into force on 1 May 2009.[1610] The second was the Agreement on Investment, which was signed on 2 June 2009 and became operative on 1 September 2009.[1611] Subsequently, AKFTA came into effect on 1 January 2010. In November 2015, the Third Protocol to Amend the AKTIG Agreement was signed by all contracting parties.[1612] It aimed at boosting bilateral trade through new commitments and trade facilitation. The last party to enter into force was Vietnam on 28 November 2023.[1613]

1607. For more details, *see ASEAN Integration Report 2019* (Jakarta: ASEAN Secretariat, 2019, 127 et seq.).
1608. Framework Agreement on Comprehensive Economic Cooperation Among the Governments of the Member Countries of the Association of Southeast Asian Nations and the Republic of Korea, signed in Kuala Lumpur on 13 Dec. 2005, came into force on 1 Jul. 2006, at: https://investmentpolicy.unctad.org/international-investment-agreements/treaty-files/3094/download. The Agreement on Dispute Settlement Mechanism was also concluded on 13 Dec. 2005; its terms extend to all sectoral instruments to be adopted pursuant to the Framework Agreement.
1609. The Agreement was signed in Kuala Lumpur on 24 Aug. 2006, at: https://akfta.asean.org/index.php?page=asean-korea-trade-in-goods-agreement. Protocols of Amendment were signed on 30 Nov. 2010, on 17 Nov. 2011, and on 22 Nov. 2015, *see* at: https://akfta.asean.org/index.php?page=trade-in-goods.
1610. Text at: https://akfta.asean.org/index.php?page=agreement-on-trade-in-services-under-the-framework-agreement.
1611. At: https://investmentpolicy.unctad.org/international-investment-agreements/treaty-files/3339/download.
1612. At: https://akfta.asean.org/uploads/docs/agreements/TIG-Third-Protocol-to-Amend.pdf.
1613. See 'Overview of ASEAN-Republic of Korea Comprehensive Strategic Partnership As of October 2024', at: https://asean.org/wp-content/uploads/2024/10/Overview-Paper-of-ASEAN-ROK-Comprehensive-Strategic-Partnership-as-of-October-2024.pdf.

460. Article 2 of the Agreement on Trade obliges each contracting party to accord national treatment to the goods of all the other contracting parties (i.e., among ASEAN Member States as well) pursuant to Article III of the General Agreement on Trade and Tariffs (GATT 1994).[1614] To that extent, the provisions of Article III GATT 1994 are to be understood as having been incorporated into the Agreement and form an integral part thereof. The gist of Article III is that GATT contracting parties recognise that all taxes, charges, etc., which are imposed under their domestic laws and regulations, and which affect the domestic sale, purchase, etc. of products as well as any domestic quantitative restrictions should not be applied to imported goods or to domestic products (in the latter case for the purpose of offering protection to domestic production).

461. Two particular aspects of the Agreement on Trade in Goods merit attention. The first is Article 21, the entry into force clause. The first paragraph of Article 21 stipulates that the Agreement shall enter into force on 1 July 2006, if at least one ASEAN Member State and Korea 'are among the Signatory Countries that have by then notified all the other parties in writing of the completion of their internal procedures'. And in case this proves to be untenable, on the first day of the second month following the latter date on which at least one ASEAN Member State and Korea have notified that their ratification process has been completed. Given that the Agreement was signed in August 2006 the obvious question is how it could have ever come into force almost two months before its signing. A possible explanation might be that the Agreement was originally scheduled to have been signed at a much earlier date. However, this is not a very satisfactory explanation because the Framework Agreement had been signed in mid-December 2005. In the event, the Agreement on Trade in Goods came into force on 1 June 2007, while 2024 has been earmarked as the year for its full implementation.

462. The second aspect is the stance adopted by Thailand, which refused to sign it because it was decided to exclude rice from the ambit of the Agreement.[1615] Thailand's displeasure was no doubt to be expected and is understandable considering that it is one of the largest rice exporters in the world. However, Thailand was offered the opportunity to sign it at a later date if it so wished. Thailand acceded to the Agreement on the basis of a Protocol of Accession, which was signed in Cha-am, Thailand, on 27 February 2009,[1616] even though the Agreement does not contain any provisions on accession.

463. Finally, it is of interest to note that, notwithstanding the existence of the ASEAN-Korea Free Trade Agreement, there have been FTAs and other economic

1614. All ASEAN countries are Member States of the WTO.

1615. *See* D. Park, I. Park & G.E.B. Estrada, *Is the ASEAN-Korea Free Trade Area (AKFTA) an Optimal Free Trade Area?* (Asian Development Bank, Working Paper Series on Regional Economic Integration No. 21, November 2008), p. 2.

1616. At: https://cil.nus.edu.sg/wp-content/uploads/2019/06/2009-Protocol-on-Accession-of-Thailand-to-AKFTA-TIG.pdf.

treaties concluded between Korea and individual ASEAN countries. More specifically, a bilateral FTA with Singapore,[1617] a bilateral FTA with Vietnam,[1618] and a bilateral economic agreement with Indonesia.[1619] And this even though both South Korea and all ASEAN countries participate in the Regional Comprehensive Economic Partnership, which is discussed *infra*. As regards the remaining ASEAN countries, on 1 December 2002, the Korea–Cambodia FTA came into force having been signed on 26 October 2021,[1620] in September 2023 the Philippines and South Korea signed an FTA on the sidelines of the 43rd ASEAN Summit (it entered into force on 31 December 2024[1621]), while in March 2024 Malaysia and South Korea decided to resume negotiations for the conclusion of a Malaysia-Korea Free Trade Agreement (MKFTA), which go back to 2019; the 7th round of negotiations was held in February 2025.

§2. The FTA with Australia and with New Zealand

464. On 27 February 2009, the Agreement establishing the ASEAN-Australia-New Zealand Free Trade Area (AANZFTA) was concluded in Cha-am, Petchaburi, Thailand. It came into force on 1 January 2010 (for some States, it came into force in 2011 and in 2012).[1622] Its provisions are meant to be fully compliant with WTO law,[1623] and include a dispute settlement mechanism. The issues covered in this regional trade regime comprise, *inter alia*, the following: (a) specific goods and services (e.g., construction, mining-related services, education, financial services, and telecommunications); (b) investments and investor protection (including a dispute resolution mechanism between investors and contracting parties); (c) temporary movement of specific categories of individuals (services suppliers, sellers of goods as well as investors); (d) e-commerce; (e) intellectual property (a regime to enforce intellectual property rights is also laid down); (f) economic cooperation (with the prospect of furthering economic integration); and (g) competition. It should also be noted that the AANZFTA Agreement has been complemented by bilateral FTAs concluded between Australia, on the one hand, and Indonesia (IA-CEPA), Malaysia (MAFTA), Singapore (SAFTA) and Thailand (TAFTA), on the other hand. The

1617. Free Trade Agreement between the Republic of Korea and Singapore, signed on 4 Aug. 2005, entered into force on 2 Mar. 2006, at: https://investmentpolicy.unctad.org/international-investment-agreements/treaty-files/2709/download.
1618. Free Trade Agreement between Vietnam and Korea (VKFTA), signed on 5 May 2015, entered into force on 20 Dec. 2015, at: https://wtocenter.vn/chuyen-de/12689-vkfta-full-content.
1619. Indonesia–Korea Comprehensive Economic Partnership Agreement (IK-CEPA), signed on 18 Dec. 2020, entered into force on 1 Jan. 2023.
1620. Text at: https://investmentpolicy.unctad.org/international-investment-agreements/treaty-files/6388/download.
1621. All Korea's FTAs are available at: https://www.customs.go.kr/engportal/cm/cntnts/cntntsView.do?mi=7308&cntntsId=2332#.
1622. Text at: https://www.dfat.gov.au/trade/agreements/in-force/aanzfta/official-documents/agreement-establishing-the-asean-australia-new-zealand-free-trade-area-aanzfta.
1623. The AANZFTA Agreement was modified by virtue of a Protocol, which was signed in Nay Pyi Taw, Myanmar, on 26 Aug. 2014, entered into force on 1 Oct. 2015, available at: https://www.treaties.mfat.govt.nz/search/details/t/3825/500. Two Chapters of the Agreement were amended, the Trade in Goods and the Rules of Origin.

implementation as well as the operation of AANZFTA are supervised by a Joint Committee (FJC), which is composed of senior officials from the twelve contracting parties. It meets at least once a year.[1624]

465. The AANZFTA Agreement is meant to be a living instrument. To that end, it contains a provision for its review, which allows contracting parties to ensure that it is always up-to-date and reflects developments relevant to the business sector. As has been mentioned in an official document: 'AANZFTA needs to remain responsive to the needs of businesses'.[1625] The so called Terms of Reference for Conducting General Review of AANZFTA were adopted on 27 July 2016 and contracting parties endorsed them on 4 August 2016.[1626] Based on the outcome of the first General Review, which was carried out in 2017,[1627] certain recommendations were made to and accepted by participating States.[1628] Later on, these recommendations led to the negotiations for a second amending Protocol, which should allow the regulation of additional areas, including consumer protection, government procurement and sustainable development.[1629]

466. The second Protocol to amend the AANZFTA Agreement ought to have been concluded by the end of 2019. It was finally signed in August 2023, in the margins of the 28th ASEAN Economic Ministers – Closer Economic Relations (AEM-CER) consultations.[1630] The second Protocol adds new provisions to the Agreement facilitating trade of essential goods during humanitarian crises; expands the scope to include education services; enhances electronic commerce and facilitates electronic payments; etc. Overall, the second Protocol upgrades thirteen Chapters of the original Agreement and adds three new Chapters (on Government Procurement; on Micro, Small and Medium Enterprises (MSMEs); and on Trade and Sustainable

1624. For the Joint Committee Meetings' Reports, *see* https://aanzfta.asean.org/statements-reports/fta-joint-committee-meeting-reports/.
1625. *See* ASEAN-AU-NZ 10th Anniversary of AANZFTA Ministerial Statement, adopted by the 24th Meeting of the ASEAN Economic Ministers held in Bangkok on 9 Sep. 2019, https://www.dfat.gov.au/sites/default/files/10th-anniversary-of-aanzfta-ministerial-statement.pdf.
1626. Text at: https://www.dfat.gov.au/sites/default/files/terms-of-reference-for-conducting-general-review-of-aanzfta.pdf.
1627. *See* Report of the FTA Joint Committee, General Review of AANZFTA Stage One: Review of Implementation 2010–2017, October 2017, at: https://aanzfta.asean.org/uploads/2016/04/AANZ-FTA-General-Review-Stage-One-report_FINAL-public.pdf.
1628. *See* AANZFTA General Review: Recommendations for the 23rd AEM-CER Consultations (endorsed by Ministers on 1 Sep. 2018), at: https://aanzfta.asean.org/uploads/2017/12/AANZFTA-GR-Stage-2-Rec-PUBLIC.pdf.
1629. It was agreed during the 23rd AEM – Closer Economic Relations (CER) Consultations, Singapore, 1 Sep. 2018, *see* the Joint Media Statement, para. 3, at: https://aanzfta.asean.org/uploads/2016/12/FINAl-JMS-AEM-CER-23.pdf.
1630. *See* The Twenty-Eighth AEM – Closer Economic Relations (CER) Consultation, 22 Aug. 2023, Semarang, Indonesia, *Joint Media Statement*, para. 7, at: https://asean.org/wp-content/uploads/2023/08/Adopted-Joint-Media-Statement-AEM-CER-28.pdf. *See* further, *The Melbourne Declaration – A partnership for the future*, *supra*, para. 31.

Development).[1631] The second Protocol the time of writing had not entered into force; it requires ratification by Australia, New Zealand and at least four ASEAN Member States.

§3. The Regional Comprehensive Economic Partnership (RCEP)

467. As was mentioned in the previous paragraphs, over and above the FTAs that ASEAN, as an international organisation, has been promoting with third states, its Member States have been concluding separate bilateral trade agreements with the same third states as well as with REIOs.[1632] Suffice to mention that Indonesia has entered into four bilateral FTAs, namely with Australia, Chile, the European Free Trade Association (EFTA), and Japan,[1633] while on 31 July 2024, it launched negotiations for the conclusion of an FTA with the GCC (I-GCC FTA), the latest round of which was held in February 2025.

468. Moreover, four ASEAN countries (Brunei, Malaysia, Singapore and Vietnam) participate in a trans-regional FTA, the Trans-Pacific Partnership (TPP), which is now governed by the Comprehensive and Progressive Agreement for Trans-Pacific Partnership (CPTPP).[1634] It entered into force on 30 December 2018: Singapore is an original contracting party while, on 14 January 2019, Vietnam became the seventh contracting party.[1635] On 1 February 2021, the United Kingdom formally requested accession to CPTPP, and in June 2021 CPTPP countries agreed to start the accession negotiations.[1636] They were concluded on 31 March 2023.[1637] The UK Protocol of Accession was signed on 16 July 2023.[1638] Britain ratified it on

1631. For the text of the consolidated Agreement, *see* https://www.dfat.gov.au/trade/agreements/in-force/aanzfta/official-documents/second-protocol-to-amend-the-agreement-establishing-asean-australia-new-zealand-free-trade-area-aanzfta.

1632. A list of these FTAs is available at: https://www.bilaterals.org/?-south-south-ftas-.

1633. *See* R. Syarip, *Defending Foreign Policy at Home: Indonesia and the ASEAN-Based Free Trade Agreements*, 39 J. Current Southeast Asian Aff. 405 (2020).

1634. Text at: https://www.dfat.gov.au/trade/agreements/in-force/cptpp/official-documents.

1635. The entry into force clause in the original TPP Agreement, which was signed in February 2016, effectively necessitated its ratification by the USA; however, because on 30 Jan. 2017 the US Administration notified the other signatory parties that it did not intend to become a contracting party, *see* https://ustr.gov/sites/default/files/files/Press/Releases/1-30-17%20USTR%20Letter%20to%20TPP%20Depositary.pdf, the remaining eleven signatories agreed to proceed with a modified Agreement, the negotiations for which were completed successfully on 23 Jan. 2018 and the CPTPP Agreement was signed.

1636. *See* Decision by the Commission of the Comprehensive and Progressive Agreement for Trans-Pacific Partnership regarding the United Kingdom's Formal Request to Commence the Accession Process, CPTPP/COM/2021/D001, 2 Jun. 2021, https://www.dfat.gov.au/sites/default/files/cptpp-decision-uk-accession-request-2-june-2021.pdf.

1637. For details, *see* UK Parliament, House of Commons Library, *The Comprehensive and Progressive Agreement for Trans-Pacific Partnership (CPTPP)*, Research Briefing, 22 Mar. 2024, at: https://commonslibrary.parliament.uk/research-briefings/cbp-9121/.

1638. *See* UK Parliament, House of Commons Library, *UK accession to the Comprehensive and Progressive Agreement for Trans-Pacific Partnership*, 12 Mar. 2024, at: https://lordslibrary.parliament.uk/uk-accession-to-the-comprehensive-and-progressive-agreement-for-trans-pacific-partnership/#fn-15.

17 May 2024. The Protocol will enter into force when the UK and the majority of CPTPP contracting parties have ratified it.[1639]

469. Finally, it should be noted that the EU has viewed the bilateral agreements it has concluded with ASEAN Member States as steps towards achieving the final objective of establishing a region-to-region trade and investment regime.[1640] New momentum to this goal was given when, at the beginning of the 2020s, the EU and ASEAN became 'Strategic Partners'. More specifically, during the 23rd ASEAN-EU Ministerial Meeting (AEMM), in December 2020, the two sides agreed to establish the ASEAN-EU Strategic Partnership.[1641] The modalities of this Partnership were agreed at the 24th AEMM, which was held in February 2024 in Brussels.[1642] Already, for the period 2021–2027, the EU has earmarked 180 million Euro for regional cooperation with ASEAN. The Plan of Action implementing the ASEAN-EU Strategic Partnership for the years 2023 to 2027 (it replaced the previous Plan of Action that run from 2018 to 2022)[1643] was concluded in July 2023.[1644]

470. Parallel to ASEAN, collectively, and its Member States, individually engaging in multilateral and bilateral FTAs, during the 19th ASEAN Summit, which was held in Indonesia in November 2011, the initiative towards an ASEAN Framework for Regional Comprehensive Economic Partnership (RCEP) was announced.[1645] The idea was to engage the ASEAN FTA partners and other states (the ASEAN Charter refers to them as the 'external partners')[1646] in broad economic agreements covering trade in goods, trade in services as well as investment. These agreements would be guided by the general principles which are outlined in the text of RCEP as well as by the specific principles which were to be defined by ASEAN itself. Arguably, RCEP was written in rather imprecise terms; for example, it is not apparent whether the aim was to have one (general) agreement or several

1639. See UK Department for Business and Trade, 'The UK and the Comprehensive and Progressive Agreement for Trans-Pacific Partnership 'CPTPP)', Last updated 24 December 2024, at: www.gov.uk.

1640. *See* K. Binder, *EU-Singapore Trade and Investment Deals Pass Major Milestone*, European Parliament, European Parliamentary Research Service, Briefing, April 2019, PE 637.940, at: https://www.europarl.europa.eu/RegData/etudes/BRIE/2019/637940/EPRS_BRI(2019)637940_EN.pdf.

1641. *See* 23rd ASEAN-EU Ministerial Meeting, Co-Chairs' Press Release, 1 Dec. 2020, at: https://asean.org/wp-content/uploads/23rd-AEMM-Co-Chairs-Press-Release.pdf. *See* further, ASEAN-EU Joint Ministerial Statement on Connectivity, 1 Dec. 2020, at: ASEAN-EU Joint Ministerial Statement on Connectivity, at:

1642. *See* 24th ASEAN-EU Ministerial Meeting, Joint Ministerial Statement, 2 Feb. 2024, at: https://asean.org/wp-content/uploads/2024/02/FINAL-Joint-Ministerial-Statement-24th-ASEAN-EU-Ministerial-Meeting.pdf.

1643. Text at: https://www.eeas.europa.eu/sites/default/files/documents/Plan%20of%20Action%20to%20Implement%20the%20ASEAN-EU%20Strategic%20Partnership%20%282023-2027%29.pdf.

1644. *See* ASEAN Post Ministerial Conference (PMC) 10+1 Sessions with the Dialogue Partners and Trilateral Meetings, Jakarta, Indonesia, 13–14 Jul. 2023, Chairman's Statement, para. 72, at: https://asean.org/wp-content/uploads/2023/07/FINAL-Chairmans-Statement-PMC-101-with-DPs-and-Trilateral-.pdf.

1645. Text at: https://asean.org/asean-framework-for-regional-comprehensive-economic-partnership/.

1646. Cf. Art. 1(15) of the ASEAN Charter stipulating that one of ASEAN's purposes is to maintain its centrality and proactive role as the primary driving force in the relations and cooperation with external partners and to engage in an open, transparent, and inclusive regional architecture.

(bilateral) agreements. But what is clear is that the ASEAN Member States will be the principal beneficiaries of this project. In particular, the text stated: 'The agreement shall contribute to ASEAN economic integration, equitable economic development and strengthening economic cooperation between ASEAN Member States as well as between ASEAN and its partners.' It is submitted that what RCEP does not explain are (a) which will be the benefits and the advantages for the third states and (b) how will it connect with the existing FTAs and/or with those which were at the time in the making or those that were to be negotiated at a later time. Finally, what might have also confused the goal of ASEAN was the Statement issued by the ASEAN Chair after the 19th Summit: it referred to a 'partnership agreement' that offered a framework for ASEAN and its external partners to address trade and investment issues that might emerge in the future.[1647]

471. Negotiations on the RCEP were launched in Phnom Penn, Cambodia, on 20 November 2012 at a special ceremony attended by the ASEAN Member States and the six FTA partners. They also endorsed the Guiding Principles and Objectives for Negotiating the Regional Comprehensive Economic Partnership.[1648] According to this document, negotiations were to commence in early 2013 and be completed by the end of 2015. Moreover, the scope of RCEP was considerably augmented to cover, additionally, technical cooperation, intellectual property, competition, dispute settlement, and other (unnamed) issues. The FTAs between ASEAN and the individual third partners (referred to in the document as 'ASEAN+1 FTAs') as well as the bilateral/plurilateral FTAs between and among participating states would continue to exist. Finally, the RCEP would 'include appropriate forms of flexibility including provision for special and differential treatment, plus additional flexibility to the least-developed ASEAN Member States'.

472. RCEP negotiations started in May 2013. Initially, India, one of the ASEAN's FTA partners, participated but withdrew in November 2019. Until today, India has abstained citing concerns over opening up its agricultural and manufacturing sectors to more foreign competition. However, it has been allowed to join the deliberations at any time.[1649] After thirty-one rounds of negotiations (the last one was on 9 June 2020), ten RCEP Inter-sessional Ministerial Meetings (the last one was on 23 June 2020) and eight RCEP Ministerial Meetings (the last one was on 27 August 2020),[1650] the RCEP was finalised in the autumn of 2020. It was signed on 15 November 2020 by the ten ASEAN countries as well as by five other countries

1647. *See* Chair's Statement of the 19th ASEAN Summit, Bali, Indonesia, 17 Nov. 2011, para. 45, at: https://www.eria.org/2011_1118_Chairs%20Statement%2019th%20ASEAN%20Summit.pdf. The Summit's theme, which was chosen by Indonesia, as the Member State holding the annual Chairmanship, was 'ASEAN Community in a Global Community of Nations'.

1648. Available at: https://www.mofa.go.jp/mofaj/press/release/24/11/pdfs/20121120_03_03.pdf.

1649. *See* Ministers' Declaration on India's Participation in the Regional Comprehensive Economic Partnership (RCEP), 5 Nov. 2020, at: https://www.dfat.gov.au/trade/agreements/not-yet-in-force/rcep/news/ministers-declaration-indias-participation-regional-comprehensive-economic-partnership-rcep.

1650. *See* Joint Media Statement of the 8th Regional Comprehensive Economic Partnership (RCEP) Ministerial Meeting, 27 Aug. 2020, at: https://asean.org/wp-content/uploads/2020/08/RCEP-MM-8-JMS.pdf.

of the Asia–Pacific region, namely China, Japan, South Korea, Australia and New Zealand.[1651] It took effect on 1 January 2022 and became the largest free trade area in the world.[1652] Considering that the RCEP stands as an alternative to the Trans-Pacific Partnership – this explains why it has been so heavily promoted by China – these two FTAs could possibly end up being in direct competition with each other, even though seven States are parties to both of them.[1653] It should be mentioned that RCEP is characterised by originality as it introduced several new features compared to previous FTAs.[1654] Even though it is too early to judge whether it will be a successful project, already four countries (Bangladesh, Hong Kong, Sri Lanka, and Chile) have applied for accession.[1655]

1651. It was signed while the 37th ASEAN Summit was ongoing, *see* Chairman's Statement of the 37th ASEAN Summit, Hanoi, 12 Nov. 2020, 'Cohesive And Responsive', para. 65, at: https://asean.org/wp-content/uploads/43-Chairmans-Statement-of-37th-ASEAN-Summit-FINAL.pdf. Text at: https://www.dfat.gov.au/trade/agreements/in-force/rcep/rcep-text.
1652. *See* Joint Media Statement of the Inaugural RCEP Ministers' Meeting, 17 Sep. 2022, Siem Reap, Cambodia, at: https://asean.org/wp-content/uploads/2022/09/Inaugural-RCEP-MM-Joint-Media-Statement-17-September-2022.pdf.
1653. Generally, *see* K. Shimizu, *The ASEAN Economic Community and the RCEP in the World Economy*, 10 J. Contemp. East Asia Stud. 1–23 (2021).
1654. Generally, *see* F. Kimura et al. (eds), *Dynamism of East Asia and Regional Comprehensive Economic Partnership (RCEP): The Framework for Regional Integration*, Economic Research Institute for ASEAN and East Asia (ERIA), November 2022, at: https://www.eria.org/uploads/media/Books/2022-RCEP-Book2/Dynamism-of-East-Asia-and-RCEP.pdf.
1655. *See* Joint Media Statement of the 2nd RCEP Ministers' Meeting, 21 Aug. 2023, Semarang, Indonesia, para. 5, at: https://asean.org/wp-content/uploads/2023/08/ADOPTED-RCEP-MM-2-Joint-Media-Statement.pdf, which reaffirmed that 'RCEP is an open and inclusive regional engagement' and noted that progress has been made in the discussions 'pertaining to the procedures for accession to the RCEP Agreement'.

Part VI. Appraisal

473. In 1967, ASEAN was established as a regional international organisation dedicated to cooperation and integration in the economic, political, socio-cultural, and security spheres by five Asian states (Indonesia, Malaysia, the Philippines, Singapore and Thailand). Since then, ASEAN has come into its own as a major and influential presence in Southeast Asia. ASEAN started life as a loose association of states committed to dialogue and promoting as close as possible collaboration. It lacked any real institutional structure, but this was outweighed by the desire of the original membership to achieve a meaningful cooperation among them and to tackle common problems in unison. The key founding principles of this regional institution, one of the very first to emerge in Asia, have been the non-interference in the internal affairs of participating states, a non-confrontational approach as regards their relations as well as decision-making by consensus. At the same time, these have been the constituent elements of the so-called ASEAN Way. However, the drawback with the ASEAN Way is that progress is contingent on agreement between all parties. This could and has often institutionalised delay in moving forward by handing power to the obstructionist state. However, in the twenty-first century, ASEAN has allowed those members seeking faster cooperation to go their own way, especially in the economic field, and in that way obstructionist states can be sidestepped.

474. The adoption of the Treaty of Amity and Co-operation (TAC) in 1976 constituted a major milestone: not only did it institutionalise the ASEAN Way, but it set out ASEAN's commitment to the peaceful settlement of disputes. What should be noted and remembered is how, over the years, a very large number of states and international organisations from all parts of the world have decided to join this Treaty as contracting parties. Presently, TAC has fifty-one parties from all continents (in 2004 there were nineteen).

475. The end of the conflicts which had traumatised Southeast Asia in the second half of the twentieth century, allowed ASEAN to extend the prospect of membership to other states as well. It also sought deeper economic cooperation, no doubt with the future goal of regional economic integration in mind. However, the very serious economic and financial setbacks that took place in the late 1990s led to the realisation that, if ASEAN were not to stagnate, it needed to boost its drive for greater political, social and economic cohesion and, ultimately, integration. It hence committed itself to becoming an ASEAN Community encompassing different fields of activities.

476. The adoption of the ASEAN Charter in November 2007 was the landmark in its transition towards a rules-based international organisation and towards the institutionalisation of its operation and activities. Its principles, aims and objectives are now set out in treaty-form, in the constituent instrument of an international organisation which has also been given a proper formal legal framework. However, despite making ASEAN a more 'strict' multilateral institution, its structure has remained comparatively slight. Significantly, there is no court of justice or a principal legal organ for that matter, with Member States retaining all significant powers and the ability to determine impetus in ASEAN, still an association of national sovereigns, more a 'League of Nations' than an 'European Union'.

477. In time, ASEAN should evolve into the ASEAN Community to be built on three interrelated elements: economic, political, and socio-cultural. Close economic and market cooperation leading to integration is being driven forward by the AEC.[1656] However, it should not be overlooked that regional cooperation among the Southeast Asian economies is also effected through three sub-regional initiatives: the Greater Mekong Subregion (GMS), the

478. Indonesia–Malaysia–Thailand Growth Triangle (IMT-GT), and the Brunei Darussalam–Indonesia–Malaysia–Philippines East ASEAN Growth Area (BIMP-EAGA). These programmes, which complement each other, could be also seen as building stocks for the much bigger and significant ASEAN regional initiative.[1657]

479. At the same time, socio-cultural cooperation aims at improving socio-economic development and creating a shared sense of identity among the populations of the region. The Political-Security Community seeks to improve internal and external stability by pursuing common goals on transnational threats such as terrorism, human trafficking and drug trafficking, by providing enhanced dispute settlement mechanisms, and by engaging with major regional and global powers. Indeed, the links established with other Asian states but also states outside the continent as well as with third international organisations are quite impressive and ASEAN is always on the lookout to cultivate them further. One strategy to promote the ASEAN Community is through the promotion and protection of human rights and fundamental freedoms, which heretofore had never featured as a priority in the region. Nevertheless, ASEAN's stance on human rights can best be described as cautious: the yardstick, the ASEAN Human Rights Declaration, is not a legally binding instrument. Indeed, there is no monitoring or a mechanism to rule authoritatively on alleged violations of human rights and fundamental freedoms, let alone an

---

1656. For evaluation of the progress, *see*, *inter alia*, K. Ishikawa, *The ASEAN Economic Community and ASEAN Economic Integration,* 10 J. Contemp. East Asia Stud. 24–41 (2021); K. Shimizu, *The ASEAN Economic Community and the RCEP in the World Economy*, 10 J. Contemp. East Asia Stud. 1–23 (2021); D. Hew, 'Is it realistic to achieve the ASEAN Economic Community (AEC) by 2025?', Hinrich Foundation, 27 Jun. 2023, at: https://www.hinrichfoundation.com/research/article/ftas/achieve-the-asean-economic-community-by-2025/.

1657. *See* Asian Development Bank, *Asian Economic Integration Report 2024 - Decarbonizing Global Value Chains*, February 2024, 9 et seq., at: https://aric.adb.org/pdf/aeir/AEIR2024_complete.pdf.

enforcement machinery of human rights obligations. Inevitably, this state of affairs raises serious questions about the credibility of the human rights system.

480. ASEAN has made, and continues to make, a positive and major contribution to the prosperity and stability of the region, not only among its membership but wider afield. This is not to make light of the challenges with which ASEAN has been and still is confronted. The diverse political and economic nature of its Member States poses its own trials in the pursuit of economic and political integration. The idea of (almost absolute) sovereignty and non-interference in the internal affairs of the membership still remain sensitive subjects, and, arguably, there is no real willingness to address them by recognising that the international community of nations is not stagnant but always changing and there is no insulation from it. Progress is therefore slower than may be hoped for, but then development in international organisations is always dictated by Member States. It is submitted that any frank discussion on these matters as well as on other issues that are characteristic of ASEAN (e.g., the extremely wide use of consensus) should lead to the revision of the ASEAN Charter. Interestingly enough, the Charter makes no mention of revision but only of the process of amendment (Article 48), the successful completion of which requires ratification by all Member States. And experience from other regional international organisations where unanimity is also demanded for amendments to enter into (the prime example is the European Union) shows how tricky and unpredictable the whole process can be.

481. Presently, ASEAN has to address and manage several challenges and issues of contention. Reference will be made to the following three, whose nature and content is different from each other. The first concerns the military regime in power in Myanmar, its treatment of the population which is in violation of basic human rights and fundamental freedoms, including whether it has perpetrated acts of genocide against the Rohingyas. Even though the latter, as explained *supra*, has been brought before the International Court of Justice for adjudication (Case of the *Application of the Convention on the Prevention and Punishment of the Crime of Genocide* (*The Gambia v. Myanmar*)), this does relieve ASEAN from the duty to be directly involved and, if necessary force the military regime and any other political entity in the country to accept and implement a resolution to the situation. As argued *supra*, the Five-Point Consensus is not a solution but merely a description of actions to be undertaken that appeared relevant when the ASEAN Summit first came to include the situation in Myanmar in its agenda following the military coup of 1 February 2021.

482. The insistence to rely on the clearly inadequate Five-Point Consensus probably shows the inability of ASEAN to come to terms with the fact of hard realities and the realisation that it is not enough to proclaim lofty principles and ideals: they must also be applied. One does not expect that ASEAN will adopt sanctions and measures of a punitive nature against those who are responsible for overthrowing the democratically elected government and for the human rights violations in Myanmar. And this despite the fact that a third regional international organisation, the

European Union, has already taken eight packages of restrictive measures targeting Myanmar's military regime[1658] in pursuing its Common Foreign and Security Policy.[1659]

483. The second concerns the process for accepting to full membership Timor-Leste, which has put to the test the provisions of the ASEAN Charter on admission of new members. As has been explained, a Statement issued in 2022 by the 40th and 41st ASEAN Summits approved Timor-Leste's application to become the eleventh Member State in principle. However, there was some confusion at the time whether this constituted the act of admission to the Organisation that is provided for in Article 6(3) of the Charter and requires the prior recommendation of the ASEAN Coordinating Council, which apparently has not been given thus far. Arguably, what in reality this Statement did was to grant the status of observer status to Timor-Leste, to permit its participation in all ASEAN Meetings including the most senior ones, and to open the process towards eventual admission, which, pursuant to Article 6(4), shall only be completed when Timor-Leste has signed the 'Instrument of Accession to the ASEAN Charter'.

484. Presently, there is no specific timeframe for Timor-Leste becoming the eleventh Member State, although 2025 or 2026 has been given as possible dates. It transpires from the last ASEAN Summit (October 2024) that what has been happening over the last two years or so are rather preparatory activities towards fulfilling the requirements and prerequisites for membership.[1660]Even though ASEAN Leaders seem to be committed to Timor-Leste's application process, the repeated call on their 'external partners to continue providing capacity building assistance to Timor-Leste'[1661] arguably shows the incapacity of the Organisation to handle a rather straightforward matter. Unless the present membership does not want to see Timor-Leste accede but rather offers it an upgraded observer status that would allow it to participate in the various organs and bodies and have access to certain benefits but without having any rights and privileges.[1662]

1658. They include travel bans for individuals, assets freeze for individuals and legal entities, an arms embargo, an export ban on dual-use goods, etc. In total, over one hundred individuals and twenty-one legal entities are presently sanctioned. The restrictive measures were last extended until 30 Apr. 2025, *see* Council Implementing Regulation (EU) 2024/1249 of 26 Apr. 2024 implementing Regulation (EU) No 401/2013 concerning restrictive measures in view of the situation in Myanmar/Burma, O.J. L, 2024/1249, 29.4.2024.
1659. *See* Council of the European Council, *Basic Principles on the Use of Restrictive Measures (Sanctions)*, Brussels, 7 Jun. 2004, 10198/1/04 REV 1, at: https://data.consilium.europa.eu/doc/document/ST-10198-2004-REV-1/en/pdf.
1660. *See* Chairman's Statement of the 44th and 45th ASEAN Summits, Vientiane, Lao PDR, 9 Oct. 2024, paras 56–59, at: https://asean.org/chairmans-statement-of-the-44th-and-45th-asean-summits/.
1661. *Ibid.*, para. 57.
1662. To that extent, note that the adoption of the Revised Guidelines for the Implementation of the Observer Status Granted to Timor-Leste in ASEAN by the 35th ASEAN Coordinating Council Meeting in 2024, which was 'welcomed' by the Foreign Ministers, *see* Joint Communiqué of the 57th ASEAN Foreign Ministers' Meeting, Vientiane, 25 Jul. 2024, para. 27, at: https://asean.org/wp-content/uploads/2024/07/Final-Joint-Communique-of-the-57th-AMM.pdf.

485. The third issue of contention is the confrontation with China in relation to the South China Sea. In reality, this is not an antiparathesis between ASEAN and China. However, since five of its Member States (Brunei, Indonesia, Malaysia, the Philippines, and Vietnam) have competing claimants in a vast sea area whose economic exploitation would benefit ASEAN, it is only natural that it would be discussed, especially when specific Member States feel threatened by actions undertaken by China. There is no doubt that the South China Sea dispute still has the potential to cause serious trouble (at the time of writing, violent clashes between Chinese and Philippine vessels were reported).[1663] What is more worrisome is that Member States do not speak with one voice on this issue, which could question whether Member States exercise unity and solidarity as demanded under Article 41(4) of the ASEAN Charter. In particular, this provision provides that, in the conduct of external relations, Member States shall, on the basis of unity and solidarity,[1664]

486. develop common positions and pursue joint actions. Even though the question of balancing within any international organisation the interests and priorities of Member States with those of the organisation is perennial, the South China Sea situation could also be viewed from the perspective of whether ASEAN is presently in the position to develop a common foreign policy. However, what is interesting, from an institutional point of view, is that ASEAN has established two entities, the ASEAN-China Senior Officials on the Implementation of the DOC (SOM-DOC) and the ASEAN-China Joint Working Group on the Implementation of the DOC (JWG-DOC), which meet regularly, respectively, to review the implementation of the 2002 Declaration on the Conduct of Parties in the South China Sea (DOC) and to negotiate the Code of Conduct in the South China Sea (COC), reference to both documents has been made *infra*.

487. In weighing up the balance, ASEAN must ultimately be considered an ongoing success story, and it could offer valuable lessons to other sub-regional alliances and multilateral institutions not only in Asia but in other parts of the world as well. Despite some of the criticisms expressed in the present monograph, there can be no doubt that ASEAN has to be proud of a large number of achievements and successes. Perhaps the magnitude of its accomplishments could be better understood if one tried to imagine the status of the Southeast Asia region if ASEAN had not existed.

1663. *See* 'Philippines challenges China over South China Sea at ASEAN meet', 10 Oct. 2024, at: https://news.abs-cbn.com/news/2024/10/10/philippines-challenges-china-over-south-china-sea-at-asean-meet-1332.

1664. *See* further, the Preamble of the ASEAN Charter, which talks of the need to strengthen existing bonds of regional solidarity to realise an ASEAN Community.

Part VII. Addresses and Networks

ASEAN Secretariat
70A Jalan Sisingamangaraja
Jakarta 12110
Indonesia
Tel: +62 21 724-3372, 726-2991
Fax: +62 21 739-8234, 724-3504
E-mail: public@asean.org
Website: http://www.asean.org
ASEAN Commission on the Implementation of the ASEAN Declaration on the Protection and Promotion of the Rights of Women and Children (ACWC)
70A Jalan Sisingamangaraja
Jakarta 12110
Indonesia
Tel: +62 21 724-3372, 726-2991
E-mail: public@asean.org Website: https://acwc.asean.org/
ASEAN Intergovernmental Commission on Human Rights (AICHR)
70A Jalan Sisingamangaraja
Jakarta 12110
Indonesia
Phone: +62 21 726 2991
Fax: +62 21 739 3504
Website: https://aichr.org/
E-mail: aichr@asean.org

Appendix 1. Charter of the Association of Southeast Asian Nations (2007)

PREAMBLE

WE, THE PEOPLES of the Member States of the Association of Southeast Asian Nations (ASEAN), as represented by the Heads of State or Government of Brunei Darussalam, the Kingdom of Cambodia, the Republic of Indonesia, the Lao People's Democratic Republic, Malaysia, the Union of Myanmar, the Republic of the Philippines, the Republic of Singapore, the Kingdom of Thailand and the Socialist Republic of Viet Nam;

NOTING with satisfaction the significant achievements and expansion of ASEAN since its establishment in Bangkok through the promulgation of The ASEAN Declaration;

RECALLING the decisions to establish an ASEAN Charter in the Vientiane Action Programme, the Kuala Lumpur Declaration on the Establishment of the ASEAN Charter and the Cebu Declaration on the Blueprint of the ASEAN Charter;

MINDFUL of the existence of mutual interests and interdependence among the peoples and Member States of ASEAN which are bound by geography, common objectives and shared destiny;

INSPIRED by and united under One Vision, One Identity and One Caring and Sharing Community;

UNITED by a common desire and collective will to live in a region of lasting peace, security and stability, sustained economic growth, shared prosperity and social progress, and to promote our vital interests, ideals and aspirations;

RESPECTING the fundamental importance of amity and cooperation, and the principles of sovereignty, equality, territorial integrity, non-interference, consensus and unity in diversity;

ADHERING to the principles of democracy, the rule of law and good governance, respect for and protection of human rights and fundamental freedoms;

RESOLVED to ensure sustainable development for the benefit of present and future generations and to place the well-being, livelihood and welfare of the peoples at the centre of the ASEAN community building process;

Appendix 1

CONVINCED of the need to strengthen existing bonds of regional solidarity to realise an ASEAN Community that is politically cohesive, economically integrated and socially responsible in order to effectively respond to current and future challenges and opportunities;

COMMITTED to intensifying community building through enhanced regional cooperation and integration, in particular by establishing an ASEAN Community comprising the ASEAN Security Community, the ASEAN Economic Community and the ASEAN Socio-Cultural Community, as provided for in the Bali Declaration of ASEAN Concord II;

HEREBY DECIDE to establish, through this Charter, the legal and institutional framework for ASEAN;

AND TO THIS END, the Heads of State or Government of the Member States of ASEAN, assembled in Singapore on the historic occasion of the 40th anniversary of the founding of ASEAN, have agreed to this Charter.

CHAPTER I

PURPOSES AND PRINCIPLES

Article 1

Purposes

The Purposes of ASEAN are:

1. To maintain and enhance peace, security and stability and further strengthen peace-oriented values in the region;
2. To enhance regional resilience by promoting greater political, security, economic and socio-cultural cooperation;
3. To preserve Southeast Asia as a Nuclear Weapon-Free Zone and free of all other weapons of mass destruction;
4. To ensure that the peoples and Member States of ASEAN live in peace with the world at large in a just, democratic and harmonious environment;
5. To create a single market and production base which is stable, prosperous, highly competitive and economically integrated with effective facilitation for trade and investment in which there is free flow of goods, services and investment; facilitated movement of business persons, professionals, talents and labour; and freer flow of capital;
6. To alleviate poverty and narrow the development gap within ASEAN through mutual assistance and cooperation;
7. To strengthen democracy, enhance good governance and the rule of law, and to promote and protect human rights and fundamental freedoms, with due regard to the rights and responsibilities of the Member States of ASEAN;

8. To respond effectively, in accordance with the principle of comprehensive security, to all forms of threats, transnational crimes and transboundary challenges;
9. To promote sustainable development so as to ensure the protection of the region's environment, the sustainability of its natural resources, the preservation of its cultural heritage and the high quality of life of its peoples;
10. To develop human resources through closer cooperation in education and life-long learning, and in science and technology, for the empowerment of the peoples of ASEAN and for the strengthening of the ASEAN Community;
11. To enhance the well-being and livelihood of the peoples of ASEAN by providing them with equitable access to opportunities for human development, social welfare and justice;
12. To strengthen cooperation in building a safe, secure and drug-free environment for the peoples of ASEAN;
13. To promote a people-oriented ASEAN in which all sectors of society are encouraged to participate in, and benefit from, the process of ASEAN integration and community building;
14. To promote an ASEAN identity through the fostering of greater awareness of the diverse culture and heritage of the region; and
15. To maintain the centrality and proactive role of ASEAN as the primary driving force in its relations and cooperation with its external partners in a regional architecture that is open, transparent and inclusive.

Article 2

Principles

1. In pursuit of the Purposes stated in Article 1, ASEAN and its Member States reaffirm and adhere to the fundamental principles contained in the declarations, agreements, conventions, concords, treaties and other instruments of ASEAN.
2. ASEAN and its Member States shall act in accordance with the following Principles:
   a. respect for the independence, sovereignty, equality, territorial integrity and national identity of all ASEAN Member States;
   b. shared commitment and collective responsibility in enhancing regional peace, security and prosperity;
   c. renunciation of aggression and of the threat or use of force or other actions in any manner inconsistent with international law;
   d. reliance on peaceful settlement of disputes;
   e. non-interference in the internal affairs of ASEAN Member States;
   f. respect for the right of every Member State to lead its national existence free from external interference, subversion and coercion;
   g. enhanced consultations on matters seriously affecting the common interest of ASEAN;

h. adherence to the rule of law, good governance, the principles of democracy and constitutional government;
i. respect for fundamental freedoms, the promotion and protection of human rights, and the promotion of social justice;
j. upholding the United Nations Charter and international law, including international humanitarian law, subscribed to by ASEAN Member States;
k. abstention from participation in any policy or activity, including the use of its territory, pursued by any ASEAN Member State or non-ASEAN State or any non-State actor, which threatens the sovereignty, territorial integrity or political and economic stability of ASEAN Member States;
l. respect for the different cultures, languages and religions of the peoples of ASEAN, while emphasising their common values in the spirit of unity in diversity;
m. the centrality of ASEAN in external political, economic, social and cultural relations while remaining actively engaged, outward-looking, inclusive and non-discriminatory; and
n. adherence to multilateral trade rules and ASEAN's rules-based regimes for effective implementation of economic commitments and progressive reduction towards elimination of all barriers to regional economic integration, in a market-driven economy.

CHAPTER II

LEGAL PERSONALITY

Article 3

Legal Personality of ASEAN

ASEAN, as an inter-governmental organisation, is hereby conferred legal personality.

CHAPTER III

MEMBERSHIP

Article 4

Member States

The Member States of ASEAN are Brunei Darussalam, the Kingdom of Cambodia, the Republic of Indonesia, the Lao People's Democratic Republic, Malaysia, the Union of Myanmar, the Republic of the Philippines, the Republic of Singapore, the Kingdom of Thailand and the Socialist Republic of Viet Nam.

Article 5

Rights and Obligations

1. Member States shall have equal rights and obligations under this Charter.
2. Member States shall take all necessary measures, including the enactment of appropriate domestic legislation, to effectively implement the provisions of this Charter and to comply with all obligations of membership.
3. In the case of a serious breach of the Charter or noncompliance, the matter shall be referred to Article 20.

Article 6

Admission of New Members

1. The procedure for application and admission to ASEAN shall be prescribed by the ASEAN Coordinating Council.
2. Admission shall be based on the following criteria:
   a. location in the recognised geographical region of Southeast Asia;
   b. recognition by all ASEAN Member States;
   c. agreement to be bound and to abide by the Charter; and
   d. ability and willingness to carry out the obligations of Membership.
3. Admission shall be decided by consensus by the ASEAN Summit, upon the recommendation of the ASEAN Coordinating Council.
4. An applicant State shall be admitted to ASEAN upon signing an Instrument of Accession to the Charter.

CHAPTER IV

ORGANS

Article 7

ASEAN Summit

1. The ASEAN Summit shall comprise the Heads of State or Government of the Member States.
2. The ASEAN Summit shall:
   a. be the supreme policy-making body of ASEAN;
   b. deliberate, provide policy guidance and take decisions on key issues pertaining to the realisation of the objectives of ASEAN, important matters of interest to Member States and all issues referred to it by the ASEAN Coordinating Council, the ASEAN Community Councils and ASEAN Sectoral Ministerial Bodies;

c. instruct the relevant Ministers in each of the Councils concerned to hold ad hoc inter-Ministerial meetings, and address important issues concerning ASEAN that cut across the Community Councils. Rules of procedure for such meetings shall be adopted by the ASEAN Coordinating Council;
d. address emergency situations affecting ASEAN by taking appropriate actions;
e. decide on matters referred to it under Chapters VII and VIII;
f. authorise the establishment and the dissolution of Sectoral Ministerial Bodies and other ASEAN institutions; and
g. appoint the Secretary-General of ASEAN, with the rank and status of Minister, who will serve with the confidence and at the pleasure of the Heads of State or Government upon the recommendation of the ASEAN Foreign Ministers Meeting.

3. ASEAN Summit Meetings shall be:
   a. held twice annually, and be hosted by the Member State holding the ASEAN Chairmanship; and
   b. convened, whenever necessary, as special or ad hoc meetings to be chaired by the Member State holding the ASEAN Chairmanship, at venues to be agreed upon by ASEAN Member States.

Article 8

ASEAN Coordinating Council

1. The ASEAN Coordinating Council shall comprise the ASEAN Foreign Ministers and meet at least twice a year.
2. The ASEAN Coordinating Council shall:
   a. prepare the meetings of the ASEAN Summit;
   b. coordinate the implementation of agreements and decisions of the ASEAN Summit;
   c. coordinate with the ASEAN Community Councils to enhance policy coherence, efficiency and cooperation among them;
   d. coordinate the reports of the ASEAN Community Councils to the ASEAN Summit;
   e. consider the annual report of the Secretary-General on the work of ASEAN;
   f. consider the report of the Secretary-General on the functions and operations of the ASEAN Secretariat and other relevant bodies;
   g. approve the appointment and termination of the Deputy Secretaries-General upon the recommendation of the Secretary-General; and
   h. undertake other tasks provided for in this Charter or such other functions as may be assigned by the ASEAN Summit.
3. The ASEAN Coordinating Council shall be supported by the relevant senior officials.

Article 9

ASEAN Community Councils

1. The ASEAN Community Councils shall comprise the ASEAN Political-Security Community Council, ASEAN Economic Community Council, and ASEAN Socio-Cultural Community Council.
2. Each ASEAN Community Council shall have under its purview the relevant ASEAN Sectoral Ministerial Bodies.
3. Each Member State shall designate its national representation for each ASEAN Community Council meeting.
4. In order to realise the objectives of each of the three pillars of the ASEAN Community, each ASEAN Community Council shall:
   a. ensure the implementation of the relevant decisions of the ASEAN Summit;
   b. coordinate the work of the different sectors under its purview, and on issues which cut across the other Community Councils; and
   c. submit reports and recommendations to the ASEAN Summit on matters under its purview.
5. Each ASEAN Community Council shall meet at least twice a year and shall be chaired by the appropriate Minister from the Member State holding the ASEAN Chairmanship.
6. Each ASEAN Community Council shall be supported by the relevant senior officials.

Article 10

ASEAN Sectoral Ministerial Bodies

1. ASEAN Sectoral Ministerial Bodies shall:
   a. function in accordance with their respective established mandates;
   b. implement the agreements and decisions of the ASEAN Summit under their respective purview;
   c. strengthen cooperation in their respective fields in support of ASEAN integration and community building; and
   d. submit reports and recommendations to their respective Community Councils.
2. Each ASEAN Sectoral Ministerial Body may have under its purview the relevant senior officials and subsidiary bodies to undertake its functions as contained in Annex 1. The Annex may be updated by the Secretary-General of ASEAN upon the recommendation of the Committee of Permanent Representatives without recourse to the provision on Amendments under this Charter.

Appendix 1

Article 11

Secretary-General of ASEAN and ASEAN Secretariat

1. The Secretary-General of ASEAN shall be appointed by the ASEAN Summit for a non-renewable term of office of five years, selected from among nationals of the ASEAN Member States based on alphabetical rotation, with due consideration to integrity, capability and professional experience, and gender equality.
2. The Secretary-General shall:
   a. carry out the duties and responsibilities of this high office in accordance with the provisions of this Charter and relevant ASEAN instruments, protocols and established practices;
   b. facilitate and monitor progress in the implementation of ASEAN agreements and decisions, and submit an annual report on the work of ASEAN to the ASEAN Summit;
   c. participate in meetings of the ASEAN Summit, the ASEAN Community Councils, the ASEAN Coordinating Council, and ASEAN Sectoral Ministerial Bodies and other relevant ASEAN meetings;
   d. present the views of ASEAN and participate in meetings with external parties in accordance with approved policy guidelines and mandate given to the Secretary-General; and
   e. recommend the appointment and termination of the Deputy Secretaries-General to the ASEAN Coordinating Council for approval.
3. The Secretary-General shall also be the Chief Administrative Officer of ASEAN.
4. The Secretary-General shall be assisted by four Deputy Secretaries-General with the rank and status of Deputy Ministers. The Deputy Secretaries-General shall be accountable to the Secretary-General in carrying out their functions.
5. The four Deputy Secretaries-General shall be of different nationalities from the Secretary-General and shall come from four different ASEAN Member States.
6. The four Deputy Secretaries-General shall comprise:
   a. two Deputy Secretaries-General who will serve a non-renewable term of three years, selected from among nationals of the ASEAN Member States based on alphabetical rotation, with due consideration to integrity, qualifications, competence, experience and gender equality; and
   b. two Deputy Secretaries-General who will serve a term of three years, which may be renewed for another three years. These two Deputy Secretaries-General shall be openly recruited based on merit.
7. The ASEAN Secretariat shall comprise the Secretary-General and such staff as may be required.
8. The Secretary-General and the staff shall:

a. uphold the highest standards of integrity, efficiency, and competence in the performance of their duties;
b. not seek or receive instructions from any government or external party outside of ASEAN; and
c. refrain from any action which might reflect on their position as ASEAN Secretariat officials responsible only to ASEAN.

9. Each ASEAN Member State undertakes to respect the exclusively ASEAN character of the responsibilities of the Secretary-General and the staff, and not to seek to influence them in the discharge of their responsibilities.

Article 12

Committee of Permanent Representatives to ASEAN

1. Each ASEAN Member State shall appoint a Permanent Representative to ASEAN with the rank of Ambassador based in Jakarta.
2. The Permanent Representatives collectively constitute a Committee of Permanent Representatives, which shall:
   a. support the work of the ASEAN Community Councils and ASEAN Sectoral Ministerial Bodies;
   b. coordinate with ASEAN National Secretariats and other ASEAN Sectoral Ministerial Bodies;
   c. liaise with the Secretary-General of ASEAN and the ASEAN Secretariat on all subjects relevant to its work;
   d. facilitate ASEAN cooperation with external partners; and
   e. perform such other functions as may be determined by the ASEAN Coordinating Council.

Article 13

ASEAN National Secretariats

Each ASEAN Member State shall establish an ASEAN National Secretariat which shall:

a. serve as the national focal point;
b. be the repository of information on all ASEAN matters at the national level;
c. coordinate the implementation of ASEAN decisions at the national level;
d. coordinate and support the national preparations of ASEAN meetings;
e. promote ASEAN identity and awareness at the national level; and
f. contribute to ASEAN community building.

Article 14

ASEAN Human Rights Body

1. In conformity with the purposes and principles of the ASEAN Charter relating to the promotion and protection of human rights and fundamental freedoms, ASEAN shall establish an ASEAN human rights body.
2. This ASEAN human rights body shall operate in accordance with the terms of reference to be determined by the ASEAN Foreign Ministers Meeting.

Article 15

ASEAN Foundation

1. The ASEAN Foundation shall support the Secretary-General of ASEAN and collaborate with the relevant ASEAN bodies to support ASEAN community building by promoting greater awareness of the ASEAN identity, people-to-people interaction, and close collaboration among the business sector, civil society, academia and other stakeholders in ASEAN.
2. The ASEAN Foundation shall be accountable to the Secretary-General of ASEAN, who shall submit its report to the ASEAN Summit through the ASEAN Coordinating Council.

CHAPTER V

ENTITIES ASSOCIATED WITH ASEAN

Article 16

Entities Associated with ASEAN

1. ASEAN may engage with entities which support the ASEAN Charter, in particular its purposes and principles. These associated entities are listed in Annex 2.
2. Rules of procedure and criteria for engagement shall be prescribed by the Committee of Permanent Representatives upon the recommendation of the Secretary-General of ASEAN.
3. Annex 2 may be updated by the Secretary-General of ASEAN upon the recommendation of the Committee of Permanent Representatives without recourse to the provision on Amendments under this Charter.

CHAPTER VI

IMMUNITIES AND PRIVILEGES

Article 17

Immunities and Privileges of ASEAN

1. ASEAN shall enjoy in the territories of the Member States such immunities and privileges as are necessary for the fulfilment of its purposes.
2. The immunities and privileges shall be laid down in separate agreements between ASEAN and the host Member State.

Article 18

Immunities and Privileges of the Secretary-General of ASEAN and Staff of the ASEAN Secretariat

1. The Secretary-General of ASEAN and staff of the ASEAN Secretariat participating in official ASEAN activities or representing ASEAN in the Member States shall enjoy such immunities and privileges as are necessary for the independent exercise of their functions.
2. The immunities and privileges under this Article shall be laid down in a separate ASEAN agreement.

Article 19

Immunities and Privileges of the Permanent Representatives and Officials on ASEAN Duties

1. The Permanent Representatives of the Member States to ASEAN and officials of the Member States participating in official ASEAN activities or representing ASEAN in the Member States shall enjoy such immunities and privileges as are necessary for the exercise of their functions.
2. The immunities and privileges of the Permanent Representatives and officials on ASEAN duties shall be governed by the 1961 Vienna Convention on Diplomatic Relations or in accordance with the national law of the ASEAN Member State concerned.

CHAPTER VII

DECISION-MAKING

Article 20

Consultation and Consensus

1. As a basic principle, decision-making in ASEAN shall be based on consultation and consensus.
2. Where consensus cannot be achieved, the ASEAN Summit may decide how a specific decision can be made.
3. Nothing in paragraphs 1 and 2 of this Article shall affect the modes of decision-making as contained in the relevant ASEAN legal instruments.
4. In the case of a serious breach of the Charter or noncompliance, the matter shall be referred to the ASEAN Summit for decision.

Article 21

Implementation and Procedure

1. Each ASEAN Community Council shall prescribe its own rules of procedure.
2. In the implementation of economic commitments, a formula for flexible participation, including the ASEAN Minus X formula, may be applied where there is a consensus to do so.

CHAPTER VIII

SETTLEMENT OF DISPUTES

Article 22

General Principles

1. Member States shall endeavour to resolve peacefully all disputes in a timely manner through dialogue, consultation and negotiation.
2. ASEAN shall maintain and establish dispute settlement mechanisms in all fields of ASEAN cooperation.

Article 23

Good Offices, Conciliation and Mediation

1. Member States which are parties to a dispute may at any time agree to resort to good offices, conciliation or mediation in order to resolve the dispute within an agreed time limit.
2. Parties to the dispute may request the Chairman of ASEAN or the Secretary-General of ASEAN, acting in an ex-officio capacity, to provide good offices, conciliation or mediation.

Article 24

Dispute Settlement Mechanisms in Specific Instruments

1. Disputes relating to specific ASEAN instruments shall be settled through the mechanisms and procedures provided for in such instruments.
2. Disputes which do not concern the interpretation or application of any ASEAN instrument shall be resolved peacefully in accordance with the Treaty of Amity and Cooperation in Southeast Asia and its rules of procedure.
3. Where not otherwise specifically provided, disputes which concern the interpretation or application of ASEAN economic agreements shall be settled in accordance with the ASEAN Protocol on Enhanced Dispute Settlement Mechanism.

Article 25

Establishment of Dispute Settlement Mechanisms

Where not otherwise specifically provided, appropriate dispute settlement mechanisms, including arbitration, shall be established for disputes which concern the interpretation or application of this Charter and other ASEAN instruments.

Article 26

Unresolved Disputes

When a dispute remains unresolved, after the application of the preceding provisions of this Chapter, this dispute shall be referred to the ASEAN Summit, for its decision.

Article 27

Compliance

1. The Secretary-General of ASEAN, assisted by the ASEAN Secretariat or any other designated ASEAN body, shall monitor the compliance with the findings, recommendations or decisions resulting from an ASEAN dispute settlement mechanism, and submit a report to the ASEAN Summit.
2. Any Member State affected by non-compliance with the findings, recommendations or decisions resulting from an ASEAN dispute settlement mechanism, may refer the matter to the ASEAN Summit for a decision.

Article 28

United Nations Charter Provisions and Other Relevant International Procedures

Unless otherwise provided for in this Charter, Member States have the right of recourse to the modes of peaceful settlement contained in Article 33(1) of the Charter of the United Nations or any other international legal instruments to which the disputing Member States are parties.

CHAPTER IX

BUDGET AND FINANCE

Article 29

General Principles

1. ASEAN shall establish financial rules and procedures in accordance with international standards.
2. ASEAN shall observe sound financial management policies and practices and budgetary discipline.
3. Financial accounts shall be subject to internal and external audits.

Article 30

Operational Budget and Finances of the ASEAN Secretariat

1. The ASEAN Secretariat shall be provided with the necessary financial resources to perform its functions effectively.

2. The operational budget of the ASEAN Secretariat shall be met by ASEAN Member States through equal annual contributions which shall be remitted in a timely manner.
3. The Secretary-General shall prepare the annual operational budget of the ASEAN Secretariat for approval by the ASEAN Coordinating Council upon the recommendation of the Committee of Permanent Representatives.
4. The ASEAN Secretariat shall operate in accordance with the financial rules and procedures determined by the ASEAN Coordinating Council upon the recommendation of the Committee of Permanent Representatives.

CHAPTER X

ADMINISTRATION AND PROCEDURE

Article 31

Chairman of ASEAN

1. The Chairmanship of ASEAN shall rotate annually, based on the alphabetical order of the English names of Member States.
2. ASEAN shall have, in a calendar year, a single Chairmanship by which the Member State assuming the Chairmanship shall chair:
   a. the ASEAN Summit and related summits;
   b. the ASEAN Coordinating Council;
   c. the three ASEAN Community Councils;
   d. where appropriate, the relevant ASEAN Sectoral Ministerial Bodies and senior officials; and
   e. the Committee of Permanent Representatives.

Article 32

Role of the Chairman of ASEAN

The Member State holding the Chairmanship of ASEAN shall:

1. actively promote and enhance the interests and wellbeing of ASEAN, including efforts to build an ASEAN Community through policy initiatives, coordination, consensus and cooperation;
2. ensure the centrality of ASEAN;
3. ensure an effective and timely response to urgent issues or crisis situations affecting ASEAN, including providing its good offices and such other arrangements to immediately address these concerns;
4. represent ASEAN in strengthening and promoting closer relations with external partners; and
5. carry out such other tasks and functions as may be mandated.

Article 33

Diplomatic Protocol and Practices

ASEAN and its Member States shall adhere to existing diplomatic protocol and practices in the conduct of all activities relating to ASEAN. Any changes shall be approved by the ASEAN Coordinating Council upon the recommendation of the Committee of Permanent Representatives.

Article 34

Working Language of ASEAN

The working language of ASEAN shall be English.

CHAPTER XI

IDENTITY AND SYMBOLS

Article 35

ASEAN Identity

ASEAN shall promote its common ASEAN identity and a sense of belonging among its peoples in order to achieve its shared destiny, goals and values.

Article 36

ASEAN Motto

The ASEAN motto shall be: ‘One Vision, One Identity, One Community’

Article 37

ASEAN Flag

The ASEAN flag shall be as shown in Annex 3.

Article 38

ASEAN Emblem

The ASEAN emblem shall be as shown in Annex 4.

Article 39

ASEAN Day

The eighth of August shall be observed as ASEAN Day.

Article 40

ASEAN Anthem

ASEAN shall have an anthem.

CHAPTER XII

EXTERNAL RELATIONS

Article 41

Conduct of External Relations

1. ASEAN shall develop friendly relations and mutually beneficial dialogue, cooperation and partnerships with countries and sub-regional, regional and international organisations and institutions.
2. The external relations of ASEAN shall adhere to the purposes and principles set forth in this Charter.
3. ASEAN shall be the primary driving force in regional arrangements that it initiates and maintain its centrality in regional cooperation and community building.
4. In the conduct of external relations of ASEAN, Member States shall, on the basis of unity and solidarity, coordinate and endeavour to develop common positions and pursue joint actions.
5. The strategic policy directions of ASEAN's external relations shall be set by the ASEAN Summit upon the recommendation of the ASEAN Foreign Ministers Meeting.
6. The ASEAN Foreign Ministers Meeting shall ensure consistency and coherence in the conduct of ASEAN's external relations.
7. ASEAN may conclude agreements with countries or sub-regional, regional and international organisations and institutions. The procedures for concluding such agreements shall be prescribed by the ASEAN Coordinating Council in consultation with the ASEAN Community Councils.

Article 42

Dialogue Coordinator

1. Member States, acting as Country Coordinators, shall take turns to take overall responsibility in coordinating and promoting the interests of ASEAN in its relations with the relevant Dialogue Partners, regional and international organisations and institutions.
2. In relations with the external partners, the Country Coordinators shall, inter alia:
   a. represent ASEAN and enhance relations on the basis of mutual respect and equality, in conformity with ASEAN's principles;
   b. co-chair relevant meetings between ASEAN and external partners; and
   c. be supported by the relevant ASEAN Committees in Third Countries and International Organisations.

Article 43

ASEAN Committees in Third Countries and International Organisations

1. ASEAN Committees in Third Countries may be established in non-ASEAN countries comprising heads of diplomatic missions of ASEAN Member States. Similar Committees may be established relating to international organisations. Such Committees shall promote ASEAN's interests and identity in the host countries and international organisations.
2. The ASEAN Foreign Ministers Meeting shall determine the rules of procedure of such Committees.

Article 44

Status of External Parties

1. In conducting ASEAN's external relations, the ASEAN Foreign Ministers Meeting may confer on an external party the formal status of Dialogue Partner, Sectoral Dialogue Partner, Development Partner, Special Observer, Guest, or other status that may be established henceforth.
2. External parties may be invited to ASEAN meetings or cooperative activities without being conferred any formal status, in accordance with the rules of procedure.

Article 45

Relations with the United Nations System and Other International Organisations and Institutions

1. ASEAN may seek an appropriate status with the United Nations system as well as with other sub-regional, regional, international organisations and institutions.
2. The ASEAN Coordinating Council shall decide on the participation of ASEAN in other sub-regional, regional, international organisations and institutions.

Article 46

Accreditation of Non-ASEAN Member States to ASEAN

Non-ASEAN Member States and relevant inter-governmental organisations may appoint and accredit Ambassadors to ASEAN. The ASEAN Foreign Ministers Meeting shall decide on such accreditation.

CHAPTER XIII

GENERAL AND FINAL PROVISIONS

Article 47

Signature, Ratification, Depository and Entry Into Force

1. This Charter shall be signed by all ASEAN Member States.
2. This Charter shall be subject to ratification by all ASEAN Member States in accordance with their respective internal procedures.
3. Instruments of ratification shall be deposited with the Secretary-General of ASEAN who shall promptly notify all Member States of each deposit.
4. This Charter shall enter into force on the thirtieth day following the date of deposit of the tenth instrument of ratification with the Secretary-General of ASEAN.

Article 48

Amendments

1. Any Member State may propose amendments to the Charter.
2. Proposed amendments to the Charter shall be submitted by the ASEAN Coordinating Council by consensus to the ASEAN Summit for its decision.

3. Amendments to the Charter agreed to by consensus by the ASEAN Summit shall be ratified by all Member States in accordance with Article 47.
4. An amendment shall enter into force on the thirtieth day following the date of deposit of the last instrument of ratification with the Secretary-General of ASEAN.

Article 49

Terms of Reference and Rules of Procedure

Unless otherwise provided for in this Charter, the ASEAN Coordinating Council shall determine the terms of reference and rules of procedure and shall ensure their consistency.

Article 50

Review

This Charter may be reviewed five years after its entry into force or as otherwise determined by the ASEAN Summit.

Article 51

Interpretation of the Charter

1. Upon the request of any Member State, the interpretation of the Charter shall be undertaken by the ASEAN Secretariat in accordance with the rules of procedure determined by the ASEAN Coordinating Council.
2. Any dispute arising from the interpretation of the Charter shall be settled in accordance with the relevant provisions in Chapter VIII.
3. Headings and titles used throughout the Charter shall only be for the purpose of reference.

Article 52

Legal Continuity

1. All treaties, conventions, agreements, concords, declarations, protocols and other ASEAN instruments which have been in effect before the entry into force of this Charter shall continue to be valid.
2. In case of inconsistency between the rights and obligations of ASEAN Member States under such instruments and this Charter, the Charter shall prevail.

Article 53

Original Text

The signed original text of this Charter in English shall be deposited with the Secretary-General of ASEAN, who shall provide a certified copy to each Member State.

Article 54

Registration of the ASEAN Charter

This Charter shall be registered by the Secretary-General of ASEAN with the Secretariat of the United Nations, pursuant to Article 102, paragraph 1 of the Charter of the United Nations.

Article 55

ASEAN Assets

The assets and funds of the Organisation shall be vested in the name of ASEAN.
DONE in Singapore on the Twentieth Day of November in the Year Two Thousand and Seven, in a single original in the English language.

Appendix 1

Appendix 2. ASEAN Human Rights Declaration (2012)

WE, the Heads of State/Government of the Member States of the Association of Southeast Asian Nations (hereinafter referred to as 'ASEAN'), namely Brunei Darussalam, the Kingdom of Cambodia, the Republic of Indonesia, the Lao People's Democratic Republic, Malaysia, the Republic of the Union of Myanmar, the Republic of the Philippines, the Republic of Singapore, the Kingdom of Thailand and the Socialist Republic of Viet Nam, on the occasion of the 21st ASEAN Summit in Phnom Penh, Cambodia.

REAFFIRMING our adherence to the purposes and principles of ASEAN as enshrined in the ASEAN Charter, in particular the respect for and promotion and protection of human rights and fundamental freedoms, as well as the principles of democracy, the rule of law and good governance;

REAFFIRMING FURTHER our commitment to the Universal Declaration of Human Rights, the Charter of the United Nations, the Vienna Declaration and Programme of Action, and other international human rights instruments to which ASEAN Member States are parties;

REAFFIRMING ALSO the importance of ASEAN's efforts in promoting human rights, including the Declaration of the Advancement of Women in the ASEAN Region and the Declaration on the Elimination of Violence against Women in the ASEAN Region;

CONVINCED that this Declaration will help establish a framework for human rights cooperation in the region and contribute to the ASEAN community building process;

HEREBY DECLARE AS FOLLOWS:

GENERAL PRINCIPLES

1. All persons are born free and equal in dignity and rights. They are endowed with reason and conscience and should act towards one another in a spirit of humanity.

23. Every person has the right to freedom of opinion and expression, including freedom to hold opinions without interference and to seek, receive and impart information, whether orally, in writing or through any other medium of that person's choice.
24. Every person has the right to freedom of peaceful assembly.
25.
    1. Every person who is a citizen of his or her country has the right to participate in the government of his or her country, either directly or indirectly through democratically elected representatives, in accordance with national law.
    2. Every citizen has the right to vote in periodic and genuine elections, which should be by universal and equal suffrage and by secret ballot, guaranteeing the free expression of the will of the electors, in accordance with national law.

ECONOMIC, SOCIAL AND CULTURAL RIGHTS

26. ASEAN Member States affirm all the economic, social and cultural rights in the Universal Declaration of Human Rights. Specifically, ASEAN Member States affirm the following:
27.
    1. Every person has the right to work, to the free choice of employment, to enjoy just, decent and favourable conditions of work and to have access to assistance schemes for the unemployed.
    2. Every person has the right to form trade unions and join the trade union of his or her choice for the protection of his or her interests, in accordance with national laws and regulations.
    3. No child or any young person shall be subjected to economic and social exploitation. Those who employ children and young people in work harmful to their morals or health, dangerous to life, or likely to hamper their normal development, including their education should be punished by law. ASEAN Member States should also set age limits below which the paid employment of child labour should be prohibited and punished by law.
28. Every person has the right to an adequate standard of living for himself or herself and his or her family including:
    a. The right to adequate and affordable food, freedom from hunger and access to safe and nutritious food;
    b. The right to clothing;
    c. The right to adequate and affordable housing;
    d. The right to medical care and necessary social services;
    e. The right to safe drinking water and sanitation;
    f. The right to a safe, clean and sustainable environment.
29.
    1. Every person has the right to the enjoyment of the highest attainable standard of physical, mental and reproductive health, to basic and affordable health-care services, and to have access to medical facilities.

2. The ASEAN Member States shall create a positive environment in overcoming stigma, silence, denial and discrimination in the prevention, treatment, care and support of people suffering from communicable diseases, including HIV/AIDS.

30.
1. Every person shall have the right to social security, including social insurance where available, which assists him or her to secure the means for a dignified and decent existence.
2. Special protection should be accorded to mothers during a reasonable period as determined by national laws and regulations before and after childbirth. During such period, working mothers should be accorded paid leave or leave with adequate social security benefits.
3. Motherhood and childhood are entitled to special care and assistance. Every child, whether born in or out of wedlock, shall enjoy the same social protection.

31.
1. Every person has the right to education.
2. Primary education shall be compulsory and made available free to all. Secondary education in its different forms shall be available and accessible to all through every appropriate means. Technical and vocational education shall be made generally available. Higher education shall be equally accessible to all on the basis of merit.
3. Education shall be directed to the full development of the human personality and the sense of his or her dignity. Education shall strengthen the respect for human rights and fundamental freedoms in ASEAN Member States. Furthermore, education shall enable all persons to participate effectively in their respective societies, promote understanding, tolerance and friendship among all nations, racial and religious groups, and enhance the activities of ASEAN for the maintenance of peace.

32. Every person has the right, individually or in association with others, to freely take part in cultural life, to enjoy the arts and the benefits of scientific progress and its applications and to benefit from the protection of the moral and material interests resulting from any scientific, literary or appropriate artistic production of which one is the author.
33. ASEAN Member States should take steps, individually and through regional and international assistance and cooperation, especially economic and technical, to the maximum of its available resources, with a view to achieving progressively the full realisation of economic, social and cultural rights recognised in this Declaration.
34. ASEAN Member States may determine the extent to which they would guarantee the economic and social rights found in this Declaration to non-nationals, with due regard to human rights and the organisation and resources of their respective national economies.

Appendix 2

RIGHT TO DEVELOPMENT

35. The right to development is an inalienable human right by virtue of which every human person and the peoples of ASEAN are entitled to participate in, contribute to, enjoy and benefit equitably and sustainably from economic, social, cultural and political development. The right to development should be fulfilled so as to meet equitably the developmental and environmental needs of present and future generations. While development facilitates and is necessary for the enjoyment of all human rights, the lack of development may not be invoked to justify the violations of internationally recognised human rights.
36. ASEAN Member States should adopt meaningful people-oriented and gender responsive development programmes aimed at poverty alleviation, the creation of conditions including the protection and sustainability of the environment for the peoples of ASEAN to enjoy all human rights recognised in this Declaration on an equitable basis, and the progressive narrowing of the development gap within ASEAN.
37. ASEAN Member States recognise that the implementation of the right to development requires effective development policies at the national level as well as equitable economic relations, international cooperation and a favourable international economic environment. ASEAN Member States should mainstream the multidimensional aspects of the right to development into the relevant areas of ASEAN community building and beyond, and shall work with the international community to promote equitable and sustainable development, fair trade practices and effective international cooperation.

RIGHT TO PEACE

38. Every person and the peoples of ASEAN have the right to enjoy peace within an ASEAN framework of security and stability, neutrality and freedom, such that the rights set forth in this Declaration can be fully realised. To this end, ASEAN Member States should continue to enhance friendship and cooperation in the furtherance of peace, harmony and stability in the region.

COOPERATION IN THE PROMOTION AND PROTECTION OF HUMAN RIGHTS

39. ASEAN Member States share a common interest in and commitment to the promotion and protection of human rights and fundamental freedoms which shall be achieved through, inter alia, cooperation with one another as well as with relevant national, regional and international institutions/organisations, in accordance with the ASEAN Charter.

40. Nothing in this Declaration may be interpreted as implying for any State, group or person any right to perform any act aimed at undermining the purposes and principles of ASEAN, or at the destruction of any of the rights and fundamental freedoms set forth in this Declaration and international human rights instruments to which ASEAN Member States are parties.

Adopted by the Heads of State/Government of ASEAN Member States at Phnom Penh, Cambodia, this Eighteenth Day of November in the Year Two Thousand and Twelve, in one single original copy in the English Language

Appendix 2

Appendix 3. ASEAN Community Vision 2025

1. We, the Heads of State/Government representing the peoples of the Member States of the Association of Southeast Asian Nations (hereinafter referred to as ASEAN), gather here today at the 27th ASEAN Summit in Kuala Lumpur, Malaysia, to celebrate the formal establishment of the ASEAN Community 2015 and to chart the ASEAN Community Vision 2025.
2. We recall the ASEAN vision of an integrated, peaceful and stable community with shared prosperity built upon the aspirations of and commitment to the Treaty of Amity and Cooperation in Southeast Asia, the ASEAN Vision 2020, the Declaration of ASEAN Concord II, the ASEAN Charter, the Roadmap for an ASEAN Community (2009–2015) and the Bali Declaration on ASEAN Community in a Global Community of Nations.
3. We are pleased that the positive progress made since 2009 in implementing the Roadmap for an ASEAN Community comprising the ASEAN Political-Security Community, ASEAN Economic Community and ASEAN Socio-Cultural Community Blueprints, as well as the Initiative for ASEAN Integration (IAI) Strategic Framework and the IAI Work Plan II (2009–2015) and the Master Plan on ASEAN Connectivity has led us to another important milestone in ASEAN development, namely, the formal establishment of the ASEAN Community 2015.
4. We resolve to consolidate our Community, building upon and deepening the integration process to realise a rules-based, people-oriented, people-centred ASEAN Community, where our peoples enjoy human rights and fundamental freedoms, higher quality of life and the benefits of community building, reinforcing our sense of togetherness and common identity, guided by the purposes and principles of the ASEAN Charter.
5. We envision a peaceful, stable and resilient Community with enhanced capacity to respond effectively to challenges, and ASEAN as an outward-looking region within a global community of nations, while maintaining ASEAN centrality. We also envision vibrant, sustainable and highly integrated economies, enhanced ASEAN Connectivity as well as strengthened efforts in narrowing the development gap, including through the IAI. We further envision ASEAN empowered with capabilities, to seize opportunities and address challenges in the coming decade.

6. We underline the complementarity of the United Nations 2030 Agenda for Sustainable Development with ASEAN community building efforts to uplift the standards of living of our peoples.

ASEAN Political-Security Community

7. Our ASEAN Political-Security Community by 2025 shall be a united, inclusive and resilient community. Our peoples shall live in a safe, harmonious and secure environment, embrace the values of tolerance and moderation as well as uphold ASEAN fundamental principles, shared values and norms. ASEAN shall remain cohesive, responsive and relevant in addressing challenges to regional peace and security as well as play a central role in shaping the evolving regional architecture, while deepening our engagement with external parties and contributing collectively to global peace, security and stability.
8. We, therefore, undertake to realise:
   - 8.1. A rules-based community that fully adheres to ASEAN fundamental principles, shared values and norms as well as principles of international law governing the peaceful conduct of relations among states;
   - 8.2. An inclusive and responsive community that ensures our peoples enjoy human rights and fundamental freedoms as well as thrive in a just, democratic, harmonious and gender-sensitive environment in accordance with the principles of democracy, good governance and the rule of law;
   - 8.3. A community that embraces tolerance and moderation, fully respects the different religions, cultures and languages of our peoples, upholds common values in the spirit of unity in diversity as well as addresses the threat of violent extremism in all its forms and manifestations;
   - 8.4. A community that adopts a comprehensive approach to security which enhances our capacity to address effectively and in a timely manner existing and emerging challenges, including non-traditional security issues, particularly transnational crimes and transboundary challenges;
   - 8.5. A region that resolves differences and disputes by peaceful means, including refraining from the threat or use of force and adopting peaceful dispute settlement mechanisms while strengthening confidence-building measures, promoting preventive diplomacy activities and conflict resolution initiatives;
   - 8.6. A region that remains free of nuclear weapons and other weapons of mass destruction, as well as contributes to global efforts on disarmament, non-proliferation and peaceful uses of nuclear energy;
   - 8.7. A community that enhances maritime security and maritime cooperation for peace and stability in the region and beyond, through ASEAN and ASEAN-led mechanisms and adopts internationally accepted maritime conventions and principles;
   - 8.8. A community that strengthens our unity, cohesiveness and ASEAN centrality as well as remains the primary driving force in shaping the evolving regional architecture that is built upon ASEAN-led mechanisms; and

8.9. A community, in the interest of developing friendly and mutually beneficial relations, that deepens cooperation with Dialogue Partners, strengthens engagement with other external parties, reaches out to potential partners, as well as responds collectively and constructively to global developments and issues of common concern.

ASEAN Economic Community

9. Our ASEAN Economic Community by 2025 shall be highly integrated and cohesive; competitive, innovative and dynamic; with enhanced connectivity and sectoral cooperation; and a more resilient, inclusive, and people-oriented, people-centred community, integrated with the global economy.
10. We, therefore, undertake to achieve:
    10.1. A highly integrated and cohesive regional economy that supports sustained high economic growth by increasing trade, investment, and job creation; improving regional capacity to respond to global challenges and mega trends; advancing a single market agenda through enhanced commitments in trade in goods, and through an effective resolution of non-tariff barriers; deeper integration in trade in services; and a more seamless movement of investment, skilled labour, business persons, and capital;
    10.2. A competitive, innovative and dynamic community which fosters robust productivity growth including through the creation and practical application of knowledge, supportive policies towards innovation, science-based approach to green technology and development, and by embracing the evolving digital technology; promotion of good governance, transparency and responsive regulations; effective dispute resolution; and a view towards enhanced participation in global value chains;
    10.3. Enhanced connectivity and sectoral cooperation with improvements in regional frameworks, including strategic sectoral policies vital to the effective operationalisation of the economic community;
    10.4. A resilient, inclusive, people-oriented and people-centred community that engenders equitable development and inclusive growth; a community with enhanced micro, small and medium enterprise development policies and cooperation to narrow the development gaps; and a community with effective business and stakeholder engagement, sub-regional development cooperation and projects, and greater economic opportunities that support poverty eradication; and
    10.5. A global ASEAN that fosters a more systematic and coherent approach towards its external economic relations; a central and foremost facilitator and driver of regional economic integration in East Asia; and a united ASEAN with an enhanced role and voice in global economic fora in addressing international economic issues.

Appendix 3

ASEAN Socio-Cultural Community

11. Our ASEAN Socio-Cultural Community by 2025 shall be one that engages and benefits the peoples, and is inclusive, sustainable, resilient, and dynamic.
12. We, therefore, undertake to realise:
    12.1. A committed, participative and socially-responsible community through an accountable and inclusive mechanism for the benefit of our peoples, upheld by the principles of good governance;
    12.2. An inclusive community that promotes high quality of life, equitable access to opportunities for all and promotes and protects human rights of women, children, youth, the elderly/older persons, persons with disabilities, migrant workers, and vulnerable and marginalised groups;
    12.3. A sustainable community that promotes social development and environmental protection through effective mechanisms to meet the current and future needs of our peoples;
    12.4. A resilient community with enhanced capacity and capability to adapt and respond to social and economic vulnerabilities, disasters, climate change as well as emerging threats and challenges; and
    12.5. A dynamic and harmonious community that is aware and proud of its identity, culture, and heritage with the strengthened ability to innovate and proactively contribute to the global community.

Moving Forward

13. In order to achieve our ASEAN Community Vision 2025, we shall realise a community with enhanced institutional capacity through improved ASEAN work processes and coordination, increased effectiveness and efficiency in the work of ASEAN Organs and Bodies, including a strengthened ASEAN Secretariat. We shall also realise a community with increased ASEAN institutional presence at the national, regional and international levels.
14. We, therefore, task the ASEAN Community Councils to fully and effectively implement the commitment contained in the ASEAN 2025: Forging Ahead Together and to submit their reports to the ASEAN Summit, in accordance with the established procedure.
15. We pledge to our peoples our resolve to realise a rules-based, people-oriented, people-centred ASEAN of 'One Vision, One Identity, One Community'.

Adopted during the 27th ASEAN Summit, Kuala Lumpur, Malaysia, 22 November 2015

Appendix 4. ASEAN Leaders' Statement on the 55th Anniversary of ASEAN

WE, the Association of Southeast Asian Nations (ASEAN), namely Brunei Darussalam, Kingdom of Cambodia, the Republic of Indonesia, the Lao People's Democratic Republic, Malaysia, the Republic of the Union of Myanmar, the Republic of the Philippines, the Republic of Singapore, the Kingdom of Thailand, and the Socialist Republic of Viet Nam, gathered in Phnom Penh, Kingdom of Cambodia, on the occasion of the 55th Anniversary of ASEAN;

RECALLING the establishment of ASEAN by its five founding Member States in 1967, where the ASEAN Declaration (Bangkok Declaration) stressed aspiration of shared responsibility for promoting peace, prosperity and stability in the region through abiding respect for justice and the rule of law and adherence to the principles of the Charter of the United Nations (the UN Charter), the successful expansion to ten Member States in 1999, and the entry into force of the ASEAN Charter in December 2008;

RECOGNISING the significant achievements over the past 55 years in maintenance of peace, security and stability in the region as evidenced by the accession to the Treaty of Amity and Cooperation in Southeast Asia (TAC) by 39 non-ASEAN Member States and growing interest from other external partners to engage in peaceful and constructive dialogue, and develop strong cooperation with ASEAN;

REITERATING our strong commitment to upholding regionalism and multilateralism; and EMPHASISING the importance of adhering to key principles, shared values and norms enshrined in the UN Charter, the ASEAN Charter, the Declaration on Zone of Peace, Freedom and Neutrality (ZOPFAN), the TAC, the 1982 United Nations Convention on the Law of the Sea (UNCLOS), the Treaty on the Southeast Asia Nuclear Weapon-Free Zone (SEANWFZ), the 2011 Declaration on the East Asia Summit on the Principles for Mutually Beneficial Relations and the ASEAN Outlook on the Indo-Pacific (AOIP);

ACKNOWLEDGING the substantive progress of ASEAN Community-building process and the narrowing of development gap within and among ASEAN Member States, including through the implementation of ASEAN Community Vision 2025, the Master Plan on ASEAN Connectivity (MPAC) 2025, the IAI Work Plans, and effective engagement between ASEAN and sub-regional cooperation frameworks in contributing to an ASEAN Community that is fully integrated, well-connected, highly competitive, people-oriented and people-centred;

FURTHER RECOGNISING the strong commitment and shared aspiration to speedily mitigate and overcome the impacts caused by the COVID-19 pandemic, through various initiatives such as the COVID-19 ASEAN Response Fund, the ASEAN Comprehensive Recovery Framework and its Implementation Plan, the ASEAN Regional Reserve of Medical Supplies for Public Health Emergencies (RRMS), the ASEAN Centre for Public Health Emergencies and Emerging Diseases (ACPHEED) and the ASEAN Travel Corridor Arrangement Framework (ATCAF);

UNDERSCORING the importance of the spirit of 'ASEAN A.C.T.: Addressing Challenges Together', which aims to further inspire ASEAN Member States to uphold the spirit of collective endeavour and togetherness in line with the ASEAN's purposes and principles as enshrined in the ASEAN Charter, to address challenges with a view to further advancing the ASEAN Community where all people live in harmony, peace, stability and prosperity;

DO HEREBY AGREE TO:

ASEAN COMMUNITY-BUILDING

1. RESOLVE to strengthen further the principles of ASEAN as enshrined in the ASEAN Charter to support ASEAN's continued development into a peaceful, stable resilient and economically competitive region.
2. STRENGTHEN ASEAN Centrality in the ASEAN-led mechanisms in promoting peace, security and prosperity, and shaping an open, transparent, inclusive and rules-based regional architecture.
3. MAINTAIN the momentum of ASEAN's progress and development; and FURTHER ENHANCE ASEAN's collective efforts to strengthen the ASEAN Community, including through the development of the ASEAN Community's Post 2025 Vision.
4. CONTINUE TO BUILD a harmonious ASEAN Community that is peaceful, stable, and prosperous, underpinning ASEAN's engagement with the wider region and regional responses to the impacts and uncertainties posed by regional and global challenges.
5. RESOLVE to realise ASEAN Connectivity through the effective implementation of the MPAC 2025 and the promotion of greater synergies amongst various connectivity strategies, including through the Connecting the Connectivities Initiative.

POLITICAL AND SECURITY COOPERATION

6. WORK to maintain peace, security and prosperity in the region in accordance with the ASEAN's objectives and principles, especially those outlined in the

ASEAN Charter, the TAC, the Bali Principles, the AOIP and the Joint Statement on Promoting Women, Peace and Security (WPS) in ASEAN and the Joint Statement on Promoting Youth, Peace and Security Agenda at the ASEAN Regional Forum.

7. STRIVE to build a united, inclusive, resilient and rules-based ASEAN Political Security Community where all our peoples live in a safe, harmonious and secure environment; embrace the values of tolerance and moderation; fully respect the differences of our peoples; and uphold ASEAN principles, shared values and norms in the spirit of unity in diversity.
8. COMMIT to the ASEAN Community which shall remain cohesive, responsive and relevant in addressing challenges to regional peace and security as well as playing a central role in shaping the evolving regional architecture that is built upon ASEAN-led mechanisms, while deepening our engagement with external partners and contributing collectively to global peace, security and stability.
9. MAINTAIN the region free of nuclear weapons and other weapons of mass destruction and contribute to global efforts on disarmament, non-proliferation and peaceful uses of nuclear energy; and REAFFIRM our commitment to continuously engage the Nuclear Weapon States (NWS) and intensify the ongoing efforts of all parties to resolve all outstanding issues in accordance with the objectives and principles of the SEANWFZ Treaty.
10. FURTHER STRENGTHEN our efforts to address key regional and global challenges, including non-traditional security issues and transnational challenges, such as illicit drug trafficking, trafficking-in-persons, terrorism, and violent extremism; as well as other transboundary challenges such as maritime related issues, in collaboration with the international community.
11. FURTHER ENHANCE maritime security and promote maritime cooperation in ASEAN region and beyond, through the strengthening of ASEAN-led mechanisms and the adoption of internationally accepted maritime conventions and principles.

ECONOMIC COOPERATION

12. SEEK to ensure equitable economic development to narrow development gaps in the region with a view to providing the peoples with inclusive growth and equal opportunities to benefit from economic development and integration.
13. LEVERAGE the implementation of initiatives and obligations under ASEAN economic agreements and arrangements to maximise ASEAN's collective efforts in realising the region's goal as a single market and production base, a highly competitive region, with equitable economic development, and fully integrated into the global economy; and MAINTAIN ASEAN Centrality in advancing the region's economic growth and effectively implementing ASEAN's Free Trade Agreements (FTAs) and comprehensive economic partnership agreements (CEPs) with external partners, such as the Regional Comprehensive Economic Partnership (RCEP) Agreement.

14. IMPROVE the economic participation and contribution of women and vulnerable and marginalised groups.
15. ENHANCE regional cooperation in promoting the digital economy and preparing for the 4IR, particularly for MSMEs and start-up, through digital technology and e-commerce, sharing of experience and best practices and expertise in artificial intelligence and 5G technologies to transform the ASEAN region into a leading digital economy, narrowing the digital divide and strengthening regional digital integration and transformation through an ASEAN Digital Economy Framework Agreement.
16. INTENSIFY efforts to comprehensively address the socio-economic impacts of COVID-19 and to build back stronger from the crisis with a view to maintaining inclusive, resilient, competitive and sustainable growth, particularly through the implementation of the ASEAN Comprehensive Recovery Framework (ACRF), as well as to further leveraging the Global ASEAN Agenda through, among others, deepening regional market integration; promoting gender equality, circular economy, MSMEs, energy transition, regional interconnectivity, financial inclusion, digital transformation and cooperation on the blue economy; pursuing an ASEAN strategy for carbon neutrality; ensuring food and energy security; exploring a cross-border payment system; stimulating digitalisation and innovation; as well as further enhancing regional integration following the successful commencement of the Lao PDR-Thailand-Malaysia-Singapore Power Integration Project (LTMS)-PIP.

SOCIO-CULTURAL COOPERATION

17. PROMOTE the 'we feeling' and a sense of belonging to the ASEAN Community and pride among ASEAN peoples; and ENCOURAGE the continued promotion of ASEAN values, awareness and identity to heighten the ASEAN's visibility and relevance at the national, regional and international levels through the implementation of the Narrative of ASEAN Identity.
18. UNDERTAKE a whole-of-society approach in strengthening ASEAN values, awareness and identity among the peoples of ASEAN through education, youth engagement, women empowerment, sports and cultural exchanges.
19. ENHANCE health, well-being, and social protection for the peoples of ASEAN, and further strengthen their capacity and capability in realising an inclusive and resilient ASEAN Community to respond to challenges of common concern without leaving anyone behind.
20. STRENGTHEN the institutional capacity, effectiveness and human resources development of the ASEAN Socio-Cultural Community through the adoption and use of digital technology and innovation.

EXTERNAL RELATIONS

21. UNDERSCORE the importance of strengthening ASEAN Centrality and unity in our engagement with ASEAN's external partners, including through ASEAN-led mechanisms such as the ASEAN-Plus One, ASEAN Plus Three (APT), East Asia Summit (EAS), ASEAN Regional Forum (ARF), and ASEAN Defence Ministers Meeting Plus (ADMM-Plus), in order to build mutual trust and confidence as well as reinforce an open, transparent, inclusive, and rules-based regional architecture with ASEAN at the centre.
22. PROMOTE further the profile and active contributions of ASEAN to the global efforts to achieve peace, stability and sustainable development through a multilateral approach as reflected in the ASEAN Leaders' Declaration on Upholding Multilateralism, in line with the principles and objectives laid out in the UN Charter, the ASEAN Charter, the TAC, the Bali Principles, the AOIP and the Joint Statement on Promoting WPS in ASEAN.
23. CONTINUE to intensify our cooperation and partnerships with other regional and international organisations, including the UN and regional groupings, to address global concerns, enhance economic ties, and promote sustainable development for the benefit of all our peoples.
24. MAINTAIN ASEAN as an outward-looking region within a global community of nations, in the interest of developing friendly and mutually beneficial relations, that deepens cooperation with external parties; and LOOK FORWARD to engagement with new external parties based on shared interest, constructive engagement, mutual benefits and comprehensive approach for ASEAN in the conduct of its external relations in order to respond collectively and constructively to global development and issues of common concern.
25. CALL upon all external partners of ASEAN to demonstrate their cooperative efforts to achieve regional peace, security, stability and prosperity through the ASEAN-led mechanisms and frameworks.

Adopted during the 40th and 41st ASEAN Summits, Phnom Penh, Cambodia, on 11 November 2022

Appendix 4

Selected Bibliography

Includes Both Works Which Were Cited in this Monograph, and Works Which Were Not Cited.

§1. Books, Book Chapters & Monographs

Acharya, A. 'The Evolution and Limitations of ASEAN Identity'. In *ASEAN@50: Retrospectives and Perspectives on the Making, Substance, Significance and Future of* ASEAN. *Volume 4. Building ASEAN Community: Political-Security and Socio-cultural Reflections*, edited by A. Baviera & L. Maramis. Jakarta: Economic Research Institute for ASEAN and East Asia, 2017, 25.

Albert, D. 'Staying the Course: From a Southeast Asian Community to an ASEAN Community'. In *An Evolving Asian: Vison and Reality*, edited by J. Menon & C. Lee. Manila: Asian Development Bank, September 2019, 36.

Beckman, R, L. Bernard, H.D. Phan, T. Hsien-Li @ R. Yusran. *Promoting Compliance: The Role of Dispute Settlement and Monitoring Mechanisms in ASEAN Instruments*. Cambridge: Cambridge University Press, 2016.

Bora, M. 'The 1993 Cambodian Constitution and International Law: A Normative Perspective'. In *Cambodian Constitutional Law*, edited by H. Peng, K. Phallack & J. Menzel. Phnom Peng: Konrad-Adenauer-Stiftung, 2016, 69.

Caballero-Anthony, M. 'From Comprehensive Security to Regional Resilience: Coping with Nontraditional Security Challenges'. In *ASEAN@50: Retrospectives and Perspectives on the Making, Substance, Significance and Future of ASEAN. Volume 4. Building ASEAN Community: Political-Security and Socio-cultural Reflections*, edited by A. Baviera & L. Maramis. Jakarta: Economic Research Institute for ASEAN and East Asia, 2017, 123.

Chesterman, S. *From Community to Compliance?: The Evolution of Monitoring Obligations in ASEAN*. Cambridge: Cambridge University Press, 2015.

Cremona, M., D. Kleimann, J. Larik, R. Lee, P. Vennesson. *ASEAN's External Agreements: Law, Practice and the Quest for Collective Action*. Cambridge: Cambridge University Press, 2015.

Duxbury, A. & T. Hsein-Li. *Can ASEAN Take Human Rights Seriously?*. Cambridge: Cambridge University Press, 2019.

Ewing-Chow, M. & L. Bernard. 'The ASEAN Charter: The Legalization of ASEAN?'. In *Global Administrative Law: The Casebook*, edited by S. Cassese et al. New York: Institute for International Law & Justice, 2012, 115.

Haider, N. *Radical Regional Cooperation: ASEAN and SAARC*. New Delhi: Axis Books, 2014.

Selected Bibliography

Hara, A.E. 'The Concerns and Sustainability of ASEAN Intergovernmental Commission on Human Rights (AICHR)'. In *Sustainable Future for Human Security*, edited by B. McLellan. Singapore: Springer Nature Singapore Pvt Ltd., 2018, 49.

Inama, S. & E.W. Sim. *The Foundation of the ASEAN Economic Community: An Institutional and Legal Profile*. Cambridge: Cambridge University Press, 2015.

Jovanovic, M. *Comparison of Anti-Trafficking Legal Regimes and Actions in the Council of Europe and ASEAN: Realities, Frameworks and Possibilities for Collaboration*. Strasbourg: Council of Europe, 2018.

Koh T., R.G. Manalo & W. Woon (eds). *The Making of the ASEAN Charter*. Singapore: World Scientific, 2009.

Li X. & L. Tianyi. 'ASEAN Community Vision 2025 with the Belt and Road Initiative'. In *Routledge Handbook of the Belt and Road*, edited by C. Fang & P. Nolan. London and New York: Routledge, 2019, 439.

Lim, M. *et al* (eds). ASEAN's Critical Assessment and Practical Reforms. Cambodia: Konrad-Adenauer-Stiftung & Asian Vision Institute, 2023.

Magliveras, K. *Exclusion from Participation in International Organisations: The Law and Practice Behind Member States' Expulsion and Suspension of Membership*. The Hague: Kluwer Law International, 1999.

Magliveras, K. 'Membership in International Organisations'. In *Research Handbook on International Organisations*, edited by J. Klabbers & A. Wallendahl. London: Edward Elgar Publishing, 2011.

Muntarbhorn, V. 'Enlarging the Space for the People: Whither Human Rights and Governance in ASEAN'. In *ASEAN@50: Retrospectives and Perspectives on the Making, Substance, Significance and Future of* ASEAN. *Volume 4. Building ASEAN Community: Political-Security and Socio-cultural Reflections*, edited by A. Baviera & L. Maramis. Jakarta: Economic Research Institute for ASEAN and East Asia, 2017, 208.

Nasu H., R. McLaughlin, D.R. Rothwell & S.S. Tan. *The Legal Authority of ASEAN as a Security Institution*. Cambridge: Cambridge University Press, 2019.

Neo D., P. Sauvé & I. Streho. *Services Trade in ASEAN - The Road Taken and the Journey Ahead*. Cambridge: Cambridge University Press, 2019.

Pelkmans, J. *The ASEAN Economic Community: A Conceptual Approach*. Cambridge: Cambridge University Press, 2016.

Pisanò, A. 'The ASEAN Commission on the Promotion and Protection of the Rights of Women and Children'. In *International Human Rights of Women*, edited by N. Reilly. Springer, 2019, 155.

Southgate, L. *ASEAN Resistance to Sovereignty Violation: Interests, Balancing and the Role of the Vanguard State*. Bristol: Bristol University Press, 2019.

Spandler, K. *Regional Organizations in International Society - ASEAN, the EU and the Politics of Normative Arguing*. Cham: Palgrave Macmillan, 2019.

Sukma, R. *ASEAN Beyond 2015*: *The Imperatives for Further Institutional Changes*, Economic Research Institute for ASEAN and East Asia, Discussion Paper Series, ERIA-DP-2014-01, January 2014.

Tan, S. 'Not Quite Beyond the "ASEAN Way": Southeast Asia's Evolution to Rules-Based Management of Intra-ASEAN Differences'. In *ASEAN@50: Retrospectives and Perspectives on the Making, Substance, Significance and Future of*

ASEAN. *Volume 4. Building ASEAN Community: Political-Security and Socio-cultural Reflections*, edited by A. Baviera & L. Maramis. Jakarta: Economic Research Institute for ASEAN and East Asia, 2017, 67.

Venzke I. & Thio L. *The Internal Effects of ASEAN External Relations*. Cambridge: Cambridge University Press, 2016.

Wahyuningrum, Y. *The ASEAN Intergovernmental Commission on Human Rights: Origins, Evolution and the Way Forward.* Stockholm: IDEA International, 2014.

Woon, W. *The ASEAN Charter – A Commentary*. Singapore: National University of Singapore Press, 2016.

Yamakage, S. 'Evolving ASEAN and the Changing Roles of the TAC'. In *ASEAN@50: Retrospectives and Perspectives on the Making, Substance, Significance and Future of* ASEAN. *Volume 4. Building ASEAN Community: Political-Security and Socio-cultural Reflections*, edited by A. Baviera & L. Maramis. Jakarta: Economic Research Institute for ASEAN and East Asia, 2017, 39.

§2. Journal Articles

Ahmad, A. 'The ASEAN Convention on Counter Terrorism 2007'. *Asia-Pacific Journal on Human Rights and the Law* 14 (2013): 93.

Allison–Reumann L. 'EU Narratives of Regionalism Promotion to ASEAN: A Modest Turn?'. *Journal of Common Market Studies* 58 (2020): 872.

Amer, R. 'The Association of Southeast Asian Nations and the Management of Territorial Disputes'. *Boundary & Security Bulletin* 9 (1999): 81.

Azis, I.J. 'ASEAN Economic Integration: Quo Vadis?'. *Journal of Southeast Asian Economics* 35 (2018): 2.

Ba, A.D. 'Regionalism's Multiple Negotiations: ASEAN in East Asia'. *Cambridge Review of International Affairs* 22 (2009): 345.

Ba, A. 'Institutional Divergence and Convergence in the Asia-Pacific? ASEAN in Practice and in Theory'. *Cambridge Review of International Affairs* 27 (2014): 295.

Ba, A.D. 'ASEAN's Constructed Dichotomies: The Ongoing Need for Complexity-Sensitive Research Agendas'. *The Pacific Review* 33 (2020): 582.

Bagulaya, J.D. 'ASEAN as *Wayang Kulit*: A Critique of the Constitutional, Extra-Constitutional, and Practical Fetters of ASEAN'. *Asian Journal of International Law* 9 (2019): 175.

Basham-Jones, D. 'ASEAN's Intergovernmental Commission on Human Rights: A Pale Shadow of What It Could Have Been'. *Asia-Pacific Journal on Human Rights and the Law* 13 (2012): 1.

Beeson, M. 'Decentered? ASEAN's Struggle to Accommodate Great Power Competition'. *Global Studies Quarterly* (2022) 2: 1.

Berkofsky, A. 'The East Asia Summit (EAS) — Really Towards an East Asian Community (EAC)?'. *Asia-Pacific Journal of EU Studies* 4 (2006): 95.

Bui, H. 'The ASEAN Human Rights System: A Critical Analysis'. *Asian Journal of Comparative Law* 11 (2016): 111.

Burchill, R. 'Regional Integration and the Promotion and Protection of Democracy in Asia: Lessons from ASEAN'. *Asian Yearbook of International Law* 13 (2007): 51.

Selected Bibliography

Butt, S. 'The Position of International Law Within the Indonesian Legal System'. *Emory International Law Review* 28 (2014): 1.

Cerna, C.M. 'Introductory Note to the Terms of Reference for the Establishment of the ASEAN International Commission on Human Rights (AICOHR)'. *International Legal Materials* 48 (2009): 1161.

Chen, Z. 'ASEAN and Its Problematic Treaty-Making Practice: Can International Organizations Conclude Treaties "on Behalf of" Their Member States?'. *Asian Journal of International Law* 4 (2014): 391.

Chesterman, S. 'Does ASEAN Exist?: The Association of Southeast Asian Nations as an International Legal Person'. *Singapore Yearbook of International Law* 12 (2008): 199.

Chesterman, S. 'Asia's Ambivalence About International Law and Institutions: Past, Present and Futures'. *European Journal of International Law* 27 (2016): 945.

Ciorciari, J.D. 'ASEAN and the Great Powers'. *Contemporary Southeast Asia: A Journal of International and Strategic Affairs* 39 (2017): 252.

Clarke, G. 'The Evolving ASEAN Human Rights System: The ASEAN Human Rights Declaration of 2012'. *Northwestern Journal of International Human Rights* 11 (2012): 1.

Cornellier, E.A. 'In the Zone: Why the United States Should Sign the Protocol to the Southeast Asia Nuclear-Weapon-Free Zone'. *Pacific Rim Law & Policy Journal Association* 12 (2003): 233.

Cribb, R. 'Burma's Entry into ASEAN: Background and Implications'. *Asian Perspective* 22(3) (1998): 49.

Davies, M. 'Explaining the Vientiane Action Programme: ASEAN and the Institutionalisation of Human Rights'. *The Pacific Review* 26 (2013): 385.

Desierto, D.A. 'Universalizing Core Human Rights in the "New" ASEAN: A Reassessment of Culture and Development Justifications Against the Global Rejection of Impunity'. *Göttingen Journal of International Law* 1 (2009): 77.

Desierto, D.A. 'ASEAN's Constitutionalization of International Law: Challenges to Evolution under the New ASEAN Charter'. *Columbia Journal of Transnational Law* 49 (2010–2011): 268.

Devan, J. 'The ASEAN Preferential Trading Arrangement: Some Problems, Ex ante Results, and a Multipronged Approach to Future Intra-ASEAN Trade Development'. *ASEAN Economic Bulletin* 4 (1987): 197.

Dewansyah, B. & I. Handayani. 'Reconciling Refugee Protection and Sovereignty in ASEAN Member States'. *Central European Journal of International and Security Studies* 12 (2018): 473.

Doyle, N. 'The ASEAN Human Rights Declaration and the Implications of Recent Southeast Asian Initiatives in Human Rights Institution-Building and Standard-Setting'. *International and Comparative Law Quarterly* 63 (2014): 67.

Durbach, A., C. Renshaw & A. Byrnes. '"A Tongue But No Teeth?": The Emergence of a Regional Human Rights Mechanism in the Asia Pacific Region'. *Sydney Law Review* 31 (2009): 211.

Engle, K. 'Culture and Human Rights: The Asian Values Debate in Context'. *New York University Journal of International Law & Politics* 32 (2000): 291.

Funston, J. 'ASEAN: Out of Its Depth?'. *Contemporary Southeast Asia* 20(1) (1998): 22.

Ghai, Y. 'Human Rights and Governance: The Asia Debate'. *Australian Yearbook of International Law* 15 (1994): 1.
Ghani, F.A., N.I.N. Redzuan, N.F.M. Nasir & M. Salamat. 'Review on ASEAN Agreement on Transboundary Haze Pollution Agreement 2002: Problems and Solutions'. *Journal of Humanities, Language, Culture and Business* 1 (2017): 153.
Ginbar, Y. 'Human Rights in ASEAN – Setting Sail or Treading Water'. *Human Rights Law Review* 10 (2010): 504.
Harris, S.R. 'Asian Human Rights: Forming a Regional Covenant'. *Asian-Pacific Law & Policy Journal* 1(2) (2000).
Heilmann, D. 'After Indonesia's Ratification: The ASEAN Agreement on Transboundary Haze Pollution and Its Effectiveness as a Regional Environmental Governance Tool'. *Journal of Current Southeast Asian Affairs* 34 (2015): 95.
Hidetaka, Y. 'Political Leadership, Informality, and Regional Integration in East Asia: The Evolution of ASEAN Plus Three'. *European Journal of East Asian Studies* 4 (2005): 205.
Hitoshi, N. 'Revisiting the Principle of Non-Intervention: A Structural Principle of International Law or a Political Obstacle to Regional Security in Asia?'. *Asian Journal of International Law* 3 (2013): 25.
Hung, L.C. 'ASEAN Charter: Deeper Regional Integration under International Law?'. *Chinese Journal of International Law* 9 (2010): 821.
Indorf, H.H. 'The Kuala Lumpur Summit: A Second for ASEAN'. *Southeast Asian Affairs* (1978): 35.
Ishikawa K. 'The ASEAN Economic Community and ASEAN economic integration'. *Journal of Contemporary East Asia Studies* (2021) 10: 24.
Jetschke, A. 'What Drives Institutional Reforms in Regional Organisations? Diffusion, Contextual Conditions, and the Modular Design of ASEAN'. *Trans-Regional and- National Studies of Southeast Asia* 5 (2017): 173.
Jones, W.J. 'Universalizing Human Rights The ASEAN Way'. *International Journal of Social Sciences* 3 (2014): 72.
Karuppana, I. 'The ASEAN Community and ASEAN Charter: Toward a New ASEAN'. *The Journal of Diplomacy and Foreign Relations* 7 (2005): 49.
Khushalani, Y. 'Human Rights in Asia and Africa'. *Human Rights Law Journal* 4 (1983): 403.
Koh, T. 'International Law and the Peaceful Resolution of Disputes: Asian Perspectives, Contributions, and Challenges'. *Asian Journal of International Law* 1 (2011): 57.
Koga, K. 'ASEAN's Evolving Institutional Strategy: Managing Great Power Politics in South China Sea Disputes'. *The Chinese Journal of International Politics* 11 (2018): 49.
Koo, O. 'Regional Approaches to Trafficking in Women in South-East Asia: The Role of National Human Rights Institutions and the New ASEAN Human Rights Body'. *Australian Journal of Human Rights* 15 (2010): 59.
Kurus, B. 'The ASEAN Triad: National Interest, Consensus-Seeking, and Economic Co-operation'. *Contemporary Southeast Asia* 16 (1995): 404.
Leviter, L. 'The ASEAN Charter: ASEAN Failure or Member Failure?'. *New York University Journal of International Law & Politics* 43 (2010–2011): 159.

Lin, C.H. 'ASEAN Charter: Deeper Regional Integration under International Law?'. *Chinese Journal of International Law* 9 (2010): 821.

Linton, S. 'ASEAN States, Their Reservations to Human Rights Treaties and the Proposed ASEAN Commission on Women and Children'. *Human Rights Quarterly* 30 (2008): 436.

Malanczuk, P. 'Regional Protection of Human Rights in the Asia-Pacific Region'. *German Yearbook of International Law* 52 (2009): 107.

Meijknecht, A. & B.S. de Vries. 'Is There a Place for Minorities' and Indigenous Peoples' Rights Within ASEAN?: Asian Values, ASEAN Values and the Protection of Southeast Asian Minorities and Indigenous Peoples'. *International Journal on Minority and Group Rights* 17 (2010): 75.

Moller K., 'Cambodia and Burma: The ASEAN Way Ends Here'. *Asian Survey* 38 (1998): 1087.

Moretti, S. 'Keeping Up Appearances: State Sovereignty and the Protection of Refugees in Southeast Asia'. *European Journal of East Asian Studies* 17 (2018): 3.

Mueller, L.M. 'ASEAN Centrality under Threat – The Cases of RCEP and Connectivity'. *Journal of Contemporary East Asia Studies* 8 (2019): 177.

Mushkat, R. 'Creating Regional Environmental Governance Regimes: Implications of Southeast Asian Responses to Transboundary Haze Pollution'. *Washington and Lee Journal of Energy, Climate and the Environment* 4 (2012): 103.

Naldi, G.J. & K.D. Magliveras. 'International Court of Justice Indicates Provisional Measures in the Rohingya Genocide Case'. *International Enforcement Law Reporter* 36 (2020): 49.

Naldi, G.J. & K.D. Magliveras. 'The ASEAN Human Rights Declaration'. *International Human Rights Law Review* 3 (2014): 183.

Naldi, G.J. 'The ASEAN Intergovernmental Commission on Human Rights: A 'Damp Squib'?'. *Sri Lanka Journal of International Law* 22(2) (2010): 1.

Naldi, G.J. 'The ASEAN Protocol on Dispute Settlement Mechanisms: An Appraisal'. *Journal of International Dispute Resolution* 5 (2014): 105.

Narine, S. 'ASEAN in the Twenty-First Century: A Sceptical Review' *Cambridge Review of International Affairs* 22 (2009): 369.

Pattanaik, S.S. 'Transforming Eastern South Asia: Relevance of BIMSTEC'. *Journal of Strategic Analysis* 42 (2018): 422.

Petcharamesree, S. 'The ASEAN Human Rights Architecture: Its Development and Challenges'. *Equal Rights Review* 11 (2013): 46.

Phan, H.D. 'Towards A Rules-Based ASEAN: The Protocol To The ASEAN Charter on Dispute Settlement Mechanisms'. *Yearbook on Arbitration and Mediation* 5 (2013): 254.

Phan, H.D. 'The Association of Southeast Asian Nations: International Legal Personality and Its Treaty-Making Power'. *International Organisations Law Review* 13 (2016): 273.

Phan, H.D. 'Promotional Versus Protective Design: The Case of the ASEAN Intergovernmental Commission on Human Rights'. *International Journal of Human Rights* 23 (2019): 915.

Pisanò, A. 'Human Rights and Sovereignty in the ASEAN Path Towards a Human Rights Declaration'. *Human Rights Law Review* 15 (2014): 391.

Pisanò, A. 'Towards an ASEAN Human Rights Mechanism: The ASEAN Commission on the Promotion and Protection of the Rights of Women and Children'. *International Journal of Human Rights* 20 (2016): 321.

Renshaw, C.S. 'Democratic Transformation and Regional Institutions: The Case of Myanmar and ASEAN'. *Journal of Current Southeast Asian Affairs* 32 (2013): 29.

Renshaw, C.S. 'The ASEAN Human Rights Declaration 2012'. *Human Rights Law Review* 13 (2013): 557.

Renshaw, C. 'Human Trafficking in Southeast Asia: Uncovering the Dynamics of State Commitment and Compliance'. *Michigan Journal of International Law* 37 (2016): 611.

Rose, G. & D. Nestorovska. 'Towards an ASEAN Counter-Terrorism Treaty'. *Singapore Yearbook of International Law* 9 (2005): 157.

Sale, J. 'Harmonisation of Labour Laws: An Arduous Journey for ASEAN'. *Labour & Industry: A Journal of the Social and Economic Relations of Work* 30 (2020): 34.

San Juan, D.M.M. 'Premises, Perils and Promises of ASEAN Integration'. *Journal of Developing Societies* 34 (2018): 325.

Seah, D. 'The ASEAN Charter'. *International and Comparative Law Quarterly* 58 (2009): 197.

Seah, D. 'The Treaty of Amity and Cooperation in Southeast Asia: The Issue of Non-Intervention and Its Accession by Australia and the USA'. *Chinese Journal of International Law* 11 (2012): 785.

Shuaib, F.S. 'The Status of International Law in the Malaysian Municipal Legal System: Creeping Monism in Legal Discourse?'. *International Islamic University Malaysia Law Journal* 16 (2008): 181.

Stubbs, R., 'ASEAN Sceptics Versus ASEAN Proponents: Evaluating Regional Institutions'. *The Pacific Review* 32 (2019): 923.

Sim, E.W. 'ASEAN Further Enhances Its Dispute Settlement Mechanism'. *Indonesian Journal of International & Comparative Law* 7 (2020): 279.

Tan, E.K.B. 'The ASEAN Charter as "Legs to Go Places": Ideational Norms and Pragmatic Legalism in Community Building in Southeast Asia'. *Singapore Yearbook of International Law* 12 (2008): 171.

Tan, L.H. 'Will ASEAN Economic Integration Progress Beyond a Free Trade Area?'. *International and Comparative Law Quarterly* 53 (2004): 935.

Tan, L.H. 'Intergovernmental Yet Dynamically Expansive: Concordance Legalization as an Alternative Regional Trading Arrangement in ASEAN and Beyond'. *European Journal of International Law* 33 (2022): 341.

Tan, S.S. & H. Nasu. 'ASEAN and the Development of Counter Terrorism Law and Policy in Southeast Asia'. *University of New South Wales Law Journal* 39 (2016): 1219.

Tay, S.S.C. 'The ASEAN Charter: Between National Sovereignty and the Region's Constitutional Moment'. *Singapore Yearbook of International Law* 12 (2008): 151.

Thio, L.-A. 'Implementing Human Rights in ASEAN Countries: Promises to Keep and Miles to Go Before I Sleep'. *Yale Human Rights & Development Law Journal* 2 (1999): 1.

Umpai, K. 'Judicial Decision and Rethinking the Constitutional Principles Concerning Treaty Making Power and Process of Thailand'. *Brawijaya Law Journal* 4 (2017): 1.

Vanoverbeke, D. & M. Reiterer. 'ASEAN's Regional Approach to Human Rights: The Limits of the European Model?'. *European Yearbook on Human Rights* 14 (2014): 185.

Woon, W. 'Dispute Settlement in ASEAN'. *Korean Journal of International & Comparative Law* 1 (2013): 92.

Yahya, F. 'BIMSTEC and Emerging Patterns of Asian Regional and Interregional Cooperation'. *Australian Journal of Political Science* 40 (2005): 391.

Yazid, S. & I. Septiyana. 'The Prospect of ASEAN Migration Governance'. *Journal of Indonesian Social Sciences and Humanities* 9 (2019): 95.

York, M. 'ASEAN's Ambiguous Role in Resolving South China Sea Disputes'. *Indonesian Journal of International Law* 12 (2015): 286.

Yun, X. 'Asia's Reticence Towards Universal Jurisdiction'. *Groningen Journal of International Law* 4 (2016): 54.

Yukawa, T. 'The ASEAN Way as a Symbol: An Analysis of Discourses on the ASEAN Norms'. *The Pacific Review* 31 (2018): 298.

Yusran, R. 'The ASEAN Convention Against Trafficking in Persons: A Preliminary Assessment'. *Asian Journal of International Law* 8 (2018): 258.

Table of Cases

African Commission on Human and Peoples' Rights

Centre for Minority Rights Development (Kenya) and Minority Rights Group International on behalf of Endorois Welfare Council v. Kenya, Communication No. 276/2003 (2009) AHRLR 75

Social and Economic Rights Action Center v. Nigeria, Communication No. 155/96 (2001) AHRLR 60

African Court on Human and Peoples' Rights

Application 006/2012, African Commission on Human and Peoples' Rights v. Republic of Kenya, Judgment (Merits), 26 May 2017 (2017) 2 AfCLR 9

Community Court of Justice of the Economic Community of West African States

Hadjiatou Mani Koraou v. Republic of Niger, Judgment No. ECW/CCJ/JUD/06/08, 27 October 2008

Constitutional Council of Cambodia

Royal Message of His Majesty Preah Bath Samdech Preah Boromneath Norodom Sihamoni, King of Cambodia, requesting the Constitutional Council to review the constitutionality of the Article 8 of the Law on the Aggravating Circumstances of Felonies, Decision No. 092/003/2007 CC.D, 10 July 2007

Court of Justice of the European Union

Case C-173/99, *BECTU v. Secretary of State for Trade & Industry*, Judgment, 26 June 2001, [2001] E.C.R. I – 4881

Case 6/64, *Flaminio Costa v. ENEL*, Judgment, 15 July 1964, [1964] E.C.R. 585

Case C-660/13, *Council of the European Union v. European Commission*, Judgment, 28 July 2016, ECLI:EU:C:2016:616

Case C-540/03, *European Parliament v. Council of the European Union (Family Reunification)*, Judgment, 27 June 2006, [2006] E.C.R. I – 5769

Case C-275/06, *Productores de Música de España Promusciae v. Telefónica de España SAU*, Judgment, 29 January 2008, [2008] E.C.R. I – 271, ECLI:EU:C:2008:54

Table of Cases

Economic Community of West African States (ECOWAS) Court of Justice

Hadijatou Mani Koraou v. Republic of Niger, Judgment No. ECW/CCJ/JUD/06/08, 27 October 2008

European Court of Human Rights

Abdulaziz, Cabales and Balkandali v. United Kingdom, Application no. 9214/80; 9473/81; 9474/81 (1985) 7 E.H.R.R. 471

Hirsi Jamaa and Others v. Italy, Application no. 27765/09, Judgment of 23 February 2012

Johnston and Others v. Ireland, Application no. 9697/82, Judgment, 18 December 1986 (1987) 9 E.H.R.R. 203

M.S.S. v. Belgium and Greece, Application no. 30696/09, Judgment, 21 January 2011 (2011) 53 E.H.R.R. 2

Saadi v. Italy, Application no. 37201/06, Judgment, 28 February 2008 (2009) 49 E.H.R.R. 30

Germany

German Federal Constitutional Court, Brunner and Others v. European Union Treaty, [1994] 1 C.M.L.R 57

Inter-American Court of Human Rights

Case of the Xucuru Indigenous Peoples and its members v. Brazil, Judgment (Preliminary Objections, Merits, Reparations, and Costs), 5 February 2018, Series C, No. 346

Interpretation of the American Declaration of the Rights and Duties of Man Within the Framework of Article 64 of the American Convention on Human Rights, Advisory Opinion, 14 July 1989, OC-10/89, Series A, No. 10

Juridical Condition and Rights of Undocumented Migrants, Advisory Opinion, 17 September 2003, OC-18/03

Velásquez-Rodríguez v. Honduras, Merits, Judgment, 29 July 1988, Series C, No. 4

International Arbitration

Arbitration between the Republic of Croatia and the Republic of Slovenia, PCA No. 2012-04, Partial Award, 30 June 2016

Arctic Sunrise Arbitration (Netherlands v. Russia), Award on Jurisdiction, 26 November 2014, 32 R.I.A.A. 185 (2014)

Arctic Sunrise Arbitration (Netherlands v. Russia), Award on the Merits, 14 August 2015, 32 R.I.A.A. 205 (2015)

Case Concerning Delimitation of Maritime Area between Canada and the French Republic (St Pierre et Miquelon) (*Canada v. France*), Award, 10 June 1992, I.L.M. 31 (1992) 1149; 95 I.L.R. 645

Dispute Concerning the Detention of Ukrainian Naval Vessels and Servicemen (*Ukraine v. Russian Federation*), PCA Case No. 2019-28, Decision on Challenges, 6 March 2024

Clipperton Island Case (France v. Mexico), Award, 28 January 1931, 2 R.I.A.A. 1105 (1931)

Eritrea-Ethiopia Claims Commission, 135 I.L.R. 519
Island of Palmas Case (*United States of America v. Netherlands*), PCA Case No. 1925-01, Award, 3 May 1928, 2 R.I.A.A. 829 (1928)
Lake Lanoux (France v. Spain), 12 R.I.A.A. 281 (1957)
Land Reclamation by Singapore In and Around the Straits of Johore (Malaysia v. Singapore), PCA Case No. 2004-05, Award, 1 September 2005, 27 R.I.A.A. 133 (2008)
Maritime Boundary Delimitation (Guinea v. Guinea-Bissau), Award, 14 February 1985, 25 I.L.M. (1986), 251
Mauritius v. United Kingdom, Procedural Order No. 2, Application to Bifurcate Proceedings, 15 January 2013
Mauritius v. United Kingdom, Reasoned Decision on Challenge, 1 December 2011
Naulilaa Case (Portugal v. Germany), Arbitral Awards, 31 July 1928, 30 June 1930 and 16 February 1933, 2 R.I.A.A. 1012 (1928)
Rainbow Warrior (*New Zealand v. France*), Award, 30 April 1990, 20 R.I.A.A. 215 (1990)
South China Sea Arbitration (*Republic of the Philippines v. People's Republic of China*), Award, 33 R.I.A.A. 153 (2015-16)
South China Sea Arbitration (*Republic of Philippines v. People's Republic of China*), Award on Jurisdiction and Admissibility, 29 October 2015, 33 R.I.A.A. 1 (2015-16)
Trail Smelter Case (*United States, Canada*), Award, 16 April 1938 and 11 March 1941, 3 R.I.A.A. 1905

International Court of Justice

Accordance with International Law of the Unilateral Declaration of Independence in Respect of Kosovo, Advisory Opinion, 22 July 2010, I.C.J. Reports 2010, p. 403
Application of the Convention on the Prevention and Punishment of the Crime of Genocide (The Gambia v. Myanmar), Provisional Measures, Order, 22 July 2020, I.C.J. Reports 2020, p. 3
Application of the Convention on the Prevention and Punishment of the Crime of Genocide (*The Gambia v. Myanmar*), Preliminary Objections, Judgment, 22 July 2022, I.C.J. Reports 2022, p. 477
Application of the International Convention on the Elimination of All Forms of Racial Discrimination (*Georgia v. Russian Federation*), Preliminary Objections, Judgment, 1 April 2011, I.C.J. Reports 2011, p. 70
Arbitral Award Made by the King of Spain on 23 November 1906 (Honduras v. Nicaragua), Judgment, 18 November 1960, I.C.J. Reports 1960, p. 192
Arbitral Award of 31 July 1989 (Guinea-Bissau v. Senegal), Judgment, 12 November 1991, I.C.J. Reports 1991, p. 53
Barcelona Traction, Light and Power Company, Limited (Belgium v. Spain), Judgment, 5 February 1970, I.C.J. Reports 1970, p. 3
Certain Expenses of the United Nations (Article 17, paragraph 2, of the Charter), Advisory Opinion, 20 July 1962, I.C.J. Reports 1962, p. 151
Corfu Channel (United Kingdom of Great Britain and Northern Ireland v. Albania), Judgment, 9 April 1949, I.C.J. Reports 1949, p. 4

East Timor (Portugal v. Australia), Judgment, 30 June 1995, I.C.J. Reports 1995, p. 90

Effect of Awards of Compensation made by the U.N. Administrative Tribunal, Advisory Opinion, 13 July 1954, I.C.J. Reports 1954, p. 47

Fisheries Jurisdiction (United Kingdom v. Iceland), Merits, Judgment, 25 July 1974, I.C.J. Reports 1974, p. 3

Gabčíkovo-Nagymaros Project (Hungary/Slovakia), Judgment, 25 September 1997, I.C.J. Reports 1997, p. 7

Kasikili/Sedudu Island (Botswana/Namibia), Judgment, 13 December 1999, I.C.J. Reports 1999, p. 1045

Land and Maritime Boundary between Cameroon and Nigeria (Cameroon v. Nigeria: Equatorial Guinea intervening), Preliminary Objections, Judgment, 11 June 1998, I.C.J. Reports 1998, p. 275

Land, Island and Maritime Frontier Dispute (El Salvador /Honduras: Nicaragua intervening), Application to Intervene, Judgment, 13 September 1990, I.C.J. Reports 1990, p. 92

Legal Consequences for States of the Continued Presence of South Africa in Namibia notwithstanding Security Council Resolution 276 (1970), Advisory Opinion, 21 June 1971, I.C.J. Reports 1971, p. 16

Legality of the Threat or Use of Nuclear Weapons, Advisory Opinion, 8 July 1996, I.C.J. Reports 1996, p. 226

Legality of the Use by a State of Nuclear Weapons in Armed Conflict, Advisory Opinion, 8 July 1996, I.C.J. Reports 1996, p. 66

Maritime Delimitation and Territorial Questions between Qatar and Bahrain (Qatar v. Bahrain), Merits, Judgment, 16 March 2001, I.C.J. Reports 2001, p. 40

Military and Paramilitary Activities in and Against Nicaragua (Nicaragua v. United States of America), Merits, Judgment, 27 June 1986, I.C.J. Reports 1986, p. 14

North Sea Continental Shelf (Germany/Denmark; Germany/Netherlands), Judgment, 20 February 1969, I.C.J. Reports 1969, p. 3

Nottebohm (Liechtenstein v. Guatemala), Preliminary Objections, Judgment, 18 November 1953, I.C.J. Reports 1953, p. 111

Pulp Mills on the River Uruguay (Argentina v. Uruguay), Judgment, 20 April 2010, I.C.J. Reports 2010, p. 14

Reparations for Injuries Suffered in the Service of the United Nations, Advisory Opinion, 11 April 1949, I.C.J. Reports 1949, p. 174

Request for Interpretation of the Judgment of 15 June 1962 in the case concerning the Temple of Preah Vihear (Cambodia v. Thailand) (Cambodia v. Thailand), Provisional Measures, Order, 18 July 2011, I.C.J. Reports 2011, p. 537

Request for Interpretation of the Judgment of 15 June 1962 in the case concerning the Temple of Preah Vihear (Cambodia v. Thailand) (Cambodia v. Thailand), Judgment, 11 November 2013, I.C.J. Reports 2013, p. 281

Sovereignty over Pedra Branca/Pulau Batu Puteh, Middle Rocks and South Ledge (Malaysia / Singapore), Judgment, 23 May 2008, I.C.J. Reports 2008, p. 12

Sovereignty over Pulau Ligitan and Pulau Sipadan (Indonesia v. Malaysia), Judgment, 17 December 2002, I.C.J. Reports 2002, p. 625

Sovereignty over Pulau Litigan and Pulau Sipadan (Indonesia v. Malaysia), Application for Permission to Intervene, Judgment, 23 October 2001, I.C.J. Reports 2001, p. 575
Temple of Preah Vihear (Cambodia v. Thailand), Merits, Judgment, 15 June 1962, I.C.J. Reports 1962, p. 6
Territorial Dispute (Libyan Arab Jamahiriya/Chad), Judgment, 3 February 1994, I.C.J. Reports 1994, p. 6
United States Diplomatic and Consular Staff in Tehran (United States of America v. Iran), Judgment, 24 May 1980, I.C.J. Reports 1980, p. 3

International Criminal Court

Situation in the Republic of the Philippines, Warrant of Arrest for Mr Rodrigo Roa Duterte, ICC-01/21, P.-T. Ch. I, 7 March 2025

International Tribunal for the Law of the Sea

Arctic Sunrise (Netherlands v. Russia), ITLOS Case No. 22, Provisional Measures, Order, 22 November 2013, I.L.M. 53 (2014), 607
Detention of Three Ukrainian Naval Vessels (Ukraine v. Russia), ITLOS Case No. 26, Provisional Measures, Order, 25 May 2019, I.L.M. 58 (2019), 1150
Case concerning Land Reclamation by Singapore in and around the Straits of Johor (Malaysia v. Singapore), ITLOS Case No. 12, Provisional Measures, Order, 8 Oct. 2003, ITLOS Reports 2003, p. 10
Responsibilities and Obligations of States Sponsoring Persons and Entities with respect to Activities in the Area, ITLOS Case No. 17, Advisory Opinion, 1 Feb. 2011, I.T.L.O.S. Reports 2011, p. 10
Southern Bluefin Tuna Cases (New Zealand v. Japan; Australia v. Japan), ITLOS Case Nos. 3 and 4, Provisional Measures, Order, 27 Aug. 1999, 38 I.L.M. (1999) 1624

Permanent Court of International Justice

Article 3, Paragraph 2, of the Treaty of Lausanne (Frontier between Turkey and Iraq), Advisory Opinion, 21 November 1925, Series B, No. 12
Competence of the ILO to Regulate Incidentally the Personal Work of the Employer, Advisory Opinion, 12 August 1922, Series B, No. 3
Status of Eastern Carelia, Advisory Opinion, 23 July 1923, Series B, No. 5
Interpretation of the Greco-Turkish Agreement of 1 December 1926 (Final Protocol, Article IV), Advisory Opinion, 28 August 1928, Series B, No. 16
Jurisdiction of the European Commission of the Danube between Galatz and Braila, Advisory Opinion, 8 December 1917, Series B, No. 14
Mavrommatis Palestine Concessions (Greece v. Great Britain), Judgment, Jurisdiction, 30 August 1924, Series A, No. 2
S.S. Lotus (France v. Turkey), Judgment, 7 September 1927, Series A, No. 10
S.S. Wimbledon (France, Great Britain, Italy, and Japan v. Germany), Judgment, 17 August 1923, Series A, No. 1
Nationality Decrees Issued in Tunis and Morocco, Advisory Opinion, 7 February 1923, Series B, No. 4

Table of Cases

Singapore

Civil Aeronautics Administration v. Singapore Airlines Limited, Case CA 92/2003, Appeal, Decision, 14 January 2004, [2004] SGCA 3
Magistrate's Appeals No 97 of 2011/01 and 97 of 2011/02, Public Prosecutor v. Tan Cheng Yew and another appeal, High Court, Judgment, 30 November 2012, [2012] SGHC 241; [2013] 1 SLR 1095
Criminal Appeal No 11 of 2013, Yong Vui Kong v. Public Prosecutor, Court of Appeal, Judgment, 4 March 2015, [2015] SGCA 11; 55 I.L.M. (2016) 307

Southern African Development Community (SADC) Tribunal

Mike Campbell (Pvt.) Ltd. et al. v. The Republic of Zimbabwe, SADC (T) Case No. 2/2007, Judgment, 28 November 2008, I.L.M. 48 (2009) 534

United States of America

Filartiga v. Peña Irala, 630 F.2d 876 (2d Cir. 1980), I.L.M. 19 (1980) 966

Index

The numbers here refer to paragraph numbers.

2030 Agenda for Sustainable Development, 67, 192, 394
Abdulaziz, Cabales and Balkandali v. United Kingdom, 308
Accordance with International Law of the Unilateral Declaration of Independence in Respect of Kosovo, 291
Afghanistan, 104
African Charter on Human and Peoples' Rights, 295, 357
African Commission on Human and Peoples' Rights v. Kenya, 301
African Union (AU)
  Constitutive Act, 22, 25
Agreement on ASEAN Preferential Trading Arrangements (PTA), 195
Agreement on the Common Effective Preferential Tariff Scheme for the ASEAN Free Trade Area
  Protocol to Amend the Agreement on the Common Effective Preferential Tariff Scheme for the ASEAN Free Trade Area, 5
Agreement on the Establishment of the Association of Southeast Asian Nations Secretariat, 4
Agreement on the Privileges and Immunities of the Association of Southeast Asian Nations, 211
American Convention on Human Rights, 291, 303
American Declaration of the Rights and Duties of Man, 289, 291
Application of the Convention on the Prevention and Punishment of the Crime of Genocide, 1, 50, 58, 189, 287, 481
Application of the International Convention on the Elimination of All Forms of Racial Discrimination, 246
Arbitral Award Made by the King of Spain on 23 November 1906, 279
Arbitral Award of 31 July 1989 (Guinea-Bissau v. Senegal), 278, 279
Arctic Sunrise Arbitration, 271
Arctic Sunrise, Provisional Measures, 271
Article 3, Paragraph 2, of the Treaty of Lausanne (Frontier between Turkey and Iraq), 262
ASEAN
  consensus, 3, 4, 20, 24, 36, 37, 52, 55, 70–77, 83, 97, 99, 104, 120, 141, 150, 152, 155, 160, 162–176, 183, 185, 192, 216, 222, 237, 238, 240, 244, 259, 330, 331, 353, 358, 360, 368, 404, 421, 431, 443, 444, 473, 480–482
  democracy, 1, 9, 11, 16, 23, 41, 47–52, 56, 67, 68, 85, 86, 88, 103, 152, 161, 163, 166, 172, 285–287, 311, 312, 319, 377, 405, 406
  non-interference, 5, 9, 16, 23, 42, 60, 67, 103, 106, 118, 166, 172, 237, 285, 358, 362, 372, 380, 473, 480
  peaceful settlement of disputes, 5, 12, 16, 42, 43, 67, 237, 244, 245, 248, 249, 282, 474
  rule of law, 11, 16, 22, 25, 40, 41, 47, 48, 50, 67–69, 78–90, 129, 131, 152, 161, 163, 166, 167, 176, 285, 287, 377, 405, 406, 414
  sovereignty, 5, 6, 9, 12, 16, 20, 22, 23, 26, 28, 29, 42, 44, 48, 50, 54, 60, 61, 67, 80, 118, 122, 125, 130, 135, 137, 159, 185, 189, 237, 247, 273, 285, 299, 308, 320, 358, 362, 371, 372, 376, 380, 391, 418, 419, 480
  supranationality, 9, 46

Index

territorial integrity, 5, 12, 16, 42, 60, 67, 103, 106, 118, 125, 185, 358, 380
terrorism, 12, 45, 103, 106, 116, 190, 201, 205, 208, 213, 370–373, 375, 377–384, 399, 406, 479
ASEAN 2025: Forging Ahead Together, 10, 15, 43, 67, 218, 238, 446
ASEAN Action on Marine Debris, 394–397
ASEAN Agreement for the Promotion and Protection of Investments, 434
ASEAN Agreement on Customs (1997) / ASEAN Agreement on Customs (2012), 454
ASEAN Agreement on Medical Device Directive, 450, 456
ASEAN Agreement on Electronic Commerce, 191, 457
ASEAN Agreement on the Conservation of Nature and Natural Resources, 385
ASEAN Agreement on the Movement of Natural Persons, 454
ASEAN Agreement on Transboundary Haze Pollution, 216, 386–393
ASEAN Co-ordinating Centre for Transboundary Haze Pollution Control Conference of Parties, 392
ASEAN Centrality, 7, 12, 55, 230, 236
ASEAN Chairman, 120, 154, 155, 173, 181, 182, 352, 424, 431, 448
ASEAN Charter
Chapter VIII, 38, 42, 43, 146, 180, 244
consensus, 4, 20, 24, 36, 37, 52, 55, 70, 77, 83, 120, 150, 152, 160, 163, 164, 167, 170, 173, 237, 238, 244, 259, 353, 358, 360, 431, 444, 480
democracy, 1, 9, 23, 41, 47–52, 56, 67, 85, 86, 88, 152, 161, 163, 285, 311, 319
dispute resolution and settlement, 237–284, *see* also ASEAN Charter, dispute resolution and settlement
economic development, 2, 46, 47, 285, 470
equality, 33, 42, 118, 152, 352, 358, 360
expulsion, 28, 149, 159
good governance, 41, 47, 48, 67, 85, 86, 88, 161, 285
human rights, 1, 4, 21–25, 35, 41, 47–50, 53–59, 61, 63, 64, 67, 81, 82, 84–86, 88, 89, 152, 161, 210, 215, 246, 248, 285, 288, 290, 293, 310, 311, 319, 323, 352, 353, 358, 360, 362
independence, 23, 33, 40, 42, 49, 50, 63, 67, 80, 118, 125, 163, 266, 352, 358, 360
national identity, 42, 118, 358
non-interference, 9, 23, 42, 60, 67, 118, 237, 285, 358, 362, 480
peace and security, 21, 42, 66, 111, 118, 173, 237, 411
people-oriented approach, 41
preamble, 10, 27, 41, 42, 70, 82, 84, 113, 161, 285, 429, 485
Protocol to the ASEAN Charter on Dispute Settlement Mechanisms, 40, 44, 144, 212, 213, 237, 244–246, 249, 252, 256, 262, 263, 265, 280, 282–284, 293
reservations, 27, 120, 164, 248
rule of law, 22, 25, 40, 41, 47, 48, 50, 67, 81–86, 88, 89, 152, 161, 163, 167, 285
Rules of Procedure for the Interpretation of the ASEAN Charter, 38, 144
sanctions, 9, 147, 149, 150, 153
social development, 25, 46
sovereignty, 6, 9, 20, 22, 23, 26, 28, 29, 42, 44, 48, 50, 54, 60, 61, 67, 80, 118, 122, 125, 159, 237, 247, 273, 285, 358, 362, 480
supranationality, 9, 46
suspension, 24, 28, 147, 149
sustainable development, 6, 41, 47, 67, 209, 228, 385
territorial integrity, 42, 60, 67, 118, 125, 358
withdrawal, 28, 29, 90, 111, 113, 114, 116
ASEAN Commission for the Promotion and Protection of the Rights of Women and Children, 210
ASEAN Committees in Third Countries, 66
ASEAN Committee of Permanent Representatives, 267
ASEAN Committee on the Implementation of the ASEAN Declaration on the

Protection and Promotion of the Rights of Migrant Workers, 367–369
ASEAN Community
ASEAN Community 2015, 15, 67
ASEAN Community Vision 2025, 15, 17, 62, 67, 85, 192, 218, 227, 400, 446
ASEAN Political-Security Community, 7, 43, 62, 218, 230, 238, 352, 400, 445
ASEAN Political-Security Community Blueprint 2025, 43, 218, 238, 400
ASEAN Economic Community (AEC), 428–472
ASEAN Economic Community Council (AECC), 232
ASEAN Economic Community Blueprint, 209, 218
ASEAN Economic Community Blueprint 2025, 218
ASEAN Socio-Cultural Community, 7, 97, 218, 430, 445
ASEAN Socio-Cultural Community Blueprint, 218
ASEAN Socio-Cultural Community Blueprint 2025, 218
Roadmap for an ASEAN Community 2009–2015, 285
ASEAN Comprehensive Investment Agreement
Fourth Protocol, 191
ASEAN Comprehensive Plan of Action on Counter Terrorism, 382
ASEAN Consensus on the Rights of Migrant Workers, 330
ASEAN Convention Against Trafficking in Persons, specifically Trafficking of Women and Children, 333
ASEAN Convention on Counter Terrorism, 45, 106, 116, 208, 370–381
ASEAN Co-ordinating Centre for Humanitarian Assistance on Disaster Management, 62, 284
ASEAN Coordinating Council, 20, 30, 70, 97, 173, 178, 180, 228, 233–236, 245, 247, 252, 259, 264, 267, 272, 483, 484
ASEAN Declaration against Trafficking in Persons, specifically Trafficking of Women and Children, 333
ASEAN Declaration on Environmental Sustainability, 209
ASEAN Declaration on Formation of the Association, 2
ASEAN Declaration on Joint Action to Counter Terrorism, 201
ASEAN Declaration on Unity in Diversity, 214
ASEAN Declaration to Prevent and Combat Cybercrime, 371
ASEAN Declaration on the Commitments for Children in ASEAN, 326
ASEAN Declaration on the Elimination of Violence Against Women, 364
ASEAN Declaration on the Elimination of Violence against Women and Children, 364
ASEAN Declaration on the Protection of Children from All Forms of Online Exploitation and Abuse in ASEAN, 326, 413
ASEAN Declaration on the Protection of the Rights of Migrant Workers, 285
ASEAN Declaration on the Rights of Children in the Context of Migration, 332, 413
ASEAN (Manila) Declaration on the South China Sea, 1–487
ASEAN Development Fund, 202
ASEAN Framework Agreement for Visa Exemption for ASEAN Nationals, 215
ASEAN Framework Agreement on Services, 433
ASEAN Framework for Regional Comprehensive Economic Partnership, 470
ASEAN Framework of Action on Marine Debris, 394, 396
ASEAN Free Trade Areas
ASEAN+1 FTAs, 471
ASEAN – Korea Free Trade Area, 462
ASEAN Human Rights Declaration, 23, 124, 215, 229, 285, 288–325, 479
ASEAN Intergovernmental Commission on Human Rights (AICHR)
consensus, 353, 358
Guidelines on the AICHR's Relations with Civil Society Organisations, 355
Terms of Reference (TOR), 35, 210, 229, 285, 351–360, 362, 364, 366, 413
ASEAN Intergovernmental Commission on the Promotion and Protection of the Rights of Women and Children (ACWC)
Consensus, 360

Index

Terms of Reference (TOR), 188, 210, 285, 328, 359–365
ASEAN international agreements
Rules of Procedure for Conclusion of International Agreements by ASEAN, 407
ASEAN Inter-Parliamentary Assembly, 39
ASEAN Leaders' Vision Statement on a Cohesive and Responsive ASEAN: Rising Above Challenges and Sustaining Growth, 18, 224, 227
ASEAN Meeting of Foreign Ministers, 398, 403
ASEAN Meeting of Ministers on Social Welfare and Development, 360
ASEAN Minus X formula, 436, 443, 444
ASEAN Mutual Legal Assistance in Criminal Matters Treaty, 348
ASEAN Mutual Recognition Arrangement, 454
ASEAN Multilateral Agreement on the Full Liberalisation of Air Services, 455
ASEAN Plus Three, 2, 204
ASEAN Plus Six, 2, 204, 209
ASEAN Regional Forum (ARF), 3, 8, 420
ASEAN Secretariat, 4, 7, 10, 18, 38, 42, 61, 69, 81, 94, 99, 100, 120, 156, 162, 167, 183, 192, 200, 202–205, 207, 211, 213, 214, 218, 228, 229, 234, 262, 358, 367, 392, 402, 407, 416, 426, 438, 441, 445–447, 450, 454, 458
ASEAN Secretary-General, 197, 228, 264, 265, 267
ASEAN Sectoral Ministerial Bodies, 180
ASEAN Six-Point Principles on the South China Sea, 422
ASEAN Summit
Rules for Reference of Non-Compliance to the ASEAN Summit, 44, 245
ASEAN Tourism Agreement, 201
ASEAN Trade in Goods Agreement, 100, 225, 226, 433
ASEAN Trade in Services Agreement, 191, 457
ASEAN Vision 2020, 6, 7, 199, 200, 202
ASEAN Way, 4, 20, 22, 37, 40, 43, 55, 60, 68, 70, 83, 131, 223, 237, 244, 282, 285, 290, 296, 353, 473, 474
Australia, 2, 3, 54, 91, 100, 102, 105, 175, 185, 195, 204, 232, 238, 247, 355, 389, 400, 402–406, 419, 458, 464–467, 472
ASEAN-Australia Strategic Partnership 2020–2024
Ayeyawady - Chao Phraya - Mekong Economic Cooperation Strategy, 223
Bali Declaration of ASEAN Concord (Bali Concord I), 7, 195
Bali Declaration of ASEAN Concord II (Bali Concord II), 7, 13, 202, 428, 429, 435
Bali Declaration on ASEAN Community in a Global Community of Nations (Bali Concord III) Plan of Action, 9, 44, 214
Bandar Seri Begawan Declaration on the ASEAN Community's Post-2015 Vision, 217
Bangkok Declaration, 54, 56, 61, 69, 70, 78, 114, 198, 285, 294, 296, 299, 354, 396
Bangkok Declaration on Combating Marine Debris in the ASEAN Region, 396
Bangkok Declaration on Human Rights (1993), 22, 68, 82, 103, 124, 208, 285, 287, 289, 294, 296, 299, 300, 310, 354
Bangkok Summit Declaration (1995), 2, 5, 47, 54, 68, 70, 103, 186, 198, 208, 216, 237, 247, 291, 324, 389, 418, 433
Bangladesh, 3, 103, 106, 165, 168, 189, 221, 472
Barcelona Traction, Light and Power Co., 54
Bay of Bengal Initiative for Multi-Sectoral Technical and Economic Cooperation (BIMSTEC), 103, 106–109
BECTU v. Secretary of State for Trade & Industry, 291
Bhutan, 103, 106
Brunei Darussalam, 1, 49, 76, 81, 82, 134, 164, 182, 183, 207, 216, 217, 223, 229, 306, 415, 478
Brunei Darussalam - Indonesia – Malaysia - Philippines East ASEAN Growth Area (BIMP-EAGA), 223, 478
Brunner and Others v. European Union Treaty, 28
Burma, *see* Myanmar
Cairo Declaration on Human Rights in Islam (1990), 103, 207, 208, 216, 273, 281, 287, 289, 295, 310, 324
Cairo Declaration on Human Rights (2020), 1, 6, 7, 18, 48, 58, 73, 79, 80, 97, 103, 112, 115, 130, 156, 162, 181, 182, 186, 190–192, 199, 200, 202, 205,

210, 216, 220, 222–230, 239, 287, 289, 307, 317, 324, 368, 399, 402, 403, 406, 412–414, 417–420, 423, 435, 444, 450, 452, 457, 463, 467, 469, 472
Cambodia
Khmer Rouge, 63, 287
Canada, 2, 3, 82, 207, 238, 275, 280, 387, 400
Case of the Xucuru Indigenous Peoples and its members v. Brazil, 324
Cebu Declaration on the Acceleration of the Establishment of an ASEAN Community by 2015, 7, 207, 437
Centre for Minority Rights Development (Kenya) and Minority Rights Group International on behalf of Endorois Welfare Council v Kenya, 301, 324
Certain Expenses of the United Nations, 149
Cha-am Hua Hin Declaration on the Intergovernmental Commission on Human Rights, 285, 352
Cha-am Hua Hin Declaration on the Roadmap for an ASEAN Community 2009–2015, 10, 209
China, 2, 71–76, 79, 99, 105, 165, 174, 175, 185, 189, 195, 204, 205, 228, 236–238, 246, 254, 271, 273, 275, 399, 400, 402, 418–427, 458, 472, 485, 486
Civil Aeronautics Administration v. Singapore Airlines Limited, 80
Clawback clauses, 297
Clipperton Island Case, 280
Cold War, 3, 88
Common Effective Preferential Tariff (CEPT) Scheme, 5, 13, 197, 432
Commonwealth, 48–50, 88, 100, 287
Competence of the ILO to Regulate Incidentally the Personal Work of the Employer, 149
Comprehensive and Progressive Agreement for Trans-Pacific Partnership, 468
Convention on the Protection of the Rights of All Migrant Workers and Members of Their Families, 208, 287
Corfu Channel Case, 42
Costa v. ENEL, 30
Council of the European Union v. European Commission, 121
Cultural variation / relativism, 296, 300
Cybercrime, 45, 213, 371
Cyber terrorism, 371
Declaration on Friendly Relations and Co-Operation Among States, 42, 237
Declaration on Conduct of Parties in the South China Sea, 421
Declaration on Drug-Free ASEAN 2015, 214
Declaration on Institutionalizing the Resilience of ASEAN and its Communities and People to Disasters and Climate Change, 217
Declaration on the Commitments for Children in ASEAN, 326
Declaration on the Inadmissibility of Intervention in the Internal Affairs of States, 42
Declaration on the Right and Responsibility to Promote and Protect Universally Protected Human Rights and Fundamental Freedoms, 50
Declaration on the Rights of Persons Belonging to National or Ethnic, Religious or Linguistic Minorities, 57
Declaration on the Right to Development, 320
Delimitation of Maritime Area between Canada and the French Republic (St Pierre et Miquelon), 275
Democracy, 1, 9, 11, 16, 23, 41, 47–52, 56, 67, 68, 85, 86, 88, 103, 152, 161, 163, 166, 172, 285–287, 311, 312, 319, 377, 405, 406
Detention of Three Ukrainian Naval Vessels, 271
Development Partner, 66, 400
Dialogue Partners, 16, 66, 67, 100, 238, 247, 355, 371, 400, 402, 424, 469
East Asia Summit (EAS), 204–206, 209, 213
East Timor (Portugal v. Australia), 54, 91, 92, 95, 97, 101, 247
Eastern Carelia, 247
Effect of Awards of Compensation made by the U.N. Administrative Tribunal, 149
Environment, 7, 47, 187, 205, 209, 216, 303, 314, 315, 317–319, 332, 371, 385–397, 402, 412, 413, 417, 424, 440
Eritrea-Ethiopia Claims Commission, 61
European Convention for the Peaceful Settlement of Disputes, 237, 245, 248, 249
European Convention of Human Rights Protocol No. 12, 300

Index

European Convention on Action against Trafficking in Human Beings, 334
European Convention on Preventing and Combating Violence against Women and Domestic Violence, 329
European Economic Community / European Union (EU)
  Charter of Fundamental Rights, 291
  Lisbon Treaty, 22
European Free Trade Association, 467
European Parliament v. Council of the European Union (Family Reunification), 291
External partners, 12, 19, 36, 65, 100, 165, 168, 173, 176, 212, 230, 400, 470, 484
Extradition, 190, 220, 230, 347, 373, 374
Extraordinary Chambers of the Courts in Cambodia, 63
Filartiga v. Peña Irala, 54
Fisheries Jurisdiction (United Kingdom v. Iceland), 271
Forced labour, 304, 307, 315, 334, 335, 368
Framework Agreement on Enhancing ASEAN Economic Cooperation, 197, 198, 239, 432, 436, 444
  Protocol to Amend the Framework Agreement on Enhancing ASEAN Economic Cooperation, 198
Framework Agreement on the ASEAN Investment Area, 434
Fund for ASEAN, 202
Gabčíkovo-Nagymaros Project, 47
General Act, 237, 248, 249, 259, 263, 273
Geneva Conventions
  Additional Protocols, 61
Geneva Convention Relating to the Status of Refugees, 61
Group of 77, 3
Gulf Cooperation Council
  ASEAN-GCC Framework of Cooperation 2020–2024
Hadjiatou Mani Koraou v. Republic of Niger, 53
Ha Noi Declaration (1998), 50, 61, 63, 68, 93, 195, 199, 200, 228, 238, 251, 285, 287, 316, 328, 410, 432–434
Ha Noi Declaration on the Enhancement of Welfare and Development of ASEAN Women and Children, 328
Ha Noi Plan of Action, 225
Hirsi Jamaa v. Italy, 308
India, 2, 103, 106, 174, 185, 204, 238, 400, 402, 458, 472
Indonesia, 1, 2, 47, 61, 76, 81, 100, 111, 126, 127, 172, 173, 181, 183, 192, 195, 202, 205, 207, 208, 211, 213, 214, 216, 223, 231, 232, 236–238, 247, 273, 287, 317, 327, 369, 370, 386, 393, 399, 412, 414, 417–419, 424, 428, 463, 464, 466, 467, 469, 470, 472, 473, 478, 485
Indonesia - Malaysia - Thailand Growth Triangle (IMT-GT), 223, 478
Inter-American Convention on the Human Rights of Older Persons, 301
Inter-American Court of Human Rights, 291, 306, 324, 331
International Convention for the Protection of All Persons from Enforced Disappearance, 287, 306
International Convention on the Protection of the Rights of All Migrant Workers and Members of their Families, 208, 287
International Court of Justice
  Statute, 273, 287
International Covenant on Economic, Social and Cultural Rights (ICESCR), 287, 295, 315, 317
International Covenant on Civil and Political Rights (ICCPR)
  Second Optional Protocol, 306
ILO Domestic Workers Convention, 208
ILO Convention No. 138 concerning Minimum Age for Admission to Employment, 316
ILO Convention No. 182 on the Worst Forms of Child Labour, 316
Interpretation of the American Declaration of the Rights and Duties of Man Within the Framework of Art. 64 of the American Convention on Human Rights, 291
Interpretation of the Greco-Turkish Agreement of 1 December 1926, 149
Island of Palmas Case, 280
Japan, 2, 54, 92, 105, 185, 196, 202, 204, 389, 400, 402, 449, 458, 467, 472
Japan-ASEAN Solidarity Fund, 202
Japan-ASEAN Integration Fund, 202
Johnston v. Ireland, 309
Joint Statement on Reaffirmation of Commitment to Advancing the Rights of the Child, 326, 413
Juridical Condition and Rights of

Undocumented Migrants, 331
Jurisdiction of the European Commission of the Danube between Galatz and Braila, 149
Kasikili/Sedudu Island, 247
Kuala Lumpur Declaration on ASEAN 2025, 10, 15, 67, 446
Kuala Lumpur Declaration on a People-Oriented, People-Centered ASEAN, 217
Kuala Lumpur Declaration on the Establishment of the ASEAN Charter, 8, 85, 285
Kuala Lumpur Declaration on the Establishment of the ASEAN Community, 203
Kuala Lumpur Declaration on the Zone of Peace, Freedom and Neutrality, 2
Land and Maritime Boundary between Cameroon and Nigeria, 251
Land, Island and Maritime Frontier Dispute, 273
Land Reclamation by Singapore In and Around the Straits of Johore, 237
Langkawi Declaration on the Global Movement of Moderates, 217
Laos, 1, 2, 5, 13, 47, 49, 61, 68, 74, 82, 95, 100, 135, 176, 181, 182, 186, 202, 205, 207, 223, 229, 247, 287, 316, 412, 414, 447, 457, 484
Legal Consequences for States of the Continued Presence of South Africa in Namibia, 53, 67, 291
Legality of the Threat or Use of Nuclear Weapons, 9, 47, 254
Malaysia, 1, 2, 44, 47, 48, 54, 61, 73, 74, 100, 128, 176, 188, 192, 196, 199, 202, 203, 206, 207, 216–218, 223, 229, 237, 247, 273, 287, 324, 399, 415, 418, 436, 446, 447, 454, 463, 464, 468, 473, 478, 485
Maldives, 103
Manila Declaration on the Peaceful Settlement of Disputes, 43, 237
Manila Declaration (1987), 43, 54, 93, 103, 129, 185, 195, 196, 237, 238, 250, 251, 254, 261, 293, 309, 317, 432, 434
Manila Protocol on Enhanced Dispute Settlement Procedure, 239-243
Maritime Boundary Delimitation, 263
Maritime Delimitation and Territorial Questions between Qatar-Bahrain, 262
Master Plan on ASEAN Connectivity (MPAC) 2025, 18, 230, 447
Mauritius v. United Kingdom, 266, 267, 270
Mauritius v. United Kingdom Procedural Order No. 2 (Application to Bifurcate Proceedings), 270
Mauritius v. United Kingdom (Reasoned Decision on Challenge), 266, 267, 270
Mavrommatis Palestine Concessions, 246
Mike Campbell (Pvt.) Ltd. et al. v. The Republic of Zimbabwe, 53
Military and Paramilitary Activities in and Against Nicaragua, 48, 61, 391
Millennium Declaration, 21, 22, 48
Minorities, 1, 57, 58, 64, 222, 246, 313, 323, 324
M.S.S. v. Belgium and Greece, 299, 308
Myanmar (Burma)
  Rakhine State, 162, 165, 167, 168, 175, 176
  Rohingya, 160, 168
Naulilaa Case, 280
Nay Pyi Taw Declaration on Realisation of the ASEAN Community by 2015, 445
Nepal, 103, 106
New Zealand, 2, 3, 185, 204, 281, 389, 400, 405, 458, 464–466, 472
Non-Aligned Movement, 3
North Korea, 3, 406
North Sea Continental Shelf, 251
Nottebohm, 273
Organisation of African Unity
  Charter, 23, 80
  Western Sahara, 80
Organization of American States Charter, 48, 291
Pacific Alliance and ASEAN relations with, 416-417
Pact of Bogotá, 237, 245, 249, 261
Pakistan, 3, 103, 400
Papua New Guinea, 1, 3, 91, 400
PCA Arbitration Rules, 262–264, 266–271, 273, 275–279
PCA Optional Conciliation Rules, 258, 259, 261
Philippines, 1, 2, 47, 57, 61, 71–73, 76, 99, 129, 130, 173, 186, 192, 196, 207, 208, 220, 223, 237, 238, 247, 254, 271, 273, 275, 287, 317, 319, 324, 334, 369, 370, 400, 417–419, 433, 434, 437, 454, 456, 457, 463, 473, 478, 485
Philippines v. China, Jurisdiction and

Index

Admissibility, 73, 271
Phnom Penh Statement on the Adoption of the ASEAN Human Rights Declaration, 215
Phnom Penh Agenda for ASEAN Community Building, 445
Productores de Música de España Promusciae v. Telefonica de España SAU, 291
Protocol to Prevent, Suppress and Punish Trafficking in Persons, Especially Women and Children, supplementing the UN Convention against Transnational Organized Crime, 307
Protocol to the Treaty establishing the Establishing the African Economic Community Relating to the Pan-African Parliament, 39
Public Prosecutor v. Tan Cheng Yew and another appeal, 138
Rainbow Warrior, 281
Regional Economic Integration Organisations, 122, 152
Reparation for Injuries Suffered in the Service of the United Nations, 4
Report of the Eminent Persons Group on the ASEAN Charter, 2, 147, 237, 285
Request for Interpretation of the Judgment of 15 June 1962 in the case concerning the Temple of Preah Vihear, Provisional Measures and Judgment, 237
Revised General Act for the Pacific Settlement of International Disputes, 237
Russia, 2, 3, 185, 246, 271, 402
Saadi v. Italy, 308, 330
Sanctions, 9, 68, 140, 147, 149, 150, 153, 240, 393, 482
Sectoral Dialogue Partner, 66, 400
Singapore, 1, 2, 8, 13, 44, 47–49, 54, 61, 80, 82, 83, 96, 97, 99, 100, 123, 137, 138, 153, 164, 175, 185–187, 191, 197, 198, 201, 207, 209, 220, 223, 229, 237, 287, 296, 306, 326, 402, 416, 417, 423, 432–434, 438, 441, 457, 463–465, 468, 469, 473
Singapore Declaration (1992), 5, 13, 22, 48, 57, 59, 61, 79, 131, 175, 194, 197, 198, 209, 237, 239, 275, 287, 291, 387, 400, 420, 432, 444
Singapore – Johor – Riau Growth Triangle, 223
Social and Economic Rights Action Center v. Nigeria, 357
South Asian Association for Regional Cooperation (SAARC), 103–106, 109, 401
South China Sea Arbitration, 73, 237, 238, 254, 271
South China Sea dispute, 73, 237, 418–427, 485
South Korea, 2, 3, 103, 175, 185, 204, 400, 458–463, 472
Sovereignty over Pedra Branca/Pulau Batu Puteh, Middle Rocks and South Ledge, 44, 237
Sovereignty over Pulau Litigan and Pulau Sipadan, 247, 273
Special Observer, 66, 400
Sri Lanka, 3, 102, 103, 106, 107, 352, 472
S.S. Lotus, 60
S.S. Wimbledon, 54
Stockholm Declaration on the Human Environment, 387
Taiwan, 79, 80, 418
Temple of Preah Vihear, 237
Territorial Dispute (Libya v. Chad), 71, 247
Terrorism, 12, 45, 103, 106, 116, 190, 201, 205, 208, 213, 370–384, 399, 406, 479
Thailand, 1, 2, 23, 42, 43, 47, 49, 51, 54, 57, 61, 67, 73, 93, 106, 136, 174, 191, 198, 207, 209, 210, 223, 230, 237, 244, 285, 287, 306, 316, 324, 327, 352, 370, 396, 413, 417, 431, 433, 445, 454, 457, 462, 464, 473, 478
Timor Leste, 208
Trail Smelter Arbitration, 280, 387
Trans-Pacific Partnership, 468, 472
Treaty of Amity and Co-operation in Southeast Asia (TAC), 2, 5, 7, 8, 12, 43, 93, 94, 195, 204, 229, 236, 238, 244, 247, 250, 282, 474
Treaty on the Non-Proliferation of Nuclear Weapons (1968), 47, 451
Treaty on the Southeast Asia Nuclear Weapon-Free Zone, 2, 198
Tunis and Morocco Nationality Decrees, 54
United Communist Party of Turkey v. Turkey, 50
United Nations (UN)
  ASEAN relations with, 414

Joint Declaration on ASEAN-UN Collaboration in Disaster Management, 412
UN 2030 Agenda for Sustainable Development, 67
UN Basic Principles on the Independence of the Judiciary, 50
UN Charter, 21, 42–44, 53, 60, 66, 69, 70, 73, 108, 111, 117, 118, 124, 128, 143, 158, 173, 175, 215, 228, 229, 237, 238, 244, 250, 291, 358
UN Convention on the Elimination of Discrimination against Women (CEDAW), 361–363
UN Convention on the Law of the Sea, 73, 228, 271, 418, 419
UN Convention on the Prevention and Punishment of the Crime of Genocide, 287
UN Convention on the Rights of Persons with Disabilities, 1078
UN Convention on the Rights of the Child
Optional Protocol to the Convention on the Rights of the Child on the Involvement of Children in Armed Conflict, 316
Optional Protocol to the Convention on the Rights of the Child on the Sale of Children, Child Prostitution and Child Pornography, 316
UN Transitional Authority in Cambodia, 287
Universal Declaration of Human Rights, 124
USA, 2, 3, 68, 105, 185, 195, 204, 238, 400, 418, 468
US Diplomatic and Consular Staff in Tehran, 271
Velasquez Rodriguez v. Honduras, 306
Vienna Convention on the Law of Treaties, 27, 28, 244, 247
Vienna Declaration on Human Rights, 22, 289
Vientiane Action Plan, 8
Vientiane Declaration on the Adoption of the Master Plan on ASEAN Connectivity 2025, 18, 447
Vientiane Protocol on Enhanced Dispute Settlement Mechanism, 43
Vietnam, 1, 2, 5, 49, 51, 59, 61, 68, 73, 131–133, 181, 186, 195, 198, 200, 205, 207, 212, 213, 223, 225, 226, 228, 247, 273, 275, 287, 316, 412, 414, 418, 423, 432, 433, 457, 459, 463, 468, 485
World Summit Outcome, 22, 48, 57, 320
Yong Vui Kong v. Public Prosecutor, 138

www.ingramcontent.com/pod-product-compliance
Ingram Content Group UK Ltd.
Pitfield, Milton Keynes, MK11 3LW, UK
UKHW020133290926
15471UKWH00003B/456

9 789403 534190